Mencius

Mencius

Contexts and Interpretations

Edited by Alan K. L. Chan

University of Hawai'i Press
Honolulu

© 2002 University of Hawai'i Press
All rights reserved
Printed in the United States of America
07 06 05 04 03 02   6 5 4 3 2 1

Library of Congress Cataloging-in-Publication Data
Mencius : contexts and interpretations / edited by Alan K. L. Chan.
    p. cm.
   Includes bibliographical references and index.
   ISBN 0-8248-2377-X (alk. paper)
   1. Mencius. Mengzi.   I. Chan, Alan Kam-leung
PL2474.Z7 M43 2002
181'.112—dc21   2001040661

University of Hawai'i Press books are printed on acid-free
paper and meet the guidelines for permanence and durability
of the Council on Library Resources.

Designed by Kenneth Miyamoto
Printed by The Maple-Vail Book Manufacturing Group

Contents

v

Acknowledgments

THE PRESENT VOLUME grew out of a workshop entitled "Mencius and His Legacy," organized by the Department of Philosophy, Faculty of Arts and Social Sciences, National University of Singapore, in January 1999. Some twenty scholars from Asia and North America participated in the workshop, which attracted a large audience and considerable public attention. Colleagues, students, and administrative staff at the Department of Philosophy contributed much time and effort in bringing about the event and ensuring its success. The Office of the Dean also provided generous assistance. We would like to place on record our sincere thanks to the following sponsors, without whose support the workshop would not have been possible: the Kwan Im Thong Hood Cho Temple; the Lee Foundation; the East West Cultural Development Centre; and the Centre for Advanced Studies, Faculty of Arts and Social Sciences, National University of Singapore.

All but one of the essays in this volume were first presented, albeit in a much shorter and preliminary form, at the Mencius workshop. I would like to thank the authors and others who have helped with the publication process. Patricia Crosby, Cheri Dunn, and at an earlier stage Sharon Yamamoto at the University of Hawai'i Press provided invaluable advice and support. Rosemary Wetherold, the copy editor of the volume, made helpful suggestions and attended carefully to every detail. Above all, I am greatly indebted to Jiuan Heng, my colleague at the Department of Philosophy, who worked tirelessly in bringing the workshop, and at a crucial stage the manuscript, to fruition.

Introduction

ALAN K. L. CHAN

THE THIRTEEN ESSAYS in this volume bring into view the complex world of the *Mencius,* a classic in the full sense of the word with few rivals in Chinese history. From the fourteenth to the early twentieth century, as is well known, it was revered as one of the "Four Books" (*sishu* 四書), which formed the basis of traditional Chinese education.[1] Its influence, of course, extends beyond China, as Confucian learning makes its presence felt in East Asia at large. Today, the *Mencius* again commands considerable intellectual attention, as debates on "Asian values" rage from the classroom to the boardroom, in both East Asia and the West. Variously interpreted, its vision of a common humanity, insights into the ethical life, and concern for the welfare of the people appeal to both conservatives and revolutionaries. A concerted effort to bring the *Mencius*—or *Mengzi* 孟子, to use its Chinese title—under fresh scrutiny seems timely.

The present offering, however, does not attempt to provide a general account of Mencius' philosophy. Students of the classic are indebted to the translations and studies of James Legge, W. A. C. H. Dobson, and D. C. Lau.[2] The works of Feng Youlan (Fung Yu-lan), Benjamin Schwartz, A. C. Graham, David Nivison, and others have further helped chart the contours of the field.[3] Kwong-Loi Shun's *Mencius and Early Chinese Thought* furnishes an important milestone, combining sinological rigor with analytic precision to arrive at a nuanced reading of the work.[4] Reflecting the current state of Mencian scholarship, the essays presented here traverse contested territories and explore new perspectives from which to approach the classic.

1

Although the role the *Mencius* played in shaping East Asian thought and culture falls outside their purview, the essays that follow afford ample opportunities for debate concerning its background, interpretation, and continued relevance.

According to the *Shiji* 史記 (Records of the Historian), Mencius —Master Meng, whose name was Meng Ke 孟軻—studied under a disciple or disciples of Confucius' grandson, Zisi 子思. There is a tradition that identifies Zisi as Mencius' teacher, but this view has been largely discarded in modern scholarship. Mencius was at one time an officer at the state of Qi 齊; as the *Shiji* "biography" relates, he taught "the virtues of the Tang 唐, Yu 虞, and Three Dynasties," unlike his contemporaries, who directed their talent to advising rulers on military affairs.[5] Mencius was not successful in his political career and toward the end of his life retired with his disciples to teach the *Shi* 詩 (Classic of Poetry), *Shu* 書 (Classic of History), and the thought of Confucius and "composed the *Mengzi* in seven books."[6] The "Grand Historian," indeed, intimates that he had firsthand knowledge of the work. While some scholars argue that the *Mencius* was compiled by the disciples of Mencius after his death, others maintain that Mencius had at least a hand in formulating its content.[7] The question of authorship and how it bears on our understanding of the *Mencius* is evidently important and receives innovative treatment in the study by Bruce Brooks and Taeko Brooks in this volume.

The text as it now stands contains the conversations of Mencius with various rulers and disciples, debates with rival philosophers, and sayings attributed to Mencius. It is divided into seven books, or chapters (*pian* 篇), each comprising two parts. This arrangement can be traced to Zhao Qi 趙岐 (d. 201 C.E.), whose commentary on the *Mencius* is the earliest extant. In the "bibliographical" section of the *Hanshu* 漢書 (History of the Former Han Dynasty), the *Mencius* is listed as having eleven books.[8] According to Zhao Qi, in addition to the seven "inner" books of *Mencius* there were also four "outer" pieces (*waishu* 外書), which he considered later forgeries. The "outer" documents seem to have been lost from an early time; some quotations attributed to Mencius that are not found in the present *Mencius* do exist, but as Lau puts it, they are few in number and not "significant in content."[9] Zhao Qi's commentary remains an important guide and is cited in many of the papers assembled here. Other important commentaries date to the Song period and after.

Chief among them are Zhu Xi's *Mengzi jizhu* 孟子集注 and the *Mengzi zhengyi* 孟子正義 of Jiao Xun 焦循 (1763–1820). Special mention should also be made of the *Mengzi ziyi shuzheng* 孟子字義疏證, by Dai Zhen 戴震 (1724–1777), which forms the focus of Kwong-Loi Shun's contribution.

Numerous legends surround the life of Mencius, who is known as the "second sage" of the Confucian tradition. However, little is known of the historical Mencius, apart from what we can gather from the classic itself. While some scholars continue to rely on the traditional view that Mencius was born in 371 B.C.E. and died about eighty years later in 289, an increasing number now follow the reconstruction of Qian Mu 錢穆, who places Mencius between 390 and 305 B.C.E.[10] In either case, Mencius arrived on the Chinese scene in the thick of the Warring States period (480–221 B.C.E.), which has an important bearing on understanding his thought. Like other philosophers in those turbulent years, Mencius was keenly concerned with the deterioration of the Zhou empire and sought ways to bring peace and order to the land. The way of the "true king" was one main concern, but there were also rival philosophers to contend with. Human nature, ethical self-cultivation, and their implications for politics—these were issues close to Mencius' heart and were hotly debated by his contemporaries.

These remarks bring forth a familiar picture, but they are not likely to satisfy students of the *Mencius* today, who seek a finer delineation of its intellectual and political compass. Comparison with other Warring States writings, including recently excavated texts, promises to shed new light on Mencius' teachings. With the help of the Guodian 郭店 bamboo texts unearthed in 1993, Ning Chen attempts to pinpoint several views of human nature (*xing* 性) that precipitated Mencius' response. The Mohist conception of human nature—"inegalitarian" insofar as it holds that inborn nature can be either good or evil—posed a strong challenge to Mencius and other Confucians, who believed that *xing*, endowed by Heaven (*tian* 天), is common to all. But perhaps even more troubling to Mencius was the view, held by some Confucians, that human nature is morally "ambivalent," containing both good and evil in incipient form. Against this background, Mencius not only defended an "egalitarian" view of nature against the Mohists but also defined what to him was the correct Confucian view—namely, that human nature is originally good, although its incipient goodness requires cultivation to blossom into a full-fledged moral nature. Chen also finds evidence of a close connection between nature and the emotions (*qing* 情). This raises the question whether the Mencian account of moral nature presupposes the idea that *xing* is fundamentally affective and social.

The Guodian material, which dates to around 300 B.C.E., is important because it contains a number of hitherto unknown texts that are quite clearly Confucian in orientation. One group of eight bamboo strips, for example, relates a conversation between Zisi and Duke Mu 穆 of Lu 魯 on what constitutes a "loyal minister" (*zhong-chen* 忠臣).[11] Although the *Hanshu* records a work by Zisi in twenty-three books, there is little reliable knowledge of Zisi's thought until the Guodian find gives us a first glimpse of it.[12] A "loyal minister," Zisi explains, is someone who constantly draws attention to the shortcomings of the ruler. Whether this is developed further in the *Mencius* need not concern us at this point; suffice it to say that the Guodian material, arguably the most exciting find in recent years after the Mawangdui silk manuscripts, promises fresh insight into early Chinese philosophy.

The Guodian material also features prominently in A. Chan's discussion of the concept of "vital energy" (*qi* 氣) in the *Mencius*. Focusing on *Mencius* 2A2, a key passage in which Mencius puts forth his view on the tending of the "heart" (*xin* 心), Chan argues that a common understanding of vital energy as constitutive of the heart, or "heart-mind," underlies the accounts of ethical development in the works of Mencius and his contemporaries. What distinguishes Mencius from his opponents—in particular, Gaozi 告子—is that he locates in vital energy an inherent ethical tendency. Constituted by *qi,* the heart has a natural "taste" for *yi* 義, or rightness. Although the immediate focus is on the concept of *qi,* this analysis has implications for an understanding of the debate on human nature and Mencius' moral psychology as a whole.

The essays by Roger Ames and Irene Bloom continue a well-known debate on the concept of human nature in the *Mencius*. Is nature essentially a "biological" concept, an "achievement" concept, or both? Ames and Bloom are equally concerned about challenging the tacit assumption of many scholars and translators that human nature in the *Mencius* denotes an essential property of human beings. Ames contends that a range of key Chinese philosophical terms, when cleansed of "essentialist" assumptions, would lend themselves to a "process" interpretation that characterizes not only Mencian philosophy but also early Chinese thought in general. Against the common understanding of *jie* 皆 as the universal "all," for example, Ames suggests that it should be taken as what is common to "all" within a particular community. To take but one more example, *shan* 善 should be read not as "good-in-itself" but rather as "effective relations: 'good at,' 'good to,' 'good for,' 'good with,' 'good in.'" Using John Dewey's process philosophy as a conceptual bridge to early Chinese thought, Ames proposes that we think of Mencian nature not as given but as a process achieved over a lifetime of actions and experience. Moreover, human nature should be seen as embedded in situations and social roles; as such, personhood is socially constructed.

Bloom also cautions against importing a metaphysical notion of an "essential" human nature that would have been alien to Mencius. Yet the Mencian problematic cannot be resolved by rejecting nature as "innate" for an achievement that is "acquired." Rather, Bloom argues that the perceived disjunction between what is "innate" and what is "acquired" must itself be subject to careful examination. The *Mencius* does not seem to envisage a conceptual divide between the biologically given and cultural achievement. While human nature is not to be limited to what is "given" or "shared," it develops from it. In Mencian terms, the predisposition to goodness is indeed biologically given, but it requires cultivation to bring it to fruition. As distinguished from a "narrow" biological view that identifies nature with selfish desires to be eradicated by cultural achievements, the Mencian position sees nature and culture mutually influencing and reinforcing each other, which calls to mind the theory of "gene-culture coevolution" put forward by the contemporary sociobiologist E. O. Wilson. Notably, Donald Munro also draws on Wilson's work in his paper, with which, however, Bloom finds reason to disagree on several points. More will be said on this below; what is critical, for Bloom, is that neither biology nor culture alone captures fully Mencius' "dynamic" view of human nature. Moral failure poses a serious challenge, and the *Mencius* gives full attention to it; but, Bloom maintains, this does not undermine the Mencian faith in a common human nature that aspires to full ethical attainments.

The Mencian view of human nature can hardly be understood without reference to Mencius' debate with Gaozi. The debate centers on the sources of morality, whether *ren* 仁 (benevolence or humanity) and *yi* 義 (rightness) are "internal" (*nei* 內) or "external" (*wai* 外). It is often asserted that although Mencius agrees with Gaozi that *ren* is "internal," he disagrees that *yi* is "external." Kim-Chong Chong challenges this widely held interpretation. Rather, according to Chong, Mencius wishes to show that Gaozi's usage of "internal" and "external" betrays certain "sensory and appetitive assumptions," which when applied to *ren* and *yi* would lead to "absurd consequences." This reading, as Chong further asserts, affords a clearer picture of Mencius' moral psychology, which traces *xing* (nature) to the heart-mind (*xin*). Not limited to appetitive desire, the heart-mind harbors a deep "moral awareness" that renders possible the development of *ren*, *yi*, and other Confucian virtues.

Mencius' moral psychology also forms the focus of Antonio Cua's discussion. Specifically, the question of moral failure, which exerts pressure on the Mencian doctrine of the original goodness of human nature, provides an avenue to understanding Mencius' thought. Distinguishing between various types of moral failure, Cua compares Mencius with Xunzi 荀子 in order to reinforce a fundamental point—that human nature is an incipient potential whose development centers on *xin*, the heart-mind. The question of moral failure brings into sharp relief the importance of cultivating a "constant *xin*" (*hengxin* 恆心). This involves constant self-examination and crucially, according to Cua, the necessary material support, without which morality can hardly be expected to flourish. Equally important, Mencian ethics presupposes the exercise of *quan* 權, the judicious weighing of circumstances, which requires creativity and cannot be reduced to a rule-based ethics. The issues are complex, and although they have been raised in different contexts in Cua's earlier writings, they cohere here to provide a considered point of entry into Mencius' moral psychology. From a different perspective, as we shall see, the portrayal of ethical authority in the *Mencius* also comes under scrutiny in Robert Eno's essay.

A central theme in both the *Lunyu* and the *Mencius* concerns the ability of the ethically accomplished person to "understand words" (*zhiyan* 知言). *Yan* 言 has been taken to mean "doctrines." This may describe aptly Gaozi's position, but as Jiuan Heng argues, it misses an important point in the *Mencius*. *Yan* (words and speech) expresses a person's *zhi* 志, the aims and direction of the heart-mind. In a political context, "knowing words" (*zhiyan*) becomes a way of "knowing men" (*zhiren* 知人); insight into a person's inner-most orientation of mind enables a statesman to recognize and employ men of moral worth and ability. At a deeper level, Heng suggests, the Mencian conception of the self rests on a prior distinc-tion between an "inner" ethical resource and its "outer" manifesta-tion. This recalls Kim-Chong Chong's discussion of *nei* and *wai* in Mencius. Heng takes the argument one step further, however. The logic of self-manifestation bears directly on self-cultivation, for when one judges the words and speech of another, one's own ethical re-sources are also put to the test. In the final analysis, understanding aims at self-understanding; *zhiyan,* in this sense, reflects ethical at-tainment.

Sor-Hoon Tan addresses a contentious sociopolitical concern in Chinese thought: what happens when one's allegiance to the family conflicts with one's obligations to society? Does Confucian ethics amount to a kind of "familism" that favors the family at the expense of social justice and equality? It is true that the family occu-pies a privileged position in Confucian ethics. The *Mencius* under-lines the importance of filial piety and sharply criticizes the Mohist doctrine of equal concern or love for all. Yet, as Tan argues, this must not be confused with a rigid authoritarian misappropriation of Confucian familism designed to serve particular political ends. The Confucian conception of familial relations is dynamic—defined by *ren* 仁, the relational network secures stability at the center and reaches out to a larger, ever growing group that includes non-kin. Tensions do arise; but as Tan's examples from a number of Confu-cian classics and dynastic histories illustrate, the point remains that Confucianism holds sufficient resources to negotiate the conflicts between state and family. Tan's discussion is not restricted to the *Mencius,* but the issues it raises are certainly important to an under-standing of the Mencian enterprise. In the contemporary context, the importance of familial relations continues to inform Confucian sensibilities; nevertheless, as Tan argues, the changing circum-stances of modernity render renegotiating one's relations to pre-serve an entire network an urgent undertaking.

The studies outlined above by and large assume a high de-gree of coherence in the present *Mencius.* They also focus on the ethical "core" of Mencius' teachings. Yet, as Robert Eno points out, much of the *Mencius* seems concerned not with philosophical coher-ence but rather with the "character of ethical authority." As a compilation, the *Mencius* aims primarily at presenting a portrait of Mencius the "great man," whose exemplary responses to ethically challenging circumstances provide a model and focus for ethical development. The text highlights Mencius' "casuistic" approach to ethical issues, case-specific and context-sensitive, which cannot be limited by rules. Indeed, far from being "inconsistent," departure from established moral rules testifies to the sage's ability to weigh circumstances and come up with a judicious response appropriate to the situation. Eno distinguishes different types of "casuistry" in the *Mencius* and forces the reader to confront passages that are often neglected because they do not address or cohere with the perceived doctrinal core of the text.

The question of coherence invites a different mode of interrogation. If certain "inconsistencies" such as the portrayal of the legendary figure Yi Yin 伊尹 cannot be explained, then the assumed coherence, or unity, of the work may be questioned. Bruce Brooks and Taeko Brooks, fresh from their groundbreaking and controversial research on the authenticity and structure of the *Lunyu*, propose an accretional model for the composition of the *Mencius*. Judging from the reception of *The Original Analects* (New York: Columbia University Press, 1998), their effort here would undoubtedly bring further excitement to the field.

The views of the historical Mencius have, according to Brooks and Brooks, been preserved in a series of interviews in Book 1. *Mencius* 2A2 also affords a rare glimpse of the Master's original teachings. The rest of the book contains several layers of material added to the original "transcripts"; they reflect the involvement of not one but two Mencian schools in contributing to the formation of the *Mencius* until the conquest of the state of Lu in 249 B.C.E. The detailed argument rewards careful reading. Besides explaining the apparent textual inconsistencies, the theory also provides an account of the ideas of the historical Mencius, which are closely allied with those preserved in Books 12 and 13 of the *Lunyu* and relate primarily to economic issues. The later material reflects the gradual loss of "rural mobility" and the tightening "autocratic" political structure in the Warring States. Does this mean that the more "philosophical" analysis of nature and the heart-mind comes from the "successor Mencians"? One of the most tantalizing suggestions is that whereas the "earlier" material seems to support a view of human nature that is endowed, the "later" material in Book 7 sees *xing* as an achievement concept. The implications of the Brookses' historical-critical reconstruction are far-reaching.

Alleged inconsistencies, however, may be viewed in other ways. While Brooks and Brooks argue that *Mencius* 3B9 and 4B21 offer two distinct accounts of Confucius' writing of the *Chunqiu* (Spring and Autumn Annals), David Nivison sees them as indicative of Mencius' "critical" approach to history. The figure of Yi Yin, in contrast, is presented in a more "speculative" light, in the sense that the view of history taken by Mencius is shaped by his larger philosophical vision, especially his belief in kingship as endowed by Heaven (*tian*) and his aversion to military force. Indeed, as Nivison succinctly puts it, "Mengzi's views are implications of his moral psychology."

To understand how Mencius understood the past, one needs to consider the different accounts of ancient history that were available to him and how he navigated through them. This is what Nivison attempts to do, contrasting Mencius' historical "speculations" with such sources as the *Zuozhuan* 左傳 and especially the *Bamboo Annals* (*Zhushu jinian* 竹書紀年). The chronology of the "Three Dynasties," the idea that a "true king" arises every five hundred years, and the treatment of the paradigmatic figures of Yao 堯, Shun 舜, Yi Yin, and King Wu 武 of Zhou provide important clues to reconstructing Mencius' philosophy of history. Although Mencius may have departed from the available accounts in many instances, it does not necessarily follow that he was deliberately fabricating or manipulating history, as it were, to score philosophical points. Different narratives competed for attention and served to legitimize events of the present. Mencius participated in the process of "idealization" of history and gave what to him was the "true" account. Political developments in the second half of the fourth century B.C.E., especially the declaration of kingship by rulers in several states, probably played an important role in crystallizing in Mencius' mind both the need to present the "correct" version and what that version is. Nivison's discussion, rich in details, presupposes some background in ancient Chinese history and may be read profitably with D. C. Lau's "Ancient History as Understood by Mencius," which is appended to his translation (appendix 4).

The reception of the *Mencius* marks an important topic in the study of Chinese intellectual history and is of critical interest to interpreters of the work today. As mentioned, Zhao Qi's commentary provides a valuable historical and hermeneutical guide. According to Zhao Qi, Emperor Wen (r. 180–157 B.C.E.) of Han appointed official scholars, or "academicians" (*boshi* 博士), to teach the *Lunyu,* the *Xiaojing,* and the *Mencius.*[13] The *Mencius,* however, was not recognized as a canonical classic at this time. It is perhaps ironic that when Confucianism triumphed over the other schools during the reign of Han Wudi (r. 141–87 B.C.E.), the post of *boshi* for the *Mencius* was dropped. According to the Qing commentator Jiao Xun, this would have taken place in 136 B.C.E., when Wudi established academicians solely for the "Five Classics."[14] Nevertheless, philosophers throughout the Han period commonly cited the *Mencius.* It may be true that the *Xunzi* exerted a strong influence on Han Confucian scholars, but it does not follow that the *Mencius* was therefore neglected.

During the Tang dynasty, thanks to the efforts of Han Yu 韓愈 (768–824 C.E.) and others, Mencius was gradually recognized as the "true" successor of Confucius. At the beginning of the Song period, stelae were made for "eleven classics," including the *Mencius.*[15] Thus, even before Zhu Xi and the establishment of the "Four Books," the *Mencius* had already attained its canonical status as a classic of Confucianism. The commentary by Zhu Xi, however, plays an important role in this development, for it established not only that the *Mencius* should be read but also how it should be read. This is not the place to discuss Zhu Xi's philosophy and its development; suffice it to say that the Neo-Confucian emphasis on *li* 理 (pattern or principle) and its apparent distrust of *qi,* from which desires are seen to derive, provided an agenda for later interpreters of the *Mencius.* Zhu Xi's own view of *li* and *qi* is a separate issue. By the time of Dai Zhen in the Qing period, it is nonetheless clear that approaches to the *Mencius* must pass through the portals of Cheng-Zhu Neo-Confucianism. Thus, Dai Zhen's influential work, the *Mengzi ziyi shuzheng,* is as much a reading of the *Mencius* as a confrontation of the Cheng-Zhu Neo-Confucian orthodoxy.[16] This serves as a background to Kwong-Loi Shun's study of Dai Zhen.

In defending Mencius' view that human nature is good and that rightness (*yi*) is internal, Dai Zhen criticizes Xunzi. Yet, as Shun shows, Dai Zhen seems to be "guided by two ideas that are more characteristic of Xunzi's rather than Mencius' thinking." These ideas concern the concepts of *qing* 情 and *yu* 欲 (desire), and the role of "understanding" (*zhi* 知) in Confucian self-cultivation. For Dai Zhen, following the Principle of Heaven (*tianli* 天理) means not the suppression or elimination of desire but rather the appropriate attainment or proper balance of *qing* and *yu*. This seems to agree more with Xunzi's understanding of the Confucian Way, which relies on ritual propriety to regulate and thus satisfy in due measure basic human desires.

In contrast, Mencius seems to take the heart-mind as having an inherent ethical direction, which ideally commands the "lesser parts," or biological desires, of a person. Moreover, Dai Zhen regards reflective understanding (*zhi* 知) to be crucial to removing "becloudedness" of the mind, which leads to excessive desire, and to guiding behavior. This, according to Shun, is again closer to Xunzi's conception of the heart-mind and self-cultivation than to Mencius'. Although its main concern is to present Dai Zhen's interpretation of Mencius, Shun's analysis also provides a useful discussion on the meanings of some of the most important concepts in Confucian philosophy.

In the last essay of the volume, Donald Munro assesses the continued relevance of Mencian ethics. The normative significance of the *Mencius* for the Chinese and other communities should be recognized, but its value will be affected by advances in knowledge and globalization. In the twenty-first century, Munro argues, no ethical theory could afford to ignore the contribution of sociobiology and evolutionary psychology. The Mencian account of human nature, in fact, gains support from sociobiological research. This eliminates any "essentialist" residue from an outmoded metaphysics and places the Mencian theory on the path of evolutionary biology and psychology. The use of empirical argument in the *Mencius* also puts it in a favorable position as ethics adopts the methods of science. Further, the Mencian emphasis on the moral import of the emotions, the recognition that kinship bonds are primary, and the analysis of the heart-mind as an "evaluative process" would all contribute to the enduring appeal of the *Mencius*.

Munro's argument recalls Ames' eschewal of "essentialism" and Bloom's reformulation of Mencian human nature. Indeed, the three papers may well be placed together; I have decided against it principally because Munro also raises other general issues in the study of Mencius. Both Bloom and Munro, as mentioned, find a

rich store of insights in the sociobiological research of E. O. Wilson.
For Bloom, however, Munro seems to have tipped the scale in favor
of "biology" at the expense of "culture." This requires adjudication:
does Munro neglect the "developmental" aspect of Mencius' view of
human nature? The larger question, of course, remains Mencius'
conception of human nature itself. According to Munro, furthermore, the *Mencius* does not take into sufficient account the distinction between "in-group" and "out-group," which affects behavior.
This bears on Sor-Hoon Tan's thesis, which credits Confucian ethics
more charitably with a dynamic view of familism. Munro's contribution will fuel debate on yet another front. The religious dimension
of Mencius' thought, as Munro throws down the gauntlet, would not
be a relevant part of the Mencian heritage in the new century. One
may question whether predictions of the death of "Heaven" are perhaps premature. Even if a theistic interpretation were deemed irrelevant, which is itself a debatable proposition, the Neo-Confucian interpretation of *tian* as "principle" (*li*) may be able to preserve a
measure of spirituality as the *Mencius* and Confucian philosophy in
general engage new generations of readers. These questions render
Munro's wide-ranging reflections a fitting finish to a volume that
aims not at closing debates but rather at investigating anew both
contexts and interpretations of the *Mencius*.

The *Mencius* is richly difficult. Intersecting at many points, the
essays presented here agree that the *Mencius* resists facile generalization. They offer no expedient consensus but rather intensify
the debate about its context and interpretation. The concept of
human nature (*xing*) likely will continue to dominate discussion, but
it must now be viewed with sharper conceptual and historical focus.
Mencius arrived on the Chinese philosophical scene when *xing* already formed a focal point for debate among Mohists, Confucians,
and other Warring States philosophers. Ning Chen's reading of the
Mozi and the Guodian material may be disputed, but it establishes
clearly the need to recover the ideological background of Mencian
discourse. Similarly, the concepts of *qi* and *qing* demand close inspec-
tion. What role does vital energy (*qi*) play in Mencian ethics? Does
qing refer to the emotions, to the "essence" of a thing (that which
makes it what it is), or to both? According to Kwong-Loi Shun, "there
is little evidence that the *Mencius* uses '*qing*' to refer to feelings, or
emotions." Given the etymological and conceptual link between na-

ture (*xing*) and life (*sheng* 生), any study of the *Mencius* cannot but be concerned with its understanding—both constitutive and functional—of the "self" and how that understanding compares with the views of other Warring States sources. The operation of *qi* and *qing* highlights the centrality of the heart or heart-mind (*xin*), which seems to rule out any bifurcation of mind and body in the Cartesian manner. The "evaluative" heart is characterized by a fundamental "moral awareness" (Chong) and constantly engages in ethical judgment, piercing through "becloudedness," weighing circumstances to find the right response, and in so doing enabling the four "germs" (*siduan* 四端) of virtue to flourish (Cua, Shun, Munro). This in turn brings to the fore the expression of "will" (*zhi* 志) and "speech" (*yan*). In this context, it may be asked, as Bloom does, whether the sociobiological and social constructivist perspectives cannot be brought closer together to yield an integral account of Mencian moral psychology.

These remarks serve to identify one conceptual cluster that invites further analysis; they do not make light of the differences in interpretation that emerge from these studies. For example, while Eno seems to support the view that Mencian ethics is a form of "intuitionism," Cua explicitly denies it, notwithstanding their agreement concerning, in Eno's words, the "rule-free character of moral perfection." Chong's view of the "internal" workings of the heart, rising above the sensory or appetitive, crosses paths but ultimately parts company with Heng's analysis of the inner and the outer in Mencius. The studies by Eno, Brooks and Brooks, and Nivison converge on several issues—for example, the treatment of Yi Yin and the sage-king Shun—but reach very different conclusions. For Nivison, the evidence suggests that Mencius was responding to real and pressing events as he articulated his views on ancient history. In Eno's interpretation, the *Mencius* does not deliver a body of coherent and systematically worked-out ethical doctrines; rather, it aims to showcase the sagelike character and ethical authority of Mencius. Inconsistencies, rhetorical flourishes, and seemingly indefensible arguments have their role to play in the light of this larger textual design. For the Brookses, these same passages attest rather to the absence of a single or uniform "authorial intent"; the different layers of material must be carefully distinguished before the *Mencius* can be understood.

By any standard, the *Mencius* is a rare achievement. It opens up a world in which human beings struggle to make sense of fast-changing circumstances, mend relationships, and seek to reclaim a measure of dignity and purpose. I have no doubt that the *Mencius* will continue to attract scholarly interest and act as a source of inspiration for both Asian and Western readers, whether or not it is seen to accord with the latest scientific findings. The only point that needs to be emphasized is that both contexts and interpretations are important to understanding. To do justice to the *Mencius,* one must pay careful attention to its background, discern its ideological rivals, ascertain its textual design, determine its composite nature, explain its key concepts, and show how these concepts such as *xing, xin,* and self-cultivation contribute to a coherent philosophical venture. Regardless of the position one takes, students of the *Mencius* would do well to encourage and bring together diverse historical and conceptual approaches. Even in revisiting familiar ground, it may yet be possible to gain new insights or greater depth in understanding.

In bringing this collection of essays to press, I considered it important to respect the authors' wishes in matters of translation and transliteration. Thus, while generally *hanyu pinyin* is preferred, the paper by Brooks and Brooks uses a different romanization system, complete with tonal marks, which the authors believe would facilitate pronunciation of Chinese terms for Western readers. However, in case it may prove useful, I have added in parentheses the *hanyu pinyin* equivalent when a term is first introduced. The Brookses' paper also adopts a different system of representing dates, without using the notations C.E. and B.C.E. as in the other essays. I retain the name "Mencius" for convenience, although some authors favor the Chinese, Mengzi. The same goes for "Confucius," "Confucian," "Mencian," "Confucianism," and other labels. Similarly, no editorial imposition has been made on translation of Chinese terms. Although different translations for the same term in different essays —for example, "heart," "heart-mind," or "mind" for *xin*—might not be conducive to easy reading, they reflect an academic judgment and as such should be put forward for criticism and debate. All authors, however, agree that if translations are deemed inadequate and transliterations are to be preferred, an explanation of the Chinese terms must be clearly given.

Notes

1. The great Neo-Confucian scholar Zhu Xi 朱熹 (1130–1200) established the "Four Books"—*Lunyu* 論語, *Mengzi* 孟子, *Daxue* 大學, and *Zhongyong* 中庸—as the new canon of Confucian learning, rivaling the older "Five Classics." From 1313 to 1905, with the rise of the Cheng-Zhu—i.e., Cheng Yi 程頤 (1033–1107) and Zhu Xi—school of Neo-Confucianism as the state orthodoxy, the "Four Books" together with Zhu Xi's commentaries formed a mainstay of the civil service examinations. For this development, see, for example, Liu Ts'un-yan, "Chu Hsi's Influence in Yuan Times," in *Chu Hsi and Neo-Confucianism,* ed. Wing-tsit Chan (Honolulu: University of Hawai'i Press, 1986), 521–550.

2. James Legge, *The Works of Mencius,* vol. 2 of *The Chinese Classics* (Oxford: Clarendon Press, 1895; reprint, New York: Dover Publications, 1970). W. A. C. H. Dobson, *Mencius* (Toronto: University of Toronto Press, 1963). D. C. Lau, *Mencius* (Harmondsworth: Penguin Books, 1970); references to Lau's translation are to the two-volume edition with the Chinese text published in 1984 (Hong Kong: Chinese University of Hong Kong Press). See also D. C. Lau, "Meng tzu," in *Early Chinese Texts: A Bibliographical Guide,* ed. Michael Loewe (Berkeley, Calif.: The Society for the Study of Early China, 1993), 333–334, for a list of translations in English, French, and German. In Chinese, the critical annotated edition by Yang Bojun 楊伯峻, *Mengzi yizhu* 孟子譯注 (Beijing: Zhonghua shuju, 1984), is invaluable.

3. Fung Yu-lan, *A History of Chinese Philosophy,* vol. 1, trans. Derk Bodde (Princeton, N.J.: Princeton University Press, 1952; reprint, 1983). Benjamin Schwartz, *The World of Thought in Ancient China* (Cambridge: Harvard University Press, 1985). A. C. Graham, "The Background of the Mencian Theory of Human Nature," in his *Studies in Chinese Philosophy and Philosophical Literature* (Singapore: Institute of East Asian Philosophies, 1986; reprint, Albany: State University of New York Press, 1990), 7–66. David S. Nivison, *The Ways of Confucianism,* ed. Bryan Van Norden (La Salle, Ill.: Open Court, 1996). This list is neither exhaustive nor exclusive. All works on early Chinese philosophy would include a discussion of Mencius and have their contribution to make. For example, see Arthur Waley, *Three Ways of Thought in Ancient China* (London: George Allen and Unwin, 1939; reprint, Stanford, Calif.: Stanford University Press, 1982); Donald Munro, *The Concept of Man in Early China* (Stanford, Calif.: Stanford University Press, 1969); and Chad Hansen, *A Daoist Theory of Chinese Thought* (New York: Oxford University Press, 1992). See also the next note.

4. Kwong-Loi Shun, *Mencius and Early Chinese Thought* (Stanford, Calif.: Stanford University Press, 1997). Special mention should also be made of I. A. Richards, *Mencius on the Mind: Experiments in Multiple Definition* (London: Routledge and Kegan Paul, 1932); P. J. Ivanhoe, *Ethics in the Confucian Tradition: The Thought of Mencius and Wang Yang-ming* (Atlanta: Scholars Press, 1990); and Lee Yearley, *Mencius and Aquinas: Theories of Virtue and Conceptions of Courage* (Albany: State University of New York Press, 1990). There is no lack of journal articles on the *Mencius*; for example, see the bibliography in Shun's book and the essays collected here.

5. *Shiji, juan* 74.1b, Sibubeiyao ed. (Taipei: Zhonghua shuju, 1970). The Tang 唐 "dynasty" is traditionally associated with the sage-king Yao 堯, and Yu 虞 with Shun 舜. On Mencius' view of ancient Chinese history, see Lau, *Mencius,* app. 4, "Ancient History as Understood by Mencius," and David S. Nivison's discussion in this volume.

6. *Shiji, juan* 74.1b; an English translation is available in Lau, *Mencius,* app. 1, "The Dating of Events in the Life of Mencius," 309.

7. On this question, see, for example, James Legge, *The Works of Mencius,* 9–13; and Lau, *Mencius,* app. 3, "The Text of the *Mencius,*" 321. Yang Bojun, *Mengzi yizhu,* 4–7, summarizes concisely the views of traditional Chinese scholars on the authorship of the *Mencius.*

8. *Hanshu, juan* 30 (Beijing: Zhonghua shuju, 1983), 6.1725.

9. Lau, *Mencius,* 322–323. The Later Han work *Fengsu tongyi* 風俗通義, by Ying Shao 應劭, also refers to the "outer" documents; see Wang Liqi 王利器, ed., *Fengsu tongyi jiaozhu* (reprint, Taipei: Mingwen shuju, 1988), 319. A couple of Song dynasty sources give the impression that the "outer" documents were still extant at that time, but most scholars doubt whether these sources reflect a real knowledge of the documents. The current "Outer Writings of Mencius" (*Mengzi waishu*), compiled during the Ming period, is generally reckoned a forgery. See also Yang Bojun, *Mengzi yizhu,* 7–8.

10. Qian Mu, *Xian Qin zhuzi xinian* 先秦諸子繫年 (Taipei: Dongda tushu, 1986; orig., 1935; rev. and enl., 1956), 187–188, 617.

11. *Guodian Chumu zhujian* 郭店楚墓竹簡 (Beijing: Wenwu, 1998), 141.

12. *Hanshu,* 6.1724. The *Hanshu* entry indicates that Zisi was a "teacher" of Duke Mu of Lu. Traditional Chinese bibliographic sources up to the Song dynasty record a *Zisi* in 7 fascicles (*juan* 卷), but the work has not survived. Other fragments from the Guodian corpus may also be associated with Zisi. On these texts and how they may relate to the *Liji* 禮記 (Book of Rites) chapters that are traditionally ascribed to Zisi, see the relevant essays in *Zhongguo zhexue* 中國哲學 20 (1999), which is devoted to the Guodian find. Another collection of essays given entirely to the Guodian texts, which appeared only after the present manuscript had been completed and submitted for publication, is *Guodian Chujian guoji xueshu yantaohui lunwenji* 郭店楚簡國際學術研討會論文集, special issue of the *Renwen luncong* 人文論叢 (Humanities Journal), ed. Wuhan Daxue Zhongguo Wenhua Yanjiushuo (Hubei: Hubei renmin, 2000).

13. Zhao Qi made the comment in the "Preface" (*Mengzi tici* 孟子題辭) to his commentary.

14. Jiao Xun, *Mengzi zhengyi* (Taipei: Shijie shuju, 1966), 1.10, commenting on Zhao Qi's "Preface."

15. Jiang Boqian 蔣伯潛, *Shisanjing gailun* 十三經概論 (Shanghai: Shanghai guji chubanshe, 1983), 612–613.

16. Ann-ping Chin discusses "Tai Chen's [Dai Zhen] Life and Times" and his thought in *Tai Chen on Mencius: Explorations in Words and Meaning,* trans. Ann-ping Chin and Mansfield Freeman (New Haven, Conn.: Yale University Press, 1990).

1

The Ideological Background of the Mencian Discussion of Human Nature
A Reexamination

NING CHEN

THE BACKGROUND to the Mencian discussion of human nature (*xing* 性) has been the subject of considerable scholarly attention because it helps explain the central Mencian argument that "human nature is good." A study of this background should take into account at least the following concerns. How many views of *xing* had been advanced before Mencius joined the debate? To what extent are they similar to or different from Mencius' own conception of *xing*? Which of these views presents the greatest challenge to him, and why? Not all of these questions have been satisfactorily answered in the relevant literature, though there have been significant contributions. For instance, thanks to A. C. Graham and Irene Bloom, attention has been drawn to the fact that Mencius wrestled with the Yangists, Mohists, Legalists, and Legalist-leaning rulers.[1] Of particular importance to an understanding of Mencius' view is the Mohist conception of *xing*, on which, however, there is little consensus among scholars. It is described as a "narrow biologism" by Bloom and a "neutralism" by Wu Yujiang, but these labels misconstrue the Mohist view for reasons that I will identify and address here.[2]

A second and more important reason provokes this reexamination. In 1993 a large number of bamboo slip texts were excavated from a Chu tomb at Guodian, Jingmen. The tomb is generally dated sometime between the late fourth century and the early third century B.C.E. These bamboo slips, assigned the title *Guodian Chumu zhujian*, are copies of ancient writings, including the *Laozi* and

17

treatises in the tradition of early Confucian moral government and cultivation. Some scholars believe that these Confucian works were closely associated with the *Liji* 禮記, because they display similarity in content, argument, and wording.[3] Photographs of these bamboo texts, with preliminary annotations, became available in 1998 and have generated intense interest among scholars of early Chinese thought.[4]

Among the Confucian texts in this collection, three address the subject of human nature. It is discussed at great length in the *Xing zi ming chu* 性自命出; one passage in the *Cheng zhi wen zhi* 成之聞之 and some of the fragments in the *Yucong er* 語叢二 also refer to it. It is not clear whether these three texts were composed by the same author.[5] As far as the subject matter is concerned, the three texts display a considerable degree of contextual and theoretical coherence, though they seem to be somewhat different in handwriting. *Xing* is spoken of in terms of "emotions" (*qing* 情) and is seen as shared by all, being morally ambivalent (possessing both good and bad elements), and having dimensions that are both normative and factual, as well as being both incipient and accomplished. The Guodian bamboo texts were probably available to Mencius and offer fresh insight into the ideological background of the Mencian discussion of human nature.[6]

Inegalitarian Conceptions of *Xing*

We begin with the question of the Mohist conception of human nature. A survey of the standard literature on *xing* by such great scholars as Fu Sinian, Xu Fuguan, Tang Junyi, Mou Zongsan, and Mori Mikisaburo reveals little.[7] They have all overlooked an important passage in the *Mozi;* or more precisely, they did not take the word *xing* found in that passage to mean "nature." They may have been influenced, in this regard, by Sun Yirang, a renowned annotator of the *Mozi* during the late Qing period, who suggested that the word *xing* should be read as *wei* 惟. Sun's own explanation does not throw much light on the text; indeed he acknowledges that difficulties remain even with his interpretation.[8] This controversial passage and my English translation, based largely on Wu Yujiang's annotation, are given below.

> 為暴人語天之為是也而性為暴人,歌天之為非也.諸陳執既有所為,而我為之,陳執執之所為,因吾所為也.若陳執未有所為,而我為之陳執,陳執因吾所為也.暴人為我,為天之以人非為是也,而性不可正而正之.[9]

To say on behalf of evil people that "being evil is determined by Heaven and so it is their nature to be evil," is to say that what Heaven does is wrong.[10] (If) it is held that these *chenzhi* have impact (on our conduct), and yet I can act (voluntarily), then the effects of the *chenzhi* are subject to my decision.[11] If it is held that they make no impact at all and that I can create them, then it can be said that the *chenzhi* are (still) subject to my decision. Evil people act for their own sake, but what Heaven has imparted to humans is not so.[12] Nature, though seemingly incorrigible, can be set aright anyway.

A.C. Graham has provided a close reading of this passage, but his interpretation differs so significantly from mine that I feel it is necessary to defend my position at some length. Following some traditional Chinese annotators, Graham takes *tian zhi* 天之 to mean *tianzhi* 天志 (the Will of Heaven), one of Mozi's fundamental doctrines.[13] He further argues that the moral Mohists were thus facing a metaphysical challenge: "To expound as a canon the Will of Heaven merely encourages the selfish man to indulge his natural egoism."[14]

As I understand it, *tian zhi* has nothing to do with the "Will of Heaven"; nor were the Mohists caught in a dilemma between the doctrine of Will of Heaven and that of a fixed nature of human beings. The Mohist recognition of human voluntarism, which is also emphasized elsewhere in the *Mozi,* may be compared to the Western concept of "free will." Arthur Waley was probably the first to point out that in the *Mozi* "we find the doctrine of Free Will."[15] Clearly articulated in the "Will of Heaven" chapter in the *Mozi* is the idea of man's power to choose his course of action and of a reciprocal relationship between Heaven and human beings in terms of reward and punishment. The *Mozi* states, "If I do what Heaven desires me to, Heaven will do what I desire," and "If I do what Heaven does not desire, then Heaven will do what I do not desire."[16]

Returning to the *Mozi* passage under discussion, Graham reads the words *shi* 是 and *fei* 非 in the sense of "right" and "wrong."[17] This explanation and its concomitant punctuation would, however, fail to make sense of the statement on human free will that follows immediately.[18] It is more reasonable to interpret the first *shi* in the way Wu Yujiang does, as a pronoun referring to the act of doing evil things.[19] The second *shi* plays the same grammatical role, referring to doing things for the sake of oneself. Therefore, here *shi* and *fei* are not used as two antithetical terms.[20] Graham's interpretation misses the Mohist conception of nature as being alterable, which comes out clearly in the assertion *xing bu ke zheng er zheng zhi* 性不可

正而正之. To be consistent, Graham punctuated the phrase as *xing bu ke zheng* ("His nature is incorrigible" in his translation), hence not only placing *er zheng zhi* ("can be set aright anyway" in my translation) inappropriately at the beginning of the succeeding sentence but also incorrectly denying the conception of alterable nature held by the Mohists. There is no doubt that the whole sentence ends with the phrase *er zheng zhi*, which carries the real argument of the Mohists.

Because Graham regards the Mohist view of nature as incorrigible, he perceives a metaphysical challenge confronting the Mohists. The Mohists may have believed that certain people are endowed with an evil nature at birth by Heaven, but the evil nature can be altered, and that the decision to change, which is also endowed by Heaven, lies with the individuals concerned. Like everyone else, such individuals have been given an evaluating and prioritizing mind, or free will, to control their conduct. For the Mohists, it is our ability to exercise moral judgment and control over our actions, perhaps against the inclination of inborn nature, that enables us to follow Heaven's will to become morally good.

According to Wu Yujiang, the Mohist view of human nature is morally neutral, that is, it is neither good nor evil; but one can develop it into something good or evil at will in the same way that one dyes cloth. Wu's connecting of the metaphor of dyeing cloth to human nature is based on his treatment of the word *xing* as "nature," which appears in the sentence *xing li xing yu ran dang* 行理性於染當 in the chapter "Suo ran."[21] However, judging from the context, *xing* in that passage is more reasonably taken to mean *sheng* 生 (to generate) as some traditional commentators have noted.[22] In addition, the Mohist assertion that nature "can be set aright" indicates pointedly that what is given to human beings is something already morally oriented.

From Irene Bloom's perspective, the Mohists seem to have perceived the problem of human nature as a "treacherous and intractable issue." This, as Bloom continues, is suggested by the idea that if the evil man "believes that egoism (*wei-wo*) is the Will of Heaven, his nature will be incorrigible." It seems clear that Bloom has adopted Graham's position, but she went further in ascribing this egoistic argument to the Mohists.[23] Consequently, Bloom regards the Mohist conception of nature as "narrow biological," a view shared by Gaozi, who bears the brunt of Mencius' attack.[24]

In all likelihood, the Mohist view of human nature greatly disturbed Mencius, for the Mohists appeared as one of the two major ideological rivals of the Confucians in Mencius' time. However, I would hesitate to follow Bloom in regarding the Mohist view as "narrow biological" and "incorrigible." The Mohists were opposing, rather than presenting, the assertion that nature, once it is given at birth, is impervious to one's will. *Xing* may be good or evil; but this "strong inegalitarianism," as Bloom calls it,[25] does not detract from the central Mohist argument that a person is responsible for his or her conduct. The emphasis on the changeability of nature suggests that, for the Mohists, the nature of human beings is evil in some and good in others; if the evil nature imparted to some people is set aright by their own effort, they can become morally good.

The point I would like to make is as follows. Bloom has perceptively suggested that our study of Mencius' argument on human nature should extend to an assessment of "what compelled him to argue."[26] One of the views of human nature that Mencius had to challenge came from the Mohists. The Mohist challenge is neither "narrow biologism" (Bloom) nor "neutralism" (Wu Yujiang); rather, it is "inegalitarianism," to adopt Bloom's term, which conflicts sharply with Mencius' fundamental convictions.[27]

An inegalitarian conception of *xing* was adopted not only by the Mohists, and those reported by Gongduzi in the *Mencius* (6A6), but also by many others in pre-Qin times. In the *Zuozhuan*, for instance, reference is made to the *xing* of mean persons.[28] Since the concept of a "mean person" (*xiaoren*) is formulated in contrast to that of a "gentleman" (*junzi*), it points to a dichotomy in the *xing* of human beings. Consider also the opening lines of the "Outer Chapters" in the *Zhuangzi:* "Two toes webbed together, a sixth finger forking off—these come from the inborn nature (*xing*) but are excretions as far as virtue (*de* 德) is concerned."[29] As Qian Mu has shown, here the word *xing* refers to the particularity of individuals while *de* is what all human beings share.[30] With the discovery of the Guodian texts, we now know that there were still others who spoke of this inegalitarianism in terms of "the *xing* of sages" and "the *xing* of the common people," which I will deal with shortly.

Against this background, we can understand better Mencius' argument for the universal similarity of innate human characteristics. However, as the Guodian texts show, Mencius was not the first one, much less the only one, to take issue with the inegalitarian argument. He might have been carrying on a task initiated by certain Confucians before him.

Egalitarian Conceptions of *Xing*

"In virtually every culture," as Bloom reminds us, "there is reflection about how human beings are alike and how they differ."[31] In pre-Qin China, it was the inegalitarian view supported by Mohists, Daoists, and other unidentified individuals that highlighted the dissimilarity in human nature. This drew a sharp response from the early Confucians, who championed an egalitarian view of *xing*.

This egalitarian doctrine is articulated in a passage in the *Cheng zhi wen zhi* of the Guodian texts. The following are my annotations and translation (the numbers in parentheses refer to the slip numbers of the bamboo manuscripts).[32]

> (26) 聖人之性與中人之性,其生而未有非之節於而(天)[33]也,(27)則猶[34] 是也.雖其於善道也,亦非有譯婁[35]以多也.及其博長而厚(28)大也,則 聖人不可由(容)與[36]罩(擅)[37]之.此以民皆有性而聖人不可慕也.

> The *xing* of the sage and the *xing* of the common people (literally "mid-ranked men") are with no exception determined at birth by Heaven, and they are equally the same. With respect to (carrying on) the moral Way, no one receives more of it (the *xing*) by means of *yilou*. When it (the *xing*) grows and extends to a large degree, even a sage cannot easily claim a monopoly of such an achievement. This is because all humans have *xing*, and the sage is not worthy of admiration.

The nature of the sages and that of the common people do not differ; the context conspicuously displays a rebuff to the kind of "inegalitarianism" that was rampant in pre-Qin times. Heaven does not favor the sage at birth, and thus there is no cause for envy. With an equal endowment of nature, everyone is capable of self-cultivation and has the potential to achieve the same moral attainments of the sage.

Interestingly, this egalitarianism is also echoed by Xunzi: "Thus, where the sage is identical to the common mass of men and does not exceed their characteristics, it is his inborn nature." Moreover, "as a general rule, the nature men share is one and the same whether they be a Yao and Shun or a Jie and Robber Zhi. The gentleman and the petty man share one and the same nature." Elsewhere, Xunzi states, "Heaven did not bestow any special favor on Zeng Shen, Fu Zijian or Filial Yi that it withheld from the common mass of men."[38] These statements strongly suggest that the *Cheng zhi wen zhi* had made an impact on Xunzi, who continued the battle against the inegalitarian view of *xing*.

Affirming the egalitarian view, the *Xing zi ming chu* says, "Within the four seas, we share one and the same nature" (slip 9). The Guodian material thus confirms that prior to Mencius, some Confucians had already taken upon themselves to assert the universal similarity of human nature. They must have been alarmed by the prevalence of the inegalitarian view.

This anti-inegalitarian thrust is continued by Mencius, who in one of his most famous arguments points to the heart-mind of sympathy or compassion that all human beings experience at the sight of a child about to fall into a well (2A6). It also informs his views on the universal human inclination to desire something more than one's own life (6A10), the impartiality of natural endowment from Heaven, the similarity in kind between the sage and ordinary human beings, and finally, the attraction of the mouth, the ears, and the eyes to certain things, which we all share (6A7).[39]

As is well known, for Confucius human beings are only "close" to one another by nature.[40] However, in their staunch adherence to the notion of a universally shared nature, the Guodian Confucians developed the master's view to a higher degree, constituting a tradition from which emerged the *Mencius* and the *Xunzi*.[41] Of great importance is that they all addressed the issue of a shared nature by emphasizing the innate equivalence between "the sage" and "the common people," as if to argue against someone who had used these terms as a basis for an argument supporting inegalitarianism.[42]

Xing as Morally Ambivalent

Our next question concerns whether the universally shared nature in the Guodian texts is good or evil, or some combination of the two. It is true that the opening lines of the *Xing zi ming chu* distinguish *xing* from *xin* (heart-mind) and place the former in a subordinate position to the latter with respect to moral cultivation. This seems to suggest a notion of nature as being uncivilized or even evil, but as I shall argue, this oversimplifies the case. Slips 9–14 of the *Xing zi ming chu* depict human nature as morally ambivalent, that is, containing both good and evil elements. In what follows, I offer a reading of certain characters on etymological and phonetic grounds and provide an English translation.

(9) 四海之內其性一也.其用心各異,教使然也.凡性(10) 或動之,或迖
(達)之,或交(矯)之,或厲之,或出之,或養之,或長之.凡動性(11) 者,物也;
迖(達) 性者,悦也; 交(矯) 性者,故也;厲性者,義也;出性者,埶(藝) 也;養
性(12) 者,習也;長性者,道也.

凡見者之謂物,快於己者之謂悦,物(13) 之埶(藝) 者之謂埶(藝),有為也
者之謂故.義也者,群善之絕也.習也(14) 者,又有以習其性也.道者,群物
之道.[43]

In this passage there are three characters that deserve special attention, namely, *da* 迖 and *jiao* 交 in slips 10 and 11, and *yi* 埶 in slips 11 and 13. Let us begin with the character *yi* 埶 It has been identified and transcribed as *shi* 勢 by the scholars who first studied the Guodian manuscripts. It can be better understood, however, as *yi* 蓺 or 藝, "to plant," "to cultivate," or "cultivation," because according to the *Jingji zuangu, yi* 藝 can be written as either 埶 or 蓺 in early texts.[44]

As for the character *da* 迖, I would hesitate to follow the annotators of the Guodian texts in recognizing it (with uncertainty) as *feng* 逢, which does not seem to agree with the context. An alternative is available: 迖 might be another form for the word *da* 達. In cases where a compound Chinese character is made up of two main parts, one for its meaning and the other for its phonetic value, it is not uncommon that the phonetic radical may take on different forms on the condition that they are homophonous or nearly so. In the case of the character *da* 達, its meaning is indicated by the radical *chuo* 辵, or 辶 in simplified form, pertaining to walking, and its phonetic radical is the graph 幸, which can be replaced by a couple of graphs, such as 大 and 隹. Therefore, the three characters 达, 迖, and 達 can be used interchangeably.[45] Since the graph 丯 belongs to the same *yue* rhyme group (月部) as do 大, 奎, and 隹, it very likely combines with 辶 to make up an alternative form for *da* 達.

To identify 迖 as 達 and hence its concomitant phrase 迖性 as *da xing* 達性 allows us to draw a parallel with *da sheng* 達生, which appears in the *Zhuangzi* and is a term favored by Daoists. However, *da xing* 達性 in the Guodian text might be used to mean "removing barriers from *xing*" or "making *xing* go smoothly," which is quite different from the Daoist sense of "mastering" *sheng*.[46] If so, the sentence in slip 11 *da xing zhe yue ye* 達性者悦也 should be rendered as "that which removes barriers from *xing* is happiness," or "that which makes *xing* goes smoothly is happiness."

   Turning to the character *jiao* 交, I would like to propose taking it as a loan graph for *jiao* 矯, for two reasons. First, both 交 and 矯 belong phonetically to the *jian* group of initial consonants (見母) and to the *xiao* rhyme group (宵部), which renders them suitable variants for each other under the rules of graph loaning in archaic Chinese. The second reason is that *jiao* 矯, with its explicit meaning of "to straighten" or "to set aright," is used by Xunzi to express the idea of altering human nature from evil to good. In his words, "In antiquity the sage kings took man's nature to be evil.... For this reason they invented ritual principles.... Through these actions they intended to 'straighten out' (*jiao* 矯) and develop man's essential nature and to set his inborn nature aright."[47] The similarity in expression between the author of the Guodian passage and Xunzi is striking. Just as the former describes the object that "straightens" human nature as "antique things" (*gu* 故), defined as "things of achievement" (*youwei* 有為, referring, later in slips 10–18, to such Confucian works as the *Book of Poetry*, the *Book of Documents,* the *Book of Rites,* and the *Book of Music*),[48] Xunzi regards ritual principles as having been created by the sage kings to set people's nature aright.

   With the etymological investigation presented above, the whole passage from the *Xing zi ming chu* can be translated as follows.

   Within the four seas, we share one and the same nature. The reason for the working of the heart-mind's differing from person to person lies in the fact that learning determines it to be so. Generally speaking, there is something that excites the nature, something that makes it go smoothly, something that straightens it, something that grinds it, something that pushes it out, something that nurtures it, and something that helps it to grow. What excites the nature are objects; what makes it go smoothly is happiness; what straightens it is something antique; what grinds it is rightness; what pushes it out is cultivation; what nurtures it is practice; what helps it to grow is the Way. What manifests itself is called "object"; what makes one joyful is called "happiness"; what has been cultivated among things is called the "cultivated"; what is of achievement is called the "antique"; "right-ness" is the most consummate among all that are good; "practice" is that which puts nature to practice; and the "Way" is the way of all things.

The seven verbs and their explications hint at an ambiguous conception of human nature. When nature is said to be "set aright" by such "antique" things as the Confucian classics, to be "ground" by "rightness," and to be "pushed out" by "cultivation," we seem to be presented with a very negative account of nature. Yet the same na-ture may become infused with morality, for it can be "nurtured" by effective practice and "helped to grow" by the Way. The implications of *dong* (to excite) and *da* (to go smoothly) are more difficult to de-cipher. Nevertheless, given that the author recognizes one universally shared nature, the language here points to a notion of human na-ture as being both good and evil.

This ambivalent conception is also spelled out in slips 39–41 of the *Xing zi ming chu*.

> (39) 仁,性之方也;性或生之.忠,信(40) 之方也;信,情之方也.情出於性.
> 愛類七,唯性愛為近仁.智類五,唯(41) 義道為近忠.惡類三,唯惡不仁為
> 近義.

> Benevolence is the orientation of *xing*, and it is perhaps engen-dered by *xing*. Conscientiousness is the orientation of sincerity, and sincerity is the orientation of *qing; qing* derives from *xing*. There are seven types of love, of which only the original love is close to benev-olence. There are five types of wisdom, of which only the way of rightness is close to conscientiousness. There are three types of dis-like, of which only the disliking of what is not benevolent is close to rightness.[49]

This passage alludes to several types of *qing* that are believed to have derived from *xing*. Although a detailed taxonomy is not available, it is clear that some types of emotions are contrary and detrimental to benevolence, conscientiousness, and rightness, form-ing part of a complex. In other words, the term *xing* appears to have a "binary" meaning.

In this respect, we see a remarkable similarity to the second view in Gongduzi's report in 6A6 and to Shi Shuo's proclamation quoted by Wang Chong (27–100 C.E.) in the *Lunheng*. Gongduzi's second view is as follows: "Human nature can become good or it can become bad, and that is why with the rise of King Wen and King

Wu, the people were given to goodness, while with the rise of King Yu and King Li, they were given to cruelty."[50] As Kwong-Loi Shun points out after a thorough analysis, this statement means that there are both good and evil in human nature.[51] Shi Shuo's argument reads, in Graham's translation, "Shi Shuo, a man of Zhou, thought that there is both good and bad in man's nature. If we pick out what is good in man's nature and by nourishing develop it, the good grows; if we nourish and develop the bad nature, the bad grows."[52] The two accounts regard human nature as binary and emphasize that education or nourishment is essential to its direction of development.

An immediate question can be asked: from the point of view of a binary nature, what is the ratio of goodness to nongoodness in our shared nature? This is important because it involves the attitude humans should take toward their inborn nature. Although nothing reveals this ratio in Gongduzi's report and Shi Shuo's statement, it is evident that the author of the *Xing zi ming chu* does not regard human nature as equally constituted by good and evil tendencies. Instead, he recognizes only a small part of endowed nature as good. The evidence is slight but unmistakable. There is only one kind of love out of seven, one kind of wisdom out of five, and one kind of dislike out of three that are considered close to goodness. As we shall see, the *Xing zi ming chu* makes a sharp distinction between the heart-mind and nature, which suggests a degree of conflict between the former's goodness and the latter's nongoodness. It is difficult to say whether the Guodian text is connected with the school of Shi Shuo or with the proponents of the view mentioned in Gongduzi's report to Mencius. But it certainly points to the prevalence of a conception of *xing* as morally ambivalent, with which Mencius had to take issue.

Against this background, we find Mencius defending the doctrine of shared nature and affirming that human nature is exclusively good. Even basic desires for food and sex as part of nature are justified. Irene Bloom has already argued convincingly that Mencius' view of human nature is fundamentally biological, a view "in which body and mind are not separated and in which the needs and potentialities of the entire human species are acknowledged."[53] Bloom cites examples from passages in 1A and 2A, where Mencius discusses the relation between constant means of material support made available by a humane ruler and the possession of a "constant mind" on the part of the common people.[54] While in full agreement with her, I think several passages from 1B offer a better illustration, where Mencius justifies the ruler's enjoyment, on the condition that he let the common people take joy together with him, in music (1B1), beauty (1B5), the Snow Palace (1B4), and, by extension, physical ease. These correspond in part to the five human biological dispositions forming part of *xing* as delineated in 7B24.

Xing as the Emotions

Most pre-Qin philosophical works discuss the concept of *xing* in connection with that of *qing*, and the Guodian Confucian texts are no exception. It is generally acknowledged that the meaning of *qing* in pre-Qin literature varies considerably and can be determined only by context. Kwong-Loi Shun has observed that the word *qing* in the *Mencius* refers to either "what is genuine" or *xing*, rather than to "emotions."[55] However, *qing* seems to be used in the sense of emotions in the Guodian texts, for many a time it refers to happiness, anger, sorrow, love, hatred, like, dislike, and so on.[56] This point comes out clearly in the following passage from the *Xing zi ming chu*.[57]

> (1) 凡人雖有性,心無定志,待物而後作,待悦而後行,待習而後(2)定.喜怒哀悲之氣,性也.... 性自命出,命(3)自天降.道始於情,情生於性.始者近情,終者近義.知□□□(4)出之,知義者能納之.好惡,性也.所好所惡,物也.善不□□□(5)所善所不善,埶(藝)也.凡性為主,物取之也.金石之有聲,□□□(6)□□□雖有性,心弗取不出.

> Every human being has *xing*, but since the direction of the heart-mind is subject to change, one starts (doing things) only after having been excited by objects, takes action only after having become pleased, and reaches a fixed personality (mind-heart) only after having practiced. The *qi* of joy, anger, sorrow, and grief is *xing*.... *Xing* comes from *ming*, and *ming* descends from Heaven. The Way begins with *qing*, and *qing* is engendered by *xing*. The beginning is close to *qing*, and the end is close to rightness. (Those who) understand (*qing* are able to)[58] push it out, and those who understand rightness are able to take it in. Like and dislike are matters of *xing*. What is liked and what is disliked are material things. Being good or not being (good has to do with the heart-mind).[59] What is regarded as good and what is regarded as not good are due to cultivation. Whenever one acts under the sway of *xing*, one is controlled by material

things. Bronze and stone musical instruments produce sound (but they do so only when struck by a stick).[60] Though anyone possesses *xing*, no one should let (it) manifest itself in the absence of decision from *xin*.

This passage begins with a distinction between the unlearned nature and the learned heart-mind, with the latter being more important in controlling one's conduct, which reminds us of the notion of "free will" advocated by the Mohists. The passage proceeds to discuss the origin and constitution of *xing* in relation to *qing*. Especially noteworthy is that "emotions" (*qing*) are said to constitute fundamentally what is bestowed on humans as their *xing*.

Yet the relation between emotions and nature seems ambiguous in that emotions are equated with nature in one statement and described as its product in another. The latter proposition is again affirmed in slip 40, quoted earlier: "*qing* comes from *xing*." It also appears in many fragments of the *Yucong er,* where various emotions such as "love" (*ai* 愛), "desire" (*yu* 欲), "mercy" (*ci* 慈), "dislike" (*wu* 惡), "happiness" (*xi* 喜), "resentment" (*yun* 慍), and "fear" (*ju* 懼) are said to have been "engendered by *xing*" (*sheng yu xing* 生於性).[61] All these characters can be written with the heart radical, like *qing* and *xing*.

The sense in which *qing* is "engendered" by *xing* can be clarified by Han Yu's (768–824) observation, though he might not have had access to the Guodian material, that "*xing* comes into being at one's birth, while *qing* comes into existence as one becomes involved in things (性也者,與生俱生;情也者,接於物而生也)."[62] From this perspective, the relationship between *xing* and *qing* can be further explained as follows. The various human emotions constitute a major, if not the only, part of the content of nature; it is in this sense that they are tantamount to nature. At a deeper level, because nature is abstract in the sense that it is itself invisible, and because emotions are concrete in the sense that they can always find channels to express themselves, the latter are manifestations or the "product" of nature.

Given that *qing*, or manifestations of one's attitudes and feelings toward others, form an essential part of human nature, the Guodian view of *xing* is implicitly social and reflects a moral orientation. In contrast, Gaozi's interpretation of human nature as desires for food and sex carries little moral weight, because they are more physical and individual than psychological and social. For this reason, Mencius rejects Gaozi's account. Human beings are born with *qing*. This seems to be the assumption underlying the Guodian view that *qing* (emotions) constitute *xing*. Indeed, it seems likely that the word *ming* in the phrase *xing zi ming chu* refers to "life," reflecting the idea that nature begins with life. In early Chinese philosophy, *xing* is generally regarded as the natural endowment that human beings are born with. A notable phenomenon in early Chinese texts is the association of certain key terms with *xing: qing*, in the sense of emotions; *de* 德, in either a moral or an amoral sense; and *ming* 命, morally understood or otherwise. All these can be associated with the word *xing* to form such compound words as *dexing* 德性, *xingming* 性命, and *xingqing* 性情.[63] In many instances *xing* can be used interchangeably with any of these three terms. Consequently, it is clear that the meanings conveyed by these four words involve what is believed to be a given element present in human beings from birth.

To regard *qing* as either the constitution or the product of *xing* is to reject the argument that *xing* is the content of *xin* (heart-mind). A major theme that percolates through the entire *Xing zi ming chu* text is the contrast between nature and the heart-mind. As slip 4 implies, while the capacity of liking and disliking is attributed to *xing*, the ability to make a choice between good and evil depends entirely on *xin*. Again, slip 6 tells us that one should rely on the evaluating and prioritizing heart-mind and not act simply by following one's natural inclinations. Moreover, parallel to the idea in slip 5 that "whenever one acts under the sway of *xing*, one is controlled by material things," slip 14 states, "Whenever (one is with) the Way, it is the principle of *xin* that holds sway (凡道,心術為主)." Here the author seems to argue that to follow one's nature is to surrender to immoral inclinations, whereas to resort to one's heart-mind is to, successfully or not, resist them.

Nevertheless, the distinction between *xing* and *xin* is by no means absolute; rather, it is relative because emotions as the content of nature are not entirely morally negative. We should be mindful of the "ambivalent" nature of *xing* discussed in the previous section. Given that emotions such as the "love of life" and one's "disliking what is not benevolent" are deliberately expressed in slips 40 and 41 as being "close" to benevolence and rightness, respectively, they must be understood as being in perfect harmony with the propensities for goodness on the part of the heart-mind. Under-standably, it is only when morally negative emotions are involved that they are seen to be in direct conflict with the moral inclina-tions of the heart-mind. To restate this argument in another way, al-though emotions as the content of nature are construed as morally ambivalent, a majority is viewed negatively, which explains why na-ture is often delineated in the Guodian texts as being in conflict with the heart-mind.

Xing as Incipient and as Full-fledged Moral Nature

One of Graham's great contributions to the study of the con-cept of human nature in early Chinese philosophy is his discussion of whether *xing* is construed as "a dynamic process" or that which "a thing has to start with."[64] Interpreting the notion of human nature in the Guodian texts in this light, one can say that it seems to be un-derstood both as "that which one starts with" and as "a dynamic process" seeking to reach an inherent fulfillment.

One cannot miss the important passage previously quoted in this essay from the *Cheng zhi wen zhi* that speaks of *xing* in terms of two stages. The first is "at birth," when the sage and the common people share one and the same nature; the second, the moment "when it (nature) grows and extends to a large degree." This second stage indicates an achievement that all human beings are capable of but only a few successfully accomplish. The words to "grow" and to "extend" used to describe the second stage as a moral achieve-ment strongly suggest an awareness that morality, however small, has already been planted incipiently in nature.

The notion of two stages can also be gleaned from slip 39: "Benevolence is the orientation of *xing,* and it is perhaps engen-dered by *xing.*" Implicitly, nature is depicted as a dynamic process with an onset and a destination. Moreover, benevolence seems to have been present at both the beginning and the final stage of this process. As such, this passage suggests a "normative" nature. But if we take the text as a whole, there is a second meaning to *xing,* which is "factual" (Graham) or "biological" (Bloom), subject to develop-ment and susceptible to diverse influences.[65] As slips 9–12 show, the final status of *xing* differs from person to person, because its process of development can be affected by seven different influences, either moral or immoral.

Slip 39 contains one of the most important statements in the whole Guodian collection of Confucian writings, for the argument together with its language is unmistakably analogous to the notion of the "four sprouts" of virtues, which has been attributed exclusively to Mencius. I am of the opinion that the Guodian notion of nature as a process with two stages found tangible expression in Mencius' writing. Indeed, the idea of two stages is already implied in the word *sheng* 生—in the sense of "being born" and of "life"—from which *xing* derives. Whereas some early Chinese philosophers emphasize the incipient stage in their conception of *xing*, others—including Mencius—take both stages into consideration. At this point it may be helpful to digress for a moment to undertake an etymological survey of the word *sheng*. The character *sheng* is used in the Shang oracle bone inscriptions to designate a variety of meanings—as verb, noun, or adjective—such as "to give birth," "offspring" and "surname," and "living."[66] As Chen Mengjia notes, a great number of the Shang oracle texts pertaining to the word *sheng* are records of the Shang's appeals for women to become pregnant (*shousheng* 受生) and for offspring (*qiusheng* 求生).[67] In Western Zhou literature the meaning of *sheng* extends to "life," especially when it appears in prayers for longevity. Following Fu Sinian, it can be argued that whereas the Shang aristocrats had prayed for descendants, or the beginning of a new life, their early Zhou counterparts extended their concern to the end of life.[68] The Shang and early Zhou evidence thus suggests that both life and life span are given and controlled from above; this notion clearly suggests two stages of life, a beginning and a destination. When the word *xing* in the sense of human nature came to be distinguished from *sheng*, presumably during Eastern Zhou times (for the earliest extant references are found in the *Zuozhuan*, the *Guoyu*, and the *Analects*), it inherited from *sheng* both the notion of an endowment from Heaven and the notion of two stages.

To return to the argument that, for Mencius, nature is both incipient and full-fledged, I will focus only on the first stage, given that the second is well recognized by modern scholars. The idea of an incipient nature is especially emphasized in *Mencius* 4B26. This passage is both problematic and controversial. At issue is the question of whether Mencius sides with or opposes the statement presented at the beginning of the passage, which in Graham's translation reads,

> As for what the world in general says about our nature, it is simply *appealing to how things were before.* Those who appeal to *how we were before* take things going smoothly (/benefit) as the basic consideration.[69]

For Graham, the Yangists were the ones who were "appealing to how things were before" (*gu* 故) and pursued only "benefit" (*li* 利) for themselves; they were thus taken to task by Mencius. Similarly, Xu Fuguan interprets *gu* as "habits" and *li* as "physical desires of humans."[70] Although their interpretations differ in some respects (e.g., Xu takes the second *gu* at the end of that passage in a different sense), they and many other scholars as well agree on one crucial point: that Mencius' view of nature rejects the *gu* perspective.

I find this interpretation problematic. In Graham's case, there is insufficient evidence that Mencius was criticizing the Yangist position, centering on *li,* or "benefit." Granted that this passage has to do with a notion of nature under Mencius' attack, it could be referring to a number of views about nature, with which, as the Guodian texts testify, Mencius had to wrestle. Likewise, Xu Fuguan's interpretation involves too many interpolations. For instance, those who speak of *xing* in terms of *gu,* Xu asserts, "do not reject benevolence and rightness"; they simply use their immoral "wisdom" for other purposes, as does Gaozi. This does not seem to follow from the original passage.

The arguments of Graham and Xu Fuguan seem to rest on taking *li* to mean either "benefit" or "human physical desires." Certainly, *li* is often used with negative connotations, in contrast with the values Mencius upholds. According to Jiao Xun (1763–1820), however, the word *li* in this context refers to "harmony" (*he* 和) and Mencius is speaking of *xing* in terms of *gu* in the sense of "things that happened in the past."[71] Although I have reservations about his interpretation of *gu,* Jiao Xun is looking in the right direction. It seems to me that the word *gu* is used in the sense of "roots" (*ben* 本) or "originality," referring to that which humans are born with, or something incipient and unlearned. It is on the basis of the "roots" residing in human nature that Mencius argues for its incipient goodness. The passage consequently should be rendered: "In talking about human nature, people in the world merely follow what is original. Hence, we should take being harmonious with its original condition as our basic consideration."

We can furnish proof for this interpretation by citing Xunzi's response to the Mencian notion of inborn nature. A noteworthy aspect of Xunzi's criticism of Mencius is that he attacks directly the latter's assertion that human nature is "originally" good. He states, "As a general rule, ritual principles and moral duty are born of the acquired nature of the sage and are not the product of what was originally (gu) in man's inborn nature."[72] At greater length, he writes,

> Mencius said: "Now, the nature of man is good, and all men will lose what is original in their nature (xinggu 性故)." ... Those who say man's inborn nature is good admire what does not depart from his original simplicity (pu 樸) and harmonize (li 利) with what is not separated from his childhood naiveté.... Now it is the inborn nature of man that when hungry he desires something to eat, that when cold he wants warm clothing, and that when weary he desires rest—such are essential qualities inherent in his nature.[73]

If Xunzi understands Mencius correctly, he can lend support to our argument that Mencius does emphasize the incipient goodness of human nature. Viewing the issue in a larger context, the incipient aspect of nature is common in Warring States literature: in the notion of an evil xing in the Mozi; in Gaozi's interpretation of xing as what is inborn;[74] in the Guodian conception of xing; and in the Mencian notion. Therefore, Mencius is not wrong in saying in 4B26 that "in talking about human nature, people in the world merely follow what is original." He knows of no counterexample.

Conclusion

When Mencius put forward his argument about human nature, several conceptions were available to him. These conceptions are motivated by the following concerns: Who determines human nature? What is the content of human nature? Is the given nature subject to change? Is the inborn nature equally imparted to all? Does it have to do with morality? If yes, then is the shared nature exclusively moral?

I believe that all these concerns about xing have to do with its related and inseparable notion of sheng. Sarah Allan has already pointed out that "just as sheng is usually understood as meaning to 'be born' or 'live,' xing is interpreted as that which is 'inborn' or 'innate' and explained as referring to the qualities with which one is endowed at birth."[75] This conceptual connection between *sheng* and *xing* also manifests itself in other ways. Just as *sheng* in the sense of life is determined by Heaven, *xing* in the sense of inborn nature is believed to be imparted by Heaven, whether it be biological desires, emotions, physical features, mental status, or propensities for virtue. Just as *sheng* in the sense of life can be prolonged (and by extension, altered) through human activities such as prayer, *xing* in the sense of inborn nature can be changed through human effort. Just as *sheng* in the sense of being born can be applied to any infant, *xing* in the sense of inborn nature can be taken as shared by all. Just as *sheng* in the sense of life span, as expressed particularly in the term *misheng* 彌生, differs from person to person, *xing* in the sense of inborn nature can be viewed as inegalitarian. Finally, just as *sheng* in the sense of life implies both its beginning and its destination, *xing* in the sense of inborn nature can be spoken of in terms of two stages.

Prior to Mencius, all the above-mentioned concerns pertaining to the notion of *xing* had more or less been raised. Hence, he was neither the first to inject morality into the content of *xing* nor the first to argue for its universal similarity. Among the views of *xing* available to Mencius, it is apparent that the inegalitarian view and the ambivalent view posed to him a far more powerful challenge than the others. Following the lines of argument by certain Confucians, Mencius launched a severe attack against inegalitarianism, but he had to combat the ambivalent position on his own. This is because it was held by a number of people, including some Confucians such as Shi Shuo and the author of the *Xing zi ming chu*. Given this, we can conclude that among his rivals there were Confucians as well as Mohists, Yangists, and other unidentified individuals.

In addition to the argument of shared nature, other tangible ideological linkages between the Guodian texts and the *Mencius* can be observed, indicative of possible influence of the former on the latter. The statement in the *Cheng zhi wen zhi* (slips 27–28) that "when it (the *xing*) grows and extends to a large degree, even a sage cannot easily claim a monopoly of such an achievement" is evidently redolent of the Mencian argument that one must know how to "enlarge" (*kuo* 擴) and "fulfill" (*chong* 充) the four sprouts in human nature (2A6). As mentioned earlier, the attribution of *ren* (benevolence), *zhi* (wisdom), and *yu* (desires) to *xing* by the author of the

Xing zi ming chu anticipates Mencius' more refined and integrated notion of human nature with propensities for such virtues as benevolence, rightness, propriety, and wisdom, as well as biological desires, as its constitution.

On the other hand, the description of the ambivalent nature, often in strong negative terms, and the concomitant stress on the conflict between *xing* and *xin* in the Guodian texts do not mirror the view of the *Mencius*. Rather, the Guodian statements are more comparable to many statements made by Xunzi, who entertains the belief that human nature is evil, completely at odds with the learned and acquired virtues. In this regard, the Guodian position can be seen as a forerunner of Xunzi's theory of human nature as being evil.

Notes

The author wishes to thank Alan Chan, Jiuan Heng, Laurent Pfister, Irene Bloom, Kim-Chong Chong, and David Nivison for their help with the writing of this essay.

1. A.C. Graham, "The Background of the Mencian Theory of Human Nature," in his *Studies in Chinese Philosophy and Philosophical Literature* (Singapore: Institute of East Asian Philosophies, 1986; reprint, Albany: State University of New York Press, 1990), 7–66. Irene Bloom, "Mencian Arguments on Human Nature (*Jen-hsing*)," *Philosophy East and West* 44 (1994): 19–53.

2. Wu Yujiang 吳毓江, *Mozi jiaozhu* 墨子校注 (Beijing: Zhonghua, 1993), chap. 3, "Suo ran" 所染, 27 n. 38; chap. 44, "Da qu" 大取, 621.

3. Li Xueqin 李學勤, "Guodianjian yu *Liji*" 郭店簡與禮記, *Zhongguo zhexueshi* 中國哲學史 24 (1998): 29–32.

4. Jingmenshi bowuguan 荊門市博物館, *Guodian Chumu zhujian* 郭店楚墓竹簡 (Beijing: Wenwu chubanshe, 1998). Hereafter cited as *GDCMZJ*.

5. Chen Lai asserts that the *Xing zi ming chu* text might be associated with three Confucians, namely, Ziyou 子游, Zisi 子思, and Gongsun nizi 公孫尼子. See Chen Lai 陳來, "Guodian Chujian zhi *Xing zi ming chu* pian chutan" 郭店楚簡之性自命出篇初探, *Kongzi yanjiu* 孔子研究, no. 3 (1998): 52–60. Guo Yi believes that the *Cheng zhi wen zhi* is a product of the Zisi School. See Guo Yi 郭沂, "Guodian Chujian *Tian jiang dachang* (*Cheng zhi wen zhi*) pian shuzheng" 郭店楚簡天降大常(成之聞之)篇疏證, *Kongzi yanjiu*, no. 3 (1998): 61–69.

6. This is the view of a group of Chinese scholars who held a conference discussing the Guodian find. See *Guangming Daily* 光明日報, *Xueshu dongtai* 學術動態, 19 June 1998.

7. Fu Sinian 傅斯年, *Xingming guxun bianzheng* 性命古訓辨證, in *Fu Sinian quanji* 傅斯年全集 (Taipei: National University of Taiwan Press, 1952), vol. 2, 346; Xu Fuguan 徐復觀, *Zhongguo renxinglun shi* 中國人性論史 (Taipei: Shangwu yinshuguan, 1990), 313–324; Tang Junyi 唐君毅, *Zhongguo zhexue yuan-*

lun yuanxing pian 中國哲學原論原性篇 (Taipei: Xuesheng, 1989); Mou Zong-san 牟宗三, *Xinti yu xingti* 心體與性體 (Taipei: Zhengzhong, 1968); Mori Mikisa-buro 森三樹三郎, *Jōko yori kandai ni itaru seimeikan no tenkai* 上古より漢代に至る性命觀の展開 (Tokyo: Sōbunsha, 1971), 74.

8. Sun Yirang 孫詒讓, *Mozi jiangu* 墨子閒詁 (Beijing: Zhonghua shuju, 1954), 254.

9. Wu Yujiang, *Mozi jiaozhu*, "Da qu" 大取, chap. 44, 611–612. Punctuation is altered.

10. The word *baoren* 暴人 is used several times by Mozi in opposition to *shanren* 善人, "good person"; therefore it is appropriate to render it as "evil person." See Wu Yujiang, *Mozi jiaozhu*, "Shang tong xia" 尚同下, chap. 13, 138–140.

11. The meaning of *chenzhi* 陳執 defies any precise interpretation. Zhang Chunyi's interpretation of it as *xiguan* (habits or "behavioral customs") is somewhat agreeable with the context. See Zhang Chunyi 張純一, *Mozi jijie* 墨子集解, in *Mozi jicheng* 墨子集成, ed. Yan Ling-feng 嚴靈峰 (Taipei: Chengwen, 1975), vol. 24, 508. Whatever the exact meaning, the term must be understood as something in comparison with or subject to man's decision.

12. The meaning of *wei* 為 in *wei tian zhi yi ren* 為天之以人 should be taken as *ze* 則 (but). Evidence for such usage of *wei* can be found in Wang Yin-zhi 王引之, *Jingzhuan shici* 經傳釋辭 (Changsha: Yuelu shushe, 1984), 46.

13. A. C. Graham, *Later Mohist Logic, Ethics, and Science* (Hong Kong: Chinese University of Hong Kong Press, 1978), 245–246; Graham, "Background of the Mencian Theory," 19.

14. Graham, *Later Mohist Logic, Ethics, and Science*, 244.

15. Arthur Waley, *Three Ways of Thought in Ancient China* (Stanford, Calif.: Stanford University Press, 1982), 122.

16. Wu Yujiang, *Mozi jiaozhu*, "Tianzhi shang," chap. 7, 293. The doctrine of "free will" also appears in the chapter "Attack on Fatalism." From Mozi's perspective, as Arthur Waley observes, "If people believe in Fate, they say 'The rich are fated to be rich, the poor are fated to be poor. What is the use of bestirring oneself?' And then what will happen? 'The countryman will be lazy at his ploughing and reaping, his planting and tilling, the wife at her twisting and spinning, her stitching and weaving, the king and his ministers at the hearing of lawsuits and handling of public affairs. The world will soon be in a great muddle.'" Waley, *Three Ways of Thought*, 122.

17. Graham, "Background of the Mencian Theory," 19.

18. Ibid. Perhaps for this reason, Graham left out that statement.

19. Wu Yujiang, *Mozi jiaozhu*, 621.

20. Further evidence of such usage comes from other pre-Qin texts. For example, in the *Zhuangzi* we read, 是非以仁義易其性與—"Isn't this because benevolence and rightness have altered their *xing*?" See Guo Qingfan 郭慶藩, *Zhuangzi jishi* 莊子集釋, chap. 8, "Pianmu" 駢拇 (Beijing: Zhonghua shuju, 1982), 323.

21. Wu Yujiang, *Mozi jiaozhu*, 27, n. 38, 621.

22. Ibid.

23. Bloom, "Mencian Arguments," 26, 47 n. 20.

24. Ibid., 45; Bloom, "Human Nature and Biological Nature in Mencius," *Philosophy East and West* 47.1 (1997): 26–27.

25. Bloom, "Human Nature and Biological Nature," 27.

26. Bloom, "Mencian Arguments," 27.

27. Ibid., 41.

28. Jame Legge, *The Ch'un Ts'ew with the Tso Chuen*, vol. 5 of *The Chinese Classics* (Hong Kong: Hong Kong University Press, 1966), Duke Seang (Xiang), year 26, 527.

29. Burton Watson, *The Complete Works of Chuang Tzu* (New York: Columbia University Press, 1968), chap. 8, "Webbed Toes," 98. Of course, this is not to say that the *Zhuangzi* was available to Mencius; the point is simply that the "inegalitarian" view of *xing* was current and posed a serious challenge to Mencius and other Confucians.

30. Qian Mu 錢穆, "Zhuangzi waizapian yan xingyi" 莊子外雜篇言性義, *Dongfang xuebao* 東方學報 1.1 (1957): 233.

31. Bloom, "Human Nature and Biological Nature," 21.

32. *GDCMZJ*, 168.

33. Qiu Xigui asserts that the character *er* 而 is a mistake for another character. See *GDCMZJ*, 170 n. 26. Professor Liu Jiahe 劉家和 offers me his suggestion that the correct character should be *tian* 天, which appears like the character *er* in pre-Qin written forms. Prof. Liu's argument is very convincing because elsewhere in the Guodian manuscripts *er* is mistaken for *tian* on three occasions and *tian* for *er* on another three. See *GDCMZJ, Laozi shiwen zhushi (jia)* 老子釋文注釋(甲), 112–113, slips 18, 27, 30; and *Wuxing shiwen zhushi* 五行釋文注釋, 150, slips 19, 26, 30.

34. Here *you* 猶 refers to *jun* 均, "equally" or "similarly." Examples can be found in *Jingzhuan shici*, 10–11.

35. The meaning of *yilou* 譯婁 is uncertain; as such, it is better to leave it untranslated.

36. The term *youyu* 由與 might be referring to *youyu* 猶豫 or *rongyu* 容與, for they are phonetically similar. The latter carries the meaning of a facial appearance of relaxation and comfort. See Huang Chengji 黃承吉, *Zigu yifu hean* 字詁義府合按 (Beijing: Zhonghua shuju, 1984), 193.

37. Qiu Xigui recognizes and transcribes the character 壼 as *shan* 墠. See *GDCMZJ*, 170 n. 27. If Qiu is correct, *shan* 墠 can be taken as a loan graph for *shan* 擅, "to monopolize."

38. John Knoblock, trans., *Xunzi*, vol. 3 (Stanford, Calif.: Stanford University Press, 1994), 23.2a, 154; 23.4a, 157; 23.4b, 158.

39. The last instance requires some clarification. Kwong-Loi Shun states, "In *Mencius* 6A7, Mencius himself contemplated (though he eventually rejected) the possibility of *hsing* [*xing*] being different from person to person with regard to the disposition of palates toward tastes." Kwong-Loi Shun, "Mencius on *Jen-hsing*," *Philosophy East and West* 47.1 (January 1997): 9. From Shun's perspective, then, Mencius expresses himself inconsistently, presenting an argument that he soon rejects. This is a misconception, for the subordinate clause *ru shi kou zhi yu wei ye, qi xing yu ren shu* 如使口之於味也,其性與人殊 is a hypothesized statement to be criticized, not an argument of Mencius'. D. C. Lau has

correctly rendered the whole sentence as "Were the nature of taste to vary from man to man in the same way as horses and hounds differ from me in kind, then how does it come about that all palates in the world follow the preferences of Yi Ya?" This is immediately followed by the assertion that "The fact that in taste the whole world looks to Yi Ya shows that all palates are alike," which undoubtedly displays the coherence of Mencius' fundamental argument.

40. D. C. Lau, trans., *The Analects* (London: Penguin Classics, 1979), 17.2, 143.

41. It is worth mentioning in this context that the early Confucian consensus concerning a shared nature surprisingly lost its momentum in Han Confucian writings. The idea of inegalitarianism, expressed in the terms "the nature of sages" and "the nature of ordinary people," was adopted wholesale by Dong Zhongshu 董仲舒 (197–104 B.C.E.), a leading figure of Han Confucianism, in a lengthy discussion on human nature. See Su Yu 蘇輿, *Chunqiu fanlu yizheng* 春秋繁露義證 (Beijing: Zhonghua shuju, 1992), chap. 10, "Shixing" 實性, 311.

42. Reference to the nature of the sage is also made in the *Zhuangzi:* "The sage penetrates bafflement and complication, rounding all into a single body, yet he does not know why—it is his inborn nature." Watson, *Chuang Tzu,* chap. 25, "Tse-yang," 281.

43. *GDCMZJ,* 179.

44. *Jingji zuangu* 經籍纂詁, ed. Ruan Yuan 阮元 (Beijing: Zhonghua shuju, 1995), chap. 67, under the entry "*yi,*" 1498, 1511.

45. This conclusion is based on the reading in the *Jingji zuangu,* chap. 96, under the entry of "*da,*" 2023.

46. Watson's translation; see Watson, *Chuang Tzu,* chap. 19, "Mastering Life," 197.

47. Knoblock, *Xunzi,* vol. 3, 23.1b, 151.

48. *GDCMZJ,* 179.

49. Ibid., 180.

50. D. C. Lau, trans., *Mencius* (London: Penguin Books, 1970), 162.

51. Shun, "Mencius on *Jen-hsing,*" 7–8.

52. Graham, "Background of the Mencian Theory," 21.

53. Bloom, "Human Nature and Biological Nature," 24.

54. Ibid., 25.

55. Kwong-Loi Shun, *Mencius and Early Chinese Thought* (Stanford, Calif.: Stanford University Press, 1997), 214–215.

56. The meaning of *qing* in the *Xing zi ming chu* is controversial, as can be seen in the discussion among members of the Warring States Working Group. It denotes "emotions" to some scholars, and "conditions" to others. I believe that among the three meanings conveyed by *qing*—"what is genuine," "nature," and "emotions"—it is the last one that agrees most with the context of the Guodian text.

57. *GDCMZJ,* 179.

58. Qiu Xigui fills in the three blanks with *qing zhe neng* 情者能, taking the reconstructed phrase to mean "those who understand emotions are able to." See *GDCMZJ,* 182 n. 3.

59. I propose that the three missing characters are *shan xin ye* 善心也, in light of the fundamental contrast between *xing* and *xin* in the text. The sentence thus reads *shan bu shan xin ye* 善不善, 心也.

60. The translation of this sentence is based on Guo Yi's hypothesis, which takes the six missing words to be "*chui fu ji bu ming; ren*" (槌弗擊不鳴; 人). See Guo Yi 郭沂, "Shitan Chujian *Tai yi sheng shui* jiqi yu jianben *Laozi* de guanxi" 試談楚簡太一生水及其與簡本老子的關係, *Zhongguo zhexueshi* 中國哲學史 24 (1998): 33.

61. *GDCMZJ, Yucong er*, 203–204; slips 8, 10, 20, 23, 25, 28, 30, 32.

62. Qu Shouyuan 屈守元 and Chang Sichun 常思春, eds., *Han Yu quanqi jiaozhu* 韓愈全集校注 (Chengdu: Sichuan daxue chubanshe, 1996), vol. 5, "Yuan xing," 2686.

63. Qian Mu has noted that in the "Outer Chapters" of the *Zhuangzi, de* and *xing* are often used together, for both are seen as natural endowment in human beings. See Qian Mu, "Zhuangzi waizapian yan xingyi," 227.

64. Graham, "Background of the Mencian Theory," 8.

65. Bloom, "Mencian Arguments," 34.

66. Yu Shengwu 于省吾, ed., *Jiagu wenzi gulin* 甲骨文字詁林 (Beijing: Zhonghua shuju, 1996), vol. 2, 1309–1325.

67. Chen Mengjia 陳夢家, *Yinxu buci zongshu* 殷墟卜辭綜述 (Beijing: Kexue, 1956), 493–494.

68. Fu Sinian, *Xingming guxun bianzheng*. At this stage, *sheng* or *xing* in the sense of "nature" had yet to be conceptualized. Against Fu Sinian, Xu Fuguan asserts that human nature in the sense of human desires was already conceptualized in Western Zhou times; it was connoted by *sheng*. As evidence, Xu examines the meaning of the phrase *mijuesheng* 彌厥生, a prayer or supplication (*guci* 嘏辭) appearing together with other prayers such as *meishou* 眉壽, *chuowan* 綽綰, *yongling* 永令, and *lingzhong* 令終 on a bronze vessel. According to Xu, if *mijuesheng* was used in the sense of "fulfilling one's term of life" as Fu had believed, it would have been a repetition of *meishou* and *lingzhong*, both of which refer to "long life." Therefore, Xu concludes that *sheng* must be understood as nature. See Xu Fuguan, *Zhongguo renxinglun shi*, 7–11. Mou Zongsan supports this view—see his *Xinti yu xingti*, 197—but it seems to me that the evidence suggests otherwise. All the prayers appearing together with *mijuesheng* in Xu's illustration convey one and the same meaning: "having a long life." As Xu Zhongshu's study of prayers in the Zhou bronzes strongly suggests, phrases such as *meishou* 眉壽, *shoukao* 壽考, *shoulao* 壽老, *wannian* 萬年, *wanshou* 萬壽, *wujiang* 無疆, *wuqi* 無期, *yongling* 永令, *misheng* 彌生, *lingzhong* 令終, *nanlao* 難老, and *chuowan* 綽綰—no matter how different in wording—are all prayers for longevity. See Xu Zhongshu, "Jinwen guci shili" 金文嘏辭釋例, *Bulletin of the Institute of History and Philology Academia Sinica* 6.1 (1936): 15–26, 39. Mou Zongsan's discussion of the usage of *xing* in pre-Confucian literature relies heavily on such forged materials as the *Xibo kanli* 西伯戡黎, *Zhonghui zhi gao* 仲虺之誥, *Taijia* 太甲, and *Lüao* 旅獒, all interpolated into the *Book of Documents* at much later times.

69. Graham, "Background of the Mencian Theory," 52. Emphasis is Graham's.

70. Xu Fuguan, *Zhongguo renxinglun shi*, 169.

71. Jiao Xun 焦循, *Mengzi zhengyi* 孟子正義 (Beijing: Zhonghua shuju, 1996), 584–586.

72. Knoblock, *Xunzi*, vol. 3, 23.2a, 153. My translation here is slightly different from Knoblock's rendering.

73. Ibid., 23.1d–23.1e, 152–153; modified.

74. Gaozi's statement in *Mencius* 6A3 that "the inborn (*sheng*) is what is meant by nature" has been differently interpreted and hence stands in need of clarification. It is rendered, for instance, as the "inborn" by D. C. Lau, as "everything that is born and grows" by Roger Ames, and as "being alive" by Bloom. Though *sheng* does convey these meanings, it is best to interpret *sheng* in the way Lau does, for Gaozi's further explanation of the content of *xing* is "appetite for food and sex," in the sense of precisely what is given at birth, a far cry from "being alive" and everything that "grows."

75. Sarah Allan, *The Way of Water and Sprouts of Virtue* (Albany: State University of New York Press, 1997), 108.

2

A Matter of Taste
Qi (Vital Energy) and the Tending of the Heart (*Xin*) in *Mencius* 2A2

ALAN K. L. CHAN

MENCIUS 2A2 offers an intriguing account of the relationship between the "heart" (*xin* 心) and *qi* 氣—the "vital energy" that engenders and sustains life—and their role in self-cultivation. On the one hand, it portrays an ethical ideal marked by a heart—or "heart-mind," as some translators prefer, taking into consideration both the affective and cognitive concerns that the concept of *xin* encompasses—that is firm and unwavering in its aims and direction. The assumption seems to be that *qi* acts as an unruly or prejudicial influence that would disturb the heart and, as such, must be tightly controlled and made to serve moral ends. On the other hand, the *Mencius* also discloses that a "floodlike *qi*" (*haoranzhiqi* 浩然之氣) informs the ethically accomplished person. How is this different from *qi*, which presumably is not "floodlike" for most people, and how can it be attained? Is it the case that when the heart is ethically determined, *qi* would become "floodlike"?

In this essay, I propose to examine *Mencius* 2A2 afresh, building on the works of D. C. Lau, David Nivison, Jeffrey Riegel, Kwong-Loi Shun, and others, and in the light of some of the recently discovered Guodian texts.[1] While the concept of *qi* is generally recognized to have an important role in Mencian ethics, the question remains whether it is viewed as a negative or positive influence and consequently how it relates to the process of self-cultivation. It is my submission that Mencius shared with his contemporaries a basic understanding of *qi* as constitutive of the person, but he differed from them in locating in it a source of moral excellence. Following the

42

structure of *Mencius* 2A2, the first part of the essay introduces the theme of courage and the "unmoved" heart. The cultivation of courage rests on nourishing one's *qi*. This brings into view the complex relationship between *qi* and *xin*. Ideally, the heart "commands" the vital energy in pursuing the way of rightness and propriety (*yi* 義).[2] In practice, however, *qi* often moves the heart in ethically undesirable directions. What, then, does nourishing *qi* entail?

Comparison with other early Chinese texts on this issue helps establish a general framework in which Mencius' approach to self-cultivation can be understood. Mencius distinguishes his position from that of Gaozi, who seeks knowledge from without to shape one's heart and to quell the *qi* within. In contrast, Mencius highlights the ethical resources that are found within the person. Just as one naturally delights in pleasing colors and good food, leaving aside the measure of quality in these instances, the heart has a natural "taste" for rightness. Fundamentally, this is a function of *qi*, which informs the heart in setting its aims and direction. It is in this context, I suggest, that Mencius makes use of the idea of a "flood-like vital energy" to signify the kind of moral vigor that characterizes the sage. The concept of *qi*, in this view, thus forms a basic point of departure in Mencius' thinking. The heart is formed and shaped by *qi;* this is the fundamental insight that underlies the approach to the ethical life. If this interpretation is correct, though my main concern is to make sense of the concept of *qi* in *Mencius* 2A2, it would affect our understanding of Mencius' moral psychology as a whole, in particular the assertion that rightness is "internal" and the nature of the "four beginnings" (*siduan* 四端).

The Heart That Cannot Be Moved

Mencius 2A2 begins with a question.

> Gongsun Chou asked, "If you, Master, became a senior official of Qi and were able to put the Way into practice, it would not be surprising that Qi would become the leader of the feudal lords and carry out the kingly way. If this were the case, would your heart not be moved?"[3]

I leave aside the questions of whether Gongsun Chou was a disciple of Mencius and whether the question he posed was a hypothetical one.[4] The philosophically challenging issue lies in the meaning of *dongxin* 動心, or "movement of the heart."

What causes the heart to "stir," "move," or become "per-turbed," as the character *dong* has been variously translated? Presumably a host of factors can be considered. In this context, however, Zhu Xi's (1130–1200) comment that "fear (*kongju* 恐懼) and doubt (*yihuo* 疑惑)" act to move the heart probably serves to summarize traditional commentators' understanding of the term.[5] According to Jiao Xun (1763–1820), the Han scholar Gao You 高誘 defines *huo* 惑 (doubt, uncertainty, or perplexity) as *dong;* the lack of mental and physical strength, as Jiao Xun further explains, would lead to doubt or uncertainty, which in turn would engender fear.[6]

Mencius replies that he has not experienced any such movement of the heart (*budongxin* 不動心) since the age of forty. There is some agreement that this harks back to Confucius' famous "autobiographical" statement in the *Lunyu* (2.4): "At forty I came to be free from doubts (*huo*)."[7] To be in a state of *huo* means at a minimum, and without privileging the intellect over the emotions, that the heart is confused; *budongxin*, in contrast, leaves no room for confusion.

Impressed, Gongsun Chou offers that Mencius surpassed Meng Ben, who is known for his courage. Zhu Xi explains that Meng Ben's is the courage of the "*qi* of the blood" (*xueqi* 血氣), for reportedly he took no caution in traveling to avoid wild beasts.[8] According to the *Lüshi chunqiu,* his anger and fierce look was enough to bring a boatful of people into such a frightful stir that they all fell into the water.[9] According to the *Hanfeizi,* commenting on *Laozi*'s idea (in chapter 67) that courage stems from kindness or affection (*ci* 慈), "Not in doubt (*buyi* 不疑) is what is meant by courage."[10] Once a person is free from doubt, fear gives way to courage and determination, which characterizes a person whose heart cannot be moved.

To attain *budongxin*, the *Mencius* continues, is "not difficult." "Gaozi was ahead of me (in attaining) *budongxin*." This sets up the question whether there is a "way" (*dao*) to attain the state in which one's heart cannot be moved or stirred. Mencius replies in the affirmative and points to the example of two presumably well-known figures—Beigong You and Meng Shishe—who excel in courage.

Quite literally, the *Mencius* suggests, Beigong You would not bat an eyelid when threatened, whether it came from a powerful lord or a common person. However slight the affront might be, he would retaliate without fail. Meng Shishe, on the other hand, was different in that he focused on "not having fear" (*wuju* 無懼) in his own heart, as distinguished from whether he could engineer certain victory against an opponent.[11]

There is probably little to choose between the two, for neither takes into account ethical issues that most would tend to associate with courage. It is thus not surprising to find Mencius saying that he could not say which form of courage is superior. Nevertheless, in being able to cultivate a heart that knows no fear, Meng Shishe guards, defends, or secures (*shou* 守) what Mencius considers more "important" (*yue* 約).

It is noteworthy that courage is explicitly said to require cultivation or nurturing (*yang* 養). It is, however, not entirely clear what the expression *shouyue* means. The generally accepted view is that *yue* suggests what is important or essential, although some commentators take the phrase to mean that Meng Shishe's method of cultivation is "simpler."[12] It has also been suggested that *yue* may be a mistake for *qi* in this context.[13] *Shouyue* may connote securing or preserving what is important, but some account must be given as to why it is important. Judging from the ensuing discussion, it is likely that Mencius was talking about some form of cultivation of *qi*. We will return to this point later.

Mencius further likens Beigong You to Confucius' disciple Zixia, and Meng Shishe to Zengzi. The last is said to have had an opportunity to hear about "great courage" from Confucius himself: "If, on looking within (*zifan* 自反), one finds oneself to be in the wrong, then even though one's adversary be only a common fellow coarsely clad, one is bound to tremble with fear. But if one finds oneself in the right, one goes forward even against men in the thousands" (Lau, trans.; cf. *Lunyu* 12.4 and *Mencius* 1B3). Lau's translation is open to debate, but it seems safe to assume that the focus of discussion is now shifted to the moral plane.[14] In comparison, Mencius concludes, "Meng Shishe's guarding his *qi* is not as good as Zengzi's *shouyue*."

Zixia is noted for his wide learning, while Zengzi pursues filial piety single-mindedly. Jiao Xun gives a general account of the point of comparison.

> Beigong You seeks to triumph over others in everything he does. He is thus like Zixia, who knows the many (manifestations) of the Dao [i.e., commands a vast knowledge of the classical texts, with the im-

plication that he sought to excel over others in learning]. Meng Shishe does not ask whether he is able to win for sure, but concentrates on defending his own being without fear. He is thus like Zengzi, who has attained the great (substance) of the Dao [i.e., through his devotion to filial piety, the most basic of all Confucian virtues]....Beigong You takes constant victory as strength. This is not as good as Meng Shishe in taking fearlessness as strength. But in being fearless, Meng Shishe only applies *qi* to secure himself, and does not ask whether what he does is right or not right. The strength of Zengzi, on the other hand, lies in his applying rightness to secure himself.[15]

The concept of *qi* makes its first appearance in *Mencius* 2A2 here, in the contrast between Meng Shishe and Zengzi. The connection is presumably well understood by the audience. The *Shuowen* defines courage (*yong* 勇) simply as *qi*, with the added note that in the ancient script the character *yong* was written with the *xin* radical.[16] Courage in the case of Beigong You and Meng Shishe is an expression of strength, a "forcing" of *qi* on an object (*qiang* 強). While challenging the conventional understanding of "strength," the *Laozi* testifies to the connection between courage, *xin*, and *qi*: "The heart exerting *qi* is what is called strength (心使氣曰強)" (chap. 55). The cultivation of courage is evidently a matter of nourishing and applying one's *qi*. It follows also that the kind of *budongxin* exemplified by Beigong You and Meng Shishe results from the same process. Is the kind of *budongxin* embodied by Mencius and Gaozi, then, in any way different from those discussed so far?

Qi, Zhi 志, and *Yan* 言

Gongsun Chou goes on to inquire about Mencius' *budongxin* and Gaozi's *budongxin*. It would appear that he had in mind not so much two different methods to arrive at *budongxin*, as a distinction between two competing conceptions of *budongxin*. Mencius answers: "Gaozi said, 'If you do not get it from words, do not seek it in the heart; if you do not get it from the heart, do not seek it in *qi*' (告子曰,不得於言,勿求於心;不得於心,勿求於氣)."

The relationship among *yan*, *xin*, and *qi* is crucial to understanding Mencius' approach to self-cultivation. According to Mencius, while the second half of Gaozi's maxim is admissible, the first is not. The text continues, "*Zhi* is the commander of *qi*; and *qi* is that which fills the body. When *zhi* arrives, *qi* is sure to follow. Thus it is said, 'take hold of your *zhi* and do not abuse your *qi*' (夫志,氣之帥也,氣,體之充也.夫志至焉,氣次焉.故曰,持其志,無暴其氣)."

I follow Kwong-Loi Shun in taking the word *zhi* 志, often rendered "will," to mean aims or direction of the heart.[17] The concept of *zhi* serves to clarify the relationship between *qi* and *xin*. Well-nourished *qi* is necessary to set the heart in a firm direction. But this is evidently not sufficient, for the heart could be set in the wrong direction. The *Lunyu* points out that "the Three Armies can be deprived of their commanding officer, but even a common man cannot be deprived of his purpose (*zhi*)" (9.26; Lau, trans.). This seems to imply that once the heart is set, it is not easily moved. The perceived strength of *zhi* thus makes it all the more important to set the right direction for the *xin*, so that correct words and deeds would follow.

To pursue this line of questioning further, consider first Mencius' account of the relationship between *qi* and *zhi*. The claim that *qi* "fills" (*chong* 充) the body can be regarded as generally accepted in early Chinese thought. Commentators generally refer to the *Guanzi* in this regard, where *qi* is similarly defined as that which fills the body.[18] The more general account in the *Zhuangzi* (chap. 22) should also help establish a baseline for understanding the *Mencius* in this context: "Man's life is a coming together of breath (*qi*). If it comes together, there is life; if it scatters, there is death."[19] At this point, suffice it to say that in being filled—the word *chong* also gives the sense of "developing" something, according to the *Shuowen*[20]—the body, including the *xin*, grows.

The claim that the heart through its *zhi* commands *qi* is more complex. In emphasizing that *zhi* is the commander of *qi*, is Mencius saying that *qi* would always follow where the heart directs it to go? If this were the case, as Gongsun Chou goes on to ask, why must one hold fast to *zhi* and at the same time not abuse one's *qi*? Mencius' reply reveals his concern with nourishing *qi*: "If *zhi* is concerted or concentrated (*yi*), then it moves *qi*. If *qi* is concerted, then it moves *zhi*. Now stumbling and hurrying is *qi*, but it turns back to move the heart (志壹則動氣,氣壹則動志也.今夫蹶者趨者,是氣也.而反動其心)."

The meaning of *yi* 壹 has been disputed. D. C. Lau, following Zhao Qi, translates, "The will, when blocked (*yi*), moves the *qi*. On the other hand, the *qi*, when blocked, also moves the will." According to Zhu Xi, if *zhi* is "concentrated" or "focused" (*zhuanyi* 專一) in one direction, *qi* would follow; but if *qi* acts in concert or concentrates on one thing, it would in turn affect *zhi*. I follow Zhu Xi's reading, although the two interpretations are perhaps not as far apart as they seem. The *Shuowen* links *yi* to the character *hu* 壺, a flasklike container, which yields the image of *qi* bottled up.[21] There is thus a sense of enclosure, but the more basic meaning seems to be that of a convergence or concentration of *qi*. Thus, in "stumbling and hurrying" the *qi* gathers, generates vigor—as if armed guards rushing to the same spot and charging at the same target—and takes control of the heart. Is the *Mencius* saying that the heart and *qi* must be "unified," in the sense that the heart through a resolute *zhi* exercises complete control over *qi*? The *Zhuangzi* (chap. 19) at one point discusses the "perfect" person, who among other things "can travel above the ten thousand things without being frightened." He can do this because "he guards the pure breath (*chunqi* 純氣)—it has nothing to do with wisdom, skill, determination, or courage";[22] he "unifies his nature" (*yi qi xing* 壹其性) and "nourishes his *qi*." Although this conveys a critique of the Mencian position, I take the nourishing of *qi* and its effect on the heart and "nature" to be a crucial issue in *Mencius* 2A2.[23]

The evidence presented so far suggests that Mencius is keenly concerned with nourishing one's *qi*, without which it would not be possible to attain *budongxin*. However, this is fundamentally different from the conception of *budongxin* exemplified by Meng Ben, Beigong You, and Meng Shishe, where *qi* is overpowering. The firmness of *zhi* is not in question; in all cases, the condition that *zhi* commands *qi* is met. But theirs is essentially a matter of manipulating "the *qi* of the blood," against which the *Lunyu* has already warned.[24] In the case of Beigong You, whether the motivation was to avoid social disgrace or simply to overwhelm one's opponents—both of which are *qi*-driven—the resultant domination of *qi* would only induce violence. Meng Shishe's courage shifts focus from a display of force to self-control. It is still a matter of nourishing and securing one's *qi*; but whereas Beigong You's strength centers on directing *qi* outward to overcome others, Meng Shishe's is a self-directed cultivation that focuses on overcoming one's own fear. The idea of *yue* 約 introduced earlier may well be used in this sense, pointing to an exercise that is "binding"—the basic meaning of the word seems to be to tie or bind something with a rope (e.g., *Laozi*, chap. 27)—as opposed to *bo* 博 (wide application)[25] or *zhang* 張 (extend widely).[26] That is to say, whereas Beigong You aims to extend his powerful *qi* to the widest possible extent, Meng Shishe ropes it in, restrains it, corralling or harnessing the vital energy, thereby rendering it more focused and in this sense "binding" in the heart.[27] It is more "important" compared with Beigong You's indiscriminate application of raw power because, in Mencius' estimation, it reflects a tighter command of *qi*.

The introduction of Zengzi (cf. *Mencius* 4A19) brings into view an ethical dimension in the cultivation of courage or *qi*, the underlying stuff of courage. An "unmoved heart" can mean a heart that is unfeeling or indifferent to ethical judgment. This is now shown to be inadequate. In Zengzi's case, *budongxin* is not just a sheer concentration of *qi* but rather *qi* with a moral focus. The process is accomplished through reflection and introspection (*zifan*), a function of the heart that is lacking in Meng Shishe's cultivation of courage.[28] Ethical reflection, in comparison with the kind of *shouqi* aimed at removing fear, is even more focused and binding, guiding *qi* in the direction of rightness. Gaozi's *budongxin* is presumably superior to Beigong You's and Meng Shishe's. The implication thus seems to be that Gaozi's *budongxin* also has an ethical dimension.

The first half of Gaozi's maxim—"If you do not get it from words, do not seek it in the heart"—articulates a view of the ethical ideal that is based on "words" (*yan*). *Yan* may mean teachings or doctrines, as Nivison points out.[29] But what can one possibly "get" (*de* 得) from *yan*? The primary function of *yan* is to "know things" (*yan yi zhi wu* 言以知物), according to the *Zuozhuan*.[30] This seems straightforward enough, but the role of *yan* poses a serious question in early Chinese philosophy. The *Zhuangzi*, for example, has this to say: "Words are not just wind. Words have something to say. But if what they have to say is not fixed, then do they really say something?"[31] "Wind"—or, in A. C. Graham's translation, "blowing breath" —can refer only to *qi*.[32] In this instance, Zhuangzi's challenge is that "*yan* has no constancy"; failing to recognize this, "we have the rights and wrongs of the Confucians and the Mohists."[33]

Words are expressions of the aims and direction of the heart. The relationship between *yan* and *zhi* is well attested in the *Lunyu* (e.g., 5.26, 11.26). *Zhi* is defined in the *Shuowen* as *yi* 意 (intention, meaning, or idea). The Qing dynasty scholar Duan Yucai comments that *zhi* was interchangeable with *shi* 識, which means primarily to know (*zhi* 知).[34] The *Shuowen* also links "poetry" (*shi* 詩) to *zhi* and adds, according to one commentator, that "*zhi* finds expression in words" (*zhi fa yu yan* 志發於言).[35] According to the *Da Dai Liji*, "food forms tastes; tastes form *qi; qi* forms *zhi*; expressing *zhi,* words are formed; issuing words, names are established; names serve to bring forth trust (食為味,味為氣,氣為志,發志而言,發言定名,名以出信)."[36] The *Zuozhuan* also states, "Tastes (i.e., food) serve to animate *qi; qi* serves to firm *zhi; zhi* serves to establish words; and words serve to issue commands."[37]

The sources of moral and political order must be clearly delineated. Words are important because the knowledge they purvey is instrumental to the flourishing of the state. These pronouncements obviously assume that the consequent decrees or commands would in fact bring order. Like Zhuangzi, however, Mencius is acutely aware that the desired outcome is by no means assured. This is because the concept of *zhi* specifies not only the way in which the heart directs *qi* but also how the heart can be moved by *qi.* The relationship between *zhi* and *qi,* in other words, runs in two opposite directions. On the one hand, *qi* is understood as having the power to move the heart, in the sense of setting its aims and direction, which in turn would find expression in thoughts, words, appearance, deeds, commands, policies, and other practical outcomes. On the other hand, *zhi* is ideally in command of *qi,* leading it in a direction that the heart deems desirable. Mencius and Gaozi, I believe, were equally concerned with this problem. In their own way, recognizing the power of *qi,* they each sought to demonstrate that the heart could command the vital energy in its pursuit of the ethical life. In Mencius' view, as we shall see, Gaozi fails because he fundamentally misjudges the role of *qi* in the tending of the heart.

The Heart That Commands *Qi*

Provided that it is not starved, *qi* finds expression in *zhi,* which in turn directs words and behavior. Physical exertion, emotional influences, mental labor, and other forms of *qi* movements can be assumed to play a role in the shaping of *zhi.* Hurrying and stumbling will affect the *xin;* the blood quickens, as it were, and one breathes harder as *qi* concentrates in response. Eating hot chili pepper, being slapped in the face, being afraid of making a fool of oneself in a learned conference, and practically everything we do or that is done to us will have an impact on our *qi,* which in turn would move the heart in certain ways. At this level, there is little to disagree about; *dongxin* is simply part of the human condition.

According to the *Zuozhuan,* heaven gave rise to the "six *qi,*" which laid the foundation of the cosmos.[38] I will not dwell on this point, for cosmological speculation does not appear to be a main concern in the *Mencius.* The *Zuozhuan,* however, also indicates that if the "six *qi*" were in excess, the people would lose their "nature" (*xing*). Further, "people have likes, dislikes, pleasure, anger, sorrow, and joy, which are born of the six *qi*"; to prevent excess, the sage ruler would need to carefully regulate the "six *zhi.*"[39] The *Mencius* cannot but be seriously concerned about this.

The "six *qi*" may have derived from an original energy, as the *Zhuangzi* implies.[40] They give rise to the five tastes, the five colors, and other phenomena. In the human body, the "six *qi*" form the basis of six main affective-cognitive tendencies, which can move the heart in different directions. Among the six, the natural tendency to "like" (*hao* 好) or "dislike" (*wu* 惡) certain things is the most basic. Being of "one heart" (*yixin* 壹心) with another person, according to the *Zuozhuan,* means that one's "likes and dislikes are the same" as the other's. Further, "pleasure or gladness is born of likes, and anger is born of dislikes.... The things one likes [referring especially to life] bring joy, and the things one dislikes [especially death] bring sorrow (喜生於好,怒生於惡 ... 好物樂也,惡物哀也)."[41] One of the bamboo texts discovered recently in Guodian, the *Yucong er* 語叢 二, also affirms that dislikes arise from one's "nature," which in turn give rise to anger (惡生於性,怒生於惡).[42] To be the commander of *qi,* the heart must therefore exercise full "control" over its affective and cognitive movements, particularly as regards what it likes or dislikes. The kind of control that is required and the way to achieve it would distinguish Mencius' approach to self-cultivation from Gaozi's.

If the "six *qi*" are not properly balanced, serious consequences can be expected. Just as disasters would result from imbalance or excesses in the "six *qi*" at the macrocosmic level, illness arises from *qi* excesses in the body. The *Zhuangzi,* for example, reckons that if *qi* rises "without coming back down," it would make one prone to anger; and if it stagnates in the heart, it would cause serious diseases.[43] Since *Mencius* 2A2 is set in the state of Qi, it is perhaps worth noting that these remarks are attributed to a "gentleman of Qi."

The *Zuozhuan* makes it clear that excesses in *qi* produce different diseases; in particular, excesses in the "dark" *qi* associated especially with sexual desires would lead to diseases of the heart marked by doubt and uncertainty (*huoji* 惑疾).[44] The greatest problem with doubt or uncertainty (*huo*) is that it destroys one's *zhi* (*huo yi sang zhi* 惑以喪志).[45]

Mencius would not dispute that *qi* must be well nourished, not "starved," so as to ensure one's physical and mental well-being. Food is evidently one important concern; rest, another. The *Zuozhuan,* for example, explains that health is a matter of one's "coming and going, food and drinks, sorrow and joy." A carefully regulated daily routine, including proper rest at night, would ensure that one's *qi* is expended in due measure, so that it would not stagnate or become exhausted. Should it be concentrated on one (*yi* 壹) activity without due measure, illness is certain to follow.[46] Mencius was probably aware of the kind of breathing exercises and calisthenics designed to enhance one's life span that were gaining popularity and reported, for example, in the *Zhuangzi* (chap. 15). Although there may be different techniques in nourishing *qi,* most would agree that the two extremes of stagnation and overreaching are both harmful.[47] The *Mencius* itself testifies that a person's character can be judged from his words and eyes, both of which reflect one's *qi* constitution.[48] Moreover, Mencius recognizes that one's surroundings can also affect one's *qi.*[49] There is little reason not to believe that Mencius shared with his contemporaries a general understanding of the person as constituted by *qi. Budongxin* describes a firm *zhi,* free from uncertainty and anxiety (*huo*), but this whole conceptual edifice is predicated on the belief that *qi* "fills" the body and makes possible the workings of the heart. This serves as a point of departure for Mencius to develop his insight into human nature, the way of the true king, and other interests.

Beyond physical nourishment, generally a process of taming, forcing, or channeling the powerful energy that informs the heart marks the first step in self-cultivation. The heart is capable of guiding or forcing *qi* into a focused, concentrated form. There does not appear to be any disagreement among early Chinese philosophers on this score. Some may argue that it should not be done, or that it should be done only in certain ways, but not whether it can be done. The simplest operation would be to hold one's breath (cf. *Lunyu* 10.4). If *qi* dictates the direction of one's heart, a heavy blow

to the face may produce a loud cry, which would be a form of utter-
ance, if not *yan* at the most rudimentary level. Being hit on the face
is not something one likes; one possible consequence is that *qi*
would "rise" and generate anger. (In modern Chinese, of course,
shengqi, "being angry," literally means giving rise to *qi*.) In the case
of Beigong You, likes and dislikes, pleasure and anger, sorrow and
joy, and other affective-cognitive concerns would be ordered into
one overriding *qi* response to retaliate. In the case of Meng Shishe,
fear, pain, and other disturbances cannot move the heart, which remains focused in its concentrated effort to secure *qi*. At a higher
level, a blow to the face would necessitate ethical reflection, which
not only puts *qi* under control but also brings into focus the aims
and direction of the heart and gives voice to them in words and action. I see little disagreement between Gaozi and Mencius on this
account of the operation of the heart as commander of *qi*.

The problem is that the heart does not have a fixed direction.
This is brought out clearly in the Guodian fragment entitled *Xing zi
ming chu* 性自命出: "Although all human beings have *xing,* the heart
does not have a fixed direction. It is formed after it has come into
contact with things (凡人雖有性,心無定志,待物而後作)."[50] From
Gaozi's perspective, knowledge and discrimination thus prove decisive. To cultivate *budongxin,* one should start with acquiring knowledge, which would inform the heart and set its direction. Recall
Gaozi's saying, "If you do not get it from words, do not seek it in the
heart; if you do not get it from the heart, do not seek it in *qi*." If one
does not "get" a sense of direction from words—that is, does not
know where one should be headed in the ethical life—then there is
little point seeking it in the heart, and still less in *qi*. To arrive at a
xin that is set in the direction of rightness, cannot be moved, and is
in total command of *qi*, one must learn.[51]

Huang Zongxi 黃宗羲 (1610–1695) makes a fine point when
he argues that for Gaozi, *qi* is essentially the operation and movement of *xin*—consciousness or one's capacity to know (*zhijue* 知
覺).[52] Gaozi would agree with Mencius that, when unified or concerted, *qi* can move the heart and dictate one's words and action.
For this reason, the heart must be firm in its aims and direction. But
the "internal" operation of *xin* and *qi* cannot by itself establish the
proper course that one should take. This has to do with knowledge
derived from contact with things. Some knowledge of the main features of the cosmos, for example, would be necessary. One would

need to know that imbalance of *qi* would bring ruin to nature and oneself. The importance of establishing trust and proper policies must also be recognized. All these can be acquired only from "words," which bridges the gap between the "internal" and the "external." Guarding one's *qi* would be pointless if it were not informed by knowledge.[53]

For both Gaozi and Mencius, as Huang Zongxi and Jiao Xun equally emphasize, there is little difference between the training of *zhi* (*chizhi* 持志) and the cultivation of *qi* (*yangqi* 養氣). But for Mencius, Gaozi is only half-correct. It is admissible that if one does not find the proper direction in one's heart, one should not expect to find it in *qi*. The reason for this will be explained later. It is not admissible, however, to say that if one does not know the proper direction from words, one should not seek it in one's heart. This is because the heart knows. What does the heart know?

From the Guodian material, one gathers that "human nature" (*xing*) was understood primarily in terms of the affective-cognitive tendencies generated by *qi*. The *Xing zi ming chu* states, "The *qi* of pleasure, anger, sorrow, and grief is *xing* (喜怒哀悲之氣, 性也)." The heart always has a certain *zhi*, as the text also relates, and thus it is crucial that *zhi* be regulated carefully so that it does not succumb to the dictates of excessive *qi*.[54] In this regard, there seems to be wide agreement among the *Zuozhuan*, *Zhuangzi*, Gaozi, and the Guodian texts.

"Human nature," in this view, is thus essentially a "biological" construct.[55] Without *qi*, life ceases; starved or not nourished properly, *qi* would lose its energy, become confused, or dissipate. In this framework, one can then talk about the formation of basic tendencies or characteristic features that all human beings share. Collectively these are referred to as *xing;* in relation to things, they are called *qing* 情, the most prominent of which are the emotions. The same picture is reflected in the *Xunzi*, where *xing* is defined as "what characterizes a man from birth" (生之所以然者謂之性) and *qing* as the "feelings of liking and disliking, of delight and anger, and of sorrow and joy that are inborn in our nature" (性之好惡喜怒哀樂謂 之情). *Xing* stems from heaven, the *Xunzi* further explains; and *qing* "are the substance of that nature" (性者天之就也, 情者性之質也).[56] Both the Guodian *Xing zi ming chu* and *Yucong er* fragment also confirm that whereas *xing* stems from *qi*, "*qing* are born of *xing*" (情生 於性).[57] These references point to a generally shared view, which philosophers can refine and develop further. The suggestion here is that Mencius also subscribed to this basic understanding. However, for Mencius, there is an important distinction. Whereas Gaozi identifies *qi* in human beings with the "*qi* of the blood," Mencius argues that *qi* can be nourished in such a way as to become one with rightness and propriety.

The "Floodlike *Qi*" (*Haoranzhiqi*)

"I know words," Mencius says, in reply to Gongsun Chou's question as to what his "strong points" are, "and I am proficient in nourishing my floodlike *qi* (我知言, 我善養吾浩然之氣)." It is difficult to explain, as Mencius continues, but the "floodlike *qi*" is nonetheless a form of *qi*. How is it different from other forms of *qi*? It is "extremely vast and unyielding" (*zhida zhigang* 至大至剛). If it is nourished with "straightness" (*zhi* 直) and suffers no harm, then it would "fill the space between heaven and earth." As a form of *qi*, it "joins with rightness and the Way" (*pei yi yu dao* 配義與道); if not, it will "starve" and "shrivel up" (*nei* 餒).[58] It is, in Lau's translation,

> born of accumulated rightness and cannot be appropriated by anyone through a sporadic show of rightness. Whenever one acts in a way that falls below the standard set in one's heart, it will collapse. Hence I said Gaozi never understood rightness because he looked upon it as external. (是集義所生者, 非義襲而取之也. 行有不慊於心, 則餒矣. 我故曰告子未嘗知義, 以其外之也.)

The usage of *da* 大 (great or vast), *gang* 剛 (unyielding, vigorous, or resolute), and *zhi* 直 (straight or upright) may point to a conception akin to the *yangqi* 陽氣—assuming that the *yinyang* theory was current by Mencius' time—that generates heaven and light. This would distinguish Mencius' view from especially the Daoist conception of *qi*, which tends to emphasize yieldingness (e.g., *Laozi*, chap. 10). But the more important point is that the floodlike *qi* cannot survive without the sustenance of rightness and the Dao. Given the general view that tastes serve to animate *qi*, the imagery is apt. Taking the metaphor one step further, the floodlike *qi* can flourish only if it is nourished consistently by rightness. Evidently Gaozi represents the view that the cultivation of *qi* depends on learning about the ethical life from "outside" sources, which in Mencius' view amounts to a piecemeal, haphazard, and unsustainable approach to ethical development.

Since Mencius is disputing Gaozi's assertion, the source of rightness must be "inside." The heart seems a logical candidate. This raises three possibilities. First, Mencius could be saying that the heart possesses certain ethical dispositions, which it uses, as it were, to feed *qi*. When sufficiently nourished, one's *qi* would become strong and morally excellent—*haoran* qualifies both the strength and moral character of this highly developed form of *qi*. In this sense, one can even speak of a moral transformation of *qi*, which ensures compliance with rightness and propriety in every step one takes.

This interpretation highlights the centrality of the heart but may not fully capture Mencius' understanding of *xin* and *qi*. The *xin* is *qi*, as Huang Zongxi bluntly puts it.[59] This is a substantive definition, which in the strong reading offered here precludes any non-*qi* stuff forming a part of the original heaven-endowed heart. If human beings were endowed with certain ethical dispositions, they would themselves be formed by *qi*. This brings us to a second interpretation of Mencius' *haoranzhiqi*, which tries to avoid the kind of circular reasoning that is evident in the first.

Although the body as a whole is formed by *qi*, different parts are characterized by specific functions. No one in early China would dispute that the eyes, for example, are the organ of sight and that the important thing is to see clearly. The heart is the seat of both cognitive and affective functions. The *Mencius* emphasizes that the heart is uniquely empowered to "think" (*si* 思). Whereas the organs of sight and hearing cannot think and are thus easily misled by things, the heart thinks and is able to "get it."[60] The usage of "get" (*de* 得) recalls Gaozi's maxim, and one may assume that the object of one's reflection is rightness. In other words, the heart can manage the influences of things on *qi* and set a proper direction because it is able to discern what is right and wrong. In this way, Mencius offers a functional account of the heart, which recognizes the special role the *xin* plays in the ethical life without denying its constitutive root in *qi*.

Still, this does not seem to give the whole picture. The problem with this interpretation is that it does not distinguish Mencius' position sufficiently from Gaozi's. The discerning power of the heart is not in contention. Gaozi could easily have made the same distinction between the heart and the various organs of sense. Precisely because the heart can think, it is able to learn from words and set itself in the direction of rightness. Not to be misled by things is good, but the point is moot if there were no contact with things in the first instance. The heart may be a powerful receptacle, but it is ultimately dependent on the external world for ethical knowledge and discipline. The *Mencius* itself distinguishes between prereflective and reflective thinking and suggests that there is a deeper ethical resource in the process of self-cultivation (7A15).

A third possibility focuses on the operation of *qi* itself. My suggestion is that in the context of 2A2, Mencius was probably referring to the *qing* of liking and disliking, which gives rise to pleasure, anger, and other emotions. In other words, the *xin* "likes" rightness or propriety, is naturally inclined toward it, just as it naturally prefers certain tastes. It is in this sense that one's feeling of commiseration or respect, which is generated by *qi*, is said to arise naturally from the heart. This seems to find support from two other passages in the *Mencius*.

Mencius 6A6, first of all, seems to suggest that "goodness" (*shan* 善) stems ultimately from one's *qing*, the basic "facts" or affective-cognitive tendencies of the heart. Rightness, in particular, can be traced to the heart of shame and dislike. Forming part of one's natural constitution, and discernible if one cares to think about it, *qing* itself makes possible ethical development. If one seeks it—that is, in one's heart—one will "get" it.[61] *Mencius* 6A7 concludes that just as human beings share certain basic tastes, they have the same preference in their heart for order and rightness: "The way in which order and rightness please my heart is like the way meat is pleasing to my palate." Both passages seem to support the claim that a sense of rightness and propriety, or more precisely a "taste" for rightness, informs the *qing* of human beings, in particular the natural tendency to be drawn to or repulsed by certain things.

If rightness can be traced to *qing*, and given that *qing* arises from *qi*, why did Mencius agree with Gaozi that if one does not get proper direction from the heart, it would be futile to find it in *qi*? If the argument is that one's *qi* endowment includes certain moral tastes or sensibilities, why not go to the source and seek them there? The answer may be that likes and dislikes compete to dominate the heart. The heart "knows" what it likes, but it likes many things; without cultivation it is thus not in a position to command the many forces of *qi*. Through cultivation, the heart knows not only what it likes but, more importantly, also why it should like certain things over others that it equally likes, and consequently it attains *budong-xin* and moves in a firm direction. But this does not detract from the fact that *qi* can pull one in different directions, and for that reason *qi* cannot be relied upon in determining the proper direction of the heart. Relying on one's likes and dislikes alone, one would find it confusing, would find oneself in a state of *huo*, unable to decide between fish and bear's paw, or between life and rightness, all of which one likes (*Mencius* 6A10).

Further, the natural preference for rightness and order cannot easily withstand the many influences from without. This interpretation seems to find support from *Mencius* 6A8. Just as the Ox Mountain faces the prospect of deforestation, the heart, though gifted with an inherent liking for the good (*liangxin* 良心), is constantly under attack from external demands. *Dongxin* is a fact of life; in the ethical sense it is deemed undesirable and requiring of a remedy. There is apparently a natural remedy, for just as the Ox Mountain can regain its former beauty if given the necessary respite, the heart can also rely on the sustenance of nature to allow it to recover its original *xing* and *qing*. In the quiet of the night or early morning, before the daily onslaught on one's heart begins anew, the natural inclination toward propriety and aversion toward impropriety has perhaps the best chance of being preserved. The heart that naturally favors rightness and propriety marks the "slight" element that distinguishes human beings from animals, according to Mencius (see also 4B19). Still, given the reality of the social life-world, the healing "*qi* of the night" (*yeqi* 夜氣) is not likely to be sufficient.[62] If one cannot rely on "outside" sources or *qi* itself for ethical direction, and given that the heart is constantly moved by competing interests, what must one do to secure rightness? The solution, of course, lies in nourishing one's *haoranzhiqi*.

As is well known, the assertion that the floodlike *qi* would fill heaven and earth has been taken to support a "mystical" strain in Mencius' philosophy.[63] The interpretation put forward here emphasizes Mencius' understanding of the heart as constituted by *qi* and may be regarded as "reductionistic" in this light. Ethics and spirituality are not mutually exclusive; nevertheless, the concept of a transcendental ego remains alien to Mencius, and *haoranzhiqi* arises out of "accumulated rightness," not meditation or mystical contemplation. More fundamentally, the nature of Mencian ethics cannot be understood unless we recognize that Mencius was not immune from the *qi* "theories" that captured the elite imagination—if not at the level of popular culture also—in his time. After all, heaven produces the "six *qi*"; the nature of the vital energy that fuels life, including the ethical life, must be properly understood and articulated. Mencius clearly believed that one's natural delight in rightness and propriety can be nourished to such an extent that it defines the whole person. Only then would one be able to remain unmoved in the face of new challenges. Indeed, the floodlike energy would radiate from the heart and find expression in one's face and bearing (*Mencius* 7A21). Of course, if one acts in any way that proves distasteful to the discerning moral palate of the heart, one's *haoranzhiqi* would starve, lose force, and collapse.

In contrast with Gaozi's model, Mencius offers an integral and holistic approach to self-cultivation. What Gaozi did was to reverse the chain of *qi, xin/zhi,* and *yan,* so that *yan* would discipline the heart and force the willful *qi* into order. It is a kind of force-feeding in the sense that the heart must be given its direction based on an objective assessment of what ought to be the case. Perhaps this is also what the *Xing zi ming chu* has in mind when it announces that the "beginning" is close to *qing,* and the "end" is close to *yi* (始者近情, 終者近義).[64]

The *Mencius* cannot but start from the same premise that *qi* energizes the heart and manifests itself in words and action; but it gives wider scope to nature. While one naturally prefers and thus easily indulges in fine tastes and pleasing colors, it is just as natural for the heart to prefer order and rightness. The problem of *dongxin* is not the fact that the heart moves—animated by *qi,* it is always moving in certain directions—but that it may move contrary to rightness, that it may lose its taste for rightness. Conversely, *budongxin* does not mean that the heart is not moving or that one should avoid contact with things. As the *Mencius* itself suggests, "greatness" can hardly be accomplished if the heart is not put through the most trying tests (6B15). Yet, the cultivation of *budongxin* cannot rely on artificial means. Precisely because the heart and the person as a whole is constituted by *qi*—substantively in forming the body and functionally in generating thought and action—self-cultivation cannot involve any violent uprooting or suppression of *qi*. The heart may be more important than the tongue, and it would be foolish to indulge in the desires of the "lesser parts" of the body at the expense of the heart (*Mencius* 6A14), but self-cultivation does not mean

doing violence to one's tongue. The Mencian approach thus seeks
to unify *qi, xin,* and *yan* into one single orientation toward rightness
and propriety.

Mencius 2A2 continues with the famous story of the man from
Song, who pulled up his plants to help them grow, which drives
home that self-cultivation is a natural process. Cultivation is crucial,
but artificial manipulation,[65] neglect, or discipline by force would
equally damage the "slight" element that distinguishes human beings from animals. Not eating is bad; force-feeding is also bad.
Artificial dieting is misguided; nothing short of a consistently whole-
some diet and regular exercise would do to nourish the floodlike *qi.*
This is the significance of "accumulating rightness," as distinguished
from any "sporadic show of rightness." The natural taste for rightness must be nourished into a profound moral vigor that would
triumph over temptations in every instance and guide the heart in
the direction of rightness. With the help of ritual and careful deliberation of case-specific circumstances, one would then be able not
only to do the right thing but also to do it right. The natural basis of
rightness was likely a hotly debated topic at that time.[66] The Guodian
text *Tang Yu zhi dao* 唐虞之道, for example, is quite clear in its recommendation that one should curb the *qing* of the blood-*qi* (*xueqi zhi
qing* 血氣之情) so that one can nourish the "right" nature and destiny (*xingming zhi zheng* 性命之正).[67]

Once the heart is in command of *qi*—or, better, when *qi* becomes *haoranzhiqi*—"knowing words" (*zhiyan* 知言) would follow. Although Mencius spoke of his strength in "knowing words" before introducing the idea of "nourishing the floodlike *qi*," it is probably no
accident that he proceeded to discuss the latter first. The *Mencius*
then concludes,

> From biased words I can see wherein the speaker is blind; from im-
> moderate words, wherein he is ensnared; from heretical words,
> wherein he has strayed from the right path; from evasive words,
> wherein he is at his wits' end. What arises in the mind (*xin*) will in-
> terfere with policy, and what shows itself in policy will interfere with
> practice. Were a sage to rise again, he would surely agree with what
> I have said. (Lau, trans.)

This confirms the general relationship between *yan, xin,* and *qi*
discussed earlier. It also highlights Mencius' disagreement with
Gaozi, who places "words" in a privileged position in the shaping of

the heart. Like Zhuangzi perhaps, Mencius was wary of the many doctrines that are evasive, immoderate, biased, and contrary to rightness and propriety (see also *Mencius* 3B9).

Conclusion

Huang Zongxi observes astutely that for Mencius *zhiyan* is in fact an item on the *yangqi* agenda.[68] Holistically understood, "knowing words" presupposes a heart that is ethically in command. Having few desires would be crucial in this regard (*Mencius* 7B35).[69] The work of "preserving the heart" (*cunxin* 存心), according to the *Mencius,* focuses on nourishing one's nature (7A1). This is but another way of saying that one's *qi* must be guarded and carefully nourished so that its natural preference for rightness would tower above all other likes and dislikes and thus be in a position to direct the heart in all its activities. *Budongxin* does not entail that one would no longer delight in pleasing food or sound; but rather that the desire for rightness would always have the final say. In this sense, the heart can be said to be the commander of *qi*. At this level, however, there is also a sense in which the distinction between leader and follower breaks down. The heart is certainly not a harsh ruler whose orders the forces of *qi* grudgingly obey. Rather, the *xin* and the entire issue of *qi* merge into a powerful, unified, "floodlike" energy that would render possible the way of the true king. In 2A6, Mencius likens the "four beginnings" to a fire starting to spread or a stream starting to flow. If they could be extended to "fill" the entire person, they would be powerful enough to defend the realm and indeed to allow the ruler to govern the world as if it were an object in his palm. Without turning the metaphoric into the mystical, this seems a fitting commentary on the *haoranzhiqi*.[70]

Mencian self-cultivation is a large topic and falls outside the scope of this paper. These remarks serve only to show that *Mencius* 2A2 should be read in the larger context of the Mencian enterprise. No doubt, Mencius was concerned to distinguish his views from his opponents';[71] but it would be a mistake to disregard his indebtedness to the beliefs current in his time. The concept of *qi* had already made its mark on the Chinese intellectual scene. To cite but one more example, the Guodian text *Taiyi sheng shui* 太一生水 states categorically that what is "above is *qi,* and is called heaven" (上,氣也,而謂之天).[72] One could interpret the concept of *qi* in different ways or dispute others' conceptions of it, but by the time of Mencius one could certainly not afford to ignore it.

The meaning of rightness or propriety can be rigorously debated; yet at least from the Han period onward it has always been understood substantively as *qi*. Neo-Confucians of the Song-Ming period, in particular, devoted considerable energy to debating whether the floodlike *qi* was already existent at the beginning of heaven and earth and inherent in human nature. Huang Zongxi, for example, supports the view that human beings are already endowed with the *haoranzhiqi* at birth and accuses Zhu Xi of having confused the issue.[73]

The argument presented here would disagree with Huang's account; in the context of *Mencius* 2A2, it seems more likely that Mencius was thinking of a process of self-cultivation that would distinguish the "great man" from the ordinary people. What is endowed is the taste for rightness, but the kind of moral vigor that is "extremely vast and unyielding" is the result of a lifelong process of nourishing *qi* and tending the heart. Nevertheless, the point remains that no Neo-Confucian has ever doubted Mencius' understanding of rightness as having to do with the *xin* and therefore with *qi*. In the preface to his commentary on the *Mencius*, Zhu Xi recounts Cheng Yi's view that whereas Confucius spoke only of *zhi*, Mencius articulated a whole theory of nourishing one's *qi*.[74] This insightful comment lies very much at the root of the present inquiry. *Yiqi* 義 氣, the "*qi* of rightness," is still a significant value term in modern Chinese. I submit that this represents an important aspect of the Mencian legacy.[75]

Notes

I would like to thank Kim-Chong Chong for his insightful comments on an earlier version of this paper.

1. In late 1993, the excavation of a tomb (identified as M1) in Guodian, Jingmen city, Hubei province, yielded 730 inscribed bamboo strips, containing more than thirteen thousand characters. Some of these, amounting to about two thousand characters, match the *Laozi*, whereas the others are generally Daoist and Confucian in outlook. The tomb is located near the old capital of the state of Chu and is dated to around 300 B.C.E. Unfortunately, it suffered damage as a result of two robberies in 1993, so that some bamboo strips may have been stolen. A transcribed version was recently published under the

title *Guodian Chumu zhujian* 郭店楚墓竹簡 (Beijing: Wenwu chubanshe, 1998). Some thirty essays on the Guodian find have been collected in *Zhongguo zhexue* 中國哲學 20 (1999). See also the essay by Ning Chen in this volume. The works by Lau and others will be cited separately later. All Chinese terms are given in pinyin, except for a few names, published titles, and quotations cited in the notes.

2. There is probably no single word in English that could capture fully the meaning of *yi*. It may be prudent to leave the term untranslated, but because this essay already makes use of a full complement of transliterations, I adopt Lau's translation, "rightness," or in some cases "rightness and propriety." Rightness represents a key condition necessary for the flourishing of the ethical ideal. In this discussion, the question that needs to be addressed concerns not so much the content as the source of rightness.

3. Compare D. C. Lau, trans., *Mencius,* vol. 1 (Hong Kong: Chinese University of Hong Kong Press, 1984), 54. Translations from the *Mencius* are based on Lau's, with modification on the basis of my own reading of the text. Unless otherwise stated, translations from other Chinese texts are my own.

4. See Jeffrey Riegel, "Reflections on an Unmoved Mind: An Analysis of *Mencius 2A2*," in *Studies in Classical Chinese Thought*, ed. Henry Rosemont Jr. and Benjamin I. Schwartz (*Journal of the American Academy of Religion* 47.3, Thematic Issue S [1980]: 433–457), for a different translation and discussion of these issues. Also see Robert Eno's discussion in this volume.

5. Zhu Xi, *Mengzi jizhu* 孟子集注, in his *Sishu jizhu* 四書集注 (Sibubeiyao 四部備要 ed.) 2.3a (Taipei: Zhonghua shuju, 1973). All quotations from Zhu Xi's commentary on the *Mencius* are from this edition.

6. Jiao Xun, *Mengzi zhengyi* 孟子正義 (Taipei: Shijie shuju, 1966), vol. 1, 111.

7. D. C. Lau, trans., *Confucius: The Analects* (Harmondsworth: Penguin Books, 1979).

8. Zhu Xi did not give any reason, but Meng Ben is cited as a "classic" example of courage in many early texts. This is the account in the *Shiji, juan* 101.2a, commentary (Taipei: Zhonghua shuju, 1970); also cited in *Mengzi zhengyi*. See also Wang Chün-chieh 黃俊傑, "Zhuzi dui Mengzi zhiyan yangqi shuo de quanshi jiqi huixiang" 朱子對孟子知言養氣說的詮釋及其迴響, in his *Mengxue sixiangshi lun* 孟學思想史論, vol. 2 (Taipei: Academia Sinica, 1997), 202–203. This essay was first published in *Qinghua xuebao* (Taiwan) 18.2 (1988). See also Wang's related effort, "Mengzi zhiyan yangqi zhang jishi xinquan" 孟子知言養氣章集釋新詮, *Guoli Taiwan daxue lishixuexi xuebao* 國立臺灣大學歷史學系學報, 14 (1988): 85–120. This essay has been collected in Wang's *Mengxue sixiangshi lun*, vol. 1 (Taipei: Dongda tushugongsi, 1991).

9. *Lüshi chunqiu*, Sibubeiyao ed. (Taipei: Zhonghua shuju, 1979), *Biji* 必己, 14.20b. See also *Zhuangzi*, chap. 17, where the courage of the sage is contrasted with that of the "fisherman," the "hunter," and the "man of ardor" (Burton Watson, trans., *The Complete Works of Chuang Tzu* [New York: Columbia University Press, 1968], 185). The description of the courage of the fisherman and the hunter is the same as that applied to Meng Ben. Bryan Van Norden

likens him to the Hollywood construct "Rambo." See Bryan Van Norden, "Mencius on Courage," *Midwest Studies in Philosophy* 21 (1997): 237–256.

10. *Hanfeizi,* chap. 20, 6.10b. Chen Qiyou 陳奇猷, *Hanfeizi jishi* 韓非子集釋 (Shanghai: Shanghai renmin chubanshe, 1974), vol. 1, 376.

11. This calls to mind the formulation in the *Lunyu,* "The man of courage is never afraid (*buju* 不懼)" (9.29, Lau, *Analects;* the numbering follows Lau's. This saying is repeated in 14.28). Confucius' remark on courage is made in connection with "knowledge" (*zhi* 知) and "benevolence" (*ren* 仁) and should not perhaps be linked to Meng Shishe's courage, which is devoid of ethical content. I mention it here, however, because Zhu Xi evidently has *Mencius* 2A2 in mind in his commentary on *Lunyu* 9.29 (9.28 in Zhu's numbering): "The *qi* is full or sufficient to join with the Way and rightness (氣足以配道義); thus, 'not afraid'." The idea that the *haoranzhiqi* "joins with *yi* and *dao*" will be discussed later.

12. For example, see Yang Bojun 楊伯峻, *Mengzi yizhu* 孟子譯注 (Hong Kong: Zhonghua shuju, 1984), 64–65.

13. See Kwong-Loi Shun's discussion on this point, in his *Mencius and Early Chinese Thought* (Stanford, Calif.: Stanford University Press, 1997), 73–74; and Wang Chün-chieh, "Mengzi zhiyan yangqi zhang jishi xinquan" (1988), 105. Riegel, "Reflections," 438, argues that *yue* in this context should mean something of "psycho-physiological import," a kind of "tension or tightness" resulting from "the absence of nervous trembling or agitation."

14. The problem lies in the character *suo* 縮 and its opposite, *busuo,* which Lau renders "right" and "wrong," respectively. This reading has the support of Zhao Qi 趙歧 (d. 201 C.E.), whose commentary on the *Mencius* is the oldest extant, and Zhu Xi—who defines *suo* as *zhi* 直, "straight"—but I suspect that the passage is better understood in terms of movements of one's *qi*. The *Shuowen jiezi,* the earliest extant Chinese lexicon dating to the Han period, defines *suo* as *luan* 亂, "disorder"; and commentators have emphasized the sense of straightening something or putting things in order. See Duan Yucai 段玉裁, *Shuowen jiezi zhu* 説文解字注 (Shanghai: Shanghai guji chubanshe, 1988), 13a, 646. My sense is that *suo* is likely related to the idea of *yue* 約, that *shouyue* is characterized by or results in orderliness in one's *qi*. The opposite, *busuo,* would lead to *zhui* 惴, which also describes movements of *qi* and which Lau translates deftly as "tremble with fear." Admittedly, however, there is insufficient evidence to confirm this line of interpretation.

15. *Mengzi zhengyi:* 北宮黝事事皆求勝人,故似子夏知道之眾.孟施舍不問能必勝與否,但專守己之不懼,故似曾子得道之大 ... 黝以必勝為強,不如施舍以不懼為強.然施舍之不懼,但以氣自守,不問其義不義也.曾子之強,則以義自守.   Also see Riegel (n. 4 above) and Van Norden (n. 9 above) for comments on Zixia and Zengzi. Xu Fuguan 徐復觀 points out that Zixia's school is known for its emphasis on courage and that Beigong You could be a member of a Confucian school. See his "Mengzi zhiyan yangqi zhang shishi" 孟子知言養氣章試釋, in *Zhongguo sixiangshi lunji* 中國思想史論集 (Taipei: Zhongyang shuju, 1951), 143. Wang Chün-chieh discusses this point further in "Mengzi zhiyan yangqi zhang jishi xinquan," 93 and 99. It is possible, as Kim-Chong Chong pointed out to

me, that what characterizes Beigong You is his attitude toward winning, as distinguished from actual victory in every case; but this does not affect the main argument presented here.

16. *Shuowen jiezi zhu,* 13b, 701.

17. Kwong-Loi Shun, *Mencius and Early Chinese Thought,* 66.

18. For example, chap. 37, *Xinshuxia* 心術下: "*Qi* is that which fills the body ... if it is not filled properly, then the heart would not obtain (its proper function) (氣者身之充也 ... 充不美，則心不得)." *Guanzi jinzhu jinyi* 管子今註今譯 (Taipei: Shangwu yinshuguan, 1990), vol. 2, 647. Whether the *Mencius* was "influenced" by the *Guanzi* or other sources is not the issue here; rather, the assertion is more simply that Mencius shared with his contemporaries certain basic ideas about the constitution of the human being. On the *Guanzi,* see W. Allyn Rickett, trans., *Guanzi: Political, Economic, and Philosophical Essays from Early China,* 2 vols. (Princeton, N.J.: Princeton University Press, 1985 and 1998), and Russell Kirkland, "Varieties of Taoism in Ancient China: A Preliminary Comparison of Themes in the *Nei Yeh* and Other Taoist Classics," *Taoist Resources* 7.2 (1997): 73–86. See also Harold D. Roth, *Original Tao: Inward Training (Nei Yeh) and the Foundations of Taoist Mysticism* (New York: Columbia University Press, 1999), for a fascinating account of "inner cultivation" in the *Guanzi* and other early Daoist sources. Riegel notes the similarities between *Mencius* 2A2 and the *Nei Ye* chapter of the *Guanzi* but argues that "in his discussion of *ch'i* [*qi*] Mencius nowhere adopts the purely physiological conceptualization found in the *Nei Yeh*"; see Riegel, "Reflections on an Unmoved Mind," 449. Jiao Xun, *Mengzi zhengyi,* cites the *Huainanzi,* chap. 1: "*Qi* is that which fills living things (氣者生之充也)"; but some have argued that the word *chong* is a mistake here. See also D. C. Lau's discussion of 2A2 in the introduction, xxii–xxv, to his translation of the *Mencius.*

19. Watson, *Complete Works of Chuang Tzu,* 235; cf. A. C. Graham, trans., *Chuang Tzu: The Inner Chapters* (London: George Allen and Unwin, 1981), 160. Compare the *Guanzi,* chap. 12, *Shuyan* 樞言 ("Cardinal Sayings"), "When the vital force (*qi*) is present, things live; when not, things die. What lives does so by virtue of its vital force." As translated in Allyn Rickett, *Guanzi,* vol. 1, 216.

20. *Shuowen jiezi zhu,* 8b, 405.

21. *Shuowen jiezi zhu,* 10b, 495–496. Yang Rubin 楊儒賓 draws attention to a passage in one of the Mawangdui manuscripts, the *Shi da jing* 十大經 (to follow the older title cited by Yang; more recent scholarship generally concurs that it should be read as *Shiliu jing* 十六經), in which the word *yi* is used to describe one's words and conduct. The context seems to suggest a contrast between words and action that are *yi* and those that are superficially colorful or ornamental. This implies that *yi* conveys a sense of fullness or something substantial. See Yang Rubin, "Lun Mengzi de jianxing guan" 論孟子的踐形觀, *Qinghua xuebao* 清華學報, n.s., 20.1 (1990), 93 n. 23.

22. Watson, trans., 198. See also Graham, 137: The "utmost man ... walks high above the myriad things but does not tremble." "It is by holding fast to his purest energies, it has nothing to do with knowledge, skill, resolution, daring."

23. The *Guanzi* (chap. 37, *Xinshuxia*) also offers that the sage "concentrates on his thoughts and focuses on his heart (*zhuan yu yi, yi yu xin* 專於意一於心)." The language, especially the usage of *zhuan* and *yi* ("one"), recalls *Laozi*, chap. 10, where the concept of *qi* assumes a central role in Daoist self-cultivation.

24. 16.7. Lau translates, "Confucius said, 'There are three things the gentleman should guard against. In youth when the blood and *ch'i* [*qi*] are still unsettled he should guard against the attraction of feminine beauty. In the prime of life when the blood and *ch'i* have become unyielding, he should guard against bellicosity. In old age when the blood and *ch'i* have declined, he should guard against acquisitiveness.'"

25. For example, *Mencius* 7B32: "*shouyue er shibo* 守約而施博"; cf. 4B15.

26. For example, *Huainanzi*, chap. 1 (Sibubeiyao ed., 1.1a): "*yue er nang zhang* 約而能張". The word *suo* (see n. 14 above) also has the sense of binding something with a rope. A poem in the *Shijing*, for example, contains the metaphor of using a rope to mark a straight line for building and tying (*suo*) wooden planks to poles in constructing a wall. James Legge translates: "With the line they made everything straight; / They bound (*suo*) the frame-boards tight, so that they should rise regularly." James Legge, trans., *The She King*, vol. 4 of *The Chinese Classics*, (Hong Kong: Hong Kong University Press, 1970), 439.

27. The word *yue* appears several times in the *Zhuangzi* in the sense of what "binds" or "ties" things together, often in the context of a discussion of what is genuine or authentic of things. For example, chapter 5 of the *Zhuangzi* observes that *yue* (Graham, 82: "commitment"; Watson, 75: "promises") is like a kind of glue for which the sage has no use. Chapter 8 ("Webbed Toes") seems to suggest that benevolence (*ren*) and rightness (*yi*) do not form a part of "human nature" (*xing*); in the ideal, "constant" (*chang* 常) state, things are *yue* (Graham, 201: "tied"; Watson, 101: "bound") not by ropes. *Ren* and *yi* are like "glue and ropes," which only "confuse" (*huo*) the world. The *Zhuangzi* goes on to say, "A little confusion can alter the sense of direction (*fang* 方)" and "a great confusion can alter *xing*" (Watson, trans.). Chapter 12 features the "hundred-year-old tree ... hacked up to make bowls" (Watson, 141). The passage mentions Zengzi, Yang Zhu, and Mozi. It identifies the sensory desires of sight, sound, smell, taste, and likes and dislikes as the culprits that bring about the loss of *xing*. With desires blocking what is "inside" (*nei*) and social artifacts and conventions restraining (*yue*) what is "outside" (*wai*), one is hopelessly lost. In "Knowledge Wandered North" (chap. 22), "Non-action" (*wuwei*) said, "I understand that the Way can exalt things and can humble them; that it can bind (*yue*) them together and can cause them to disperse" (Watson adds, "i.e., cause them to be born and to die"; Graham [163] translates *yue* as "knot together"). The word *yue* appears also in chapter 17 (Graham, 150: "tied up"), but its meaning there is not clear. Other references use the word in the sense of being frugal and sparing. *Yue* also refers to a treaty or covenant in early Chinese.

28. It is interesting that whereas Beigong You always retaliates (*fan* 反), Zengzi concentrates on self-reflection (*zifan*). The contrast between *fan* and *zifan*, however, may be coincidental.

29. David Nivison, "Philosophical Voluntarism in Fourth-Century China," in *The Ways of Confucianism,* ed. Bryan Van Norden (La Salle, Ill.: Open Court, 1996), 127. See also Kwong-Loi Shun's discussion in *Mencius and Early Chinese Thought,* 112–119.

30. Zhao 1; see James Legge, trans., *The Ch'un Ts'ew with the Tso Chuan,* vol. 5 of *The Chinese Classics* (Hong Kong: Hong Kong University Press, 1970), 568 (Chinese text) and 576: "From words you know things."

31. Chap. 2; Watson, trans., 39.

32. Graham, 52.

33. Chap. 2; Watson, trans., 43, 39.

34. *Shuowen jiezi zhu,* 10b, 502.

35. As cited in Zhu Ziqing 朱自清, *Shiyanzhi bian* 詩言志辨 (Shanghai: Huadong shifan daxue chubanshe, 1996), 2. The present *Shuowen* does not contain these words, which are restored on the basis of a quotation.

36. *Da Dai Liji, juan* 9, *Sidai* 四代; in Wang Pinzhen 王聘珍, *Da Dai Liji jiegu* 大戴禮記解詁 (Beijing: Zhonghua shuju, 1983), 171. "Trust," the passage goes on to say, carries *yi,* "rightness," in action. Wang, a Qing dynasty scholar, also cites here that *ming,* "names," should be read in the sense of orders or commands. See also *Guoyu* 國語, *juan* 3 (Zhouyu, pt. C): "sounds and tastes give birth to *qi*. Qi in the mouth forms *yan* (聲味生氣,氣在口為言)" (Shanghai: Shanghai shudian, 1987), 43. Two useful volumes devoted to the concept of *qi* are Onozawa Seiichi, Fukunaga Mitsuji, and Yamanoi Yu, eds., *Ki no shisō* (Tokyo: University of Tokyo Press, 1978); and Zhang Liwen, ed., *Qi* (Beijing: Renmin daxue chubanshe, 1990). The pioneering effort of Kuroda Genji (1886–1957), *Ki no kenkyū* (Tokyo, 1977), should also be mentioned.

37. Zhao 9: 味以行氣,氣以實志,志以定言,言以出令. See Legge, trans., *The Chinese Classics,* vol. 5, 624–626.

38. Zhao 1; Legge, 573, 580–581. The six *qi* are identified as *yin, yang,* wind, rain, darkness, and light.

39. Zhao 25; Legge, 708. See also the *Guanzi,* chap. 26, *Jie* 戒 ("Admonitions"). Rickett (*Guanzi,* 379) translates: "Liking and disliking, pleasure and anger, sadness and joy are fluctuations (*bian* 變) in life.... For this reason the sages were temperate in satisfying their tastes and timely in their movement and repose. They controlled fluctuations in the six moods (six *qi*)."

40. The *Zhuangzi* mentions the "one *qi*" in chaps. 6 (Watson, 87) and 22 (Watson, 236). See also the *Chuci,* "Far-off Journey," in David Hawkes, trans., *The Songs of the South* (Harmondsworth: Penguin Books, 1985), 195. Probably, the idea that the "one *qi*" came to be differentiated through the transformation of *yin* and *yang* was already established by the time of Mencius and Zhuangzi. The *Zhuangzi,* for example, states that one "receives *qi* from *yin* and *yang*" (chap. 17; cf. Watson, 176) and that "*yin* and *yang* are *qi* that is large" (chap. 25; cf. Watson, 291). The term "six *qi*" is mentioned in chaps. 1 and 11 in the *Zhuangzi.* The original vital energy may have arisen from the transformation of "nonbeing" (*Zhuangzi,* chap. 18), but this does not affect the argument pursued here.

41. Zhao 25; Legge, 704, 708–709.

42. *Guodian Chumu zhujian* (Beijing: Wenwu chubanshe, 1998), 204. The text goes on to say, *xi* 喜 is born of *xing; le* 樂 (joy) is born *xi; bei* 悲 (grief) is born of *le*. Perhaps *xi* (to be pleased) is here taken in the sense of *hao* (to like something). Another fragment, the *Yucong yi* 語叢一 (193), states, "When there is life and consciousness, then likes and dislikes are born (有生有知而後好惡生)." The *Xunzi*, chap. 2, considers "unifying one's likes" to be key to controlling *qi* and nourishing one's heart; this passage is cited in Roth, *Original Tao*, 33. The *Hanfeizi*, on several occasions, stresses that the ruler must not reveal his "likes" and "dislikes," so that his ministers would not be able to discern his true feelings and disguise their *qing;* for example, see the chapter "Zhu Dao" 主道, in Chen Qiyou, *Hanfeizi jishi*, vol. 1, 67.

43. Chap. 19; Watson, 203. See also *Zhuangzi*, chap. 11, which raises the concern that the six *qi* are not in harmony at the macrocosmic level (Watson, 121).

44. Zhao 1; Legge, 573, 581.

45. Zhao 1; Legge, 573, 580; cf. *Lunyu* 14.36, where *huozhi* 惑志 is traced to calumny.

46. Zhao 1; Legge, 573, 580.

47. The *Guoyu, juan* 3 (Shanghai: Shanghai shudian, 1987), 35, for example, describes the ideal *qi* formation in nature in these terms.

48. *Mencius* 4A15; cf. 7A21. According to the *Zuozhuan* also, ill-formed speech, not looking at others properly, and other kinds of defective appearance can all be traced to impoverished *qi*, or more precisely to not having secured one's *qi* (Zhao 11; Legge, 632, 634). Similarly, the *Guoyu* (*juan* 3, 43) singles out one's words and eyes as the key expression of *qi*. Cf. *Lunyu* 8.4. The *Da Dai Liji* (see n. 36 above), after indicating that *zhi* rises from *qi*, also concludes that appearance reflects one's inner "substance."

49. *Mencius* 7A36. See Kwong-Loi Shun's discussion in *Mencius and Early Chinese Thought*, 158–163.

50. *Guodian Chumu zhujian*, 179. Also see Ning Chen's discussion in this volume.

51. This is close to Kwong-Loi Shun's interpretation. Shun writes, "Kao Tzu [Gaozi] believed that having to know *yi* [rightness] through ethical doctrines, one's knowledge of *yi* helps set the directions of the heart. These directions then guide the vital energies to shape them in an ethical direction" (*Mencius and Early Chinese Thought*, 118). The point I wish to emphasize, however, is that the debate between Mencius and Gaozi in 2A2 hinges on their understanding of the operation of *qi* and the heart as commander of *qi*. It is significant that two of the Guodian fragments, the *Yucong yi* (194) and the *Liude* 六德 (188), indicate that whereas *ren* stems from within, *yi* comes from without. Ning Chen also discusses this point in his paper.

52. *Mengzi shishuo* 孟子師説, in *Huang Zongxi quanji* 黃宗羲全集, vol. 1 (Zhejiang guji chubanshe, 1985), 61.

53. Both Nivison and Shun emphasize that Gaozi turns to the "external" to find a moral anchor for the heart. On the distinction between "inner" and "outer," see also Kim-Chong Chong's discussion in this volume.

54. *Guodian Chumu zhujian*, 179. The *Yucong yi* (195) also spells out that

"all things that have blood-*qi* have pleasure as well as anger" (凡有血氣者皆有喜
又有怒); their "body" (*ti* 體) all "have *qi* and *zhi*" (有氣有志).

55. See Irene Bloom, "Human Nature and Biological Nature in Men-cius," *Philosophy East and West* 47.1 (1997): 21–32; and Kwong-Loi Shun, *Mencius and Early Chinese Thought*, 119–123. This is, of course, a much-debated point. Space constraint does not allow a discussion of the various approaches to the concept or how the term is used in the *Mencius;* the discussion here will con-centrate on how *qi* forms the basis of an understanding of the person.

56. *Xunzi*, chap. 22 (*Zhengming* 正名); as trans. in John Knoblock, *Xun-zi: A Translation and Study of the Complete Works*, vol. 3 (Stanford, Calif.: Stanford University Press, 1994), 127, 136. On this point, see especially A. C. Graham, "The Background of the Mencian Theory of Human Nature," in his *Studies in Chinese Philosophy and Philosophical Literature* (Singapore: Institute of East Asian Philosophies, 1986; reprint, Albany: State University of New York Press, 1990), "Appendix: The Meaning of *Ch'ing*," 59–65. Graham, as is well known, argues that in pre-Han works *qing* refers to the "fact" or "essence" of something and does not mean "emotions." See also Chad Hansen, "Qing (Emotions) in Pre-Buddhist Chinese Thought," in *Emotions in Asian Thought*, ed. Joel Marks and Roger Ames (Albany: State University of New York Press, 1995), 181–211. The Guodian texts, however, support a more inclusive interpretation of *qing* as in-volving the emotions. See also Ning Chen's discussion in this volume. The im-portant point, it seems to me, is to find an adequate way to express the per-ceived integral functioning of the heart in early Chinese philosophy, which does not isolate the intellect from the emotions. The contributions by Mary Bockover and Robert Solomon in *Emotions in Asian Thought* are helpful on this question.

57. *Guodian Chumu zhujian*, 179, 203; or *qing chu yu xing* 情出於性, *Xing zi ming chu*, 180.

58. The translation "starve" is taken from Nivison; "shrivel up," from Riegel. See also Wang Chün-chieh's (1997) discussion of this line, 203–207. Of interest also is Lee Rainey, "Mencius and His Vast, Overflowing *Qi*," *Monumenta Serica* 46 (1998): 91–104.

59. *Mengzi shishuo*, 60.

60. *Mencius* 6A15. On the concept of *si*, see Kwong-Loi Shun, *Mencius and Early Chinese Thought*, 149–153; and David Hall and Roger Ames, *Thinking through Confucius* (Albany: State University of New York Press, 1987). 46–50. See also the *Xing zi ming chu*, which links *si* directly to the movement of the heart (*dongxin*) and distinguishes between *si* that is directed to "worries" (*yousi* 憂思) and that directed to "joy" (*lesi* 樂思). *Guodian Chumu zhujian*, 180.

61. The concept of *shan* deserves closer attention. See Kwong-Loi Shun, *Mencius and Early Chinese Thought*, 210–212. The Guodian material links it to both *ren* (benevolence) and *yi* (rightness). *Yucong san* 語叢三, for example, defines it as the method or direction (*fang* 方) of *yi* (*Guodian Chumu zhujian*, 210). In *Yucong yi* (ibid., 198), it is said that to love *shan* is what is called *ren* (*ai shan zhi wei ren* 愛善之謂仁). The *Shuowen* defines *shan* simply in terms of propriety and what is beautiful (*mei* 美), relating the character to the "sheep" radical. In the Guodian texts, the cognate *shan* 膳, a good "meal," is used inter-

changeably with *shan* ("good"). This may suggest that goodness was also understood in terms of "taste." Incidentally, the word *ai* ("love") is etymologically related to *qi*. In the Guodian material, both *ren* and *yi* (and *de* 德, "virtue," and *yong* 勇, "courage") are written with the *xin* radical.

62. See Yang Rubin, "Lun Mengzi de jianxing guan," *Qinghua xuebao* 20 (1990): 104. The idea of "night *qi*" also appears in the poem "Far-off Journey" in the *Chuzi;* see Hawkes, *Songs of the South,* 195. In his commentary, Zhu Xi states to the effect that the most numinous of *qi* would stay in the person in the quiet of the night. See Zhu Xi, *Chuzi jizhu* 楚辭集注 (Shanghai: Shanghai guji chubanshe, 1979), 108.

63. A recent work is Julia Ching, *Mysticism and Kingship in China* (Cambridge: Cambridge University Press, 1977); see esp. pp. 99, 170.

64. *Guodian Chumu chujian,* 179. It is tempting to link Confucius' remark on "human nature" to this as well. Lau translates, "The Master said, 'Men are close to one another by nature. They diverge as a result of repeated practice'" (17.2).

65. The *Mencius* here is difficult. I follow Huang Zongxi in taking the phrase *wuzheng* 勿正 to mean that artificial manipulation or correction should be avoided. See *Mengzi shishuo,* 63. It is possible that the text is corrupt, in which case the *Mencius* would be simply saying that both neglect and artificial inducement would be detrimental to the process of nourishing one's *qi.*

66. Nivison draws attention to a similar concern in *Zhuangzi,* chap. 4. Rather than forcing *qi* into a particular direction or nourishing its natural preference for order and propriety, the *Zhuangzi* highlights the need to "fast" the heart so that it would not be swayed by external influences. Given the prominence of the imagery of food in *Mencius* 2A2 and elsewhere, the contrast is highly suggestive. "Knowledge" (*zhi* 知) is an instrument of contention, the *Zhuangzi* argues, and cannot be relied upon to gain an insight into the *qi* and *xin* of human beings (Watson, 55; Graham, 67). The passage here is difficult. Although "knowledge" is certainly deemed problematic, the meaning of *weida renqi* 未達人氣 and *weida renxin* 未達人心 is not clear. Nevertheless, the point seems to be that any vain effort in setting the direction of the heart and unifying one's nature is futile. It argues also against the expansion of *yang* energy. The secret to the fasting of the heart lies in "making the will one," which involves abandoning the wrongly assumed certainty of sensory perception and the imposition of the heart. This would allow the *qi* to remain "vacuous" and to "await" or receive the arising of things (*xu er daiwu* 虛而待物) without prejudice. This should be read in the light of the *Xing zi ming chu* passage cited earlier, which suggests that the heart's direction is formed only after it comes into contact with things (*daiwu er hou zuo* 待物而後作). The fasting of the heart centers on being "vacuous," for the Dao is realized when vacuity "accumulates" (*jixu* 集虛)—I take this to be a direct criticism of Mencius' *haoranzhiqi,* which is "born of accumulated rightness" (*jiyi* 集義).

67. *Guodian Chumu zhujian,* 157.

68. *Mengzi shishuo,* 64. For a different interpretation of "knowing words" in *Mencius* 2A2, see Jiuan Heng's paper in this volume.

69. The *Hanfeizi,* chap. 20, 6.6b, commenting on chap. 60 of the *Laozi,* specifies that, having few desires, the *"qi* of the blood" would be in order. See Chen Qiyou, *Hanfeizi jishi,* vol. 1, 356. The *Lüshi chunqiu* laments that people do not take care to nourish their nature but instead abuse their nature in indulging in things; consequently, confusion (*huo*) arises. See *Lüshi chunqiu,* Sibubeiyao ed. (Taipei, 1979), *Bensheng* 本生, 1.4a: 今世之人惑者,多以性養物.

70. Interestingly, in explaining why the virtue of "trust" is not included among the four beginnings, Zhu Xi says that it does not have its own distinctive *qi* (*zhuanqi* 專氣). See *Mengzi jizhu,* 2.12b.

71. In 4B26, Mencius criticizes the various views of *xing* as having to do with "artificial effort" (*gu* 故) based on concerns for "profit" (*li* 利). The word *gu* has given rise to numerous interpretations. The debate should now be laid to rest, as the *Xing zi ming chu* (179) defines *gu* explicitly in terms of "effort" (有為也者之謂故). See Kwong-Loi Shun's excellent discussion on this point (*Mencius and Early Chinese Thought,* 193–198). Shun arrives at the same conclusion, based on a close reading of the usage of *gu* in the early texts, without the help of the Guodian material. See also Shun's discussion in this volume, on Dai Zhen's interpretation of the Mencian assertion that things have "one root" (*Mencius* 3A5). On my interpretation, this "root" would be *qi.* Insofar as the four "germs" or "sprouts" of virtue stem from the heart, they, too, arise from *qi.*

72. *Guodian Chumu zhujian,* 125.

73. *Mengzi shishuo,* 65. Although it is well known that Zhu Xi takes "knowing words" to be the key to interpreting *Mencius* 2A2, he recognizes that in its pristine state the universe is filled with the *haoranzhiqi.* It has been "lost," however, and must therefore be recovered by accumulating rightness. On this point, see the study by Wang Chün-chieh (1997) cited in n. 8 above.

74. *Mengzi jizhu,* Preface.

75. The concept of *yiqi* appears in the commentary section of the *Wuxing* (or *Wuheng,* according to Pang Pu), one of the lost texts discovered at Mawangdui, which may reflect the influence of the *Mencius.* See Pang Pu, *Zhubo Wuheng pian jiaozhu ji yanjiu* (Taipei: Wanjuanlou tushu, 2000), 47, 63, 67. At one point, the commentary also mentions Meng Ben (47). A shorter version of the *Wuxing,* without the commentary, is also found among the Guodian bamboo texts.

3
Mencius and a Process Notion of Human Nature

ROGER T. AMES

MICHAEL SANDEL, in his *Liberalism and the Limits of Justice*, reflects on the variety of names we use to express our self-understanding, one of them being "human nature." "To speak of human nature," he observes, "is often to suggest a classical teleological conception, associated with the notion of a universal human essence, invariant in all times and places."[1] This "essentialist" and "invariant" (or, in other words, "transcendent") conception of human nature not only has been influential as a cultural dominant in the way in which we in the West are inclined to think about ourselves but also has quite naturally colored our best readings of those cultural traditions that we would interpret, including classical China.[2] Specifically, with the responsibility of interpreting Mencius' notion of *renxing* 人性 for the Western academy, if we fail to make it clear that we are *not* ascribing an essentialist understanding of human nature to Mencius by providing guidance to some alternative reading, I expect that many if not most of our readers will tacitly default to this understanding.

Against an "Essentialist" Reading of Mencius

This essentialist interpretation of Mencius has been further encouraged by what seems at first blush to be a familiar nature/nurture distinction in Xunzi's critique of Mencius. Xunzi, in pressing his distinction between (what John Knoblock has translated as) "inborn nature" (*xing* 性) and "conscious activity" (*wei* 偽), is adamant that *renxing* can mean only what is given in the human experience prior to conscious application: in the language of substance ontology, *xing* is something you are; *wei* is what you do about it.[3] It is on the basis of this distinction that Xunzi (unfairly) accuses the Mencian position of asserting that everyone is already fully moral by virtue of his or her natural endowment.[4]

Two important features of Xunzi's philosophical contribution need to be considered in evaluating his critique of Mencius. First, the subtext of Xunzi's critique of Mencius that is reminiscent of the *Analects* is his commitment to hard work. Confucius probably did not speculate on *renxing* because he gave priority to the love of learning (*haoxue*) as an active process for becoming authoritative in one's conduct.[5] For Confucius and for Xunzi too, acting in an exemplary manner requires real application and exertion. Xunzi's position, more extreme than Confucius' perhaps, is that becoming moral requires a substantial redirection and reshaping of our initial conditions along the lines of straightening a piece of wood. It would seem that one of Xunzi's basic concerns about Mencius is that, in failing to make a clear distinction between *xing* and *wei*—what we are and what we do—Mencius' seeming "naturalization" of what it takes to be moral makes acting morally too easy, like water running downhill. The question is, In insisting that Mencius has failed to appreciate the effort needed to become a person, is Xunzi giving short shrift to Mencius' conception of *renxing* and the rigorous demands of self-cultivation that are entailed in achieving it?

Second, it is seldom advertised that Xunzi's powerful and effective method of promoting Confucianism was to co-opt the vocabulary of those lineages that would compete with him and to revise their major tenets along his own Confucian lines. This process of appropriation is pervasive and can be illustrated by two examples: the absorption of later Mohist ideas in the chapter "Using Language Properly" (*zhengming* 正名), and the Confucianization of militarist ideas in the chapter "Discussing the Military" (*yibing* 議兵). In accomplishing this appropriation, it was not beyond Xunzi to revise heavily his opposition to suit his own ends. The question then is, To what extent and, importantly, in what way is Xunzi promoting a revised and much truncated reading of his competition, Mencius, on *renxing*?

The problem with an essentialist reading of *renxing,* by my lights at least, is that it makes Mencius into a relatively uninteresting philosopher. For me, the view that our highest nature is full obedience to and compliance with some invariant and univocal nature endowed in all human beings by something other than themselves ("Thy will be done"), thus making the very possibility of human dignity dependent upon compliance with something transcendent, is repugnant. The horticultural analogy understood as a fair explanation for self-realization—"the human being as a stalk of corn"—leaves little room for the kind of creative social intelligence that I am able to find in an alternative reading of early Confucianism.

In any case, as a basis for an alternative understanding, Angus Graham rejects any essentialist interpretation of Mencius. In Graham's own words, he cautions that "the translation of *xing* by 'nature' predisposes us to mistake it for a transcendent origin, which in Mencian doctrine would also be a transcendent end."[6] In setting aside this possible misunderstanding, Graham suggests as an alternative reading that "*xing* is conceived in terms of spontaneous development in a certain direction rather than of its origin or goal" and, further, that "*xing* will be spontaneous process with a direction continually modified by the effects on it of deliberate action."[7] If I might paraphrase Graham here, *xing* is a spontaneous process that is continually being altered through changing patterns of human conduct. Distinguishing this from an essentialist reading, Graham's interpretation would make *xing* historicist, particularist, and genealogical. In other words, it would locate Mencius' notion of *renxing* within the generic features of a process or "event" ontology, a worldview that, as David Hall and I have argued at length elsewhere, is most appropriate for understanding classical Confucianism.[8]

Now, in the *Analects,* Confucius has warned us that contentiousness is not consistent with exemplary character.[9] Even the condescending and often disagreeable Xunzi recommends to us "the art of accommodation" (*jianshu* 兼術) in our engagement with other scholars.[10] Why then must I be perverse and return once again to the "does *renxing* mean human nature?" question, which has given rise to some debate and occasionally offense among the current students of classical Confucian culture?

My answer would be that there is an awful lot at stake here philosophically. Nathan Sivin, insisting that cultures are too subtle and complex to allow for overly heavy-handed assertions, has prudently warned against the wholesale "rather than" approach to cultural comparisons.[11] With such a caution in mind, however, the careful Sivin still allows, and I think rightly so, that the "fundamental claim, which we usually refer to as appearance vs. reality, has no counterpart in China."[12] What Sivin does not say is that the philosophical entailments of this observation are truly enormous, one of the casualties being specifically the possibility of invoking an essentialist reading of human nature. Several implications of this absence of the distinction between reality and appearance are noted by Sivin himself in his further reflections on "Comparing Greek and Chinese Philosophy."

For example, Sivin observes:

> Much effort has been wasted by comparativists straining to find logic in early Chinese philosophy, but no one has yet come to grips with the complementarity of Greek logic and Chinese semantics.[13]

Logic conceived as the invariant and essential "form" of thinking is analogous to essential nature as the invariant "form" of the human being. The relative unimportance of logic in China and the key importance of semantics (or perhaps better, "pragmatics") reflect the fact that this tradition does not privilege some unchanging formal aspect as being more "real" than what is in flux. The semantic preoccupation with "using names properly" (*zhengming*) in its many variations, however, does reflect a worldview that accepts the always processional and hence always provisional character of natural, social, and cultural order.[14] In fact, it is arguably the continuous need to renegotiate order within this processional experience that explains why it was the pursuit of consensus (orthodoxy, canonical core) that was regarded as having high value in the classical Chinese world. Dialectical dispute is driven by the possibility of certainty and is characteristic of people who would ask, What is the Truth? The "art of accommodation" (*jianshu*), on the other hand, is driven by a sense of melioration and is characteristic of people who, recognizing the performative and perlocutionary force of communication, would ask, How do we, most harmoniously and productively, make our way together?[15]

In sum, the irrelevance for classical China of the ontological reality/appearance distinction together with "essence/accident" and all of its corollary dualisms (form/matter, fact/value, soul/body, reason/experience, and so on) locates us within a radically different "process" worldview.

Renxing as Process

In this essay, I want to offer a strategy for guiding the discussion away from the default essentialist assumptions about *renxing*. One entirely reasonable approach to getting clearer on this issue has been analytical: let's look at each passage in the *Mencius* and make our determination on the evidence found in the text. This is the approach taken with considerable effort and much profit by scholars such as David Nivison, P.J. Ivanhoe, Irene Bloom, Kim-Chong Chong, and Kwong-Loi Shun. In particular, Shun's recent work has produced a more nuanced, developmental interpretation of Mencius on *renxing*, where *ren* is distinguished by the social (as opposed to biological) capacity for certain cultural accomplishments, and *xing* is the development of the ethical predispositions of the heart-and-mind.[16]

I want to try to push this understanding a bit further, by using a different, more synoptic strategy. In fact, truly appreciating the accomplishments of rigorous analytic work as one important approach, I want to follow Confucius' suggestion that we bang on the question from both ends.[17] In clarifying this issue of *renxing*, there is another step that I believe should be taken prior to or at least simultaneously with this kind of careful analysis. We must, with imagination, locate the issue of *renxing* within its own worldview. After all, a further implication of the absence of the reality/appearance distinction is that although analysis—the "logical" approach that looks for what is true behind what appears to be—might be the privileged method for "truth seekers," it does not have pride of place for "way seekers."[18] "Way seekers" are more inclined to look to a narrative rather than to an analytical understanding—that is, to give an issue context by locating it within a particular time and place, and only then to trace out its particular associations.[19]

The nub of the problem is that if we do not locate the discussion of *renxing* within a particular worldview, we do not know with sufficient precision what the cluster of terms defining of the issue are saying to us. For example, does *jie* 皆 operate as the verbalized equivalent of the universal quantifier as found in formal logic, so that Mencius is speculating on *humanitas,* an essential definition of each member of the set "humanity" that by definition precludes the possibility of any revision by, in Graham's words, "the effects on it of deliberate action"?[20] Or does *jie,* as a process worldview would require, refer to a generalized yet still particular community, a graduated "all of us," or "all together"? The *Shuowen* defines *jie* as a particle meaning *ju* 俱, "all together," and the etymology of *jie* with *bi* 比, for its signific suggests "combined, assembled, several together." The cognates of *jie* such as "steps, stairs, graduations" (*jie* 階) and "in harmony with" (*xie* 諧) suggest an aggregation of things rather than universal predication. Philosophically, there is an important difference between the weight and ambition of a universal claim and that of a much more modest generalization.

In a world without assumptions about the invariance of logical propositions, does *tong* 同 mean "the same" as a marker of strict identity among natural kinds, referencing some self-same, identical characteristic, or does it, as a process worldview would entail, mean only "similar" (*si* 似)?[21] This would certainly be the inference in *Mencius* 6A7.

故凡同類者舉相似也

Thus generally speaking, things of a kind are similar to each other.

If there is no Being behind the beings, no One behind the many, then all we have is a world of the myriad things (*wanwu*), each unique, all continuous, some more similar to this one than to others. In this world, everything does taste more or less like chicken.

In what sense does *lei* 類 mean "kind"? Mary Tiles has discussed the Aristotelian genera/species mode of classification in some detail.

> The kind of rational structure which is given prominence in Aristotle's works is the structure of a classificatory system—a hierarchy of kinds of things organized successively by kinds (or genera) and forms of those kinds (or species). (In turn, species become in effect genera to be divided into [sub]species and genera grouped into more comprehensive genera.) Definitions were not in the first instance thought to be accounts of words but of the "what-it-is-to-be" a thing of that kind, in other words accounts of essence. To define an object—give its name a precise or correct use—was to locate it in a classificatory system.[22]

Commenting on the assumptions behind Aristotle's method of classification, Tiles further observes,

> This is a hierarchical order based on qualitative similarities and differences. A key assumption underlying such an order is that a thing cannot both have and lack a given quality—the requirement of non-contradiction. Non-contradiction is therefore fundamental to this kind of rational order.... Knowledge of definitions (or essences) coupled with the principle of non-contradiction can serve as the foundation for further, rationally demonstrable, knowledge.[23]

Reasoning thus understood is the mental process of uncovering univocal essences of which particulars are instances.

Turning to the classical Chinese world, how do we understand the elements in *Mencius* 6A7, which D. C. Lau translates as follows?

心之所同然者何也謂理也義也

> What is it, then, that is common to all hearts (*xin*)? Reason (*li*) and rightness (*yi*).

Should *xin* be nominalized formally (might we say, anatomically) as "heart-mind," or should we approach it more processionally (might we say, physiologically) as "thinking and feeling," where *xin* is only abstractly considered a dense center of complex functions intimately and inseparably related to the other major visceral systems? The medical anthropologist Judith Farquhar, viewing this "organ" from a medical point of view, insists that

> Chinese medicine, after all, sees the brain as the product—not the cause or source—of a whole-body process of production, dissemination, accumulation, and elimination.[24]

And what is the implication of this functional perspective in considering and locating the "four beginnings" (*siduan*)? On this reading, would these tendencies be more properly conceived as some generalizable inchoate stirrings within regular patterns of the human experience rather than as some superordinate formal structure located psychologically within the human heart-and-mind, some Chinese analogue to the rational faculties, the emotions, a priori categories of the mind, the individuated will? In fact, the terms used to define the *siduan* are the feelings of compassion, shame, deference, and affirmation, all of which presuppose a social context and which themselves conduce to effective social behaviors: "authoritative conduct" (*ren* 仁), "appropriateness" (*yi* 義), "the observance of ritual-ized roles and relationships" (*li* 禮), and "wisdom" (*zhi* 智).

Would we understand this passage differently were we to translate it as

> Wherein are the thoughts and feelings of the heart-mind similar? I would say in their taste for coherence and appropriateness.

This second translation would at least be more consistent with Mencius' appeal to the flow of *qi* 氣 and with the analogies of taste, hearing, and sight that are offered in this same passage as illustrations of human similarities.

And if *li* 理 refers to one's sense of "coherence" rather than some faculty of impersonal reason, how should it be understood? In contrast to reasoning as the process of uncovering essences, *li* identified by Mencius as a function of heart-and-mind involves tracing out correlated details forming the pattern of relationships that obtain among specific things and events. Confucian thinking has as its goal a comprehensive and unobstructed awareness of interdependent conditions and their latent, vague possibilities, where the meaning and value of each element is a function of the particular network of relationships that constitute it.

Such "reasoning" permits noninferential access to concrete detail and nuance. One appeals to the categories of correlative rather than natural "kinds" (*lei*) to organize and explain items in the world. The correlations one pursues among the welter of concrete details foreground similarities among them. Inclusion or exclusion in any particular "kind" is a function of analogical activities rather than logical operations that depend on notions of identity or contradiction.[25] Such correlations are meant to provide a sense of continuity and regularity in the world and are more or less effective as coherent orders to the extent that some juxtapositions tend to maximize difference, diversity, and opportunity and, hence, are more productive of harmony than others.

Li 理 is both descriptive and normative. As a dynamic pattern of experience inclusive of subject and object, it suggests how things ought to be realized. This prescriptive aspect of *li*, however, does not appeal to any order beyond that which is available by analogy to historical models. Ideals reside in history. In this sense, *li* is not "metaphysical" and must be distinguished from assertions about some a priori structure or transcendent aim.

Does *shan* 善 mean essentially "good," "good-in-itself," or, as a process worldview would require, does it refer to effective relations—"good at," "good to," "good for," "good with," "good in" (that is, *shanyu* 善於)? And what are the implications of this active, relational understanding when we use *shan* to predicate *xing*? Does it entail an existential assumption that experience is defining of whatever "essence" we might construct constituted by efficacious, constitutive relationships?

Is the distinction "inner/outer" (*neiwai* 內外) exclusive, entailing a doctrine of external relations as required by a coherent notion of strict transcendence?[26] Or is *neiwai* inclusive and mutually entailing (like *yinyang*) and thus simply a matter of emphasis, more or less subjective, more or less objective, in a world in which constitutively related "things" are at once distinct and continuous, unique and many?[27]

Is *tian* 天 as the putative "source" of *xing* to be construed as a divine and transcendent "other," precluding any robust sense of self-determination from the human experience, or like *yinyang* and *neiwai*, are *tian* and *ren* continuous, as is suggested by the often cited peculiar feature of classical Chinese religiousness, *tianren heyi* 天人合一, "the continuity between *tian* and the human experience"? If the human being, while being "endowed" by *tian*, also contributes to the content of *tian*, then in some degree at least, perhaps in the persons of exemplary models, the human being has a role in negotiating and renegotiating what it means to be human. Perhaps there are performative implications in the Mencian 7A1 dictum.

> 盡其心知其性也知其性則知天矣

> To express fully the thoughts and feelings of one's heart-and-mind is to realize one's *xing*, and if one realizes one's *xing*, one is realizing *tian*.

In fact, to appreciate the difference between "human nature" understood within a substance (or essence) ontology and the term understood within a process ontology requires a gestalt shift, a rethinking of our philosophical language. Fortunately, we do not have to reinvent the wheel. To assist us in considering a process understanding of *renxing*, we have available as analogy the process philosophy of thinkers such as John Dewey. Indeed, it is because Dewey uses a cluster of seemingly familiar terms in such an unfamiliar way that it is only very recently, within the last decade in fact, that the radical nature and the contribution of his philosophy are at last coming to light. I want to identify in Dewey several of the terms that have a bearing on what he would call human nature and to see if they do not suggest a new direction for understanding Mencius. This is not to reduce Mencius to Dewey or to provide a "Deweyan" reading of Mencius but is rather an attempt to use a Deweyan vocabulary to stimulate us to think differently about Mencius.

The Dynamics of Self-realization: Gleanings from Dewey

For Dewey, "individuality" is not a given but rather arises qualitatively out of ordinary human experience. "Experience" itself will not resolve into the categories of "subjective" and "objective." Situation for Dewey is prior to any abstracted notion of agency. Experience, like the terms "life" and "history," is both the process and the content of the interaction between human organism and the social, natural, and cultural environments.

> "Experience" ... includes *what* men do and suffer, what they strive for, love, believe and endure, and also *how* men act and are acted upon, the ways in which they do and suffer, desire and enjoy, see, believe, imagine—in short, processes of *experiencing*.[28]

For Dewey, "individuality" is not quantitative; it is neither a presocial given nor a kind of isolating discreteness. Rather, it is qualitative, arising through distinctive service to one's community. Individuality is "the realization of what we specifically are as distinct from others,"[29] a realization that can take place only within the context of a flourishing communal life. "Individuality cannot be opposed to association," said Dewey. "It is through association that man has acquired his individuality, and it is through association that he exercises it."[30] An individual so construed is not a "thing" but an "event," describable in the language of uniqueness, integrity, social activity, relationality, and qualitative achievement.

How radical is Dewey in this social construction of the person? He certainly rejects the idea that the human being is in any way complete outside of the association one has with other people. But does he go too far in asserting, "Apart from the ties which bind him [the human being] to others, he is nothing"?[31] This passage is easily and often misunderstood as a negation of human individuality.[32]

But as we have seen with Dewey's emergent notion of "individuality," to say that persons are irreducibly social is for Dewey not to deny the integrity, uniqueness, and diversity of human beings; on the contrary, it is precisely to affirm these conditions.

In commenting on Dewey and the social processes in which persons are created, James Campbell avers Aristotle's vocabulary of potential and actual.

> Dewey's point is not just that what was potential becomes actual when provided with the proper conditions, as, for example, the growth of a seed into a plant is sometimes understood.... His point is rather that persons are incomplete without a social component and develop into what they are—individual members of groups, socially grounded selves—in the ongoing process of living in a social environment.[33]

How does the community grow its persons? Dewey invests enormously in the centrality of language (including signs, symbols, gestures, and social institutions).

> Through speech a person dramatically identifies himself with potential acts and deeds; he plays many roles, not in successive stages of life but in a contemporaneously enacted drama. Thus mind emerges.[34]

For Dewey, mind is "an added property assumed by a feeling creature, when it reaches that organized interaction with other living creatures which is language, communication."[35] In reflecting on Dewey's emergent mind, Robert Westbrook observes that "it is not because they had minds that some creatures had language, but because they had language that they had minds."[36]

For Dewey, then, heart-and-mind is created in the process of realizing a world. Heart-and-mind, like world, is *becoming* rather than *being,* and the question is, How productive and enjoyable are we able to make this creative process? The way in which heart-and-mind and world are changed is not simply in terms of human attitude but in real growth and productivity, and in the efficiency and pleasure that attend them.

Dewey's notion of "equality" is also interesting. As we would expect, given his qualitative notion of "individuality," equality is active participation in communal life forms that allows one the full contribution of all one's unique abilities. Commenting on this departure from the common meaning of the term, Westbrook allows that Dewey advocated neither an equality of result in which everyone would be like everyone else nor the absolutely equal distribution of social resources.[37]

Dewey instead insists,

> Since actual, that is, effective rights and demands are products of interactions, and are not found in the original and isolated constitution of human nature, whether moral or psychological, mere elimination of obstructions is not enough.[38]

Equality so construed is not an original possession. Again, attaching a most unfamiliar interpretation to a familiar term, Dewey insists,

> Equality does not signify that kind of mathematical or physical equivalence in virtue of which any one element may be substituted for another. It denotes effective regard for whatever is distinctive and unique in each, irrespective of physical and psychological inequalities. It is not a natural possession but the fruit of the community when its action is directed by its character as a community.[39]

In interpreting this passage, Raymond Boisvert underscores that, for Dewey, "equality is a result, a 'fruit', not an antecedent possession." It is growth in contribution. Further, like freedom, it has no meaning in reference to a discrete and independent person and can assume importance only when "appropriate social interactions take place." Finally, equality is parity rather than identity. In Dewey's own words, equality can take place only by

> establishing the basic conditions through which and because of which every human being might become all that he was capable of becoming.[40]

The Deweyan alternative to teleology, which by definition entails a means/end-driven dialectic, is again novel. In place of some predetermined and preassigned design, Dewey's notion of ideals are aspirational ideas projected as meliorative goals for social action that "take shape and gain content as they operate in remaking conditions."[41] As James Campbell observes,

> For Dewey, ideals like *justice* or *beauty* or *equality* have all the power in human life that the proponents of "abstract," "fixed," or "remote" senses of such ideals claim for them. The problem that he sees is with their interpretation, one that presents ideals as some sort of finished and unchanging Existents placed in a realm other than the natural world of hunger and death, secure from the problems and confusions of day-to-day existence.... Our ideals are connected to

> the ongoing processes of living: they are rooted in particular difficulties and draw upon presumptive solutions.[42]

How is direction identified and secured within a Deweyan world? For Dewey, it is not ideals that guide conduct as ends in themselves, but rather the consummatory experiences in which such ideals are revealed. And consummatory experiences are themselves a shared expression of social intelligence dealing with unique situations as they may arise within the communicating community.

Process philosophy takes change seriously. And relentless temporality vitiates any notion of perfection or completion. Rather, the world of experience entails genuine contingency and the emergent possibilities that always-changing circumstances produce. It is the pursuit of the as yet only possible that makes the end inhere in the means for achieving it.

Dewey in presenting his understanding of human nature uses John Stuart Mill's individualism as his foil. He cites Mill at length, who asserts that "all phenomena of society are phenomena of human nature"; that is, "human beings in society have no properties but those which are derived from and may be resolved into the laws of the nature of individual man." Expressing appreciation for Mill's motives in liberating the common man from a powerful landed aristocracy, Dewey wants to invert Mill's assumptions about the relationship between the person and the society. For Dewey, discussion of the fixed structure of human nature independent of particular social conditions is a nonstarter because it "does not explain in the least the differences that mark off one tribe, family, people, from another —which is to say that in and of itself it explains no state of society whatever."[43]

For Dewey, then,

> ... the alleged unchangeableness of human nature cannot be admitted. For while certain needs in human nature are constant, the consequences they produce (because of the existing state of culture —of science, morals, religion, art, industry, legal rules) react back into the original components of human nature to shape them into new forms. The total pattern is thereby modified. The futility of exclusive appeal to psychological factors both to explain what takes place and to form policies as to what *should* take place, would be evident to everybody—had it not proved to be a convenient device for "rationalizing" policies that are urged on other grounds by some group or faction.[44]

For Dewey, the human being is a social achievement, an adaptive success made possible through the applications of social intelligence. Given the reality of change, this success is always provisional, leaving us as incomplete creatures with the always new challenge of contingent circumstances. And yet this success is progressive and programmatic. "We *use* our past experiences to construct new and better ones in the future," Dewey writes.[45]

The final topic that I want to explore briefly is Dewey's sense of religiousness. While rejecting "religion" as institutionalized dogmatism competing with equally misguided modern science in its claims about "Truth," Dewey again insisted on retaining the term "religious" to connote "the sense of the connection of man, in the way of both dependence and support, with the enveloping world that the imagination feels is a universe."[46]

Again, with the term "religious," Dewey inverts popular wisdom. Rather than beginning from a conception of Deity that infuses social forms with religious meaning, standing as the ultimate arbiter and guarantor of truth, beauty, and goodness, Dewey begins from social practices that, when they achieve a certain breadth and depth of meaning, reveal a religious sensibility that connects a cultured human community to humanity more broadly, and importantly, to the natural world. What dissuades Dewey from secular humanism is the radicalness of his contextualism. Although Dewey specifically rejects "atheism" because it pretends to too much confidence in human understanding, Dewey's sense of religiousness might be fairly described as an "a-theistic naturalism" that has no need for positing the existence of a supernatural supreme being.

> Nature, as the object of knowledge, is capable of being the source of constant good and a rule of life, and thus has all the properties and the functions which the Jewish-Christian tradition attributed to God.[47]

In fact, although Dewey does rarely refer to "God" as a sense of continuity, any notion of a temporarily prior, transcendent source and architect of the human experience, lawgiver, and judge is anathema to the substance of Deweyan pragmatism. What Dewey wants to preserve of traditional religiousness is natural piety—a sense of awe and wonder and modesty that precludes any temptation to seek control and, in its stead, encourages an attitude of cooperation and coordination with the natural complexity that surrounds us.

Conclusion

Now, for me at least, there is much in Dewey's vocabulary that I find resonating with the way in which I have come to understand the cluster of terms defining the classical Confucian sensibilities: "experience" and *dao*, "consummatory experience" and *he* 和, "individuality and equality" and *ren* 仁, "religiousness" and *li* 禮, "human nature" and *renxing*. There are many points of convergence: the irreducibly social nature of human experience, the priority of situation to agency, the central importance of effective communication, melioristic continuity as the alternative to teleology. And there are many more interesting differences, both substantial and in terms of emphasis.

The real value that this discussion of Mencius and particularly his notion of *renxing* has is its immediate contemporary relevance as China moves ineluctably toward some Chinese version of democracy. The essentialist interpretation promises many of the prerequisites for liberal democracy, certainly notions such as autonomy and equality, which provide a basis for individually conceived political rights.

The process interpretation of Mencius, on the other hand, would recommend to China the more communitarian model of democracy grounded in the process philosophy of John Dewey, where the greatest guarantee of human liberty is not entitlements but a flourishing community.[48] And liberty is not the absence of constraint but full participation in self-governance. Can Chinese democracy best be served by an appeal to the kind of communitarianism ubiquitous in classical Confucianism, or need China abandon its cultural center and import a Western conception of liberal democracy?

Notes

1. Michael Sandel, *Liberalism and the Limits of Justice* (Cambridge: Cambridge University Press, 1982, 2d ed., 1998), 50.

2. Perhaps philosophers who regularly teach Leslie Stevenson's *Seven Theories of Human Nature* (Oxford: Oxford University Press, 1974, recently rev. to *Eleven Theories*) are less inclined to be overwhelmed by this cultural dominant, but our best interpreters of the Chinese tradition would seem to begin here. See, for example, Don Munro, in commenting on *Zhongyong* 1 in his *Concept of Man in Contemporary China* (Ann Arbor: University of Michigan Press, 1979).

This means that a person's nature being so decreed, cannot be altered through human action; it is a "given" that exists from birth. The Neo-Confucians also affirmed the fixed character of man's essential nature .... The Chinese immediately associate the panhuman with the innate and the innate with the unchangeable. (19–20, 57)

See also B. Schwartz, *The World of Thought in Ancient China* (Cambridge: Harvard University Press, 1985), who appeals to this conventional interpretation in describing *xing* as "a 'heavenly endowed' or 'heavenly ordained' tendency, directionality, or potentiality of growth in the individual," an innate tendency toward growth or development in a given, predetermined direction (179).

In *A Taoist Theory of Chinese Thought* (New York: Oxford University Press, 1992), Chad Hansen, concerned that "most of Graham's appreciative herd of Mencius worshipers still think that the problems of moral reform dictate Mencius' status-quo solution" (194), argues that Mencius' "innatist" interpretation of *xing* precludes the possibility of moral reform all together: "The content —the detailed structure of the nature of the moral plant—is not the result of external factors.... Morality is internal in this sense" (174). Hence, as Hansen insists, "There is an absolutely correct thing to do in each situation" (178) because "Nature programs the *xin* to generate that action" (177). Hansen summarizes his innatist position in the following terms.

We could understand Mencius as arguing that humans have an entire innate moral grammar. That moral grammar enables them to process any morally neutral external structure and produce the morally right line of behavior. But moral rightness has no metaphysical basis other than its situational production by the heart. That would preserve Mencius' claim that morality is *metaphysically* internal rather than external. (187)

P.J. Ivanhoe in his *Ethics in the Confucian Tradition* (Atlanta: Scholars Press, 1990) acknowledges the merit of Angus Graham's novel insistence that "*the proper course of development* defines human nature" (34). However, he insists that morality is not "existential" in any sense of being dependent upon human choices but rather is simply "the manifestation of human nature" (33). "Human nature has a specific *content*.... These different parts are arranged in a very special structure and the shape of this structure emerges as an individual matures" (47).

3. In the formative years of Confucianism as a state ideology, it was Xunzi's ritual-centered Confucianism rather than the personal cultivation of Mencius that held sway. This was emphatically the case during the first century of the Han dynasty, when the empire was founded and consolidated. I believe that the interpretation of Xunzi in this way is to metaphysicalize a mere generalization about initial conditions by a philosopher who self-consciously develops the idea that the moral heart-and-mind is a human construction.

4. See *Xunzi* 88/23/29–50, and Kwong-Loi Shun's discussion in *Mencius and Early Chinese Thought* (Stanford, Calif.: Stanford University Press, 1997), 229.

5. When in *Analects* 5.13 it is said of Confucius that "we do not hear him discourse on subjects such as *xing* and *tiandao* 天道," we recall the assertion that Confucius was not given to speculation or conjecture (*Analects* 9.4).

6. Angus C. Graham, "Reflections and Replies," in *Chinese Texts and Philosophical Contexts: Essays Dedicated to Angus C. Graham*, ed. H. Rosemont Jr. (La Salle, Ill.: Open Court, 1991), 287.

7. Ibid., 288–289.

8. See David L. Hall and Roger T. Ames, *Thinking through Confucius* (Albany: State University of New York Press, 1987) and, continuing the argument most recently, *Thinking from the Han: Self, Truth, and Transcendence in China and the West* (Albany: State University of New York Press, 1998).

9. *Analects* 3.7: "The Master said: 'Exemplary persons (*junzi*) are not competitive, except where they have to be in the archery ceremony. Greeting and making way for each other, the archers ascend the hall, and returning they drink a salute. Even in contesting, they are exemplary persons.'"

10. *Xunzi* 14/5/49: "Exemplary persons with their superior character are able to tolerate the vacuous, in their wisdom are able to tolerate the stupid, with their breadth of understanding are able to tolerate the superficial, and in their purity are able to tolerate the tainted. It is this that is called the art of accommodation."

11. Nathan Sivin, *Medicine, Philosophy, and Religion in Ancient China: Researches and Reflections* (Aldershot, UK: Variorum, 1995), viii.

12. Ibid., 3.

13. Ibid. Chad Hansen begins his entry on "Chinese logic" in the *Routledge Encyclopedia of Philosophy* (London: Routledge, 1998) by denying its existence.

14. See John Makeham's survey of these variations in his *Name and Actuality in Early Chinese Thought* (Albany: State University of New York Press, 1994) and Carine Defoort's *Heguanzi* in *The Pheasant Cap Master: A Rhetorical Reading* (Albany: State University of New York Press, 1997).

15. A.C. Graham, *Disputers of the Tao* (La Salle, Ill.: Open Court, 1989), 3. See our discussion in Hall and Ames, *Thinking from the Han* (1998), pt. 2.

16. Kwong-Loi Shun, *Mencius and Early Chinese Thought*, 187–207. Given the quality of Shun's work, it is disappointing that so far he has declined to take a position on some of the more interesting questions: Is *tian* transcendent? Is *xingshan* a claim about "original goodness" (*benshan* 本善) or a proclivity, a direction? See Shun, 207–212.

17. *Analects* 9.8: "... if a simple peasant puts a question to me, and I come up empty, I bang the question from both ends until I have gotten to the bottom of it."

18. I.A. Richards surmises, I think correctly, that if conceptual "analysis" is introduced as a methodology for understanding traditional Chinese culture, it smuggles in with it a worldview and a way of thinking that is alien to the tradition itself. See his *Mencius on the Mind* (New York: Harcourt, Brace and Co., 1932), esp. 84–94.

19. Much of the comparative work of Tang Junyi, Mou Zongsan, and Li

Zehou, for example, is directed at a search for generic differences between the Chinese and Western cultural experience.

20. Ivanhoe, *Ethics,* associates Mencius' *xing* and Wang Yangming's *tianli* 天理, where "principle described human nature in a way remarkably close to Mencius' view" (47).

21. An argument can be made that the "*datong* 大同" idealized community of the *Liji* is really what Confucius means by "*he er butong* 和而不同."

22. Mary Tiles, "Idols of the Market Place—Knowledge and Language" (unpub. ms.), 5–6. A revised version is available in Tiles, "Images of Reason in Western Culture," in *Alternative Rationalities,* ed. Eliot Deutsch (Honolulu: Society for Asian and Comparative Philosophy, 1992).

23. Tiles, "Images of Reason," 7–8.

24. Judy Farquhar, "Chinese Medicine and the Life of the Mind," *North Carolina Medical Journal* 59.3 (1998): 190.

25. Antonio S. Cua in his work on Xunzi is sensitive to this basic meaning of *lei* when he states that "a *lei* is formed by way of comparison or analogy between similarities and differences." See Cua, *Ethical Argumentation: A Study in Hsun Tzu's Moral Epistemology* (Honolulu: University of Hawai'i Press, 1985), 55. He further qualifies his usage of *lei* when he states, "In this essay, I have used 'sort', 'kind', and 'class' interchangeably without implying that *lei* is a set-theoretical notion. So also, my occasional use of 'category' must not be construed as an ascription of a general doctrine of categories to Hsun Tzu [Xunzi]" (178–179).

26. See the attempt of Charles Hartshorne to develop a coherent doctrine of external relations in Hartshorne, *The Divine Relativity: A Social Conception of God* (New Haven, Conn.: Yale University Press, 1964). This has been more difficult to express than one might think. The moment one begins to articulate the consequences of epistemological or ontological independence, incoherences and inconsistencies begin to multiply. How might one characterize a being externally related to oneself? Surely independence in this sense suggests complete ignorance of the object or entity. Whether Kant's noumenal realm, externally related to the phenomenal at the epistemological level, is populated by things-in-themselves or is one giant *Thing*-in-Itself, or whether "thing" language even applies in that realm, is, of course, unknowable.

27. Tang Junyi's *yi duo bu fen guan* 一多不分觀, in the introduction to his *Zhong xi zhexue sixiang zhi bijiao lunwenji* 中西哲學思想之比較論文集,導言: 中國文化根本精神之一種解釋 (Taipei: Student Book Store, 1988), esp. 16–19.

28. John Dewey, *Later Works* 1925–1953, in 17 vols., ed. Jo Ann Boydston (Carbondale, Ill.: Southern Illinois University, 1981–1990), vol. 1, 18.

29. *Outlines of a Critical Theory of Ethics* (1891), in John Dewey, *Early Works,* 1892–1898 in 5 vols., ed. Jo Ann Boydston (Carbondale, Ill.: Southern Illinois University Press, 1969–1972), vol. 3, 304.

30. "Lecture Notes: Political Philosophy, 1892," Dewey Papers, 38.

31. Dewey, *Later Works,* vol. 7, 323.

32. James Campbell, *Understanding John Dewey* (La Salle, Ill.: Open Court, 1995), 53–55.

33. Ibid., 40.

34. Dewey, *Later Works*, vol. 1, 135.

35. John Dewey, *Experience and Nature* (New York: Norton, 1929), 133.

36. Robert B. Westbrook, *John Dewey and American Democracy* (Ithaca, N.Y.: Cornell University Press, 1991), 336.

37. Ibid., 165.

38. Dewey, *Later Works*, vol. 3, 99.

39. John Dewey, *Middle Works 1899–1924,* in 15 vols., ed. by Jo Ann Boydston (Carbondale, Ill.: Southern Illinois University Press, 1976–1983), vol. 12, 329–330.

40. Dewey, *Later Works*, vol. 11, 168. For Raymond D. Boisvert's discussion, see *John Dewey: Rethinking Our Time* (Albany: State University of New York Press, 1998), 68–69.

41. John Dewey, *The Political Writings* (Indianapolis: Hackett, 1993), 87.

42. Campbell, *Understanding John Dewey,* 152–153.

43. Dewey, *Political Writings,* 223.

44. Ibid., 223–224.

45. Dewey, *Middle Works,* vol. 12, 134.

46. Dewey, *Later Works,* vol. 9, 36.

47. Ibid., vol. 4, 45.

48. For a discussion of the irrelevance of the liberal model for Chinese democracy, and the possibilities (in Dewey's sense) of communitarianism, see David L. Hall and Roger T. Ames, *The Democracy of the Dead: Dewey, Confucius, and the Hope for Democracy in China* (La Salle, Ill.: Open Court, 1999).

4

Biology and Culture in the Mencian View of Human Nature

IRENE BLOOM

IN TWO PREVIOUS ESSAYS on the Mencian conception of *renxing* 人性, I have argued (1) that the term *renxing* in the *Mencius* is aptly translated and understood as "human nature"; (2) that *renxing* expresses Mencius' notion of what is both universally and distinctively human; and (3) that it is fundamentally a biological concept.[1] It is the third argument that is perhaps most controversial and that I would like to develop further here. In doing so, I will refer in passing to an ongoing disagreement that I have had with my friend Roger T. Ames, as well as to a more recent disagreement with another friend, Donald J. Munro, whose fascinating and provocative essay "Mencius and an Ethics of the New Century" appears in this volume.

My contention in this essay is that we do a disservice to Mencius if we discount either the biological dimensions of his thought (as, I believe, Ames does, choosing to put his entire emphasis on culture) or his views on culture (as Munro seems to do when he tries to weed the Mencian garden of elements that appear not to conform to current perspectives in sociobiology and evolutionary psychology). The genius of Mencius, I will argue, was that, as early as the fourth century B.C.E. he saw with remarkable clarity the importance of both biology and culture.

"Innate" versus "Acquired"?

Before attempting to elaborate the earlier argument about the Mencian view of the nature as a biological conception, I need

to draw attention to a terminological question—a problem reminiscent of the Confucian concern for *zhengming*, the rectification of
terms, but in this case involving both a conceptual issue and a problem of translation. There are any number of as yet unrectified English terms and translations that have come up in recent debates over
the Mencian concept of *renxing*. However, for present purposes,
I shall focus on "innate" versus "acquired." This distinction (like
"nature versus nurture") is so familiar to readers of English that it is
sometimes difficult to see that, deriving as it does from Western
usage, it may be a misplaced marker that draws us off the path on
our way through the great philosophical forest of the *Mencius*.
The dichotomy of "innate" versus "acquired" signals a style of analysis that seems fundamentally un-Mencian; it has the unfortunate
effect of laying an added argumentative burden on the case that I
would like to make, requiring more heavy lifting than would otherwise be necessary to complete a relatively unproblematic conceptual
portage.

Suppose that I were to disagree with the suggestion that, for
Mencius, *renxing* is to be understood not as "human nature" but as
an "achievement concept," and to disagree also with the notion that
"human beings are unimportantly similar and importantly distinct
cultivated achievements"[2]—two of the central assertions made by
Roger Ames in his reflections on the Mencian concept of *renxing*.
The burden of the dissent under these circumstances would be to
show (1) that human beings are, in Mencius' view, *both* importantly
similar *and* importantly distinct biological and cultural achievements; (2) that their distinctness derives from the development and
refinement of *the same qualities* that make them similar in the first
place; and (3) that it makes sense to see Mencius' view of human nature as a remarkable case for both a common humanity and the
human potential for creative development. To accomplish this particular portage, given the strong support of the unmistakable carry-
over from *Analects* 17.2, it would be necessary only to demonstrate
(1) that Mencius believed that all human beings have minds that
are similar and capacities that enable them realistically to aspire to
become good; and (2) that the possession of such minds and capacities, which are bestowed by *Heaven,* was what he had in mind when
he spoke of human nature as "good."

The argument takes another turning, however, when the suggestion is put forward that a concomitant of the view of *renxing* as an

achievement concept is the notion that this achievement goes on "against the background of what is unlearned and shared."[3] I have no difficulty with the word "shared," which resonates with the Mencian theme that "all human beings have ..." (*ren jie you ...*) certain moral propensities. Nor is "unlearned" a word without an obvious Chinese equivalent or a prominent place in the *Mencius*. There it is, prominently deployed in the famous passage in *Mencius* 7A15, which affirms,

> What human beings are able to do *without having to learn it* is their original, good ability (*liang neng* 良能); what they know *without having to ponder it* is their original, good knowing (*liang zhi* 良知). There is no child carried in the arms who does not know to love his parents or who, having grown older, does not know to respect his older brother. To love one's parents is humaneness; to respect those who are older is rightness. It is nothing more than this—to be extended to all-under-Heaven. (Emphasis added.)

This is, of course, among the passages often cited in support of the view that Mencius thought in terms of a common humanity: "there is *no child* ... who does not know to love his parents or who, having grown older, does not know to respect his older brother."[4] Clearly, this statement, though it does not include the term *xing*, must be related to human nature and meant to be inclusive; it echoes 2A6 and 6A6 in invoking humaneness and rightness, two of the four developed capacities to be brought to fullness through the cultivation of the "beginnings" (*duan* 端) of pity and commiseration and shame and dislike, respectively.

Given the uncertainty surrounding what Mencius meant by the term *liang* 良, I have been cautious in translating *liang neng* and *liang zhi* and have opted for "original, good ability" and "original, good knowing" in order to avoid using the more familiar "innate ability" and "innate knowledge."[5] However, the need to steer clear of this translation prefigures a larger issue lurking along the way ahead. "Innate" is, of course, not necessarily a *mis*translation of *liang*, but it is subject to misunderstanding all the same. Entering English from the Latin *innatus*—past participle of *innasci*, to be born—"innate" has been assigned the following spectrum of primary meanings:

> (a) existing in or belonging to some person or other living organism from birth; (b) belonging to the essential nature of some-

thing; inherent; (c) originating in, derived from, or inherent in the
mind or the constitution of the intellect rather than derived from
experience—compare a priori, intuitive.[6]

Meaning (a)—"belonging to some person ... from birth"—may or
may not be consistent with an understanding of the Chinese word
liang, depending on the conception one has of just what it is that
"belongs" to the person from birth and how static or dynamic such a
conception is. But meaning (b), which introduces the idea of the
"essential nature of something," is, many scholars would now agree,
off target in terms of early Confucianism.[7] Meaning (c), which con-
traposes "the constitution of the intellect" with "experience" is out
of the picture entirely in terms of early Chinese thought, in which
reason (or reflectiveness) and experience are generally not distinguished and certainly not contraposed. The point here is that to interpret the Chinese word *liang* to mean "innate" in either sense (b)
or sense (c) would involve importing a metaphysical notion of an
"essential nature" and an epistemological distinction between reason and experience (or reason and intuition). Neither appears to
have been part of its meaning in the *Mencius*.

Equally important, however, is that the dichotomy of "innate"
and "acquired" suggests a disjuncture between a biological given
and a cultural achievement—a disjuncture that is never actually signaled in the *Mencius* text. This is perhaps something that our contemporaries, inclined to make a sharp distinction between biology
and culture, and perhaps steeped in the longstanding debate over
"nature" versus "nurture" (or, in Edward O. Wilson's terms, a stand-
off between the nurturists and the hereditarians),[8] have brought to
the text rather than taken from it.

But beyond the issue of translation is a deeper issue. The
more serious problem with this discussion of *liang neng* and *liang zhi*
is that it is not at all clear what *liang* means, and commentators
across the centuries have disagreed. Just what does it suggest about
the nature of the bonding between parents and children other than
that it is universal and morally formative? Does it represent an early
example of a developmental concept? If what is *liang* represents a
"given," what is "given" and who or what is the giver?

In 7A15, for example, Mencius speaks of children carried in
the arms (*haiti zhi tong*), among whom there is none "who does not
know to love his parents or who, having grown older, does not know
to respect his older brother." Is this an instance of nature or of nur-

ture? Apparently, it is both. It is biologically natural (for humans and other mammals, at least) to require and to respond to nurturing and, over the course of the life cycle, to nurture other generations in turn. Is this behavior unlearned and shared, or is it achieved and acquired? Apparently, it is both. (Are we humans not by nature nurturing?) The real message of the passage seems to come in the closing lines: "To love one's parents is humaneness; to respect those who are older is rightness. It is nothing more than this—to be extended to all-under-Heaven." Though what Mencius understood by *liang* admittedly remains a matter of conjecture, my own conjecture is that what is *liang* in Mencius is believed, like the capacities (*cai* 才), to involve a gift from Heaven, but one that can either be developed and fulfilled or lost and destroyed.[9] One might say that the culture itself will be built on and sustained by recognizing and sacralizing what is biologically natural.

The point I would like to make here is that no serious account of the conception of *renxing* found in the *Mencius* should be seen as limited to what is "given" or "shared." This would be a reductio of a complex idea. As we have seen in 7A15 (and could see in other passages as well), the distinctive feature of Mencian thought is a belief in the natural endowment "given to" or "bestowed on" every human being by Heaven. But there is also a Mencian confidence in the possibility that morally dedicated individuals *will* develop this endowment, which is, after all, described by Mencius as a potentiality, a predisposition toward goodness, rather than a fully developed capacity. The child, carried in the arms and knowing to love his parents, is at one stage of development; Shun, living in the depths of the mountains and responding to a single good word or a single good deed "like water causing a breach in the dykes of the Yangtse or the Yellow River,"[10] is at quite another. One child—all children; Shun—the supremely filial son. Potential; development. As I have suggested, the distinctiveness of the high moral achievers seems clearly to derive from their ability to develop the same energies and to refine the same dispositions that make them similar to others in the beginning.

Biology and Culture

In describing recent work in biology, psychology, and anthropology contributing to the conception of a process known as gene-culture coevolution, Edward O. Wilson explains, "In essence, the conception observes, first, that to genetic evolution the human lineage has added the parallel track of cultural evolution, and, second, that the two forms of evolution are linked."[11] He continues,

> Culture is created by the communal mind, and each mind in turn is the product of the genetically structured human brain. Genes and culture are therefore inseverably linked. But the linkage is flexible, to a degree still mostly unmeasured. The linkage is also tortuous: Genes prescribe epigenetic rules, which are the neural pathways and regularities in cognitive development by which the individual mind assembles itself. The mind grows from birth to death by absorbing parts of the existing culture available to it, with selections guided through epigenetic rules inherited by the individual brain.[12]

Although Mencius obviously had no conception of genes or genetic inheritance, he, with his remarkable integration of the bodily and the spiritual, the practical and the sacred, did have a conception of the importance of the biological continuity of life. An example of this is found in the two instances in the text in which Mencius explains that the duty to ensure posterity overrides all other filial concerns; this, of course, is what justified Shun in marrying without telling his parents (4A26, 5A2).

There are a number of examples in which caring by a son for the physical survival needs of parents and caring by a ruler for the physical survival needs of the common people are seen as one aspect of honoring the role of parents and respecting the human dignity of the people, respectively. In the case of parents, physical support is required as a minimum condition of filiality, whereas in the case of the common people, their physical support is an undeniable concomitant of humane government (e.g., *Mencius* 1A3, 1A4, 1A7; 3A3, 4A19, 7A23, 7A37). The point here is not simply to draw attention to the concern for survival needs, which is obvious to any student of the *Mencius*, but to highlight the characteristic interrelatedness of the biological and the cultural, the physical and the moral, the practical and the sacred.

Biology and Human Nature

What bearing has the foregoing on our understanding of *renxing*? First, please recall Angus Graham's view of the Mencian project in transforming an earlier notion of *renxing*. According to the reconstruction elaborated in Graham's classic article "The Background of the Mencian Theory of Human Nature," Mencius was responding to Yang Zhu's hedonism and to a view of the nature that involved simply "the natural tendency of human development over the course of a lifetime"—absent any moral propensities—by retaining the dynamic view of *xing* and *adding* the notion of moral inclinations and potential as fundamental to it.[13]

The context of controversy within which Mencius was working is, of course, outlined by Gongduzi at the beginning of 6A6, and it is here and in the ensuing passages in 6A that we see Mencius responding to three alternative views of the nature—those views, rejected by Mencius, I have called "narrow biologism," "strong environmentalism," and "radical inegalitarianism."[14] Representing Mencius' view takes several tellings and retellings, employing different metaphorical contexts: the sowing of barley under unequal conditions, illustrating the degree to which Mencius judiciously accepts environmental influences (6A7); Ox Mountain, providing an ecological metaphor for moral breakdown and failure (6A8); the success and failure of the *weiqi* master's two students, accounting for inequality of achievement in terms of differences of effort and concentration (6A9); the choice between fish and bear's paws, life and rightness, followed by the anecdote of the principled refusal of food by the hungry wayfarer, providing images of the strength of the human sense of dignity as well as the possible loss of that sense (6A10); strayed chickens and dogs being a more present worry than a strayed heart (6A11) or a damaged finger being more of a concern than a damaged heart (6A12), showing the dangers of letting inconsequential concerns crowd out what is of ultimate consequence.

Note that every one of these passages provides some perspective on moral failure, some way of anticipating it, and, presumably, a provoking of some reflection on how to avert it. Several also deal directly with the issue of equality and inequality. Mencius clearly knew there would be moral failures and foreclosures. He knew there would be questions about why some succeeded and others failed. Had he not been putting forward such an expansive concept, such a powerful assertion of a common human nature, the need to explain apparent inequality and evident failure might not have required such sustained effort.

Back in the philosophical hub of 6A6, which is notably more direct and less metaphorical than many other passages, Mencius explains in straightforward (if not wholly unambiguous) language the natural resources human beings possess that can be developed in the direction of moral fulfillment. The major terms are *qing* 情 and *cai*—"characteristic tendencies" and "capacity." I will not repeat here the analysis already provided in the painstaking work of Kwong-Loi Shun. Suffice it to say that the *qing* to which Mencius referred, whether or not it can be associated with emotional dispositions, is understood to pertain to or to describe *every* human being, and *cai* is understood to be possessed—and, ideally, developed—by *every* human being. If a response is required to the argument that not every human being was actually considered by Mencius to be a *ren* 人,[15] the quotation from Ode 260 and the quotation ascribed to Confucius with which the passage draws to a close make quite clear that the *min* 民 also share in a "common disposition."

> Heaven in giving birth to humankind,
> Created for each thing its own rule.
> The people's common disposition (*bingyi* 秉彝)
> Is to love this admirable virtue (*yide* 懿德).
> Confucius said, "How well the one who made this ode knew the Way!"
> Therefore for each thing there must be a rule, and people's common disposition is therefore to love this admirable virtue.

It has been suggested that certain passages in *Mencius* 2A and 6A are most likely to support a view of the Mencian idea of *xing* as shared by all human beings, whereas certain passages in *Mencius* 7A and 7B, especially those in which *xing* is used as a verb (7A21, 7A30, and 7B33), are most likely to support a view of *xing* as a cultural accomplishment attained by high moral achievers (sages, the ideal kings of antiquity, and noble persons). I would only note here that although these three passages do relate to high achievers (in 7A21, "the noble person"; in 7A30, sage kings Yao and Shun and dynastic founders Tang and Wu; and in 7B33, the same cast as in 7A30), they are represented as regarding the process of "fully developing their capacity" for humaneness, rightness, propriety, and wisdom in just the way any other person would (based on the package instructions in 2A6 and 6A6) but, of course, with more reliable success. The noble person of 7A21 derives his satisfaction, in fact, not from possessions or influence, or even that visibility that enables others to recognize him as a "noble person," but from a nature that has been fulfilled in such a way that he is at peace with himself, as reflected even (or, rather, especially) in his physical appearance and kinesics. What more striking signs could there be of a common humanity and of the relation between biology and culture?

Biology and Ethics: "Filtering the Heaven out of Mencius"?

Donald Munro suggests that parts of the ethical theory found in the *Mencius* may survive and have relevance in the twenty-first century, while others will not. In his view, "those aspects that are compatible with evolutionary biology will survive a sifting to become for the new century the essence of the *Mencius* text, separated from what will then be disregarded as the dross." Professor Munro indicates that his starting point in anticipating how this process of philosophical sifting "essence" from "dross" might work is a "theory about an innate nature from which the moral concepts derive." He continues,

> In simple terms, the contemporary Darwinian and Mencian theories share the position that ethical rules derive from biology, that is, from our hereditary or inborn human nature.... The *Mencius* also implies that human nature is in turn derived from Heaven: "a man who knows his own nature will know heaven."[16] This claim has no Darwinian counterpart. It would be rejected today, along with similar claims that base ethics on God's commands.

Munro proposes a distinction between "a biological claim (a testable claim about an innate response) and a religious claim (not testable)." He writes, "This means that someone today can filter the heaven out of Mencius (the religious claims) and still retain a justification for much of his ethics."

This line of argument prompts several questions. One, already discussed above, has to do with the difficulty of determining with any clarity whether there is an "innate nature from which the moral concepts derive" or whether the relation between "innate" and "acquired" characteristics (or between genes and culture) is not more subtle than this formulation might imply. Though Mencius obviously contemplated the effects of environment on human development,[17] he would almost certainly have resisted a classic Western distinction between "nature" versus "nurture," precisely because his conception of the nature was developmental rather than essentialist, dynamic rather than static.

Another obvious question involves the relation between the nature and culture, an issue closely related to the issue of "nature" versus "nurture." Much of what we understand of Mencius' biological thought is, as I have suggested above, intimately bound up with his views on culture. Culture involves, among other things, the way people go about developing their natural potentialities, their moral capacity, their ability to care for and cooperate with one another. When Mencius speaks of what is endowed in human beings by Heaven (and, of course, the word *tian* in Mencius may in most cases be more aptly translated as "Nature" rather than "Heaven") he is giving voice to a deep yet untestable sense for what the world is like—and why—and to an equally untestable sense of what we can make it through our efforts. Fortunately, most people do not go about in the world predicating their own actions on the basis of what other people are statistically likely to do, and to base our actions on claims that are testable could be expected to yield very poor moral results indeed. I am inclined to think that Mencius, who lived in such an unstable and violent time, was keenly aware of this.

Finally, a word about that child in *Mencius* 2A6, still teaching us about ourselves while teetering for all these centuries on the brink of the well. Professor Munro suggests that certain parts of the Mencian theory of human nature "can last because they are compatible with the standard of empirical testing." As he says,

> This is the case with one of the most famous arguments Mencius presents, namely, the automatic response of an observer to seeing a child in danger of falling into a well. Mencius predicts immediate acts to save the child, devoid of any cost-benefit calculations.

In fact, Mencius makes no predictions of acts to save the child. (We fill these in out of our own frequently tested but ultimately untestable humanity.) He simply says that when "all of a sudden" any of us sees a child in peril, our immediate response will be that of pity and commiseration. We will respond thus because, insofar as we are human, we have a mind that cannot bear to see the suffering of others. But Mencius is subtle enough to leave open the possibility that the pity and commiseration may not issue in action. For whatever reason, we may not act to save the child. Empirically speaking, any of us may fail the test, occasionally or even repeatedly. If we do so, however, we must know that we are damaging ourselves and our own human nature as well as failing the child—or the children.

Beyond territoriality, beyond the incest taboo, there are moral instincts or propensities that seem to tell us not only what we should do or refrain from doing in a given instance but also how we are located in a larger human context, what difference we may make in the world. I think Mencius had something like this in mind when he said that "by fully developing one's mind one knows one's nature, and by knowing one's nature one knows Heaven (or Nature)."[18] That untestable but undeniable sense of being part of a whole is not something I think should be filtered out, lest what we lose in Mencius we lose in ourselves as well. Why not just keep the whole of the *Mencius*?

Notes

1. Irene Bloom, "Mencian Arguments on Human Nature (*Jen-hsing*)," *Philosophy East and West* 44.1 (1994): 19–53; and "Nature and Biological Nature in Mencius," *Philosophy East and West* 47.1 (1997): 21–32.

2. This is the assertion of Roger T. Ames in "The Mencian Conception of *Ren Xing*: Does It Mean Human Nature?" in *Chinese Texts and Philosophical Contexts: Essays Dedicated to Angus C. Graham*, ed. Henry Rosemont Jr. (La Salle, Ill.: Open Court, 1991), 158. My article "Mencian Arguments," cited in n. 1, is a response to Ames on this issue.

3. Kwong-Loi Shun, "Mencius on *Jen-Hsing*," *Philosophy East and West* 47.1 (1997), 1.

4. Can a child carried in the arms be "an importantly distinct cultural achievement"?

5. I have translated here according to Zhu Xi's commentary, which glosses *liang* as "*benran*" (original, natural) and "*shan*" (good), though I am aware of Kwong-Loi Shun's observation, after reviewing the major commentarial literature, that "the interpretation of '*liang*' as 'good' allows us to make sense of many occurrences of '*liang*' in both the *Meng-tzu* and in other early texts.... But as far as I can tell, none of the occurrences of '*liang*' in early texts requires our taking the character to mean what is original" (Shun, "Mencius on *Jen-Hsing*," 10). Other translators have also tried to avoid the use of "innate." W. A. C. H. Dobson: "The abilities men have which are not acquired by study are part of their endowment of good. The knowledge men have which is not acquired by deep thought is part of their endowment of good." D. C. Lau: "What a man is able to do without having to learn it is what he can truly do; what he knows without having to reflect on it is what he truly knows."

6. *Webster's Third New International Dictionary of the English Language Unabridged* (1971), s.v. "innate."

7. Kwong-Loi Shun has argued to this effect against A. C. Graham in re-

lation to the concept of *qing*. Graham's argument in "The Background of the Mencian Theory of Human Nature," in his *Studies in Chinese Philosophy and Philosophical Literature* (Singapore: Institute of East Asian Philosophies, 1986; reprint, Albany: State University of New York Press, 1990), is as follows: "The *ch'ing* [*qing*] of X is what makes it a genuine X, what every X has and without which it would not be an X; in this usage *ch'ing* is surprisingly close to the Aristotelian 'essence'" (33). In "Mencius on *Jen Hsing*," Kwong-Loi Shun writes, "I would hesitate ... to follow Graham in taking the further step of translating '*ch'ing*' as 'essence' and interpreting *ch'ing* in terms of Aristotelian essence, since it is unclear that early Chinese thinkers drew a distinction between essential and accidental properties" (7). I am assuming that the same argument that Shun applied to the understanding of *qing* as "essence" would have to apply also to the understanding of *liang* in essentialist terms.

8. Edward O. Wilson, *Consilience—The Unity of Knowledge* (New York: Alfred A. Knopf, 1998), 142–143.

9. I have raised only the problem of translation. Psychologist Paul E. Griffiths suggests that there are problems inherent in the English word "innate" itself as it is often used. In a chapter on the psychoevolutionary approach to emotional expression, he writes, "The experiments I have reviewed might be thought to show not only that emotional expressions can be given evolutionary explanations, but also that they are innate. Indeed, it might be thought that if the expressions have evolutionary explanations, then they *must* be innate. Both these implications should be rejected. The psychoevolutionary theory of emotion (and evolutionary theory in general) need not be committed to any particular view of the developmental mechanisms which create emotional expressions. Innateness is a fundamentally confused concept. It confounds under one term several independent properties. These include the properties of having an evolutionary explanation, being insensitive to variation in 'extrinsic' factors in development, being present at birth, and being, in various senses 'universal.' Traits are often said to be innate because they have one sort of property, and then assumed without sufficient warrant to have the other properties associated with innateness." Paul E. Griffiths, *What Emotions Really Are: The Problem of Psychological Categories* (Chicago: University of Chicago Press, 1997), 59–60.

10. *Mencius* 7A16, trans. D. C. Lau, *Mencius* (Harmondsworth: Penguin Books, 1970), 184–185.

11. Wilson, *Consilience*, 127.

12. Ibid.

13. This essay was originally published in the *Tsing Hua Journal of Chinese Studies* 6.12 (1967) and was reprinted in Graham, "Background of the Mencian Theory," 7–66.

14. Bloom, "Mencian Arguments," 35–38.

15. See Shun, "Mencius on *Jen-Hsing*," 11–12.

16. *Mencius* 7A1.

17. See esp. *Mencius* 6A7 and 6A8.

18. *Mencius* 7A1; in this case the translation is my own.

5

Mengzi and Gaozi
on *Nei* and *Wai*

KIM-CHONG CHONG

THE DEBATE between Mengzi and Gaozi in Book 6 of the *Mengzi* has been controversial. For instance, D. C. Lau has argued that it is wrong to think that "Mencius ... could have indulged consistently in what appears to be pointless argument or that his opponents were always effectively silenced by *non sequiturs*."[1] But it is precisely this that Mengzi is guilty of, according to Chad Hansen.[2] More famously, Arthur Waley states, "As a controversialist he [Mengzi] is nugatory. The whole discussion (Book VI) about whether Goodness and Duty are internal or external is a mass of irrelevant analogies, most of which could equally well be used to disprove what they are intended to prove."[3] A. C. Graham credits Lau with converting him from sharing this point of view.[4]

Given these contradictory views, it is timely to look at the debate afresh. A major feature of it is the use of analogies by both Mengzi and Gaozi. I shall draw out certain assumptions and implications of these analogies that have not been sufficiently clarified. As we shall see, Mengzi fails to refute Gaozi in 6A1, 6A2, and 6A3. But the real issue emerges in 6A4 and 6A5, where the terms *nei* 內 and *wai* 外, or "internal" and "external," are prominent.[5] It is crucial to note that they are introduced by Gaozi and questioned by Mengzi. Through the analogies of food and drink, Mengzi exposes the sensory and appetitive assumptions behind Gaozi's use of these terms.[6] This throws doubt on whether *nei* and *wai*, as understood by Gaozi, can be applied to show that *ren* 仁 is internal and *yi* 義 is external. As far as I am aware, no commentator has seen the debate in this light.

Instead, they have simply assumed that Mengzi agrees with Gaozi that *ren* is internal, but disagrees that *yi* is external. On my interpretation, however, Mengzi is questioning Gaozi's application of "internal" and "external" to both *ren* and *yi* and showing that it has absurd consequences.[7]

I shall assume some familiarity with the debate on the part of the reader and shall not reproduce the passages in full. There is a progression of argument that is best displayed in terms of paraphrase. Although reference shall be made to Lau's paper because of its centrality in the controversy, my aim is to analyze the arguments between Gaozi and Mengzi so as to reveal their philosophical underpinnings. Thus, it is essential to Mengzi's rebuttal of Gaozi that we understand his own application of "internal" and "external." But as an important preliminary to this, we need to see that Mengzi provides a moral psychology of the heart-mind (*xin* 心), which describes the possibilities of relationships and attitudes based on responses other than desire. Gaozi, on the other hand, emphasizes the biological processes of life (*sheng* 生), and this limits him to a psychology of desire. Ultimately, as we shall see, it is Mengzi's description of what it is to be human that allows him a conception of *xin* and *xing* 性 (nature).[8]

The Willow Analogy (6A1)

In 6A1, Gaozi draws an analogy between *xing* and the *qi* willow (*qiliu* 杞柳): to make *renyi* 仁義 out of the *xing* of human beings is like making cups and bowls out of the willow. Some commentators have taken Gaozi to imply that *xing* is bad. Zhu Xi (1130–1200), for instance, has commented that according to Gaozi, human *xing* originally has no *renyi*. It must be worked upon before *renyi* can be established, and this is similar to Xunzi's saying that *xing* is originally bad.[9] But contrary to Zhu Xi, this last comparison does not follow, for two reasons. First, the belief that *renyi* is constructed need not imply that human *xing* is originally bad. Nothing is implied one way or another, about the original state of human *xing*. Second, as recent scholarship has shown, the sense in which Xunzi says that human *xing* is bad may have nothing to do with any original nature. Instead, badness or evil is a result of the nonregulation of desires in human interaction and the limited supply of material resources.[10]

In response, Mengzi poses two questions. First, would making cups and bowls out of the willow not involve doing violence to it? Second, on this analogy, would it not mean doing violence to human beings to make them *renyi*? To be consistent with Gaozi's analogy, Mengzi should speak of doing violence to the *xing* of human beings and not to human beings per se. Perhaps it would be fair to say that this is what he has in mind, as he had prefaced the above questions by asking whether one could follow the *xing* of the willow in making cups and bowls. As Kwong-Loi Shun has shown,[11] whereas Gaozi compares *xing* to the willow, emphasizing that human *xing* is pliable and can be molded in a good or bad direction, Mengzi, on the other hand, compares human *xing* to the *xing* of the willow: because making the willow into cups and bowls involves going against its *xing* (to grow into a full-grown plant), Mengzi argues that Gaozi's analogy commits him to saying that making humans moral also involves going against their *xing*.

But in any case, there is so far no real argument between Gaozi and Mengzi. We have an analogy and its construal. There is no telling whether Gaozi accepts this construal. If he accepts it, no contradiction need arise vis-à-vis his analogy. It may be that making *renyi* out of the *xing* of human beings would involve force or violence. However, the extent of "violence" depends on how pliable the *xing* of the willow is. Similarly, the extent of "violence" to human *xing* depends on its pliability. In this sense, violence need not imply a "violation" of anything.

There are two possible replies here, in support of Mengzi. One is that in order to make cups and bowls out of the willow, one would have to kill the tree first. Another is that "pliability" does not imply nonsuffering—a "pliant" person can be made to suffer terribly, in which case violence may increase with pliability.[12] Perhaps it is objections like these that lead Gaozi to his next analogy of water, where no damage is done no matter how one forces it.

Mengzi's comment on Gaozi's willow analogy is that "Surely, it will be your *yan* 言 (words, teachings) which lead people of the world to *huo* 禍 (bring disaster upon, regard as a disaster) *renyi*." But this is a consequence that Gaozi could accept. After all, there is no saying that Gaozi wishes to uphold *renyi*. On the other hand, Gaozi may want to uphold *renyi*. Still, he could dispute the consequence.

However, D. C. Lau has developed two arguments for Mengzi.[13] First, by implying that it is necessary to do violence to man's nature in making him moral, one is saying that it is bad to do so—that it is unnatural and artificial to make man moral. But, according to Lau, these *are* moral judgments. Gaozi cannot escape making moral judgments, and this shows that they cannot be artificial and unnatural. Second, Gaozi's position implies that it would be just as much a violation of man's nature if he were to be made immoral. But it would be easy for anyone "hostile to morality" to argue that "since it is unnatural for man to be moral it must be natural for him to be immoral." It is in this sense that Gaozi's saying would be disastrous for morality.[14]

In Gaozi's defense, we may deny that he is making any moral judgment about the badness of making man moral or that he is committed to any such judgment. Another sense of "inescapably" making moral judgments would be that Gaozi has to make such judgments in his everyday life. Nonetheless, we may invoke the distinction between first-order and second-order levels of discourse here. Thus, the fact that Gaozi inescapably makes moral judgments is logically distinct from how he views the nature of such discourse, that is, at the second-order level. Gaozi is proposing the theory that *renyi* is established through the process of working upon *xing*. This is consistent with either upholding or not upholding *renyi*, at the first-order level of moral discourse. This distinction also enables us to look at Lau's second argument as simply a reiteration of the moral anxiety felt by Mengzi, at the first-order level, reflective of Mengzi's earnest moral faith. Interestingly, Lau himself does not say that Gaozi is hostile to morality. Instead, he thinks that Gaozi may be "misrepresented," given that it is easy for anyone hostile to morality to argue that it would be natural to be immoral.[15]

The Water Analogy (6A2)

In 6A2, perhaps sensing a misunderstanding on Mengzi's part, or wishing to circumvent Mengzi's objections to his willow analogy, Gaozi resorts to an analogy with water. Human *xing* is, like whirling water, directionless until it is channeled. The fluidity of water allows Gaozi to bypass the earlier objection that to make *renyi* out of human *xing* would involve a violation. Water being fluid, no violence is done to it when channeled. It could be said that human *xing*, like water, does not have any inherent direction.

Mengzi replies that although water may be indifferent to east or west, it cannot be indifferent to up or down. He asserts that the

goodness of human *xing* is like the tendency of water to flow downward—there is no human being who is not-good (*bu shan* 不善), just
as it can never be the case that water does not tend to flow downward. Further, just as water may be forced upward by splashing and
damming, human beings may be made to be not-good. But this state
of affairs may not be said to constitute the *xing* of water or humans.
Commenting on this, Sarah Allan has argued, "Mencius won his argument with Gaozi not for the trivial reason that his rhetoric was
more ingenious than that of his opponent, but *because he had a better
understanding of water than Gaozi.* Mencius—unlike Gaozi—truly understood water; therefore, he knew that, just as water goes down, human nature tends toward the good."[16] (Allan's emphasis.)

If the comparison between the tendency of water to flow
downward and the tendency of human nature to be good were only
a metaphor, it would be harmless, although it would not be doing
any work. However, situated as they are within the context of an argument, there is no logical connection whatsoever between the former and the latter tendencies. Contrary to Allan, one could assert
that it is Gaozi who had a better understanding of the nature of
water. But more to the point, it is not so much a matter of the superior understanding of water as it is the appropriate use of metaphor
or analogy within the terms of an argument.[17] There is a dynamism
to water that makes it hard to accept that any damage is done to it
in the process of splashing and damming. We noted earlier that
Gaozi could accept Mengzi's construal of his willow analogy. The
notion of violence being done to the willow need not imply a "violation" of anything, because the suitability of the willow for making
cups and bowls depends on its pliability. The water analogy extends
this point, because the dynamic fluidity of water enables it to be
shaped and channeled in any direction whatsoever.[18] Again, there
need be no connotation that man is naturally and originally bad.
The emphasis is still on *renyi*'s being a construction.

Xing as *Sheng*: Mengzi's Attempted Reductio (6A3)

Gaozi next gives a definition of *xing: sheng zhi wei xing* 生之謂
性. Mengzi's questions about the tautologous nature of whiteness as
applied to various things show that *sheng* and *xing* are taken by Gaozi
tautologously. Mengzi further asks whether, in this regard, there is
any difference between the *xing* of a hound and that of an ox, and

the *xing* of an ox and that of a man. This is meant as a reductio ad absurdum of Gaozi's assertion that there is nothing more to human *xing* than *sheng*, the life process, or the related biological processes of food and sex, as given in Gaozi's statement in 6A4, *shi se xing ye* 食色性也.

Although there is no indication in the text that Gaozi is floored by this attempted reductio, commentators like Lau and Graham take this as the clincher, thinking that Gaozi himself has no choice but to accept the argument.[19] But there is no reason why Gaozi cannot accept the conclusion that human *xing* is the same as that of animals. To make this more reasonable, we need to look closely at Gaozi's overall position. His belief that *xing* is without inherent direction is spelled out more explicitly in 6A6 by Mengzi's disciple, Gongduzi (Kung-tu Tzu), as *xing wu shan wu bu shan* 性無善無不善. This should be rendered not simply as "*Xing* is neither good nor bad," but instead as "*Xing* is without good and without not-good." In other words, the category of *shan*, or goodness, is wholly inapplicable to *xing*. The assertion that *xing* and *sheng* are tautologous reinforces this decategorization, bringing into focus instead the animal and biological instincts of man.

The reason why Mengzi's reductio fails is that it simply reiterates Gaozi's view, that the *xing* of man is to be seen in terms of the necessary animal and biological processes of life. To say that human *xing* is the same as the animal and biological processes of life seems to imply that there is no difference between man and animal. This is shocking. However, this merely begs the question. Neither does it follow that Gaozi believes there is no difference between man and animal. The assertion that *xing* and *sheng* are equivalent is still consistent with the view that *renyi* is constructed out of *xing*. For even if *xing* consists of the sensory and appetitive desires, it may still be shaped, constructed, or enculturated into *renyi*, and this is what differentiates man from animal. Later, we shall see how Mengzi provides an argument for the difference between man and animal in terms of the possibilities of human relationships and reflective thought, but that argument does not belong here.[20]

Gaozi on Internal and External (6A4, 6A5)

In 6A4, Gaozi says: "Appetite for food and sex is *xing* (*shi se xing ye*). *Ren* is internal, not external; *yi* is external, not internal." He is asked by Mengzi to clarify the latter of the two statements. Evidently, *ren* is thought to be internal in some sense similar to the sensory and appetitive desires. An example of *ren* is given further in the passage, in terms of love or affection for one's brother, as against the brother of a man from Qin whom one would not love. The word *yue* 悦 is used here, indicating that in loving my brother and not another's, I am doing what "pleases" me.[21] This, together with the examples of food, sex, and affection, shows that, by "internal," Gaozi is referring to the motivational basis for action, as arising from the sensory and appetitive desires. Quite literally, the motivational source lies *in* me, and this is precisely what is meant by *nei*, "internal."

This is reinforced by the contrast with *yi*. The externality of *yi* is described by Gaozi in terms of the concept of elderliness and respect for elders. An analogy is made with whiteness. Elderliness is said to be an external quality in the same way as whiteness is. Just as it is on account of something's being white that I regard it as white (*bai zhi* 白之), Gaozi states that it is on account of someone's elderliness that he respects him (*bi zhang er wo zhang zhi* 彼長而我長之). Respect, in other words, is due to someone in relation to his position. One is fulfilling *yi* if one pays attention to the circumstances under which it is due, and shows respect accordingly. *Yi*, in this sense, is a social construct and, hence, external.

Mengzi replies that admittedly there is no difference between the "whiteness" of a white horse and of a white person, but is there no difference between the *zhang* of *zhang ma* 長馬 (old horse) and the *zhang* of *zhang ren* 長人 (old or elderly person)? The ambiguity of *zhang* either as adjectival (attributing oldness) or as verbal (to treat with respect) is brought out in his next question: Whether we say that it is the object of respect—that is, the elderly person (*zhang zhe* 長者)—or the person evincing respect (*zhang zhi zhe* 長之者), who is *yi*?

Mengzi is drawing attention to the fact that the *yi* that is shown in respecting the elderly comes from the person who shows respect, not from the object of respect. Gaozi's reply is that since there is no difference between respecting an elder from Chu and my own elder, this is due to the quality of being elderly and hence it is called external. Presumably, in the case of one's own elder, there is affection as well as respect. But because the respect shown is identical in both cases, this is *yi* and it is an external source that identifies whether respect is due.

The Roast and Drink Analogies

In reply, Mengzi asks, Although there is no difference between enjoying the roast of a person from Qin, and enjoying my own roast, does it follow that there is externality in my enjoying a roast? A similar question is asked in 6A5: Respect or reverence may vary depending on the ceremonial context, but does this show that the respect or reverence evincing *yi* is external? Thus, although one may take a hot drink in winter but a cold drink in summer, does it follow that the desire for food and drink is external?

Both replies may seem puzzling. But in both passages, Mengzi is ridiculing Gaozi's argument, this time to greater effect. Referring to Mengzi's arguments here, Lau says,

> The arguments are obviously not conclusive, but this is in part due to Mencius' limited purpose. All he set out to do, in both cases, was to show that his opponents failed to establish the externality of *yi*. He did not attempt to go beyond this and to establish positively that *yi* was internal.[22]

This is an important observation. Mengzi is seeking a clarification of the terms "internal" and "external," extending the question he had posed earlier in 6A4: "Why do you say that *ren* is internal and *yi* is external?" Mengzi was pointing to a difficulty with "internal" and "external," because the evincing of respect is not just an external quality like whiteness or being elderly (whether it be an old horse or an old man). The roast and drink analogies bring out further difficulties.

These analogies are consistent with the form of the arguments of both Gaozi and Meng Jizi (Meng Chi-tzu, presumably a disciple of Gaozi's) in 6A4 and 6A5. The roast analogy parallels Gaozi's argument that because the respect shown for both a family member and a nonfamily member is the same in virtue of position, this shows that respect for the elderly must be external. Mengzi points out that by the same token, because there is no difference between enjoying my own roast or another's, my enjoyment would be deemed external. This is of course absurd, for enjoyment of a roast must be internal in the sensory and appetitive sense. This problem is heightened by the drink analogy. Thus, Meng Jizi's assertion that respect varies with the circumstances shows that respect is external. Mengzi's reply, through the proxy of Gongduzi, is that by the same token the variation of hot or cold drink with the seasons shows that thirst must be deemed external.

Mengzi's choice of these "absurd" analogies would seem to have been deliberate. Together, they show that variation or non-variation in the circumstances has nothing to do with whether something is to be regarded as internal or external, in any sense of "internal" and "external." Gaozi's claim that *yi* is external is therefore invalidated. At the same time, we are made aware that this does not mean that *yi* is internal either, *in the sense that taste and thirst are internal.* The same holds for *ren.* All the commentators I have come across have failed to appreciate this last point. They have assumed that since Gaozi holds that *ren* is internal, Mengzi does not question this but instead questions only the assertion that *yi* is external.[23] However, as already stated in the introduction to this essay, Mengzi is not counterasserting that *yi* is internal, as most readers believe. Instead, he asks whether *yi,* in this case evincing respect, may not also be "internal" in the sense used by Gaozi, as something that comes from "within" the agent, just like the sensory and appetitive desires. This construal of "internal" (and, correspondingly, "external" too) leads to absurd consequences, as we have just seen.

Having shown the absurdity of Gaozi's position, the onus is on Mengzi to provide his own understanding of "internal" and "external." Although this is not a stated task in the context of the debate with Gaozi, it is necessary to complete the argument and may be seen as lying in the background. Thus, another way of looking at the debate with Gaozi is to see it as preparing the way for an account of Mengzi's own understanding of "internal" and "external." But before discussing this, we need to analyze his concept of *xin* first.

Xin: The Heart-Mind

In 6A6, Mengzi is asked by Gongduzi to elaborate on his position that *xing* is good (*xing shan* 性善). According to Mengzi, it is not the fault of a man's native endowment (*cai* 才) if he does not perform good. All men have the heart-mind (*xin*) of compassion, shame, respect, and right and wrong (*ceyin zhi xin, xiuwu zhi xin, gongjing zhi xin, shifei zhi xin*). It is clear from 2A6 that these are *duan* 端 (germs or beginnings). Mengzi says in 6A6 that these four *duan* "do not give me a lustre from the outside, they are in me originally. It is only that I have not reflected (*si* 思) upon this" (Lau, trans.; modified). Mengzi's denial of a luster can be taken as a direct rebuttal of Gaozi's emphasis on *renyi* as having an external source.

He is disagreeing with Gaozi that *renyi* is a social construct, and internality for him has to do with a potential goodness, consisting of the four *duan*, which require reflective thought (*si*) and nurturance or nourishment (*yang*) for their development into the virtues of *ren, yi, li* 禮, and *zhi* 智.

The example in 2A6 of the child about to fall into a well is regarded by most commentators as evidence for the existence of the heart of compassion. It has to be said that, as evidence, this is rather thin. The sudden feeling one has may be of alarm, not amounting to compassion.[24] Instead, it would be better to regard this and other examples as providing a descriptive moral psychology that, when expanded upon, is more sophisticated than Gaozi's.

Mengzi is especially careful to differentiate the feeling of compassion from wishing to please the child's parents, winning the praise of others, or even disliking the cry of the child. In other words, the compassion is a direct concern for the child. It is not indirect or secondary, as a means to pleasing the parents. Neither is it for the anticipated pleasure of winning the praise of others. And lastly, it is not a deflection of an unpleasant sensory state. These are various modes of desire. Suppose one describes the compassion as a desire for the welfare of the child. Even so, it is clear that it is not like the desire for a pleasurable state or for deflecting an unpleasurable state. In the latter cases, the focus is on consummating a desire-state. Compassion, on the other hand, is outward directed. The difference can be accentuated by considering that an unfulfilled sensory state may yet be fulfilled by "transferring" one's desire elsewhere; for example, frustrated in my attempt to buy a piece of property, I can look for another with similar characteristics. On the other hand, what would it mean to recommend that I "transfer" my compassion for the child elsewhere?

Consider the following example. In George Eliot's *Middlemarch*, Dorothea is disappointed to find that the villagers in her parish are not so poor as to need her charitable work. We might recommend that she should transfer her "compassion" elsewhere. This contrasts with the "nontransferability" of compassion, the point being that the phenomenological description of (genuine) compassion precludes such transference; that is, my compassion is for *you*, not for some substitute, and this is precisely what Mengzi is getting at in his contrast of the compassion for the child with other motives.[25]

Mengzi can also be construed as describing the relations that can obtain between oneself and others or certain states of affairs, on the basis of certain primitive responses. Again, these are not relations of desire. In 2A6, Mengzi associates having the four germs with having the four limbs. A lack of any of these would cripple one. In other words, the capacity to uphold oneself and to relate to others in certain ways would be absent. As Mengzi says,

> For a man possessing these four germs to deny his own potentialities is for him to cripple himself; for him to deny the potentialities of his prince is for him to cripple his prince. If a man is able to develop all these four germs that he possesses, it will be like a fire starting up or a spring coming through. When these are fully developed, he can tend the whole realm within the Four Seas, but if he fails to develop them, he will not be able even to serve his parents.

Earlier in the same passage, Mengzi says that anyone who lacks any of the four germs would not be a human being. Clearly, the germs are said to define the human being in terms of enabling one to relate to others in certain ways, which, if developed, would be the relations of *ren, yi, li,* and *zhi*. Although not mentioned in this passage, there is also the upholding of oneself in relation to certain things.

Two examples are given in 6A10 of this last relation. Referring to the fact that the heart-mind loathes (*wu* 惡) certain things more than death, Mengzi states that this attitude is not confined to the virtuous person but is common to all men. It is simply that the virtuous person (*xian zhe* 賢者) never loses this heart. Given that it would not only be loathsome (*wu*) but also shameful (*xiu* 羞) to do something that is worse than death, one develops the virtue of *yi* by maintaining this sense of shame and loathing (*xiuwu*). The second example makes the same point. When getting food means life instead of death, even a beggar would not accept the food if it is given only after being trampled upon. Mengzi goes on to say, however, that people seem to forget the proprieties of *liyi* 禮義 when they accept certain things improperly, such as beautiful houses, concubines, and the gratitude of others, although like the beggar, they believe that they would rather die than accept food that has been trampled upon. Mengzi concludes by saying, "This way of thinking is known as losing one's original heart (*benxin* 本心)."

Environmental factors play a role in the failure to nourish, nurture, and sustain one's heart-mind. This is described, for example, in 6A8: it would be mistaken to think that the denuded state of Ox Mountain constitutes its original nature (see also 6A9). But the failure is also attributed to the failure to think or reflect (*si*), in several places (6A6, 6A13, 6A15, 6A17).

In 6A7 Mengzi says that there is something possessed in common by all hearts:

> All palates have the same preference in taste; all ears in sound; all eyes in beauty. Should hearts (*xin*) prove to be an exception by possessing nothing in common (*du wu suo tongran hu* 獨無所同然乎)? What is it, then, that is common to all hearts? Reason and rightness (*wei li ye yi ye* 謂理也義也). Thus reason and rightness please my heart (*yue wo xin* 悅我心) in the same way as meat pleases my palate (*yue wo kou* 悅我口).

Our earlier analysis has shown that it would be wrong to construe Mengzi as suggesting that the heart-mind is a sensory organ in the way that the palate is. Instead, he is making a naturalistic assumption that just as there is something that pleases my palate, there is also something that pleases my heart-mind. It is clear, however, that it is *li* 理 and *yi* that please the heart-mind, not the sensation of taste. Lau translates *li* as "reason." Together with his translation of *tongran* 同然 as "common," this may suggest that reason and rightness are distinctive of the heart-mind, to the extent that they bind the four germs together. But alternative translations of *tongran* are "agreed upon" and "agree in approving of."[26] And *li,* which occurs only in three passages in the *Mengzi,* seems more appropriately translated as "pattern" or "principle."[27] In 5B1, it occurs as order, or *tiaoli* 條理, in the context of the orderly progression of music from beginning to end and, analogously, the beginning and end of wisdom and sageness.[28]

In the light of these other translations, we may read Mengzi as saying that the contents of the heart-mind, that is, the four germs, are such that they affirm and are pleased with pattern, order or principle, and rightness. In other words, they are able to distinguish and judge what is right, on their own principles of feeling. We may say that Mengzi is asserting the ability of the four germs to register certain modes of awareness, that is, both cognitively and affectively at once.[29]

Thus, the perception of the child about to fall into a well is not a mere cognition; it registers a moral awareness of an alarming situation. The compassion or feeling of concern for the child is not a concomitant part of the cognition but constitutes the mode in which the situation is registered. This applies also to the other examples discussed in 6A10. The perception that something is both loathsome and shameful is a direct mode of awareness, not something added on to a pure cognition. In 3A5, Mengzi gives the example of people in earlier times who threw the bodies of their deceased parents into the gullies. Later observing that the bodies were eaten by creatures and flies, they broke into a sweat and returned home for baskets and spades to bury them. Mengzi comments, "The sweating was not put on for others to see. It was an outward expression of their innermost heart (*zhongxin da yu mianmu* 中心達於面目)." Again, we have a mode of cognition that brings about a particular form of action. This is not confined to a single case, but as Mengzi says, "(If in this case) burying them is the thing to do (*yan zhi cheng shi ye* 掩之誠是也), then the burying of their own parents by filial sons and *ren* persons also must have (a) *dao* (*ze xiaozi renren zhi yan qi qin yi bi you dao* 則孝子仁人之掩其親亦必有道)."[30] The perception of the thing to do here is a function not of reason but of what all heart-minds *tongran,* that is, what they would all affirm.

Through his usage of organic and developmental terms in his description of the heart-mind, Mengzi would be hard put to explain why it is that some people fail to nourish their heart-mind. As we have seen, he has referred to environmental interference, and he also mentions the failure of people to reflect, both cognitively and affectively, on their priorities. This last is not an explanation but, nonetheless, a realistic psychological observation. Time and again, Mengzi laments that many people are imprudent, neglecting the greater part of themselves for the smaller. Comments are made about the person knowing how to tend to various things, such as a tree, one's animals, one's body, or parts of one's body such as the mouth and belly, but neglecting the greatest or most precious part of oneself, the heart-mind (6A11, 6A12, 6A14).

Mengzi on Internal and External

With this picture of Mengzi's account of moral psychology, we are now in a position to appreciate his understanding of "internal" and "external." As we have seen, the germs of compassion, shame and loathing, respect, and right and wrong are not sensory and appeti-

tive desires. The latter are transferable, and their objects substituta-
ble and negotiable. To use Mengzi's example in 6A10, if I cannot get
both delicacies of fish and bear's palm, then I will settle for bear's
palm. Similarly, the desire to remain alive could be such that a man
may resort to any means to keep alive. But Mengzi goes on to say,

> Yet there are ways of remaining alive and ways of avoiding death to
> which a man will not resort. In other words, there are things a man
> wants more than life and there are also things he loathes more than
> death. This is an attitude not confined to the moral man but com-
> mon to all men. The moral man simply never loses it.

The want or desire (*yu* 欲) in this case must surely be different from an appetitive desire. Rather than being of a piece with any
desire that one will go to any length to satisfy, the want of not avoiding death at any cost puts a stop to certain desires. In other words, it
judges the desires. We now see why Gaozi's definition of *xing* as
sheng, the biological processes of life, and his insistence that the appetite for food and sex is *xing,* are unacceptable to Mengzi. The sensory organs, which are attracted to external objects, function differently from the four germs and their corresponding virtues. In 6A15,
Mengzi says,

> The organs of hearing and sight are unable to think (*bu si* 不思) and
> can be misled by external things. When one thing acts on another,
> all it does is to attract it. The organ of the heart can think. But it will
> find the answer only if it does think; otherwise, it will not find the
> answer. This is what Heaven has given me. If one makes one's stand
> on what is of greater importance in the first instance, what is of
> smaller importance cannot displace it. In this way, one cannot but
> be a great man.

The sensory organs are part of *xing,* but their nature is such that
they are simply attracted or drawn toward (*yin zhi* 引之) external objects. The heart-mind, given its ability to distinguish, judge, and
reflect, is able to prioritize and as such can judge the suitability of
external objects and not be drawn by them. *Ren* and *yi,* insofar as
they are developed from the germs of the heart-mind,[31] are internal,
in a deeper moral sense. This sense is heightened by the constant
contrast between man and the brutes. Mengzi is giving us a definition of what it means to be human. There are two passages in particular that spell this out, 4B19 and 7B24.

In 4B19, Mengzi says,

> Slight is the difference between man and the brutes. The common man loses this distinguishing feature, while the gentleman retains it. Shun understood the way of things and had a keen insight into human relationships. He followed the path of morality. He did not just put morality into practice (*you renyi xing fei xing renyi ye* 由仁義行非行仁義也).

Certain remarks in 2A6 referred to earlier may help us understand what Shun is said to have known. Shun's understanding about things in general and his insight into human relationships amount to understanding the basic constituents of the heart-mind and their nurturance. As we have seen, the person who denies the four germs is incapacitated for human relationships. Shun's understanding of this allowed him to flow from *renyi*. In other words, he acted and moved naturally from within the basic contents of the heart-mind, instead of instituting or imposing principles of conduct. Gaozi's emphasis on the sensory and appetitive desires made him insist that *renyi* could be only an enforced social construct and, as such, an imposition on natural desires. Mengzi is asserting that *renyi* is a natural mode of conduct, albeit one that arises from principles of the human psyche different from the principle of desire.

In 7B24, Mengzi says,

> The way the mouth is disposed towards tastes, the eye towards colours, the ear towards sounds, the nose towards smell, and the four limbs towards ease is human nature, yet therein also lies the Decree (*ming* 命). That is why the gentleman does not describe it as nature. The way benevolence (*ren*) pertains to the relation between father and son, duty (*yi*) to the relation between prince and subject, the rites (*li*) to the relation between guest and host, wisdom (*zhi*) to the good and wise man, sageness (*sheng* 聖)[32] to the way of Heaven, is the Decree, but therein also lies human nature. That is why the gentleman does not describe it as Decree.

This describes the attitude of the gentleman, or superior person. Again, Mengzi does not deny that the sensory organs and their objects are part of nature. His statement that therein lies *ming* is the idea that the external objects toward which the sensory organs are drawn are contingent. In this regard, the gentleman, though recognizing that they are part of his *xing*, nonetheless takes the attitude that they are not *xing* or nature.

This reading takes *ming* in a descriptive sense, pertaining to the contingency of events.[33] It is consistent with the above analysis of the externality of objects of desire. When Mengzi describes the relations of *ren, yi, li, zhi,* and *sheng* (in 7B24), on the other hand, it is difficult to read *ming* as a contingency, given that Mengzi sees them as arising out of the germs of the heart-mind. As we have seen, Mengzi has argued against Gaozi that, as human beings, we have the potentiality of relations other than the relation of desire. These are relations that may instead judge the objects of desire, and "That is why the gentleman does not describe it as Decree." But if we are to be consistent in the use of *ming* in the same passage, Mengzi does seem to be saying that nonetheless, there is contingency in human relations too. Despite our efforts in maintaining the forms of relationships, things may go awry.

This is as it should be. Mengzi does speak of Heaven as the source of *xin* (6A15). Fully realizing *xin*, one knows *xing*, and through this, one knows and serves Heaven (7A1). In this sense, not only does Heaven endow one with some potentialities, but there is also a proper destiny, *zhengming* 正命.[34] This is a normative sense of *ming*, which enables one to take a steadfast attitude toward death and to cultivate one's character (7A1). Both *ming* and *zhengming* seem to be described in 7A2—understanding that there is nothing that is not *ming*, one does not stand under a wall on the verge of collapse. This implies a cautious attitude to the contingency of events. But if one dies "after having done his best in following the Way," he would have followed *zhengming*.

This difference between *zhengming* and *ming* reiterates and heightens our understanding of "internal" and "external" as Mengzi sees it. The four germs enable us to relate to others and to act in ways that are proper, ultimately defining us as human beings who can stand to others and to things in terms of the virtues[35] of *ren, yi, li,* and *zhi*. This is to follow what is internal both literally and normatively, that is, the heart-mind. In doing so, one is obeying what has been decreed by Heaven, *zhengming*. The internality here may also be described in terms of the relation between seeking and getting. Thus, in 7A3, Mengzi says, "Seek and you will get it; let go and you will lose it. If this is the case, then seeking is of use to getting and what is sought is within yourself." We may add that the seeking is a constitutive part of the getting.[36] In other words, the effort to cultivate oneself involves modes of awareness described earlier. These modes of awareness are not means to an end that one may discard after the getting but are an important part of what it means to be a human being. There cannot be a stronger sense of "internal" than this, because it goes right to the heart of one's identity as a human being. The relation between seeking and getting, we may say, is essential. By contrast, the external objects that one seeks even if arrived at properly may elude one, depending on *ming*. In this sense, there is no essential relation between seeking and getting. As Mengzi says in the same passage, "then seeking is of no use to getting and what is sought lies outside yourself."

Conclusion

Mengzi fails to rebut Gaozi's assertion that morality is a construction in 6A1 to 6A3. Mention was made of how Gaozi could escape the charge of inviting disaster to morality (*renyi*), given his belief that it is constructed. That is, Gaozi could make a distinction between the second- and first-order levels of discourse. His theorizing at the second-order level need not imply that he cannot engage in first-order moral discourse like anyone else.

It is only when Gaozi mentions that *ren* is internal whereas *yi* is external that Mengzi manages to pin him down, given the incoherence of the appetitive sense of "internal" and "external" when applied to the virtues. The development of Mengzi's account of moral psychology enables us to see why the distinction we have made for Gaozi between first- and second-order levels of discourse cannot be maintained for morality, or *renyi*. For Mengzi, denial of the heart-mind and its contents would mean denying the basis on which human relationships are built. You can maintain *renyi* only if you have a deep faith in it as arising out of your deeper self, not as something artificially imposed.

The debate with Gaozi enables us to appreciate more fully Mengzi's philosophy of the human being. We see its basis in a sophisticated moral psychology, which goes beyond the psychology of desire as emphasized by Gaozi. In the final analysis, for Mengzi, *xing* or nature rests on *xin*. And *xin*, as Mengzi states in 6A6 is a potentiality for the virtues of *ren*, *yi*, *li*, and *zhi*. My analysis has shown that Mengzi is in fact stressing the potential for relating to others and to things in terms of certain modes of moral awareness when he talks of *xin*. This stands in contrast to the psychology of desire as advocated by Gaozi, where the emphasis is on consummating a desire-state. In other words, it is definitive of human beings that they do not stand in relation to others as consumers, and neither are they objects that are helplessly drawn toward other objects.

My analysis has shown that we can interpret Mengzi to be stressing the potential for relationships that are relations not of desire but of compassion, shame, respect, and a sense of right and wrong. These are different modes of moral awareness. Mengzi is reminding us that it is within the human capacity to have these modes of awareness. We should not forget, however, that these are only potentialities. It is their development into the virtues that give them their worth. There is a feedback effect here. The manifestation of the virtues enables us to talk of potential capacities and their cultivation. Mengzi sometimes talks as if what prevents moral growth is the lack of appropriate environmental conditions. Thus, it could be said that one cultivates the seeds of the virtues by providing the conditions for moral growth. But there is another sense of "cultivation" that is nonvegetative and that he emphasizes. This involves thought and reflection of what it is to be human. In this sense, nothing is given and talk of what is potential is worthless if nothing is achieved. The debate with Gaozi enables us to take a particular view of what Mengzi is doing when he describes examples to illustrate *xin*—namely, he has provided us with a moral psychology of the possibilities of human relationships. One advantage of this reading is that it alleviates the problem mentioned earlier, that Mengzi would find it difficult to explain why some people fail to nourish their *xin*. If we see *xin* from within the framework of what it is to be human and the possibility of human relations, then it becomes an existential possibility, one that some individuals may fail to live up to.

There is a case for saying that Mengzi would find it difficult to argue for the contents of *xin* without a prior picture of what it is to be human and the relationships and virtues that are involved. Undoubtedly, the picture Mengzi paints of the human being represents a cultural achievement, and the sense of internality that he describes is ultimately normative. Ironically, Gaozi may have been right after all—what we have is a sociocultural construct. Nonetheless, the construction Mengzi gives us is much richer in describing human possibilities than Gaozi's limited picture of human—and animal—desires.

Notes

I am very grateful to Alan Chan, Don Munro, and Kwong-Loi Shun for their comments on earlier versions of this essay. Some of these comments are acknowledged in the body of the essay, as well as in the notes below.

1. D.C. Lau, "On Mencius' Use of the Method of Analogy in Argument," in Lau trans., *Mencius*, vol. 2 (Hong Kong: Chinese University Press, 1984), 334. This essay originally appeared in *Asia Major*, n.s., 10 (1963). In what follows, quotations of passages from the *Mengzi* are taken from Lau's two-volume translation, unless otherwise stated. Except for quotations, I have consistently used *hanyu pinyin* romanization in my discussion. This includes the spelling of names, e.g., Mengzi for Mencius, Gaozi for Kao Tzu, Gongduzi for Kung-tu Tzu, and so on.

2. Chad Hansen, *A Daoist Theory of Chinese Thought: A Philosophical Interpretation* (New York: Oxford University Press, 1992), 188.

3. Arthur Waley, *Three Ways of Thought in Ancient China* (London: George Allen and Unwin, 1939; reprint, New York: Doubleday and Co., 1956), 145.

4. A.C. Graham, "The Background of the Mencian Theory of Human Nature," in Graham, *Studies in Chinese Philosophy and Philosophical Literature* (Singapore: Institute of East Asian Philosophies, 1986), 27.

5. To make it easier for the reader, I shall henceforth use "internal" and "external" instead of *nei* and *wai*.

6. I shall use the term "sensory and appetitive desires" throughout to refer to two broad phenomena of desires: the inclinations stimulated by the sensations of taste, sight, sound, and so forth (as mentioned in *Mengzi* 6A7, e.g.); and the appetite for food and sex (as mentioned by Gaozi to be definitive of *xing* in 6A4).

7. *Ren* and *yi* have been translated as "Goodness" and "Duty" by Waley (see passage quoted above in the text) and as "benevolence" and "right", "righteous," "rightness," "duty," "dutiful," by Lau. The combination of the two terms, *renyi*, is translated by Lau as "morality" (see Lau, "On Mencius' Use of the Method of Analogy," 334–335 nn. 1, 2) but by James Legge as "benevolence and righteousness." See Legge, *The Chinese Classics*, vols. 1 and 2 (Taipei: Southern Materials Center, 1985), 395. I shall follow Lau in taking *renyi* as "morality" but generally leave it untranslated, just as I shall leave *ren* and *yi* untranslated.

8. Although *xing* means "nature," I shall largely leave it untranslated. It may mean human nature or the nature of certain specific things, depending on the context. But as we shall see, Gaozi wishes to argue that it is no different from *sheng*, or the biological life process. As Graham has noted, for Gaozi, "there is no *hsing* [*xing*] other than *sheng*, the life process itself" (Graham,

"Background of the Mencian Theory," 42). Leaving *xing* as it is will allow us to follow the arguments more closely.

9. Zhu Xi, *Sishu zhangju jizhu* 四書章句集注 (Taipei: Changan chuban-she, 1990), 325.

10. See for instance, Donald J. Munro, "A Villain in the *Xunzi*," and David B. Wong, "Xunzi on Moral Motivation," both in *Chinese Language, Thought, and Culture: Nivison and His Critics*, ed. Philip J. Ivanhoe (Chicago: Open Court, 1996), 193–201 and 202–223, respectively.

11. Kwong-Loi Shun, in his comments on an earlier version of this essay. See also Shun, *Mencius and Early Chinese Thought* (Stanford, Calif.: Stanford University Press, 1997), 88.

12. Alan Chan posited these replies. I have not seen the *qiliu* and should add that we do not know the process involved here, whether it is necessary to cut the whole trunk of the *qiliu* or just its branches. If it is the former, perhaps we are killing it; if the latter, then not necessarily. But presumably the branches of the *qiliu* may not be thick enough?

13. Lau, "On Mencius' Use of the Method of Analogy," 336.

14. Don Munro, in correspondence, offers another interesting interpretation here: "Chinese thinkers of many schools use the behavioral implications of a doctrine as grounds for accepting or rejecting it (i.e. the psychological impact it is likely to have on people who hear it). The behavioral implication of saying that it is unnatural to be moral (or a violation of the nature) is that people will not act morally, namely, they will have no incentive to do the right thing."

15. Lau, "On Mencius' Use of the Method of Analogy," 338.

16. Sarah Allan, *The Way of Water and Sprouts of Virtue* (Albany: State University of New York Press, 1997), 42.

17. If a contemporary scientist understands the nature of water better than Mengzi (who had no conception of H_2O), what has that to do with the understanding of human nature?

18. A comparison may be made here with Xunzi's image of molding clay when describing the production of *liyi* 禮義. Gaozi's image of water, however, is more dynamic. See the chapter "Man's Nature is Evil," in *Xunzi,* trans. John Knoblock (Stanford, Calif.: Stanford University Press, 1994), vol. 3, 157.

19. See Lau, "On Mencius' Use of the Method of Analogy," 340: "If we insist on saying that this [the appetite for food and sex] constitutes the whole of human nature then we will have to accept the logical conclusion that the nature of a man is no different from that of a dog or an ox and this not even Kao Tzu was prepared to accept." And Graham, "Background of the Mencian Theory," 46: "Kao-tzu has committed himself to much more than he has bargained for; if *hsing* [*xing*] in general is merely *sheng* there is no inherent tendency in the development of any specific thing, and nothing to distinguish the natures of ox, dog and man."

20. In a wider context, it may be necessary to bring out the early Confucian concern with *xiao* 孝 or *xiaoti* 孝弟 (filial piety), having to do with the innate love of parents, and the duties that derive from it, when discussing the differences between man and animal. *Lunyu* (*Analects*) 1.2, for instance, mentions

xiaoti as the root of *ren*. In *Mengzi* 7A15 we have the identification of *qin qin* 親親 (love of parents) with *ren*, as well as in 7A45, where the gradation of loving parents, people, and things in descending order is spelled out. I thank Don Munro for pointing out the relevance of these passages. We ought to be careful, though, not to equate the discussion of *ren* in the *Lunyu* with that in the *Mengzi*. In the latter text, *ren* is integrally connected with the discussion of human nature, whereas in the former this is not the case. I discuss the differences in "The Practice of *Jen*," *Philosophy East and West* 49.3 (1999).

21. My rendering of *yue* in 6A4 as what "pleases" is contextual, and I believe it captures what Gaozi is thinking of in his explanation of "*ren* is internal." Both Alan Chan and Kwong-Loi Shun have pointed out the need to mention D. C. Lau's different translation of *yue* here as "explanation," in the sense of *shuo* 說. Thus, Lau translates *shi yi wo wei yue zhe ye gu wei zhi nei* 是以我為悅者也故謂之內 as "This means that the explanation lies in me. Hence I call it internal." And similarly, a few sentences later, *shi yi zhang wei yue zhe ye gu wei zhi wai ye* 是以長為悅者也故謂之外也 is translated as "This means that the explanation lies in their elderliness. Hence I call it external." The first use of *yue* as "the explanation lies in me" is consistent with my rendering of it as what "pleases," but not the second use, "the explanation lies in their elderliness." Note that in 6A7, we have *gu liyi zhi yue wo xin you chuhuan zhi yue wo kou* 故理義之悅我心猶芻豢之悅我口, which Lau renders as "Thus reason and rightness please my heart in the same way as meat pleases my palate." Although both instances of *yue* are translated as "please(s)," I show below that the pleasure of the heart-mind in *liyi* is different in kind from the sensory pleasure of taste.

22. Lau, "On Mencius' Use of the Method of Analogy," 351.

23. David Nivison, for instance, states, "Gao and Mencius are agreed about *ren*, exemplified by loving: I won't show love unless I am disposed to, in virtue of the relation of the object to me. They disagree about *yi*, exemplified by behavior showing respect for elderliness, because Gao thinks of the occasional cause as the decisive one: It is what is 'out there' that counts, every time, no matter where, including the applicable public standard." See David Nivison, *The Ways of Confucianism: Investigations in Chinese Philosophy,* ed. Bryan W. Van Norden (Chicago: Open Court, 1996), 162–163. Nivison notes the absurd consequence of Gaozi's having to say that his enjoyment of roast is external, but Nivison does not make the point that Mengzi is rejecting the internal-external distinction that Gaozi is working with. Lau perhaps sees the point dimly, but does not quite exploit it, when he says of Mengzi, "All he set out to do . . . was to show that his opponents failed to establish the externality of *yi*. He did not attempt to go beyond this and to establish positively that *yi* was internal." (Quoted above in the text; see n. 22.)

24. Alan Chan has drawn my attention to the following: Lau translates *bu ren ren zhi xin* 不忍人之心 in 2A6 as "a heart sensitive to the suffering of others" and "a sensitive heart." W. T. Chan translates this as "the mind which cannot bear to see the suffering of others." Mentioning the example, Mengzi attributes this capacity to something more basic, *ceyin zhi xin*. Lau translates this as "compassion," and Chan as "a feeling of alarm and distress." It could be argued that Lau's "sensitive heart" and "compassion" are no different, and one cannot as

such be the basis of, or serve as evidence for, the other. On the other hand, Chan's "feeling of alarm and distress" could be seen as a more rudimentary form of response, necessary (but not sufficient) for the "mind which cannot bear to see the suffering of others." See W. T. Chan, *A Source Book in Chinese Philosophy* (Princeton, N.J.: Princeton University Press, 1963), 65.

25. For a detailed discussion of the nontransferability of compassion or concern, see my book *Moral Agoraphobia—the Challenge of Egoism* (New York: Peter Lang, 1996), 50–51, where the case of Dorothea is described more fully. Alan Chan has brought up the following interesting case: I see a child killed in a car accident; contrary to what I normally do, I might give some money to a child begging further down the road. There is no denying that this constitutes a psychological phenomenon of "transference," but it should not affect what I mean by the "nontransferability" of compassion or concern.

26. See Shun, *Mencius and Early Chinese Thought*, 137; Ann-ping Chin and Mansfield Freeman, trans., *Tai Chen [Dai Zhen 戴震] on Mencius: Explorations in Words and Meaning (Mengzi ziyi shuzheng 孟子字義疏證)* (New Haven, Conn.: Yale University Press, 1990), 74.

27. Shun, *Mencius and Early Chinese Thought,* 150, 265. According to Tang Junyi (T'ang Chün-i 唐君毅), the pre-Qin thinkers largely used *li* in the sense of *wenli,* or "pattern." See his study of the concept of *li* in "*Lun Zhongguo zhexue sixiangshi zhong li zhi liu yi* 論中國哲學思想史中理之六義," in *Xinya xuebao* 新亞學報 1.1 (1955): 45–98, esp. 47. The three passages where *li* occurs are 5B1, 6A7, and 7B19. In the last, someone called Mo Ji (Mo Chi) says, "*Ji da bu li yu kou* 稽大不理於口*,*" which Lau renders as "I am not much of a speaker." Yang Bojun 楊伯峻 takes *li* here as *shun* 順 (agreeable, smooth-going). Thus he gives the modern Chinese equivalent of the passage as "I am badly spoken of by others." See Yang Bojun, *Mengzi yizhu* 孟子譯注 (Hong Kong: Zhonghua shuju, 1984).

28. Lau's translation of the relevant passage in 5B1 reads, "Confucius was the one who gathered together all that was good (*ji da cheng* 集大成). To do this is to open with bells and rally with jade tubes. To open with bells is to begin in an orderly fashion (*shi tiaoli ye* 始條理也); to rally with jade tubes is to end in an orderly fashion (*zhong tiaoli ye* 終條理也). To begin in an orderly fashion pertains to wisdom while to end in an orderly fashion pertains to sageness." Note Wing-tsit Chan's as well as Chin and Freeman's translation of *ji da cheng* as a "complete concert." See W. T. Chan, *Source Book,* 711; Chin and Freeman, *Tai Chen on Mencius,* 69.

29. See David Wong, "Is There a Distinction between Reason and Emotion in Mencius?" *Philosophy East and West* 41.1 (1991): 31–44, for an extended argument of this point. Much earlier, Don Munro made the same point in his *The Concept of Man in Contemporary China* (Ann Arbor: University of Michigan Press, 1977); see esp. chap. 2, 26 ff.

30. Translation is my own. Compare Lau: "If it was truly right for them to bury the remains of their parents, then it must also be right for all dutiful sons and benevolent men to do likewise." As Lau often uses "right" for a translation of *yi,* and *yi* does not occur in this passage, it is better not to use the term "right" here.

31. Note that in 6A6, Mengzi seems to identify *ren, yi, li,* and *zhi* with the four germs: *ceyin zhi xin ren ye, xiuwu zhi xin yi ye,* and so on. Lau's translation, however, leaves it ambiguous: "The heart of compassion *pertains* to benevolence, the heart of shame to dutifulness...." (My emphasis.)

32. The original text has *sheng ren* (sage) instead of *sheng* (sageness). I have adopted "sageness" instead of "sage" because it allows for a more consistent reading of *ren, yi, li, zhi, sheng.* This is a possible reading as noted after the Chinese text of 7B24 in Lau. Lau cites Pang Pu (P'ang P'u 龐樸) in this regard. This refers to Pang's *Boshu wuxing pian yanjiu* 帛書五行篇研究 (Jinan: Qilu shushe, 1988), 19–21. As Kwong-Loi Shun explains, "P'ang P'u argues for the emendation on the grounds that *sheng* is grouped along with *jen* [*ren*], *yi, li,* and *chih* [*zhi*] in the 'Essay on the Five Processes' in the Ma-wang-tui [Mawangdui] silk manuscripts." See Shun, *Mencius and Early Chinese Thought,* 203–204.

33. The distinction between the descriptive and normative senses of *ming* is made by Kwong-Loi Shun, *Mencius and Early Chinese Thought,* 78–79. Shun gives quite an exhaustive discussion of different possible interpretations of 7B24 on pp. 203–205 of his book.

34. The term *zhengming* occurs in 7A2. In 7A1, we have *li ming* 立命, which Lau translates as "stands firm on his proper Destiny."

35. Not to be confused with *de* (*te*) 德, often translated as "virtue" and/or "power." See Kwong-Loi Shun, *Mencius and Early Chinese Thought,* 48, for his preference in using the term "ethical attributes" in referring to *ren, yi, li,* and *zhi* in the *Mengzi,* because it is "unclear that the use of '*te*' had evolved by Mencius's time to allow references to particular desirable attributes as different *te.*"

36. Lau makes a related distinction between instrumental and constitutive means in his discussion of *Mengzi* 4A17, although I would not describe what I have said as a constitutive relation between seeking and getting in terms of "means." Asked why he would save a drowning sister-in-law (contrary to the ritual rule of *nan nü shou shou bu qin* 男女授受不親) but not the empire, Mengzi replies, "When the Empire is drowning, one helps it with the Way (*dao*); when a sister-in-law is drowning one helps her with one's hand. Would you have me help the Empire with my hand?" To Waley (*Three Ways of Thought,* 146), this is a "cheap debating point." Lau replies that one may use anything to save a drowning woman; the means is purely instrumental. But one may save the empire only through the proper way, the *dao.* He adds, "[The Way] becomes part of the end it helps to realize, and the end endures so long as the means remains a part of it. Remove the Way at any subsequent time, and the Empire will revert to disorder." See Lau, "On Mencius' Use of the Method of Analogy," 341–342.

6

Xin and Moral Failure
Notes on an Aspect of Mencius' Moral Psychology

ANTONIO S. CUA

THE FOLLOWING is a study of an aspect of Mencius' moral psychology. The first section deals with *xin* 心 as the seat of the "four beginnings" (*siduan* 四端) of the four Confucian cardinal virtues (*ren* 仁, *yi* 義, *li* 禮, *and zhi* 智). This discussion presupposes the vision of the Confucian *dao,* an ethical ideal of the unity and harmony of Heaven and humanity (*tianren heyi*). The second section examines Mencius' account of moral failure with a Xunzian supplement. The essay concludes with some remarks on Mencius' contributions to Confucian ethical theory.

Xin as the Seat of Virtues

In an earlier essay, I proposed that the contrasting positions of Mencius and Xunzi on human nature are versions of internalism and externalism.[1] At issue is the question of the connection between morality and human nature. For Mencius, an internalist, the connection is intrinsic, for the intelligibility of moral achievement depends on certain inherent moral capacities. For Xunzi, an externalist, the connection is extrinsic. When we focus on the regulative aspect of morality, we readily think of morality as a system of rules, which aims to counteract a certain problematic basic motivational structure, particularly the native human tendency to create problems for one another. However, if we focus on the ideal aspect of morality, or *ren* (in the broad sense), as an ideal of the good human life as a whole, it is an object of sentiment as well as an object of volition for a committed agent. This moral ideal furnishes a way of seeing persons as having moral import. It is a perspective, a point of orientation, an ideal theme rather than a norm for assessing conduct.[2] Given the commitment to the ideal, compliance with rules and principles of morality has ethical significance only when these rules and principles are invested with the ideal of humanity. For this sort of moral achievement, morality can have nothing to do with benefits extrinsic to personal commitment. Perhaps this is the basis for the familiar characterization of the difference between Mencius and Xunzi as located in their respective emphasis on *renyi* 仁義 and *liyi* 禮 義. Mencius' doctrine of *siduan* makes an important contribution to the problem of the connection between morality and human nature.

If we look at the four cardinal virtues as general specifications of the Confucian ideal of *dao*, Mencius' doctrine of *siduan* provides an insightful account of the possibility of realizing this holistic ideal of the good human life. Consider Mencius' doctrine as an answer to the question, How can I become a Confucian agent? In some ways, this is reminiscent of Kierkegaard's question, How can I be a Christian? Notably, this is a question of self-transformation, of the actuating import of the Confucian ideal of *dao* or *ren* in the broad sense. However, in classical Confucian ethics, *ren* is often used in a narrow sense.[3] The distinction between the broad and the narrow senses of *ren* is clear, for example, in Zhu Xi's view that *ren* embraces the four virtues, which includes *ren* in the narrow sense (*ren bao si de* 仁包四德).[4] *Xin* is the seat of *siduan*. The proper development of *siduan* into virtues or ethical attributes depends on preserving the constancy of *xin* (*hengxin* 恒心).[5]

Recall that the *siduan* are the *xin* of (1) compassion, (2) aversion to shame, (3) courtesy and modesty, and (4) right and wrong. If we regard the *siduan* as sentiments, we can say that *xin*, while expressive of a feeling, has both cognitive and emotive aspects. The adoption by many Sinologists of "mind-heart" as a translation of *xin* rightly presumes a Mencian rejection of an exclusive disjunction between "reason/judgment" and the "passions/emotions." This notion of sentiment captures the sense of Butler's apt characterization of "moral faculty" as "a sentiment of the understanding or perception of the heart."[6] More importantly, implicit in the notion of sentiment is prereflective judgment. As Reid points out,

> Our moral determinations may, with propriety, be called *moral senti-ments.* For the word *sentiment,* in the English language, never, as I conceive, signifies mere feeling, but judgment accompanied with feelings.... So we speak of sentiments of respect, of esteem, of grati-tude. But I have never heard the pain of the gout, or any other mere feeling, called a sentiment.[7]

Plausibly, these sentiments embody prereflective judgments subject to reasoned refinement.[8] In this light, Mencius' doctrine of *siduan* is a doctrine of moral sentiments.

More formally, the *xin* of compassion, for instance, is expressed as a *qing,* or feeling, which pragmatically implies an epistemic atti-tude, that is, belief, thought, or judgment.[9] Thus, the *xin* of compas-sion involves the following: (a) a feeling of alarm and distress, (b) an implicit belief, thought, or judgment that one ought to help the person in distress, and (c) a disposition to act accordingly. Because the *siduan,* the germs of virtue, are spontaneously expressed, these epistemic attitudes are subject to reasoned evaluation. I take this to be the purport of Mencius' remark that reason and rightness (*liyi* 理義) are common to all *xin.* Says Mencius, "The sage is simply the man first to discover this common element in my heart (*xin*). Thus reason and rightness please my heart in the same way as meat pleases my palate" (6A7).[10] On this interpretation, *ren* (in the narrow sense of benevolence), for example, is a fruition of the *xin* of compassion, presuming that it is properly expressed and that the epistemic atti-tude is reasonably justified. If this point is acceptable, we can say that for Mencius, expressing the four *xin* does not automatically lead to the acquisition of the four virtues (*ren, yi, li,* and *zhi*), unless the expression is mediated by reason (*li* 理).

As germs of the cardinal virtues, the *siduan* are capacities for ethical achievement. Basically, they are capacities of agency (e.g., capacities to initiate and bring about changes in current states of affairs, changes that are explainable by the notion of practical rather than theoretical causation).[11] The Confucian cardinal virtues are achievements. This interpretation is based on a retrospective view of Confucian virtues as the successful development of the *si-duan.* In this way, moral virtues are qualities of character. Conse-quently, we can depict the Mencian cardinal virtues as ethical attri-butes or qualities of persons.[12] This is consistent with a prospective view of virtues as goals of action. These two conceptions are comple-mentary, given that the former depends on learning the moral significance of the virtues as having actuating or transformative import in human life.[13]

In sum, for Mencius, expressing the four *xin* does not automatically lead to the ethical virtues of *ren, yi, li, and zhi,* unless their expression is mediated by reason and a sense of rightness (*liyi* 理義). Among other factors, the exercise of *quan* 權 (weighing of circumstance) in exigent situations plays a crucial role. In the next section, we will discuss the other factors.

In normal situations, informed by Confucian culture and in the absence of the interfering factors to be explored later, one would expect, say, compassion to be expressed fairly spontaneously. Mencius stresses *quan* as a standard: "It is by weighing a thing that its weight can be known and by measuring it that its length can be ascertained. It is so with all things, but particularly with the heart" (1A7). The exercise of *quan*—consider, for example, the case of the drowning sister-in-law (4A17)—implies a reasonable prereflective judgment of rightness in an exigent situation.[14] Moreover, the proper exercise of *quan* presupposes that the agent has an open mind. As Mencius (7A26) reminds the Confucian agent, he must not hold on to any one particular moral doctrine even if it represents a moderate position between extremes (*buzhiyi* 不執一). Apart from the case of the drowning sister-in-law, we find suggestions of other features—for example, Mencius' characterization of Confucius (5B1) as a sage of timeliness (*sheng zhi shizhe* 聖之時者), and his saying that reason and rightness are common to all *xin* (6A7). These remarks provide partial support for our interpretation of the cognitive-emotive nature of *siduan*. If this interpretation is correct, we must reject the philosophical attribution of ethical intuitionism to Mencius.[15]

I assume that Mencius' ethical ideal of *ren* in the broad sense is an ideal theme, an ideal of the good human life that has a concrete specification in particular human lives, regardless of their stations in society. The rich and the poor, the eminent and the mean, must have the same opportunity for realizing *ren*. The actuating force of Confucian aretaic notions presupposes a reflective capacity of the committed Confucian agent to make reasonable judgments in particular circumstances. I take this to be the force of Mencius' remark on *buzhiyi* (not holding to one thing): "Holding on to the middle (*zhong* 中) is closer to being right, but to do this without moral discretion (*quan*) is no different from holding to one extreme. The reason for disliking those who hold to one extreme is that they cripple the Way. One thing is singled out to the neglect of a hundred others" (7A26).[16] Mencius, as mentioned, admired Confucius as a timely sage (5B1). This stress on timeliness underlies Mencius' example of the drowning sister-in-law, where *quan* is exercised. In contrast, where a situation permits time for reflection and decision, Xunzi would say that this is a case for using *yi* to cope with changing circumstances (*yiyi bianying* 以義變應).[17]

The development of *xin* presupposes an extension of *ren,* an affectionate concern for human beings and ultimately for all things in the world. Says Mencius,

> If a man is able to develop all these four germs that he possesses, it will be like a fire starting up or a spring coming through. When these are fully developed, he can take under his protection the whole realm within the Four Seas, but if he fails to develop them, he will not be able even to serve his parents. (2A6)

The realization of this vision presupposes the "constancy of *xin*" (*hengxin*). For example, Am I willing, as a Confucian committed to *ren* as an ideal of the good human life, in the current difficult case, to forgo self-interest? An affirmative answer to this question requires the Confucian agent to harmonize his or her thought, feeling, words, and deeds. In this light, the realization of the Confucian ideal of the good human life is a personal achievement.

Moral Achievement and Failure

For Mencius' conception of moral achievement, that is, the full development of the four germs into the four cardinal virtues, I propose the following schema for explication.

> The *xin* of X (for example, compassion) is the capacity to feel X and be mindful of the situation that calls for performing X-act. If X is appropriately expressed in the current case and certain deficiencies are not present, then the Confucian agent may be ascribed the virtue V. Alternatively, an act cannot be properly described as a V-act, unless it is an exercise of X as an inherent human capacity.

Failure to develop *xin* is due to failure to overcome certain deficiencies of moral agency. I distinguish six such deficiencies in this context:

D1. Lack of will. The agent may be unwilling to subject his or her desires to reasoned assessment or does not appreciate the import of extending *xin* (e.g., in the case of extending beneficence [*tui-en* 推恩]).

D2. Lack of a constant *xin* (*hengxin*). This may be due to the enticement of personal gain at the expense of *yi*, or failure in preserving moral integrity.

D3. Lack of a sense of moral priority or importance, especially when there is a conflict of goods.

D4. Lack of constant self-examination, leading to failure in correcting moral faults.

D5. Lack of means to support a constant *xin*.

D6. Lack of appreciation of the nature of the current situation.

In the proposed schema, we assume a negative approach to understanding moral achievement, that is, the full development of *xin*, through an inquiry into the possibility of moral failure. This approach makes no claim to completeness or adequacy, for it gives only the principal, necessary, and not the sufficient conditions for understanding Mencius' conception of moral achievement as a full development of *xin* as the seat of the cardinal virtues.

(D1) Lack of Will. When King Xuan of Qi inquired about a virtuous person becoming a true king, Mencius cited the incident when the king could not bear to see the blood of an ox in a sacrifice and suggested the use of a lamb instead. Mencius remarks, "The heart behind your action is sufficient to enable you to become a true king ... your failure to become a true king is due to a refusal to act (*buwei* 不為), not to an inability to act (*buneng* 不能)." Mencius explains the difference between refusal to act and inability to act as follows.

> If you say to someone, "I am unable to do it," when the task is one of striding over the North Sea with Mount T'ai [Tai] under your arm, then this is a genuine case of inability to act. But if you say, "I am unable to do it," when it is one of massaging an elder's joints for him, then this is a case of refusal to act, not of inability. Hence your failure to become a true king is not the same in kind as "striding over the North Sea," but the same as "massaging an elder's joints for him."
>
> ... In other words, all you have to do is take this very heart here and apply it to what is over there. Hence one who extends his bounty (*tui-en*) can bring peace to the Four Seas; one who does not cannot bring peace even to his own family. (1A7)

The foregoing passage provides a basis for discussing the sources of moral failure. Moral failure may be a failure owing to lack of willingness to extend *xin,* which reflects a failure to appreciate the distinction between *buneng* and *buwei. Buneng,* the inability to act in an appropriate way, construed as incapacity, may be an exculpating circumstance for excuse or justification of moral failure. *Buwei,* the refusal to act, however, is an expression of resolve. Because it manifests the agent's character, it is subject to ascription of ethical responsibility, even though the agent may not be conscious of the nature of his act. Given the native moral capacity, the agent—in this case, the king—can extend beneficence (*tui-en*) to the people, thus bringing peace to the realm. More fundamentally, every sincere committed Confucian must extend *ren* and *yi* (7B31). With Xunzi, we may want to make a related distinction between *neng* 能 (actual capacity) and *ke* 可 (theoretical possibility). It is theoretically possible that everyone can become (*ke yi wei* 可以為) a sage, yet as a matter of actuality, some cannot (*buneng*) become one: "Thus, there is a wide distance between *neng bu neng* 能不能 and *ke bu ke* 可不可. We must not confuse the distinction."[18] Mencius' case of *buwei* (not doing) is perhaps more clearly read as *buken* 不肯 (an unwillingness), implying deliberate intention not to do something or a deliberate negative action as the Daoist *wuwei* 無為.

(D2) Lack of Hengxin. At issue then is the importance of preserving *hengxin* (a constant *xin*).[19] For if a person does not do (*buwei*) the right or good thing in a particular situation, it may be that he or she was unwilling (*buken*) to do so. Following Confucius, Mencius draws a fairly sharp contrast between *yi* (rightness) and profit or personal gain (1A1). The envisaged conflict between *yi* and concern with personal gain provides a partial ground for construing *yi* as reflecting the Confucian moral point of view as contrasted with the point of view of self-interest.[20] For Mencius, an agent's lack of *hengxin,* the constant or persevering *xin,* may well be a result of preoccupation with personal gain without attending to the relevance of *yi* as a basis for assessment, or the exercise of *quan* particularly when the situation is one that promises personal gain.

Alternatively, lack of *hengxin* is a failure to appreciate *xin* as a weighing standard for determining the ethically proper course of action. Moreover, the failure may also be a result of the corruption of moral integrity. Mencius once said that a great man "cannot be led into excesses when wealthy and honoured or deflected from his purpose when poor and obscure, nor can he be made to bow before superior force" (3B2). On another occasion, Mencius was insistent on the ethical integrity of the sages: "The conduct of the sages is not always the same. Some live in retirement, others enter the world; some withdraw, others stay on; but it all comes to keeping their integrity intact (*guijie qishen* 歸潔其身)" (5A7). Indeed, integrity is not limited to the sages; no self-respecting villager would sell himself into slavery "in order to help one's prince toward achievement" (5A9). More important, a wayfarer, or even a beggar, would not accept a bowl of soup if it were tendered in an abusive manner, particularly when the behavior violates the requirements of propriety and *yi* (6A10).

Ordinarily, failure to preserve one's ethical integrity is a failure of *cheng* 誠 (being true to oneself). Says Mencius, "Being true (*cheng*) is the Way of Heaven; to reflect upon this is the Way of man. There has never been a man totally true to himself who fails to move others. On the other hand, one who is not true to himself can never hope to move others" (4A12). Indeed, the utmost of the development of *xin* (*jinxin* 盡心) presupposes knowing one's nature (*xing*). Elsewhere, Mencius states,

> For a man to give full realization to his heart (*jin qi xin* 盡其心) is for him to understand his own nature and a man who knows his own nature will know Heaven. By retaining his heart (*cun qi xin* 存其心) and nurturing his nature (*yang qi xing* 養其性), he is serving Heaven. Whether he is going to die young or live to a ripe old age makes no difference to his steadfastness of purpose. It is through awaiting whatever is to befall him with a perfected character that he stands firm on his proper Destiny. (7A1)

Since moral integrity lies in a genuine commitment to the actuating force of *ren* and *yi*, the agent must be prepared to sacrifice his or her life for the sake of that commitment. Recall Confucius' saying, "A scholar dedicated to *dao* or a *ren*-person would not seek to stay alive at the expense of *ren*. He would accept death in order to have *ren* actualized."[21] Mencius is more elaborate on this spirit of sacrifice, as depicted in his well-known statement of inner moral conflict (6A10).

> Fish is what I want; bear's palm is also what I want. If I cannot have both, I would rather take bear's palm than fish. Life is what I want;

doing what accords with *yi* is also what I want. If I cannot have both, I would rather take *yi* than life. On the other hand, though death is what I loathe, there is something I loathe more than death. That is why there are troubles I do not avoid. If there is nothing a man wants more than life, then why should he have scruples about any means, so long as it helps him to avoid troubles? Yet there are ways of remaining alive and ways of avoiding death to which a man will not resort. In other words, there are things a man wants more than life and there are also things he loathes more than death. This is an attitude not confined to the good person but common to all men. The good person simply never loses it. (6A10)

Here we have the familiar Confucian emphasis on *yi* as a guide to one's moral life: "The ethically paradigmatic individual (*junzi*) considers *yi* as the most important thing in life" (*Lunyu* 17.23). Mencius' remark is especially noteworthy because it draws attention to the importance of making an autonomous choice when the agent confronts, so to speak, the ultimate predicament, whether to sacrifice life or *yi*. Notably, the ethical attitude depicted in 6A10 refers to a natural, innate ethical capacity of all humans. Sagehood is simply the culmination of the development of *xin* of common humanity (4A2), not the exclusive attainment of a few elites who have dedicated their lives to the actualization of *siduan*.

(D3) Lack of a Sense of Moral Priority. The lack of a sense of moral priority or importance is connected with (D2) in the sense that it may be influenced by the factors that interfere with the preservation of *hengxin*. However, for Mencius, given his view on the inherent goodness of human nature, (D3) is a fairly typical human experience. According to Mencius, one can distinguish the degrees of ethical worth of persons by their choices, because their choices reflect concern with the greater or smaller import of the different aspects of personhood (*dati* 大體 and *xiaoti* 小體). Human beings are creatures of the same kind, but some are greater than others because of the choices they make. Those who follow and nurture *dati* (the more important and more valuable aspects of personhood) become great men and those who follow *xiaoti* (the less important and less valuable aspects of personhood) become small men.

> Now consider a gardener. If he tends the common trees while neglecting the valuable ones, then he is a bad gardener. A man who takes care of one finger to the detriment of his shoulder and back

without realizing his mistake is a muddled man. A man who cares only about food and drink is despised by others because he takes care of the less important and less valuable aspects of himself (*xiaoti*) to the detriment of the more valuable aspects (*dati*). If a man who cares about food and drink can do so without neglecting any other aspects of his person, then his mouth and belly are much more than just a foot or an inch of his skin. (6A14)

What explains the difference between great and small persons? Mencius replies that, though equally human, some are guided by *dati* and some by *xiaoti*.

The organs of hearing and sight are unable to think and can be mis-led by external things. When they interact, they merely attract one another. The organ of *xin* can think. But it will succeed in perform-ing its function only if it thinks. If it does not, it will not function properly. This is what Heaven has given me. If one makes one's stand on what is of greater importance in the first instance, what is of smaller importance cannot displace it. In this way, one cannot but be a great man. (6A15)

The above passages from 6A14 and 6A15 provide important insights into the task of moral theory and agency. First, Mencius' conception of agency presupposes the idea of the freedom of choice. Indeed, it is difficult for moral theorists to make sense of their subject matter unless moral agents are presumed to have freedom of choice and their choices are subject to reasoned evaluation. Mencius is em-phatic that *xin* is a standard of evaluation (1A7). Thus Mencius' use of *xin,* in the light of 6A15 and 1A7, pertains to *xin* as an "evaluative mind."[22] This use supports our earlier interpretation that *xin* has a cognitive aspect, which appertains primarily to evaluation. An elabo-ration of the *xin* of aversion to shame (*xiuwu zhi xin*) and the *xin* of right and wrong (*shifei zhi xin*) is hardly intelligible without the cog-nitive aspect of *xin*. The former as the root of the virtue *yi* implies that the agent can know and appreciate the distinction between shame and honor and can identify the sort of situations to which the distinction applies. The latter, the *xin* of right and wrong, is the rudimentary capacity to distinguish right from wrong conduct, though the agent may make mistakes in such an identification.[23] Generally, we may say that, for Mencius, the successful actualization of the four *xin* or *siduan* depends crucially on reflective mediation.

Pondering Mencius' notion of freedom of choice, one may ask whether this notion conveys the idea of autonomy. If one proffers an affirmative answer, the autonomy must be understood in the value-neutral sense of self-government, a notion that has nothing to do with issues of the validity of Kantian and post-Kantian conceptions of moral autonomy.[24] This sense of autonomy of *xin* is explicit in *Xunzi*.

> *Xin* is the ruler of the body and the host of godlike insights (*shenming zhi zhu* 神明之主). It gives commands but does not receive commands. [Of its own volition] it prohibits or permits, renounces or selects, initiates or stops. Thus the mouth can be forced to speak or to be silent; the body can be forced to crouch down or to stretch out. But *xin* cannot be forced to change its opinions. What it considers right it will accept; what it considers wrong it will reject. Hence, we have the saying: "The salient features of mind (*xinrong* 心容) are these: Its choices are not subject to any external control. Inevitably it manifests its own choices."[25]

Here we have a statement of *xin*'s freedom of volition. Thus *xin* must be guided by reason (*li* 理). Without such guidance, it would be incapable of resolving doubts concerning right or wrong conduct. Because of its volitional freedom, without knowing and accepting the ideal of *dao* as the ethical standard for evaluating conduct, *xin* may even reject *dao* as a guide to right conduct. Xunzi agrees with Mencius that all human beings can become sages.

> The sage follows his desires, satisfies all his emotions, and at the same time is restrained, because he possesses reason (*li* 理). What has he to do with strength of will, endurance, or fearlessness? The man of *ren* practices *dao* through inaction; the sage through nonstriving. The thoughts of a benevolent man are reverent; the thoughts of the sage are joyous. This is the way to govern *xin*.[26]

Given its autonomy, from Xunzi's standpoint, the problem is the unity of *xin*, that is, coordination of its intellectual and volitional functions by way of the ethical ideal of *dao*.[27] This is a problem of self-transformation. In Confucius' view (*Lunyu* 12.1), the agent must have self-discipline and pay heed to the requirements of the rules of proper conduct.

Let us focus again on Mencius' distinction between *dati* and *xiaoti*, the greater and the lesser aspects of personhood. Without a *xin* informed by reflection and the ideal of *dao* or *ren*, the person would be unable to make proper ethical choices. The distinction between *dati* and *xiaoti* supposes that the situation an agent confronts is one of conflict between goods that are deemed desirable; that is, the available options seem to the agent to be benefit producing. Recall our earlier citation of 6A10 involving the choice between fish and bear's palm, and in the more extreme case the choice between *yi* and life. More generally, in any situation that presents live options between desirable states of affairs, Confucian agents may make the wrong choice, because they fail to weigh adequately their comparative value in the light of their ethical commitments. Among other things, moral theory should be concerned with this sort of ordinary human experience of conflict of goods or values rather than with conflict between goods and evils.[28] Moreover, in the light of the role of reflection guided by an ethical ideal, the proper evaluation of the degree of importance among competing options would require reasoned judgment. Because this judgment may differ from that imposed by established rules of conduct, it acknowledges implicitly the distinction between the customary and reflective morality.[29] We may add that moral theory must also deal with exigent cases that call for the exercise of *quan* discussed above.

Before proceeding further, we must note a profound difference in attitude between Mencius and Xunzi toward human desires, quite apart from their different conceptions of human nature. Although both recognize the problematic tendency of some of our desires and the importance of distinguishing ethical from nonethical desires (7B25), Mencius would advocate a reduction of desires in self-cultivation. Says Mencius,

> There is nothing better in nourishing *xin* than to reduce the number of one's desires. When a man has but few desires (*guayu* 寡欲), even if there is anything he fails to retain in himself, it cannot be much; but when he has a great many desires, then even if there is anything he manages to retain in himself, it cannot be much. (7B35)

Compare this attitude with Xunzi's critique of two prevailing theories of desires.

> Those who advocate the elimination of desires before there can be orderly government fail to consider whether the desires can be guided, but merely deplore the fact that they exist at all. All those who advocate the reduction of desires (*guayu*) before there can be orderly government fail to consider whether desires can be

regulated, but merely deplore the fact that they are so numerous. Beings that possess desires and those that do not belong to two different categories—the living and the dead. But the possession or nonpossession of desires has nothing to do with good government or bad.[30]

Here perhaps lies Xunzi's greater emphasis on *li* 禮 as rules of proper conduct, for in addition to their regulative and ennobling functions, crucially *li* have also a supportive function. In Xunzi's view, *li* also provide channels for the satisfaction of desires (*gei ren zhi qiu* 給 人之求). As suggested in his remark on the good (*shan*) as that which is (ethically) desirable (7B25), Mencius would agree with Xunzi that those desires that counter the realization of the Confucian *dao* must be transformed into ethically desirable ones.[31] In other words, one must distinguish between natural, occurrent desires and reflective desires. Indeed, this distinction is implicit in Mencius' statement of moral conflict (6A10). Yet he does not seem to appreciate fully the supportive function of *li* 禮.

One might object that Mencius advocated the reduction of desires because of his concern with "distorted desires."[32] To this rejoinder, Xunzi would point out that at issue is the development of reflective desires in accord with the guidance of reason and invested with a concern with *li* 禮 and *yi*.[33] Again, we find grounds for the common distinction of emphasis on government by *ren* in Mencius and government by *li* in Xunzi. A reasonable solution may lie in reconciling internalism and externalism on the connection between morality as a regulative system and human nature. This issue in Confucian ethical theory has its counterpart in Western ethical theory, in the debate between Kantianism and Utilitarianism, though the Confucian issue is more complex, for it involves questions concerning the viability of a moral tradition (*daotong* 道統). With few exceptions, post-Kantian Western ethical theory rejects moral tradition as being an uncritical guide to conduct, although pre-Kantians like Shaftesbury and Reid would emphasize sensus communis, the sense of common interest in a moral community.[34] The anti-tradition moral theory fails to distinguish intelligent, critical adherence to tradition from blind adherence to the prevailing understanding of the living significance of tradition. As Pelikan succinctly states: "Tradition is the living faith of the dead, traditionalism is the dead faith of the living."[35]

Before we take up (D4), let us also observe that value conflict does not pertain only to the conflict between moral and nonmoral values. Perhaps the more difficult cases involve conflict between moral goods. Notably our *xin* of compassion (*ceyin zhi xin*) may conflict with our sense of honor or aversion to shame (*xiuwu zhi xin*). Such cases give rise to the question of the unity of *siduan* and, consequently, the unity of the four cardinal virtues. Zhu Xi's doctrine of *ren* (in the broad sense) as the virtue of *xin* (*xinzhide* 心之德) and as embracing the four virtues is one attempt worthy of further inquiry. At any rate, without a doctrine of the hierarchy of values, the burden is placed upon the Confucian agent to exercise *quan* carefully. For one committed to *ren,* the task involved is the burden of *ren* (*Lunyu* 8.7), a burden of moral creativity.

(D4) Lack of Self-examination. Obviously the exercise of moral creativity depends on self-cultivation, which involves constant self-examination, so that the agent can correct his or her character faults and misconduct. Thus (D4) is a familiar Confucian concern. In the *Lunyu* (1.4), we have this remark of Zengzi's: "Everyday I examine myself on three counts. In what I have undertaken on another's behalf, have I failed to do my best? In my dealing with my friends have I failed to be trustworthy? Have I passed on to others anything that I have not tried out myself?"

Self-examination may also be described, following *Daxue,* as a process of attaining *chengyi* 誠意, or sincerity of thought, which significantly requires avoidance of self-deception. Ideally the result of self-examination is freedom from self-reproach. As Confucius reminds his pupils, "If, on examining himself, a man finds nothing to reproach himself for, what worries or fear can he have?" (*Lunyu* 12.4). Mencius concurs: "A *junzi* differs from other men because he examines his heart (*xin*). He examines his heart by means of *ren* and *li* 禮."[36] Suppose he is treated by someone in an outrageous manner. He will turn around and examine himself (*zifan* 自反) and say to himself, "I must be lacking in *ren* and *li,* or how could such a thing happen to me?" When self-examination discloses that he has done nothing contrary to *ren* and *li,* and yet the outrageous treatment continues, he will say to himself, "I must have failed to do my best for him" (4B28). It must be noted that the possibility of others' reproach or the concern with honor or one's "face" (*mianzi* 面子) is also a proper subject of self-examination. We find this point in an apt comment on *chengyi* in *Daxue* (sec. 6).

> What is true in a man's heart will be shown in outward appearance.
> Therefore the *junzi* must be watchful when he is alone. Tseng Tzu
> [Zengzi] said, "What ten eyes are beholding and what ten hands are
> pointing to—isn't it frightening?" Wealth makes a house shining
> and virtue makes a person shining. When one's mind is broad and
> his heart generous, his body becomes big and is at ease. Therefore a
> *junzi* always makes his thought sincere.[37]

Ideally, intrinsic honor (*yirong* 義榮) coincides with circumstantial
honor (*shirong* 勢榮).[38] In the end, if frequent self-examination is
successful, one can claim with justification to have a modicum of self-
knowledge (*zizhi* 自知). One hopes the process of self-examination,
in conjunction with the constant practice of *ren, li,* and *yi,* will culminate in personal attainment, or realization of *dao* (*zide* 自得).

However, this process requires the person to engage in reflection detached from preoccupation with personal gain, especially in
the context when one is predisposed to violate the requirement of *yi*
(rightness). Earlier we cited Confucius' reminder that a *junzi* considers *yi* to be of the highest importance (*Lunyu* 17.23). The aim of
self-examination is self-knowledge. At a minimum, self-knowledge
consists in acknowledging one's knowledge and ignorance. This is
perhaps the force of Confucius' saying: "To say you know when you
know, and to say you do not when you do not, that is knowledge (*zhi*
知)" (*Lunyu* 12.17). Self-knowledge enables the moral agent to prevent the recurrence of misconduct and, in so doing, to preserve
one's *xin* (*cunxin* 存心).

(D5) Lack of Means to Support a Constant *Xin.* We must
note the frequent interplay of the above conditions of deficiency
(D1–D4). Take, for example, the lack of concern with moral priority. Crucially this depends on circumstances occasioned by the
presence of things cherished by the agent. Failure to preserve *hengxin,* despite the agent's sincere efforts, may simply be a result of inaccessible and/or unavailable means to support it. Says Mencius,

> Only a *junzi* can have a constant heart (*hengxin*) in spite of a lack of
> constant means of support. The people, on the other hand, will not
> have constant hearts if they are without constant means. Lacking
> constant hearts, they will go astray and fall into excesses, stopping at
> nothing. To punish them after they have fallen foul of the law is to
> set a trap for the people. How can a benevolent man in authority
> allow himself to set a trap for the people? Hence when determining

what means of support the people should have, a clear-sighted ruler ensures that these are sufficient, on the one hand, for the care of parents, and, on the other, for the support of wife and children, so that the people always have sufficient food in good years and escape starvation in bad; only then does he drive them toward goodness; in this way the people find it easy to follow him (1A7).

Mencius' concern for human welfare as a prerequisite for the pursuit of the Confucian *dao* is an important insight for moral theory. It is unreasonable for any moral theory to require compliance with its principles or ideals without a clear understanding of the defeasible conditions. What is the point of asking ordinary people to follow the commands of the presumably *ren* ruler unless they are provided with the necessary means to do so? Even if one wants to do the good and the right thing as required by the Confucian cardinal virtues, one must have adequate means for sustaining at least a decent standard of living. Confucius' attitude in *Lunyu* (12.7) does not fully appreciate this point about good government. He seems to advocate trust of the people over providing sufficient food for them, though subsuming arms to these concerns. Admittedly a *junzi* would sacrifice his life for the sake of *ren* (*Lunyu* 15.9). For ordinary people, on the contrary, the lack of constant means of support is one major source of moral failure.

I think Mencius would agree with Xunzi that handicapped or incapacitated persons such as the dumb, the deaf, and the crippled deserve special consideration and protection for welfare: "The government should gather them together, look after them, and give them whatever work they are able to do. Employ them, provide them with food and clothing, and take care to see that none are left out."[39] Claims of disability must be demonstrated, for those who are capable of working even in menial tasks must assume some responsibility. Economic goods for maintaining a morally decent life need not be extensive in quantity; but minimal economic sustenance and accessibility to goods are preconditions of moral conduct. Were these goods unavailable or inaccessible, anticipation of virtuous and/or right conduct is hardly reasonable. Moral requirements for action are thus subject to defeat by the absence of resources, the necessary means to moral performance. Although a few laudable moral agents are capable of self-sacrifice and even giving up their life for the sake of *ren*, we cannot reasonably expect ordinary humans to do the same. In my youth I was impressed by someone saying,

"You cannot preach morality to a starving man." This serves as a constant reminder in my decades of teaching ethics: Ethics is vacuous of moral significance unless it acknowledges the intimate connection between scarcity and moral evils. Today when we ponder the woeful poverty of millions of people throughout the world, it is difficult not to acknowledge our responsibility to ameliorate their predicament.[40]

(D6) Lack of Appreciation of the Situation. The lack of appreciation of the nature of the situation at hand is a common human failing. One reason for this failure is the tendency of most human beings to adhere to fixed ideas. Because of this tendency, many rigid adherents of Confucian orthodoxy often fail to appreciate the importance of *quan* and the exercise of *yi* in exigent circumstances.[41] These Confucians seem oblivious to Mencius' reminder that persons dedicated to the fulfillment of *ren* do not always traverse the same paths: "All that is expected of a *junzi* is *ren*. Why must he be exactly like other *junzi*?" (6B6). In the pursuit of *ren,* or the ideal of the good human life, sincere and thoughtful persons (*chengzhe* 誠者) would pursue different paths to realize the ideal. After all, *ren* (in the broad sense) is an abstract ideal of the good human life that requires concrete specification in the lives of ordinary humans. Because of differences in temperament, experience, and stations in society, persons devoted to *ren* will respond to changing circumstances in quite different ways. Because *ren* is an ideal theme, it has polymorphous actualization in the human world. If my interpretation of this aspect of Mencius' thought is disputed, consider my reading as a response to those Kantian interpreters of Mencius.[42] Issues of universality of moral principles or moral autonomy are alien to Confucian ethics, though I do not deny that Kantian ethics can contribute to the development of Confucian ethics. In Mencius and Xunzi, and later Song-Ming Confucianism, we find a predominant idea of reason (*li* 理) as reasonableness rather than rationality.[43]

One aspect of reasonableness is the ability to size up the situation, to consider whether moral notions have appropriate application in a current situation. I take this to be the point of Zixia's remark in *Lunyu* (19.6): "Learn widely and be steadfast in your purpose, inquire earnestly and reflect on what is at hand (*jinsi* 近思), and there is no need for you to look for *ren* elsewhere."[44] Among

Confucians influenced by Mencius, Wang Yangming especially stresses the importance of reflection of things at hand: "The sage does a thing when the time comes.... The study of changing conditions and events is to be done at the time of response. The thing to do is to keep the mind clear as a mirror and engage in moral reflection."[45] Note that this Confucian notion of reasonableness does not deny the use of reason (*li* 理) in deductive or inductive inferences, though it favors informal, practical reasoning that employs a variety of plausible considerations in support of a conclusion.[46] If this Confucian theory of argumentation is deemed plausible, the study of the logic of *quan* is one important task of contemporary Confucian philosophy.

Conclusion

This essay on Mencius' conception of moral failure is a prolegomenon to a larger project on Confucian moral psychology. Among other things, we need a more elaborate treatment of *siduan* and the factors or sources of moral failure,[47] correction of character flaws and misconduct, and shame as an internal monitor of moral thought and action. Perhaps, more important is the Confucian problem of conflict of values.[48] This essay articulates some of Mencius' insights concerning creative moral agency. Morality, in its ideal aspect, is a personal creative achievement. For this reason, Confucian paradigmatic individuals (*junzi*), committed to *dao* or *ren,* will always have a role to play in character education and self-cultivation.

Moreover, it is difficult to make sense of moral achievement unless something like the *siduan* provides the roots for moral growth. The interfering factors in the successful exercise of moral agency will always be a source of concern. One thing perhaps stands out, unless our mind (*xin*) is free from obscurations (*bi* 蔽) and attendant delusions (*huo* 惑), as Xunzi points out, it is unlikely that our *siduan* will flourish into the Confucian cardinal virtues. Without a clear mind guided by reason (*li* 理), our *siduan* are easily subverted and misdirected, leading to a life contrary to *ren*. In addition to desires and aversion, there are other sources of *bi* that lead to moral failure, for example, inordinate concern with the beginning or end, the breadth or shallowness of knowledge, and the authority of the past or the present. When our mind is not functioning properly, we make distinctions among myriad things and unreasonably place more value on one thing than another, thus leading to misconduct. This is a common human affliction, according to Xunzi. Even reflective moral desires, modified by varieties of satisfaction provided by popular culture, may become a source of moral failure. This is the human condition. No moral theory can provide an assurance of the success of its guidance. For Confucius and Mencius, this is a matter of fate (*ming* 命), a consequence of one's ethical commitment to *ren, yi,* and *li.* Confucian ethics does not provide a definitive guidance to the good human life. What really matters for a committed Confucian is *cheng* 誠, a sincere, serious, and unwavering concern for *dao* or *ren,* and overcoming the deficiencies of moral agency.

Issues of universality of moral principles or universalizability of personal moral decisions have little relevance to Confucian ethics. As a Confucian moral philosopher, I wonder whether these issues, rooted in Western philosophical traditions inspired by Plato, are an example of *bi* (obscurations) or obsession with a Western philosophical tradition. If one is committed to something like the Confucian *dao* or Daoist *dao,* why must the person insist that there is only one way to understand moral concepts and their application to human life? Without a serious study of other moral traditions, the search for one philosophical moral theory that applies to all moral traditions, as Xunzi would say, is a delusion, a result of *bi,* a darkening or blindness of *xin* to the ethical significance of other moral traditions and moral theories. Of course, for a genuine understanding and interaction of philosophical traditions rooted in different cultures, as Xunzi reminds us, one must deploy the art and skill of accommodation (*jianshu* 兼術); that is to say, parties in disputation must have a spirit of accommodation and mutual respect, for self-respect and respect for others are complementary qualities of participants in ethical argumentation, which is a form of reasoned discourse aiming at resolving problems of common interest. For Xunzi, a *junzi* practices the art of accommodation: "he is talented but can embrace those who are incapable of assuming duties; he is intelligent but can embrace the stupid; he has extensive learning but can embrace those with limited learning; he is pure in dedication to his task but can embrace those with diverse purposes."[49] Recall again Mencius' remark (6B6), "All that is expected of a *junzi* is *ren.* Why must he be exactly like other *junzi?*" For ideals of the good human life are basically abstract notions or ideal themes that call for concrete, individual specification and realization.

Notes

1. Antonio S. Cua, "Morality and Human Nature," *Philosophy East and West* 32.3 (1982): 279–294; also in Cua, *Moral Vision and Tradition: Essays in Chinese Ethics* (Washington, D.C.: Catholic University of America Press, 1998), essay 6.

2. Antonio S. Cua, *Dimensions of Moral Creativity: Paradigms, Principles, and Ideals* (University Park: Pennsylvania State University Press, 1978), chap. 8.

3. See Wing-tsit Chan, "The Evolution of the Confucian Concept *Jen* [*Ren*]," *Philosophy East and West* 4 (1955): 295–319; Cua, *Dimensions of Moral Creativity;* and Kwong-Loi Shun, *Mencius and Early Chinese Thought* (Stanford, Calif.: Stanford University Press, 1997).

4. See *Renshuo* 仁説; trans. in W. T. Chan, *A Source Book in Chinese Philosophy* (Princeton, N.J.: Princeton University Press, 1963), 394; Zhu Xi, *Zhuzi yulei* 朱子語類, 8 vols. (Taipei: Zhengzhong, 1962), 6.10a.

5. On *siduan* as "ethical attributes," see Shun, *Mencius and Early Chinese Thought,* 48.

6. In "A Dissertation Upon the Nature of Virtue," Butler writes, "It is manifest great part of common language, and of common behavior over the world, is formed upon the supposition of such a moral faculty; whether called conscience, moral reason, moral sense, or divine reason; whether considered as a *sentiment of the understanding or as a perception of the heart*; or, which seems the truth, as including both." Joseph Butler, *Five Sermons* (Indianapolis: Bobbs-Merrill, 1950), 82; my emphasis. James Legge quotes extensively from Butler's first three sermons in discussing Mencius' *siduan* with emphasis on "conscience" or "the principle of reflection" and maintains that the substance of Butler's reasoning "is to be found in Mencius." See James Legge, trans., *The Works of Mencius,* in *Chinese Classics,* vol. 1 (Oxford: Oxford University Press, 1893), 58–62; see also D. C. Lau, trans., *Mencius* (Baltimore: Penguin Books, 1970), 12.

7. Thomas Reid, *Essays on the Active Powers of the Human Mind* (Cambridge: MIT Press, 1969), 468–469.

8. This is a qualification of Reid's notion of moral sentiments. Similar qualification would apply to Solomon's assertion: "The heart of every emotion is its value judgments, its appraisals of gain and loss, its indictments of offences and its praise of virtue, its often Manichean judgments of 'good' and 'evil,' 'right' and 'wrong.'" See Robert Solomon, *The Passions: The Myth and Nature of Human Emotion* (New York: Anchor Books, 1977), 267. More concisely, Solomon writes, "emotions are judgments—normative and often moral judgments"; in *What Is an Emotion? Classic Readings in Philosophical Psychology,* ed. Cheshire Calhoun and Robert Solomon, (New York: Oxford University Press, 1984), 312. Arguably, one of the difficulties of such a thesis is that it fails to acknowledge the "conceptual gulf between 'emotion' and 'belief'" (Calhoun and Solomon,

What Is an Emotion?, 330–331). For linguistic facility, perhaps it is better to regard Mencius' doctrine as a doctrine of moral senses. In this way, we can simply speak of the *xin* of compassion as "the sense of compassion," the *xin* of modesty and courtesy as "the sense of modesty," and so forth.

9. In Xunzi, we find a sharper distinction between *xin* and *qing* 情 (passions/feelings). *Xin* has a primary cognitive function that is distinct from *qing*. When this function is guided by *li* 理 (reason), *xin* can provide a reliable ethical guide to the expression of *qing*. This notion of *xin* is best rendered as "mind" in the sense of mental capacity of remembering, thinking, judging, and reasoning, rather than a sort of mental feeling or affection as seems to be implicit in Mencius' doctrine of *siduan*. It must be noted that Xunzi's conception of *xin* also embraces a volitional function, which may counter its intellectual or cognitive function, resulting in different sorts of cognitive delusion (*huo* 惑). However, when it approves of *dao* and is guided by *li*, *xin* can provide a reliable ethical guide to conduct. For a fuller discussion, see Antonio S. Cua, *Ethical Argumentation: A Study in Hsün Tzu's Moral Epistemology* (Honolulu: University of Hawai'i Press, 1985), chap. 4; and Cua, "The Possibility of Ethical Knowledge: Reflections on a Theme in the *Hsün Tzu*," in *Epistemological Issues in Ancient Chinese Philosophy*, ed. Hans Lenk and Gregor Paul (Albany: State University of New York Press, 1993).

10. Translations from the *Mencius* are based on Lau (1970), with modification in some cases. For the Chinese original, see Shi Ciyun 史次耘, *Mengzi jinzhu jinyi* 孟子今註今譯 (Taipei: Shangwu, 1974).

11. For the distinction between theoretical and practical causation, see R. G. Collingwood, *An Essay on Metaphysics* (Oxford: Clarendon Press, 1962), 287. For the role of practical causation in Confucian ethics, see Antonio S. Cua, "Practical Causation in Confucian Ethics," *Philosophy East and West* 25 (1975): 1–10. In this connection, ethical capacities may also be called "active powers" in Reid's sense (Reid, *Essays*, 11): "The term *active power* is used … to distinguish it from speculative powers, the same distinction is applied to the powers by which they are produced. The powers of seeing, hearing, remembering, distinguishing, judging, reasoning are speculative powers; the power of executing any work of art or labour is active power.... The exertion of active power is called *action;* and as every action produces some change, so every change must be caused by some exertion, or by the cessation of some exertion of power."

12. Shun, *Mencius and Early Chinese Thought*, 48.

13. Cua, *Dimensions of Moral Creativity*, chap. 2; Cua, *The Unity of Knowledge and Action: A Study in Wang Yang-ming's Moral Psychology* (Honolulu: University Press of Hawai'i, 1982), chap. 1.

14. A study of the notion of *quan* in *Zhuzi yulei* discloses some salient features. Concisely put: (a) As a metaphorical extension of the basic sense of a steel yard for measuring weight, *quan* pertains to assessment of the importance of moral considerations to a current matter of concern. Alternatively, the exercise of *quan* consists in a judgment of the comparative importance of competing options answering to a current problematic situation. (b) The situation is such that it presents a "hard case," that is, a case falling outside the scope of operation of normal standards of conduct (*jing* 經). These standards of conduct

provide insufficient guidance for the situation at hand. (c) *Quan* is an exercise of moral discretion and must conform to the requirement of *yi* (rightness, righteousness). (d) The judgment must accord with *li* 理 (reason, principle), that is, be a principled or reasoned judgment. (e) The immediate objective of *quan* is to attain timely equilibrium (*shizhong* 時中), namely, to do the right thing (*yi*) as appropriate to the demand of the current situation. (f) The ultimate objective of *quan* is to further the realization of *dao* or *ren* as the holistic ideal of the good human life. See Chan, *Source Book;* and Cua, *Dimensions of Moral Creativity.*

15. Appeal to *liangzhi* 良知 and *liangneng* 良能 (7A15) does not support an intuitionist interpretation. "Intuition" in Western ethical theory is a technical term with various philosophical uses. Unless one clearly stipulates its use, the attribution of ethical intuitionism to Mencius is uninformative and highly misleading. My emphasis on the cognitive aspect of *siduan* does not imply acceptance of any version of ethical intuitionism.

16. For an insightful discussion of *buzhiyi*, see Chen Daqi 陳大齊, *Mengzi de mingli sixiang ji qi bianshuo shikuang* 孟子的名理思想及其辨説實況 (Taipei: Shangwu, 1968), chap. 2. Lau translates *quan* as "proper measure" in this instance.

17. See *Bugou pian* 不苟篇, 43; *Zhishi pian* 致士篇, 306. The Chinese text I used is Li Disheng 李滌生, *Xunzi jishi* 荀子集釋 (Taipei: Xuesheng, 1979).

18. *Xingwu pian* 性惡篇, 554, cf. Burton Watson, trans., *Hsün Tzu: Basic Writings* (New York: Columbia University Press, 1963), 167–168; John Knoblock, *Xunzi: A Translation and Study of the Complete Works*, 3 vols. (Stanford, Calif.: Stanford University Press, 1989–1994), 3: 159–160.

19. I construe *hengxin* as an agent's commitment to Confucian *dao* or *ren*. For a discussion of the creative aspect of Confucian agency focusing on Wang Yangming, see Cua, *Unity of Knowledge and Action.*

20. Cua, *Dimensions of Moral Creativity,* 67–68.

21. *Lunyu* 15.9. Translations from the *Lunyu* are based on D. C. Lau, trans., *Confucius: The Analects* (Baltimore: Penguin Books, 1978), with modification when necessary. For the Chinese text, see Mao Zishui 毛子水, *Lunyu jinzhu jinyi* 論語今注今譯 (Taipei: Shangwu, 1975).

22. Donald J. Munro, *The Concept of Man in Ancient China* (Stanford, Calif.: Stanford University Press, 1969).

23. Indeed, Mencius' *liangzhi,* however it is rendered, implies *liangneng,* which, as Wang Yangming points out, is the innate capacity to appreciate moral distinctions or an expression of *shifei zhi xin*. See, for example, Wang Yangming, *Instructions for Practical Living and Other Neo-Confucian Writings*, trans. Wing-tsit Chan with notes (New York: Columbia University Press, 1963), sec. 162; and Cua, *Moral Vision and Tradition*, essay 9.

24. Perhaps, to avoid misleading association with the ideal of moral autonomy, it may be better to adopt the term "autarchy," as suggested by Benn. Among other things, ascription of autarchy to any person depends on whether the agent is capable of recognizing the evidential and inferential grounds for justifying changes in belief, capable of making decisions in the light of preferences, and capable of formulating policies that will actualize present prefer-

ences. See S. I. Benn, "Freedom, Autonomy, and the Concept of a Person," *Proceedings of the Aristotelian Society* 76 (1976), 116. Though a matter of constructive interpretation, Benn's notion of autarchy may be ascribed to Mencius in an inchoate form. Most of Benn's requirements of autarchy are much more explicit in Xunzi; see, for example, Cua, *Ethical Argumentation*, and Cua, "The Possibility of Ethical Knowledge." For the notion of constructive interpretation as one of finding the best explanation and justification of a topic for explication, see Ronald Dworkin, *Law's Empire* (Cambridge: Harvard University Press, 1985).

25. *Jiebi pian* 解蔽篇, 488. This translation is an emendation of Watson, trans., 129, and Knoblock, trans., vol. 3, 105. My translation differs from both with respect to the italicized expressions, which is a critical interpretation of Machle's discussion of the beginning of the passage. See Edward Machle, "The Mind and the '*Shen-ming*' in Xunzi," *Journal of Chinese Philosophy* 19 (1992): 361–386. For justification of my rendering of *shenming zhi zhu*, see Antonio S. Cua, "Ethical and Religious Dimensions of *Li*," in *Confucian Spirituality*, ed. Tu Wei-ming and Mary Ellen Tucker (New York: Crossroads, 1999).

26. *Jiebi pian*, 494; Watson, trans., 133; modified.

27. Cua, *Ethical Argumentation*, 138–141.

28. John Dewey, *Theory of the Moral Life*, ed. Arnold Isenberg (New York: Holt, Rinehart and Winston, 1963), 3–7. This is a redaction of pt. 2 of Dewey and Tufts' *Ethics*, rev. ed. (1932).

29. Dewey argues, "[Moral theory] emerges when men are confronted with situations in which different desires promise opposed goods and in which incompatible courses of action seem to be morally justified. Only such a conflict of good ends and of standards and rules of right and wrong calls for personal inquiry into the bases of morals.... For what is called moral theory is but a more conscious and systematic raising of the question which occupies the mind of any one who in the face of moral conflict and doubt seeks a way out through reflection" (ibid., 5).

30. *Zhengming pian* 正名篇, 527; Watson, trans., 151; modified. Elimination of desires is advocated in the *Laozi*, chap. 37; and by Song Xing 宋鈃, criticized by Xunzi in the *Zhengming pian*. For further discussion of Xunzi's view on this issue, see Antonio S. Cua, "Dimensions of *Li* (Propriety): Reflections on an Aspect of Hsün Tzu's Ethics," *Philosophy East and West* 29 (1979): 373–394; and Cua, *Moral Vision and Tradition*, essay 13.

31. Cua, *Moral Vision and Tradition*, essay 13.

32. Shun, *Mencius and Early Chinese Thought*, 174–175.

33. The distinction between natural and reflective desires seems implicit in the following perplexing passage in *Xunzi*: "A single desire which one receives from nature (*tian*) is regulated and directed by the mind in many different ways; consequently, it may be difficult to identify and distinguish it from its original appearance.... If the guidance of the mind accords with reason (*zhongli* 中理), although desires are many, what harm will this be to good government?" (*Zhengming pian*, 527; Watson, trans., 151; modified). This interpretation by way of Frankfurt's distinction between first-order and second-order

desires (Harry G. Frankfurt, "Freedom of the Will and the Concept of Person," *Journal of Philosophy* 68 [1971]), corresponding to the distinction between natural and reflective desires, was proposed in my "Dimensions of *Li*," 380–381. After publication, I discovered a similar interpretation of this problematic passage in Liang Qixiong's 梁啟雄 annotated text. Liang remarks that the contrast lies in the distinction between *tianxing yu* 天性欲 (desires as endowed by nature, or natural desires) and *lixing yu* 理性欲 (desires as guided by reason, or reflective desires). Because of this distinction, it is difficult to classify all desires in the same way. See Liang Qixiong, *Xunzi jianshi* 荀子簡釋 (Taipei: Shangwu, 1978), 323.

    34. Cua, *Moral Vision and Tradition,* essay 12.

    35. Jaraslov Pelikan, *The Vindication of Tradition* (New Haven, Conn.: Yale University Press, 1982), 65. The most important exception is Alasdair MacIntyre, *After Virtue* (Notre Dame, Ind.: University of Notre Dame Press, 1981); and *Whose Justice? Which Rationality?* (Notre Dame, Ind.: University of Notre Dame Press, 1988).

    36. *Mencius* 4B28. My translation here reads *cun* 存 as *cha* 察 (examine) in accordance with Jiao Xun's gloss. See Shi Ciyun, *Mengzi jinzhu jinyi,* 233 n.

    37. W. T. Chan, *Source Book,* 90; modified.

    38. It is often said that modern Chinese are concerned with "face." But as Hu Hsien Chin points out, there is a distinction between *mianzi* and *lian* 臉. The former pertains to social standing and does not necessarily have moral implications. The latter implies satisfaction of the moral standards of the society. A person concerned with *lian* is one who possesses a sense of decency and regard for moral virtues. See Hu Hsien Chin, "The Chinese Concepts of 'Face,'" *American Anthropologist,* n.s., 46 (1944): 45–64. This distinction between social and ethical standards is implicit in Mencius' conception of shame (see Shun, *Mencius and Early Chinese Thought,* 58–53). More explicit is Xunzi's distinction between intrinsic shame (*yiru* 義辱), i.e., shame justly deserved because of an agent's misconduct, and circumstantial shame (*shiru* 勢辱), i.e., shame experienced as a result of external circumstances, such as poverty, lowly social position, and the like. Also, for the Confucian, concern for one's name (*ming* 名) or reputation is always a reasonable concern except, according to Xunzi, in the case of circumstantial shame, i.e., when one is in a shameful situation that has nothing to do with one's moral fault. In this way, Xunzi may concur with Hume's insightful remark on the love of fame: "By our continual and earnest pursuit of a character, a name, a reputation in the world, we bring our own deportment and character frequently in review and consider how they appear in the eyes of those who approach and regard us. This constant habit of surveying ourselves, as it were, in reflection, keeps alive all the sentiments of right and wrong, and begets in noble natures a certain reverence for themselves as well as others, which is the surest guardian of every virtue." David Hume, *An Inquiry concerning the Principles of Morals* (Indianapolis: Bobbs-Merrill, 1957), 96.

    39. *Wangzhi pian* 王制篇, 161; Watson, trans., 34.

    40. In James' suasive words, "Whether we are empiricists or rationalists, we are ourselves parts of the universe and share the same one deep concern in

its destinies. We crave alike to feel more truly at home with it, and to contribute our mite to its amelioration." William James, *Essays in Radical Empiricism and a Pluralistic Universe* (New York: E. P. Dutton, 1971), 128.

41. For an informative study of Song-Ming orthodoxy in Confucianism, see Wm. Theodore de Bary, *Neo-Confucian Orthodoxy and the Learning of Mind-and-Heart* (New York: Columbia University Press, 1981).

42. Li Minghui 李明輝, *Kangde lunli xue yu Mengzi daode sikao zhi chongjian* 康德論理學與孟子道德思考之重建 (Taipei: Zhongyang yanjiu yuan, 1994).

43. For further discussion of *li*, see Cua, *Dimensions of Moral Creativity*, 96–98; Cua, *Unity of Knowledge and Action*, 91–100; and Cua, "Reason and Principle in Chinese Philosophy," in *A Companion to World Philosophies*, ed. Eliot Deutsch and Ron Bontekoe (Oxford: Blackwell, 1997).

44. This remark inspired the title of Zhu Xi and Lü Zuqian's anthology of Song Confucianism, *Jinsi lu* 近思錄. W. T. Chan, trans., *Reflections of Things at Hand: The Neo-Confucian Anthology Compiled by Chu Hsi and Lü Tsu-ch'ien* (New York: Columbia University Press, 1967).

45. Wang Yangming, *Instructions for Practical Living*, sec. 21; modified.

46. Cua, *Ethical Argumentation*, chap. 2; Cua, *Moral Vision and Tradition*, essays 1 and 10.

47. Shun, *Mencius and Early Chinese Thought*, 173–179.

48. Tang Junyi 唐君毅, *Renwen jingshen zhi chongjian* 人文精神之重建 (Taipei: Xuesheng, 1977).

49. *Feixiang pian* 非相篇, 86.

7

Understanding Words and Knowing Men

Jiuan Heng

THIS PAPER SEEKS to resituate Mencius' celebration of *zhiyan yangqi* 知言養氣 in 2A2 in a political context by proposing that "*zhiyan*" should be translated as "understanding words" or "understanding speech" as opposed to "understanding doctrines," as Nivison and Riegel have argued.[1] To understand how to decipher words is to draw upon a powerful resource for reading persons and situations, a key to knowing how to employ men and how to remonstrate. It is an aspect of self-cultivation that draws the political and the personal into a dialectic of mutual implicature and enhancement, to paraphrase Sor-Hoon Tan.[2] I trace "understanding speech" to the assumption that everything within is manifest without and show how it relates to Mencius' conception of the relation of the inner and the outer.

Zhiyan: Setting the Context

It is a rare thinker who has enough insight into his own strengths to limit himself to two, when asked what they are, and to be able to capture them in a pithy one-liner:

我知言, 我善養吾浩然之氣.

I have an insight into words. I am good at cultivating my floodlike *qi*.[3]

Whatever the enigmatic phrase *wo zhiyan* 我知言 means, we can be sure that Mencius is absolutely sure of his own powers, and of what

151

distinguishes him from other men, when he rises to the challenge of issuing a self-apology. Recall the occasion for Gongsun Chou's question. The cheeky disciple constructs a hypothetical scenario: Mencius, the philosopher-statesman, is appointed to the highest political office and secures for his political master the prize trophy—dominion over the feudal lords. Would this cause his heart to stir?

The entire passage 2A2 may be read as an exploration of the varieties of the unperturbed heart-mind and ways of cultivating it. The stakes are not entirely personal; the context, established right from the beginning, is political. I will argue, in the course of this essay, that Mencius raises it a notch higher. He suggests that excellence in governance is a precondition of sagehood, and he suggests, if not in so many words, that he has what it takes to be a sage. For he understands *yan* (speech), and he is able to cultivate his floodlike *qi*. Both these qualities would enable him to take political office without losing his ethical bearings. But it is even more interesting that of his dual strengths singled out for posterity, it is *zhiyan* that immediately connects him to Confucius. Not one to miss a beat, Gongsun Chou tries to force upon Mencius the upshot of his account of what he means by understanding *yan*. Of the immediate Confucian disciples who had a way with words, some excelled in this but not that, and Confucius, in his characteristically modest fashion, denied having any such knack. Yet Mencius, it would seem, has covered every possible ground—he must already be a sage!

An adequate interpretation of *wo zhiyan* should take into account this broader context, where Mencius not only proffers his fitness for political office but also establishes his claim to be the direct spiritual descendant of Confucius. The question to be revisited is, What does Mencius understand when he understands *yan*? And how does this understanding serve his rhetorical aims—to prove that he can be the maker of a true king and to prove that he shares with Confucius this uncommon ability?

Background to the Debate on "Understanding Words"

The most elegant, persuasive proposal, courtesy of David Nivison, is that we should understand *yan* as moral doctrines. His arguments, intricately set out in the essay "Philosophical Voluntarism in Fourth-Century China," are informed by two considerations.[4] First, our interpretation of *yan* must illuminate the differences between Gaozi and Mencius on the matter of how to attain the "unperturbed mind." The interpretation pivots on the first half of Gaozi's maxim, which in Nivison's translation reads,

不得於言, 勿求於心, 不得於心, 勿求於氣.

What you do not get from "words," do not seek in the mind. What you do not get from the mind, do not seek in the vital energy (*qi*).[5]

Moreover, as Huang Zongxi had pointed out, we should take that maxim as the kernel of Gaozi's ethical position in general.[6] Hence, we should find the consequences of its application throughout the literature, whenever we encounter that philosopher. Within the scope of the *Mencius,* it should explain why Gaozi holds that *yi* 義 (dutifulness) is external (6A4), that human nature is ethically neutral (it's what you make of it) and has no inherent direction (6A1–6A6).

Second, our understanding must be supported by the general pattern of the usage of *yan* in the literature. The motivation behind Nivison's arguments in that paper, if not elsewhere, is a question that may be put in the form of a paradox: How do we become good, if we weren't already, in some sense, good? It underlies his focus on so-called moral psychology, even, perhaps, to the neglect of the politics of governance.

Although Nivison's interpretation of *yan* as "doctrines" captures beautifully Gaozi's position—the inner and the outer are distinct sources of moral energy—it misses the point of Mencius' choice of the same term *yan* to define his own distinction.[7] Mencius is playing with words, exploiting the elastic sense of *yan,* which Gaozi associates with the outer, to mean not doctrines but words and speech, in order to advance a diametrically opposed thesis. That is, *yan* (words and speech) are the outward manifestation of the inner. Inner and outer are not distinct categories of the moral life but are seamlessly bound together in and through self-cultivation.

Mencius and the Master: Knowing Words and Judging Men

When offering his own version of self-cultivation to attain the unperturbed mind, Mencius alludes to the closing passage of the *Lunyu:*

不知言, 無以知人也.

A man has no way of judging men unless he understands words.[8]

But words are not merely words in the Confucian tradition. Mencius must have had in mind the teaching delivered from father to son in *Lunyu* 16.13—incidentally, the only instance where Confucius assumes the role of both biological father and teacher:

不學詩, 無以言.

Unless you study the Odes, you will be ill-equipped to speak.[9]

Both passages refer to schooling in speech and rites as the twin pillars of self-cultivation. In the former, an understanding of speech enables one to know others; in the latter, speech enables others to know oneself. The elusive link, which the *Book of Documents* (*Canon of Shun*) formulates explicitly, connects the Odes and, by extension, speech, directly to *zhi* 志 (the intent of the heart-mind): *shi yan zhi* 詩言志. Speech indicates the tendencies of the heart-mind.

The consideration given in the *Lunyu* to speech as a means of knowing someone is immense. The qualification in *Lunyu* 15.23, that the gentleman neither recommends a man on account of what he says, nor dismisses what is said on account of a speaker, does not undermine it; rather, it affirms that this notion must have been widely accepted and practiced. To understand when to speak, to whom one should speak, and how one should speak is the mark of wisdom. It is indispensable to the aspiring statesman. It should neither be wasted on those who fail to benefit from it nor, conversely, withheld from those who may so benefit (*Lunyu* 15.8). Speech—remonstration—is potentially dangerous, even while it is a duty: it demands a nuanced reading of the political situation (*Lunyu* 14.3, 2.8). The keynote is caution. We often think of moral virtues in terms of dispositions to act, but here virtue takes the form of the power of judgment. The Master urges his disciples to appraise men and contexts with care. Numerous conversations are devoted to making distinctions between personalities and their ethical qualities. The sage emerges as the ultimate reader and critic, as Mencius acknowledges in 2A2 when he pays homage to the Master with the words of Zigong:

> Through the rites of a state he could see its government; through its music, the moral quality of its ruler. Looking back over a hundred generations he was able to appraise all the kings, and no one has ever been able to show him to be wrong in a single instance.[10]

When speech is so revealing as to deserve such extended notice in the recorded conversations of the Master, even the lowest-ranking official must have watched his speech assiduously. It is unlikely that one could count on knowing a man by "knowing doctrines" as such. Doctrines and maxims, crafted with care, are unlikely to give us the kind of portrait of a man that will enable the statesman to judge him, in order to know how to employ him. It is equally unlikely that Mencius, given the opportunity to write his own epitaph, as it were, would have cited an ability that even a bright undergraduate possesses. More likely, he is saying that he is able to hear in a man's turns of phrase, his slips of tongue, the incipient tendencies of his heart-mind—his *zhi*—even before he acts. In a political system where responsibility, if not always power, concentrates at the top, knowing how to delegate responsibility is a crucial knack. The man at the top must know the complexities and complications of his aides and subordinates, in order to determine whom to trust, to what extent, and with what responsibilities. Otherwise, he compromises the business of government.

Notice that when asked to explain what he meant by "*zhiyan*," Mencius cites different kinds of phrases, not entire maxims, as revelations of different turns of mind.

> 詖辭知其所蔽, 淫辭知其所陷, 邪辭知其所離, 遁辭知其所窮.

> From biased words I can see wherein the speaker is blind; from immoderate words, wherein he is ensnared; from heretical words, wherein he has strayed from the right path; from evasive words, wherein he is at his wits' end.[11]

Mencius is speaking in general terms about knowing a man in depth, in spite of what the other wishes to reveal of himself. The assumption, as Stephen Owen, among others, has pointed out, is that of manifestation: "Everything that is inner ... has an innate tendency to become outward and manifest."[12] Owen traces the source of this central assumption to *Lunyu* 2.10.

> 子曰, 視其所以, 觀其所由, 察其所安. 人焉廋哉? 人焉廋哉?

> Look to how it is. Consider from what it comes. Examine in what a person would be at rest. How can a person remain hidden? How can someone remain hidden?[13]

And Mencius reiterates this assumption at 6B6.

> 有諸內, 必形諸外.

> What is within must manifest itself without.[14]

Language is one form of outward manifestation; the body is another. The body harbors the depths of the self and should be read with as much care as speech. Mencius teaches in a striking instance of judging a book by its cover in 4A15.

> There is in man nothing more ingenuous than the pupils of his eyes. They cannot conceal his wickedness. When he is upright within his breast, a man's pupils are clear and bright; when he is not, they are clouded and murky. How can a man conceal his true character if you listen to his words and observe the pupils of his eyes?[15]

And again, in 7A21, where we get to the root of the matter.

> That which a gentleman follows as his nature, that is to say, benevolence, rightness, the rites and wisdom, is rooted in his heart, and manifests itself in his face, giving it a sleek appearance. It also shows in his back and extends to his limbs, rendering [it: his nature] without words.[16]

This remarkable passage expresses the highest hope for a hermeneutic of the self, the art of interpreting, perhaps primarily for oneself, the word-event that is the enactment of the self when another communicates symbolically. Perhaps, too, when we are attentive to the involuntary communication that occurs as the subtext of speech, speech becomes symbolic even at its most direct, and symbolic gestures become speech in that they communicate intent. For Mencius, the deeper the intent, the more unintentional it becomes, as the intent works its way from conscious thought to unconscious embodiment, with "nature" mediating the two. Since virtue is luminous and beauty radiates from within, there should be no misleading appearances, if one knows where to look. Mencius also relates that hermeneutic to the desire for effortless, wordless communication that Confucius had expressed[17] and that Mencius, disputatious in spite of himself, later echoes. It tells us how Mencius views the relation between the internal and the external. We can now clarify it by contrasting it with Gaozi's.

Internal and External: Gaozi and Mencius

In Gaozi's view, the internal is that which is within me.[18] The picture we form of Gaozi's conception of the inner, admittedly sketchy, is remarkably consistent. It equates the inner with what one feels immediately. For instance, the feeling of *ren* 仁, an affective concern, which I act upon in caring for my immediate family, or the hunger that I appease with food, is internal. The external is what is not rooted in myself; it may have its source in teachings, customs, or doctrines, which I consult and adopt as a guide for action. Thus, he sees *yi* (dutifulness) as an external source of action. And thus, too, he sees *yan:* doctrines, as an external resource for moral sustenance. With this simple distinction, Gaozi can distinguish between two kinds of dispositions. There are spontaneous, uneducated disposi- tions he deems "inner." How I am disposed to act is directly con- nected to how I feel. The other kind of dispositions—the outer— has to be inculcated through socialization or by indoctrination. With such "external" causes, one need not feel in order to be moved to act. Because there are, for Gaozi, two distinct sources of morality, the internal and the external, each motivating action in different ways, there is no point in looking within myself when I fail to get the support that a doctrine is supposed to give me—*bude yu yan, wu qiu yu xin* 不得於言, 勿求於心.

Not so, says Mencius. There is really no external source of the ethical life; all that is required is already within us, implanted by Heaven as our nature, and rooted in the heart-mind.[19] To follow our nature is to manifest it, to bring it out, as it were.[20] I am not ex- ternally related to my moral source through the tenuous connection of others' doctrines or social conventions. Look within you to find the strength you need, Mencius exhorts. This rejoinder to Gaozi's teaching on how to attain the unperturbed heart-mind heralds a new way of thinking about the relation between the inner and the outer, and a radically new conception of interiority as the locus of one's energy. The internal and the external, for Mencius, are or- ganically related as core and periphery of the same person. It is not a distinction between self and other. My heart-mind is the deepest source of myself, yet it is simultaneously connected to my speech and my body. To say that it is deep is not to say that it is hid- den, but that it is authentic and subtle. It is truly there, as Mencius explains in 6A8, yet it is easy to lose sight of it, because the incipient tendencies can be obscured by distractions and dissipation.

Inner and Outer: What the Debate Is Not About

Accustomed as we are to variations on the Cartesian cut be- tween the inner and the outer, we may well ask what the interiority of the Mencian conception of the inner consists in. For Descartes, the division between the inner and the outer corresponds to the distinction between mind and body. The mind is inner in the sense that it is accessible through introspection alone. It is not located within the body, for mind is a different kind of thing from body; it has neither spatial location nor extension. The Cartesian distinction between inner and outer, ontologically and epistemologically, turns on this difference; the outer has extension in space, which allows it to be objectively quantified, whereas the inner exists and can be known by being an active subject. Its classic (and purest) formulation is "I think; therefore I am." Moreover, the inner is by its nature private—only I can know the contents of my mind.

Neither Mencius nor Gaozi subscribes to any of these Cartesian claims: the ontological claim that the inner is mental; the epistemological, that it is available to introspection alone; and the thesis that minds are atomistic. Descartes wants to define essential differences between the mental and the physical in order to establish a methodology appropriate to each. First philosophy of this kind is far from the concerns of the Chinese disputants.

When Mencius and Gaozi debate whether a particular disposition is internal or external, they are both trying to explain the disposition in question by tracing it to its origin, the better to know how to cultivate the disposition.[21] Put another way, it is an inquiry into ethical resources. They share a conception of the inner as the source of a person's manifest expression. That is to say, the nascent states of the heart-mind—inclinations, desires, and feelings—explain the genesis of one's thoughts, actions, and speech. They differ on the scope of the inner. As we have seen, Mencius traces all virtuous dispositions to the heart-mind, whereas Gaozi restricts the domain of the inner to one's affects. Whereas Gaozi believes that external factors can explain one's dispositions, Mencius implies that only internal factors can be genuinely explanatory. We treat the elderly with respect not because they are old, as Gaozi holds, but because of our latent sense of shame (xiuwu zhi xin 羞惡之心) that, properly nurtured, develops into the disposition to do what is yi (right). Gaozi mistakes the condition under which a disposition is activated—that is, being in the presence of an older person—for its explanation.

Given that the inner is functionally related to our dispositions to act in certain ways, it is not necessarily the case that the inner is intrinsically private or that it is unfathomable by another person.

This begs a question. If everything inner has a tendency to become manifest, how is the distinction between the inner and the outer maintained? Is there an inner life that is not exhibited in the public, social roles that the self enacts? In short, how do we make sense of an inner life that is not intrinsically private?

Without an ontological wedge that will define the essence of the inner, in virtue of which the inner is what it is, and can subsist independently of the outer, we do better to ask instead, What is the function of the inner? Mencius' account, rich and justifiably famous, repays revisiting. The heart-mind is a master organ, capable of reflecting, of setting priorities, of overriding the spontaneous desires, and of self-direction. Exercising the heart-mind enables one to "get it."[22] These are functions we would recognize as "self-reflection" or "introspection." This exercise may even take the form of having silent conversations with oneself. The *Mencius* relates, for instance, Yi Yin's deliberations about whether to accept office in the form of an internal monologue.[23] The point of keeping alive the inner life is spiritual and not just pragmatic; it is to grow into one's "larger self" (*dati* 大體),[24] to realize the destiny that Heaven has implanted in one's heart-mind as one's nature. Self-realization is reflected outward and enlarges, even as it gives substance to a gift of potential. Heaven bestows upon us our body and complexion, yet only the sage can give it complete fulfillment.[25]

If one's inner life is not different in kind from the life one leads as child, parent, student, teacher, citizen, friend, how is it related to these roles? Perhaps more than any other Chinese philosopher, it is Mencius who gives voice to the complexities of an ethical life grounded in multiple roles and responsibilities. Sometimes roles come into conflict,[26] and sometimes assuming a role may involve personal sacrifice.[27] Often, one risks being misunderstood. Choices have to be made, courses of action deliberated, deeds timed, not from the point of view of any agent but from the orientation of my agency, my *zhi*. Compare the conduct of the altogether different sages Bo Yi, fastidiously avoiding contamination; Yi Yin, indiscriminating about whom he served; and Liuxia Hui, easygoing in his acceptance of prince and position. Each acted very differently under conditions that were not very dissimilar. Why were they revered as sages? We cannot understand the ethical significance of their actions unless we refer the man's action to his inner quality. Mencius exalts the decision of Yi Yin to emerge from the obscurity of farming to become kingmaker by reconstructing Yi Yin's inner deliberation, in which his sense of noblesse oblige triumphs over his contentment with his secluded life. But as Robert Eno points out, Mencius is taking liberties with historical facts; he does not know what Yi Yin actually thought when the messenger arrives in the field with the king's offer of office.[28] Mencius claims to know what makes Yi Yin's manner of public service, apparently so self-serving, a sagely enterprise because he knows Yi Yin's *zhi* (his inner orientation of intent) and thus knows what Yi Yin must have thought under those circumstances. Indeed, the *Mencius* juxtaposes these bewilderingly different attitudes to political participation in 5B1 precisely to drive home the point that there is no universal prescription for sageliness, nothing that constitutes the role of conscientious subject. The sage unifies his *zhi* and acts according to the orientation of his heart-mind in all situations. And we, apprehending the sage's *zhi*, are able to infer his thoughts and actions from his *zhi*, insofar as they manifest his *zhi*. Word and deed are examined, recounted, and held up as model insofar as they embody the inner condition of the man.

By contrast, the village worthy, beyond reproach in his conduct and speech, is singled out as "the enemy of virtue" precisely because his deeds align perfectly with what society expects of him. His orientation is entirely external. The apparent absence of friction, of a different kind from the sagely paradigms discussed above, between the social role and an individual's conduct is an indication to the wise that the man lacks inner direction. The sage harmonizes his social role with his *zhi;* the village worthy conforms his social role to what he thinks society expects of him or what his society does expect of him. He adjusts his acts and desires before the mirror of social approbation, acting out of a distorted sense of self that Jean Jacques Rousseau baptizes "*amour de soi.*" The tragedy is that the village worthy has lost his *zhi* and has no true sense of self. Or as some folk might put it, he lacks integrity. The sage inhabits his social role with his *zhi* and thus inflects the social role. This contrast between two modes of aligning with social roles suggests that the authentically ethical person may have to flout conventional morality when a situation calls for it. That is a judgment call, demanding an improvisation, not performance from a score.

Mencius' most significant contribution to Chinese philosophy is his insistence that the heart-mind harbors the germinal shoots of the four virtues (*siduan*) and that tending to these inner resources will enable the virtues to become manifest. He takes special care to refute the possibility that the virtues can come from anywhere but within.

> Benevolence, dutifulness, observance of the rites and wisdom do not give me a lustre from the outside; they are in me originally.[29]

I mention this passage, which has been much discussed only to draw attention to the sentence that follows immediately.

> It is only that we no longer heed it.[30]

Taken together, we can conclude that the inner has an inherent energy. But its presence is subtle. That is why the inner needs to be actively cultivated. Heeding the call of the heart-mind is a matter of "seeking" and never "letting go"; and "one never knows the time it comes or goes, neither does one know the direction."[31]

The Inner and Self-cultivation

With this conception of the inner as the source of one's moral energy and self-direction, self-cultivation should be seen as being rooted in the cultivation of the inner. Once established, these roots enable one to develop in radiating networks of human relationships. The cultivation of the Five Relationships would, on this Mencian account, be a manifestation of the cultivation of the heart-mind.

Let us consider a possible objection. Suppose someone were to argue that on a relational conception of the self, where the self is constituted by its particular network of relationships, self-cultivation is equivalent to cultivating one's relations with others. There is no inner that is left over from the self that thinks and acts in relation to others, and hence, no outer either. Inner and outer are inappropriate categories of the immanent self; to the extent that one cultivates one's relations with others, one cultivates oneself, and in order to cultivate oneself, one cultivates one's relationships.[32]

This would be a beguiling account that takes seriously the central notion of a relational self in Chinese civilization and then proceeds to misconstrue, if not quite to ignore, the key texts that spell out the relations between self-cultivation and human relationships. The most explicit of them, the *Great Learning*, speaks of the interlocking affairs of man and world in terms of "roots and branches," "beginnings and ends," and the importance of knowing what comes before and what comes after. The relationships are structured on the imagery of root and branch, which conveys the idea that once the root system is established, the branches naturally will flourish as a result. And conversely, the branches will be very vulnerable if the roots are weak. It describes self-cultivation as a systematic journey toward the core of personhood and identifies that pivotal core as the heart-mind, from which one can venture outward toward larger circles of society.

> When the will is sincere, the mind is rectified; when the mind is rectified, the personal life is cultivated; when the personal life is cultivated, the family will be regulated....[33]

The text insists on the different stages of self-cultivation without explaining why it is so structured. I think it anticipates a phenomenon around which contemporary psychotherapy revolves. It is especially important for the relational self to cultivate its inner resources in order to prevent mutual dependence from degenerating into "codependence." When we draw on our own sources of strength, we do not feed off the insecurities and weaknesses of others, entangling ourselves in webs of mutual exploitation whereby each party deprives the other of the ability to grow into his or her fully realized self. When we enter into relationships from positions of strength, we make it possible for the other person to be free within the context of role-governed, interdependent relationships. This is yet another way of seeing the distinction between internal and external, albeit one that is not broached by Gaozi: the person who has cultivated his own resources is self-contained; the one who has not derives his energy from others.

Although the opportunity for mutual self-enhancement and self-realization is equally available to both parties in a relationship, the senior partner has more opportunity to exercise a creative influence, while the duty of exerting a mitigating influence lies with the junior party. It is all the more important, then, for the more powerful party to cultivate himself. As his sphere of influence ranges further, he is instrumental in effecting global social transformation by enabling the self-realization of the junior members of his web of relationships. The key relationships are conceived, not as discrete pairs, but as interlocking relationships. Relationships are *gang* 綱— knots that constitute the net of society and individual. Perhaps this calls for further study of the relative ranking of the Five Relations. To the extent that the husband-wife relationship is central in enabling a person to grow into a socialized self, it should be placed at the center, a notion that the *Great Learning* gestures toward.

From Hermeneutic to Self-cultivation: An Organic Conception of Inner and Outer

In the remaining part of this essay, I want to sketch an account of what I call the organic conception of the inner and the outer, with respect to Mencius' assertion that he understands speech. We are left with a puzzle: what does understanding another person have to do with my own self-cultivation?

When we understand speech as the outer aspect of the heart-mind, vitally connected to its source in the heart-mind, speech cannot be mere signs by which to understand another. For that understanding is self-reflexive; it tells us to develop the inner resources that will enable us to speak mindfully. In an organic conception of speech as the external manifestation of the heart-mind, speech is depth rendered on the surface. Heart-mind is embodied in speech, in other words. When Mencius proclaims his two advantages, he sees them as a circuit of ethical energy: to understand speech as he does is to know how to cultivate it, and to be able to cultivate his *haoranzhiqi* is to nourish his powers of expression. Han Yu, the Tang Confucian, uses the metaphor of water enabling things to float to elucidate the relation of *qi* to speech.

氣, 水也. 言, 浮物也. 水大而物之浮者, 大小畢浮. 氣與言猶是也. 氣盛則言之長短與聲之高下皆宜.

Qi is like water; and speech, the floating object. With a large body of water, all things that float in water will float. *Qi* is related to speech as water is to the floating object. When *qi* is abundant, the length of speech and the pitch of sound will all be appropriate.[34]

To get objects that are naturally buoyant to float, all we need to do is to provide the "supporting" condition: a sufficiently large body of water. Water supports the floating object, enables the natural capacity to manifest. In the same way, by cultivating *qi*, which speech draws on, we enhance our powers of speech.

Speech articulates the condition of the heart-mind, specifically *zhi*—a person's ambition, the goal toward which he directs

himself. In the celebrated teaching that earns Mencius his status as
second sage, *zhi* (the heart-mind in its focused state) commands *qi*
(the vital energy), which in turn supports *zhi*. Because speech is intrinsically connected to the heart-mind, to maintain a balance between the enabling vital energy and the focal energy of the heart-
mind is to nourish the spiritual resources for self-expression.
Speech, lying at the interface of the inner and the outer, is the most
direct avenue of self-expression. But self-expression does not stop
there. The direction one sets oneself—one's *zhi*—manifests itself, in
increasingly broader and more public domains, in the family, in affairs of state, in the conduct of life in general. This conception of
the self binds the private and the public seamlessly. Speech is critical because it serves as a barometer of the heart-mind. It indicates
the extent to which a person is ready for participating in public life.
It predicts the outcome of his self-cultivation. It is a general truth
that

生於其心, 害於其政. 發於其政, 害於其事.

What arises in the mind will interfere with policy, and what shows itself in policy will interfere with practice.[35]

Yet in that truth the statesman must draw a particular lesson: to listen
to how a man speaks and decide what his sphere of influence
should be. In the telling phrases of a man's speech, you will hear an
echo of his future accomplishments and his downfall. Words are not
just words—they are the living signs of the man, connected to his *qi*
(breath), produced by his breath, and nourished by his breath.
Precisely because it is spontaneous, changing, ephemeral, and contextual, speech is invaluable to the reader who needs fresh clues to
the living heart-mind of another. It may be worth noticing, at this
point, that the various types of deviant language that Mencius
mentions—the biased, the immoderate, the heretical, and, especially,
the evasive—presuppose an interlocutor, with another point of view,
and a speaker. Moral doctrines, as thoughts crystallized and em-
balmed in words, prima facie would be concerned with addressing
these faults. Mencius is telling the disciple Gongsun Chou how he
judges, and why it is important to judge, in explaining what he
means by *zhiyan* (understanding words). To fail to appreciate a man
of ability and virtue is a waste of gifts. To employ someone who has
ability but not virtue is to risk abuses of power. In any case, these

errors of judgment reflect badly on the judge. In the chief minister, they are not merely errors of moral judgment; they are miscarriages of duty. The statesman who is a superlative judge of character may be assured that the tasks of government are in good hands, having entrusted them to the right men; he can save himself a sleepless night or two.

I do not mean to trivialize the notion of cultivating the unperturbed mind. I think that Mencius must have thought through the question of how it is possible to incorporate morality into effective government, so that the latter is not just realpolitik, while at the same time uncompromised by the priggish and the smug, the so-called men of principle. His response in this passage, which sees him assuming the hypothetical position of a chief minister, relies on the notion of understanding and employing men: *zhiyan* and, thereby, *zhiren* 知人.

The flip side of self-cultivation, then, is *yan*. For what is within, what is cultivated, will manifest itself. I have, for rhetorical reasons, focused on the judgment of persons. But *yan*, of course, is also remonstration. Both judgment and remonstration are political functions, correlating roughly (though not perfectly) with the ruler-minister division of responsibilities. But is judging others properly understood as an aspect of self-cultivation?

Two considerations are pertinent to this problem. First, the self is not an atomic self. In the Confucian scheme of things, one has specific duties to others owing to one's different functional roles. It is a given that those who govern must manage their human resources in order to administer successfully to the business of state. This presupposes knowledge of those with whom one is dealing. Second, the judgment is only as good as the judge; we can understand others only as far as our own understanding reaches. Janus-like, a judgment reaches out to knowledge of another, at the same time as it reflects on oneself. My judgment is only as sound as my own understanding, and it resounds with my biases, my immoderation, my heresies, my limitations. In other words, in judging others, I am being judged. The only way to rise above these potential errors is to cultivate oneself. The deeper my own reservoir of resources, the better can I live ethically.

That Mencius has this conception of the inner life as being intrinsically and directly related to its external manifestation, and Gaozi does not, can be traced to Mencius' novel idea, that *qi* is not just physical energy but also ethical and spiritual energy. Thus, *qi* is not just the vital energy that sustains life; in its ethicized version, it is discharged and displayed in every domain of life, from the biological to the political to the religious. To put it in another way, the expression of all forms of life is contingent upon the quantity and quality of our *qi*. The consequence of ethicizing the *qi*, as Mencius explains in 2A2, is that the intent of the heart-mind cannot be alienated from our resources for carrying out the intent. If the spirit is willing but the body weak, the agent has failed to honor the circuit of heart-mind, its vital energy, and its expression in word and deed (*zhi* 志, *qi* 氣, *yan* 言, *shi* 事, *zheng* 政). The mirror image of such failure of self-cultivation is the case of the man who has formidable physical energy but a frail spirit—Beigong You—the character who illustrates the least desirable way of cultivating the unperturbed heart-mind, that is, by refusing to discriminate. In the ideal case, the creative source of action flows from within, and the agent honors his creative, executive resources by acting in accordance with the authentic desires of the heart-mind.

What Is at Stake in the Interpretation of *Zhiyan*?

I have tried to locate Mencius within a moral tradition that articulates what it is for one to be a self, and how that self is articulated in speech and nonverbal gestures. With his conception of self-cultivation as an ongoing process of self-development, it follows that a person's character is mutable. His speech and his physical body serve as indices of the care of the heart-mind that he undertakes. Both must be read carefully, sensitively. To understand Mencius as an insightful reader of a person's words is to understand him as making a claim about his spiritual insight. To understand him as someone who understands doctrines is to place him within the context of the intellectual debates of his day. But this fails to capture his unique contribution to the tradition.

That tradition is itself a hermeneutic construction. Let me end by indicating one strand of the Mencian tradition. It is remarkable that the tradition of Chinese aesthetic criticism has, from the very beginning, focused on the idea that *shi yan zhi* (poetry articulates intent) and subsumed every form of artistic creativity under its rubric. The aesthetic is irksome in its restrictions, insisting that the work *is* the man, manifests his ethical qualities, and can be appreciated only by those with the necessary cultivation. It is also very rich and integrates the aesthetic coordinates of universe, man, work, and audience in a particularly interesting way with spirituality. Moreover, in its emphasis on receptive skills, we have the germ of the idea that subjectivity, which can exist apart from intersubjectivity, can also emerge in intersubjective encounters. My suspicion is that Mencius provided the philosophical foundations for the poetics of the lyric tradition in 2A2.[36]

Notes

1. David Nivison, "Philosophical Voluntarism in Fourth-Century China," *The Ways of Confucianism: Investigations in Chinese Philosophy*, ed., Bryan van Norden (Chicago: Open Court, 1996), 121–132; Jeffrey Riegel, "Reflections on an Unmoved Mind: An Analysis of *Mencius* 2A2," in *Studies in Classical Chinese Thought*, ed. Henry Rosemont Jr. and Benjamin I. Schwartz (*Journal of the American Academy of Religion* 47.3, Thematic Issue S [1980]: 433–457).

2. See Sor-Hoon Tan, "Between Family and State: Relational Tensions in Confucian Ethics," in this volume.

3. D. C. Lau, trans., *Mencius* (Hong Kong: Chinese University Press, 1984), 2A2, 56–57.

4. Nivison, "Philosophical Voluntarism."

5. Ibid., 122.

6. Huang Zongxi, "Mengzi shishuo" 孟子師説, *juan* 2, in *Huang Zongxi quanji*, vol. 1, 61. I thank Alan Chan for this reference.

7. Nivison has since communicated to me that he did not mean that *yan* should be interpreted as doctrines throughout 2A2. Because his essay was not explicit on that point and, perhaps more important, did not discuss its hermeneutic significance, I would still maintain that the oversight is serious enough to warrant a rebuttal.

8. D. C. Lau, trans., *Confucius: The Analects* (Hong Kong: Chinese University Press, 1992; orig., 1983), 20.3, 204–205. The idea of judging men by their words is reiterated by Zigong in *Lunyu* 19.25: "The gentleman is judged wise by a single word he utters; equally he is judged foolish by a single word he utters. That is why one really must be careful of what one says (君子一言以為知, 一言以為不知, 言不可不慎也)" (196–197).

9. Ibid., 16.13.

10. *Mencius*, 61.

11. Ibid., 58–59.

12. Stephen Owen, ed., *Readings in Chinese Literary Thought*, Harvard-Yenching Institute Monograph Series, no. 30 (Cambridge: Council on East Asian Studies, Harvard University, 1992), 21.

13. Ibid., 19.

14. I have adapted D. C. Lau's translation for consistency and economy of expression.

15. *Mencius,* 150–151.

16. Ibid., 270–271.

17. *Lunyu* 17.19.

18. I have found Charles Taylor, *Sources of the Self* (Cambridge: Cambridge University Press, 1989) very helpful in my formulation of the inner/outer distinction in Mencius and Gaozi. See esp. his pt. 2.

19. *Mencius* 7A1, 264–265.

20. Notice that Mencius encounters a problem: how to explain the lack of "spontaneous responses" if the sources of morality are indeed inner.

21. *Mencius* 2A2, 6A4.

22. *Mencius* 6A15.

23. *Mencius* 5A7. I am indebted to David Nivison for this reference.

24. *Mencius* 6A14, 6A15.

25. *Mencius* 7A38.

26. *Mencius* 7A35.

27. *Mencius* 5A7.

28. See Robert Eno, "Casuistry and Character in the *Mencius,*" in this volume.

29. *Mencius* 6A6, 228–229.

30. Adapted from A.C. Graham's translation in his *Disputers of the Tao* (La Salle, Ill.: Open Court, 1989), 128.

31. *Mencius* 5A6, 5A8.

32. See David L. Hall and Roger T. Ames, *Thinking from the Han: Self, Truth, and Transcendence in China and the West* (Albany: State University of New York Press, 1998), 39–43, for a version of such a conception of selfhood.

33. Wing-Tsit Chan, *A Source Book in Chinese Philosophy* (Princeton, N.J.: Princeton University Press, 1963), 86.

34. Han Yu, "Da Liyi shu," *Han Yu sanwen quanji* (Beijing: Jinri zhongguo chubanshe, 1996), 95; my translation. I thank Kim-Chong Chong for his help with the translation.

35. *Mencius* 2A2, 58–59.

36. See also Tu Wei-ming, "Inner Experience: The Basis of Creativity in Neo-Confucian Thinking," in *Artists and Traditions: Uses of the Past in Chinese Culture,* ed. Christian Murck (Princeton, N.J.: Art Museum, Princeton University, 1976), 9–15.

8

Between Family and State
Relational Tensions
in Confucian Ethics

SOR-HOON TAN

IN THE *MENCIUS,* when asked what the sage-king Shun would
do if his father killed a man and was about to be apprehended for
the crime, Mencius replied,

> Shun looked upon casting aside the Empire as no more than dis-
> carding a worn shoe. He would have secretly carried the old man on
> his back and fled to the edge of the sea and lived there happily,
> never giving a thought to the Empire.[1]

This recalls a passage in the *Lunyu* where Confucius informed the
governor of She that in his village "a father covers for his son, and a
son covers for his father. And being true lies in this."[2] Both passages
are symptomatic of what has been called Chinese familism,[3] which
prompted Bertrand Russell to wonder what concern is left over for
society and strangers, in the face of such an inordinate investment
in immediate human relations.[4] Chinese scholars such as Liang
Shuming and Lin Yutang also considered limiting one's concern to
one's family as an undesirable Chinese characteristic.[5]

Confucian attitudes to the family are complex and constantly
evolving. Even between the *Lunyu* and the *Mencius,* there are both
similarities and differences in this area. Some of Mencius' pronouncements seem more inflexible when it comes to the prior
importance of family relations; yet in some instances, Mencius also
interpreted this importance in such ways as to allow for practical
flexibility. Such casuistic moves became increasingly important, as
the orthodoxy of filial piety propagated by the imperial state ideology

grew more extreme and rigid. This essay will consider whether, and how far, Confucian emphasis on the ethical importance of the family is at the expanse of the state, by examining passages from the *Mencius* and comparing them with other texts belonging to different historical periods. These passages might focus on different issues within their specific historical contexts, but I have juxtaposed them to illuminate, each in its own way, a problem that the *Mencius* addressed and is still of contemporary interest. My aim then is not detailed textual exegesis but rather an attempt to draw on the varied resources within the Confucian tradition in examining the problem of conflicts between what family and state require of a person who is a member of both.

Relational Ethics in the Confucian Tradition

There is no denying the centrality of the family in Confucian ethics. As Tu Wei-ming points out, "families imbued with Confucian values are perhaps still the single most important social institution in imparting ways of learning to be human in East Asian societies."[6] But the basic model of Confucian relational ethics is not familistic in a way that is incompatible with concern for the wider society. Mencius said, "There is a common expression, 'The Empire, the state, the family (*tianxia guojia* 天下國家)'. The Empire has its basis in the state, the state in the family, and the family in one's own self."[7] A person is not an isolated individual; she is constituted by a network of human relations.[8] Cultivation of the person (*xiushen*) is the extension and enhancement of this relational network. In Confucianism, moral progress begins with the recognition that biological bonds provide authentic opportunities for personal realization.[9] We first learn to relate to others in our most immediate relations, that is, within the family: "Treat the aged of your own family in a manner befitting their venerable age and extend this treatment to the aged of other families; treat your own young in a manner befitting their tender age and extend this to the young of other families."[10] The method of ethical development, of becoming an authoritative person (*ren,* often translated as "benevolence") is "correlating one's conduct with those near at hand."[11] An authoritative person is one who, loving others, is able to take their concerns as her own.[12] By extending one's love and concern for others, one is able to take care of all within the Four Seas, to bring peace to all under heaven: "As for filial and fraternal responsibility (*xiaoti* 孝悌), it is, I suspect, the root of authoritative conduct."[13] But the root is not the entire plant; for personal cultivation to be truly fruitful, one must go beyond the family. One's ethical achievement is measured by how far one's concern for others, one's *ren,* extends. The whole world turns to one who is *ren;* the sage is more than a *ren* person because he "is broadly generous with the people and is able to help the multitude."[14]

Both the *Lunyu* and the *Mencius* are preoccupied with the art of effective (i.e., ethical) governing, which is not the sole responsibility of rulers. Rulers cannot rule alone, and their success in part lies in recognizing and promoting the right kind of talents.[15] The character for "ruler" (*jun* 君) is also the character for the "exemplary person" (*junzi*). The "exemplary person" is etymologically associated with personal order that expands through political participation. Three of the four aspects of the exemplary person's way mentioned in the *Lunyu* are sociopolitical.[16] Personal cultivation and effecting sociopolitical order are mutually implicated and mutually reinforcing.[17] Consequently, a perennial theme of Confucianism is the ethical requirement to take office in order to serve the people.

Both Confucius and Mencius spent a significant part of their lives trying to find a ruler who would accept their advice on governing. The only good reasons for not taking up political office were if one had inadequate ability[18] or if the political situation of the time rendered taking office an ineffective way to bring about sociopolitical order: "Qu Boyu was indeed an exemplary person! When the way prevailed in the state, he gave of his service, and when it did not, he rolled it up and tucked it away."[19] One does not withdraw from public life just to preserve life and limb. The point is to serve only where one could make a difference.[20] The Confucian tradition is full of praise for those who not only risk but even sacrifice their lives attempting to influence bad rulers for the benefit of the people.[21] In the *Lunyu,* we see a buildup of the pressures for participation in government. Initially, Confucius seemed content for his contribution to be made through the immediate circle of family and friends.[22] Later, he was prepared to offer his counsel even to rebels and to one whose character was questionable.[23] When commenting on those ancients who retired from government to preserve their ideals and integrity, he considered himself as different in not having "presuppositions about what may or may not be done."[24] Even when the way does not prevail, one must do one's best to reconstitute the situation instead of simply withdrawing.[25]

Compatibility between Familism and Concern for Society

The *Lunyu* sometimes presents family relations as contributing to, rather than conflicting with, nonfamily relations: "It is rare for one who has a sense of filial and fraternal responsibility to have a taste for defying authority; and it is unheard of for those who have no taste for defying authority to be keen on initiating rebellion"[26] and "A filial son is good at serving his ruler."[27] Proper cultivation of filial and fraternal responsibility enables one "to be broadly generous with the people and to help the multitude," that is, to become a sage.[28] As Mencius said, "The way of Yao and Shun is simply to be a good son and a good younger brother."[29] According to the *Great Learning*, "Those in ancient times who wanted their pure and excellent character to shine in the world would first bring proper government to the empire; desiring to bring proper government to the empire, they would first bring proper order to their families; desiring to bring proper order to their families, they would first cultivate their persons."[30] Tu Wei-ming sees this as a "process which enables us to embody the family, community, nation, world, and cosmos in our sensitivity."[31]

In a study of visual arts, Rudolf Arnheim remarks that a center is a position of stability; in a relational network, this stability is the strength of relations.[32] A geometric center is a point; a relational center extends as far as the condition of stability holds. This elasticity of the center is another reason Confucianism, despite the centrality of the family, is much less familistic than it appears at first sight. To the Chinese, *jia* 家 sometimes includes only members of a nuclear family, sometimes all members of a lineage or a clan, and sometimes even servants and other dependents who are not related by blood. Feng Youlan [Fung Yu-lan] asserts that, in the past, what is meant by *guo* (the state) is in fact *jia*.[33] At one extreme, the classical usage of *jia* includes reference to a single person of high rank, such as a noble, a high official, or the "son of heaven"; at the other, it can be extended to an unlimited number of people so that "all under heaven belongs to one family" (*tianxia yijia*).[34] The conceptual ambiguity is not limited to classical usage but is also an issue in contemporary sociological studies of Chinese societies.[35] To this day, the common expression "our family people" (*zijiaren*) can refer to any person one wishes to include—"family" can be expanded or contracted, depending upon the circumstances.[36] It is tempting to argue that use of *jia* to apply to people who are not blood relatives is simply a figure of speech; but such an argument already assumes that the concept should, in its primary meaning, apply only to blood relatives (or even the nuclear family), which is precisely what is doubtful in the Chinese context.

Although there are no pre-given limits to the extension of one's ethical consideration, of one's *ren*, Confucianism does not advocate equal love for everyone. That is the doctrine for which Mencius vehemently attacked the Mohists: by loving everyone equally, one fails to acknowledge the ethical significance of family relationships (*wufu*, "doing away with the father") and thereby sinks to the level of beasts.[37] An authoritative person practices "graduated love." Her network of relations is like a ripple; no matter how far it extends, the energy is always greatest at the center, decreasing proportionally to the distance from the center. How far a ripple could extend depends on the amount of energy at the center.[38] According to this model of ethical relations, instead of precluding concern for those outside the family, investment in immediate relations enables us to include those further afield in our ethical consideration and influence. Lack of concern for those outside our immediate relations would be condemned in Confucianism as inhibited ethical development.

Tension between Family and State: Confucian Responses

It is questionable how often the ideal of mutual enhancement between family and other relations is attained, if ever. Some might feel that an approach that insists fundamentally on harmony cannot deal adequately with the conflictive aspects of social interactions. Although Confucianism resists a depiction of social life as fundamentally conflict-ridden, it does not deny that at any one time there could be conflicts that are beyond our abilities to resolve, and the best we could do is damage control. Confucian acknowledgment of the reality of conflicts, however, is different from some Western views that perceive conflicts as consisting in a clash of absolute

moral duties, or categorical imperatives, that are in principle irrec-
oncilable.[39] Hence one has to be careful about comparing Confucian treatment of relational conflicts with apparently similar problems in Western philosophy such as found in Plato's *Euthypro*.[40]

The problem in the *Mencius* passage quoted at the beginning
of this essay is not whether Shun had undermined the rule of law.
The role of law in Confucianism differs radically from its role in
Western thinking. According to Aristotle, "the laws in their enactment in all subjects aim at the common advantage of all."[41] In Confucianism, the laws are viewed as a poor way of achieving the common good.

> Lead the people with administrative injunctions and keep them or-
> derly with penal law, and they will avoid punishments but will be
> without a sense of shame. Lead them with excellence and keep
> them orderly through observing ritual propriety (*li*) and they will
> develop a sense of shame, and moreover, will order themselves.[42]

To achieve what is good for the community, persuasion and transformative education, as befitting an ethics that centers on "model-
ing," are always preferred to the sanction of law.[43] One resorts to
laws only when one has failed in effecting genuine sociopolitical
order through *li* 禮. Henry Rosemont has argued that concept clus-
ters embedded in Western law-governed morality, such as "autonomy," "principles," "rationality," "rights," "duties," and "ought," pru-
dential or obligatory, are absent in Confucian ethics.[44] The general
evaluative discourse on human conduct found in Confucianism is
based on human relations rather than moral laws. Confucianism is a
relations-based ethics rather than a law-governed morality, and the
conflict between family and state is between situational demands of
the two kinds of relations.

With increased complexity of modern life, conflicts among
relational demands have not merely persisted but increased. Even
where there is no direct conflict, people may focus so much on their
families that public life suffers, for example, when capable people
refuse to enter politics or to engage in community services because
of the cost to their families. Even after granting that Confucianism
has no room for absolute conflicts, its ideal of relational mutual enhancement, persuasive as far as it concerns emotional, intellectual,
and ethical resources that grow with use, encounters problems when
resources—time, material, economic resources, and even our physical energies—are limited and exhaustible.

When limited resources have to be distributed, and a situation makes it impossible for us to fulfill everyone's needs or demands, relations may cease to be mutually enhancing and some decision on priority has to be made. This does not mean that relational tensions are always destructive or a zero-sum game. Tensions could prompt us to review our circumstances and see each relation in a fresh light; they could give rise to new insights that lead to better employment of existing resources or even result in the acquisition of new resources. A relation is stretched and expanded by another in tension with it. This effect of relations on one another is not unilateral as implied by the ripple metaphor, with the more immediate relation enhancing the less immediate. Unilateral enhancement may be characteristic of the initial stages of our development; but with growing maturity, experience becomes more complex, so that it is quite possible that what we learn and acquire in a less immediate relation could enhance a more immediate relation, and relations could mutually enhance one another.[45] As Rudolf Arnheim points out, a center could be both a focus of energy from which vectors radiate into environment, and the place where vectors act concentrically.[46] Each person, or family, may constitute a center, but not the only center—other persons and families are centers, foci of energy in their own right. Each center acknowledges the existence of other centers by acting upon them and being acted upon by them—the end result, and hence the resolution of any tension arising from the crisscrossing interaction of centers, depends on the quality of the centers involved and the quality of the relations among them.

If one fails to distinguish between what Confucianism advocates as ideals worth pursuing and the imperfect status quo at any one time, one might fall into the trap of trying to explain away conflicts among the demands of different relations. Although this weakness is at times discernible in the literature on relational conflict, Confucian attempts to resolve conflicts between family and state still provide some evidence that family does not always have priority. The answers to dilemmas created by conflict of situational demands of different relations are neither simple nor absolute. Confucius himself provides a model of resistance to dogmatism; he refused to insist on certainty, and he refused to be inflexible.[47]

Commenting on the sages Yu and Ji "passing their doors three times without entering" while serving the community, Mencius attributed their actions to the closeness of their relations with the people.[48] But one might point out that Yu and Ji did not allow their concern for their families to distract them while serving the people; that is, family relations did not have priority for them. There is some support for such a stand in the *Lunyu.* We find a student rejoicing that Confucius, in his teaching, did not show any partiality toward his own son.[49] When his favorite student, Yan Hui, died, Confucius' grief exceeded his grief at his own son's death.[50]

In the *Mencius,* Shun's filiality goes beyond a reciprocation of his father's love. His father had treated him very badly, even tried to kill him on at least two occasions.[51] Mencius' view of Shun's behavior toward his father makes the important point that one must not give up too easily on family relations even when they are dysfunctional. Dysfunctional family relations are often the source of deep-rooted psychological problems that handicap a person in other relations. Healing should start with the family relations. When someone rejects family relations with little qualm, we question the value she places on human relations in general. Having said that, we must recognize that there are times when families are so dysfunctional that clinging to those relations becomes self-destructive. Flexibility is necessary.

In the *Lunyu,* Sima Niu disowned his brother because of the latter's very bad conduct. When he lamented that he had no brother, Zixia consoled him with these words, "Since exemplary persons are respectful and impeccable in their conduct, are deferential to others and observe ritual propriety (*li*), everyone in the world is their brother; why would exemplary persons worry over having no brothers?"[52] It is immediate relations with ethical significance that have priority. Although it is true that traditionally the Chinese set great store by blood (and marriage) ties, the link between genetic relations and ethical significance in human relations is not pre-given or absolute. Ethical significance in relations is invested by actions of the interacting parties. It can also be eroded in the same way. Thus, it becomes possible for our relations with those genetically unconnected with us to become more immediate, ethically speaking, than family relations. Confucian persons are not simply locked from birth into hierarchical and cohesive family networks; construction of relations through interactive practices has always played an important role in Confucian societies.[53]

Does the importance of immediate relations translate into

shielding those closest to us from the consequences of their own unethical conduct? Heiner Roetz remarks that an often-overlooked
major aspect of the value of filiality in Confucianism is the requirement of "moral vigilance."[54] This oversight is due partly to conflicting messages found in the Confucian texts. When asked about
Shun's rewarding his villainous brother with a fiefdom when less villainous people were punished harshly, Mencius justified the partiality
in terms of the personal love Shun bore his brother, though he
added that Shun ensured that the people of the fiefdom did not
suffer from his brother's position. Although the upright people of
Confucius' village would agree with Shun, Sima Niu's case suggests
a different answer. For Mencius, even taxing one's parents with their
ethical failings, though not one of the five primary ways of being
unfilial, was deemed a matter at which parents could justifiably take
offense, and the offender was deemed deserving of punishment.
Hence, Mencius' defense of Kuang Zhang against condemnation of
being unfilial rested not only on the estrangement between father
and son being due to an ethical argument but also on Kuang
Zhang's punishing himself for the offense to his father.[55]

Confucius, on the other hand, believed that one should remonstrate with one's parents when they err, though this must be
done in a gentle and respectful manner. However, when they refuse
to listen, one should not become disobedient, nor should one complain about being worn out in the process.[56] We get a different picture in the *Xunzi:* "Being filial at home and respectful to one's
elders outside the home is the minimal ethical practice (*xiaoxing* 小
行).... Following the way (*dao*) instead of one's ruler and following
what is appropriate (*yi*) instead of one's father constitute the highest
ethical practice (*daxing* 大行)."[57] Among the later Confucian texts,
Confucius' recommendation of "obedience" when remonstration
fails is repeated in the *Liji* (Book of Rites).[58] In contrast, the *Xiaojing*
(Classic of Filiality), following the *Xunzi,* devotes a whole chapter to
the need not only to remonstrate but also to oppose parents and
rulers when they are contemplating unethical conduct—according
to this text, it is unfilial to obey one's parents when they are ethically
wrong.[59]

Introducing the additional consideration of whether the parents' wishes and actions are ethical or not sets a limit on what children should tolerate from parents. The *Book of Rites* elaborated on
Confucius' comment about "not complaining" to include occasions

when parents, in a rage, beat their children until they bleed.[60] In contrast, the "Narratives of the Confucian School" (*Kongzi jiayu* 孔子家語) and the *Shuoyuan* 説苑 both tell the story of Zeng Shen who, when he behaved as recommended in the *Book of Rites,* was reprimanded by Confucius as "entrapping his father in unethical practices" (*xian fu yu buyi* 陷父于不義).[61] Whereas relatively light beatings may be tolerated, one should evade any beatings that would cause serious injury; for if one's parents cause harm to oneself, they would be acting unethically, and the consequences would be detrimental to themselves. Hence, a filial child should not allow her parents to injure her. In an interesting reversal of paternalism, one finds that children's disobedience and curbs on parents' action can be justified on the grounds that what the parents want is not good for the parents.

Not only are there different currents, some contradicting one another, in Confucian literature regarding the extent to which family relations should dictate one's life, but we should also remember that the historical contexts often involve a social structure wherein the family is the locus of most people's activities, economic and even political. The opportunities for relations completely independent of the family are extremely limited and, in some cases, nonexistent. It is different today, when both opportunities for living some or even most of one's life outside the family, and the pressures to do so, are increasing. In the current context, recommendations of a qualified obedience to parents and a tempered relative priority of family relations seem much more relevant.

According to Keith Knapp, although both the scope and the importance of filiality broaden at the end of the Warring States period and the beginning of the Western Han, so that filiality emerges as the paramount virtue and the source of all others, earlier Confucians distinguish filiality from political loyalty, and the former far outstrips the latter in importance.[62] Some Confucians may reject giving outright priority to nonfamily relations over family relations: "One who does not love her parents but loves other people is called a rebel against excellence (*beide* 悖德); one who does not respect her parents but respects other people is called a rebel against propriety (*beili* 悖禮)."[63] Even then, flexibility in dealing with relational tension and conflicts of relational demands is found in the varied interpretations of what it means to give priority to family relations. Shun did not inform his parents of his marriage, even though according to ritual propriety of the time, it would be unfilial to marry without parental permission. Mencius defended him on the grounds that, if informed, Shun's parents would have objected unjustifiably, with detrimental result to themselves.[64] Interpretations of the "detrimental result" vary. According to D.C. Lau's translation, it is "bitterness against his parents." In Legge's translation, the resentment is on the part of the parents. Dobson's interpretation appears most consistent with the rest of the text: being prevented from marrying would have led to Shun's not having any descendants, which is detrimental to his parents.[65] Mencius believed that the most serious infiliality is "to have no heir." Based on this, he argued that Shun's not informing his father of his marriage "was as good as having told his father."[66]

Following Mencius' casuistic method, one might question the way Mencius resolved the hypothetical situation of Shun's father's killing a man. By escaping, Shun's father would be condemned for cowardice, not "taking his punishment like a man," in addition to the original crime. Furthermore, the manner of his escape would also deprive the empire of a sage-king—a potentially greater crime than killing one person. Surely these consequences would be more detrimental than staying to face the music. Given that the Chinese believe that family members are responsible for one another's actions to some extent, Shun could perhaps offer to take the punishment for his father.[67] And bearing in mind his great contribution to the people's welfare, even Gao Yao might be lenient in meting out punishment to this filial replacement. The equivalent today might be to hire for his father the best lawyer available, even if it means bankrupting himself, and standing by his father regardless of the world's condemnation—not because he condones the wrongdoing but in the hope that his father would have a chance to change. This is the reason the legendary filial daughter of the Han dynasty, Ti Ying 緹縈, cited in her petition to the Emperor Xiaowen to punish her in her father's place.[68]

The Authoritarian Appropriation of Confucian Familism

The legal codes from the Han dynasty to the Qing dynasty tend to emphasize the fathers' absolute power over their children:[69] "Of three thousand crimes deserving the five punishments, none is

worse than infiliality."[70] The authoritarian interpretation of relationships seems more Legalist than Confucian. Whereas Confucians
stress the reciprocity of relations, Hanfeizi says unequivocally, "A
loyal minister does not endanger his ruler; a filial son does not contradict his father."[71] Mencius' casuistic move paved the way for flexibility in practice despite the doctrinal and legal entrenchment of
the priority of family relations, especially the father-son relation.
Although the law upheld the Confucian stance that "those under
the same roof should cover up for one another," this applied only to
petty crimes; in the case of major crimes, like treason, the people
were expected to turn in their family members, even their parents,
in the name of a higher good.[72] This notion of *dayi mieqin* 大義滅親,
or disregarding family relations in favor of a higher good, can be
found in the *Zuozhuan,* which gives an account of a minister of
Duke Huan of Wei, Shi Que 石碏, who had his son, Shi Hou 石厚,
killed for being an accomplice in the murder of the duke. Shi Que's
action is said to exemplify *dayi mieqin,* which appears to be a common idiom of the time.[73] Turning in parents who have committed a
major crime is not considered unfilial, because filiality does not include helping parents to be unethical; moreover, this virtuous act of
dayi mieqin, like all virtuous acts on one's part, may be counted as a
form of filiality.

Ironically, the fact that filiality became so important that it
encompassed various other virtues contributed to flexibility in practice, with regard to the priority of father-son relation.[74] One could
thereby justify neglecting one's family to some extent, even over-
looking certain mourning rites while serving the ruler. Mencius considered "those who were unable to attend to the needs of their parents as a result of having to attend to the king's business" as filial,
for "the greatest thing a dutiful son can do is to honor his parents,
and the greatest thing he can do to honor his parents is to let them
enjoy the empire."[75] We find throughout the *Xiaojing,* and in the
chapters on Master Zeng's filiality in the *Da Dai Liji,* the belief that
worldly success, especially in the political arena or public service, is
an important way of being filial, more important than personally
taking care of the personal needs of one's parents.[76] This belief is
still widely accepted in Chinese societies today. Although the definition of worldly success today is perhaps more economic than political, the basic idea is still that of the *Da Dai Liji:* having others envy
one's parents for having such a child.[77]

In extreme cases when loyal service to the emperor means sacrificing the lives of family members, not all Chinese, even those who would consider themselves Confucians, were prepared to follow Shun's example in the *Mencius*. The *Later Han History* tells how Zhao Bao 趙苞, a prefect of Liaoxi, sacrificed his mother and wife in a border battle—an alien tribe raiding in the Han territories had captured his family and attempted unsuccessfully to blackmail him with their lives. He defeated the raiders, buried his mother, and died of remorse for being an unfilial son.[78] The commentary beginning this section of the *Later Han History* says that though the "unique acts" recorded therein may appear extreme, "missing the mean" (*bude zhongyong* 不得中庸), these people are nevertheless able to "make a name for themselves that would be known in all directions (*cheng-ming lifang* 成名立方)." Later attempts to resolve the problem differently—by Cheng Yi, for example—do not appear anymore moderate, closer to the mean, or even practical.[79]

Unlike Confucius and Mencius who spent much of their lives in the "political wilderness," later Confucians frequently were, or looked forward to being, state officials. This probably had an effect on their views regarding the priority of family relations vis-à-vis that between ruler and minister. From the Han dynasty, it became more and more difficult to place the father-son relation above the ruler-minister relation in practice. Yet, where it does not conflict with imperial power, paternal power became even more absolute as imperial power grew, for the latter is modeled on the former. Moreover, in order to justify imperial authoritarianism, state orthodoxy prescribed paternal authoritarianism. According to a May Fourth intellectual, Wu Yu, "the effect of the idea of filiality has been to turn China into a big factory for the production of obedient subjects."[80] Against such criticism, Xu Fuguan has argued persuasively that Confucian familism, centered on love and concern for others, does not support authoritarianism and that, in practice, it has even mitigated some of the excesses of Chinese authoritarianism. In Xu Fuguan's view, that familism became a tool of despots was due to Legalist influence and the *Classic of Filiality*—both distortions of Confucianism.[81] More recently, John Schrecker has argued that "far from using filial piety to bolster governmental power, Confucius and Mencius employ it for precisely the opposite purpose—to advocate limitations on political authority and to place responsibilities on the ruler."[82]

In the current revival of Confucianism, some people suspect politicians who advocate a revival of "the traditional family" and "the way of filiality" of being motivated by a desire to foster blind obedience. I believe that the authoritarian aspects of filiality as practiced in Chinese society resulted from imperial authoritarianism's manipulating Confucianism; Confucianism itself did not give rise to authoritarianism. Although there have been serious abuses, these may have been exaggerated through overemphasis and excessive publicity relative to the cases in which filiality benefits all parties. (We see a parallel in the way the mass media pays attention almost exclusively to bad news.) Confucianism paid a high price for becoming a state orthodoxy, apart from the theoretical and practical distortions that resulted. When the dynastic system collapsed, it almost took Confucian ethics with it. Filiality, instead of being the greatest of all virtues, became the greatest of all sins; and the family was seen as "the source of all evil" during the May Fourth movement.[83]

Conclusion

Today a generation that has witnessed the consequences of the disintegration of the family in many societies is reassessing the value of family relations. Hu Shi, a leader of the May Fourth movement, in a speech given in Taiwan in 1954, admitted to a reversal of his attitude toward the classics and especially promoted the study of the *Xiaojing*.[84] What we see is not a simple revival of the old orthodoxy but various attempts to reconstruct Confucian filiality to meet the demands of the contemporary situation. For example, Tu Weiming does this by locating the psychocultural dynamics of the Confucian family "in the complex interaction of the authoritarianism of the Three Bonds and the benevolence of the Five Relationships" and distinguishing the strengths and weakness of the Confucian legacy in family ethics.[85]

Recognizing the continuing, or even increasing, importance of the family does not mean that we must give absolute priority to family relations. For one thing, we no longer live our lives almost entirely within the family and with little contact with others. This brief survey of the Confucian tradition has tried to show that even a Confucian response could incorporate considerable flexibility when tensions occur as a result of the plurality of relations constituting a person. One tries hard to find a way that preserves the conflicting relations by trying to look at the situation from new perspectives. When that is impossible, as so often happens, priority should depend on which alternative course of action would preserve more of one's entire relational network and also provide opportunities for future growth of the network. There are times when "breaking away" from a family relation is necessary for the growth of one's relational network. In becoming involved in other relations, one does not simply replace the damaged family relation with others that one attempts to make more immediate. The new resources one gains in the resulting personal growth could also enable one to repair the damaged family relation in a way that would be impossible without that earlier break.

In today's society, a family cannot flourish in isolation. Even the best parents will have difficulties bringing up their children properly if the wider social environment works against their efforts. Concern for one's family therefore entails concern for a wider community. Even when family relations are all that they should be, there could still be situations wherein it would make sense to give priority to less immediate relations. As Confucius says, "The person who does not consider what is far away will find worries much closer at hand."[86]

Notes

1. *Mencius* 13.35/71/17. *A Concordance to the Mengzi*, ICS Ancient Chinese Text Concordance Series (Hong Kong: Commercial Press, 1995). D.C. Lau, trans., *Mencius* (Hong Kong: Chinese University Press, 1984), 279.

2. *Lunyu* 13.18/35/22. *A Concordance to the Lunyu*, ICS Ancient Chinese Text Concordance Series (Hong Kong: Commercial Press, 1995). Roger Ames and Henry Rosemont, *The Analects of Confucius* (New York: Ballantine, 1998), 167.

3. The term is used in Ch'ü T'ung-tsu, *Law and Society in Traditional China* (The Hague: Mouton and Co., 1961). Many scholars, Western and Chinese, have remarked on the central position of the family in Chinese thinking and society.

4. Bertrand Russell, *The Problem of China* (London: Allen and Unwin, 1922), 40.

5. Liang Shuming, *Zhongguo wenhua yaoyi* (The Essential Features of Chinese Culture) (Hong Kong: Joint Publishing Co., 1989), 22. Lin Yutang, *My Country and My People* (New York: Halcyon House, 1938), 180.

6. Tu Wei-ming, "Probing the 'Three Bonds' and the 'Five Relationships' in Confucian Humanism," in *Confucianism and the Family*, ed. Walter H.

Slote and George A. De Vos (Albany: State University of New York Press, 1998), 135.

    7. *Mencius* 7.5/36/23. Lau, *Mencius,* 141.

    8. See Roger Ames, "The Focus-Field Self in Classical Confucianism," in *Self as Person in Asian Theory and Practice,* ed. Roger Ames, Wimal Dissanayake, and Thomas Kasulis (Albany: State University of New York Press, 1994), 187–212.

    9. Tu Wei-ming, "Probing the 'Three Bonds,'" 127.

    10. *Mencius* 1.7/5/7; Lau, *Mencius,* 17.

    11. *Lunyu* 6.30/14/17; Ames and Rosemont, *Analects,* 110. For reasons for translating *ren* as "authoritative person," see David L. Hall and Roger T. Ames, *Thinking through Confucius* (Albany: State University of New York Press, 1987), 114–125.

    12. *Lunyu* 12.22/33/5.

    13. *Lunyu* 1.2/1/7; Ames and Rosemont, *Analects,* 71.

    14. *Lunyu* 12.1/30/17, 6.30/14/16; Ames and Rosemont, *Analects,* 110, 152. See also *Mencius* 7.3/36/16.

    15. *Lunyu* 12.22/33/7, 13.2/33/23; *Mencius* 3.5/17/28.

    16. *Lunyu* 5.16/10/18. See also *Lunyu* 14.42/41/14, 19.10/54/26, 20.2/57/19.

    17. *Lunyu* 1.7/1/19. See also Hall and Ames, *Thinking through Confucius,* 183–184.

    18. *Lunyu* 11.24/28/20.

    19. *Lunyu* 15.7/42/15; Ames and Rosemont, *Analects,* 186. See also *Lunyu* 8.13/19/9.

    20. Confucius implied that he was waiting for "the right price," an appropriate appreciation of his talents in *Lunyu* 9.13/21/9. Refer to *Lunyu* 18.4/51/13 for circumstances of his departure from Qi. Mencius tended to take a more pragmatic attitude; he allowed being treated with respect as a reason for staying in office even when one's advice was ignored, and in desperate circumstances, "to ward off starvation," even accepting charity from a ruler who ignored one's advice was permissible. *Mencius* 12.14/66/30.

    21. *Lunyu* 18.1/51/5.

    22. *Lunyu* 2.21/4/12.

    23. *Lunyu* 17.5/48/7, 17.7/48/18.

    24. *Lunyu* 18.8/53/6; Ames and Rosemont, *Analects,* 216.

    25. *Lunyu* 18.7/53/4.

    26. *Lunyu* 1.2/1/6; Ames and Rosemont, *Analects,* 71.

    27. *Da Dai Liji* 4.3/29/17. *A Concordance to the Da Dai Liji,* ICS Ancient Chinese Text Concordance Series (Hong Kong: Commercial Press, 1992). My translation.

    28. *Lunyu* 6.30/14/16; Ames and Rosemont, *Analects,* 110.

    29. Mencius 12.2/62/18; Lau, *Mencius,* 245. Mencius expanded the concept of filiality to cover that which, for Confucius, is the extension of filiality. Xu Fuguan has pointed out the dangers involved in this move, which in the *Mencius* is at least mitigated by the concrete recommendations for government, showing clearly that government is more than just being filial. But the later

merging of filiality with loyalty to the ruler, especially in the *Classic of Filiality* (*Xiaojing*), which Xu Fuguan viewed as a distortion of Confucian teaching, created a tenuous relationship between filialism and authoritarianism in Chinese society. Xu Fuguan, *Zhongguo sixiangshi lunji* (Discussions on the History of Chinese Thought) (Taiwan: Donghai University, 1959), 162–175.

30. *Liji* (Book of Rites) 43.1/164/28. *A Concordance to the Liji*, ICS Ancient Chinese Text Concordance Series (Hong Kong: Commercial Press, 1992). Trans. in David L. Hall and Roger T. Ames, *The Democracy of the Dead: Dewey, Confucius, and the Hope for Democracy in China* (La Salle, Ill.: Open Court, 1999), 175.

31. Tu Wei-ming, "Embodying the Universe: A Note on Confucian Self-realization," in *Self as Person in Asian Theory and Practice,* ed. Roger Ames et al., 186. See also Tu Wei-ming, *Humanity and Self-Cultivation* (Berkeley, Calif.: Asian Humanities Press, 1979); and Tu Wei-ming, *Confucian Thought: Selfhood as Creative Transformation* (Albany: State University of New York Press, 1985).

32. Rudolf Arnheim, *The Power of the Center* (Berkeley and Los Angeles: University of California Press, 1998), 109.

33. Feng Youlan, *Xin shi lun* (New Discussions of Issues of the Practical World) (Taipei: Commercial Press, 1939), 68. Li Zehou shared this view to some extent, though he limited it to the Spring and Autumn period of China's history. Li Zehou, *Zhongguo gudai sixiangshilun* (History of Thought in Ancient China) (Taipei: Sanmin shuju, 1985), 14.

34. Ambrose King, "The Individual and Group in Confucianism," in *Individualism and Holism: Studies in Confucian and Taoist Values,* ed. Donald Munro (Ann Arbor: Center for Chinese Studies, University of Michigan, 1985), 61.

35. Myron Cohen, "Development Process in the Chinese Domestic Group," in *Family and Kinship in Chinese Society,* ed. Maurice Freedman (Stanford, Calif.: Stanford University Press, 1970), 22–36.

36. Fei Xiaotong, *From the Soil,* trans. Gary Hamilton and Wang Zheng (Berkeley and Los Angeles: University of California Press, 1992), 62.

37. *Mencius* 6.9/35/1.

38. This metaphor seems especially apt given the interesting cognate relations between the Chinese characters for ethical human relations (*lun* 倫) and a ripple (*lun* 淪). See Ames, "Focus-Field Self," 206.

39. Heiner Roetz, *Confucian Ethics of the Axial Age* (Albany: State University of New York Press, 1993), 93–100.

40. Greg Witlock, "Concealing the Misconduct of One's Own Father: Confucius and Plato on a Question of Filial Piety," *Journal of Chinese Philosophy* 21 (1994): 113–137.

41. Aristotle, *The Complete Works of Aristotle,* rev. Oxford trans., ed. Jonathan Barnes (Princeton, N.J.: Princeton University Press, 1984), 1129b15.

42. *Lunyu* 2.3/2/29. Ames and Rosemont, *Analects,* 76. See also *Mencius* 5.3/26/10 on the law as a "trap" if people are not given the means of living and education.

43. *Lunyu* 12.19/32/22.

44. Henry Rosemont, "Rights-Bearing Individuals and Role-Bearing

Persons," in *Rules, Rituals, and Responsibility*, ed. Mary I. Bockover (La Salle, Ill.: Open Court, 1991), 71–101. Liang Shuming also viewed concepts of "rights" and "autonomy" as alien and almost incomprehensible to most Chinese on first encounter. Liang Shuming, *Zhongguo wenhua yaoyi*, 15.

45. Chen Xiyuan, "Shengwang dianfan yu rujia 'neisheng waiwang' de shizhi yihan" (The Sage-King Model and the Concrete Meaning and Content of Confucian "Inner-Sage-Outer-King"), in *Mengzi sixiang de lishi fazhan* (The Historical Development of Mencian Thought), ed. Wang Junjie (Taipei: Zhongyang yanjiu yuan, 1995), 42–50.

46. Arnheim, *Power of the Center*, 13.

47. *Lunyu* 9.4/20/13.

48. Mencius 8.29/44/10–14; Lau, *Mencius*, 171. In the *Lunyu*, Confucius praised Yu for living "in humblest circumstances yet gave all of his strength to the construction of drain canals and irrigation ditches." *Lunyu* 8.21/19/29; Ames and Rosemont, *Analects*, 125.

49. *Lunyu* 16.13/47/9.

50. *Lunyu* 11.10/27/3.

51. *Mencius* 9.2/46/20.

52. *Lunyu* 12.5/31/6; Ames and Rosemont, *Analects*, 154.

53. Ambrose King and Michael Bond, "The Confucian Paradigm of Man: A Sociological View," in *Chinese Culture and Mental Health*, ed. Wen-shing Tseng and David Wu (Orlando, Fla.: Academic Press, 1985), 38–42.

54. Roetz, *Confucian Ethics*, 56.

55. *Mencius* 8.30/44/16–24.

56. *Lunyu* 4.18/8/15.

57. *Xunzi* 29.1/141/19. *A Concordance to the Xunzi*, ICS Ancient Chinese Text Concordance Series (Hong Kong: Commercial Press, 1996). My translation.

58. *Liji* 2.17/9/17. See also *Da Dai Liji* 4.5/30/26. Heiner Roetz suggests that "*wei*"—usually translated as not resisting, i.e., not disobeying—may also be understood as not abandoning one's purpose, i.e., persisting in trying to change one's erring parent's conduct. Roetz, *Confucian Ethics*, 59.

59. *Xiaojing* (Classic of Filiality) 15/4/3–7. *A Concordance to the Xiaojing*, ICS Ancient Chinese Text Concordance Series (Hong Kong: Commercial Press, 1992). Some Confucian scholars, Zhu Xi and more recently Xu Fuguan among them, had challenged the authenticity of this text and its qualification to be a "classic" and, in some cases, are very critical of its content, even going so far as to say that its doctrines distort Confucianism. Xu Fuguan, *Zhongguo sixiangshi lunji*, 176–191. I am sympathetic to these criticisms, but given the significant influence of this text on Chinese society, I have nevertheless used various citations from it as illustrating beliefs of the later Confucian tradition.

60. *Liji* 12.12/74/20–22.

61. *Kongzi jiayu* (Narratives of the Confucian School) 15.10/29/17. *A Concordance to the Kongzi Jiayu*, ICS Ancient Chinese Text Concordance Series (Hong Kong: Commercial Press, 1992). *Shuoyuan* 3.7/20/9. *A Concordance to the Shuoyuan*, ICS Ancient Chinese Text Concordance Series (Hong Kong: Commercial Press, 1992).

62. Keith Knapp, "The *Ru* Interpretation of *Xiao*," *Early China* 20 (1995): 216–219.

63. *Xiaojing* 9/2/29. Adaptation of translation by James Legge, *Sacred Books of the East*, vol. 3, pt. 1 (Oxford: Clarendon Press, 1899), 479.

64. *Mencius* 9.2/46/10.

65. Lau, *Mencius*, 181. James Legge, trans., *Life and Works of Mencius* (London: Trübner and Co., 1875), 274. W.A.C.H. Dobson, trans., *Mencius* (Toronto: University of Toronto Press, 1963), 39.

66. *Mencius* 7.26/40/12; Lau, *Mencius*, 155–156.

67. King and Bond, "Confucian Paradigm of Man," 37.

68. Ban Gu, *Hanshu* (Han History), *juan* 23 (Beijing: Zhonghua shuju, 1975), 3: 1098. For other examples of juniors punished as substitutes, see Ch'ü T'ung-tsu, *Law and Society*, 74–76.

69. Ch'ü T'ung-tsu, *Law and Society*, 20–64.

70. *Xiaojing* 11/3/12; my translation. John Wu remarked that he knew of "no other system of law which is so meticulous in enforcing the duties of filial piety." John C. H. Wu, "The Status of the Individual in the Political and Legal Traditions of Old and New China," in *The Status of the Individual in East and West*, ed. Charles Moore (Honolulu: University of Hawai'i Press, 1968), 396.

71. *Hanfeizi*, Sibubeiyao ed. (Shanghai: Zhonghua, 1927), *juan* 20.2a. To Hanfei, even citing ancient kings as examples, let alone direct criticism of the reigning ruler, is "endangering" the ruler.

72. Ch'ü T'ung-tsu, *Law and Society*, 70–74.

73. *Zuozhuan*, Duke Yin 4th year. James Legge, trans., *The Ch'un Tsew with the Tso Chuan*, vol. 5 of *The Chinese Classics* (Hong Kong: Hong Kong University Press, 1970), 15–17.

74. We can see the all-embracing nature of filiality in various passages in the *Xiaojing*, the *Liji*, and the *Da Dai Liji*.

75. *Mencius* 9.4/48/3; Lau, *Mencius*, 187.

76. *Da Dai Liji* 4.4/29/22–4.4/30/9. *Xiaojing* 2–5/1/10–30. The idea reappears frequently in the later chapters.

77. "What the exemplary person calls being filial is to have every fellow citizen wish for it, saying, 'How fortunate it is to have such a son.'" *Da Dai Liji* 4.4/29/27; my translation.

78. Ban Gu, "Duxing liezhuan" (Biographies of those who acted uniquely), in *Hou Hanshu* (Later Han History), *juan* 81 (Beijing: Zhonghua shuju, 1982), 9: 2692–2693.

79. *Lunyu* 13.21/36/6. *Hou Hanshu*, *juan* 81, 9: 2665. On later attempts to solve the problem differently, see Feng Youlan, *Xin shi lun*, 82. For other incidents of such dilemmas, see Roetz, *Confucian Ethics*, 98–100.

80. Wu Yu, "Shuo Xiao" (On Filiality), *Wu Yu wenlu* (Collection of Essays by Wu Yu) (Shanghai: Oriental Books, 1922), 15.

81. Xu Fuguan, *Zhongguo sixiangshi lunji*, 155–200.

82. John Schrecker, "Filial Piety as a Basis for Human Rights in Confucius and Mencius," *Journal of Chinese Philosophy* 24 (1997): 401. I am more skeptical of Schrecker's argument that filial piety may be viewed as a "natural right," for reasons I have explained earlier.

83. Before May Fourth, intellectuals like Kang Youwei, Tan Sitong, and Liang Qichao were very critical of the Chinese family and other institutions of their time, although they did not reject Confucianism entirely.

84. Yan Xiehe, preface to *Xiaojing baihua zhuyi* (A Modern Mandarin Translation and Commentary on the Classic of Filiality) (Taipei: Ruicheng shuju, 1980), 14.

85. Tu Wei-ming, "Probing the 'Three Bonds,'" 121–136.

86. *Lunyu* 15.12/42/29; my translation. Cf. D.C. Lau, trans., *Confucius: The Analects* (Middlesex: Penguin, 1979), 134: "He who gives no thought to difficulties in the future is sure to be beset by worries much closer at hand." Cf. also Ames and Rosemont, *Analects,* 187: "The person who does not consider what is still far off will not escape being alarmed at what is near at hand." Both temporal and spatial interpretations of *yuan* 遠 (far) and *jin* 近 (near) work—the text is richer for its polysemy.

9

Casuistry and Character in the *Mencius*

ROBERT ENO

THE *MENCIUS* PROVIDES a clear and distinctive theory of moral knowing in its doctrine of the innate and universal structure of human nature as moral, and in its identification of the four moral senses that characterize that uniquely human nature. The forceful way in which the text presents such ideas invites us to see the core of Mencian moral discourse in terms of these theories and the modified intuitionism that they imply.[1] However, a great deal of the ethical discussion in the *Mencius* seems to have little explicit connection with these theories. Although we are certainly entitled to construct from *Mencius* passages a complex architecture of moral ideas that represents an implicit theoretical basis for the text as a whole, moral discourse in the text itself seems so frequently at odds with such a structural goal that to do so may misrepresent the kind of ethical enterprise that the *Mencius* undertakes.

My intention here is to explore certain features of the *disorderliness* of ethical discourse in the *Mencius*. The importance of these features suggests that, for the authors and early readers of the text, ethical interest was not focused on the articulation of coherent theory, though theory making was clearly an activity Mencius engaged in. A more basic goal of Mencian ethical discourse seems to be to provide for members of Mencius' tradition clear insight into the character of ethical authority, as conveyed through exemplary figures essential to the teaching lineage—most importantly, Mencius himself. The methodology of such discourse I take to be principally literary, inviting readers to engage in a hermeneutic of personal exploration, approaching through imaginative acts of *verstehen* the perspective of the authoritative sage.[2]

The points of the *Mencius* on which I will focus are passages that I will call casuistic, in that they treat moral value in terms of case-specific examples. For my purposes, there are three respects in which a passage may belong to Mencian casuistry. It may defensively rationalize through moral rule invocation the behavior of a historical model or associate of the Mencian lineage; it may probe elusive perspectives of wisdom by examining specific acts of authoritative exemplars; and it may express a theory that all moral wisdom is case-specific. Such passages reveal that though the *Mencius* engages in detailed discussions of rules and virtues, it most basically reflects neither a rule ethics nor a virtue ethics, in the Aristotelian sense.[3] Rather, it promotes a view of ethical understanding achieved through personal apprehension of sage character, as exemplified by real and individualized authoritative actors, known through experience or literary re-creation. I would like to claim that, in this way, the *Mencius* seems to undertake what I will call an ethics of character, by which I mean an ethics of virtue resting on a methodology of *verstehen*, an empathetic grasp of virtue perspectives cultivated through hermeneutic probing of historical narratives. Toward the end of this discussion, I will suggest that this is an enterprise that distinguishes much of early Confucianism from the ethical discourse of competing schools.

Modes of Casuistry in the *Mencius*

Casuistic passages in the *Mencius* may rationalize ethical rule-breaking behavior by exemplary people associated with the Mencian school or may provide access to their authoritative morality by exploring their responses to morally difficult situations. I will refer to these two modes as "rationalizing" and "interpretive" casuistry. In the following passage concerning an associate of Mencius in the state of Qi, Kuang Zhang 匡章, we see both these dimensions.

> Gongduzi said, "Kuang Zhang is termed unfilial throughout the state, yet you, Master, travel in company with him and treat him with the forms of courtesy. May I ask why?"
>
> Mencius said, "There are five types of behavior that the world commonly refers to as unfilial. To be physically lazy and

ignore the welfare of one's parents is the first. To gamble and drink, and so ignore the welfare of one's parents, is the second. To be greedy for wealth that one reserves for wife and children, and so ignore the welfare of one's parents is the third. To revel in sensual pleasures and bring shame upon one's parents is the fourth. To be enamored of bravado and brawls and so endanger one's parents is the fifth.

"Does any one of these apply to Zhangzi? In his case, the son reproached the father over an issue of moral conduct and now the two have broken off relations. Reproaches are appropriate between friends, but between father and son, they are great despoilers of love. Do you think Zhangzi does not wish to have a family and be a husband with children? Yet because he offended his father and is banished from his presence, he has sent away his wife and children, to live out his days without their care and support. He reasoned that were he not to do so, his offense would be great indeed—and *that* is precisely what Zhangzi is all about."[4] (4B30)

Mencius is portrayed throughout the text as laying heavy stress on filiality, and Kuang Zhang has clearly violated this rule.[5] Yet Mencius excuses him on two grounds. The first is that he has not broken any of the five rules concerning filiality. The second is that in the manner in which he has attempted to expiate his crime, he has demonstrated "what he is all about"—that is, he has shown a moral strength of character that belies any claim that his unfilial act was sufficient grounds to treat him as an unfilial person.

For the first of these strategies, I will be ungenerous to Mencius and say that he is indulging in rationalizing casuistry. He appears willfully to misconstrue the ethical seriousness of the situation by exculpating Kuang Zhang on the basis of a spurious rule to the effect that if one does not commit any of five popularly formulated sins of unfiliality, then one is not to be treated as unfilial. Kuang Zhang was a friend and associate who appears at several points in the *Mencius*, and the text has a defensive interest in clearing him of misconduct. It does so at some cost to theoretical consistency, as Mencius' arguments diminish the moral gravity of filiality that the text elsewhere celebrates, particularly in its valorization of the exemplary figure Shun 舜. This is an instance where we see lineage interests that govern casuistic argument undermine ethical theory, and I think it is correct to note that the loyalty the text shows to certain individuals connected with Mencius and his lineage (most particularly, as we will see, Mencius himself) leads to ad hoc rule manipulation that is damaging to the philosophical coherence of the text.

But there is a richer side to the passage. Mencius goes beyond rationalizing casuistry when he gives a sensitive description of Kuang Zhang's predicament that highlights three features: Kuang Zhang's unfilial offense was the product of overcommitment to morality; Kuang Zhang has recognized that it was an offense; and he has voluntarily inflicted lifelong punishment on himself to mitigate his offense. Mencius has determined that it is these features of conduct that reveal Kuang Zhang's character, rather than his unfilial conduct. The rhetoric suggests that it is in light of this character, rather than on the narrow grounds that Kuang Zhang violated none of the five rules, that Mencius is willing to stand alone in associating with and honoring Kuang Zhang.

Presumably, everyone in Qi understands the basic facts of Kuang Zhang's situation; what they have misconstrued is his character. Mencius alone is able to identify which elements of the situation reveal who Kuang Zhang is, and having grasped whom he is dealing with, rather than the acts considered in isolation from the man, Mencius adopts an attitude toward him different from the attitude of those who attend to the acts alone. In its latter section, the passage represents interpretive casuistry, and its function operates on two levels. First, the text portrays how Kuang Zhang, as a moral exemplar, behaves in complex and morally challenging circumstances. Second, the text reveals how Mencius, himself a moral exemplar, uses his moral faculties to attend to subtle issues of context and character, rather than to rule-described behavior alone, and so is able to discover exemplary character where others detect only moral failure.

The Rule-Free Character of Moral Perfection

The search for moral character in the *Mencius* is pursued through close, casuistic analysis of the actions of real people or of legends thought to be real. Descriptions of moral rules and consideration of their competing claims on us are woven through depictions of sage exemplars in complex ways, often dominating casuistic analysis. However, as important as reasoning clearly is to moral rules at many points in the *Mencius*, it is equally clear that rules are viewed as of provisional value only. The text explicitly describes rule-transcending moral dispositions as the ultimate form of the sage character it wishes to celebrate. Passages of this nature are linked to Mencian casuistry in that they make the case-specific nature of moral knowing a principle of Mencian ethics. The clearest example is a lengthy discussion of sage models in 5B1, which belongs to a set of passages that reflect what I will call theoretical casuistry, in that they idealize moral wisdom in terms of rule-free case sensitivity.

The passage, 5B1, begins with descriptions of three sages Bo Yi 伯夷, Yi Yin 伊尹, and Liuxia Hui 柳下惠. The essential features of the personal histories of each of these men are briefly described in the form of a series of rules. For example, the description of Bo Yi begins, "Bo Yi: his eyes would not look upon a bad color; his ears would not listen to a bad sound; he would not serve one who was not his lord; he would not dispatch one who was not his subordinate; in [a context of] order he would advance; in chaos he would retreat...." His conduct is later encapsulated in a virtue epithet; he is "the sage of purity." Similar discussions of Yi Yin and Liuxia Hui characterize the former by rules that warrant the epithet "the sage of responsibility" and the latter as "the sage of harmony." In the cases of Bo Yi and Liuxia Hui, Mencius adds a phrase noting that their examples can have salutary effects on certain classes of people: "Hearing of Bo Yi's style of conduct, a greedy man becomes honest and a timid man gains resolve.... Hearing of Liuxia Hui's style of conduct, a rude bumpkin becomes tolerant and a miser becomes generous."[6]

Although 5B1 reduces these three exemplars to rules (or, alternatively, to delimited virtues that can be captured by simple rules), which can serve thematically as antidotes to certain styles of moral defect, the passage ends in a different moral dimension by offering Confucius as "the sage of timeliness," whose apparently contradictory acts cannot be reduced to a rule, because they are always direct responses to situations in all their complexity: "When speed was appropriate, he was speedy; when delay was appropriate, he delayed; where it was appropriate to remain, he remained; where it was appropriate to serve, he served.... Confucius was the sage of timeliness. We may say he was the Grand Coda that brings all together—the Grand Coda, which combines the ringing of the bronze bells and the sounding of the jade chimes."

Inscrutability

To the degree that the sage's acts are determined by contexts rather than rules, his acts may be incomprehensible to normal rule-governed moral reasoning. To penetrate the sage perspective of such actors, one needs to reconstruct the context, so as to perceive the factors that triggered moral responses. It is the detailed particularity of contexts, so much more nuanced than rules, that accounts, at times, for the inscrutability of the sage. This is illustrated in the *Mencius* by a discussion of apparently incommensurable actions by two masters of Mencius' lineage, Zengzi 曾子 and Zisi 子思.

> When Zengzi dwelt in Wucheng, there were bandit troops from Yue. "The bandits are coming!" cried someone. "Shouldn't we leave this place?" Zengzi said, "Do not allow people to lodge in our compound or to cut from our firewood groves." As the bandit troops retreated, he said, "Repair our compound walls and roofs; we are going to return." After the bandit troops had retreated, Zengzi returned. Some followers said, "The Master has been treated here with such loyalty and respect—perhaps it was not appropriate that when the bandits came, he set an example for the people by being the first to leave and then returned when they were gone." Shenyou Xing said, "This is beyond your understanding. When there was a disturbance among the field workers in my family estate, none of the seventy men who were then followers of the Master became involved."[7]
>
> When Zisi dwelt in Wei, there were bandit troops from Qi. "The bandits are coming!" cried someone. "Shouldn't we leave this place?" Zisi said. "Were I to leave, beside whom would our lord defend his state?"
>
> Mencius commented: "Zengzi and Zisi followed an identical *dao*. Zengzi was a teacher [in the one instance] and a clan leader [in the other].[8] Zisi was an officer and was of minor rank.[9] Had Zengzi and Zisi exchanged places, they would have acted identically."[10] (4B31)

Zengzi's actions appear to be self-interested rather than ethical, and the response of "some followers" articulates our intuitive ethical response. Shenyou Xing 沈猶行, viewing Zengzi's behavior in a larger context, has a clearer view of how his present conduct exemplifies a consistent moral standpoint (though the text fails to convey the specifics to us). Moreover, the apparent contradiction between the acts of two sages is reconciled through reference to second-level rules concerning role imperatives that configured the field of their ethical vision. This perfect sensitivity to moral imperatives within the complex contexts of roles is not "readable" to those who attend only to the situational features that call general rules into play. But it is precisely this shared feature of moral sensitivity in context that reveals the identity of the *dao* the two exemplars follow.[11]

There is in this type of passage a mystification of moral knowing that insulates it from criticism based on rules or, in this case, a critique of self-contradiction. In that sense, the passage seems to be an example of rationalizing casuistry, as we might label any passage that resorts to the formula, "this is beyond your understanding" (a phrase that appears also in 5A1, to privilege Mencius' understanding of Shun's actions). Yet Shenyou Xing goes beyond warding off inquiry and gives us a clue about the source of his positive judgment, and Mencius' closing comments are also designed to help us reimagine the actions of the two authoritative exemplars through thicker contextualization. In this way, we may consider the apparent inscrutability of sagehood to be a characteristic feature of both rationalizing and interpretive casuistry.

The Thematic Coherence of Character—*Zhi* 志

In 4B30 and 4B31, we have examined two passages that entail interpretive casuistry. In each case, there seems to be a notion that the actions of an exemplary person must be understood as expressions of a unified ethical perspective that embodies the character of the person in a basic and holistic way. The word "*zhi*" is sometimes used in the text to point to such a coherence or moral theme in an exemplary individual's character.

> Gongsun Chou said, "Yi Yin said, 'I will not consort with one who is obdurate!' He banished [his ruler] Taijia to Tong, and the people were very pleased. When Taijia became worthy, Yi Yin brought him back, and the people were very pleased. If a worthy man were minister to a ruler who was unworthy, is it so that he might properly banish him in this way?"
>
> Mencius said, "If he had the *zhi* of Yi Yin, then he might; if he did not have the *zhi* of Yi Yin, then this would be usurpation." (7A31)

The text's treatment of Confucius seems to reflect confidence in an a priori understanding of Confucius' *zhi*, which reveals that for both the text's protagonist and its authors, factual issues concerning Confucius' conduct were of secondary importance when using Confucius as an exemplar to convey sage character.

For example, in 5A8, Mencius is confronted with testimony that when in the states of Wei and Qi, Confucius accepted the patronage of certain men of unsavory character. Mencius denies the story, naming an alternative patron in Wei and arguing that Confucius had demonstrated by his response to other offers of patronage that, in such action, Confucius' attention would never have deviated from the moral force of ritual, right, and the demands of necessity. Mencius does not entertain the notion that the accounts of unsavory action may report timely responses to extraordinary contexts; rather, confident of his understanding of Confucius' character, he proclaims that had Confucius acted as the stories say, "How could he have been Confucius?" The claims are thus refuted.[12]

The Subversiveness of Rationalizing Casuistry

Interpretive casuistry challenges the completeness of ethical theory in principle, by denying to universalizable rules or virtue descriptions the power to convey authoritative moral knowing as it is encountered in real individuals. This is an intellectually defensible feature of Mencian moral discourse as an ethics of character, in the sense defined earlier. However, the commitment to defend authoritative lineage heroes that inspires the rationalizing casuistry of the text undermines coherence in more fundamental and less defensible ways. We have seen earlier, in considering the defense of Kuang Zhang, that the initial formulaic rationalization of Mencius' willingness to associate with his friend was maintained at some cost to the text's deep commitment to imperatives of filiality. Elsewhere, the *Mencius'* defensive concerns reveal the secondary nature of factual consistency.

As we will explore further below, the text presents a portrait of Mencius' political career that highlights Mencius' controversial behavior and provides him a forum to defend it. Among the criticisms that Mencius refutes are accusations that once given leverage to achieve moral ends through his appointment as a minister in the state of Qi, he squandered that opportunity through inactivity and an early, unforced resignation. In 6B6, Mencius responds to such a charge by citing Confucius' behavior as a precedent.

> When Confucius was Minister of Crime in Lu, his counsel was not employed. Subsequently, on the occasion of a state sacrificial rite, no meat from the sacrificial roast was delivered to him. He left the state without taking off his cap. Those who did not understand took the cause to be the meat, but those who understood knew it was because of the [breach of] *li*. Hence even with Confucius, he was willing to depart on account of a small offense but was unwilling to set off improperly. Indeed, the common man cannot understand the doings of the True Prince![13]

Now, in 5B1, the sobriquet "sage of timeliness" is given Confucius on the basis of the following conflicting action choices: "When Confucius quit the state of Qi, he set off without waiting to cook the rice he had washed. When he left Lu, he said, 'I shall go slowly' (such being the way to depart the state of one's parents)."[14] In 6B6, however, the facts in Lu have been altered, apparently to fit Mencius' case, and were we to accept this account, the basis given in 5B1 for Confucius' canonization would be removed.[15] In 4B30 we see ethical doctrine subordinated to rationalizing casuistry; in 6B6 we see factual consistency undermined. In passages such as these, it seems clear that defense of Mencius and the exemplars associated with his tradition holds priority over issues of fact and theory for the authors, and this is a major source of problems that emerge when attempts are made to delineate coherent structures governing the ideas of the *Mencius*.

We should note also that casuistic discourse in the *Mencius* bears an ambiguous relation to the intuitionist theory for which the text is best known. Theoretical casuistry, the doctrine that perfected moral wisdom entails rule-transcending case sensitivity, fits well with assertions that our moral responses are innate and spontaneous; passages of interpretive casuistry generally align well with theoretical casuistry and intuitionist theory. However, passages in which we encounter rationalizing casuistry frequently seem disengaged from this realm of discourse. For example,

> There was famine in Qi. Chen Zhen said, "The people of the state all believe that you will bring about a second distribution from the Tang granary, Master. But isn't such a distribution unlikely?" Mencius replied, "This would be like Feng Fu. In Jin there was once a certain Feng Fu, who excelled at wrestling tigers. Later he became a model

gentleman.[16] But one day, upon traveling in the countryside, he came upon a crowd that had pursued a tiger and penned it against a hillside, where no one dared attack it. Seeing Feng Fu, the crowd rushed to meet him. Feng Fu rolled up his sleeves and dismounted his carriage. The people were all delighted, but the gentlemen present laughed." (7B23)

While this passage suggests Mencius' skill at literary repartee and sophisticated understanding of the role of the courtier, which naturally entails "timeliness" in perceiving the limits of what one may achieve in the context of the court, against the background of starving people looking for a moral hero, Mencius' cool wit seems to emanate from a moral universe remote from that of the sage responding to the imperatives of the moral senses.

Understanding the Sage through Literary Imagination—Discourses on Shun

The most extended case of interpretive casuistry that the text attributes to Mencius is his discussion of the legendary emperor Shun. Among the various moral exemplars discussed in the *Mencius,* Shun is unique in serving as a detailed portrait of a sage who simply has no history of alienation from his moral responses and so, in a very real sense, has "never lost his infant heart." To the degree that we take the text as reflecting the ideas of the historical Mencius, Shun appears to have been central to Mencius' own ethical imagination. We will use the case of Shun as an extended illustration of the *verstehen* methodology of the *Mencius'* ethics of character.

In the first four passages of the *Wan Zhang* chapter, the *Mencius* addresses a series of problems concerning the legend of Shun. In each case, the problem that is raised concerns apparent contradictions between Shun's conduct and proper rules. One by one, Mencius demonstrates that in cases where we might find Shun's actions contrary to the models of sagehood we might anticipate, the reason is that we have not powerfully imagined the nature of a pure heart.

In 5A1, the disciple Wan Zhang 萬章 questions how a sage such as Shun could have cried out to Heaven in agony over his parents' immorality and hatred. He cites a rule, "If your parents hate you, just work and don't complain," and then asks, "Didn't Shun complain?" Mencius does not dispute the fact, but his response challenges the appropriateness of interpreting Shun's behavior in terms of rules. The salient fact about Shun is the depth of his love for his parents, a feature of character. Despite the fact that he had attained in the world every good of wealth, pleasure, and esteem that could be imagined, nothing could repair the primal wound of unrequited love for parents. Wan Zhang's challenge to Shun is launched on the level of normal rules for ordinary people; the response to the challenge is to illustrate how Shun was morally extraordinary.

In 5A2, Wan Zhang first addresses the contradiction between Shun's reputed filiality and the report that he married without asking his parents' permission. Mencius responds that Shun acted as he did because, knowing that in their hatred of him his parents would never allow him to marry, he realized that were he to conform to the rules of filiality, his love of his parents would be poisoned by resentment. Thus he acted to preserve the purity of his loving response to his parents. What I want to underscore in this extraordinary answer is the manner of thought that it appears to represent. Unless there existed at this time a version of the Shun legend that stipulated precisely this motive, then either Mencius or the author of this passage has allowed an imaginative reconstruction of Shun's psychology to detect in the persona of this sage motives that will explain his actions consistent with the prime feature of his legendary character: that despite the greatest of challenges, he never lost full awareness of the strength of his love of parents.[17]

What licenses the *Mencius* to elaborate Shun's thinking in this way? Clearly, Mencius is portrayed as possessing insight into who Shun actually was, insight that others did not have. Passage 5A2 continues by posing the question whether, in light of the legendary account that Shun asked his brother Xiang 象 to join him in governing the state only moments after Xiang had attempted to assassinate him, Shun was ignorant of his brother's designs. Mencius denies that Shun was ignorant and maintains instead that he was guided by a perfect brotherly love that aligned his own responses of pleasure and care with Xiang's. As in the case of filial feelings, such innate patterns of affective response in Shun remained undisturbed by events in the world. Wan Zhang is unable to see the possibility of such alignment of feelings prevailing in such circumstances and asks whether Shun's projection of pleasure on his brother's behalf was not, in fact, feigned. Mencius again reads the heart of Shun and determines that, in the instance under examination, the operative fact was that Xiang, despite his consternation at seeing Shun alive, had addressed him in a brotherly manner, and it was this to which Shun intuitively responded in offering to share his empire with Xiang.

The subsequent two passages deal with the manner in which Shun resolved conflicts between his familial feelings and political duties. They employ similar strategies of inventing a psychology for this legendary figure that will keep him aligned with ethical perfection. The ultimate instance of this occurs outside the *Wan Zhang* chapter.

> Tao Ying asked, "When Shun was Son of Heaven and Gao Yao was Minister of Crime, had [Shun's father] Gu Sou killed a man, what would have been done?"
>
> Mencius answered, "Gu Sou would have been apprehended, that's all."
>
> "Then, Shun would not have prevented it?"
>
> "How could he have prevented it? It would have been Gao Yao's mandate."
>
> "Well, then, what would Shun have done?"
>
> Mencius replied, "Shun would have viewed casting off the empire like casting off a worn-out shoe. He would secretly have borne his father on his back and fled until he came to dwell by the shores of the sea. There he would have lived in joyful contentment, having forgotten the empire." (7A35)

Here we can have no doubt that Mencius has been authorized not merely to transmit but to re-create the legend of Shun. The reasoning in this passage goes beyond a balancing of conflicting loyalties to duty on the one hand and to family on the other and reaches an act of literary creativity. We can only infer from the manner of casuistry in these passages concerning Shun that the "case" from which Mencius argues in each instance is not the unique context of events being proposed but the uniquely imagined character of Shun, to whose *zhi,* or inmost orientation of intent, Mencius, as his re-creator, has unique access.

If we view Shun as a "lineage ancestor" in whose perfection the *Mencius* has some stake, then much of the text's treatment of Shun may be viewed as rationalizing casuistry—certainly there are inconsistencies of fact and a certain distortion of doctrine in these accounts of Shun, which raise filiality to an absolute criterion. However, the empathetic imagination that animates these passages makes it more cogent to view them as sincere attempts on the part of Mencius or of the authors to make personal sense of Shun's reported ethical extremism.[18] A more complex mix of casuistic motives appears to characterize the treatment of the moral exemplar most central to the text's concerns—Mencius himself.

The Character of Mencius

The casuistic discussions of Shun in the *Mencius* reflect a quest for understanding of sage character that operates on an aesthetic plane divorced from ethical theory. The importance and complexity of this mode of discourse is best observed in the text's account of Mencius himself, which constitutes the most detailed and nuanced biographical portrait in ancient Chinese literature. The centrality to the text of Mencius the man is reflected in the extended narrative descriptions we are provided, but more importantly in the space devoted to Mencius' own casuistic rationalizations of his often questionable behavior. Many of these defensive rationalizations represent arguments so weak and obviously self-serving that they lead us to wonder whether, for the authors of the text, that Mencius could err was so far beyond possibility that they could not conceive the need to tailor their presentation of his words and conduct.

I will argue instead that the shape of the narratives suggests that the authors wished to highlight problematic and idiosyncratic features of Mencius' behavior precisely because these convey his uniqueness as a person and provide access to his character, which, for the authors, represented the closest approach to perfect sagehood in living memory, a memory that the *Mencius* itself is dedicated to preserving.

In its most lyrical passage, 2A2, the *Mencius* offers us a detailed portrait of Mencius' psychology, in which it is made clear that Mencius belongs to a rare breed of men who have gained control over and focused their *zhi*. Mencius is pictured as a warrior for righteousness, whose force of energy (*qi* 氣) is under the firm command of its general, the *zhi*, which remains in unified alignment with the *dao* of righteousness (*yi* 義). This firm grasp of a moral compass, the product of long training, has made Mencius' heart-mind impervious to potentially destabilizing situational influences. This imperturbable focal alignment with the right is reflected in this Mencian formula: "The great man will not necessarily keep his word nor see his course of action through. With him, there is only righteousness" (4A11, echoing *Analects* 4.10). The *Mencius'* portrait of the Master is thus very close in kind to the exemplary model of Confucius. Like Confucius, we can expect Mencius to be a sage without rules, one who merely responds to the unique situations of real life by means of his unwavering attentiveness to his recovered innate sense of *yi*.

At its time of composition, the *Mencius* may have been as much a tribute to Mencius' outstanding public career as to his ideas. A great deal of the text is taken up with accounts of Mencius' unusual career, and there are many occasions when Mencius is called upon to explain his actions. At each of these junctures, the real Mencius most likely articulated a variety of self-justifications of varying intellectual and ethical quality. Part of the authorial intent of the *Mencius,* I mean to argue, was to preserve these moments of Mencius' political and intellectual biography without particular regard for their philosophical or ethical coherence. In these facets of the *Mencius,* Mencius himself, the real man, is the point of the book, the object of inquiry for readers seeking access to the character of a great man.

The large body of casuistic material concerning Mencius precludes a full survey here. I propose instead to illustrate how the text approaches these issues by focusing on two long passages, both of which concern how Mencius justified the position he took early in his career that the *junzi* 君子 (gentleman, true prince) does not seek an audience with a potential employer—a feudal lord—until that lord has demonstrated recognition of the superiority of the *junzi* by seeking an audience with *him.*

Casuistry concerning Mencius' Policy of "Not Visiting the Feudal Lords"

In a number of passages, Mencius is asked to explain his rigid adherence to the policy of "not visiting the feudal lords," in light of the good that could be achieved were he to reach a position of influence by offering service. The most extensive of these passages is 5B7, which I will consider by sections.

> Wan Zhang said, "May I ask how your not visiting the feudal lords accords with right (*yi*)?" Mencius replied, "Those who dwell within the walls of the state are called subjects of the marketplace; those who dwell beyond are called subjects of the wilds. These are all com-

moners, and according to *li,* commoners do not undertake to gain audience with their lord without having first conveyed the requisite gift." Wan Zhang said, "As for commoners, when they are summoned to corvée service, they go. When their lord wishes to have them appear in audience and summons them to do so, how is it that they do not appear?" Mencius replied, "To go to fulfill one's corvée service is right. To go to appear in audience is not right. . . ."

The latter part of this section indicates that the situation at issue is not merely that Mencius is according with the rule of not visiting lords but that he is holding to that rule even after having been summoned to do so by the ruler. Wan Zhang questions the grounds for Mencius' apparent disobedience, and Mencius responds that to visit the lord would contravene ritual *li* 禮, because he has not submitted the required token of allegiance. Why he has not done so emerges in the following section, which begins by continuing Mencius' reply.

"Moreover, for what reason would a ruler wish to have such a man appear?" Wan Zhang said, "Because he has broad learning or because he is worthy." Mencius replied, "If it were a case of broad learning, then even the Son of Heaven would not send a summons to a teacher, much less a feudal lord! If the man were a worthy, then I have yet to hear of a lord who, wishing to see such a man, sent him a summons."

We learn here that Mencius' initial account for refusing to respond to the lord's summons—that Mencius had not fulfilled the prior *li* required of a man of commoner status—was a pretext. The actual reason was that the lord had violated the *li* due to a man esteemed as a teacher or worthy. This latter objection is indeed Mencius' basic position on this issue wherever it surfaces in the book. Here, after citing the authoritative example of Zisi, who rebuffed his lord for failing to maintain the proprieties between ruler and great man, Mencius continues his reply by citing an example endorsed by Confucius.

"Once, when Duke Jing of Qi was out hunting, he summoned his gamekeeper with a pennant. The gamekeeper did not come, and the duke was on the verge of executing him. 'A warrior of firm intent (*zhi*) never forgets, even if it means dying in a ditch; a warrior of valor never forgets, even if it means losing his head.' What did Confucius draw from this? That if one is not properly summoned, one should not go."[19]

Mencius goes on to note that a ruler's inappropriate conduct toward a gamekeeper is far less serious than the inappropriate conduct that Mencius, as a worthy, has been subjected to, and he thereby intensifies the justification for stubborn adherence to this rule. Finally, he concludes his reply with an appeal to general ethical values.

> "One who wishes to see a worthy but who does not employ the *dao* for this is like one who wishes to enter but closes the gate. Righteousness is the road, and *li* is the gate. Only a *junzi* can proceed along this road and go in and out through this gate!"

This position effectively requires that any ruler with whom Mencius would find it acceptable to meet would need already to be a *junzi*, a man himself well along the way toward sagehood. To reach this position, Mencius has adduced a combination of authoritative rules and authoritative exemplars. He has interpreted these as expressions of ethical intuitions that pertain on the most universal level, *li* and yi being among the four moral senses. The passage ends with this exchange.

> Wan Zhang said, "It is said of Confucius, 'When his lord sent a summons, he did not await the harnessing of the chariot to be on his way.' Do you mean to say that Confucius was wrong?" Mencius replied, "Confucius was then in service. Having assumed the duties of office, he was summoned in accord with his office."

Here Mencius turns aside an authoritative counterexample by asserting that it applied to periods of Confucius' life in which the context was fundamentally different from that in which Mencius was acting.[20]

It is the rigidity of rule adherence that is most striking in 5B7. One might expect, in light of 2A2, that a man of Mencius' confident *zhi* would feel that this particular rule could be engaged with flexibility—after all, Mencius' position appears to require that rulers acknowledge his own moral authority before meeting him. But Mencius is, indeed, inflexible. In a closely related passage, 3B1, where another disciple suggests that Mencius employ expedient means to engage a ruler's attention, Mencius explicitly rejects the suggestion. Responding to the disciple's use of the metaphor, "Bend a foot to straighten a rod," Mencius replies, "Never yet has there been one who could straighten others by bending himself."[21]

Mencius here has raised to the level of a critical test a ruler's willingness to debase himself before Mencius' reputation. Only such a man could be a *junzi*, with the potential to make use of Mencius and truly do the world some good. In the terms of analysis I have been using, Mencius holds stubbornly to this rule as the key to revealing the *zhi* of those with whom he might associate, were he to take the risks of political engagement.[22] Unless we adopt an interpretation along these lines, it would be difficult to defend Mencius against the charge of extremism in rule-based action. In a sense, Mencius has shifted the burden of moral action from himself to the ruler; only if the ruler conforms to the proper rules of engaging a worthy will Mencius respond.

In 2B2, the second passage I want to consider in detail here, we find ourselves in a context where Mencius, for reasons nowhere detailed, has previously determined that it would be appropriate to appear in audience with the king of Qi, and that he has done so on numerous occasions.[23] The passage begins with a narrative.

> Mencius was about to set off for court in Qi when a message arrived from the king saying, "I had intended to pay you a visit, but I have caught a chill and cannot venture into the morning air. I do not know whether you will allow me to see you." Mencius responded, "Unfortunately, I am ill and cannot go to court."

It will become clear later in the passage that Mencius interprets the king's message as a summons. Although he was himself preparing to go see the king, what he objects to here is the summons itself, which is what a lord must never issue to a teacher or worthy, even when phrased as an apology, as in this case. Thus, although 2B2 is not a context that engages the rule for not first visiting lords, it does engage the rule for not responding to an improper summons.

How are we to evaluate the fact that Mencius is portrayed as intentionally lying? I think that a normal reading strategy would see Mencius as employing a vehicle of etiquette, a white lie, in a manner reflective of the king's use, so as to avoid saying something abrasive while resisting an attack on principle. However, the manner in which the narrative develops indicates that we are to give unusual weight to Mencius' act of lying.

> The following day, Mencius was setting off to pay a call of condolence at the Dongguo estate. Gongsun Chou said, "Yesterday you excused yourself on the grounds of illness, but today you are off to pay a condolence call. Is this not, perhaps, inappropriate?" "Yesterday I was

ill," replied Mencius. "Today I'm better. Why shouldn't I pay a call of condolence?"

The king sent a messenger to ask after Mencius, and a doctor followed. Meng Zhongzi replied to the messenger, "Yesterday when the king's order came, the Master was suffering from a minor complaint and was unable to go to court. Today, his illness being somewhat better, he has hurried to court, but I am unsure whether he will actually be able to get there."

A number of men were sent to intercept Mencius. "Please by all means do not return home, but go directly to court!" But in the end, Mencius had no alternative but to go spend the night at the estate of Jing Chou.

The key exchange, in my view, is that between Gongsun Chou 公孫丑 and Mencius. Without that exchange—which could be omitted without damage to the narrative—this interesting account of Mencius' misadventure would locate the principal fault with the follower Meng Zhongzi, who invents an unnecessary lie that, for reasons only partially clear, forces Mencius to take refuge with a local patron. But Mencius' reply to Gongsun Chou opens a very different window. Mencius' remark is ironic, a clear show of disrespect for the ruler, exhibited both to Gongsun Chou and to us. Mencius and Gongsun Chou know that Mencius was not, in fact, ill, but Mencius is playing with his lie, showing how an extension of it can be invented, should his actions be discovered. As Meng Zhongzi's conduct indicates, the force of Gongsun Chou's remark was not the question of whether Mencius could get better in a day; it concerned the appropriateness of setting off on an activity that did not further respond to the surface graciousness of the king's initial message. Mencius' response is, in effect, to say, "What further claim of courtesy does the ruler have on me?"

The issue of disrespect becomes the focus of the latter sections of the narrative, when Mencius' host, Jing Chou 景丑, upbraids him for his conduct. "I have seen the king show respect toward you," he says, "but I have yet to see you show respect toward the king." Mencius initially responds with a sophistic argument, to the effect that he alone treats the king with respect, because he alone treats the king as worthy of listening to moral preachments. Jing Chou recognizes that Mencius has distorted the meaning of his reproach.

"No, I'm not talking about that. The *Li* says, 'When one's father summons, do not put him off with delaying assent. When one's lord summons, do not wait for the chariot to be harnessed.' Now, your intent was originally to go to court, but once having heard that it was a command from the king, you did not follow through. One can only judge this to be a contravention of the *Li*."

The author of this passage has gone to great lengths to place Mencius in a tight spot. He has gratuitously revealed Mencius' cavalier attitude toward the king. He has prevented him from evading the obvious point of Jing Chou's initial question with self-serving moralizing, and he has focused the issue on precisely the imperative that Wan Zhang raised at the close of 5B7, the ritual show of promptness that is due from a subject to his lord.

Mencius, in a long closing speech, veers among several possible responses. Initially, he invokes the authority of Zengzi, whom he quotes picturing his *ren* and *yi* as of greater worthiness than the wealth and rank of great rulers—"How could Zengzi say this if it were not right?" Then he proceeds to reason that there are three standards for respect: rank, age, and virtue; given that, on these counts, he outscores the king two to one, the king has no business treating Mencius with disrespect. Finally he returns to the rule that a worthy lord does not summon a worthy man.

> Thus it is that a ruler who will achieve great things inevitably has ministers he does not summon. When he wishes to consult with them, he goes to see them. If a ruler's respect of virtue and joy in the *dao* is not of this kind, then he is inadequate to achieve anything worthwhile.... Today the world is divided into territories of similar size with rulers of comparable virtue. That no one of them can prevail over the others is due only to one factor: rulers like appointing those whom they can teach and dislike appointing those from whom they can learn. The way Tang treated Yi Yin and Duke Huan treated Guan Zhong, they would not have dared to summon them. If even Guan Zhong could not be summoned, how much less so one who would not deign to be a Guan Zhong!

Once again, Mencius shifts the burden of action off his own shoulders and onto the ruler's. Mencius' interpretation of this entire incident is that he is free of any obligation until the ruler proves his worthiness. But here, more clearly than in any other passage, the narrative has been designed to emphasize all those aspects that work against our crediting Mencius' arguments and that push us toward a judgment that what we see in Mencius' various responses throughout this tale is "rationalizing casuistry": attempts to hide motives, rationalize actions, and exculpate oneself not just by means of weak arguments but by one weak argument after another. Given that this narrative could easily have been designed in another way or omitted altogether, it seems legitimate to ask why it was written as it was.

The simplest answer, and I think the correct one, is that it was written this way because its purpose was not to promote the arguments Mencius offers but to tell the story, which is one of the most lifelike in the book. As in many narrative sections of the *Mencius,* the principal interest of the authors is clearly in Mencius the real person rather than in the authoritative teachings of Mencius.[24] What the text seems to be sketching, in its often unflattering or ambiguous accounts of Mencius' actions and his rationalizing casuistry, is a multifaceted portrait of Mencius that can reveal to us who he really was, that is, his *zhi.* In this respect, the goals of the *Mencius* are principally literary goals, best understood through readings that are sensitive to the literary qualities that have shaped the narrative.

Such an approach applies less readily to passages that are aphoristic than to those that are narrative, and I do not mean to offer it as a key to understanding all aspects of the text. Neither do I want to deny the interest and importance of moral theory and Confucian political doctrine to Mencius the person and to the *Mencius.* I do, however, wish to claim that such interests are generally subordinate to literary ones where biographical elements of the text are concerned and that it is a fundamental error to view Mencius' words in such passages, which comprise a very substantial portion of the text, as uttered, recorded, or invented with any intent for theoretical consistency. This is not to say that these speeches are not in many cases theoretically interesting or reflective of moral and social insight—the Mencius we meet in this text is a rich individual whom it is edifying to know. But casuistic statements we hear him make are generally shaped to respond to the case, not to fit a general architecture of ethical theory.

Theoretical Casuistry as a Theme of Mencius' Biography

As noted earlier, the career of Mencius was unorthodox, and tendentiously so. The various twists in his public path gave rise to a wide variety of attacks on his actions and character; a complete inventory is well beyond the scope of this essay. Besides casuistic responses concerning the issue of visiting the lords (central to 3B1, 3B7, and 4A17, in addition to the passages analyzed above), two issues connected with Mencius' career seem particularly fruitful in generating ethical ideas in the form of casuistic responses to explicit or implicit criticism. They involve the proper grounds for accepting and ethically exploiting official position (2A1, 2B8, 2B12, 2B14, 6B6, 7B17, 7B23) and the appropriateness of accepting or refusing patronage gifts without holding office (2B3, 3B4, 5B6, 6B5).[25] There are, in addition, a range of challenges encountered only once or twice, as well as challenges to Mencius' private conduct and treatment of students.

So frequently is Mencius pictured defending his actions to an uncomprehending audience that he seems the image of the inscrutable sage, a man who has simply achieved a moral perspective beyond the reach of ethical common sense. In this regard, we may recall that Mencius' self-justifying casuistry invokes the example of Confucius to link Mencius with the rule-transcending timeliness that characterizes ultimate sagehood.[26] Mencius' defense of his behavior accordingly aligns his rationalizing casuistry with theoretical casuistry in a way that insulates him from negative judgment.

The Priority of the Search for Character

Although among ancient texts the *Mencius* may provide the most compelling example of what I am terming an ethics of character, in this respect the *Mencius* is one of a number of Confucian texts that seem to share this common enterprise to varying degrees. These texts share a central interest in probing the *zhi* of individuals through narratives that reconstruct the contexts of their actions or their words.

The most obvious of these may be the *Analects,* which seems as interested in the complex character of Confucius as in his explicit teachings. A more self-consciously formulaic example would be the *Gongyang* 公羊 tradition of *Chunqiu* exegesis, which extracts from the Lu court chronicles Confucius' supposed lexical hints of how the contours of intention (*zhi*) and action may be distinguished and evaluated.[27] Schools of *Shijing* exegesis that draw on the prefaces associated with the tradition of the Confucian disciple Zixia 子夏 also focused on hermeneutic strategies for revealing the intent of the poets, which was conceived as the ultimate level of moral meaning in the text.[28] Both the *Gongyang* and "Zixia" *Shi* schools shared a position that the words of the texts were merely gateways to the hearts of those who had embedded in them moral meanings and to the hearts of those whose actions and character were under scrutiny.[29] To employ these texts for moral self-cultivation and understanding required special reading strategies that would bypass the words and reveal the intentions of these sage writers.

It is in the *Mencius* that we first encounter such theories of these two texts. The theory that Confucius embedded in the *Chunqiu* a hidden code to guide readers past mere words to moral truth is twice reported in the *Mencius* (3B9, 4B21). Elsewhere, Mencius cautions a disciple against a literalist reading of the *Shi:* "One who explicates the *Shi* must not let the written characters distort the sense of the words they represent and must not let those words distort the poet's intent (*zhi*). One's own thoughts should meet the intent halfway; in this way, the meaning will be grasped" (5A4).

This textual hermeneutic, which asserts that we can get past words into the hearts of those who wrote the words if we can locate our level of attention beyond that of words, finds a parallel in the *Mencius'* approach to understanding people. Rather than trust their words, Mencius tells us to look them in the eyes: "Nothing is more authentic in a person than the pupils of his eyes.... Listening to his words, watch the pupils of his eyes—where can he hide?" (4A16; cf. *Analects* 2.10). Elsewhere, Mencius asserts that he is able not only to be undeluded by defective acts of speech but also to be able to see past the words and diagnose through them the defects of the speaker: "Biased words—I know what deludes them. Profligate words—I know what entraps them. Wayward words—I know what they stray from. Refractory words—I know what exhausts them" (2A2).[30] Ultimately, this level of ethical inquiry seems devoted to the cultivation of a sagely eye that can read character out of words and actions even if they are designed for self-concealment, or if their apparent contours belie the intent that generates them. This is the sagely eye that allows Mencius to penetrate the character of the "unfilial" Kuang Zhang, and allows careful readers of the *Mencius* to uncover the character of the text's protagonist.[31]

Gratuitous Casuistry and Mencius' Personality

In closing, I would like to discuss briefly a passage, one of a pair, in which casuistry is employed ironically, as a particularly subtle way of illuminating Mencius' character. In 4B6, Mencius utters this aphorism: "Rituals that contravene ritual, righteousness that contravenes righteousness: the great man does not engage in these."

Here, Mencius distances himself from those who would employ "semblances" of propriety to achieve ends skewed to the moral import of *li* and *yi*.[32] Yet in a passage not far removed in the book, we read the following account of Mencius' conduct.

> Gong Hangzi lost his son, and the Marshall of the Right went to pay his respects. When he entered the gate, some of those present went up to speak with him, while others went to speak with him after he took his seat. Mencius did not speak with him. The Marshall was displeased. "All the other gentlemen spoke with me," he said, "only Mencius did not. This was a slight to me." Mencius heard of this and said, "According to ritual, one neither cuts across the place of others in order to engage in talk or ascends from one's proper step to engage in bows. My desire was to act in accord with ritual. Zi-ao took me to be slighting him! Strange, is it not?" (4B27)

On a surface level, Mencius' response is problematic. We know from other passages (4A25) that Mencius disapproved of the Marshall of the Right, Wang Huan 王驩 (Zi-ao)—there even exists a second passage in which Mencius snubs him in a similar manner[33] —so why should Mencius be astonished at Wang Huan's response here? Moreover, Mencius justifies his behavior on the basis of a court ritual, but the event in question occurred not at court but at a private gathering. Are we to believe that Mencius is so doltish that he cannot grasp how, in light of his relations with Wang Huan, this sort of adherence to a rule of court etiquette, in a context that seems unsuited to rules of court, would give offense?

No reader sensitive to literary nuance could think so. It is plain to see that Mencius is employing rationalizing casuistry, and the unmistakable clue is Mencius' feigned astonishment. We are not meant to take Mencius' casuistry seriously; it is an ironic sneer at Wang Huan, spoken in the same voice in which, in 2B2, Mencius snapped off to Gongsun Chou his dismissal of the king of Qi.[34] Mencius is tendentiously violating the rule he utters in 4B6, distorting *li* and *yi* for counterpurposes in order to express his disdain for the buffoonish Wang Huan. But the interest of the passage lies precisely in the revelation that Mencius would do this—that he would adopt a sly subversiveness in order to engage humor in the service of expressing ethical judgment. It is passages like these that convey how interesting Mencius, the near-sage, must have been. His vividness of character, or perhaps the authors' vivid reimagining of Mencius' character, disrupts the theoretical coherence of the *Mencius'* ethics but creates new avenues of literary experience that may be as germane to the Confucian ethical enterprise. If this is so, then the principle of the *Mencius'* authors would align closely with that attributed by the *Gongyang* tradition to Confucius, who is reported to have said of his editing of the *Chunqiu,* "I believed that rather than revealing [the heart-mind of the True King] through empty words, it would be more deeply penetrating to illustrate it through action and event."[35]

Notes

1. Although the theory of innate moral senses is basically intuitionist, the *Mencius* pictures these senses in competition with innate amoral dispositions that tend to be magnified by environment and habit, at the expense of our sensitivity to moral impulses. Mencian intuitionism provides important roles for rules and moral exemplars, which help train us to recapture sensitivity to our moral intuitions.

2. In this discussion, I use the term *verstehen* (understanding) in the technical sense accorded it by Wilhelm Dilthey, as a humanistic type of empathetic understanding of (for our purposes) a historical individual's life experience, derived through extensive study of social environment and personal biography. On this sense of *verstehen,* see Dilthey, *Pattern and Meaning in History* (New York: Harper, 1962), especially the introduction by H.P. Rickman, 37–43.

3. I mean in this project to challenge two important studies of the *Mencius:* Kwong-Loi Shun's analysis of the architecture of the text's ethical doctrine (*Mencius and Early Chinese Thought* [Stanford, Calif.: Stanford University Press, 1997]), without question the most sophisticated attempt to approach a description of Mencian ethics as coherent, and Lee Yearley's interpretation of the *Mencius* in light of Aristotelian categories of virtue ethics (*Mencius and Aquinas* [Albany: State University of New York Press, 1990]), which throws light on important dimensions of moral discourse in the text. Without wishing to dispute the achievements of these studies, my claim is that major facets of the *Mencius* address an agenda significantly skewed to their lines of analysis.

4. The italics convey the heightened rhetoric of the close. Translations are my own, but I have particularly benefited by consulting D.C. Lau, *Mencius* (Harmondsworth: Penguin Books, 1979), and Yang Bojun 楊伯峻, *Mengzi yizhu* 孟子譯注. All references to both the *Mencius* and the *Analects* are according to Harvard-Yenching concordance numbers.

5. The details of Kuang Zhang's dispute with his father may be indicated in an account in the *Zhanguo ce,* which speaks of a Zhangzi's father's having killed his mother and buried her under his stables (see Lau, who notes the problems with matching the two accounts, [*Mencius,* 212–213]). Mencius elsewhere comments on the unsuitability of disputes over right conduct between father and son (4A19).

6. Elsewhere, Bo Yi and Liuxia Hui form a set of two, independent of

Yi Yin, as in 2A9 and 7B15. The phrases rendered here appear also in the latter passage, and they may have been imported into 5B1 at a late stage of editing, accounting for the lack of a parallel formula for Yi Yin. *Analects* 18.8 is parallel to 5B1.

7. Commentary is unhelpful on the most difficult aspects of this passage. In light of the conclusion of the passage, I take it that Shenyou Xing's tale indicates that whereas the followers did not become involved, Zengzi did, thus fulfilling the role of a teacher, who is surrogate family to his student. The contrasting behaviors would have indicated to Shenyou Xing, who was aware of both cases, that Zengzi did not follow a general rule of disengagement but rather followed rules that shifted according to role. Alternatively, the point may be that neither Zengzi nor his followers intervened, and this was so because they were not family members, whereas in the earlier example Zengzi was attending to his familial role (and hence unconcerned with political effects his act might have).

8. I take *fuxiong* 父兄 to refer to the role of senior member of an extended family and have translated Zengzi's remark at the outset as spoken in this role.

9. I suspect, on the basis of parallelism, that a contrastive example in the Zisi story, in which his low status is stressed, has been dropped from the current text account. If so, this sentence should read, "Zisi was an officer [in the one instance] and possessed no status [in the other]."

10. The final phrase occurs also in 4B29, which is consistent with the fact that 4B29–4B31 appear to be a text unit devoted to issues of close casuistic analysis (a major theme of the *Li Lou* chapter in general).

11. The attribution of a single *dao* standpoint to several sages who respond incommensurably due to differences of context and role is also a theme of 4B29.

12. 5A7–5A9 dispose of malicious legends concerning exemplary figures by invoking generalizable character traits that capture these men and by imagining a line of compromise they would not cross.

13. Mencius' resignation from Qi was a consequence of Qi's invasion of the state of Yan. Mencius did not resign immediately, however, deeming it inappropriate in a time of war (2B14). Although the text nowhere specifies that Mencius ultimately resigned upon a pretext, the use of Confucius' example as part of the response in 6B6 suggests that this was so.

14. In 7B17, nearly identical phrasing adds the comment that Confucius' departure from Qi was "the way to depart the state of another."

15. The celebration of timeliness in 5B1 seems itself designed, in part, to legitimize Mencius' political conduct through rationalizing casuistry. Mencius' conduct in Qi departed from Confucian norms that discouraged office holding under rulers who were not themselves ethical. Mencius rationalizes his actions on the basis of timeliness (2A1, 2B13).

16. This translation is unsatisfactory, but it appears there is a defect in the text, and I have found no better solution.

17. Note that in 4A26, Shun's reason is quite different. There Mencius tells us that his concern was that, in denying him permission to marry, his par-

ents would force him to commit the act of greatest unfiliality, having no descendants. Shun's calculus in 4A26 is somewhat more utilitarian (and less interesting) than in 5A2.

18. In an earlier version of this analysis, I treated casuistic analyses of Confucius as similarly dominated by interpretive motives. But the degree to which Confucius stands as a practical proxy for Mencius in connection with political behavior has led me to conclude that there is less imaginative probing for Confucius' character than use of him as a legitimizing model.

19. The text also appears in 3B1. The tale of the gamekeeper is found in *Zuozhuan*, Zhao 20, along with commentary attributed to Confucius. Note that Mencius' interpretation of the tale is insensitive to distinctions concerning issues of relative status in the gamekeeper's case and his own (the gamekeeper did not *presume;* Mencius does not *deign*).

20. This is not inconsistent with *Analects* 10.14, where this characterization of Confucius also appears. The line of reasoning here concerns role-appropriate conduct, as discussed earlier.

21. Here we can hear echoes of the lesson Mencius teaches when he rejects scandalous gossip about Yi Yin, Confucius, and Boli Xi 百里奚 in 5A7–5A9. If these men had been willing to demean themselves, it would have been a sign that they could not have been sages at all ("wherein would Confucius have been Confucius?"), and thus their moral authority and transformative power would have been lost. Mencius seems here to be establishing his credentials by drawing a line that he will not cross, though the stakes seem much lower than in the 5A examples.

22. In the *Mencius,* we do see several rulers make the unusual (though not unheard of) gesture of leaving the palace to meet with Mencius (King Hui of Liang in 1A1, King Xuan of Qi in 2B10), but it would be hard to say that the events recorded in the *Mencius* confirm that these men possessed the moral qualities that Mencius believed such a gesture would reveal. Duke Wen of Teng, who visited Mencius as a crown prince, would seem to be a different type of case.

23. The commentator Zhao Qi assumes that Mencius has taken office in Qi, but it may equally be that he has simply been received as a guest "persuader," as was the case, for example, in Liang.

24. Jeffrey Riegel, in an article on 2A2, has noted the sharpness with which Gongsun Chou questions Mencius in the text, and Riegel suggests that this is because Gongsun Chou was not a disciple. I think that what Riegel has spotted is, in fact, a thematic characteristic of the text, which seems willing to probe Mencius in ways that would seem inappropriate were the authorial intent one of canonization rather than of interpretive biography. Riegel, "Reflections on an Unmoved Mind: An Analysis of *Mencius* 2A2," in *Studies in Classical Chinese Thought*, ed. Henry Rosemont Jr. and Benjamin I. Schwartz (*Journal of the American Academy of Religion* 47.3, Thematic Issue S [1980]: 450).

25. It is interesting to note that two issues that recur in these discussions, lack of activism in advising rulers and inconsistent behavior with regard to gifts, are central to the attack on the person of Confucius in the *Mozi*'s "Fei ru" 非儒 chapter.

26. This was discussed in relation to a criticism of Mencius' lack of accomplishment as an official in Qi in 6B6. That challenge was leveled by Shunyu Kun 淳于髡, who, ironically, traps Mencius on just this issue in 4A17, critiquing him for lack of flexibility in his rigid refusal to meet with feudal lords. Mencius' intransigence is contrasted with his own description of "balancing" (*quan* 權), that is, employing one's acute moral eye to discern the imperatives of context when rules give conflicting answers.

27. The importance of the distinction between *zhi* and rule-described act to *Gongyang* exegesis and its Han period political applications have recently been explored by Sarah Queen, in her *From Chronicle to Canon* (Cambridge: Cambridge University Press, 1997). This general interest is equally evident in certain narratives included in the *Zuozhuan* (which frequently form the background of *Gongyang* exegesis) and in the *Zuo*'s inserted *junzi yue* 君子曰 commentary sections. It should be noted that the *Mencius* and the *Gongyang* are additionally linked in characterizing moral action in terms of rule-breaking acts of "balancing" (*quan;* see *Gongyang,* Huan 11).

28. This is explored at length by Stephen Van Zoeren in *Poetry and Personality* (Stanford, Calif.: Stanford University Press, 1991).

29. Similar interests permeate the *Analects,* both in terms of its general interest in the issue of discerning the *zhi* of others and more particularly in its interest in the person of Confucius.

30. I take the repeated pronoun *qi* 其 (them) to refer to the speakers. I differ from Kwong-Loi Shun (*Mencius,* 116) in interpreting *ci* 辭 as "words" rather than "teachings" here, noting parallels in the way that the complementary word *yan* 言, which may indeed mean "teachings," is employed in 4A16. Shun is correct that, within the context of 2A2, "teachings" is a viable reading.

31. Clearly, not all Confucian texts are devoted to this concern. The *Xunzi,* for example, is thoroughly devoted to systematizing doctrine, and neither Xunzi nor any other exemplary figure is offered to the reader as a subject for empathetic *verstehen.* The same is true for the earlier Confucian texts recently excavated at Guodian 郭店, suggesting that, even in Mencius' time, texts exploring an ethics of character represented only one of several Confucian approaches.

32. Adopting Lee Yearley's useful terminology (see *Mencius and Aquinas,* esp. 67–72).

33. 2B6. It seems unlikely that there were two such incidents, and the common element of a funeral suggests that these are variant presentations of a single event by different authors.

34. Zhu Xi reads 4B27 without sensitivity to its literary dimensions. His commentary is devoted to an exploration of relevant court rituals recorded in the *Zhou li,* and an explanation of why they apply in this case, despite the private nature of the occasion. Here, Zhu Xi construes unsystematic rationalizing casuistry as systematic doctrine.

35. *Chunqiu fanlu* 春秋繁露, "Yu-xu," 6.4/17 (ICS Ancient Chinese Text Concordance Series [Hong Kong: Commercial Press, 1994]); cf. *Shiji* 史記, 130.3297 (Beijing: Zhonghua shuju, 1975).

10

Mencius, Xunzi, and Dai Zhen
A Study of the *Mengzi ziyi shuzheng*

KWONG-LOI SHUN

IN HIS DEBATES with Gaozi, Mencius opposes Gaozi's view that there is neither good nor bad in *xing* 性 (nature) and that *yi* 義 (propriety) is external, apparently defending the view that *xing* is good (*xing shan* 性善) and that *yi* is internal (*yi nei* 義內) (*Mencius* 6A1–6A6, 2A2).[1] These two Mencian claims have come to be regarded by later Confucians as key elements in his thinking. In his *Mengzi ziyi shuzheng* 孟子字義疏證, Dai Zhen 戴震 seeks to defend these two claims, framing his discussion in terms of *li* 理 (pattern), which has become a key philosophical term by his time. In doing so, he also criticizes Xunzi, who explicitly opposes Mencius' views on *xing*. In this essay, I will examine Dai Zhen's interpretation of these two Mencian claims and argue that his interpretation is actually guided by two ideas that are more characteristic of Xunzi's than Mencius' thinking. The purpose of the essay is not to criticize Dai Zhen for misreading Mencius but to understand the distinctive form of Confucian thought that results from his combining certain ideas of Xunzi's with the Mencian framework.

The first idea concerns the role the Confucian Way plays in relation to the *qing* 情 (what is genuinely so, feelings) and *yu* 欲 (desires) of human beings. According to Xunzi, human beings share in the natural state certain *qing* and *yu* that will lead to strife and disorder if not regulated by the heart (*xin* 心). The ancient sage-kings comprehended the situation and instituted social distinctions and norms to regulate human conduct and transform the *xing* (nature) of human beings, so as to nourish their *qing* and *yu*. The details of the rites and norms of propriety, which for Xunzi extend to the whole social setup, might need to be adapted over time to cope with changing circumstances. However, *li* 理, the pattern or rationale that underlies such details and gives them a unity, is unchanging; indeed, it is by grasping the underlying *li* that one can cope appropriately with the changing circumstances of life.

The second idea concerns the importance of understanding (*zhi* 知). For Xunzi, propriety is something that the ordinary person has to learn. Through learning rituals, the ancient classics, and basically the whole cultural heritage from the past, and through repeatedly acting and shaping oneself in accordance with what one has learned, one's whole person will be transformed. It is also important to acquire a proper understanding (*zhi*) with the help of teachers, both because seeing the beauty and the underlying rationale of what one has learned will enable it to be firmly embedded in oneself, and because such understanding makes possible adjustment and adaptation in exigent or changing circumstances. Thus, according to Xunzi, it is through understanding *dao* (the Way) that one will approve of it, and it is through approving of it that one will abide by it. The becloudedness (*bi* 蔽) of the heart, which takes the form of the heart's focusing its attention on certain things at the expense of a full comprehension of *dao,* prevents the heart from acquiring the proper understanding, and so it is important to develop one's understanding to attain clarity (*ming* 明). Such clarity Xunzi relates to a spiritlike quality (*shen* 神), at times using the combination "*shenming*" 神明 to emphasize the spiritlike clarity of the heart.

Like Xunzi, Dai Zhen regards *dao* as rooted in *qing* and *yu* and emphasizes the importance of learning and understanding. For him, *li,* the pattern to which human beings should conform their behavior, is also that which makes possible the appropriate attainment (*de* 得) of *qing* and satisfaction (*sui* 遂) of *yu*. Because human beings share the same basic *qing* and *yu,* one can use oneself as a measure in fathoming the *qing* and *yu* of others, and one follows *li* by acting in a way that makes possible the appropriate attainment of *qing* and satisfaction of *yu* in both oneself and others. One needs to learn to grasp the *li* in daily affairs, and the understanding (*zhi* 知) of *li* is important in guiding behavior. The primary task in self-cultivation is to remove the becloudedness (*bi*) of the heart to let it attain clarity (*ming*) so that it can better comprehend *li;* often, sageness is characterized in terms of a spiritlike clarity (*shenming*) of the heart and linked to wisdom (*zhi* 智).

So Dai Zhen is like Xunzi in the way he views the relation between *li* and *qingyu* 情欲 and in his emphasis on the guiding role of understanding. Working under the influence of these two ideas, which are more characteristic of Xunzi's thinking than Mencius', he is at the same time very serious and sincere in his attempt to unravel the "true" meaning of the *Mencius.* What resulted is a novel and distinctive form of Confucian thought that differs from both Mencius' and Xunzi's views in interesting ways. In what follows, I will first discuss his views on the relation between *li* and *qingyu* and on understanding, next consider his interpretation of the Mencian ideas that *xing* is good and *liyi* 理義 internal, and then conclude with a comparative discussion of Mencius, Xunzi, and Dai Zhen.

Qing (What Is Genuinely So, Feelings), *Yu* (Desires), and *Li* (Pattern)

Dai Zhen regards the *xing* (nature) of a thing as that which accounts for the characteristics of the thing, including the way the thing grows and develops; for example, the *xing* of peach and almond is the innermost part of their seeds, which accounts for their development and growth (no. 27, p. 35).[2] The *xing* of an animal comprises both *qi* 氣, the vital forces that fill its body, and awareness (*zhijue* 知覺); animals of different kinds are distinguished by the differences in their *qi* and in their capabilities of awareness (no. 27, p. 35). In regard to human beings, he speaks of *xueqi* 血氣 (blood-qi) and *xinzhi* 心知 (the heart that understands) as what compose their *xing* (e.g., no. 2, p. 2; no. 9, p. 8; no. 20, p. 25; no. 21, pp. 29–30; no. 30, pp. 40–41).

Working with the distinction between an inactivated state (*jing* 靜, literally "still") and an activated state (*dong* 動, literally "moved") that has become common by his time—that is, the distinction between what is there prior to one's contact with things in the world and how one responds upon coming into contact with things—Dai Zhen views *xing* as without error in its inactivated state (no. 2, p. 2). When *xing,* or more specifically the *xueqi* that is part of *xing,* is activated upon contact with things, *yu* (desires) arises. This is the *yu* of *xing* (*xing zhi yu* 性之欲), and it is the same for all human beings (no. 2, p. 2). It includes the tendencies exhibited by different parts of the body, such as the tendencies of the senses to go after certain sensory objects (no. 8, pp. 6–7; no. 30, p. 40), and it relates to *xing* in the way that the flow of water relates to water (no. 11, pp. 10–11). These tendencies, especially the tendency to eat and drink, help to nourish physical life or, more specifically, the *xueqi* of human beings, enabling them to grow from weak to strong (no. 30, p. 40; no. 9, p. 8). Hence, knowing the *xing* of human beings is important to nourishing their growth, just as knowing the *xing* of peach and almond enables us to know what contributes to their growth and thereby to nourish them (no. 27, p. 35).

As for *qing* (what is genuinely so, feelings), Dai Zhen cites the examples of joy, anger, sorrow, and delight and also character-izes *qing* as *xing*'s response when one comes into contact with things (no. 30, p. 40). It appears that, for him, *qing* comprises one's emo-tional responses upon contact with things. The question remains, though, as to how *qing* differs from and relates to *yu*. Addressing this question is important to our understanding of his views on *li*, be-cause he explains *li* sometimes in terms of *qing* and sometimes in terms of *yu*.

Dai Zhen explains *li* in terms of *qing* by saying that *li* is a matter of *qing*'s not being in error; there is no instance of one's attaining *li* without attaining *qing* (no. 2, p. 1). *Qing* is what resides in oneself and in others, whereas *li* is a matter of not being excessive or defi-cient in relation to *qing* (no. 3, p. 2). To attain *li*, what one needs to do is to use one's *qing* to gauge others' *qing*, and then one must ensure that both attain their proper balance (*ping* 平) (no. 2, pp. 1–2). He also explains *li* in terms of *yu* by saying that it is by regulat-ing *yu* and avoiding excess that one follows *tianli* 天理 (the pattern of Nature) (no. 11, pp. 10–11). This point he illustrates with the analogy of water; having compared *xing* to water and *yu* to the flow of water, he further compares following *tianli* to the sage-king Yu's channeling water in such a way that it is regulated and not overflow-ing (no. 11, p. 10; cf. *Mencius* 4B26).

On several occasions, Dai Zhen mentions *qing* and *yu* together in his characterization of *li*. He describes the sage as someone who personally understands (*ti* 體) the *qing* of the common people and enables them to satisfy their *yu* (e.g., no. 10, pp. 9–10; no. 43, p. 59); a similar point is sometimes put in terms of *yu*'s being satisfied and *qing*'s being attained or expressed (*da* 達) (no. 30, p. 41). Elsewhere, he also refers to *qing* and *yu* in a way that presents them as intimately related. For example, by regulating (rather than eliminating) *yu*, one is able to be not excessive or deficient with regard to *qing*, thereby attaining *tianli* (no. 11, p. 11). And to regard *li* as a matter of *qing*'s not erring is also to regard *li* as residing in *yu* (no. 10, p. 8). How, then, are *qing* and *yu* related, and how do they relate to *li*?

A possible answer is suggested by Dai Zhen's elaboration on the Confucian idea of reciprocity, expressed through the notions of *shu* 恕 and *zhongshu* 忠恕. Dai Zhen follows the *Lunyu* in explaining *shu* in terms of not doing to others what one would not want done to oneself (no. 5, p. 4) and explains *zhong* sometimes as being able to devote oneself (no. 41, p. 55) and sometimes as regarding others as like oneself (no. 15, p. 18). *Zhong* and *shu* are methods of learning to be a sage, and although the sage's accomplishment cannot be adequately described by *zhong* and *shu*, it is actually the utmost attainment of *zhong* and *shu* (no. 41, p. 55). Dai Zhen links *yu* and *qing* in his further elaboration on the idea of reciprocity. With regard to the *yu* of *xing*, my *yu* is the same as others', and it is from *yu* that likes (*hao* 好) and dislikes (*wu* 惡) arise. The ethical task is to avoid indulging in one's *yu*, which involves pursuing one's likes and dislikes to the neglect of others' likes and dislikes. To do so, one should turn back on oneself (*fangong* 反躬) and think about one's own *qing* should one suffer from others' indulging in their *yu*. When *qing* attains its proper balance, it is also a matter of one's likes and dislikes being properly regulated, and a matter of following *tianli* (no. 2, pp. 1–2). *Qing* and *yu* are also related in other contexts. For example, referring to the use of "*yu*" in the *Lunyu* and "*wu*" (dislike) in the *Daxue* in connection with the idea of reciprocity, Dai Zhen says that *yu* and *wu* are the common *qing* of the people and that it is by using one's *qing* to gauge the *qing* of others that one seeks *li* (no. 5, pp. 4–5). Elsewhere, he also describes as *qing* the way one would respond if others were to treat oneself in the way one proposes to treat others (no. 11, p. 10), and he takes this to be what is involved in using one's *qing* to gauge the *qing* of others, thereby allowing *qing* to attain its proper balance (no. 2, pp. 1–2).

It appears that *qing* and *yu* are related in the following manner. Human beings share certain *yu* of *xing* that takes the form of parts of one's body being drawn toward certain things, such as the senses being drawn toward certain sensory objects. As one becomes aware of such tendencies when one comes into contact with things, one comes to form likes and dislikes, and the former can also be described as *yu* in a more reflective sense. That is, it is no longer just a matter of parts of one's body being drawn unreflectively toward certain objects but a matter of one's person as a whole liking or disliking certain things, with an awareness of what it is that one likes or dislikes. One's liking certain things moves one to go after such things; on the other hand, one's dislike is a response to certain contemplated or actual situations involving oneself, especially situations in which one is deprived of certain things by others who indulge in their own *yu*. Such likes (or *yu* of the more reflective kind) and dislikes are the *qing* of human beings. Here Dai Zhen is probably drawing on the dual connotations of *qing* as what is genuinely so and as feelings or emotions; such likes and dislikes are genuinely (*qing*) in human beings and are manifested in a variety of emotional responses (*qing*) such as joy, anger, sorrow, and delight.

As one is moved by one's likes and dislikes, there is a tendency to pursue what one likes to the neglect of others' likes and dislikes. To follow *li*, one not only has to understand that human beings share the same basic unreflective tendencies but also has to understand their more reflective responses to situations—what they like and dislike, and the associated emotional responses. To do so, one has to use one's own *qing* (namely, what is genuinely in oneself, one's feelings) to gauge the *qing* of others, and one must understand how others would react to one's treatment of them by turning back on oneself and reflecting on how oneself would react if similarly treated by others—this is presumably how the sages personally understand the *qing* of the common people (*ti min zhi qing* 體民之 情). The goal is to go beyond satisfying one's *yu* by also satisfying others' *yu*, and to go beyond attaining one's *qing* by also enabling others to attain their *qing*, so that everyone's *yu* is appropriately satisfied and *qing* appropriately attained (no. 30, pp. 40–41). By attainment of *qing*, Dai Zhen probably has in mind being able to take joy in things and avoid dissatisfaction—he sometimes cites passages in the *Mencius* about how benevolent government involves the ruler's sharing his enjoyment with the common people and ensuring that there is no dissatisfaction among them (no. 10, pp. 9–10).

With regard to both *qing* and *yu*, Dai Zhen works with some conception of a proper measure of each—he speaks of properly regulating *yu* so that one is not excessive with regard to them (*jie er bu guo* 節而不過) and of being not excessive and not deficient in regard to *qing* (*wu guo qing wu bu ji qing* 無過情無不及情) so that they attain their proper balance (*qing de qi ping* 情得其平). Probably, what constitutes the proper measure of each has to do with whether the extent of, and the means by which one secures, the satisfaction of one's *yu* and attainment of one's *qing* will prevent others from equally satisfying their *yu* and attaining their *qing*. Attaining the proper measure enables people to mutually nourish their lives (no. 11, p. 10), this being the way of the sages (no. 15, p. 18). The emphasis on nourishing life is reflected in his characterization of *ren* 仁 (humanity) in terms of the idea of giving and nourishing life (*sheng sheng* 生生) found in the *Yijing; ren* involves one's not just promoting one's own life but also working to promote everyone's life (no. 36, p. 48).

Dai Zhen sees his view of the relation between *li* and *yu* as opposed in at least two ways to Zhu Xi's thinking. Zhu Xi often speaks of a contrast between *tianli* and *renyu* 人欲 (human desires), as if the *yu* of human beings is always problematic. According to Dai Zhen, the *yu* of *xing* is itself respectable and not to be eliminated; rather, the ethical task is to regulate *yu* properly so that one is not excessive with regard to it (no. 11, p. 10–11; no. 43, pp. 57–58). Indeed, one's practice of *ren* (humanity) depends on *yu*—*ren* is a matter of promoting life in others as well as in oneself through satisfying the *yu* of *xing,* and one's understanding the *yu* in others depends on one's own possession of *yu*. Furthermore, Zhu Xi appears to regard *li* as a thing distinct from *yu* (*ru you wu yan* 如有物焉); for Zhu Xi, *yu* is based on *qi,* whereas *li* is something distinct from *qi* but residing in things and affairs and also (in a beclouded state) in the human heart. According to Dai Zhen, *li* is nothing but the proper ordering of *yu;* we should speak of the *li* of things and affairs and not, as Zhu Xi does, of *li* as something residing in them (no. 41, p. 54).

Dai Zhen's first point of criticism—that Zhu Xi advocates the elimination of *yu*—may not be entirely fair to Zhu Xi who, in his more cautious moments, does acknowledge that certain basic human desires are respectable and should be satisfied. However, the second point of criticism—that Zhu Xi regards *li* as something other than the proper satisfaction of *yu*—captures an element of Zhu Xi's thinking that differs from Dai Zhen's view. Dai Zhen's view that *li* is nothing other than the proper satisfaction of *yu* and attainment of *qing* often informs his interpretation of early Confucian texts. For example, invoking the ideas of human relations (*renlun* 人倫) (no. 32, pp. 43–44) and of daily activities (*riyong* 日用) (no. 36, p. 48) found in the *Zhongyong*, he interprets the line "following *xing* is what is meant by *dao*" from the text to mean that *dao* (the Way) resides in human relations and daily activities, which have to do with the *yu* of *xing* (no. 32, pp. 43–44; no. 38, p. 50). Referring to other ideas in the *Zhongyong*, he observes that since *dao* governs one's daily activities, it is something from which one should not depart even for a single moment (no. 33, pp. 44–45); furthermore, to seek *dao* outside of human relations and daily activities is like seeking to know taste outside of food and drink (no. 34, p. 46). For him, the various ethical attributes highlighted in the *Zhongyong* all have to do with human relations and daily activities, themselves rooted in the *yu* of *xing* (no. 38, pp. 50–51).

His view also informs his interpretation of well-known ideas in the *Mencius*. He takes Mencius' comparison of *dao* to a wide road to emphasize the fact that *dao* does not go beyond human relations and daily activities. In *Mencius* 6A6, Mencius cites the *Shijing*: "Where there are things, there are norms" (*you wu you ze* 有物有則); this Dai Zhen takes to emphasize that *liyi* is not outside of things and affairs, contrary to Zhu Xi's view (no. 8, p. 7). He sometimes takes "*wu*" 物 to refer to *yu* (desires), sometimes to human relations and daily activities; "*ze*" 則 he sometimes takes to refer to *li* and sometimes to the ethical attributes (no. 10, p. 8; no. 3, pp. 2–3; no. 34, p. 46; cf. no. 13, p. 12); in any case, the point is that *li* is nothing other than the proper ordering of human activities that leads to the appropriate satisfaction of *yu*.

Xinzhi and Understanding

Having considered Dai Zhen's view of *qing* and *yu*, which are rooted in *xueqi*, let us turn to *xinzhi* 心知 (the heart that understands), the other part of *xing*. Just as *xueqi* manifests itself as *qing* and *yu* when one comes into contact with things, *xinzhi* manifests itself in the form of understanding (*zhi*), where the objects of understanding are such things as beauty and ugliness, right and wrong (no. 30, p. 40), as well as various human relations (no. 28, p. 37). Dai Zhen views *xinzhi* as having a priority over *xueqi* in that the heart is able to and should regulate the senses, which he ascribes to *xueqi*. He illustrates this point with the analogy, also found in the

Xunzi, of the heart's standing in a relation to the senses like that of the ruler to officials (no. 8, p. 7). Although the emphasis on the priority of the heart is also part of Mencius' thinking, Dai Zhen further emphasizes the heart's ability to make the fine discriminations that constitute clarity with regard to *li* (*mingli* 明理), an idea more characteristic of Xunzi's thinking (no. 4, p. 3).

According to Dai Zhen, what distinguishes human beings from and makes them superior to animals is the understanding of the heart. The various basic desires that human beings have can also be found in animals and are not what distinguish human beings from them (no. 21, pp. 26–27). Neither does the distinctive feature of human beings reside in their capability of social relations, for some animals are apparently capable of such relations—there appears to be love between mother and child among certain animals, and some seem to observe a ruler-subordinate relation (no. 21, pp. 27–28). Rather, the distinctive feature is that whereas other animals are limited in their capability of such relations, human beings can expand their understanding of such relations to the utmost to attain a spiritlike clarity (*shenming*) (no. 6, pp. 5–6; no. 23, p. 30; no. 21, pp. 28–29; no. 27, p. 35). Accordingly, the highest ideal for human beings is to develop the understanding of the heart to attain clarity, and he explicates the four ethical attributes *ren, yi, li,* and *zhi* (仁, 義, 禮, and 智), highlighted by Mencius in these terms (no. 21, p. 29; no. 6, p. 6).

Dai Zhen recognizes that problems can arise with *qing* and *yu* (rooted in *xueqi*), as well as with understanding (rooted in *xinzhi*); *yu* can become selfish (*si* 私), *qing* one-sided (*pian* 偏), and understanding beclouded (no. 30, p. 41). Selfishness is a matter of satisfying one's *yu* to the neglect of others' *yu,* and it is opposed to *ren* (humanity), which involves satisfying the *yu* of others as well as of oneself (no. 36, p. 48). This point he takes to be implicit in *Lunyu* 12.1, in which Confucius refers to overcoming the self (*keji* 克己) as part of his explication of *ren.* According to Dai Zhen, "self" (*ji*) in this passage is contrasted with "others" (*ren* 人), and to overcome the self is to overcome the gap between self and others that characterizes selfishness (no. 42, p. 56). Selfishness is often mentioned along with becloudedness, a state of the heart that prevents it from attaining *li* (no. 10, p. 9). For example, in criticism of the Daoists and Buddhists, he opposes the idea of eliminating *qingyu* and understanding; instead, the important task is to get rid of selfishness and becloudedness, thereby attaining humanity and wisdom (no. 40, pp. 53–54; no. 43, pp. 57–58; no. 10, pp. 9–10). In criticism of Zhu Xi's contrast between *tianli* and *renyu* and the idea that the heart is beclouded by *renyu*, Dai Zhen points out that the problem with *yu* is not becloudedness but selfishness (no. 10, p. 9).

However, although Dai Zhen does talk about selfishness as a problem with *yu*, there is evidence that he gives priority to getting rid of becloudedness of the heart. For example, he criticizes views that emphasize getting rid of *yu* (no. 40, p. 54) or the selfishness of *yu* (no. 42, p. 57) without also emphasizing getting rid of becloudedness, and he makes the point that it is an error to emphasize action (*xing* 行) without first emphasizing understanding (*zhi* 知). The primary task in learning to be a sage is to acquire understanding through learning; in acting, what one does is to practice in human relations and daily activities that with regard to which one's heart is not beclouded (no. 40, p. 54; cf. no. 42, p. 57). It is only after one has attained the proper understanding that one can go beyond oneself to satisfy others' *yu* and attain others' *qing* also (no. 30, p. 41), and so it is by getting rid of becloudedness that one also gets rid of selfishness. The emphasis on understanding is also seen from the priority that Dai Zhen gives to wisdom over humanity. For him, *ren* (humanity) is the absence of selfishness, and wisdom the absence of becloudedness (no. 39, p. 51); *ren* involves giving life to and nourishing everyone, and wisdom involves understanding the *li* that underlies this process (no. 36, p. 48). Because *li* underlies the life-giving and nourishing process, it is only when one has understood *li* that one can partake in the process (no. 36, p. 48).

That developing one's understanding is the primary task in self-cultivation can also be seen from Dai Zhen's pairing of sageness with wisdom (*shengzhi* 聖智) (e.g. no. 1, p. 1; no. 13, p. 13; cf. *Mencius* 5B1) and from his describing self-cultivation as an advance from the narrow and small to the broad and large, or from dimness and hiddenness to clarity and discernment (no. 9, p. 8), until one attains clarity of *xinzhi* (no. 41, pp. 55–56). He gives two analogies to illustrate this process. Just as the body (*xingti* 形體) grows from small and weak to big and strong via the nourishment of food and drink, one's character (*dexing* 德性) grows from being obstructed and dim to being sagely and wise via learning and inquiry. Also, he compares the understanding of the heart to the brightness of fire; just as the increased brightness of fire can allow one to discern clearly both far-

away objects and the details in objects, the increase in the understanding of the heart enables one to discern the fine details of the *li*
of things (no. 8, p. 7; no. 6, pp. 5–6).

Other methods of self-cultivation are not neglected, such as
the kind of mental attentiveness that later Confucians emphasize
with the notion of *jing* 敬 (seriousness), or the notion of caution
and of watching over *du* 獨 (solitude) found in the *Zhongyong* (no.
12, p. 11), but Dai Zhen's primary emphasis is on inquiry and learning. This involves not just studying the classics but also such things
as broadening one's acquaintance with things, inquiring into details
to resolve uncertainties, and cautiously reflecting on what one has
acquired in the process (no. 40, p. 54; no. 41, p. 55). *Xue* 學 (learning) is mentioned along with *si* 思 (reflection) in the *Lunyu*, and *si*
for Mencius describes the heart's relation to *liyi* that is akin to a
form of perception (*Mencius* 6A15). Citing Mencius' remarks on *si*,
Dai Zhen interprets *si* to refer to a discernment of *li*, which is refined
and developed through learning until it attains a spiritlike clarity
(no. 6, p. 5). However, the important thing is not the accumulation
of knowledge through learning, which is superficial (no. 41, p. 55);
rather, just as food and drink have to be digested for them to nourish the growth of the body, the same is true of what one has learned
for it to nourish the growth of *xinzhi* (no. 9, p. 8). The latter involves the heart's increasing capacity to discern the fine details of *li*
in situations it confronts, even with regard to affairs about which
one has not learned (no. 41, p. 55, citing *Mencius* 4B14). The goal is
to enable the heart to attain a spiritlike clarity, just as the brightness
of the sun and moon enables them to illuminate every object (no. 6,
p. 6; cf. no. 8, p. 7). Such clarity of the heart is what enables one to
quan 權, a term used by Mencius to refer to the capacity to weigh situations and discern what is proper without abiding by general rules,
even in exigent or novel circumstances (no. 40, pp. 52–54; no. 41,
p. 56; no. 42, p. 57).

Xing Is Good and *Liyi* Is Internal

With the above discussion as background, we may return to
Dai Zhen's interpretation of the Mencian claim that *xing* is good.
First, let us consider the apparent tension between this Mencian
claim and parts of the *Lunyu* and the *Zhongyong* that highlight the
differences among human beings. The *Lunyu* describes people as

close to each other, rather than being the same, in *xing* and apparently distinguishes among different grades of people, describing those of highest and lowest intelligence as unchanging (*bu yi* 不移). It distinguishes among people with different capacities of understanding, and the *Zhongyong* similarly distinguishes among people with different capacities of understanding and action. Dai Zhen resolves this apparent tension by proposing that although there are differences among human beings in *xing*, these are insignificant in comparison with a broad similarity in the *xing* of human beings by virtue of which *xing* is good.

Drawing on ideas in *Mencius* 6A6, Dai Zhen distinguishes between *xing* and *cai* 才, taking the *cai* of something to refer to the characteristics of the thing that are discernible from the outside, and *xing* to refer to that which underlies such characteristics. The *xing* of a thing is compared to the kind of metal that a utensil is made of, and *cai* to the characteristics that the utensil exhibits by virtue of the kind of metal it is made of; it is from *cai*, the outwardly discernible characteristics, that one sees the *xing* of a thing (no. 29, pp. 39–40; cf. no. 20, p. 25). While *cai*, the outwardly discernible characteristics of a thing, may change, *xing*, the underlying constitution, does not change. Thus, although every human being starts with a good *xing* and a beautiful *cai*, *cai* can become not beautiful through inadequate nourishment and other influences, while *xing* stays good throughout (no. 30, p. 41; no. 31, pp. 42–43).

Concerning the differences among human beings referred to in the *Lunyu* and the *Zhongyong*, Dai Zhen acknowledges that there are differences in their *xing*, which explain why Confucius does not describe people as the same in *xing* (no. 21, pp. 28–29). The differences in *xing* account for the different capacities of understanding and action in people, which are differences in their *cai* (no. 22, p. 30; no. 24, p. 31; no. 39, p. 52). However, such differences are insignificant in comparison with certain characteristics that distinguish human beings as a kind from other animals, and this is why Confucius speaks of their being close to each other, rather than being different, in *xing* (no. 20, p. 25; no. 23, p. 30). What human beings share is a *xinzhi* that is absent from other animals, by virtue of which all human beings have a good *xing* (no. 21, pp. 28–29; no. 24, p. 31). Despite their different capacities, all human beings can develop their *xinzhi*, and there is no difference in what they can accomplish in this regard (no. 39, p. 52). Confucius' observation that those of the lowest intelligence are unchanging does not mean that they are incapable of developing their *xinzhi* to the same degree as others; rather, they do not change because they, by their own choosing, do not learn, despite their being able to develop their *xinzhi* through learning (no. 22, p. 30; no. 23, p. 30).

What, then, are the characteristics of *xinzhi* by virtue of which *xing* is good? At times, Dai Zhen speaks as if the goodness of *xing* consists in the capability of human beings to develop their *xinzhi* via learning. For example, when comparing the development of *xinzhi* via learning to the growth of the body via food and drink, he observes that, just as *xueqi* in the body must be receptive of food and drink for the body to grow, *xinzhi* must be receptive of learning for it to grow, and so must have some goodness to start with (no. 26, pp. 32–33). Interestingly, he says that Xunzi's view that every human being is capable of becoming good not only does not conflict with, but actually helps to explicate, the view that *xing* is good (no. 25, p. 31). On several occasions, Dai Zhen explains the goodness of *xing* in terms of the observation that human beings have a *xinzhi* that surpasses other animals' in its capacity to understand goodness (no. 21, p. 29; no. 27, p. 35; no. 28, pp. 37–38).

However, when commenting on specific Mencian ideas, Dai Zhen places greater emphasis on the heart than on the capability of developing understanding. Just as the growth of the body is the growth of something that is already there, however fragile and small, the development of *xinzhi*'s understanding starts from some understanding, however obstructed and dim it may be (no. 14, p. 15). He interprets Mencius' idea of the four germs in such a way that they exemplify the understanding that the heart has to start with. Mencius gives as an example of the germ of *ren* (humanity) the commiseration that everyone would feel toward an infant on the verge of falling into a well (*Mencius* 2A6). Dai Zhen takes such commiseration to show that everyone is already to some extent capable of taking one's own attachment to life and fear of death beyond oneself; this explains why everyone would be moved by the infant's imminent death. Some understanding of *li* is already implicit in such a response, as well as in the other three germs, and the observation that everyone has some understanding to start with provides a sense in which *xing* is good. For Dai Zhen, the expanding and filling up (*kuochong* 擴充) of the four germs that Mencius speaks of refer to the development of the understanding implicit in the four germs, until one attains a spiritlike clarity that constitutes *ren, yi, li,* and *zhi* (no. 21, pp. 28–29; cf. no. 6, p. 6; no. 7, p. 6).

The way he interprets *Mencius* 6A7 points to another sense in which *xing* is good. In that passage, Mencius observes that just as the senses share the common feature of taking pleasure in certain ideal sensory objects, there is "tongran" 同然 to the human heart, which can be interpreted to mean that all human hearts have something in common or that they agree in the objects they approve of. According to Mencius, *liyi* pleases the heart just as the ideal sensory objects please the senses. Dai Zhen adopts the second interpretation of *tongran* and elaborates on the passage as follows.

He takes the comparison of the heart to the senses to emphasize that the heart's "getting through" (*tong* 通) to *liyi* and the senses "getting through" to their respective sensory objects are both rooted in *xing* (no. 7, p. 6). This "getting through" involves, minimally, the capacity of *xinzhi* to be not perplexed with regard to *liyi,* a capacity that he links to *si* 思 and that Mencius ascribes to the heart in *Mencius* 6A15 (no. 21, p. 28). Furthermore, because all human hearts share such a capacity, everyone can come to agree on what is genuinely *li.* This he takes to be Mencius' point in speaking of *tongran;* that is, if something accords with *li,* everyone would approve of it and regard it as unalterable for ten thousand generations (no. 4, p. 3). It is only when what one approves of is also approved of by everyone else that it qualifies as *li* rather than personal opinion (*yijian* 意見); this point Dai Zhen sees as a corrective to the Song Confucians' view that *li* already resides in the heart, a view that opens the room for each person to present his or her own personal opinion as *li* (no. 5, pp. 3–5).

In addition to the shared approval of *li,* the heart also takes pleasure in it just as the senses take pleasure in certain sensory objects (no. 6, p. 5). One might not be able to discern *liyi* fully to start with, but *xinzhi* can be developed, and the heart is structured in such a way that there is a sense of ease and contentment when one acts in accordance with *tianli* and a sense of loss and discontent when one acts contrary to *tianli* (no. 8, p. 7; no. 15, p. 19). This feature of the heart provides another sense in which *xing* is good (no. 15, pp. 18–19).

So, for Dai Zhen, *xing* is good in that *xinzhi* has the capacity to understand *liyi,* takes pleasure in it, has some understanding of it to start with, and agrees in approving of it. At times, he also explains the goodness of *xing* in terms of how the "should-be-so" (*biran* 必然) is a completion of the "self-so" (*ziran* 自然)—goodness has to do with the should-be-so and *xing* with the self-so, and it is by attaining the should-be-so that one completes the self-so (no. 32, p. 44; cf. no. 26, pp. 32–33). The self-so describes *xing*, which comprises *xueqi* and *xinzhi*, whereas the should-be-so concerns *li*. Although every living animal pursues the self-so, human beings are distinguished from other animals by their ability to understand and follow the should-be-so (no. 15, p. 16).

The should-be-so completes the self-so in at least two senses. First, the should-be-so is nothing but the pattern (*fenli* 分理) that runs through human relations and daily activities, the latter having to do with *qing* and *yu,* which are rooted in *xueqi,* this being part of *xing* or the self-so (no. 2, p. 2; no. 13, pp. 12–13). That is, the should-be-so is nothing other than the proper ordering of what pertains to the self-so. Second, that *xinzhi* can discern and takes pleasure in *li,* the should-be-so, is itself part of the self-so, because this feature of *xinzhi* is part of *xing.* Therefore, when *xinzhi* fully discerns and takes pleasure in *li,* the should-be-so, the self-so is also developed to the utmost (no. 15, pp. 18–19). Stating these two points differently, to act contrary to the should-be-so is also to go against the self-so in two senses—one will not be able to properly satisfy *yu* and attain *qing,* which is part of the self-so, and one's *xinzhi* will feel a sense of loss and discontent, where *xinzhi*'s taking pleasure in *liyi* is also part of the self-so.

This interpretation of the goodness of *xing* shapes Dai Zhen's interpretation of *Mencius* 7B24, which says of the senses that "this is *xing* 性, and yet therein lies *ming* 命, and the superior person *bu wei xing ye* 不謂性也," and of the ethical attributes that "this is *ming* 命, and yet therein lies *xing* 性, and the superior person *bu wei ming ye* 不謂命也." In criticism of the Song Confucians who distinguish between *xing* pertaining to *qi* and *xing* pertaining to *li* and who emphasize the latter, Dai Zhen stresses that Mencius is not in this passage saying that the senses should not be regarded as part of *xing* (no. 28, pp. 36–38). Rather, Mencius' point is to emphasize, as a corrective to certain ways of viewing *xing* common during his time, that the heart's relation to *liyi* is as much a part of *xing* as the relation of the senses to sensory objects (no. 7, p. 6). The sensory desires are rooted in *xueqi* and are part of *xing;* however, there is *ming* in that they are subject to certain normative constraints—they should be regulated so that they do not become excessive (no. 11, pp. 10–11). There is *ming* in the ethical attributes in that human beings are not born alike in their capacity to develop these attributes, and yet there is *xing* in that everyone can develop and expand (*kuochong*) what they have to start with and embody the ethical attributes (no. 28, pp. 36–38). The character "*wei*" 謂 Dai Zhen takes to mean "use as an excuse"—Mencius is not saying that the superior person does not regard the sensory desires as *xing*; rather, the superior person does not use the fact that they are part of *xing* as an excuse for indulging in them. And Mencius does not deny that there is *ming* with regard to the ethical attributes; rather, the superior person does not take the difference in capacities among human beings as an excuse for not fully developing them.

In considering *liyi* as internal rather than external, Dai Zhen seems to regard *liyi* as part of *xing*. Thus, he takes the observation in *Mencius* 6A7 that all hearts agree in approving of *liyi* to emphasize that *liyi* is part of *xing* and to be directed against the view that *yi* is external (no. 7, p. 6; no. 21, p. 28). The observation serves as a corrective to views common in Mencius' time that regard *liyi* as something instituted by the sages to regulate *xing* (no. 7, p. 6), an example being Gaozi's position that *yi* is external in the sense that it is something that is not self-so but should shape what is self-so (no. 21, p. 27). Another example from a time later than Mencius' is the view of Xunzi, who, according to Dai Zhen, regards the rites and propriety as separate from and not rooted in *xing*, thereby missing the point that the should-be-so is just a matter of developing the self-so to its completion. Unlike Mencius who sees learning as a nourishment of what is on the inside with the help of something from the outside (namely, the teachings of the ancient sages), Xunzi emphasizes learning because he thinks there is something (namely, propriety) lacking on the inside that one needs to obtain from the outside. What Xunzi regards as part of *xing* (namely, the *qing* and *yu* of human beings) Mencius also regards as part of *xing*, but Mencius emphasizes the more important component of *xing* (namely, *liyi*), whereas Xunzi neglects it (no. 26, pp. 32–33).

On other occasions, Dai Zhen links the idea that *yi* is internal to the idea, found in *Mencius* 3A5, that things have one root (*ben* 本) rather than two. He regards *xueqi, xinzhi,* and the spiritlike clarity that is developed via learning as having one root, presumably in the sense that *xueqi* and *xinzhi* are both part of *xing* (or the self-so), whereas the spiritlike clarity is just the development of *xinzhi,* and hence also of one's *xing* (the self-so), to the utmost. To regard them as having one root is not to treat any of them as external, but to regard them as having two roots is to treat at least one of them as external. According to him, the Daoists and Buddhists, who downplay the *yu* that is rooted in the self-so of *xueqi* and who advocate nourishing *xinzhi* via quietude, ascribe two roots to *xueqi* and *xinzhi.* Xunzi and the Cheng-Zhu school, on the other hand, regard *xueqi* and *xinzhi* as having one root by grouping them together as the self-so, but they postulate two roots in that they think that the self-so should be regulated by something—the rites for Xunzi and *li* for the Cheng-Zhu school—that constitutes the should-be-so and that is not itself rooted in the self-so. Although the Cheng-Zhu school regards *li* as originating from *tian* and Xunzi regards the rites as originating from the ancient sages, they are not that different in that they both regard the should-be-so as separate from the self-so (no. 15, pp. 18–19).

Sometimes, Dai Zhen explains the idea of two roots in other ways. For example, the Song Confucian separation of *li* and *qi,* and Cheng Yi's view that *xing* (identified with *li*) is good while *cai* (one's endowment of *qi*) is responsible for what is not good, are described as treating *li* and *qi,* or *xing* and *cai,* as having two roots (no. 19, p. 24; no. 31, p. 42). Nevertheless, Dai Zhen's criticism seems directed primarily against any view that sees a discontinuity between *liyi* and the natural makeup of human beings. Fundamentally, continuous with *xueqi* and *xinzhi, liyi* is a matter of properly satisfying *yu* and attaining *qing* that are rooted in *xueqi;* it develops from the understanding implicit in *xinzhi* and is something that *xinzhi* takes pleasure in. For Xunzi, the rites serve to regulate the *xing* of the ordinary people; though everyone can understand and practice them, they need to be learned from the past with the help of teachers (no. 25, pp. 31–32; cf. no. 14, p. 14). The Cheng-Zhu school regards *li* as due to *tian* that can be obscured by the endowment of *qi* in which *xueqi* and *xinzhi* is rooted. In regarding *li* as something separate from *qi* and serving to regulate *yu,* which is rooted in *qi,* the Cheng-Zhu school is like Xunzi in seeing a discontinuity between *li* and the natural makeup of human beings (no. 14, pp. 13–15; no. 27, pp. 34–36).

Mencius, Xunzi, and Dai Zhen:
A Comparative Discussion

Let us now consider the differences between Dai Zhen and Mencius in the way they understand the two ideas under consideration —that *xing* is good and that *liyi* or *yi* is internal. There are certain differences that stem primarily from the different conceptual apparatus or constraints that Dai Zhen is working with. For example, he views the relation between *xing* and *qingyu* in terms of the distinction between an inactivated and an activated state, a distinction that is common during his but not Mencius' time. Also, since the *Lunyu* and the *Zhongyong* have by his time been accepted as canonical texts of the Confucian school, Dai Zhen has to discuss the differences in capacity among human beings mentioned in these texts, though such differences are not highlighted in Mencius' thinking. For the present purpose, I will set aside such differences and focus instead on the differences that would have remained had Dai Zhen not worked with such conceptual apparatus and constraints.

The first idea that Dai Zhen shares with Xunzi concerns the way in which *li* is related to *qing* and *yu*. Dai Zhen regards *qing* and *yu* as rooted in *xueqi*, which, along with *xinzhi*, constitutes *xing*. The term *xueqi* occurs several times in the *Xunzi* and is also paired with *zhi* 知 (e.g., 13/13a) or *zhilü* 知慮 (1/8a–8b).[3] Both Xunzi and Dai Zhen understand *qing* to refer to feelings or emotions and what is genuinely so. *Qing* is often used in the combination "*ren zhi qing*" 人之情 in the *Xunzi* to describe what human beings are genuinely like (e.g., 2/4a, 2/12a, 2/11a). *Ren zhi qing* includes certain desires (*yu*) pertaining to the senses (7/5b, 7/9a) or to the person as a whole (2/12b, 2/13b) and also refers to the fact that human beings desire to have more rather than less of what they desire (12/13a–13b). Sometimes, such desires are characterized as the *yu* of *qing* (16/9a) or in terms of what a person likes (*hao*) (17/3a–3b). Likes and dislikes, along with feelings of joy, anger, sorrow, and delight, are also described as *qing* (11/10a, 16/1b); sometimes, joy and anger are described as the responses (*ying* 應) of the *qing* of likes and dislikes (*hao wu zhi qing* 好惡之情) (14/2b). As for the relation among *xing*, *qing*, and *yu*, Xunzi sometimes characterizes *qing* as the likes, dislikes, joy, anger, sorrow, and delight of *xing* (16/1b), and he sometimes describes *qing* as the substance (*zhi* 質) of *xing* and *yu* as the responses (*ying*) of *qing* (16/9a). The combination "*qingxing*" 情性

occurs several times in the *Xunzi,* and *xing, qing,* and *yu* are mentioned together on other occasions (e.g., 16/11a).

It appears that *xing, qing,* and *yu* are related in the *Xunzi* in the following manner. The *xing* of human beings consists of what pertains to them by birth, and it includes certain facts (*qing*) about how the senses and the person as a whole are drawn toward certain objects. Such tendencies are the *yu* of human beings; because such tendencies are revealed only when one interacts with external situations, *yu* is also describable as the responses of *qing.* In its basic form, *qing* has to do with *yu* and the associated likes and dislikes. But because the emotional responses such as joy, anger, sorrow, and delight that result from one's getting what one likes or dislikes are also part of what is genuinely so in human beings, they are also describable as *qing.* Quite likely, certain occurrences of *qing* in the *Xunzi* are used both to refer to the emotions and to emphasize what is genuinely so in a person. For example, in discussing the basis of certain ritual practices, *qing* is used to refer to such emotions as remembrance (13/14b) and sorrow or joy (13/9a–9b) and is at the same time contrasted with *wen* 文 (e.g., 13/4b, 13/9a, 13/12b, 13/14a–14b), where *wen* refers to the refinement on the outside and *qing* to what is genuinely within the person (e.g., 13/6a, 19/6b).

Thus, though there are some differences in the way they spell out this relation, Xunzi and Dai Zhen are similar in regarding *qing* and *yu* as intimately related to *xing* and as part of the basic constitution of human beings. Furthermore, they both emphasize how the Confucian Way serves to promote satisfaction of *yu* and attainment or expression of *qing,* though Xunzi does not, with occasional exceptions (e.g., 3/4b), highlight the idea of reciprocity as Dai Zhen does. By contrast, there is little evidence that the *Mencius* uses *qing* to refer to feelings or emotions or emphasizes human desires in the way Xunzi and Dai Zhen do.[4] This does not mean that Mencius does not attach importance to basic human desires. He does emphasize how *ren* government involves attending to the basic needs and desires of the people, and how a ruler should share with his subjects his enjoyment of what he desires (e.g., *Mencius* 1B5). However, unlike Xunzi and Dai Zhen, who view propriety primarily as a way of satisfying the basic human desires, there is little evidence that Mencius regards *yi* as consisting primarily in the satisfaction of such desires. Consider Mencius' well-known example of the beggar who would rather die of starvation than accepting food given with abuse, which furnishes a paradigmatic example of a *yi* response (6A10). It is difficult to see how the propriety of such a response can be explained in terms of its conduciveness to satisfying the basic human desires, whether in oneself or in others.

Indeed, the kind of human desires that Dai Zhen focuses on and that he calls the *yu* of *xing* is primarily the biological desires that make living possible; as we have seen, he regards following *li* as what enables one to take part in the process of giving and nourishing life. Mencius, in redirecting attention to the heart in his explication of *xing*, appears to be ascribing to the heart a certain ethical direction that is independent of any instrumental role it plays with regard to the satisfaction of biological desires. Dai Zhen is probably correct that Mencius' emphasis on the heart in his explication of *xing* is not a denial that the biological desires are part of *xing* but serves more as a corrective to contemporary views about *xing* that focus exclusively on biological desires. Still, the way Mencius views the relation of the heart to biological desires is different from Dai Zhen's. Dai Zhen compares *xing* to water, *yu* to the flow of water, and *li* to regulating the flow of water to avoid overflowing. This analogy illustrates that *li* is nothing but the regulation of *yu* to enable the *yu* of everyone to be satisfied; the importance of the heart lies in its ability to grasp how *yu* in everyone can be satisfied and *qing* attained. Mencius, on the other hand, views *xing* as the direction of development of the whole person over a lifetime. Although biological growth is part of such development, the heart itself has an ethical direction that (as illustrated by the beggar example) has priority over biological growth. The importance of the heart lies less in its ability to grasp the means to satisfy *yu* and more in its setting an ethical direction that is independent of and should regulate the satisfaction of *yu*.

The second idea that Dai Zhen shares with Xunzi concerns the guiding role of understanding. In the *Xunzi, zhi* 知 (understanding) and *xing* 行 (action) are often mentioned together (e.g., 1/1a, 4/11a, 16/8a), and though understanding is not explicitly described as guiding action, it is assigned a guiding role in one's following the Way—it is through understanding the Way that one will approve of it, and it is through approving of it that one will abide by (15/4a–4b) or follow (16/9b) it. Indeed, like Dai Zhen, Xunzi often links understanding to *ren* (humanity) (6/4a, 8/5b, 15/4a) and to being a sage (4/4b, 15/10a, 20/8b, 20/12a). Furthermore, he also advocates developing one's understanding (1/1a; cf. 2/3a) or understanding and deliberation (*zhilü*) (11/11b, 12/12a; cf. 2/9a) to attain clarity (*ming* 明), and he uses the idea of clarity to describe both the rites (11/13a, 13/6a) and the sage (1/11b, 13/15a; cf. 3/11a). The notion of clarity is opposed to becloudedness (*bi*); in the "Jie Bi" 解蔽 chapter, the removal of becloudedness is described as that which enables one to understand and to attain purity and clarity, where clarity in its ideal state is compared to the brightness of sun and moon (15/5b; cf. 20/12a). In addition, again like Dai Zhen, clarity is related to a spiritlike quality (*shen*) (2/4a), the latter having to do with the subtle way in which certain effects are accomplished (11/10a); the term "*shenming*" is used to refer to the spiritlike clarity of the heart (1/3a, 4/12a, 5/8b, 15/5b).

By contrast, we do not find in the *Mencius* a similar emphasis on the guiding role of understanding and a similar employment of terms like *ming, bi,* or *shenming. Shen* is used in the *Mencius* to refer to the subtle way certain effects are accomplished (7A13, 7B25), and *ming* (clarity) to refer to clear understanding (2A4, 3A3, 4A12), but *ming* is not used explicitly to describe the heart or in the combination *shenming.* Similarly, although *bi* is used to characterize certain problematic teachings (2A2), the hindrance of worthy people (4B17), or the way the operation of the senses is exhausted in their being drawn by external things (6A15), it is not explicitly used in contrast to *zhi* (understanding) or *ming* (clarity) to describe the heart. As for the relation between *zhi* (understanding) and *xing* 行 (action), although understanding is related to ability (*neng* 能) (7A15, 6B2) and action to *yan* 言 (words) (4B11, 6B14, 7B37), *zhi* (understanding) is not explicitly linked to *xing* (action).

These observations suggest that Mencius probably does not emphasize the guiding role of understanding in the way Dai Zhen does, though the guiding role of the heart itself is certainly emphasized. For example, in *Mencius* 2A2, Mencius discusses at length how *zhi* 志, the directions of the heart, should guide *qi,* the vital energies that fill the body. Human conduct should ideally involve setting one's heart in certain directions that accord with *yi* and cultivating one's *qi* so that it provides the motivational strength to support the execution of the directions of the heart. Nevertheless, this is different from Dai Zhen's notion of understanding in one crucial respect. Understanding for Dai Zhen takes *li* as its object, and it involves one's having a reflective awareness of certain courses of action as being in accord with *li*. For Mencius, however, while *zhi* 志 (not to be confused with *zhi* 知, understanding) should ideally accord with *yi*, one's having the appropriate *zhi* need not by itself involve a reflective awareness of the fact that one's *zhi* accords with *yi*. The object of *zhi* (the directions of the heart) is not *li* or *yi*; rather, the object is a specific course of action (such as returning to one's home state) or an aim in life (such as learning) toward which one's heart is directed. It is possible for *zhi* to be accompanied by an awareness that the course of action toward which one's *zhi* is directed accords with *yi*. Indeed, Mencius probably thinks that, ideally, one should at least be capable of such awareness—*Mencius* 2A2 describes how ideally one should be free from fear if, upon self-reflection, one realizes that one's actual or proposed course of action is in accord with *yi*. However, unlike Dai Zhen, who emphasizes the importance of understanding in guiding action, there is little evidence that Mencius believes that one's action should always be guided by, and not just be accompanied by, the awareness that one is acting in accordance with *yi*.

Consider, for example, the *yi* responses described in *Mencius* 6A10 and 3A5—the beggar refusing food given with abuse and one's being moved to bury one's parents upon seeing their dead bodies being devoured by wild animals. The responses are described as coming spontaneously from the heart, involving one's being moved to act in the way one does without guidance from any prior conception of what the *yi* response should be. Indeed, the point of the second example is that the propriety of burying parents is itself revealed in one's response; that is, it is in being moved in the way one does that one sees that burying parents is proper, and so the former is not guided by the latter. Admittedly, some reflective conception of what is proper can play a guiding role in the process of self-cultivation—after all, such a conception is what the teachings of the ancient sages are supposed to convey. But there is little evidence that Mencius thinks that such a reflective conception should continue to play a guiding role as one makes ethical progress; it seems compatible with his view to hold that, in its ideal state, the heart's responses should at least in some situations not depend on guidance by such a conception.

These two differences between Dai Zhen and Mencius—that concerning the relation between *li* and *qingyu* and that concerning the guiding role of a reflective understanding of *liyi* or *yi*—lead to differences in the way they understand the goodness of *xing*. Dai Zhen's view that *xing* comprises *xueqi*, which is the source of *qing* and *yu*, and *xinzhi*, which is capable of understanding, is not in itself significantly different from how it is viewed by Mencius, who, in emphasizing the heart, is probably not denying that biological desires are also part of *xing*. Dai Zhen and Mencius do differ, however, in what they ascribe to the heart. Mencius' emphasis on the heart is in large part a response to the Mohist assumption that a conception of *yi* can be established independently of the way the heart is initially disposed, a conception that can be imposed on the heart to reshape it. For Mencius, *yi* is itself determined in large part by the way the heart is already disposed, and it is by reflecting on the heart's own predispositions that we arrive at a conception of *yi*. These predispositions are seen from the spontaneous responses as exemplified in the four germs and from familial attitudes such as love for parents or respect for elders, as well as from the way the heart takes pleasure in *liyi* and feels discontent at what is contrary to *liyi*. While Mencius sees an ethical direction in the heart's predispositions from which *yi* is derived, Dai Zhen emphasizes primarily the heart's capacity to understand *li*. He characterizes the four germs as themselves a form of understanding that the heart has to start with, and though he tries to accommodate Mencius' idea that the heart takes pleasure in *liyi*, this idea does not play a role in his conception of how we come to understand *li*. For Mencius, it is from the predispositions of the heart that we derive a conception of *yi*. For Dai Zhen, we come to grasp *li* by using our *qing* and *yu* to gauge the *qing* and *yu* of others, thereby finding out how *yu* can be satisfied and *qing* attained. Although this process involves the operation of the heart, the heart's contribution lies mainly in its capacity to engage in this process.

Thus, in asserting that *xing* is good, Mencius is probably ascribing more to the heart than Dai Zhen does. For Mencius, the claim conveys the point that the basic constitution of the heart has an ethical direction that has a priority over other biological tendencies; to nourish *xing* is to cultivate oneself in order to fully realize this ethical direction. For Dai Zhen, however, the claim conveys the point that being ethical is primarily a matter of satisfying *yu* and attaining *qing*, these being rooted in *xueqi*, a part of *xing*; this in turn involves developing the capacity of *xinzhi*, the other component of *xing*, to understand how *yu* can be satisfied and *qing* attained. Although he links the goodness of *xing* to the Mencian ideas of the four germs and of the heart's taking pleasure in *liyi*, these ideas are not essential to the heart's capacity to understand *li*, because *li* is not derived from the predispositions of the heart.

This discussion also bears on the different understanding of Dai Zhen and Mencius regarding the claim that *liyi* or *yi* is internal. Mencius' claim that *yi* is internal makes the point that *yi* can be derived from certain predispositions of the heart, a point also conveyed in his disagreement with Gaozi's view that *yi* is to be obtained from teachings (*yan* 言) rather than from the heart. In a debate with the Mohist Yi Zhi, Mencius makes a similar point, saying that things have one root in the sense that both the emotional resources needed for *yi* behavior and our seeing what is *yi* have their source in certain emotional predispositions of the heart. In saying that *yi* is internal, Mencius is not saying that *yi* is located in the heart rather than in things—he does speak of *yi* as something that pertains to human relations and conduct, and in citing the line "where there are things, there are norms" from the *Shijing*, he apparently sees norms as residing in things. Accordingly, Dai Zhen's difference from Mencius is not that he locates *liyi* in things rather than in the heart; rather, it has to do with how Dai Zhen views the way one arrives at an understanding of *li*. For him, although it is the heart that arrives at this understanding, it does so not by deriving *li* from the way it is itself predisposed but by attending to how *yu* can be satisfied and *qing* attained. Although he ascribes to the heart the tendency to take pleasure in *liyi*, he does not share Mencius' view that this tendency reflects a constitution of the heart from which *liyi* can be derived.

To conclude, let us consider how Dai Zhen differs from Xunzi despite the similarity in their views about how *li* relates to *qingyu* and in their emphasis on understanding. Dai Zhen criticizes Xunzi for the way he distinguishes between the ancient sages and the ordinary people—the capacity of the heart of the ancient sages surpasses that of the ordinary people so that whereas the ancient sages were able to establish the rites on the basis of the heart's deliberation about the human situation, the ordinary people have to learn them with the help of teachers. This, according to Dai Zhen, is to treat the rites and propriety on the one hand, and the ordinary people's *xueqi* and *xinzhi* on the other, as having two roots; it is also

to view propriety as external. Although this is an important difference, there are also other differences that are independent of Xunzi's
distinction between the ancient sages and the ordinary people.

For Xunzi, there is, whether in the ancient sages or in the ordinary people, nothing in the basic constitution of the heart that
points in an ethical direction. What the human heart shares is the
capacity to understand the rationale behind the rites—how strife
and disorder would have resulted from the desires that human beings have without the regulation of the rites—and to abide and be
transformed by them. Xunzi does not believe that there is any ethical dimension to the heart other than the capacity just described,
and so for him self-cultivation involves a radical reshaping of the
whole person. Now, although Dai Zhen does not ascribe to the
heart the kind of ethical predispositions that Mencius does, it appears that Dai Zhen still differs from Xunzi in ascribing something
to the heart that bears some affinity to *li*. Unlike Xunzi, he ascribes
to the heart a starting point for self-cultivation that goes beyond a
mere capacity to understand the rationale behind the social setup
and to abide by and be transformed by it. The four germs reflect
some understanding of *li* that human beings already have, and the
heart is already predisposed in a way that it takes pleasure in *li*. So
self-cultivation is a matter of nourishing and developing the understanding that one already has, however obstructed and dim, in the
way that growth of one's body is a nourishment and development of
something one has to start with, however weak and fragile. While
Dai Zhen differs from Mencius in viewing this process primarily in
terms of increasing one's understanding, he also differs from Xunzi
in seeing a greater continuity between this process and the basic
human constitution.

Notes

Ideas in this essay were presented at the International Symposium on
Confucian Currents in Japan and East Asia (National University of Singapore,
Singapore, 5–6 December 1997), International Symposium on Mencius (Academia Sinica, Taipei, Taiwan, 16 May 1998), and the International Conference
on Mencius and His Legacy (National University of Singapore, Singapore, 7–9
January 1999). I am grateful to the participants for their comments on earlier
drafts of the essay.

1. All references to the *Mengzi* (*Mencius*) are to book and passage numbers (with book numbers 1A to 7B substituted for numbers 1 to 14) in Yang
Bojun, trans., *Mengzi yizhu* (Beijing: Zhonghua shuju, 1984).

2. All references to the *Mengzi ziyi shuzheng* are to passage numbers, with the whole text divided into 43 passages. Page references are to the edition of the text published by Zhonghua shuju (Beijing), 2d ed., 1982.

3. All references to the *Xunzi* are to volume and page numbers in the edition of the text with Yang Liang's commentary published in the Sibubeiyao series.

4. See my *Mencius and Early Chinese Thought* (Stanford, Calif.: Stanford University Press, 1997), 183–186, 214–216. The discussion of Mencius that follows draws on ideas from this book.

11

The Nature and Historical Context of the *Mencius*

E. Bruce Brooks and A. Taeko Brooks

LATER AGES ASCRIBE all the sayings in the *Mencius* 孟子 (MC) equally to the historical Mèng Kē [Meng Ke] 孟軻, but the text contains differing statements of view that are not easily explained as variant statements of a single view.[1] As we shall argue, they are more plausibly seen as early and late phases in a development. That is, the text seems to have a time depth. If so, its thought will be best understood not as a unity, diverse but ultimately consistent, but rather as a sequence of positions, nourished by continued thought and perhaps also shaped by the continuing pressure of outward circumstances. This essay, though philological in nature, is thus ultimately offered as a contribution to a proper understanding of the thought of Mencius—in which term we would include the thought of those followers who preserved and continued his contribution in the years after his death.

To anticipate, we believe that the structure of the text is as follows: (1) a series of genuine official interviews by Mencius, preserved together with an equal number of later, imagined interviews in MC 1; (2) a conflated but original private discourse of Mencius in 2A2, this together with the MC 1 core constituting the heritage of the historical Mencius as it was put into text form shortly after his death in c0303; and (3) not one but two series of textual records left by posthumous Mencian schools, one comprising the rest of MC 1–3 and the other all of MC 4–7, each being added to over time and interacting with the other and with outside texts and events, and their respective final sections MC 3 and 7 being from the same period,

242

the years just before the final conquest of Lŭ in 0249.[2] We suggest that this hypothesis, together with outside evidence, not only
leads to a consistent view of the text but also can clarify some otherwise perplexing individual passages and shed light on some longstanding Mencian controversies.

In the present essay we will give reasons for doubting the
standard view (section 1), argue in general terms for our hypothesis of the text (sections 2–9), see whether that hypothesis in fact
removes the previously noted contradictions (section 10), and suggest that the hypothesis may help to clarify issues or explain anomalies that have been raised or noticed by previous scholars (section
11).[3]

1. Against the Consistency Hypothesis

Here are three observations that invite doubt as to the internal consistency and singleness of viewpoint of the *Mencius*. We will
return to them later (in section 10). We cite them here to show that
the standard hypothesis of authorial consistency fails, so as to clear
the way for an alternate hypothesis.

Yĭ Yĭn 伊尹. Yĭ Yĭn is mentioned in various Warring States
texts as an emblematic figure, that is, as one who represents a particular kind of ministerial conduct in or out of office. We are not here
concerned with the truth of any of these representations, or with
the historicity of Yĭ Yĭn himself, but only with the consistency of Yĭ
Yĭn's emblematic value in the *Mencius*. There are eight passages in
all. In MC 2A2 and 5B1, Yĭ Yĭn is invoked as an example of one who
would accept office under any ruler, and 6B6 describes him as going
to more than one ruler, whereas in 7B38 and in most other passages
he is associated only with the Shang ruler Tāng (in 7A31 he banishes
Tāng's unworthy son and, after the son's reform, restores him). This
might be rationalized by taking 2A2, 5B1, and 6B6 in a general, and
7B38 and other passages in a more focused, sense. In 5A7, Yĭ Yĭn
is said to have accepted office only reluctantly; in 6B6 he is said to
have actively sought it.[4] These passages clearly differ as to the motives
behind Yĭ Yĭn's career. In 2B2 he is said to have gained office not by
appointment but by advancing from a subordinate position (tutor);
in 5A7 an extreme version of this story (the subordinate position
being that of a cook) is explicitly denied. Not only do these two pas-

sages differ as to the history of Yī Yǐn, but the second also openly
disputes the first. As to Yī Yǐn's emblematic value, in 2A2 he is
ranked lower than Confucius, whereas in 5A6 and by implication in
7A31 he is bracketed with Confucius' ideal, Jōu-gūng [Zhou-gong],
his integrity in that role contrasting strongly with the political flexibility in 6B6. Given any of these passages, it would seem somewhat
risky to guess what position the next passage will take concerning
the life or the exemplary value of Yī Yǐn. Such a contrast might be
expected between two rival texts, but it is surely problematic when it
occurs within a single, supposedly consistent text.

Confucius and the *Chūn/Chyōu* [*Chunqiu*] 春秋**.** It is here assumed that Mencius was at the School of Lǔ (the group whose text
was the *Analects*) before embarking on his own career in 0320.[5]
If so, we should expect him to be informed about the role of Confucius in the formation of the *Chūn/Chyōu*. The subject is twice mentioned in the *Mencius,* but the two passages give different accounts.
MC 3B9 says that Confucius "made" (作) the *Chūn/Chyōu* and that,
on his completing it, evil ministers and undutiful sons were put in
fear and confusion. MC 4B21 merely says that the *Chūn/Chyōu* is
one of several chronicles written in the "historical" style (其文則史)
and that Confucius "ventured to take his principles from it" (Lau;
其義則丘竊取之矣). Legge renders this as "make its [righteous] decisions," but there is in any case no claim of authorship of the whole
Chūn/Chyōu. We feel obliged to doubt that a student in the successor school of Confucius in Lǔ would be this unclear about the nature of Confucius' supposed contribution to the *Chūn/Chyōu.*

Good Government 善政**.** In 2A1 the phrase "good government" is positive, referring to the lingering effects of the wise rule of
the Shang founders. In 7A14 the term has bitterly negative over-
tones: "He who practices good government is feared by the people;
he who gives the people good teaching is loved by them. Good government wins the wealth of the people; good teaching wins their
hearts." We might for the word "good" in this usage of "good government" substitute "efficiently rapacious." With this much oscilla-
tion in the meaning of basic vocabulary, we question whether a single-
author presumption can be maintained for the *Mencius.*

Examples might be multiplied. We take it that the point is
made or at least raised by these three.

2. The Alternate Hypothesis: Separation within MC 1

The Historical Mencius. Lau observes that the interviews of MC 1 appear to be in chronological order.[6] We would offer two amendments. (1) The final 1B16 is clearly out of sequence. It depicts Mencius as having returned from Chí [Qi] to bury his mother, and so it must be before his final departure from Chí (in 0313, following the Yēn [Yan] incident). It cannot be earlier than Lǔ Píng-gūng's [Lu Ping-gong] first year, 0317,[7] and its hope of a private rather than a full court meeting would be consistent with any mourning restrictions that may have obtained in that year, the first after Pínggūng's accession.[8] If so, then its date is 0317, and its proper chronological place in MC 1 would be after 1B1. It may have been placed last editorially because its comment about fate makes a suitable epigraph, or epitaph, for the public career of Mencius. (2) The MC 1 interviews readily divide themselves into two groups:[9]

1A1, 1A3:1–3, 1A5:1–3, 1A6, 1B1, [1B16], 1B9, 1B10, 1B12, 1B13, 1B14, 1B15 (total 12)
*1A2, *1A4, *1A7, *1B2, *1B3, *1B4, *1B5, *1B6, *1B7, *1B8, *1B11 (total 11)

Of the 1A1 group, all the following statements can be made: their implied duration is not more than three minutes; the ruler sets the theme (when it is specified who sets the theme, as it is not in 1B9) and may develop it by a further question; Mencius observes reasonable propriety; and he does not quote the *Shr̄* [*Shi*] 詩 or the *Shū* 書, nor does he assume that the ruler is familiar with them, but uses instead illustrations drawn from common experience. Of the *1A2 group (the asterisk indicates passages in MC 1 that we believe are interpolated), one or more of the following may be said: they are long; Mencius defines the theme; he is accusatory of the ruler; and he or the ruler quotes the *Shr̄* or *Shū*. This suggests that besides the modest genuine 1A1 group of interviews, we have a second, imagined *1A2 set, in which Mencius has a more dominating role, discourses freely, and occupies a learned and specifically Confucianized context characterized by familiarity with the classic writings. The two groups clearly inhabit different circumstantial and rhetorical worlds, and of them, the *1A2 group would have been far more grateful to Confucian sensibilities and in particular to the self-esteem of the followers of Mencius. We take them as imaginative retrospections and not historical transcripts.

Further Evidence for the Hypothesis. (1) Other traits divide the proposed genuine and spurious interviews. With the exception of the narrated noninterview 1B16, and some details in 1A6 to be discussed below, no genuine interview describes persons or actions, whereas in 1B6 we have the narrative line 王顧左右而言他, "The King looked left and right and spoke of other things." The use of narrative techniques suggests a retrospectively visualized, not a verbally reported, meeting. (2) The general form of interview implied by the 1A1 group (though not that of the *1A2 group) is also exemplified in the interviews in the Syẃndž [Xunzi] 荀子 (SZ). Syẃndž's interviews run a little longer but otherwise a similar situation obtains: Syẃndž speaks on an assigned theme and maintains decorum, and the interviewer is not represented as versed in Confucian culture. In SZ 15 (not an interview but a command performance), from c0250, the only expertise shared by ruler and adviser is military, represented in part by quotations from the Sūndž [Sunzi] 孫子. The expertise displayed by Lyáng Hwèi-wáng [Liang Hui-wang] in MC 1A3:1–3 and 1A5:1–3 (c0320, genuine) was also military. We conclude that these passages accurately reflect a military rather than learned outlook on the part of Warring States rulers and that they also imply a more or less standard format for Warring States interviews. (3) Separating the *1A2 group as spurious removes some contradictions in MC 1. 1B9 (genuine) advocates delegation to the talented, whereas in *1B7 (spurious) it is a last resort. The economic policy of 1A3:1–3 (genuine) differs from that of *1A7 (spurious). The ability to remove such difficulties is evidence in favor of this (as it is of any) proposed text reconstruction.

Another argument in favor of the reconstruction is a high degree of continuity in the series of Lyáng Hwèi-wáng interviews—1A1-1A3-1A5, which has been obscured by the addition of *1A2 and *1A4. In 1A1 the king, calling Mencius sǒu 叟 (old man), asks what Mencius can say that will benefit his state. Mencius objects to the term lì 利 (value, benefit, profit). In 1A3 (though not in the intervening *1A2), the king again refers to Mencius as sǒu (since in 0320 the king was more than seventy years old, apparently the threshold of "old age" in this culture, and Mencius, born in c0387, was younger than this and certainly younger than the King, this respectful epithet may have had a humorous tone). In 1A3 the king returns to the question of 1A1, but indirectly, saying what he has himself been doing to benefit his state and asking why it is not working. Mencius this time answers with an economic program: not overusing the food resources. Mencius uses a military metaphor in the course of explaining this program. In 1A5, perhaps taking the metaphor as an indication that Mencius is willing to discuss military matters, the king introduces his military efforts, again as a failed program, and invites comment. Again Mencius responds with a policy suggestion (and makes his first use of the phrase 仁政), again the policy is economic, and again it is along the lines of resource conservation, but here not only the food resources (fish and turtles) but also the revenue resource (the people) are not to be overexploited. 1A3 deals with the question of people not immigrating into Ngwèi [Wei] 魏; 1A5 discusses the question of motivating the people already resident in Ngwèi to fight for Ngwèi. The sense of progression from 1A1 to 1A3 to 1A5 is very strong.[10] It vanishes if we restore 1A2 and 1A4 to the series. That fact strongly supports the proposal that the sequence 1A1-1A3-1A5 was the whole of the original text.[11]

Partition. If on this evidence we accept the 1A1 set of twelve interviews as the only genuine ones and regard the others as later additions, then besides the line drawn across the text by Lau's observation about MC 1,

MC 1 / MC 2–7

we must also draw a second line separating the genuine MC 1 interviews from the spurious ones:

MC 1A1 etc. / MC *1A2 etc. / MC 2–7

Scenario. If the 1A1 set are genuine transcripts, how were they taken down? There is a hint in MC 1A6, the only interview with Ngwèi Syāng-wáng [Wei Xiangwang], which, uniquely in the book, remarks that Mencius emerged from the interview and told "someone" (*rún* [*ren*] 人) what had transpired. A few descriptive remarks are made, and the interview transcript itself follows. What is going on here? We note the following. (1) By the sequence of MC 1, this interview occurred soon after the death of Syāng-wáng's father, Hwèi-wáng. (2) 04-century rulers seem to have succeeded directly, without a mourning interval, but it is still reasonable to suspect that court ceremonial was for a time reduced from its normal level, and individuals meeting with the ruler might, out of respect for that reduction, have had to leave their retinues at the door. (3) 1A6 may then show Mencius emerging from a low-key interview in 0319 and repeating the gist of the interview to the amanuensis for writing down. (4) Can we test this? We believe so, as follows: 1A6 is the only interview to give Mencius' highly negative personal impression of the ruler. To whom would he have spoken such comments? Surely not to the ruler, but quite possibly to one of his own party. In 1A6, where (as we infer) that description was delivered along with Mencius' repetition of the interview proper, it might then have been atypically but naturally incorporated in the transcript of the interview. The implication is that Mencius normally had an amanuensis present at his court interviews, but when none was present, he reported the interview to his amanuensis for transcription at the first opportunity.

3. The Core Text and Its Physical Form as of c0303

The Physical Text. The hypothesis that MC 1 was originally only half its present size will also help to explain an otherwise perplexing feature of the *Mencius:* its double chapters. Many early books are divided into *pyēn* [*pian*] 篇, presumably separate rolls of bamboo strips, which in some cases (among them the *Analects* [*Lunyu;* abbr., LY] and the *Jwāngdž* [*Zhuangzi*] 莊子) take their titles from the first words of the included text (thus LY 1: 學而). This pattern also applies to the *Mencius,* with the difference that each named unit is divided into two, labeled with the *pyēn* name plus 上 or 下. Why? In particular, why is not 1B called "Jwāng Bàu" [Zhuang Bao] 莊暴 from its first-named person? We may note that the sizes of these half-chapter *pyēn* are within the rather narrow range of 2,277–2,927 characters. Depending how we imagine the text as being written (an average for the period might be 25 characters per bamboo strip), that may imply a roll of bamboo strips whose diameter is approaching its length. We have suggested that this is the limit of physical stability for such a roll.[12] That is, the original interviews as we here identify them would have made a large roll but still a manageable single one. However, any further increase in contents, such as would have occurred when the later school felt impelled to add to the genuine record, would very soon require a division into two rolls. If the second roll was split off in this way from the first by accretional pressure, it might well retain the name that had by then become familiar for the single roll. Hence we would logically have, for the title of the split-off second roll, not 莊暴 but 梁惠王下. That formal device being once adopted for the core collection of transcripts, it would very naturally be generalized to any later *pyēn*. Here the accretional hypothesis offers an explanation for a fact that is less readily explained on the standard theory.

The Position of MC 2A2. In the perception of many readers, 2A2 is unique among *Mencius* passages. It is not only among the longest (1,097 characters; second only to the 1,313 characters of *1A7), but it also conveys a uniquely intimate feeling of conversation between Mencius and his followers, who are not (as they mostly are elsewhere in the text) mere receptors for the delivery of maxims but press Mencius as to his personal preferences and practices. We believe that 2A2 may well be a record of just such informal questioning and that at one point it existed in parallel to the one-*pyēn* form of the public MC 1 as a private memoir of the school founder. We would exclude the final section (Legge, secs. 24–28, which ends with a repeat of the line that concludes sec. 23), and we would make a division between sections 1–17, which are largely taken up with breath control and related matters, and sections 18–23, which are more conventionally political. These two series look like separate remembered conversations that were combined, probably at the time of Mencius' death, c0303, into a consecutive document.[13] We presently see no intrinsic or positional reason to suspect their genuineness as Mencian memories. Accepting them as genuine, then as of Mencius' death in c0303, the complete textual repertoire of his remaining followers would have consisted of the 1A1 group of twelve interview transcripts (total 1,942 words) plus the 2A2:1–23 conversational memoir (908 words), each occupying its own generous, but stable, roll of bamboo strips.

The Ideas of the Historical Mencius. The conclusion that in the 1A1 set we have literal transcripts of the arguments of the historical Mencius may justify spending a moment to see what range of ideas we can, on that basis, firmly attribute to him. We have elsewhere suggested that the philosophy of Mencius as it is implied in the MC 1 interviews is largely derived from LY 12–13, the part of the *Analects* that we conclude was added to the text during Mencius' last years at the school of Lŭ, and in whose composition he may have been involved.[14] We feel that this philosophical agreement between

MC 1 and LY 12–13 needs no separate exposition here. We invite readers to observe, however, that the seemingly disconnected observations of LY 12–13 have a more integrated and worked-out character in MC 1. They would appear to have been subjected to considerable thought in the meantime and not to be mere reiterations of *Analects* maxims.

For example, LY 13.16 (c0322) states the basic principle of attracting new populace, which is also found in *Gwǎndž* [*Guanzi*] 管子 3[15] and was evidently familiar to Lyáng Hwèi-wáng himself. LY 13.9 prescribes that the people must first be made numerous, then made prosperous, and only then instructed. LY 13.29–30 make plain that the instruction in question is to make them viable soldiers. We can by our own further effort assemble these separate sayings into a coherent political philosophy, but LY 13 itself does not do so, and any such assemblage can be objected to as imposed on the unsystematic *Analects* material. Again, filial piety appears explicitly in 13.20 as a proper trait of the gentleman and in 13.18 as a duty of the commoner that transcends obedience to law. Since a consistent respect for law is not readily inferable from LY 13 and is indeed contradicted by the implication of 13.18, it is arguable whether filial piety forms part of the LY 13 system, if indeed LY 13 can be said to constitute a system. In MC 1, on the other hand, there is no question: filial piety is part of the system. It defines privileged needs (the support of elders) that give the people a right not only to survival rations but also to reasonable surplus (1A3). Lack of that reasonable prosperity is said to lead in turn to popular resentment and military instability in the state (1A5; cf. 1B12). A government that shows reasonable consideration for the needs of others (*rún* [*ren*] 仁), not out of charity but simply out of self-interest, and yet not under the rubric of an admitted self-interest, will find its self-interest well served. For Syāng-wáng, the next year (1A6), Mencius repeats some of these arguments and makes clear that in his view a reasonably supportive government not only will secure its own strength but also will attract the strength, that is, the people, of the opposing states, thus undermining their power to conquer or to resist conquest, and leaving the way open for a merely nominal military force (that is, for a small but virtuous state) to achieve the desired political unification.

What is new in this is the integration of some of the LY 12–13 insights into a connected body of doctrine, the quantitative terms in which that doctrine is sometimes expressed, and the explicit placing of that doctrine at the service of the large powers in their struggle to obliterate each other. Of the three, it is perhaps the quantitative aspect that is the largest departure from *Analects* precedent. LY 13.20 had ridiculed the sort of granary accountancy in which Lǔ petty officials were engaging, but Mencius clearly sees the point of grain supplies and ration equivalents. And unlike the political theorists of the *Dàu/Dv̌ Jīng* [*Daodejing*], he has no illusions about how big a country has to be before it can aspire to dominate others. For little Tv́ng [Teng] 滕, below the 100:1 minimum area (1A5), he offers no prospect other than an honorable defeat (1B13–15). Only the big states have a discussable chance.

It would be inadequate to call Mencius, the historical Mencius of the MC 1 core, a social philosopher on the strength of his use of the word "*rv́n*" 仁, just as it would be absurd to call him a domestic philosopher because he mentions *syàu* [*xiao*] 孝. He might with some justice be called an economic philosopher, since much of his program lies within that sphere, and since his acceptance of quantitative statements indicates an openness to logistic as well as moral thinking. But Mencius goes beyond economics to the insight of 1A1, that the principle of utility or benefit, though crucial in assessing the functioning of a bureaucracy, is also fatal to that functioning if it becomes a principle of open self-interest among the bureaucrats. Mencius has reflected not only on the purpose of government, like everyone else in his time, but also on the way government can work without losing its public efficiency to private greed. We might validly call him a systems philosopher, noting that his system includes, and rests on, a sense of human values and responses.

The Successor Mencians. Any summary of the thought of the remainder of the book must, on the present hypothesis, count as a characterization of the posthumous Mencian school or schools. Of the successor Mencians in general, we may at this point reasonably infer the following. (1) A successor group must have existed, because not only was the original *Mencius* preserved, but also interpolations were later made in it so as to enhance the image of Mencius and to extend and develop his ideas. This implies an active custodianship, by people for whom Mencius remained an authenticating figure, hence most probably by his successor school or schools. (2) Among their concerns was to attribute to the late 04 century a general Confucianization of culture. This goes beyond what the core

MC 1 or other slightly later texts such as the *Syŵndž* will countenance, and it indicates a degree of counterfactual thinking that may be of interpretive value at a later stage of the investigation. (3) It is reasonable to attribute to the successor school or schools not only the MC 1 interpolations (and the codicils to 1A3, 1A5, and 2A2) but all the rest of the present *Mencius*—the balance of MC 1 and MC 2 and all of MC 3–7.[16] In what follows, we will argue that there were not one but two successor schools, which evolved in parallel and came to an end at essentially the same time, namely the year 0249, when Chǔ conquered Lǔ and its satellite states.

4. The Alternate Hypothesis: The Division between MC 1–3 and MC 4–7

Despite wide agreement that the *Mencius* offers a consistent sample of Warring States language,[17] the text does show signs of internal inconsistency and thus of complex origin. Linguistic evidence suggests a division into two groups, one being the additions to MC 1 plus MC 2–3, and the other being MC 4–7. A study of the content of the respective chapter series confirms this difference and also suggests that each series shows growth over time, with the more advanced governmental theories and the more subtle philosophical insights tending to come at the ends of the respective series.

Linguistic Evidence. A line drawn between MC 1–3 and MC 4–7 defines areas that are not identical linguistically. Chinese shows a general tendency for adverbs to migrate from the postverbal, or F, position to the preverbal, or B, position in the sentence. This process can be seen during the period documented by the *Chūn/Chyōu* (0721–0481); it has gone almost to completion in modern Mandarin, where the F adverb is attested only by a few duration-of-time idioms (e.g., 坐了半天) and some analogous fossilized expressions. Over the short time depth of the *Mencius,* we have so far detected no evolution, but the two series tend to show different states of equilibrium within the larger development. The evidence does not permit concise summary here.[18] Among vocabulary traits that tend to distinguish the two series are the negatives *fút* [*fu*] 弗 (38 times, 32 of them in MC 4–7) and *vùt* [*wu*] 勿 (24 times, 20 of them in MC 1–3). These may have a phonological, and thus ultimately a dialect, basis.

Content Evidence. Most vocabulary contrasts between the two series, however, seem to reflect differing subject emphasis—MC 1–3 are chiefly governmental, whereas MC 4–7 are more theoretical. The *Chywn-shū Jr̄-yàu* [*Qunshu zhiyao*] 群書治要 of 631, compiled under imperial auspices and thus likely to represent a governmental point of view, selects equally from both series (7 from each; total 14). More philosophically inclined works show a marked preference for the MC 4–7 series; thus Dài Jv̀n's [Dai Zhen] *Mv̀ngdž Dz-yì* [*Mengzi ziyi*] 孟子字義 of 1777 discusses in all 40 different passages, of which 11 are from MC 1–3 and a preponderant 29 are from MC 4–7. Among the latter, only 9 are from MC 4–5, and the remaining 20 passages are from MC 6–7. The index locorum of any recent work on the philosophy of Mencius will also tend to list MC 4–7 (especially MC 6–7) passages more frequently than MC 1–3 passages.[19] The MC 4–7 series, and especially its later chapters, thus seems to be of greater interest to a philosophically inclined posterity.

Analects **Relations.** We assume that Mencius knew all the *Analects* through LY 13 (that is, all of the text that had been compiled before his departure from the school in 0320), and through ongoing personal contact with the Lǔ school, he might before his death in c0303 have come to know LY 2 (c0317) and even LY 14–15 (the latter c0305), but not LY 1 (c0296) or chapters beyond LY 16 (c0285).[20] If we list the latest *Analects* saying of which each chapter of the *Mencius* seems to be aware, and we distinguish the two series as two columns, we obtain the following:

	MC 2A2: LY 9.6 (c0405)
MC 4: LY 2.9 (c0317)	
MC 5: LY 10.14 (c0380)	
MC 6: LY 13.29 (c0322)	
	MC 2: LY *14.35 (c0298)[21]
MC 7: LY 17.1, 11, 16, 22 (c0270)	
	MC 3: LY *18.18, *19 (c0260)

A presumed Mencian heritage will account for all *Analects* quotations or references in MC 1 and in MC 4–6, as well as MC 2A2, but the quotation of LY *14.35 in MC 2, and of material from LY 17 and later in both MC 3 and MC 7, require the assumption of a post-Mencius contact with the *Analects* group and imply a time depth in the Mencian material that forbids the attribution of all of it to Mencius or to disciples who had cherished and recorded his sayings without adding anything from their own thought or experience.

5. The Division into Two Schools

The characterization of MC 1–3 as governmental and MC 4–7 as philosophical may seem to be contradicted by the fact that the notorious Mencian theory of the right of revolution is found in both strands. We here explore that detail and take a closer look at the interpolations in MC 1, concluding with a suggestion about the cause and the date of the division of the successor Mencians into two schools.

The right of revolution is an aspect of Mencian populism. The basic tenet of Mencian populism is that the people are the foundation of the state and that the test of a state is its ability to protect and provide for its people. As an implication, this is present in the Lyáng Hwèi-wáng dialogue in MC 1A1-1A3-1A5; in 1A1, for example, the king asks why his concern for his people is not achieving the expected condition of good order. The genuine MC 1 transcripts do not go beyond this position.

The MC 1 addenda do go beyond it. Some of the extensions to the original transcripts already show the distinctive accusatory tone of the MC additions as a whole. In MC *1A3:5 the king of Lyáng is told, "Dogs and pigs eat the food of men, and you do not know enough to stockpile; roads are filled with the corpses of the starving, and you do not know enough to distribute; if people die, you say, 'It wasn't me; it was the harvest'. How is this different from stabbing someone to death and saying, 'It wasn't me; it was the knife'?" This is already pretty strong,[22] but the newly invented passages go further, to ask what follows when the ruler fails to nurture his people or actively oppresses them. In *1B6, "Mencius" is made to ask King Sywæn [Xuan] of Chí a series of questions: what happens if a friend betrays a trust, or an officer shows himself unworthy of his commission, and finally, "If all within the four borders is not well ordered, then what?" The king glances to left and right and talks of other things. Even more aggressively, in *1B8, "Mencius" replies to a question about the bad last Shang ruler, "I have heard about the killing of the ordinary fellow Jòu 紂, but I have not heard of the assassination of any ruler." The sanctity normally attaching to the ruler's person is lost when his behavior violates the expectations that (in this theory) define a ruler. *1B11 mentions the killing of bad local rulers as a detail of the conquests of the good first Shang ruler, Tāng, at which "the people were greatly delighted." In this view of things, it is the people who shall judge.[23]

In the MC 4–7 series we find analogues to the stages just described. (1) 4A5 asserts the primacy of the people, and 4A20 notes the importance of criticizing the ruler. This does not depart significantly from the implications of the authentic Mencius interviews. (2) 4B3 introduces the note of hostility toward the ruler: "When the ruler looks on his ministers as dirt and weeds, then the ministers will look on the ruler as a thief and an enemy." (3) The following chapter has several yet more drastic statements, challenging the theoretical position of the ruler. One is 5A5, which denies the principle of succession: "The Son of Heaven cannot give the world to another.... Heaven gave it to him [Shùn]; the people gave it to him." 5B9 concludes, "If the ruler has great faults, then [the ministers related to the ruler] will remonstrate. If he repeats [his errors] and does not heed [the criticism], then they will change incumbents." The king falls silent and changes his expression. In addition to this graphic touch, the assertion of the right to replace the ruler puts this on a par with *1B8. Later references to this theory do occur in both strands, but they are much less heated.

The parallels then seem to be as follows.

MC 4A5, 4A20	MC 1A1-1A3-1A5 etc.
MC 4B3	MC *1A3:5
MC 5A5, 5B9	MC *1B6, *1B8, *1B11
[returns to mere populism]	[repeats some earlier statements]

It is easy to imagine that after the death of Mencius, the more theoretically intemperate of the posthumous school were forced to leave and founded the separate MC 4–7 school. Yet the above pattern suggests that the increasingly strident Mencian theory of rulership developed in parallel in both schools. The split between them must thus have been relatively early, and the theory itself must have developed in response to some external situation, presumably the doings of a bad contemporary ruler, which impinged on both groups. If we take it as the least unlikely possibility that one group remained in Tv́ng while another relocated slightly to the north in Dzōu [Zou] 鄒, then the obvious candidate for this bad ruler is the notorious king of Sùng [Song] 宋, whose realm lay a day's journey southward from Dzōu and shared a common border with Tv́ng. That king's excesses, doubtless in exaggerated form, have left traces in other texts and are taken as obvious in the later MC 3B5.[24] The extirpation of Sùng by Chí in 0286 (which is described as imminent in

3B5) will have removed that king from the scene, and the lower intensity of Mencian revolution statements after MC 5 and the MC 1 interpolations may well reflect that removal. Then the separation of schools probably occurred not long after Mencius' death in c0303, and MC 4–5 and its counterparts in the southern school text should occupy the period c0300–0286.

Is there any clue as to the reason for the division of the schools? We think it possible that the northern passage MC 4B3 may contain an echo of that school's own departure from Tv́ng. The relevant lines are these: "But now those who act in ministerial capacity: if their responses are not followed, and their words are not listened to, so that benefits do not descend upon the people; if they for any reason leave the state, the ruler tries to seize and detain them, and will also retaliate against them in the place to which they have gone, and on the very day of their departure will summarily take back their lands and settlements; this is what one calls a thief and an enemy." Construed as a recent memory, this suggests that the departure of the northern group was voluntary, induced by political frustration rather than forced by higher disapproval, and that it was resented by their patron in Tv́ng. The patron's retaliation may have been due to the Mencians' being considered an asset to his public image, just as benefits were showered on the Ji-syà [Jixia] 櫻下 stipendiaries in Chí, at about the same time, to show the world that Chí "knew how to treat officers."[25] That retaliation may also help explain why the northern group seems never to have gained comparable access to power in their new location.

6. The Alternate Hypothesis: Synchronicity of MC 3 and MC 7

We here take up the proposition that MC 3 and MC 7, the respective last chapters in the two strands of the *Mencius* text, are from the same absolute time period.

Among features that suggest that MC 3 and 7 are responding to the same external world are the following. (1) *Syìng* [*xing*] 性 (nature) and *tyēn* [*tian*] 天 (Heaven) are linked only in 7A1 and 3A5.[26] This ethical theory thus unites these chapters. (2) Both chapters use the self-designation Rú 儒 for the school of thought to which they themselves belong, a term that is prominent in that sense in the Syẃndzian writings but is unknown elsewhere in the *Mencius*. (3)

Both chapters, but no other *Mencius* chapter, refer to the opposing schools as Yáng 楊 (Jū) [Yang Zhu] and Mwò 墨 (Dí) [Mo Di]. Though Micianism [Mohism] was part of the scene from the early 04 century until Hàn, Yáng's movement seems more limited. His views are little known, and his background is even less known. Yángist prominence in Warring States debate was thus probably not protracted,[27] and it is likely that these chapters (and the *Jwāngdž* primitivist chaps. 8–10, which also oppose "Yáng and Mwò"), are from the same relatively short period. From the *Analects,* which has links to both the *Mencius* and the *Jwāngdž,* that period can in turn be identified as roughly the decade before the Chǔ conquest of Lǔ in 0249.[28] (4) Another vocabulary item that is unique to these two chapters is *háu-jyé jř shř* [*haojie zhi shi*] 豪傑之士, which occurs in 3A4:12 (Lau, "an outstanding scholar") and 7A10 (Lau, "an outstanding man") and nowhere else in the text. There are other common vocabulary traits that are not readily attributable to random factors but seem to imply a common discourse style. (5) That commonality does not preclude some mutual antagonisms. On the assumption that the MC 1–3 series represents the continuation of Mencius' followers in Tv́ng, whereas the MC 4–7 series reflects a separate strand whose likeliest location is Dzōu, and noting that Gūngsūn Chǒu [Gongsun Chou] figures prominently in the former chapters (he gives his name to MC 2) and Wàn Jāng [Wan Zhang] in the latter (he gives his name to MC 5), there are passages that can be construed as barbs exchanged between the two schools. MC 7A32 in effect calls Gūngsūn Chǒu (the hero of MC 1–3) a primitivist, and 7A39 brands him a Mician.[29] As though in response, 3B5 portrays Wàn Jāng as a political dunce who credits evil Sùng with good intentions ("Mencius," in a long and exasperated diatribe, will have none of this).[30] As perhaps a further rejoinder, the odd and seemingly pointless tale 7B30 records an accusation that the Mencians in Tv́ng [*sic*] are little better than thieves (for whom again "Mencius" disclaims individual responsibility). These little intergroup squabbles, as they seem to be, are much more plausible as between separate and rival groups than as among the remembered chief disciples of a single movement. In no chapters other than MC 3 and 7 does this impression of intergroup asperity arise. Neither the uniquely common features of these chapters nor the differences and the rancor that divide them are readily accounted for by the standard theory that the *Mencius* is the sayings of one man.

Those qualities suggest an outward event, one that pushed the schools into closer conjunction than previously. One candidate event is the preliminary conquest by Chŭ of the southern portion of Lŭ in 0255/0254. We may note that Syẃndž's influence on both MC 3 and 7 is visible in their use of his signature term "Rú," and recall that Syẃndž moved to Chŭ as director of Lán-líng, a town located at 34°44′ N, 117°54′ E, just south of the old Lŭ southern boundary and somewhat east of Warring States Syẃjōu [Xuzhou] 徐州, 120 km on a line southeast from the Lŭ capital Chw̄fù [Qufu] 曲阜. Syẃndž's appointment brought him close to the southern edge of Lŭ, so it could have been made only after Chŭ controlled Lán-líng, and that was true only after 0254. Then the possible dislocation of one or both Mencian schools, and the strong influence of Syẃndzian vocabulary on both, would seem to be best dated to 0254 and the few years that elapsed before 0249, when Chŭ completed its conquest and absorbed Lŭ and its satellites entirely into the Chŭ polity.[31]

7. The Alternate Hypothesis: Developments in the Proposed Text Strand MC 1–3

It has been suggested above that (1) MC 1–3 and 4–7 are separate text strands and that (2) their respective ends, MC 3 and 7, are not only near each other in time but also different in character from the rest of their groups. If this is so, we might expect to be able to detect a certain progression of ideas within each of the two proposed text strands. In this and the next section, we will cite details that tend to show that the text does not merely contain internal differences but that any developments implied by those differences tend to be in the same direction, and that this direction is toward MC 3 or 7, not the reverse. We may begin with economic matters, since for these there is sometimes corroborating text or archaeological evidence.

Rural Mobility. As noted above, Mencius, and indeed Lyáng Hwèi-wáng, envisioned a populace that was mobile and thus capable of being attracted from one state to the next by a benign government (1A5). This assumption seems to hold true as late as 2A6, but it is not present in still later economic passages such as 3A3. Archaeological and literary evidence from the period generally attests the increasing subjection of the populace and thus supports the idea of a gradual loss of what might be called residential mobility.[32]

Rural Independence. The early Mencian policy statements can be interpreted as applying to single-family farms. Late policy statements, such as the well-field proposal in 3A3, instead envision a pooling of labor within an eight-family group. Such 03-century statecraft texts as the *Gwǎndž* [*Guanzi*] show the coresponsibility principle in process of development,[33] and as is well known, coresponsibility was further extended and enforced under the Chín [Qin] empire.[34] The *Mencius* passages that we are here considering take their place without difficulty in the 03-century stage of that larger general development.

Rural Diet. Early Mencian economic passages speak of fish and turtles as endangered by overuse (1A3) but as providing an animal protein supplement to the basic grain diet. The later *1A7:24 and the very late 7A22 refer to barnyard animals but not to fish or turtles. The implication is that the ponds where these used to grow have been drained to make plowlands. The motive for doing this is obvious. Farming is several times more efficient, in terms of net caloric yield, than fishing.[35] As agriculture became more "rationalized," that is, as its caloric yield was made to increase in the 03 century, the ponds were presumably sacrificed to the goal of maximum output. By Hàn times, one scholar concludes that pigs in the rural economy functioned primarily not as a source of meat but rather as a source of manure.[36] Again, the implied development fits easily into what the scanty evidence suggests is the probable long-term developmental picture.

***Rín Jìng* [*Ren Zheng*] 仁政.** The term "*rín jìng*" turns up first in 1A5, where it means leaning easier on the people so that they can gratify their filial instincts and thus feel gratitude toward the state, which they express in willing military service.[37] The converse of this theory is expressed in 1B12, where lack of willing military service is ascribed to the resentment of the people. In none of these early and genuine pieces is there any hint of moral self-cultivation, by the people, the ministers, or the ruler. They focus instead on the basic economic needs of the people. If these are met, loyalty ensues, and the state is strong. If not, resentment ensues, and the state is weakened. This is the entire content of *rín jìng* as expounded by Mencius himself.

In the interpolated *1B11, Chí is said to have courted military intervention by annexing Yēn, doubling its area without also practicing *rún jùng*. In the authentic 1A5:1–3, *rún jùng* was recommended as strengthening the state, leaving open the possibility that this new strength might provoke preemptive attack by other states. The *1B11 *rún jùng* seems to deal with this difficulty by operating so as to prevent intervention, presumably because the people of those states (and, in the age of the mass army, thus the armies of those states) will not support a campaign against a *rún jùng* state. This goes beyond the 1A5:1–3 idea that *rún jùng* will attract population. It asserts that it will also enlist the sympathies of the people of the other states, making them willing to be conquered. This more developed view of *rún jùng* as a principle of policy is shared by 2A1.

By 3A3, *rún jùng* is defined not in terms of interstate rivalry but in terms of land distribution and the imposition of family co-responsibility. The chief responsibility is the common field that they must cultivate before beginning work on their private fields. There is no longer any idea of attracting population; rather, the mechanism for holding it in place seems to be highly developed. As attested in LY 12–13, and as admitted by MC 3A3 itself, earlier taxation was at the rate of 1 in 10. The new well-field system gives a rate of 1 in 9. The state is clearly not losing by this change. The theme of a mobile population recurs in 3A4, but it is set in a frame story designed to argue against an autonomous rural culture. The general social development that seems to be reflected in these recommendations is in the direction of an increasingly less mobile rural populace.

Remonstrance. The original *Mencius* (1A3:1–3, 1A5:1–3) uses only the device of persuasion. The *Mencius* of the interpolated *1B4 speaks of "restraining" the ruler. MC *1B8 even countenances killing a ruler on grounds that he had ceased to function as a true ruler. These are fairly extreme (and thus perhaps not literally transcribed) examples of remonstrance. After this point in the MC 1–3 series, *jyèn* [*jian*] 諫 declines. In 2A5:2 a minister resigns when his remonstrance is unheeded. 2B12:6 ridicules remonstrance as a deed of petty men. MC 3 never mentions it. That chapter criticizes policy in the presence of ministers (3B8) but attributes the shortcomings of rulers to the inadequacies of their advisers (3B6). The ruler has become unavailable to direct criticism. Instead, policy failures are attributable to ministers. This is probably a reflection not of the increasing policy role of ministers but, more likely, of an increasingly exalted and eventually uncriticizable role for rulers. The development in the political sphere is toward autocracy, just as the earlier-noted development among the people is toward increased subjugation of the people.

8. The Alternate Hypothesis: Developments in the Proposed Text Strand MC 4–7

Rv́n Jv̀ng 仁政. The term *rv́n jv̀ng* is common in MC 1–3; in MC 4–7 it is confined to 4A1 and 4A14. In neither passage is it described sufficiently closely that its content can be stated. It is praised in 4A1 as the only way to "rule the world equitably" (平治天下; Legge prefers "tranquilly"). It is mentioned almost in passing in 4A14 (essentially a commentary on LY 11.17) as defining the type of government that it is acceptable to "enrich" by collecting taxes. We may say that MC 4 regards a *rv́n* government as the only one that can rule properly and tax validly, but the content of that government, how it works and what it is supposed to achieve, is unclear. *Rv́n jv̀ng* is thus a perfunctory term in the first chapter of the MC 4–7 series and is absent altogether from the remainder of that series.

Shàn Jv̀ng [shan zheng] 善政. The phrase "*shàn jv̀ng*" should mean "good government," and in 2A1 that is what it does mean, in the most general sense: the heritage of good government left over from the past (specifically, from the good early rulers of a dynasty, such as Wǔ-dīng of the Shang). But in 7A14, where it occurs three times, the same phrase refers sarcastically to a government that is "good" at getting every ounce out of the people: "He who practices good government is feared by the people," and again, "Good government wins the wealth of the people." What 7A14 recommends instead is not *rv́n jv̀ng* and not any kind of government whatever. It recommends education as the way to win the hearts of the people. So in parallel with the increasing severity of policy recommendations toward the end of the MC 2–3 sequence, we find the end of the MC 4–7 sequence commenting adversely on a merely "efficient" government. Taking these two terms together, we may say that the tendency in MC 4–7 is to mention *rv́n jv̀ng* in passing at the beginning, drop the subject in the middle, and denounce "efficient" governments under another rubric at the end. This implies not unconcern for government but a growing revulsion for government. It makes a plausible parallel to the increasing severe limitations under which, as noted above, the MC 1–3 theorists of government apparently had to operate.

Remonstrance and Revolution. The political theory of MC 1–3 is administrative, whereas that of MC 4–7 is populistic: the latter chapters are concerned with political theory as seen from below. They parallel MC 1–3 in attesting the vanishing of remonstrance but become increasingly shrill on the topic of replacing the ruler. 4A1 (like 1A5) uses persuasion on the ruler, 4B3 implies retaliation by the ruler against remonstrance, and 5B9 limits the right of remonstrance to ministers of royal blood, thus making it acceptable only within the ruler's own family. There is no later use of the term in that text strand. MC 5B9 at the same time marks the beginning of the idea of replacing the ruler, not in ancient instances (as in *1B11) but as a possibility for the historic present. MC 7A8 and 7B35, at the end of the series, both show contempt for the ruler, and 7B14 reaffirms that a bad ruler may be replaced, this time without the 5B9 limitation to the ministers of the blood. The hostility to the ruler does not increase after MC 5, but it remains a well-remembered position in MC 7. Neither here nor in the dwindling of interest in ministerial protest in MC 1–3 is there any ground for inferring a mitigation of political conditions. Both strands rather suggest a political situation in which protest continued to be relevant but was increasingly futile.

The People. The historical Mencius (1A3, 1A5) had said that the people were the basis of state power. The related interest in rural mobility and rural independence dwindles, as noted above, throughout the course of MC 1–3. By contrast, the focus on the people as the basis, and indeed the definition, of the state increases during MC 4–7. MC 4A9, in the tradition of 1A3, ascribes winning the world to winning the hearts of the people. 5A5 makes the voice of the people the voice of Heaven, in confirming the ruler (Shùn) in possession of the world. The people rank higher even than the ruler in importance to the state in 7B14. This theoretical defense of the people contrasts and dovetails with the practical abandonment of the people as an element in the statecraft of MC 1–3. That extreme difference of principle possibly helps explain the rancor of the "good government" passage 7A14. It may well be a criticism of the harder, less populistic tendency in MC 1–3.

Jǐn Syīn [***Jin Xin***] 盡心. In 1A3, Lyáng Hwèi-wáng says that he has "done everything he can think of" (*jìn syīn*) in caring for his people, including moving both food and populace in times of famine. The phrase recurs in *1A7 as "putting all your heart and strength" (盡心力) into the pursuit of some goal, and again in 2B7, where the people "fully express their natural human feelings" (盡於 人心) in the splendor of their funerary goods. None of these usages moves much beyond the basic meaning of the phrase. When it occurs in the MC 4–7 sequence, however, namely in 7A1, it is a technical term of psychology: one who gets to the end of his heart will come to understand his nature (*syìng*). This seems to envision a conscious mind (*syīn*) beneath which, and accessible through which, is the underlying nature of the person (*syìng*), through which in turn, as the next phrase tells us, the natural order (*tyēn*) of which that *syìng* is a part may be apprehended. This geometry of the soul is unique in the *Mencius,* but its similarity to that of the meditation texts is manifest.[38]

Tsún Syīn [***Cun Xin***] 存心. A less precise geometry than that of 7A1 is implied by 6A8, on the general subject of the original ethical inclination (*syìng,* propensity), which speaks of how the original heart or disposition (*syīn*) may be kept amid the difficulties of life. In this passage, *syīn* and *syìng* are essentially synonyms. In 7A1 they have become distinct, and different actions are recommended for them ("To retain the heart, and nourish the nature, is the way to serve Heaven"). The evolution here is toward greater specificity, and greater complexity, in the way the human inward realm is perceived.[39] The larger movement, including these details, is from political populism in MC 4–5 to increasingly inward activism (and an increasing frustration with outward situation) in MC 6–7.

9. The Common Developmental Tendency

The above examples of evolution (or innovation as a special type of evolution) are, we suggest, individually coherent. They imply a reasonably consistent line of development for each of the two text strands. Taken together, they show several common qualities shared, or common situations attested, in the whole of the later *Mencius* over time. As a review of the developmental hypothesis, it will be useful to summarize and add some detail to these common qualities.

Retreat from Politics. The political strand MC 1–3 does not disengage from politics, but it does cut back on the policies it thinks it can afford to recommend; the late policies are less compassionate than the early ones. The theoretical strand MC 4–7 opens with a repetition of the *rvn jvng* phrase, and drops it thereafter; its politics is the outpolitics of the people. It develops this to a point of acrimony, in apparent opposition to the increasingly less people-centered policies of the other school, and perhaps also in contempt for the more demeaning role (5A7; compare 5A8–5A9, on the same theme) that the members of the other school may have been accepting. MC 3B6 may be a complementary gesture: a complaint by that other school, that by whatever accommodations of original theory it had been gained, their court access was not, after all, effective in influencing policy.

Discouragement. It seems fair to say of the historical Mencius, in the twelve genuine passages in MC 1, that he has the answer to the political problems facing Ngwèi and Chí and that the answer is a simple one. The rest of the text in various ways recedes from that simplicity and that assurance.

In the early layers of the text, it is asserted that the ruler has only to make the right move, and the people in response will surge toward him like an irresistible force of nature (1A6, 1B15; also 4A9) and will fight for him with mere sticks against the mailed warriors of the enemy (1A5). This assertion logically contains within it a theory providing for an immediate ethical response by the people to the ethical initiative of the ruler. By 6A8, the famous Ox Mountain passage, the text is trying to explain why the expected ethical response is lacking in some people. Many consider this to be the most beautiful passage in the book.[40] Perhaps all parties can agree on "poignant." To us it is one of the most bleak. We find in it less a theory of the goodness of human nature than an account of the loss of goodness from human nature. MC 6A8 as it stands seems to accept, and merely tries to explain, that some men are unable to respond to the good. Their nature (*syìng*) is absolved of blame (irresistible circumstance is at fault) and the theory is salvaged, but the fact of loss remains. By 7A3 the very idea of the consequences of action, and thus the efficacy of action, is called into question. The only sphere of action in which seeking leads dependably to getting is within the self. Seeking in the outer world has no guarantees; it is a matter of fate whether success follows effort. The implication is that the only quest that offers a reasonable chance of success is the inner quest. The inward turning recommended in 7A3 is echoed in the injunctions of 7A8 (forget power), 7A9 (self-cultivation in obscurity), 7A20 (abandon rulership for familial and personal satisfaction), 7A24 (Confucius regards the world as small), and 7A35 (Shùn casts aside the world for family duty).

It is an interesting world and, when properly cultivated, no doubt an admirable world, but it is surely much reduced in scope and ambition from the plan for social integration, and indeed for world conquest by the most compassionate, which had been put forward by the historical Mencius.

Social Separation. Meanwhile, what of the lyrical identity of the hearts of king and commoners that Mencius recommended in 1B1 and was elaborated in *1A7? The MC 1–3 series even at its end (3A1) continues to assert that the gentleman is of one substance with Yáu [Yao] (3A1). But less is claimed for the common people, and their difference from the gentleman comes to be emphasized. 3A3 states the famous principle that some use their minds and some use their backs and calls it "consistent throughout the world" (天下之通義). Even the right of self-determination, the core of the former assumption of a mobile population, is denied in 3A3: "On the occasion of death or removal, there will be no leaving of the country." The coresponsibility group members are fettered to each other and collectively chained to the land. If they have an idea that life would be better over the border, they cannot act on it. This in effect violates and ultimately abandons the policies of the historical Mencius.

Confucianization. It was noted that the MC 1 interpolations, unlike the original interviews, imply a world in which knowledge of the *Shr̄* and the *Shū* was shared by Mencius and the rulers he addresses. A more striking type of Confucianization is the appearance of Confucius as the historical sage in 3B9 and as one of the sequence of sage-rulers in 7B38. This amounts to a substitution of the house icon Confucius, of whom 03-century Confucians could speak and mythologize at will, for the perhaps less interpretationally tractable historical rulers cited in earlier passages.

Interiorization. A similar retreat to a zone of greater control, but one with less public influence, is the tendency toward interiorization and inner self-cultivation already noted in MC 7. The most psychologically sophisticated part of the *Mencius* (that is, MC 7) is also the most politically attenuated part of the *Mencius.*

All these trends can be seen as responses to, and in some cases protests against, the same trend toward autocracy in the state and the same frustration at the ineffectiveness of protest by the elite. The text largely abandons the people it had first championed, either by accepting their loss of social freedom (MC 1–3) or by abandoning politics altogether and taking up instead the interior quest (MC 4–7).

10. A Return to the Inconsistency Problem

Of the internal inconsistencies cited at the beginning of this essay as arguments against single authorship of the *Mencius,* we may now ask: Does the present hypothesis better account for these inconsistencies, or do problems remain? Before applying this test, we should first emphasize that the hypothesis here offered is incomplete in many respects. The date of the MC 1 interpolations, the growth patterns around each chapter core, and the exact relations between the two later chapter sequences all remain to be worked out in detail. With that qualification, it should still be possible to see if the alternate hypothesis offers a better account of the inconsistencies noted above.

Good Government. The fact that government itself is positive in MC 1–3 or the southern school, with its consistent governmental focus, will explain the casual use of *shàn-jùng* 善政 in 2A1. The indignation felt in the northern school (7A14) for increasingly severe governmental schemes (perhaps, as suggested above, the schemes such as the southern school advances in 3A3) would be in line with the increasing retreat of the northern school from all outward situations. The seeming difficulty would appear to be explained by the proposed alternate hypothesis.

Confucius and the *Chūn/Chyōu*. The contributory role of Confucius assumed by the early 4B21, and the constitutive role claimed by the late 3B9, would be consistent with a general tendency, over time, to attribute more of the authorship or preservation of earlier culture to Confucius personally. In addition to this time factor, it is also understandable that the ethical side of the *Chūn/Chyōu* should be emphasized by the philosophical school's 4B21 and that the governmental consequences of the composition of the *Chūn/ Chyōu* are instead emphasized in the governmental school's 3B9. The seeming difficulty would appear to be explained by the proposed hypothesis.

Yī Yǐn. The problem with the Yī Yǐn motif in the supposedly integral *Mencius* was that it showed an unlikely degree of thematic and emblematic variation. This problem will be reduced if arranging the data in the proposed order of composition yields either a developmental picture, showing the Yī Yǐn myth as such in the process of evolving, or a circumstantial picture, which would plausibly fit the needs of the two Mencian schools. What we seem to see is a combination of the two.

(1) The original Mencian position will have been that of 2A2, echoed in 5B1. These passages accept Yī Yǐn's willingness to benefit any ruler, or himself rule any people, as one valid type of the sagely minister persona. This is the flexible Yī Yǐn. Both the historical Mencius, with his wandering from Ngwèi to Chí and then to smaller courts, and the northern successor school, splitting off after Mencius' death from the court at which his movement seems to have become established, would have found this flexible Yī Yǐn persona congenial to their situation and supportive of their hopes. (2) 5A7 and 2B2 seem to be reacting to a development of the Yī Yǐn story, presumably outside the *Mencius,* in which Yī Yǐn's flexibility is exaggerated by having him initially accept service in a humble position. 5A7 denies that he stooped so low as to serve as a chef and thus attempts to preserve his previous statesmanly image. The seemingly later 2B2, on the contrary, accepts a variant of the new development in which Yī Yǐn's first position is that of tutor. We suggested above that the southern school may at some point have accepted a less than ministerial position in order to maintain continued access to power; if so, this humble Yī Yǐn persona may have served as a symbolic justification. Both 5A7 and 2B2, in slightly different ways, emphasize that the content of Yī Yǐn's expertise was his knowledge of the ways of the ancient rulers—essentially a preceptorial role. (3) 5A6 compares Yī Yǐn with Jōu-gūng; both served the larger interest of the state and its people but never actually held power; 7A31 emphasizes Yī Yǐn's principled and temporary stewardship. The same lack of desire for power is present in 5A7, and all these passages

(which are from the northern school sequence MC 4–7) would be congenial to the self-image of the northern school, which as far as we can discern never achieved a regular relationship with a court. (4) That the southern school never mentions Yī Yǐn after his "tutor" appearance in 2B2 would be consistent with its increasing loss of real policy influence; a strong ministerial symbol might well have been more than the group's modest status and negligible success could sustain. (5) It may seem anomalous that Yī Yǐn should continue to be mentioned in the northern school, but the details highlighted in those occurrences are different from those stressed earlier (for instance, the element of flexibility is no longer included) and are consistent with that school's continued hostility to government, its own attenuated political interests, and its final abandonment of the dream of good government. Thus, in 5B1 and 6B6, Yī Yǐn is not praised for his knowledge of the ancient rulers (the technica of government, as it had been defined in the previous 5A7 and 2B2), but for a more general knowledge of the Way (dàu [dao] 道) and the more inward quality of benevolence (rǐn 仁) toward the people. The more political elements in Yī Yǐn's legend are not mentioned (nor is the earlier term rǐn jǐng revived). In the muted protest piece 7A31, Yī Yǐn's disinterestedness qualifies him to remove a ruler if necessary; he is thus a useful spokesman for the Mencian "right of revolution" in the less assaultive but still fervent form in which we find it in these late northern chapters. In the last piece in the book, 7B38, Yī Yǐn has none of these specific attributes; he is merely one among several ancient worthies with whom the present age has somehow lost all contact and continuity.

The diverse estimates of Yī Yǐn thus become intelligible on assuming a slight mythological development in the Yī Yǐn legend itself and on noting that the emphasis on different aspects of his historical persona in different parts of the *Mencius* are appropriate to the varying political situations of the two schools. The seeming difficulty would appear to be explained by the proposed hypothesis.

11. Examples of the Practical Application of the Alternate Hypothesis

There are many other *Mencius* cruxes than the above three, some of them being vigorously debated at the present time and even in the present volume. It may also be of interest to see if the hypothesis developed above, which it may now be appropriate to refer to as a theory, can contribute anything to the resolution, or the redefinition, of those cruxes.

Syìng 性. There is a difference of opinion on whether *syìng* is innate or acquired, as asserted, respectively, in a long-running argument between Irene Bloom and Roger Ames. Kwong-Loi Shun points out cases where *syìng* is exceptionally used as a verb—in 7A30 性之 (presumably the causative "internalized as a propensity"; in Legge's translation, "were natural to"; in Lau's, "had it as their nature"), 7A21, and 7B33—as most strongly supporting the Ames position.[41] Ames cites these passages as showing that "*syìng* is not given, but is an accomplished project."[42] On the other hand, the passages chiefly relied on by Bloom for the intrinsic view of *syìng* are the 6A1 injunction not to do violence to one's *syìng* (cf. 6A6–6A7 and 6A15), which has earlier counterparts in 2A6 and the original 2A2 (where the inner quality to be let alone is *chì* [*qi*] 氣).[43] Accepting for purposes of present discussion that the respective passages have all been correctly interpreted, it is striking that the ones cited in support of an "innate" or "noninterfering" theory of nature are in MC 6 and earlier, whereas the passages attesting a concept of "acquired" or "accomplished" nature are in MC 7. On the present theory that MC 6 precedes MC 7, this implies that an early concept of intrinsic *syìng* was first asserted (2A2), then defended against opponents (6A1), and finally replaced by a concept of acquired *syìng*. The distribution of *syōu shŭn* [*xiu shen*] 脩身 (cultivate the self), which is confined to 7A1, 7A9, and 7B32, would seem to support this inference by emphasizing the act of cultivation over the earlier assumption of innate qualities. It was noted above that MC 7 emphasizes working on the self as something in which the doer has control and is sure of results, and that MC 3 and 7 lie in the zone of possible Sywndzian influence, the Sywndzian view being that our good impulses are not given but rather are acquired through personal effort. This gives a consistent picture, in which both interpretations of *syìng* are correct but refer to different stages in the philosophical development represented within the time span of the *Mencius*.

Chŭng [Cheng] 誠. The term "*chŭng*" occurs in 4A12 and 7A4 in a technical philosophical sense, not with the common meaning of "sincere." Kwong-Loi Shun notes that the progression from indi-

vidual to family to state to world is "somewhat different" in 4A12 and
the nearby passage 4A5, but he does not adjudicate the difference.[44]
Van Norden notes further that 4A12 is also found in the *Jūng Yūng*
[*Zhongyong*] 中庸, where it is not attributed to Mencius, and that the
related passage 7A4 also contains the only Mencian occurrence of
the *Jūng Yūng* term "*shù*" 恕, as well as the phrase "*wàn wù*" 萬物
(the myriad things, all things), which, however, is found in the
Jwāngdž and the *Syǔndž*.[45] The relation of 4A12 and 7A4 to each
other and to the *Jūng Yūng* and other texts, and their uniqueness in
or difference from the rest of the *Mencius,* certainly invite an explanation. Van Norden proposes that the two *Mencius* passages are interpolations, but it is not obvious how, or even why, substantive interpolations would have been added to a book that seemingly did
not circulate very widely after it was composed.[46] It will suffice if the
passages instead represent contemporary influence from the *Jūng
Yūng* (on the early 4A12) and also from the mid 03-century texts
Jwāngdž and *Syǔndž* (on 7A4).[47] This hypothesis of lateral influence,
made possible by dating the later *Mencius* to the first half of the 03
century, seems to suffice also as an explanation for the anomalous
features of MC 4A12 and 7A4.

Tyēn 天. Nivison points out that, in 2B13, Mencius is asked to
explain his seemingly dissatisfied expression on leaving Chí, despite
his previous remark that a *jywūndž* [*junzi*] 君子 neither resents Heaven
nor blames men (all commentators equate this with LY *14.35).[48]
He responds, "彼一時, 此一時也" (most naturally, "That was then;
this is now"), and after a seeming explanation of why he might indeed be dissatisfied, concludes, "吾何為不豫哉" ("Why should I be
dissatisfied?"). Legge resolves the non sequitur by reversing the final
sentence: "How could I be *otherwise than* dissatisfied?" (emphasis
added). Waley finds the reversal unjustified.[49] Nivison concurs,
though noting that in this meaning the sentence would have been
"perfectly natural." If we eliminate this "natural" conclusion, then a
conversation that seems to begin in disappointment must end in
affirmation. Ivanhoe, after reviewing commentaries, proposes two
possible solutions: (1) Mencius from the first intends to show contentment with Heaven, and hence his seeming disappointment is
specious, and (2) 2B13 shows him as "talking himself out of his initial feeling of distress."[50] Ivanhoe prefers the first, in part because it
is compatible with the Mencian "unmoved mind" of 2A2 and thus

gives a consistent Mencian persona. But the consistency comes at a price. For one thing, if the passage merely intended to elicit an affirmation from Mencius, the disciple's question could have been framed ("Do you not feel disappointed?") to do so less problematically. For another, though it also occurs in other texts, the saying about resentment is treated in 2B13 as Mencius', not Confucius'; hence interpreting 彼 with the time of Confucius is awkward, Jàu Chí [Zhao Qi] 趙岐 notwithstanding. Finally, in this interpretation, the balancing (一時) predicates must be construed to assert not contrast (the natural interpretation) but identity between the two periods. This would be more naturally expressed by a single predicate after a double subject (as A/B, 一也).

The present theory, with its different alignment of the texts, favors a version of Ivanhoe's second option. (1) By the *Analects* chronology here assumed, LY 14 (c0310) was written after Mencius had left Chí (c0313), and the interpolated *14.35 sometime later (we suggest c0296, after Mencius' death). The historical Mencius thus could not have known it as a saying of Confucius, and its presence in 2B13 makes that piece a retrospective envisioning by his followers rather than a true report of his own situation. (2) MC 2B13 seems to return to the situation of the genuine 1B16, where again confidence in Heaven is asserted against a merely circumstantial setback ("That I failed to find favor with the Lord of Lǔ is due to Heaven; how could some son of the Dzàng [Zang] 臧 clan prevent me?"). (3) This genuine comment does reflect the imperturbability that Mencius claims in 2A2—a disappointment expressed in a larger context of imperturbable acceptance. (4) Both by position and by featuring description of persons, 2B13 is a literary construct rather than a contemporary transcript. It is thus not necessary to make its Mencius consistent with the historical Mencius; the 2B13 persona may symbolize later concerns. This frees up interpretation or, more precisely, imposes a different sort of consistency constraint upon interpretation. (5) 2B13 is the next-to-last piece in the chapter. The last is 2B14, where Mencius asserts that he never meant to stay long in Chí. These are paired in a way that is frequent in the *Analects,* one saying being a complement rather than a parallel to the other. It is typical of this device that an initially expressed disappointment (2B13) should be balanced—put in a larger context—by a more comprehensive expression of ultimate unconcern for outcomes (2B14). The thread linking the pair is the idea of personal emotional engagement. (6) Jū Syī [Zhu Xi] 朱熹 has seen that the disappointment expressed at the beginning of 2B13 must be at a different level from the assertion made at the end. The contrast seems to be a disappointment that it has not happened (in contrast with the serenity of 1B16) versus a stoic confidence that if it does happen, it will be through Mencius' efforts. (7) This darker reinterpretation fits the downward developmental pattern that we have seen is present in this text strand, tending from greater to less optimism about outcomes. (8) A further stage in that same process of disengagement from optimism is seen in 7B38, the last piece in the book: "But if there isn't anybody, well, then, there *isn't* anybody" (emphasis added). The goal is, in fact, not going to be achieved. We wish to suggest that 2B13 can be intelligibly seen as a point in that trajectory of discouragement.

More generally, subsuming all the above examples, we submit that these evidences of intelligible development of ideas within the text support our theory, and that our theory in turn provides a dynamic overview against which many of the text's internal inconsistencies can be at least partly resolved, leaving for close analysis indeed a residue, but one from which considerable material not requiring or not amenable to such analysis has first been eliminated. We offer this theory, then, not in place of analysis but ultimately as an aid and precursor to analysis. The argument for the theory is its success in accounting for difficulties in the text.[51] Its proof will lie in the success of future analysis using it as a starting point.

12. Envoi

The *Mencius* is a difficult text, and apart from the text itself and a few other contemporary texts of contrasting outlook but ultimately of similar nature, we have very little knowledge of the time in which it was written. We must therefore expect that there will always be points, or whole passages, whose intent eludes us and that thus present themselves to us as having general meaning or none at all, whereas contemporary readers might have had much more specific reactions. We believe that the present theory offers the possibility of recovering, from the structure and interrelationships of the text, some sense of its original specificity. If that possibility should prove fruitful, it may lead to an increased appreciation of the evidently difficult conditions under which the authors worked, and the degree to which, despite disappointments and reverses and against the course of the mainstream of history in their own time, they persisted in their advocacy of a better world, inhabited by better people. For their insights into how society works or how it might work if it realized the best possibilities of its human material, and above all for their courage in maintaining and developing those insights until the very end of their time in the world, the present world may well be grateful.

Appendix: Diagrammatic Representation of the Present Theory

Original Mencius interviews, c0320–c0310
1A1, 1A3:1–3, 1A5:1–3, 1A6; 1B1, [1B16], 1B9, 1B10, 1B12, 1B13, 1B14, 1B15

Composite remembered Mencian conversations, c0303
2A2:1–23

Northern school separates, c0300 MC 4A	Southern school early addenda, c0300 MC 2A
Northern school extensions, post–c0300 MC 4B	Addenda to MC 1, post–c0300 *1A3:4–5, *1A5:4–6, *2A2:24–28
Northern school second chapter MC 5	Interpolated inverviews *1A2, *1A4, *1A7, *1B2, *1B3, *1B4, *1B5, *1B6, *1B7, *1B8, *1B11

Chí conquest of Sùng, 0286

Northern school third chapter MC 6	Southern school later addenda MC 2B

Sywíndž becomes director of Lán-líng, 0255

Last northern layer, c0254–c0249 MC 7	Last southern layer, c0254–c0249 MC 3

Chŭ absorbs Lŭ and surrounding territory, 0249

Note: The above diagram represents the main points of the accretional *Mencius* theory as developed in the present paper. For simplicity, we have ignored differences of date among the interpolated interviews, and instances of overlap between the layers here shown (as the sequence of the MC 1 and MC 2 addenda). This schematic view will, it is hoped, serve the purposes of the present argument. We hope to offer a more detailed account of the theory on a subsequent occasion.

Notes

The authors are grateful to the National Endowment for the Humanities for a 1996–1997 Fellowship under which part of the research reflected in the present essay was carried out.

1. Chinese words are romanized in this paper according to the Common Alphabetic convention, which is designed to exploit the existing reflexes of Latin alphabet users. It uses the standard guideline "consonants as in English, vowels as in Italian," plus the following conventions for vowels not found in Italian: *r* as in "fur," *z* as in "adz," *v* as in "up," and *yw* (after *l* and *n*, simply *w*) for "umlaut *u*." (Pinyin romanization has been supplied at a character's first appearance by the editor.) To distinguish the two states whose names are presently pronounced identically as Wèi, a lost initial *ng-* is restored for that of the larger of them, thus Ngwèi 魏 versus Wèi 衛.

2. Dates "B.C.E." are here identified, in what we feel is a more culturally neutral way, by a prefixed zero. We prefer this to Needham's solution for the same problem—namely, a prefixed minus sign—because the latter confusingly invokes astronomical usage for what are rather "historical" dates, and because it precludes the use of hyphenation for spans; cf. "Confucius, 0549–0479."

3. An anonymous reader for the University of Hawai'i Press has suggested that the integral view of the *Mencius* is a "paper tiger" that no one in fact holds and that the present argument against that view is thus superfluous. We forbear to weary our own readers by citing in extenso scholars who subscribe to some variant of the *Shř Jì* [*Shiji*] 74 statement that the text was written by Mencius in retirement, in collaboration with several disciples, and who regard our *Mencius* as "one of the best preserved texts from the Warring States period" (D.C. Lau, trans., *Mencius* [Harmondsworth: Penguin Books, 1970], 222). The same reader asserts that our alternate hypothesis, attributing to the text a significant time depth, "has been noted by others, for example Nivison and Riegel." We have been unable to verify this assertion and have referred it to the scholars in question. Professor Riegel has replied, "I have not made the claim about the *Mencius* ascribed to me," and Professor Nivison has responded, "I don't know what that guy's talking about."

4. This inconsistency is also noted, though not explained, in Lau, *Mencius*, 231.

5. For this date, see ibid., app. 1.

6. Ibid., 9, 209.

7. In Chyén Mù [Qian Mu], *Syēn-Chín Jū Dž Syì-nyén* [*Xian Qin zhu zi xi nian*], 2d ed., 2 vols. (Hong Kong: Hong Kong University Press, 1956), numbers 106 and 112 argue for 0322 as the beginning of Píng-gūng's reign; Lau also uses this date. There are several anomalies in the *Shř Jì* dates for Lǔ and other rulers that have to be resolved in a mutually compatible way; for our solution, see E. Bruce Brooks, "Chronology of the Princes of Lǔ" (Warring States Working Group [WSWG] Note 10, 1 August 1993). References to WSWG internally circulated papers are given here, though they are not presently publicly available. Conference papers by Stephen C. Angle and Manyul Im (April 1997) ex-

plored and largely confirmed, respectively, the separation here proposed between the northern and southern Mencian schools and the conjunction here asserted between MC 3 and MC 7; and an October 1997 WSWG conference paper by Dan Robins on animal imagery in Mencius further showed the fruitfulness of our proposed northern/southern contrast. It is hoped that these and other relevant results, including the WSWG internal Notes, will presently be formally published.

8. We see a parallel in the fact that when meeting with Ngwèı Syāng-wáng [Wei Xiangwang] in the first year of his rule (MC 1A6), Mencius emerged from the interview and recounted it to "someone." For details, see the text below, under the heading "Scenario."

9. In order not to burden the main argument, we summarize here briefly the reasons for regarding the final sections of MC 1A3 and 1A5 as later additions. (Asterisks relate to grouping of MC 1 interviews; see text.) (1) These passages end satisfactorily from a literary and policy point of view at 1A3:3 and 1A5:3. The proposed cores 1A3:1–3 and 1A5:1–3 are consistent with themselves, with each other, and with 1A1. With 1A1, they form a plausible series of consecutive interviews. (2) 1A3:4 presents a more elaborate farmstead than the preceding 1A3:1–3 and thus appears to be an elaboration on it. (3) 1A3:4 is a near duplicate of *1A7:24, implying some relationship between them. Since *1A7:24 is introduced by a phrase about "going back to fundamentals," it is likely that 1A3:4 existed earlier than *1A7. Then the spuriousness of *1A7 does not impugn the earlier 1A3:4. 1A3:4 still makes best sense as an evolutionary stage from the simple 1A3:1–3 to the elaborated *1A7. (4) 1A3:5 has a strident, anti-ruler tone, at variance with that of the preceding passages. (5) Coming now to 1A5:4–6, unlike the preceding 1A5:1–3 (but like 1A3:5) it is directly critical of rulers, who "rob the people of their time" and make their parents suffer from hunger and cold. (6) It also advocates military expeditions ($j\bar{i}ng$ [zheng] 征) to punish the evil rulers of other states; this agrees with the interpolated *1B11 and differs from the genuine 1B10, which sees military occupation as relieving the suffering, not punishing the guilty. The original Mencian position seems to have consisted of recommendations for one state, including its protection from enemies; it is only in what seems to be later material that we find the idea of invading other states. The more aggressive position may plausibly be seen as a later development.

10. Here and in the text that follows, where no confusion is likely, we will by "1A3" and "1A5" indicate the original cores of those passages, 1A3:1–3 and 1A5:1–3.

11. We notice that the pieces that we conclude were the original MC 1 interviews, as they stand in the text, make a perhaps intentional three-part pattern: three (MC 1A1, 1A3, 1A5) with Lyáng Hwèı-wáng followed by one (1A6) with his successor Lyáng Syāng-wáng [Liang Xiangwang]; three (MC 1B1, 1B9–10) with Chí Sywǣn-wáng [Qi Xuanwang] followed by one (1B12) with Dzōu Mù-gūng [Zou Mugong]; and three (1B13–15) with Tvng Wén-gūng [Teng Wengong] followed by one chronologically misplaced noninterview (1B16) with Lǔ Píng-gūng. Literarily, this assigns three pieces each to the two major rulers in Mencius' career (Lyáng Hwèı-wáng, Chí Sywǣn-wáng) and to

the minor ruler under whom he apparently finished his career (Tv́ng Wén-gūng). It then appends to each of these series what might be called a transition away: the unsympathetic Syāng-wáng as the end of Mencius' hopes under Hwèi-wáng, Mù-gūng as a stopover in Mencius' travels away from Chí, and Píng-gūng (as above suggested) as a comment on the failure of Mencius' career as a whole. Three hopes ending in three denials. The pattern seems intentional enough that we suspect that the compiler of the memorial text must have exercised some options of selection in order to produce it. (We may note, however, that the added MC 1 material is sufficiently different in character that it probably represents later composition and not a later insertion of unused earlier material.)

12. See E. Bruce Brooks, "The Bamboo Slip Factor" (WSWG Query 18, 24 October 1993).

13. For the dates of Mencius, which we do not believe have been adequately settled by Chyén Mù, *Syēn-Chín Jū Dž Syì-nyén*, #63, see E. Bruce Brooks, "The Dates of Mencius" (WSWG Note 99, 22 June 1996).

14. E. Bruce Brooks and A. Taeko Brooks, *The Original Analects* (New York: Columbia University Press, 1998), 97.

15. W. Allyn Rickett, *Guanzi*, 2 vols. (Princeton, N.J.: Princeton University Press, 1985 and 1998), 1/52.

16. We leave aside the difficult question of the lost four chapters of the *Mencius* and of the probity of the various reconstructed *Mv̀ngdž Wài-shū* 孟子外書. We may, however, add that the generally recognized Mencian character of the commentary to the *Wŭ-syíng* [*Wuxing*] document in the Mǎwángdwēi [Mawangdui] group of texts (whose terminus ad quem is the tomb date of 0168) would seem to prove that a Mencian point of view continued to be active, and to leave textual traces, into the early years of the Hàn dynasty. This is a much stronger result than can be deduced from the *Hán Shŕ Wài-jwàn* [*Han Shi Waizhuan*] 韓詩外傳 or the *Shŕ Jì*, which prove only that our *Mencius* text was known and favorably regarded during the reign of Hàn Wŭ-dì. They do not imply a continued active Mencian school.

17. Hán Yẁ's [Han Yu] 韓愈 famous characterization of Mencius as "the purest of the pure" (醇乎醇者; see Charles Hartman, *Han Yü and the Tang Search for Unity* [Princeton, N.J.: Princeton University Press [1986], 181, and Hán Yẁ, *Hán Chāng-lí ji* [Shangwu, 1964], 3/72) referred to his ideological continuity from Confucius, but the purity of the text is certainly implied. Jörg Schumacher, *Über den Begriff des Nützlichen bei Mengzi* (Peter Lang, 1993), 79, speaks of an "Eindruck einer fast wunderbaren Konsistenz in Mengzis Sprache," and the author himself quoted this line to us to register his surprise at the proposal summarized in section 2 above. Linguists have tended to treat the *Mencius* as a pure linguistic sample. George A. Kennedy ("Word-Classes in Classical Chinese," in Li Tien-yi, *Selected Works of George A. Kennedy* [Far Eastern Publications, 1964]) implies that opinion, and Edwin Pulleyblank (*Outline of Classical Chinese Grammar* [University of British Columbia Press, 1995], 3) treats the *Mencius* as a specimen of the Lŭ dialect "more evolved" than the *Analects*.

18. A sample complexity: The existence of both 易之以羊 and 以羊易之 (equally "change it for a sheep") in MC *1A7 does not show that the position of

the instrumental adverb is indifferently F (following the verb) or B (before the verb), because on the second occasion another B adverb interferes: 我非愛其財 而易之以羊. The better analysis is that the instrumental phrase 以羊 has been displaced from its normal B position in the second instance by a higher-ranking B-preference element.

19. In addition to the examples given in E. Bruce Brooks, "Mencius and Posterity" (WSWG Note 133, 20 March 1997), we may add the statistics of Kwong-Loi Shun, *Mencius and Early Chinese Thought* (Stanford, Calif.: Stanford University Press, 1997), which are 48 passages (27 percent) from MC 1–3 and 131 passages (73 percent) from MC 4–7; within the latter series, MC 4–5 contribute 40 percent and MC 6–7 contribute 60 percent of the total number. If we eliminate passing mentions and give full weight to repeated passages, the prominence of MC 6–7 in the discussion becomes still greater.

20. For our view of *Analects* chronology, see *Original Analects;* the argument for that view is presented briefly in app. 1.

21. It is here assumed that LY 19.21 (c0253) quotes from MC 2B9, rather than the reverse. For the awareness in LY 19 of the contemporary and competing schools of Mencius and Sywndž, see *Original Analects*, 185 (headnote), 190 ("Interpolations"), and 193 ("Reflections"). Notice also the mentions of the *Mencius* in the commentary, passim. LY 19.21, as our commentary neglects to say, extracts as an independent saying (of Dž-gùng [Zigong]) the climactic maxim of MC 2B9 (there represented as spoken by Mencius). The section of LY 19 in which Dž-gùng figures (19.20–25) generally adopts a Mencian and anti-Sywndzian position; Dž-gùng's extravagant praise of Confucius in 19.24–25 echoes the tone of such passages as the end of MC 2A2 and has a phrase in common with MC 7A41.

22. In fact, the language is so strong that translators and commentators have been reluctant to render or acknowledge its simple force as language, feeling no doubt that such a statement would have been situationally impossible before an actual ruler. With this feeling we agree; it is one of the strongest reasons for regarding these as fictive rather than transcribed interviews. But as they stand, they are among the high points of Warring States rhetoric and deserve to be rendered in all their audacity.

23. Nothing later, no passage in a higher-numbered chapter, in the series MC 1–3 sustains this level of invective. The exceptions to this statement are largely doublets of the MC 1 interpolated passages, such as *1A4 and 3B9, which have identically the following: "In your kitchen there is fat meat, in your stables there are fat horses, but on your people's faces is a hungry pallor, and in the wilds are the corpses of the starved. This is leading on animals to eat men." The audacious *1A4, developing *1A3:5, is addressed to the king of Lyáng, whereas the verbally identical 3B9 is represented as a quotation from Gūng-míng Yí [Gongming Yi] 公明儀. Beyond noticing this particular case of attenuated reuse of earlier material, we cannot here pursue the topic of the Mencian doublets. For the special climate of discouragement that seems to attend MC 3 in particular, and that may help to explain the recurrence of this theme in 3B9, see further discussion in the text below.

24. *Jàn-Gwó Ts̀v* [*Zhanguo ce*], #479 (J.I. Crump Jr., *Chan-kuo Ts'e*

[Oxford: Oxford University Press, 1970], 565) records misdeeds of King Kāng of Sùng, which have already been mythically exaggerated, but there is no reason to discount altogether the idea of misrule in Sùng (as does Arthur Waley, *Three Ways of Thought in Ancient China* [London: Allen and Unwin, 1939], 137–143, pursuing a vendetta against Mencius). "Mencius" in 3B5 (on which see further in the text below) refuses to accept a claim of Sùng's noble intentions, and it is probable that, in this text, the Mencius persona is expressing the view and the historical memory of the school. We feel safe in concluding that the king of Sùng was a bad egg, if on a less epic scale than the *Jàn-Gwó Tsv̀* makes out, and safe in relying on that conclusion for our argument at this point.

    25. *Shř Jì* 74 (5/2348).

    26. Kwong-Loi Shun, "Mencius on *Jen-hsing,*" *Philosophy East and West* 47.1 (1997): 10.

    27. Yáng Jū's name continued to be associated with a philosophical position as late as Hàn, but that position does not seem to be identical with the one held by what appears in the mid 03 century to have been the Yáng Jū movement, and the movement in any case seems not to have continued past the mid 03 century. The question is greatly complicated by the rhetoric of opposition that affects virtually all the texts that mention Yáng Jū and together constitute our entire body of evidence about him.

    28. By far the most unmistakable instance of *Jwāngdž/Analects* textual relatedness is the three anecdotes of LY 18.5–7. We deal in *Original Analects,* 183, with the notion (see Waley, *The Analects of Confucius* [London: George Allen and Unwin, 1938], 21) that these can be later hostile interpolations. They rather represent creative (if of course adversative) interactions between two texts still in process of formation—an argument at the time, not an anomaly intruded afterward.

    29. Gūngsūn Chǒu here adopts a Mician position on mourning observances similar to that of the renegade Confucian disciple Dzǎi Wǒ [Zai Wo] in LY 17.19 [17.21 in Lau's numbering]. See our *Original Analects,* 165, 258.

    30. This passage has been criticized as showing Mencius' pedantic refusal to inquire into "what is asserted to be happening now and close at hand" (Waley, *Three Ways of Thought,* 143). We are reluctant to differ with the redoubtable Waley in two successive footnotes, but 3B5 makes much more sense if its point is not Mencius' unreality (contrast the extreme reality of such populist passages as 1B15) but rather the political naivete of Wàn Jāng. Sensitive readers will not fail to see the similarity in tone between this disciple rebuke and such a prototype as LY *13.3 (which we date to a similar period, namely, c0253; see *Original Analects,* 190).

    31. This scenario puts Syẃndž in Lán-líng later than is often supposed, but it is consistent with a close reading of the biographical evidence for Syẃndž; see E. Bruce Brooks, "The Dates and Career of Syẃndž" (WSWG Note 142, 9 September 1997).

    32. For a survey of slavery as evidenced by archaeologically recovered slave chains and collars, see E. Bruce Brooks, "Warring States Slavery" (WSWG Note 90, 23 August 1995), which in turn is based on the material reported in Donald B. Wagner, *Iron and Steel in Ancient China* (Leiden: E.J. Brill, 1993).

33. As in *Gwăndž* 4.4 (c0250), Rickett 1/105.

34. For an example of the extremely detailed Chín regulations govern-ing the responsibilities and liabilities of the urban residential group of five, see A. F. P. Hulsewé, *Remnants of Ch'in Law* (Leiden: E. J. Brill, 1985), s.v. "D80–82."

35. Fish provides high-quality protein, but its final value as a supple-ment to a grain diet is a function of the effort that must be expended to obtain it. For an analysis showing the problems with relying on hunting and fishing as alternative food sources in times of poor grain yield, see Thomas W. Gallant, *Risk and Survival in Ancient Greece* (Stanford, Calif.: Stanford University Press, 1991), 119–121. Gallant usefully remarks that the input-to-output ratio is differ-ent for well-equipped elite hunters than for "the humble peasant setting a sim-ple trap for an unsuspecting hare," the effort input being greater in the latter case.

36. Francesca Bray, "Agricultural Technology and Agrarian Change in Han China," *Early China* 5 (1979): 3.

37. This is perhaps an oblique way of expressing the little people's rea-sonable desire for enough to eat. It is notable that in all 03-century writings, in-cluding the comprehensive and merciless anti-Confucian satires of the *Jwāngdž*, filial piety is the one value that is never criticized or ridiculed. It seems to have been, at any rate in the literature available to us, a cultural untouchable. That would have made it highly valuable rhetorically, as a carrier or protector of other, less self-justifying concepts.

38. The sequence of meditation texts in the *Gwăndž*—namely 49, 37, 36, and 38—goes into great and relevant detail. We date the first of these, the "Nèi Yè," to c0305 (in general agreement with Harold D. Roth, "Redaction Criticism and the Early History of Taoism," *Early China* 19 [1994]: 16; and Rickett, *Guanzi,* vol. 2, 37) and the others at intervals of approximately one gen-eration thereafter, respectively: c0290 (Syīn shù syà [Xinshu xia]), c0265 (Syīn shù shàng), and c0240 (Bái syīn [Baixin]). See A. Taeko Brooks, "The Gwăndž Meditation Texts" (WSWG Note 198, 5 September 1999).

39. The rapprochement with meditation in MC 7 is one factor that has probably made this chapter attractive to later Confucianism, in which personal self-cultivation had a central role. This may partly account for the high rate of quotation from MC 7 (and from MC 6, whose human nature emphasis pro-vides, in retrospect and probably also in historical fact, a theoretical substrate for MC 7) in later Confucian writings down to our own time, a phenomenon briefly noted above.

40. For a notably moving example, discordant in terms of the present argument but humanly beautiful, see Naomi Lewis, "The Silences of Arthur Waley," in Ivan Morris, *Madly Singing in the Mountains* (New York: Walker, 1970), 81, on Arthur Waley's funeral; and compare Waley, *Three Ways of Thought,* 115–118.

41. Kwong-Loi Shun, "Mencius on *Jen-hsing*," 3.

42. Roger Ames, "The Mencian Conception of *Ren Xing*," in *Chinese Texts and Philosophical Contexts,* ed. Henry Rosemont Jr. (La Salle, Ill.: Open Court, 1991), 159 f.

43. Irene Bloom, "Human Nature and Biological Nature in Mencius,"

Philosophy East and West 47.1 (1997): 26 f. See also Bloom, "Mencian Arguments on Human Nature," *Philosophy East and West* 44.1 (1994): 19–53.

44. Shun, *Mencius and Early Chinese Thought*, 164.

45. Bryan W. Van Norden, "Comments and Corrections to D. C. Lau's *Mencius*," ⟨http://faculty.vassar.edu/~brvannord/lau.html⟩, 1998, s.v. "4A12."

46. Kennedy ("Review of Creel, *Literary Chinese by the Inductive Method*," in Li Tien-yi, *Selected Works of George A. Kennedy*, 493) convincingly points out an included gloss that separately defines the halves of two near-reduplicative expressions in MC 1B4 (the segment is sec. 7 in Legge's text; it will be noted that 1B4 reads perfectly smoothly if sec. 7 is eliminated). The incorporation of a scholarly gloss is a not uncommon occurrence in otherwise well-preserved texts. The argument for 4A12 and 7A4 as interpolated passages is their unlikeness to the rest of the *Mencius*. We feel that they fit well with the gradual change in its tenor and with its relations to chronologically parallel texts, which we are here pointing out. See further in the text below.

47. Brooks and Brooks, *Original Analects*, 176 (s.v. "LY*6.29"), note that a similar *Jūng Yūng/Analects* overlap occurs in an *Analects* passage that, though interpolated in the relatively early chapter LY 6, is best dated to the 03 century. For contact between the unambiguously 03-century portion of the *Analects* and the contemporary *Jwāngdž* and *Syŵndž*, see, respectively, *Original Analects*, 174 f. and 190 f.

48. David S. Nivison, "On Translating Mencius," in Nivison, *The Ways of Confucianism* (La Salle, Ill.: Open Court, 1996), 188 f.

49. Arthur Waley, "Notes on Mencius," *Asia Major*, n.s., 1.1 (1949).

50. Philip J. Ivanhoe, "A Question of Faith," *Early China* 13 (1988): 158.

51. The present essay has focused on what might be called the internal argument for its view of the *Mencius*. Synchronisms with other texts, such as the *Jwāngdž* and the *Syŵndž*, have been mentioned only in passing. It is perhaps not inappropriate to add that the system of synchronisms that constitutes our working theory of the Warring States text corpus as a whole is also part of the argument, and that this larger system received confirmation in an important detail in 1998, when after years of editorial preparation the transcriptions of the Gwōdyèn [Guodian] 郭店 texts were finally made available to scholars. Following Li Xueqin's opinion ("Recently Discovered Confucian Texts from Guodian," Lecture, Dartmouth College, 22 October 1998) that the Gwōdyèn 1 tomb occupant was tutor to the Heir Apparent who later became King Kǎu-lyè [Kaolie 考烈] of Chǔ, the span of possible years for the tomb itself is from 0298 (the accession of Kǎu-lyè's father) to 0278 (the abandonment of the Jīng-mvn [Jingmen] site), with both extremes being for various reasons unlikely. The current best guess is thus c0288. The tomb includes three selections made at some time before that date from the *Dàu/Dv Jīng* [*Daodejing*] (DDJ), emphasizing (unsurprisingly, in this statecraft context) its statecraft maxims, which, as is well known, tend to be more common toward the end of the DDJ. Our general theory of the DDJ (see E. Bruce Brooks, "The Present State and Future Prospects of Pre-Han Text Studies," *Sino-Platonic Papers* 46 [1994]: 63 f., and the more detailed synchronisms in *Original Analects*, passim) is that it was undergoing grad-

ual compilation during this period and that a version of it from the year c0288 should show an incomplete state of that growth; specifically, it would probably contain DDJ 1–55 and might contain passages as high as DDJ 65, but it ought not to contain anything from the span DDJ 70 or higher; a strikingly different result would seriously challenge our general theory of the texts. We thus in effect predicted a range of DDJ 1–65 for the Gwōdyèn extracts. The actual range of chapters represented in the Gwōdyèn materials is DDJ 2–66. The very close agreement of the archaeological fact and the textual theory offers, we feel, striking confirmation of the soundness of the text theory. For a slightly more detailed statement of this situation, see E. Bruce Brooks and A. Taeko Brooks, "Response to Professor Slingerland," *Philosophy East and West* 50.1 (2000): 141–146.

12

Mengzi as Philosopher of History

DAVID NIVISON

I WILL FIRST distinguish between "critical" and "speculative" philosophy of history. I then will examine briefly some of Mengzi's critical views, which are less prominent than his speculative ones. Proceeding to the latter, I will examine his ideas about the origins of civilization, his idea that a true king must "arise" every 500 years (in Mengzi's time 700 years had passed), and the sources for these ideas. Noting then that Mengzi's overriding view of the past was the concept of the "Three Dynasties," I will consider how Mengzi participated in a contemporary discourse that was refining and changing this concept, focusing on Yao 堯 and Shun 舜, Yi Yin 伊尹, and Wu Wang 武王.

In doing this, I first will use my analysis of the *Bamboo Annals* ([*Jinben*] *Zhushu jinian* 今本竹書紀年) to establish the facts (or the earliest accounts that I can reconstruct); then I will show how the accounts changed and how Mengzi participated in the change. I will try to show how current events were motivating Mengzi, notably the rulers of the leading states claiming the title *wang* 王, and especially the events in Yan 燕, where the "king" tried to give the state to his prime minister. Then I will ask how much of Mengzi's picture of the past is his own invention, considering in particular the three-years mourning institution. Finally I will try to see how his imagination works.

"Speculative" and "Critical" Philosophy of History in Mengzi

Using the conventional terms, without intending any invidious contrast, I take "speculative philosophy of history" to be any picturing of history in the sense of what has happened (and will) or what has been done (and will be) that is guided by a nonempirical commitment, either as to what is, that is, metaphysics, or what ought to be, that is, values. And I take "critical philosophy of history" to be any examination of history in the sense of the study or account of what has happened or has been done that is guided by a nonempirical commitment, for example, as to what must count as being reasonable or honest or justifiable. Thus I distinguish the former from mere historical description or generalization, and I distinguish the latter from mere historiography.

Mengzi was doing what I am calling "critical philosophy of history," I take it, when he said (3B9) not only that Confucius wrote the *Chunqiu* (for that is merely a [doubtful] point of historiography) but also that this was "the business of the Son of Heaven," thus demanding that we either condemn Confucius for doing it or acknowledge that he had superhuman authority, and that rendering judgment as would a *tianzi* 天子 is what the historian must do. Mengzi is likewise making a "critical" point when he says of the *Chunqiu* that "its matter (*shi* 事) is the doings of Huan of Qi and Wen of Jin, and its literary form (*wen* 文) is that of the scribe, but its moral significance (*yi* 義) is what Confucius concerned himself with" (4B21) and is therefore the most important aspect of it—implying that one must recognize these three aspects of any history and must see *yi* as the most important concern of the historian. (I suspect that Mengzi here was thinking of the *Chunqiu* with its *Zuo* commentary expansion.) The *shi-wen-yi* triad was picked up in modern times by Zhang Xuecheng 章學誠 and turned into a sweeping speculative vision; but this is not in Mengzi.

Usually, however, when I consider "Mengzi as philosopher of history," I find myself looking at the ways he participated in a discourse in his time that I must call "speculative philosophy of history." One has no difficulty seeing this in what Mengzi says at 2B13. Every 500 years a true king must arise to correct the world. This is the will of Heaven, and the fact that we are having to wait more than 700 years must also be the will of Heaven. At 7B38 the idea recurs, and the intervals of 500-odd years are Yao and Shun to Tang of Shang, Tang to Wen Wang, Wen Wang to Confucius. There is a hint here of the "uncrowned king" (*suwang* 素王) conception of Confucius, suggested also in what Mengzi had said about Confucius and the *Chunqiu* in 3B9. This developed in the Han into the speculative theory of "three ages." But this too is not in Mengzi.

Another "speculative" historical theme suggested here and there briefly concerns the origins of civilization, a major interest of some of Mengzi's near contemporaries. Mengzi's views are implications of his moral psychology (which is, of course, at the center of his philosophy). If human nature contains the seeds of morality (2A6, 6A6), then the "sages," commonly thought of as the creators of civilization (explicitly so in Xunzi), must actually have simply "anticipated" what we all feel (6A7). Xunzi was to object that this kind of thinking would allow removing sages from the picture altogether, and we find Mengzi in effect doing just this in 3A5 in his critique of the Mohist Yi Zhi: human burial rites must have developed because people felt a natural revulsion when the bodies of dead parents had been "thrown into gullies" and their sons saw them "eaten by foxes and sucked by flies." To think of moral and ritual rules as mere constraints would be to make them something painful, in modern idiom "alienated" from our natural being—causing people to hate them (6A1). The operation of moral norms in human relationships should be thought of as *xing* 性, what is natural for us, not as *ming* 命, something demanded of us (7B24).

The idea is integral to Mengzi's moral and political optimism. Morality has one "root" (*ben* 本) (3A5), the human heart, whose impulses are Heaven-given (7A1). Therefore the people will react positively to "virtue" (*de* 德) in a ruler, who thus will have been successful only if he has deserved to be in Heaven's eyes, for "Heaven sees as the people see" (5A5). One implication is that success, including military success, is in effect self-validating. A contrasting implication (7B14) is that the ruler is the least important element in the political order, and the people the most important.

Mengzi conceives of past recorded history as the sequence of the "Three Dynasties," and this has, of course, some basis in fact. But the very concept of a "dynasty" is larger than fact. Heaven picks out the one man in the world best qualified to care for the people, gives this man and his successors the "Mandate," which ebbs away, perhaps to be renewed temporarily in a revival of dynastic fortunes (*zhongxing* 中興), under the guidance of wise ministers, only to expire finally in a reign of surpassing wickedness; and then the cycle of events begins anew. Part of this conception can be seen in chapters in the *Shangshu* that are probably early Zhou, such as the "Shao Gao." But the "Shao Gao" merely censures the Xia and the Shang rulers for having failed to "care for their virtue." Early Zhou propaganda probably did vilify the last Shang king—Di Xin 帝辛, or Zhou 紂. But the supposed "bad last ruler" of Xia—named Di Gui, or Jie 桀—is an invention probably of the late fifth or early fourth century B.C.E.,[1] serving to make "history" conform more closely to the dynastic concept. Mengzi recognizes Jie and sees him as paradigmatically evil but says little about him.

Regimes earlier than Xia were conceived. Chinese at least as early as the late fifth century knew about Huang Di 黃帝, followed by Zhuan Xu 顓頊 and then by Di Ku 帝嚳 and his son, Zhi 摯. These are not mentioned by Mengzi; but he has much to say about the next two archaic rulers, Yao and Shun, as well as about Yu 禹, progenitor of the following rulers of Xia, and about the Shang founder Tang 湯 and his chief minister, Yi Yin. In received Chinese history Yao and Shun are conceived as preceding Xia and indeed as each constituting a "dynasty," Yao's being "Tang" 唐 and Shun's being "Yu" 虞.[2] But in Mengzi and for much of Chinese historical thinking down at least to Six Dynasties, the reigns of Yao and Shun were conceived as the opening episodes of the story of Xia, because it was during those reigns that the career of Yu was said to begin. This is probably why Mengzi in 7B38 begins his first 500-year cycle with Yao and Shun. The point is also in evidence in the statement by Du Yu 杜預 (222–284) in his "Zuozhuan Houxu" 左傳後序 that when he examined the recently recovered *Bamboo Annals* text (ca. 280), he found that it began with Xia. This seems mysterious, when coupled with the statement by Shu Xi 束皙 (261–303; see his biography in *Jinshu*, 51) that in the *Annals* Xia (apparently 471 years) was longer than Shang (496 years). Both were taking the Xia as beginning in effect with Yao. But the attention Mengzi accorded to Yao and Shun, especially to Shun, probably did contribute to edging into place the idea that Yao and Shun are pre-Xia.

It is sometimes said that Mengzi presents essentially the Confucian idealized account of these worthies, which can be contrasted with other, cynical accounts, sometimes described as "Legalist."[3] But there are several accounts, even several "Confucian" ones, and the accounts have a history. The picture of this Chinese past was changing in the course of a century or more before Mengzi's death (just before 300 B.C.E., I assume, following Qian Mu).[4] The change amounts to a rewriting of Three Dynasties history to make it accord with an ideal; and so I must see the details of this rewriting as itself the form that philosophy of history was taking. Mengzi was taking part in this idealization. To see how he did it one must see just what he was doing; and to see this one must deduce the stages of change from a true, or at least earlier, account that obtained in the late fifth century. This requires looking at other texts that were taking shape during Mengzi's long lifetime, namely the *Zuozhuan* and especially the compound chronicle that became in the end a chronicle of Wei 魏, which we call the *Bamboo Annals* (*Zhushu jinian*).

The *Bamboo Annals* stops at 299 B.C.E., which was probably the year of death of Xiang Wang 襄王 of Wei. His successor Zhao Wang's reign began in 295, probably after an interval for formal mourning. The *Annals* text was buried at some time between 299 and 296, the burial being either in a cache of royal treasures or in the king's tomb. It had been reworked in Xiang Wang's reign, which coincided with the last years of Mengzi. This reworking exhibited the claim of Xiang's father, Huicheng, to be a king as dated exactly 700 years after 1035 B.C.E., the date that the text assigned to the founding of Jin, the parent state. It also dated to 327 the supposed loss in the Si River of the nine "cauldrons of Zhou," said in the *Zuozhuan* to embody the "virtue" (*de*) of the Zhou dynasty, this being just 700 years after 1027, the date that the *Annals* assigned to the formal placing of the cauldrons (captured from Shang, which had appropriated them from Xia) in Luoyang. The idea that the Zhou Dynasty was destined to last 700 years and no longer is also found in the *Zuozhuan,* which was being written in the course of the fourth century. A fictitious conversation is recorded for 606 B.C.E. between the ruler of the Chu state and a delegate of the Zhou king; the lord of Chu asks the weight of the Zhou cauldrons but is refused an answer, on the ground that the weight depended on the *de* of the dynasty, which was not yet exhausted. Cheng Wang 成王 had divined when the cauldrons were placed in Luoyang, getting the result that the dynasty would last 700 years and 30 generations. (Xian Wang 顯王, in the thirtieth generation, reigned 368–321.) So Mengzi in the conversation in 2B13, probably in 312 B.C.E. (as he was leaving Qi under a cloud), is echoing a common current idea in saying that it has now been more than 700 years without the appearance of a new dynastic founder.

Mengzi's idea that a true king (i.e., dynastic founder) should appear every 500 years may be a very old one. David Pankenier may well be right in suggesting that it derives from the interval of 516+ years between the planetary formation of late 1576, heralding the rise of Shang, and the conjunction of May 1059, heralding the rise of Zhou.[5] In the *Annals* for 1561 we are told that "two suns appeared at once," meaning (obviously) that there were now two kings in the world, an old one going out and a new one coming in, a situation that was against nature and could not continue. The year is the 500th counting from 2060, the year of Yu's first being received in audience by Yao, according to the *Annals*. We here see a late stage of the text, because the entire chronicle for Jie, 1589–1559, must have been invented probably in the late fifth or early fourth century.[6] The statement apparently copies another one exactly the same in the chronicle for Di Xin, the last Shang king, under the year 1055, which was the 500th year counting from 1554, the actual first year of Shang.[7] So Mengzi shows no originality in his remarks as he left Qi. His 500s and 700s are interesting, however, because it happened to be about seven centuries after the beginning of Zhou that the rulers of the more powerful states began claiming to be kings (see below), claims that signaled their belief, and everyone's, that the Zhou era had ended. "Seven hundred and more years but still not yet" was simply Mengzi's way of saying that "King" Xuan 宣 of Qi was not to be the new *tianzi*.

Mengzi on Yao and Shun, Yi Yin, and Wu Wang

I will not try to cover all of Mengzi's views of the historical past. The details of Mengzi's philosophically informed picture of the dynastic past that I want to examine are these: his picture of Yao and Shun and the relation between them; his account of Yi Yin and the beginnings of Shang; and his view of Wu Wang and the conquest of Shang. In each case I will first sketch the background facts or the earliest reconstructable account (for I don't know whether Yao and Shun are factual at all) and show how Mengzi altered this picture (or lent his support to the redrawing of it). Then I will try to determine the circumstances and events that motivated Mengzi (thus, in part, dating the relevant *Mengzi* texts). Last, I will try to probe the way he is thinking; unavoidably this will raise the question whether he is being honest.

Yao and Shun. I obtain my earliest account of Yao and Shun by analyzing the "modern text" *Bamboo Annals*.[8] Pankenier has shown that the 14th year of Shun was 1953 B.C.E., the date of a spectacular conjunction of the planets in lunar lodge Ying Shi 營室 in February.[9] I have found that in Western Zhou and in Xia there normally was a 2-year period of mourning completion after the death of a ruler, before the successor's recorded reign began. I therefore posit a 2-year calendar break for mourning completion for Yao after his death and assume that the *Annals* entry recording the exile of Yao's heir, Dan Zhu 丹朱, in Yao 58—that is, the 58th year of Yao's reign —was originally in Yao's last year as ruler. Yao 1 therefore must have been 2026 B.C.E. There was no mourning after the reign of the preceding ruler, Zhi, son of Di Ku, because the 9-year reign ended not with Zhi's death but with his overthrow by Yao. One can then count back: mourning, 2 years; Di Ku, 63 years; mourning, 2 years; Zhuan Xu, 78 years; mourning interregnum under Zuo Che 左徹,[10] 7 years; Huang Di, 100 years. Huang Di 1 then was 2287 B.C.E. In the present *Annals* the hagiographic treatment of Yao sets his first year at 2145 and gives him a 100-year reign, pushing Huang Di 1 back accordingly. Counting back similarly (positing 2-year mourning intervals, which are not in the present text), one obtains 2287 as Zhuan Xu 13, and the entry for that year is the promulgation of the Zhuan Xu calendar. One can assume then that when the chronology was pushed back to make Yao 1 the year 2145, the date 2287 was saved as a calendar first year by inventing the record of the promulgation.[11] My hypothesis is that the date 2287 was adopted as calendar year 1 because it was 31×60 years before 427 B.C.E., the first year of a *jiyou bu*—that is, *bu* 蔀 beginning with day *jiyou* (46)—used in other ways in *Annals* calculations.[12] The *Shiji* ("Wu Di Benji") yields the information that Yao spent the last 9 years of life in "retirement" (i.e., Shun's 50th through 58th years of age); and a fragment from the original *Annals* text says that Shun placed Yao under detention at the end of his life, after Yao had become incompetent, keeping him from communicating with his son Zhu.[13] I take this detail to be from the earliest stage of the *Annals,* surviving in the recovered "original," but suppressed in the extant "modern" text as too shocking. The modern text does recognize an abdication in Shun's favor in Yao 73 but does not begin Shun's year count until after Yao's death and the completion of mourning for him.

Obviously we must assume that Yao did not resign in Shun's favor but was forced out by Shun, who at the same time banished Yao's heir, taking the next year as his own year 1. This early account, which (if I am right) must have been current at least as late as 427 B.C.E., accords no honor to Yao and gives an ugly picture of Shun. There is more in the *Zuozhuan*, in which one finds a long account of Shun's career, both as a minister under Yao and afterward.[14] There Shun is put in a very favorable light, and Yao in an unfavorable light; Shun is said to have always made excellent appointments, whereas Yao was unable to recognize and dismiss evil men in his service. There is nothing said about Yao's resigning in Shun's favor; Shun is said to have become ruler only after Yao died, and this was simply because everyone in the world approved of him. Perhaps still later in the fourth century, but still prior to what we find in the *Mengzi* 5A, is the "Yao Dian" (now "Yao Dian" and "Shun Dian") in the *Shangshu*. This is laudatory without qualification to both Yao and Shun, giving them a relative chronology like that now in the *Annals*.

The *Zuozhuan* was being compiled in the course of the fourth century; Jupiter positions mentioned in the text, usually in fulfilled predictions, can be shown to be based on observed positions prior to 340 B.C.E. The redating of Yao 1 to 2145 in the *Annals* requires redating the Zhong Kang eclipse of 1876 back to 1948, and this required using *jiyou bu* 1 as base date—that is, it must have been done sometime in *jiyou bu*, 427–352.[15] Furthermore, redating Yao 1 to 2145 also requires the moving of the slip discovered by Edward Shaughnessy, which in turn affects chronological details in the *Zuozhuan*.[16] Also, one detail in the *Zuozhuan* that shows that its Jupiter positions were based on early fourth century observations (and not, as some still maintain, calculated and faked by Liu Xin 劉 歆 in the Han[17]) is the statement that Zhuan Xu died in a Chun Huo 鶉火 year[18]; and this date, 2218, requires a third stage of the *Annals* in which mourning periods except for Yao, Shun, and Xia are deleted. I will argue presently that the discussion of Yao and Shun by Mengzi is prompted by events in 318–314. The sequence perhaps then is (1) the *Annals*, stage one; (2) *Zuozhuan*, account of Shun; (3) *Annals*, stages two and three; (4) *Zuozhuan*, other details; (5) *Shangshu*; and finally (6) *Mengzi*—a development extending over about a century. The stage of the Yao-Shun story that would have been known to Confucius (if any was) would not have tempted him to talk about them; so all passages in the *Lunyu* to the contrary are interpolations.

Mengzi has much less to say about Yao than about Shun, but he treats Yao very favorably and wants us to have no doubt that both were perfect sage-rulers. At 5A4, Mengzi quotes the "Yao Dian" (the part now called "Shun Dian"): when Yao died, "it was as if the people had lost their fathers and mothers; for three years all musical instruments were silenced." Shun Mengzi makes a paragon of filial piety, through much adversity (his father tried repeatedly to kill him). But Mengzi insists more than once (5A4, 5A5) that Yao never actually abdicated to Shun; Shun did not even become emperor at Yao's death, but only after the completion of mourning for Yao, for otherwise there would have been two rulers in the world at once, and that is unthinkable: "The emperor cannot give the empire to another." Only Heaven can do that, and Heaven reveals its transfer of authority in the way the people act. Yao presented Shun to Heaven and Heaven accepted him, as shown by the fact that when Yao presented Shun to the people, the people accepted him. Likewise, a lord cannot give his fief to another; only the king can do that. In insisting on this, Mengzi differs from the *Shangshu*'s "Yao Dian"–"Shun Dian" account, which like the *Annals* does have Yao actually abdicating. (The quotation from Confucius at the end of 5A6, in which Confucius speaks of an abdication, is therefore an interpolation, easily made at the end of a section. Confucius couldn't have said it, and Mengzi wouldn't have quoted it.)

Yi Yin. The usual kind of account of Yi Yin in histories and among philosophers, notably in the *Mengzi*, gives him the appearance of a mythical sage-minister. I will offer arguments that he was quite real and quite unscrupulous. All of the accounts of him (I think) are partly wrong, and most of them are wildly wrong. Variations on the myth deserve study, but one should also try, if possible, to ascertain the facts.

Mengzi would have us believe that Yi Yin was a paragon of loyalty, wisdom, and virtue, at first working in the fields "delighting in the ways of Yao and Shun" (5A7), then serving Tang, and after Tang's death continuing to serve in sustaining the dynasty. Tang's heir was his grandson Tai Jia 太甲 (whose father, Tai Ding 太丁, had predeceased Tang). Mengzi recognizes two kings after Tang and before Tai Jia, however, namely Wai Bing 外丙, reigning for 2 years, and Zhong Ren 仲壬, for 4; but he offers no explanation for the two. According to Mengzi (5A6), Tai Jia became king after Zhong Ren, but he "upset the laws of Tang," and Yi Yin banished him to (a palace in or called) Tong 桐. After 3 years Tai Jia repented and reproached himself and, while in Tong, reformed and became a good and dutiful man. After another 3 years, since he heeded the instruction of Yi Yin, he was allowed to return to Bo 亳—that is, to resume his position and functions as king. Mengzi's disciple Gongsun Chou (7A31) asks the obvious question. Granted Yi Yin's virtuous intent, still "when a prince is not good, is it permissible for a good and wise man who is his subject to banish him?" "It is permissible," said Mengzi, in D. C. Lau's translation, "only if he had the motive of a Yi Yin; otherwise it would be usurpation." The two kings Wai Bing and Zhong Ren are not recognized in the standard received chronology, and this calls for explanation.

One finds a very different account in the *Bamboo Annals*. That book too, unlike many chronologies, recognizes as kings before Tai Jia first Wai Bing, 2 years, and then Zhong Ren, 4 years. But then,

> Tai Jia (personal name Zhi 至): First year, 1540, the king assumed his position and dwelt in Bo, appointing as minister Yi Yin. Yi Yin banished Tai Jia to Tong, and then set himself up (as king). In the seventh year, the king slipped out of Tong, and killed Yi Yin. The weather was very foggy for three days; so (the king) recognized his sons Yi Zhi 伊陟 and Yi Fen 伊奮, ordering that their father's property be restored to them and divided equally between them. In the tenth year, (the king) performed the *da xiang* 大饗 rite in the ancestral temple, and for the first time sacrificed to the Intelligences of the Four Quarters. In his twelfth year, he died. (My translation.)

The date 1540 is almost right. In *Hanshu* 21B, Liu Xin (in his *Shijing* 世經, "Canon of Generations," there included) says that Tang reigned 13 years, but Liu also treats the thirteenth year as Tai Jia's first year, and there are no reigns of Wai Bing or Zhong Ren. If Liu is right, I assume that Tang died early in the year and that in the Shang era a king's year of death counted in his own calendar only if he lived through most of it. A sacrifice is performed for Tang at the end of the year, by Yi Yin and not Tai Jia, which may suggest that Yi Yin was moving toward usurpation. David Pankenier has shown that the first year of Shang was 1554 (the *Bamboo Annals* has 1558); therefore the "first year" of Tai Jia was 1542, not 1540.[19]

Working out a consistent chronology on the basis of the *Annals* requires assuming that in the Shang, as in the Zhou (and in effect also in the Xia), a king's year count in the *Bamboo Annals* must normally be understood as preceded by a period for completion of mourning (not recognized in the *Annals* for Shang and Zhou; for Xia there are interregnums, which I regularize to 2 years each).[20] In Western Zhou this was the 2 years following the year of the predecessor's death, and so also in Shang, but in the Shang usually the year of death counted in the successor's calendar, so that in his calendar the period of mourning completion was usually 3 years; and it was so in this case. Tai Jia's dates, therefore, are 1542/1539–1528, 3 + 12 years.

But where have Wai Bing and Zhong Ren gone? I have also been able to show that a Shang king's *gan* 干 name was determined by the first day of his reign—the first day of his succession year, unless that gave a *gan* the same as his predecessor's, and in that case the first day of his postmourning accession year.[21] To find the two missing kings, we must then check first days. It will be found that the first day of 1542 was a *ren* day, and the first day of 1539 was a *jia* day. This takes care of Zhong Ren and Tai Jia: I propose as the best explanation that Yi Yin, in control, named Tai Jia's uncle Zhong Ren as acting king in 1542, while Tai Jia functioned as chief mourner. But before the year was out, Yi Yin had momentarily assumed that function himself. That couldn't continue; he needed another puppet. So in 1541, Yi Yin banished Tai Jia, and in Tai Jia's place, to function as chief mourner, he appointed another uncle, Wai Bing; for 1541 began with a *bing* day. When the mourning was finished at the end of 1540, Wai Bing, having had 2 years, was no longer needed, and Zhong Ren continued as functioning king (under Yi Yin's thumb) for the 4 years that Mengzi and other histories accord him. Then, in 1536—Tai Jia's de jure seventh year, just as in the *Annals,* and after 6 years of exile, just as in Mengzi—Tai Jia makes his escape, returns to Bo, and kills Yi Yin. A powerful person in life is very dangerous when dead, as the account in the *Annals* indicates; and this must be especially so if you yourself have killed him. It is not surprising, then, that even though Yi Yin had almost displaced the Shang royal house, still there were regular sacrifices to him throughout the remainder of the Shang dynasty, as oracle inscriptions show. Probably the *da xiang* sacrifice 3 years after Yi Yin's death marks the end of mourning for him, allowing Tai Jia then to enter upon his

formal sacrificial duties as king. That it was in the *da miao* 大廟—
"grand temple"—probably indicates that Yi Yin had a kinship relation to the Shang line of kings.

Tai Jia must have died not in 1528 but early in 1527, which
counted as the first year of his successor, Wo Ding 沃丁 (in the
Annals). The year 1527 began with a *jia* day, so Wo Ding had to use
1524, which did begin with a *ding* day. The system works as expected, from then on. In the *Annals*, of course, Wai Bing and
Zhong Ren precede all of Tai Jia's 12 years. In the *Annals*, overlaps
of reigns are never tolerated; it's one king at a time. Hence in the
Annals, Yi Yin is portrayed as making himself king, not just handling
puppets, because the two puppets had been removed into reigns of
their own. Further, Wai Bing's 2 years replace Tai Jia's 3 years of
mourning.

Skeptical doubt must focus on my hypothesis about *gan* names
of Shang kings. If it is right, then I have uncovered the facts about
the "good and wise" Yi Yin. My case against him rests on *gan* data,
determined by first days of lunar months, which are astronomical
data. If these are the facts, Mengzi has traveled far from the truth,
and one must wonder how and why.

Wu Wang. There is no sustained treatment by Mengzi of Wu
Wang and the conquest of Shang. I will single out two texts only.

In 3B5, Mengzi and his disciple Wan Zhang apparently are in
Song, probably in the capital, Shangqiu. Wan Zhang (one can suppose that he has been listening to local political talk) asks Mengzi,
"If Song, a small state, were to put into effect kingly government,
and be attacked by Qi and Chu for doing so, what could be done
about it?" Practicing "kingly government" (*wangzheng* 王政) can
have either of two senses: (1) practicing the kind of ideally good
government that a real king would practice; or (2) proclaiming that
the lord of the state is a *wang* and demanding that he be recognized
as such by other states, thus formally declaring his candidacy to
become ruler of the world. Obviously here it has the second sense,
because one cannot imagine the great neighboring states Qi and
Chu objecting to Song's putting into effect kingly government
in the first sense. But Mengzi deliberately fudges the question as
being also about *wangzheng* in the first sense and launches into a ser-
mon about real *wangzheng*, that is, benevolent behavior by a ruler.
(Mengzi uses the same strategy in talking with King Xuan of Qi in

1B5, about whether the king should keep or pull down his *ming tang* 明堂, a symbol of royal pretensions, *wangzheng*.) Consider Tang, founder of Shang, and Wu Wang, founder of Zhou; they were welcomed by the peoples of the lands they conquered, because the people recognized them as benevolent rulers. So if Song really practices kingly government, then Song will be invincible, and need not fear Qi and Chu.

7B3 needs quoting in full:

> Mengzi said, "If one believed everything in the *Shangshu* (Book of History), it would have been better for the *Shu* not to have existed at all. In the "Wu Cheng" chapter ("The Completion of the War," one of the now lost texts), I accept only two or three strips (of the bamboo text). A benevolent man has no match in the world. How could it be that 'the blood spilled was enough to carry staves along with it', when the most benevolent (i.e., Wu Wang of Zhou) waged war against the most cruel (i.e., Zhou Xin of Shang)." (Lau, 194; adapted.)

But the account of Wu Wang's conquest in the "Shi Fu" 世俘 chapter of *Yi Zhou shu* 逸周書, which has a convincing richness of detail, shows that in all likelihood the conquest was indeed a very bloody affair, which is just what one would expect. So what is Mengzi doing here?

It is tempting to read 7B3 as showing Mengzi willing and able to question the most revered authority in pursuing historical truth. But Mengzi was not a historian. While the ideal of courageous honesty on the part of official recorders is celebrated (perhaps mythically) in the *Zuozhuan* (see, e.g., Xiang 25, 5th month), the ideal of critical integrity on the part of a historian begins to appear only in the Han—for example, with Sima Qian's refraining from attempting to give absolute dates for events prior to 841 B.C.E., because he finds his sources suspiciously in conflict. Something else—very interesting—is going on in 7B3, and in 3B5 as well. I will return to this.

Chinese History in Mengzi's Times and Its Impact on Mengzi's Thought

Lau takes the view that no datable events in Mengzi's career can be identified prior to 320 B.C.E., the probable date of his interviews with "King Hui of Liang," that is, with Huicheng Wang of Wei, who died in 319. If we speak of precisely datable events, I agree.

Mengzi's dates of birth and death are not known, and there are two views, one (Qian Mu's, Lau's, and mine) that he died shortly before 300 B.C.E. and was well over 80 years old when he died; and an older (but still late) opinion that his life span was 372–289 B.C.E. The arguments, in my view, are two. First, it appears that Mengzi was older than the king of Wei (Liang) when they talked in 320–319, and the king had succeeded as lord of Wei in 369; second, Mengzi's conversation with his disciple Gongsun Chou (2A2) suggests that Gaozi, with whom Mengzi debates in 6A1–6A4, was considerably older than Mengzi (and by then already long dead). In my judgment, Gaozi's ethical voluntarism indicates that he is the same Gaozi who figures as a wayward disciple of Mozi at the end of *Mozi*, 48 ("Gong Meng").[22] Mozi perhaps died around 390 (according to Qian Mu). A young and brash Gaozi could have been a temporary follower of Mozi circa 400–395 and could later, circa 360, have been an old and respected local moralist arguing with a still-young Mengzi, if Mengzi were born circa 390–385.

Political and military events especially important in the last phase of Mengzi's life, when precise dating is possible, start in 342, when the lord of Qi won a great victory over Wei at Maling at the beginning of the year, and at once (I follow Qian Mu, except for the date of the battle) declared himself *wang*. Following this he and the lord of Wei agreed to recognize each other as *wang* in 334. The next year, Qi suffered an attack by Chu, apparently in retaliation. (The rulers of Chu had internally called themselves *wang* for centuries.) In 325 the rulers of Wei, Han, and Zhao recognized each other as *wang*, and the ruler of Qin also claimed the title *wang*, perhaps independently. In 323, the year of a major defeat of Wei by Chu, there was another mutual recognition (*xiang wang* 相王) conference, bringing in Yan and Zhongshan. And in 318, according to the *Shiji* ("Liu Guo Nianbiao"), the ruler of Song, acting alone, claimed to be a *wang*. This has been challenged by both Qian Mu and Lau, who point out that the *Shiji* has the current ruler of Song, Yan 偃 (=Kang Wang 康王), beginning his reign in 328, whereas it must have been earlier (338, thinks Qian; I would say perhaps 336).[23] The argument is that Sima Qian has made a mistake, of the same kind he makes with the kings of Qi and Wei, taking the date of the declaration of kingship as the first year of a ruler's reign; actually, they hold, Song declared kingship in 328, and nothing happened in 318.

This argument fails. Declaring kingship was dangerous, as the response of Chu in 333 shows. Such a declaration, if unqualified, could be taken as a declaration of intent to conquer all the other states. The *xiang wang* practice itself shows this; rulers needed mutual recognition for protection. Song was the weakest of the larger states. It is hardly conceivable that its ruler would have declared himself *wang* even before Qin had done it. Further, Qian Mu shows that Lord Yan of Song ("Kang Wang") had originally succeeded as a minor.[24] The date 328 that the *Shiji* uses probably was the date when he attained majority, when he might be expected to have promulgated a new calendar. Moreover, in 318 apparently there was a united attack by most of the other major states against Qin; Song could have seen the way clear while their attention was directed elsewhere.

If the *Shiji* is right in dating Song's action to 318 (necessarily effective at the beginning of the year), the matter must have been under intense discussion in Song in 319. In 319, Mengzi left Da-Liang in Wei and went to Qi and would almost certainly have traveled through Song to get there. It seems to me clear, therefore, that Wan Zhang's question in 3B5 was about the issue of declaring kingship and that the question was addressed to Mengzi late in 319. That Wan Zhang was the one who asked the question shows that he was with Mengzi at this time, and this is important, because all but one of Mengzi's discussions about Yao, Shun, and Yi Yin in 5A are in response to questions put to him by Wan Zhang. Those texts too must report conversations that occurred in 319–318; and there is a detail in one of them that goes far to prove this—and to show what was really on Mengzi's mind. Mengzi's view of the relationship between Yao and Shun is conspicuously different from the standard one, in that Mengzi emphatically denies that Yao ever resigned the position of ruler to Shun. His most forceful statement is in 5A5:

> Wan Zhang asked, "Is it true that Yao *gave* the Empire to Shun?" "No," said Mengzi. "The Emperor cannot give the Empire to another.... The Emperor can recommend a man to Heaven, but he cannot make Heaven give this man the Empire; *just as a feudal lord can recommend a man to the Emperor, but he cannot make the Emperor bestow a fief on him,* or as a Councilor can recommend a man to a feudal lord but cannot make the feudal lord appoint him a Councilor." (Lau, 143, adapted, emphasis mine.)

For the background of this, I must turn to the *Zhanguo ce*—with hesitation, because this book is on the border between history and short story, but the details it supplies in this case fit too well to be entirely fiction. The main events, as follows, are accepted also by Yang Kuan. In 318, King Kuai 噲 of Yan gave the state to his prime minister, Zi Zhi 子之 (or perhaps started the process, completing it in 315).[25] This led to great unrest in Yan, and in 315, General Shi Bei 市被 and Crown Prince Ping 平 led an armed revolt. In 314, Zi Zhi crushed the revolt, killing its leaders. Qi sent in an army—King Xuan first asking Mengzi's advice (1B10–1B11, 2B8–2B9)—and occupied the whole state in fifty days. The Zhao state then recognized another Yan prince as king of Yan, and by 312 there was an allied attack on Qi, Mengzi at that time leaving Qi permanently.[26]

If the extraordinary act of King Kuai was undertaken as of 318, this must have been the talk of the whole country, especially in Qi. The *Zhanguo ce* account supplies rich detail.[27] Qi was using Su Dai 蘇代, in league with Zi Zhi, to egg King Kuai on; others supporting the idea urged King Kuai to emulate Yao, who (in a Daoist story about him, in *Zhuangzi* 1) tried to resign his position to the hermit Xu You, who declined indignantly. If you do offer to give your state to Zi Zhi, they urged, he too will not dare accept, and you will gain a reputation for being a sage like Yao. But of course Zi Zhi did accept, and all of the high officers who were supporters of the crown prince were furious. Other versions of the episode have the king genuinely wanting to give his position to Zi Zhi and being urged not to go halfway. Consider Yu, the first Xia king, they said; he wanted his minister Yi 益 to succeed him, but after Yu died, his son Qi 啟 and his supporters killed Yi, making Qi king after all. The original text of the *Bamboo Annals* had it that Yi was aiming at Qi's position, and Qi killed him.[28] This too is taken up by Mengzi (5A6), who says that Yu presented Yi to Heaven, but after Yu's death the people followed Qi, showing that this was really Heaven's will. The present text of the *Annals* has been cleaned up, so that it is consistent with Mengzi's account: Yi, lord of Bi, withdrew to his state in Qi's second year and died 4 years later, being given posthumous honors.

The two contrasting accounts of Yi parallel the two contrasting accounts of Yi Yin in the reign of the (de jure) second Shang king, Tai Jia, who is also discussed at length by Mengzi in 5A6 and 5A7. It seems likely therefore that, in all of this, Mengzi is reflecting discussion that swirled around events in Yan, 318–315. We should take this into account in appraising Mengzi's advice to King Xuan in

315–314 on how to deal with the Yan matter. Mengzi must have been genuinely horrified by King Kuai's folly—and more, by Kuai's implied assumption that he, as ruler, owned the state of Yan and could give it away—and by Zi Zhi's behavior. With him and with others, arguments about the episode would take the form of arguments about the historical models that were being appealed to. In the following from 5A6, then, Mengzi is really talking about the events in Yan.

> A common man who comes to possess the Empire must not have only the virtue of a Shun or a Yu but also the recommendation of an Emperor. That is why Confucius never possessed the Empire. On the other hand, he who inherits the Empire is put aside by Heaven only if he is like Jie or Zhou Xin. That is why Yi, Yi Yin, and the Duke of Zhou never came to possess the Empire. (Lau, 145, adapted.)

The discussion moves seamlessly to Yi Yin. In Mengzi's mind, Zi Zhi must have been threatening the historic models of such as Zhou Gong, who were models for men like himself; and I assume that he knew perfectly well of the alternative accounts of Yi and of Yi Yin. But there is no reason to suppose that Mengzi knew of these accounts as earlier and as having a prior claim to veracity. They were simply other accounts. The world of talk in his time was full of other accounts. Those accounts must be overwritten, and he does so, with passion.

Mengzi's Inventiveness:
The Three-Year Mourning Problem

But is Mengzi making it all up? No, or anyway not quite. The *Zuozhuan* (Xiang 21.4, 552 B.C.E., Legge, 491), in the context of a persuasion has references to Yu, Yi Yin, and Zhou Gong, and the line for Yi Yin goes thus: "Yi Yin acted as minister for Tai Jia while keeping him in confinement, and in the end there was no sign of resentment on [the king's] face." The line assumes that everyone knows the story, so the story must have become well established when this was written; and it is Mengzi's story. But there is no reason to suppose that either Mengzi or the Zuo author (they were contemporaries) is copying the other; so each is using some earlier account. Somewhere along the line there was radical originality, and it

is hard to imagine its being gradual. And I do not think that the account of a bad Yi Yin is the cynical invention of unscrupulous de-
baters of the late fourth century. I think that the account that I have
extracted from my analysis of the *Bamboo Annals* is true. It coheres
too well with everything else I get from that book, in even mathe-
matical and astronomical detail, for me to put it on the table as
merely possible, though of course I recognize that it is not logically
certain.

But I think that Mengzi does make things up, though he does
not think of it that way. Sometimes you can see it happening. Of Yi
Yin: "When Tang sent a messenger with presents to invite him to
court, he calmly said, 'What do I want Tang's presents for?'" But
later (one must assume, to himself), "'Is it not better for me to make
this prince a Yao or a Shun than to remain in the fields, delighting
in the way of Yao and Shun?'" And so on. No recorder was taking
down this bit of poetry, and I have no trouble imagining Mengzi the
poet. Yi Yin must have been a person with no interest in his own
advancement—so, no interest in presents and no haste to accept
a call—but completely unselfish and wise; so farewell to the fields.
Mengzi is painting a picture, and its truth is the higher truth of art,
a sensitive response to sensed logical pressure, perhaps; but that is
not the same thing as narrative based on evidence. Mengzi is like a
folk-art storyteller; he has the rough plot in his head, and he makes
it live.

We see the same kind of thing going on, even more obviously, in Mengzi's development of the story of Shun. In 5A3, Wan
Zhang asks about Shun's treatment of his brother Xiang, who had
plotted with Shun's father to kill him. Why did Shun not have Xiang
executed, as he did other wicked persons, instead of merely banish-
ing him? On the contrary, Mengzi replies, Shun did not banish
Xiang—he enfeoffed him in You Bi! Wan Zhang objects with surprise: "What wrong had the people of You Bi done? Is that the way a
benevolent man behaves? Others he punishes, but when it comes to
his own brother, he enfeoffs him instead!" Mengzi first pursues the
suggestion of improper favor to a brother: a truly benevolent man
will love his brother no matter what and will try to provide enjoyment for him, and the way Shun chose was appropriate to Shun's
status and power as ruler. Then Mengzi, sensing the other part of
Wan Zhang's objection, adds that of course "Xiang was not allowed

to take any action in his fief." Shun appointed others to run it; "Xiang was certainly not permitted to ill use the people." Here again, I think we can see the story in the process of growing, so as to satisfy its audience.

Perhaps the most striking thing Mengzi does to the Yao-Shun story is to stress the theme of filial piety and family affection, virtually making Shun a hero of *xiao* 孝 and *ti* 悌. To make the story vivid, Shun's brother and parents are made abominable without relief. One new detail that Mengzi may not even have noticed is the treatment of Yao's two daughters, given as wives to Shun. In the *Shangshu,* Shun gains Yao's attention because of his success in achieving amicable relations with his difficult family, and it is only then that Yao says he will give Shun his daughters. But in Mengzi's retelling, the worst of Xiang's and the "blind man's" acts, their repeated schemes for Shun's destruction, have them planning the division of Shun's effects after his death—and the two wives are to go to Xiang. Yao has already given them to Shun.

Some would want to say that Mengzi's invention goes much farther. The virtue of *xiao,* it is said, enjoyed an extraordinary emphasis and development by Warring States Confucians, who maintained, and probably believed, that they were simply trying to bring past "family values" back to life. There may be truth in this. But the argument does not stop there. There are those who have argued, and are arguing, that the institution of 3 years of mourning for a deceased parent was an invention of Confucius, or of his followers in the next two centuries, who made Confucius say what they wanted him to say.[29] Mengzi has to be included, prominently, in this charge. Not only do we have his treatment of Shun; we also have his highlighting of Shun's behavior during the mourning period for Yao (5A4, 5A5) and of Yu's behavior during the mourning for Shun and Yi's during the mourning for Yu (5A6). And then there is Mengzi's detailed advice (3A2) to the heir-prince of Teng on how to mourn for his father that exasperated the duke's ministers, who objected that all this bother was unheard of in past practice. Is Mengzi making all of this up?

After my examination of his creative imagination, I certainly don't trust Mengzi's details. And we can well imagine that the obvious inconvenience of ritual mourning, even without the loving detail that Mengzi builds into it in 3A2, would have led over time to its being neglected more often than observed by busy heads of state in Warring States times. But one will notice that my entire chronological construction for fifteen centuries of Chinese history prior to Warring States posits mourning breaks between reigns and requires that assumption to make coherent sense of the *Bamboo Annals*. This construction is confirmed, over and over, by references to astronomical details—conjunctions, eclipses, beginnings of lunar months calculated to the day—in inscriptions and old texts. The institution of "3 years" (25 or 27 months) of mourning for deceased parents must have been well entrenched in prehistoric China. Mengzi was probably embellishing, but he was not participating in the invention of this institution.

Charity versus Wishful Thinking

What was Mengzi doing when he said that it would be better not to have the *Shangshu* at all than to accept all of it? He says of the "Wu Cheng" chapter that he accepts two or three slips, not the rest. He does not do this just with the "Wu Cheng." He quotes, approvingly, the "Yao Dian," about how the people mourned for Yao when Yao died. But the same chapter also says that Yao resigned his position to Shun. Mengzi rejects this statement and reinterprets: what Yao did, really, was to turn over most or all of the administration to Shun, while he, Yao, kept his position.

For Mengzi, Yao was a sage, and Wu Wang was a sage. A sage would have behaved like a sage. For me, Mengzi was a man, with a brain. A man with a brain would behave like a man with a brain. When I examine something that someone like Mengzi said or did, I begin by assuming that he was acting and thinking rationally, that is, that he had comprehensible and in his own eyes defensible reasons for what he said or did. As I try to describe and explain him, I "save" this assumption as long as I can, maybe exploiting that phrase "in his own eyes," by building a hypothetical thought-world around him, for those eyes to see, before retreating to a strategy of causal explanation, perhaps arguing that he was under duress. And I stubbornly exhaust this second possibility before giving up and saying that he must simply have been foolish (or more puzzling, that he was acting or speaking contrary to his better judgment). We call this kind of historian's behavior applying a "principle of charity."

Mengzi, especially when it came to sages, was applying a principle of charity too, only his principle of charity was thicker than mine. Mengzi had a nonempirical belief about what we call political sovereignty: it depends ultimately on the will of Heaven. It follows that its possessor cannot alienate it at will. Only Heaven can transfer it; and a sage like Yao, being all-wise because he was a sage, would know that. He would know that he, Yao, did not own the world. So he must have behaved as Mengzi said he did. Mengzi also was a pacifist and had a nonempirical belief about military force: a perfectly benevolent ruler would never have occasion to use it, because everyone would want to be his subject. Wu Wang, being a sage, must have known this and must have been perfectly benevolent. So it was inconceivable to Mengzi that Wu Wang's conquest could have involved bloodshed; and any statement to the contrary must be wrong.

Now, this matter of the relative "thickness" of principles of charity bothers me a lot. For how do I know that my own principle of charity isn't "thicker" than it ought to be? To put the matter another way, that will make it even more disturbing, it seems obvious that Mengzi wanted Yao and Wu Wang to live up to his, Mengzi's, ideal of sagehood; and so he sees in their respective pasts and behaviors what he wants to see. We have a name for this: we call it "wishful thinking."

How do I tell the difference between applying a principle of charity and indulging in wishful thinking? I cannot just give up, and say, well then, let's be done with charity; for trying to understand human behavior as thought-governed, inevitably in the process going beyond simply reading off the "evidence," is what makes history—in the sense of *shixue* 史學 (the discipline)—history. Without this, we would find that history—in the sense of *lishi* 歷史 (what has happened)—would (to borrow a metaphor) disintegrate into a dish of loose facts.

Notes

1. David Nivison, "The Key to the Chronology of the Three Dynasties: The 'Modern Text' *Bamboo Annals*," *Sino-Platonic Papers* 93 (January 1999): 12–13.

2. For example, see D. C. Lau, trans., *Mencius* (Harmondsworth: Penguin Books, 1970), 224–226.

3. See, e.g., *Hanfeizi* 51.

4. Qian Mu (Ch'ien Mu), *Xian Qin zhuzi xinian* (Chronological Studies

of the Pre-Ts'in Philosophers), 2 vols. (Shanghai: Shangwu yinshuguan, 1935; reprint, Hong Kong: Hong Kong University Press, 1956).

5. David W. Pankenier, "Astronomical Dates in Shang and Western Zhou," *Early China* 7 (1981–1982): 2–37.

6. Nivison, "Key to the Chronology," 12–13.

7. As established by Pankenier, "Astronomical Dates."

8. A summary of this analysis can be found in Nivison, "Key to the Chronology," 34.

9. David W. Pankenier, "Mozi and the Dates of Xia, Shang, and Zhou: A Research Note," *Early China* 9–10 (1983–1985): 175–181.

10. See Fan Xiangyong, *Guben Zhushu jinian jijiao dingbu* (Shanghai: Renmin, 1962), 5–6.

11. The date is confirmed by a quotation in the *Xin Tang shu* from Liu Xiang's *Hong Fan zhuan;* see David Nivison and K. D. Pang, "Astronomical Evidence for the *Bamboo Annals* Chronicle of Early Xia," *Early China* 15 (1990): 87–88 n. 2; and Nivison's response to critics in the same volume, 169–170.

12. Nivison and Pang, "Astronomical Evidence," 91–92. One *bu* equals 76 years.

13. Fan Xiangyong, *Guben Zhushu,* 6.

14. Wen Gong 18; see James Legge, trans., *The Ch'un Ts'ew, with the Tso Chuen,* vol. 5 of *The Chinese Classics* (Hong Kong: Lane Crawford, 1872), 282–283.

15. Nivison and Pang, "Astronomical Evidence," 92.

16. Edward L. Shaughnessy, "On the Authenticity of the *Bamboo Annals*," *Harvard Journal of Asiatic Studies* 46 (1986): 149–180. Also see Shaughnessy, *Sources of Western Zhou History* (Berkeley and Los Angeles: University of California Press, 1991).

17. See, e.g., Liu Tan, *Zhongguo gudai zhi xing sui jinian* (Beijing: Kexue chubanshe), 134.

18. See E. Chavannes, trans., *Les memoires historiques de Se-ma Ts'ien,* 5 vols. (Paris: Adrien-Maisonneuve, 1895–1905; reprint, Leiden: E. J. Brill, 1967), vol. 3, app. 3.

19. Pankenier, "Astronomical Dates," 7.

20. Nivison, "Key to the Chronology," 12.

21. Ibid., 13–17. And *gui* was never used; it defaulted to *jia.*

22. David Nivison, *The Ways of Confucianism: Investigations in Chinese Philosophy,* ed. Bryan W. Van Norden (Chicago: Open Court, 1996), 121–132.

23. See Qian Mu, *Xian Qin,* 274; and Lau, *Mencius,* 208–209.

24. Qian Mu, *Xian Qin,* 275.

25. Yang Kuan, *Zhanguo shi* (Shanghai: Renmin chubanshe, 1961), 100–101, 260–261; see also *Shiji,* "Yan Shijia," in Chavannes, *Memoires historiques,* vol. 4, 140–144, and *Hanfeizi,* "Wai Chu Shuo, You Xia"; see W. K. Liao, trans., *The Complete Works of Han Fei Tzu* (London: Arthur Probsthain, 1939, 1959), vol. 2, 128–131.

26. Qian Mu, *Xian Qin,* 371.

27. J. I. Crump, trans., *Chan-kuo Ts'e* (Oxford: Oxford University Press, 1970), no. 451, 517–520.

28. James Legge, trans., *The Shoo King, or Book of Historical Documents,* vol. 3 of *The Chinese Classics* (London: Henry Froude, 1865), 118. The "Prolegomena" contains Legge's translation of the *Bamboo Annals, Zhushu jinian.*

29. See, for example, K. N. Knapp, "The *Ru* Reinterpretation of *Xiao,*" *Early China* 20 (1995), especially 209–213. Knapp himself shares this view and points out that even Hu Shi held it at one time.

13

Mencius and an Ethics of the New Century

Donald J. Munro

I HAVE NEVER MET anyone who tried to use either the ethics of Plato's *Republic* or the Epicurean hedonism of Lucretius' *On the Nature of Things* as a guide for living. So I would not spend time asking if there was any compatibility between either of them, on the one hand, and some serious contemporary Western ethics, on the other. But I have met Chinese people who treat the *Mencius* as such a guide. I think that Arthur Danto was on target when he made the following comments about some non-Western literature.

> The difficulty with our approach to non-Western literature is that it fails to adequately address the issue of these texts' Otherness. I am not arguing for relativism of any sort. But in non-Western cultures there are values other than truth and ways of addressing books other than by analyzing their content. For texts are things that have to be lived, as many books of the Orient are lived—their vitality as writing bound up with their being vitally a part of the lives of their readers in a way that they cannot be with ours.[1]

I expect that some people will continue to treat the *Mencius* as a text to be lived, well into the twenty-first century. Every age picks and chooses which parts of a complicated text it wishes to emphasize. Therefore, I ask myself, How much ethical theory from within the *Mencius* do I believe will endure in the new century, in China or in other societies that may treat the Chinese texts attentively? My answer is that those aspects that are compatible with evolutionary biology will survive a sifting to become for the new century the essence of the *Mencius* text, separated from what will then be disregarded as the dross.

A Darwinian perspective dominates contemporary human biology and psychology, perspectives respectively identified as sociobiology and as evolutionary psychology. This means that both accept the principle that human behavior reflects the reciprocal impact of genes and culture. Those genes that dominate in large groups (not necessarily individuals) do so because they increase the likelihood that the people will be more fit for survival and for reproducing their genes. The psychologists refer to the genetic roots as "hard wiring." They say that hardwired within our brains are hereditary rules for mental development, for viewing the world in a certain way, and for making certain choices. Some sociobiologists call these rules "epigenetic." I assume that such principles will dominate biology and psychology well into the twenty-first century. I also assume that any ethical position that expects to be treated seriously during this time by people who accept the Darwinian trends must have essential tenets that are compatible with those principles, as fleshed out.

Edward O. Wilson is the most prominent spokesman for the sociobiological position, and so I will take his positions on relevant issues as representative. He gets off to a start that is promising to anyone who wishes to treat Mencian ethics with respect. That is, he accepts the premise that there is a human nature, a concept for which Mencius is well known. Wilson defines it as the hereditary rules for mental development that bias cultural evolution.[2] This is an age in which many scholars in the humanities and in anthropology/ sociology are so focused on the differences between people and on the uniqueness of individual cultures that they condemn belief in a human nature as "essentialism." Some call this antiessentialist perspective postmodern. But even the antipostmodernist American philosopher Richard Rorty says that we should stop asking what our nature is and instead ask, What can we make of ourselves?[3] In short, Rorty also opposes use of the expression "human nature." This is a curious position that reveals Rorty as both opposed to foundationalist ethics (where ethics would be based on human nature) and as also an acknowledged Darwinian.

The belief in a common human nature does not require belief that, correcting for environmental variations, all people's minds are the same. Describing the findings of the brain scientist Dr. Gerald Edelman, one writer says,

Thus, every person, even an identical twin, has a network of connections within his or her brain different from that in every other brain. Every person's individual network has been shaped by Darwinian rules of selection to provide a structure that will enable him or her to cope with the world.[4]

A Common Human Nature

Mencian ethics in the new century has an optimistic starting point. The biologists and psychologists to whom I referred would have no trouble with the Mencian assumption that there is a common human nature. This is important because it affirms that ethics can be grounded in the innate human condition. In other words, certain moral concepts derive from something that is inborn. They are not entirely arbitrary human inventions relative to individual communities and cultures. Whether or not they are also founded on something transcendental is another question. For now, I begin with a general description of the theory about an innate nature from which the moral concepts derive. Then I will take up its content.

In simple terms, the contemporary Darwinian and Mencian theories share the position that ethical rules derive from biology, that is, from our hereditary or inborn human nature. Just below I give an example of Mencius' use of an empirical argument on this matter. The *Mencius* also implies that human nature is in turn derived from Heaven: "a man who knows his own nature will know heaven."[5] This claim has no Darwinian counterpart. It would be rejected today, along with similar claims that base ethics on God's commands.

There is no necessary connection between a biological claim (a testable claim about an innate response) and a religious claim (not testable). Mencius gives various examples of the innate traits that he affirms exist[6] and of the religious kind of claims.[7] This means that someone today can filter the heaven out of Mencius (the religious claims) and still retain a justification for much of his ethics. So the biological basis of ethics is the first Mencian position that is likely to endure.

This basis is important as a rule of thumb for sorting through the barrage of varying ethical rules that a person may encounter today. Only those consistent with human nature will survive in the long term.[8] Those that are inconsistent, such as Shaker celibacy, will have short lives. To affirm a biological basis is to affirm the existence of transcultural moral instincts, such as territoriality and the incest taboo. Of course there are exceptions to the practice of these instincts, but they are sufficiently limited in scope so as not to contradict the basic principles of survival and reproductive success.

The Empirical Basis of a Common Human Nature

There is a general point I would make about the enduring vibrancy of the Mencian theory of human nature. Certain parts of it can last because they are compatible with the standard of empirical testing. This is the case with one of the most famous arguments Mencius presents, namely, the automatic response of an observer to seeing a child in danger of falling into a well. Mencius predicts immediate acts to save the child, devoid of any cost-benefit calculations.[9] He treats this as evidence of the existence of the moral instinct of empathy for suffering and altruistic response to do something about it. In principle, a person could set up an experiment involving children teetering on wells and see if neutral observers would so act. He is arguing that we both can (a matter that we call biological and Mencius would call an inborn heart) and should act with compassion. This is the point.

Belief in innate moral sentiments is quite compatible with evidence that under extreme conditions they can also be nonexistent in people who previously exhibited them. Auschwitz survivor Primo Levi wrote,

> In conclusion: theft in Buna, punished by the civil direction, is authorized and encouraged by the SS; is considered by the civilians as a normal exchange operation; theft among Haftlinge is generally punished, but the punishment strikes the thief and the victim with equal gravity. We now invite the reader to contemplate the possible meaning in the Lager of the words "good" and "evil," "just" and "unjust."[10]

But the moral sentiments of those same persons could return. Levi wrote of the offer of a slice of bread by some inmates to others who had been working, shortly after the SS guards had fled.

> Only a day before a similar event would have been inconceivable. The law of the Lager said: "eat your own bread, and if you can, that of your neighbor," and left no room for gratitude [for the offer of bread]. It [the offer of bread] really meant the Lager was dead.

It was the first human gesture that occurred among us. I believe that that moment can be dated as the beginning of the change by which we who had not died slowly changed from Haftlinge to men again.[11]

So the empirical argument for certain innate moral sentiments can withstand this counterexample. It does need updating, namely, acknowledgment that they may evaporate under certain circumstances.

To return to his form of argument, in fact, Mencius uses many different types of argument at various places in the text. Sometimes he argues from analogy, a technique widespread in different cultures, including our own. For example, he approves of the plant analogy to explain the potentiality of our innate moral instincts.[12] He says that his interpretation of the water analogy to explain human nature is superior to that of his debating partner, Gaozi.[13] A second type is the argument from behavioral implications. If people accept a given position, it is psychologically likely to affect their behavior in a certain positive or negative way. For example, he argues against Gaozi that if people believe that behaving dutifully is artificial or not natural to the human condition, they will not be motivated to do the right thing: "If you must mutilate the willow [by analogy, human nature] to make it into cups and bowls [to generate moral conduct], must you mutilate a man to make him moral? Surely it will be these words of yours men in the world will follow in bringing disaster upon morality."[14] There are arguments from authority, such as the practices of the sage-kings Yao and Shun.[15] And there are arguments from utility. These may include the utility of providing models to the people, for then they will follow the model: "If there is one who is not [fond of killing people], then the people of the Empire will crane their necks to watch for his coming. This being truly the case, the people will turn to him like water flowing downwards with a tremendous force."[16] Or, they may include the utility of policies, such as tax reduction, for improving the lives of the people. While acknowledging the existence of many forms of argument, I point to the explicit existence of those from empirical evidence to show the compatibility of Mencius with the standards of verification likely to dominate in our new century.

Actually, Mencius uses the argument from analogy to bolster his empirical argument for universal traits and for universal standards. His "child and the well" argument goes from establishing the existence of a trait of spontaneous compassion to treating compassion as a universal duty. Mencius would have us infer from a universal trait of human nature to a universal standard. For him, as for Xunzi, the analogy of carpentry tools conveyed the abstraction that Westerners call a universal. These are the various carpentry tools that give the same result no matter where or when they are used: the plumb line, the balance scale, the compass, and the square. Giving the same results universally, they also provide a standard. By analogy, the sage, whose nature we share, also is a universal standard of human perfection. Mencius said, "The compass and the carpenter's square are the culmination of squares and circles; the sage is the culmination of humanity."[17] The argument is that we know perfection exists from the carpenter's tools. By analogy, we know there are degrees of perfection in human nature, with the sage as the highest degree. To repeat, the existence of a common human nature is assumed.

The strength of the Mencian position thus far includes his belief in a common human nature and his use of the empirical argument. In addition, he will have three other theses that are positive from the standpoint of the ethics of the new century. One is the identification of what is innate and of primary moral significance as an emotion. The second is that the primal emotion is kinship love, on the basis of which empathy is learned. Bringing him up to date, I would suggest that the Mencian refer to "caregiver" rather than kin, because in fact persons other than kin enter into the familial roles. The third is his characterization of the mind as an evaluative process.

Emotions and Deliberation

To identify the content of the theories of human nature shared by Mencius and modern Darwinians reveals something that sets Confucian ethics apart from most previous Western ethical systems. This is the prominence of the emotions in Mencian moral deliberations and its relative absence in prominent Western systems. From the nineteenth century onward, Kantianism and utilitarianism have dominated Western ethics. In the former case, reasoning about the applicability of the categorical imperative dominates consideration of action choices. In the latter, it is cost-benefit calculations about the greatest happiness for the greatest number of persons. In both cases, the thinking is supposedly rational, devoid of much emotion. In contrast, Mencius places the emotions of compassion and shame at the center of his moral psychology. He also says that our sense of duty (*yi*) pleases the heart just as meat pleases the taste buds.[18] In other words, we find the emotion of joy joined with the cognitive sense that something is a duty.

Similarly, Edward O. Wilson affirms, "[Brain scientists] have established that passion is inseverably linked to reason. Emotion is not just a perturbation of reason but a vital part of it."[19] And, "Without the stimulus and guidance of emotion, rational thought slows and disintegrates."[20] Among other things, this means that the emotions provide the motivation that leads to action. In treating compassion and shame as among the root moral sentiments, Mencius was focusing on emotions that are basic to doing the right thing. Wilson agrees with the basic Mencian assumption that "moral concepts are derived from innate emotions."[21]

Infant Bonding and Sympathy

Infant bonding with caregivers and sympathy are among the specific emotions that are central to the innate emotions singled out by both Mencius and the Darwinians. Edward O. Wilson writes, "Among traits with documented heritability, those closest to moral aptitude are empathy with the distress of others and certain processes of attachment between infants and their caregivers."[22] Obviously, there will be considerable difference in the specifics of what the emotions involve. Mencius will focus on patriarchal emotions, such as those between father and son, though such a relationship is absent from Wilson's work.[23] The important point is the connection that both parties see between kinship and sympathy, or altruism. Mencius says that the gentleman first treats his kin as kin, and then treats the people with humaneness.[24] Also, "Loving one's kin [especially parents] is humaneness."[25] Among the hereditary rules of mental development making up Wilson's concept of human nature are the details of mother-infant bonding:[26] "Kin selection [involving the natural selection of genes and their effect on genetic relatives] is especially important in the origin of altruistic behavior."[27] Altruism is an emotion.[28]

James Q. Wilson is a social scientist who draws heavily on evolutionary theory, genetics, brain science, and primatology. He also takes his evidence from anthropology, psychology, and education. Like Mencius, he believes in an innate moral sense. And like Mencius, he finds that sympathy is rooted in kinship emotions: "For most children the ability to be affected by the emotional state of others leads to a concern for the well-being of others."[29] Again, this is a matter of an emotion. He writes,

> Much of the time our inclination toward fair play or our sympathy for the plight of others are immediate and instinctive, a reflex of our emotions more than an act of our intellect, and in those cases in which we do deliberate . . . our deliberations begin . . . with feelings —in short, with a moral sense.[30]

This moral sense is nearly universal.[31] In short, it is part of human nature. The two Wilsons do not always agree. James Q. would reject the assertion of Edward O. that investment in child care is driven only by a desire to reproduce one's genes.[32] But they both follow the 1906 finding of Edward Westermarck that "the maternal sentiment is universal in mankind."[33]

The Evaluating Mind

James Q. Wilson also argues for another aspect of the content of human nature favored by Mencius. When Mencius refers to the *shifei zhi xin*, or the mind of right and wrong, he is asserting that human beings evaluate. The human mind is an evaluating mind. Wilson says that one meaning of the claim that there is an innate moral sense is that

> virtually everyone, beginning at a very young age, makes moral judgments that, though they may vary greatly in complexity, sophistication, and wisdom, distinguish between actions on the grounds that some are right and others wrong.[34]

There is a sign that we differentiate between matters of taste and matters that carry moral praise or blame. This sign is the general feeling that if we are going to violate a standard based on a common moral impulse, we must give justifications.

Both Wilsons agree on the existence of a moral sense. E. O. Wilson says,

> Such a process [leading to the predominance of genes predisposing people toward cooperative behavior] repeated through thousands

of generations inevitably gave birth to the moral sentiments. With the exception of stone psychopaths (if any truly exist), these instincts are vividly experienced by every person variously as conscience, self-respect, remorse, empathy, shame, humility, and moral outrage.[35]

Empathy and the Out-group: The Mencian Gap

Some people may not care about the child at the well and thus may do nothing. They may even throw the child into the well. One piece of Holocaust literature can represent the countless documented instances of Nazi barbarity toward children. This is from Elie Wiesel's *Memoirs:*

> Unable to "handle" such a large number of Hungarian Jews in the crematoria, the killers were not content merely to incinerate children's dead bodies. In their barbarous madness they cast living Jewish children into specially tended furnaces.
>
> ... I see them now, and I still curse the killers, their accomplices, the indifferent spectators who knew and kept silent.[36]

Obviously, this kind of episode exhibits the existence of in-group/out-group behavior. If any group expressed it starkly, the Nazis did, and their Ukrainian guards as well. Sociobiologists base this behavior in an instinct. They would say that the instinct to differentiate in-group from out-group and to favor the former can coexist with the instincts of empathy and altruism. Sociobiologists call it a tribal instinct, but "tribal" is not in favor with anthropologists these days, except when referring to some places such as India. They generally prefer the term "ethnic group." In any case, the Darwinians would insist that there are innate dispositions to divide people into in-group and out-group categories. Such sentiments will periodically be in conflict with empathy and altruism. Our natures are not one-dimensional. The tribal instinct coexists with the altruistic. I suspect that both have proven useful over time. The tribal is probably the basis of the value of patriotism that is especially necessary when one's society is threatened. At other times, there are broad benefits to altruism. The big question is how we deal with the conflict between the altruistic and the out-group perspectives.

So Mencius is on solid ground in affirming that our ethics rests heavily on common human emotions associated with caregivers, in recognizing that sympathy grows from those emotions, on noting that our mind is an evaluating mind, and on seeing the emotional dimension of moral choice rather than treating it as exclusively cognitive. However, from a contemporary perspective, his weakness is in not dealing with in-group/out-group distinctions that limit the scope of our empathy. The solution for the modern Mencian is to study the question of the possible survival value of enlarging group cooperation. Biologists have already done some work on this matter. E. O. Wilson says that there is empirical evidence that "cooperative individuals generally survive longer and leave more offspring."[37] There are seeds, but only seeds, in the *Mencius* for developing that idea. They lie in the opposition to Yang Zhu's egoism and in the argument that productive role divisions and cooperation in the exchange of output are in the interest of people as a whole. Farmers and craftsmen trade grain for implements: "Moreover, it is necessary for each man to use the products of all the hundred crafts."[38]

How one realizes this activity is another matter. It requires both the rule of law and stable institutions, both matters neglected by Mencius. Respect for cooperation as a value can also be taught. With their highly developed educational concerns, we might hope that the modern followers of Mencius would have something to contribute here.

Notes

1. Arthur Danto, cited in *Harpers* (May 1990): 34.

2. Edward O. Wilson, *Consilience: The Unity of Knowledge* (New York: Knopf, 1998), 164.

3. See the discussion by Carlin Romano, "Rortyism for Beginners," in *The Nation*, 27 July/3 August 1998, 28. Romano is discussing the second set of essays in Richard Rorty, *Truth and Progress: Philosophical Papers*, vol. 3 (Cambridge: Cambridge University Press, 1998).

4. Steven Levy, "Dr. Edelman's Brain," in *The New Yorker*, 2 May 1994, 68.

5. *Mencius* 7A1. Translations are from D. C. Lau, *Mencius* (Harmondsworth: Penguin Books, 1976); see p. 182.

6. *Mencius* 1A7, 2A6.

7. Ibid. See 4A12 and also various passages about heaven making the crucial decisions about who should rule.

8. Wilson, *Consilience*, 249.

9. *Mencius* 2A6; Lau, 82.

10. Primo Levi, *Survival in Auschwitz and the Reawakening: Two Memoirs* (New York: Summit Books, 1965), 86.

11. Ibid., 160.

12. *Mencius* 6A7; Lau, 164.

13. *Mencius* 6A1–6A2; Lau, 160.

14. Ibid.

15. *Mencius* 3A4; Lau, 103.

16. *Mencius* 1A6; Lau, 54.

17. *Mencius* 4A2; Lau, 118.

18. *Mencius* 6A7.

19. Wilson, *Conscilience*, 106.

20. Ibid., 113.

21. Ibid., 179.

22. Ibid., 253. See also Edward O. Wilson, "The Biological Basis of Morality," *Atlantic Monthly,* April 1998, 59.

23. *Mencius* 3A4 and 7B24.

24. Ibid., 7A45.

25. Ibid., 7A15.

26. Wilson, *Conscilience*, 164.

27. Ibid., 169.

28. Ibid., 205.

29. James Q. Wilson, *The Moral Sense* (New York: Free Press, 1993), 46.

30. Ibid., 8.

31. Ibid., 11.

32. Ibid., 43.

33. Ibid., 19.

34. Ibid., 25.

35. Wilson, *Conscilience*, 253.

36. Elie Wiesel, *Memoirs All Rivers Run to the Sea* (New York: Knopf, 1995), 78.

37. Wilson, "Biological Basis of Morality," 59.

38. *Mencius* 3A4; Lau, 101.

Contributors

ROGER T. AMES is professor of philosophy at the University of Hawai'i and editor of *Philosophy East and West*. His most recent publications include *Tracing Dao to Its Source* (1997; with D. C. Lau); *Thinking from the Han: Self, Truth, and Transcendence in Chinese and Western Culture* (1997; with D. L. Hall); *The Confucian Analects* (1998; with H. Rosemont Jr.); *Democracy of the Dead: Dewey, Confucius, and the Hope for Democracy in China* (1999; with D. L. Hall); and *Focusing the Familiar: A Translation and Philosophical Interpretation of the Zhongyong* (2001; with D. L. Hall).

IRENE BLOOM is Ann Whitney Olin Professor and chair of the Department of Asian and Middle Eastern Cultures, Barnard College. Her publications include *Knowledge Painfully Acquired: The K'un-chih chi of Lo Ch'in-shun* (1987); *Religious Diversity and Human Rights* (coedited with J. Paul Martin and Wayne Proudfoot, 1996); and *Sources of Chinese Tradition* (1999, rev. ed.; coedited with Wm. Theodore de Bary).

A. TAEKO BROOKS holds B.A. and M.A. degrees in Japanese history from the University of Hawai'i. She is the co-author, with E. Bruce Brooks, of *Chinese Character Frequency Lists* (1974) and *The Original Analects* (1998) and is a research associate with the Warring States Project of the University of Massachusetts at Amherst.

317

E. BRUCE BROOKS holds a Ph.D. degree in Chinese language and literature from the University of Washington and has published studies on various aspects of textual analysis in Chinese and English, including *The Original Analects* (1998; with A. Taeko Brooks). He is research professor of Chinese at the University of Massachusetts at Amherst, and director of the university's Warring States Project.

ALAN K. L. CHAN received his Ph.D. from the University of Toronto, Canada. He is currently vice-dean, Faculty of Arts and Social Sciences, and associate professor, Department of Philosophy, National University of Singapore. With research interests in both Confucianism and Daoism, he is the author of *Two Visions of the Way* (1991) and other studies on early Chinese philosophy and religion.

NING CHEN received his Ph.D. from the University of Pittsburgh and is currently affiliated with the Departments of History and Religious Studies, Santa Clara University. His published works have appeared in such journals as *Journal of Chinese Religions, Journal of Chinese Philosophy,* and *Philosophy East and West.*

KIM-CHONG CHONG (Ph.D. London) is an associate professor in the Philosophy Department at the National University of Singapore. He specializes in moral philosophy and early Chinese philosophy. His publications include *Moral Agoraphobia: The Challenge of Egoism* (1996), "The Aesthetic Moral Personality: *Li, Yi, Wen,* and *Chih* in the *Analects*" (*Monumenta Serica* 1998), and "The Practice of *Jen*" (*Philosophy East and West* 1999).

ANTONIO S. CUA received his Ph.D. from the University of California, Berkeley, and is Professor Emeritus of Philosophy at the Catholic University of America. His major publications include *Dimensions of Moral Creativity: Paradigms, Principles, and Ideals* (1978); *The Unity of Knowledge and Action: A Study in Wang Yang-ming's Moral Psychology* (1982); *Ethical Argumentation: A Study in Hsün-tzu's Moral Epistemology* (1985); and *Moral Vision and Tradition: Essays in Chinese Ethics* (1998).

ROBERT ENO received his Ph.D. from the University of Michigan and is currently associate professor of East

Asian languages and cultures at Indiana University, Bloomington. He is the author of *The Confucian Creation of Heaven* (1990) and other studies in early Chinese thought and history.

H. JIUAN HENG received her Ph.D. from Columbia University and is an assistant professor in the National University of Singapore. She works on the foundations of Chinese scholar painting, philosophy in cross-cultural contexts, and aesthetics. Her published works include "Body and Ritual in Chinese Literati Painting" (*Analecta Husserliana* 2001) and "The Return of Pure Consciousness: The Theatre of Virtual Selves in the Age of the Internet", in *Technology and Human Values* (forthcoming; edited by Roger Ames and Peter Hershock).

DONALD J. MUNRO is Professor Emeritus of Philosophy and of Chinese at the University of Michigan. A former chair of the Department of Asian Languages and Cultures, he is the author of a trilogy of books on theories of human nature and their relation to education and social control principles in early China, the Southern Song, and Maoist China.

DAVID S. NIVISON received his Ph.D. from Harvard University and is Professor Emeritus of Philosophy at Stanford University. His major publications include *Confucianism in Action* (1959; coedited with Arthur Wright); *The Life and Thought of Chang Hsüeh-ch'eng* (1966); and *The Ways of Confucianism* (1996; edited by Bryan Van Norden).

KWONG-LOI SHUN obtained his B.Phil. from Oxford University and Ph.D. from Stanford University. He is currently professor of philosophy at the University of California, Berkeley. He is the author of *Mencius and Early Chinese Thought* (1997) and other studies in Chinese philosophy.

SOR-HOON TAN received her Ph.D. in comparative philosophy from the University of Hawai'i at Manoa. She is currently assistant professor of philosophy at the National University of Singapore. She has published works in Confucianism and pragmatism in various international journals and is a regular contributor to the *China Review International*.

Index

Citations from the *Mencius*

IMMUNITY TO ANIMAL PARASITES

CONTRIBUTORS

OLE AALUND

JOHN F. BARBARO

COLIN DOBSON

S. M. GAAFAR

M. A. GEMMELL

N. N. IZZAT

W. H. R. LUMSDEN

F. N. MacNAMARA

G. A. MAEKELT

D. F. MAHONEY

MAX MURRAY

L. J. OLSON

M. ELAINE ROSE

ELVIO H. SADUN

E. J. L. SOULSBY

W. T. WEBER

IMMUNITY TO ANIMAL PARASITES

Edited by **E. J. L. SOULSBY**

Department of Pathobiology
School of Veterinary Medicine
University of Pennsylvania
Philadelphia, Pennsylvania

 *1972*

ACADEMIC PRESS New York and London

ACADEMIC PRESS, INC.
111 Fifth Avenue, New York, New York 10003

United Kingdom Edition published by
ACADEMIC PRESS, INC. (LONDON) LTD.
24/28 Oval Road, London NW1

LIBRARY OF CONGRESS CATALOG CARD NUMBER: 72-77338

324386

PRINTED IN THE UNITED STATES OF AMERICA

CONTENTS

Chapter 7   Immune Response to Gastrointestinal Helminths

COLIN DOBSON

Chapter 8   Immune Response to Tissue Helminths
I. Nematodes

L. J. OLSON AND N. N. IZZAT

Chapter 9   Immune Response to Tissue Parasites
II. Cestodes

M. A. GEMMELL AND F. N. MACNAMARA

Chapter 10   Immune Response to Arthropods

S. M. GAAFAR

Chapter 11   **Immune Response to Hemoprotozoa**

I. Trypanosomes

W. H. R. LUMSDEN

Chapter 12   **Immune Response to Hemoprotozoa**

II. *Babesia* spp.

D. F. MAHONEY

Chapter 13   **Immune Response to Intracellular Parasites**

I. *Leishmania*

G. A. MAEKELT

Contents

Chapter 14   Immune Response to Intracellular Parasites
II. Coccidia

M. ELAINE ROSE

LIST OF CONTRIBUTORS

Numbers in parentheses indicate the pages on which the authors' contributions begin.

OLE AALUND (1), Royal Veterinary and Agricultural University, Bülowsvej, Copenhagen, Denmark

JOHN F. BARBARO (131), Department of Immunochemistry, Division of Communicable Disease and Immunology, Walter Reed Army Institute of Research, Walter Reed Army Medical Center, Washington, D.C.

COLIN DOBSON (191), Department of Parasitology, University of Queensland, St. Lucia, Brisbane, Queensland, Australia

S. M. GAAFAR (273), Department of Veterinary Microbiology, Pathology and Public Health, School of Veterinary Medicine, Purdue University, Lafayette, Indiana

M. A. GEMMELL (235), Hydatid Research Unit, Medical Research Council of New Zealand, University of Otago Medical School, Dunedin, New Zealand

N. N. IZZAT (223), Department of Dermatology, Baylor College of Medicine, Houston, Texas

W. H. R. LUMSDEN (287), Department of Medical Protozoology, London School of Hygiene and Tropical Medicine, London, England

F. N. MACNAMARA (235), Department of Microbiology, University of Otago Medical School, Dunedin, New Zealand

G. A. MAEKELT (343), Instituto de Medicina Tropical, Facultad de Medicina, Universidad Central de Venezuela, Caracas, Venezuela

D. F. MAHONEY (301), Division of Animal Health, Commonwealth Scientific and Industrial Research Organization, Long Pocket Laboratories, Indooroopilly, Queensland, Australia

MAX MURRAY (155), Department of Veterinary Pathology, Glasgow University Veterinary School, University of Glasgow, Bearsden, Glasgow, Scotland

L. J. OLSON (223), Department of Microbiology, University of Texas Medical Branch, Galveston, Texas

M. ELAINE ROSE (365), Department of Parasitology, Houghton Poultry Research Station, Houghton, Huntingdon, England

ELVIO H. SADUN (97), Department of Medical Zoology, Walter Reed Army Institute of Research, Walter Reed Army Medical Center, Washington, D.C.

E. J. L. SOULSBY (57), Department of Pathobiology, School of Veterinary Medicine, University of Pennsylvania, Philadelphia, Pennsylvania

W. T. WEBER (33), Department of Pathobiology, School of Veterinary Medicine, University of Pennsylvania, Philadelphia, Pennsylvania

PREFACE

The rapid development of immunology in the last decade has affected all areas of the biological sciences and not least the field of parasitology. The increased interest in parasitological problems by immunologists and in immunology by parasitologists has greatly assisted in placing studies of the immunology of parasitic infections on the firm bases of sound immunology and sound parasitology. A number of joint meetings of parasitologists and immunologists, arranged by various national and international agencies, have done much to foster the present healthy state of the subject, and this volume is, in part, a tribute to the foresightedness of the organizers of such meetings.

This volume represents the proceedings of the Fifth International Conference of the World Association for the Advancement of Veterinary Parasitology which was held in Mexico City in August, 1971, as a joint meeting with the Academie Nacionale de Medicina de Mexico. The invited papers of the conference, published in this volume, formed the core of the theme of the conference. They take an immunological look at the immunology of host–parasite relationships. The authors were asked for a critical appraisal of their subject areas and to place the knowledge of host–parasitic relationships into the context of modern immunology. It is increasingly possible to do this, and it is clear from the contributions to this volume that parasitologists have unfettered themselves from the mystique that immune responses to parasites are things apart from the immune responses to other antigens and infections. Nevertheless, by the very complexity of their structure, especially in the case of helminths and their developmental cycles, the responses to them are complex and multicomponent in nature. The contents of this volume though illustrating this complexity also indicate the growing strength of the effort to analyze the complexity.

The cooperation and enthusiasm shown by all the authors were an indication of the excitement that pervades the field at this time. It is hoped their efforts in providing an up-to-date statement of the situation will serve as a point of departure for others, immunologists and parasitologists, who are drawn to the challenge of the work that lies ahead.

As with the other International Conferences of the WAAVP, the local flavor of the hospitality of our hosts gave an added dimension by which the theme of the conference will be remembered and which, unfortunately, cannot be translated in any tangible way in this volume.

I wish to express my thanks to the contributors for their wholehearted cooperation, including the observance of the editorial constraints placed on them for style, length of manuscript, and delivery of the finished product. To the staff of Academic Press I extend special thanks for their willingness and competence which have led to a smooth and speedy publication.

E. J. L. SOULSBY

1 IMMUNE RESPONSE OF SHEEP, GOATS, CATTLE, AND SWINE

OLE AALUND

I. Introduction

Jerne (1967) has defined cis and trans immunologists as persons approaching the mystery of antibody formation from the side of the antigen and the antibody, respectively. In a lecture in Copenhagen in 1968 Jerne gave the following account of the development of immunological concepts since 1900. With Ehrlich as the front figure since the 1890's, cis immunology was predominant during the first golden age of immunology. By 1910 the cis philosophy led to a stagnation which lasted to the late 1950's when the trans approach took over and opened the second golden age of immunology. Jerne (1967) has emphasized that this fully copes with a statement made by Francis Crick that "if you cannot study function, study structure." This review will reflect predominantly a trans approach and will review the pertinent data on the humoral immune response and the immunoglobulins of ruminants and swine.

Chemical studies of immunoglobulins started in 1845 when the so-called Bence-Jones proteins were first recognized (Bence-Jones, 1847). These proteins were encountered in the urine from a patient with *mollities ossium*, presumably multiple myeloma. It was found that the precipitate formed in acidified urine redissolved upon boiling. Bence-Jones proteins have been intensively examined in recent studies of immunoglobulins. The existence of Bence-Jones proteins and homogeneous populations of pathological immunoglobulins, myeloma proteins, and Waldenström macroglobulins has allowed detailed information to be accumulated about the structure, synthesis, and genetics of human immunoglobulins. This is also the reason there is a lack of information about immunoglobulins in species such as ungulates since pathological immunoglobulins are absent or extremely rare in these species.

II. Historical Aspects

The practical application of immunological principles goes back to variolation in China in the fifteenth century. Thus, specific resistance against infectious diseases was recognized centuries before the demonstration of circulating antibodies. The proof of humoral substances in serum as a basis for immunity was established in 1890 by von Behring and Kitasato. Working with tetanus and diphtheria toxins they named the protective serum substances *antitoxins*. In serum from nonimmunized animals Buchner (1893) recognized a heat labile factor that accomplished lysis of bacteria in cooperation with specific antibody. Bordet used the term *alexine* (Greek: to ward off) for this factor which was later named *complement* by Ehrlich (1900).

It soon became clear that the production of antibodies was not necessarily associated with immunity against disease. Thus, Ehrlich (1897) was able to block the hemagglutinating action of ricin with goat anti-ricin serum, Tchistovitch (1899) found that anti-eel serum neutralized the hemolytic action of normal eel serum on rabbit erythrocytes and Bordet (1898) demonstrated agglutinins against erythrocytes in serum from animals inoculated with defibrinated blood. The term *antibody* (Antikörper) was invented in 1900 by Ehrlich in his famous presentation of the "side chain theory" for the production of antibodies.

Gamma globulins were defined by Tiselius in 1937 as the slowest migrating electrophoretic group of serum proteins when electrophoresis was conducted at alkaline pH. Association of antibody activity with the gamma globulin fraction was demonstrated for the first time in 1939 by Tiselius and Kabat. Subsequent experiments revealed that antibody activity also resided in the electrophoretic beta region and Heremans in 1959 therefore proposed the "immunoglobulin concept." This concept was adopted by the World Health Organization in 1964 to designate proteins of animal origin with known antibody activity as well as other chemically related normal and pathological proteins (Cohen, 1965).

III. Nomenclature

For the human immunoglobulins (Rowe, 1970) a complete set of terminology has been adopted by the World Health Organization. The terminology used in this review will conform as closely as possible to the human nomenclature. The standard requirements for applying the human terminology to a particular immunoglobulin class of another species should be antigenic cross-reactivity between the Fc portion of the human immunoglobulin and the immunoglobulin of the other species. This standardization was recently proposed for the immunoglobulins of the domesticated Bovidae at a "Symposium on the Bovine Immune System." This symposium was held on November 18–20, 1970 at the Interstate Inn, College Park, Maryland.

The nomenclature and the main characteristics of the human immunoglobulins are summarized in Table I.

IV. Immunoglobulin Structure

A. THE FOUR-CHAIN IgG UNIT

Studies on the structure of IgG started in the 1940's when Peterman (1946) papain-digested human "gamma globulin" into fragments of about one-half to one-quarter the size of the original molecule. R. R. Porter reported similar results in 1950 from studies on rabbit anti-ovalbumin. The distinction was then made between what is now known as the Fab and Fc fragments. The findings were further substantiated by R. R. Porter in 1958 and 1959 through studies employing highly purified crystalline papain. The rabbit 7 S IgG molecule was split into 2 Fab and 1 Fc fragments, each about one-third the size of the original molecule ($s_{20,w}$ 3.5) with molecular weights of 45,000 and 55,000, respectively (R. R. Porter, 1959, 1963).

A number of important biological properties are associated with the Fc fragment. Thus, the catabolic site is located on the Fc piece (Fahey and Robinson, 1963) as is the structure responsible for the persistence of IgG in the circulation (Spiegelberg and Weigle, 1965a,b). The sites involved in tissue affinity and complement fixation (Taranta and Franklin, 1961) reside in the Fc fragment and this fragment is essential for the transport of the IgG molecule across fetal membranes (Hartley, 1951; Brambell *et al.*, 1959, 1960).

Peptic digestion of 7 S rabbit IgG produces a 5 S (Fab')$_2$ fragment which upon reduction of a single and exceptionally labile disulfide bond yields two 3.5 S Fab' fragments (Nisonoff *et al.*, 1960, 1961). The human IgG subclasses are heterogeneous in their susceptibility to enzymatic digestion. Thus, IgG$_2$ is most resistant, IgG$_3$ most sensitive, and IgG$_1$ and IgG$_4$ intermediary sensitive (Virella and Parkhouse, 1971). Similarly, human secretory IgA and IgA$_1$ paraproteins have been found to be 3 to 4 times more resistant to pepsin digestion than IgA$_2$ paraproteins (Shuster, 1971).

The multichained structure of IgG was discovered in 1959 by Edelman. After reduction and alkylation of the interchain disulfide bonds, two types of polypeptide chains, light chains and heavy chains, could be isolated by cation exchange chromatography in 6 M urea (Edelman, 1959; Edelman and Poulik, 1961). However, the separated polypeptide chains were insoluble in aqueous media and had lost their biological activity. This problem was overcome by Fleischman *et al.* (1962, 1963) through reduction and alkylation in neutral aqueous media. The chains were separated by gel filtration on Sephadex G-75 or G-100 in 1 N propionic or acetic acid.

The above data allowed R. R. Porter in 1962 to present his model for the IgG molecule (Fig. 1). The IgG molecule was postulated to consist of two light and two heavy polypeptide chains held together by disulfide bonds. This model has been able to cope with the findings of numerous investigations, including electron microscopic studies.

The IgA molecule also contains two heavy and two light polypeptide

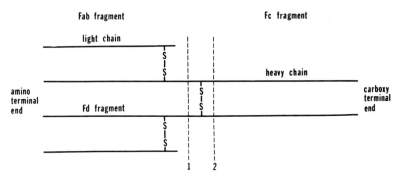

Fig. 1. Diagrammatic structure of IgG-immunoglobulin showing the terminology for polypeptide chains and enzymatic fragments. Dotted vertical lines indicate the site of papain cleavage (1) and the site of pepsin cleavage (2). After R. R. Porter, 1962.

chains held together in a molecular structure similar to IgG (cf. Butler, 1970). IgM consists of five building units similar in structure to the IgG molecule. These five units are held together in a spiderlike structure carrying ten antigen combining sites (Chesebro *et al.*, 1968). IgD and IgE exist in IgG-like monomer units with sedimentation coefficients of 7–8 S and 8 S, respectively (cf. Butler, 1970).

B. PRIMARY STRUCTURE AND ANTIGENIC DETERMINANTS

Intensive sequence studies of human and mouse Bence-Jones and myeloma proteins have revealed that the amino terminal half of the light chains varies considerably from kappa chain to kappa chain, and from lambda chain to lambda chain, while the carboxy terminal half is essentially invariable within the kappa and lambda entities, respectively (Putnam *et al.*, 1967). The recognition of these two antigenic subclasses of light chains was made in 1956 by Korngold and Lipari (1956a,b) studying Bence-Jones proteins. It was subsequently found (Mannik and Kunkel, 1962; Fahey, 1963a,b; Migita and Putnam, 1963) that each immunoglobulin class is made up of molecules carrying either kappa or lambda chains, but never both.

The class specific antigenic determinants reside exclusively in the heavy polypeptide chains (Franklin and Stanworth, 1961). In man five types, gamma, alpha, mu, delta, and epsilon, of heavy polypeptide chains have been identified. These chains belong to the IgG, IgA, IgM, IgD, and IgE classes, respectively. Also the heavy polypeptide chains contain a variable NH_4-terminal region which is about the length of the light chain variable region, while the constant COOH-terminal region is approximately 3 times as long as the constant region of the light chain (Köhler *et al.*, 1970). The sequence of the constant portion of the heavy chain is class-specific, whereas antigenic subgroups common to alpha, gamma, and mu chains (Seligmann *et al.*, 1966; Todd *et al.*, 1967) have been found to be paralleled by sequence homologies on the variable part of these chains (Köhler *et al.*, 1970; Wang *et al.*, 1970). This is in contrast to light chains where the variable region is characteristic of the kappa and lambda chains, respectively. On the basis of differences in the variable portion, three and five antigenic subgroups have been identified within the kappa and lambda chains, respectively (cf. Rowe, 1970).

Although monoclonal gamma-M and gamma-G both had kappa-1 chains with extensive variable region sequence homologies, the sequence of the variable regions of the mu and gamma chains was only 30% identical (Putnam and Köhler, 1969). In this case, then, the sequence difference between the light and heavy chains of the same molecule was of the same magnitude as between light and heavy chains of different molecules (Köhler *et al.*, 1970).

Extensive interspecies homologies have been identified in the amino acid sequence of kappa chains from man, mouse, and rabbit (Doolittle and Astrin, 1967; Titani *et al.*, 1967) and of human kappa chains and the Fc fragment from rabbit IgG (Hill *et al.*, 1966). On the basis of these findings Titani *et al.* (1967) have suggested a common ancestry of light and heavy polypeptide chains of the IgG molecule.

The kappa and lambda light polypeptide chains have been identified in a broad variety of animals, but the ratio between the two classes of chains varies considerably from species to species (Hood *et al.*, 1967). For IgG the normal ratio in man is 2:1, but 1:1, 1:8, and 1:8 in swine, ox, and sheep, respectively. Kappa chains are completely lacking in the horse.

The kappa:lambda ratio for normal human immunoglobulins is similar to the kappa:lambda ratio for the incidence of patients with multiple myeloma and Waldenström macroglobulinemia (Laurell and Singurowicz, 1967). This may be interpreted to indicate that the kappa and lambda producing cells mutate and start to produce M-components in proportion to their normal occurrence (Laurell and Singurowicz, 1967).

A variety of antibodies in man [Rh antibodies, isoagglutinins (anti-A and anti-B), thyroglobulin antibodies, dextran antibodies, and teichoic acid antibodies] have been demonstrated to be expressed in both kappa and lambda type immunoglobulins, but the kappa:lambda ratio in purified antibody preparations varies widely in different individuals and sometimes diverges markedly from the typical 2:1 kappa:lambda ratio

(Mannik and Kunkel, 1963). Gamma-M cold agglutinins have been found to be either kappa or lambda type (Mannik and Kunkel, 1963). Similar observations have been made in the guinea pig (Nussenzweig and Benacerraf, 1966) and rabbit (Knight *et al.*, 1967). Human myeloma proteins (gamma-G_1, lambda) with antibody activity were identified by Eisen *et al.* (1967), and several similar findings have been made in mice (cf. Yamada *et al.*, 1970).

Four human gamma-G subclasses have been identified corresponding to the gamma-1, gamma-2, gamma-3, and gamma-4 chains (Grey and Kunkel, 1964). Similarly three IgG subclasses are present in mice (Fahey *et al.*, 1964b). At least two IgA (Kunkel and Prendergast, 1966; Vaerman and Heremans, 1966; Feinstein and Franklin, 1966) and two IgM (Harboe *et al.*, 1965) heavy chain subclasses are known in man. The relative abundance of the gamma-G subclasses may be seen in Table I. Cases of hypogammaglobulinemia with drastically altered IgG subclass abundance have been reported (Virella *et al.*, 1970; Yount *et al.*, 1970). All the gamma-G subclasses are present in the electrophoretically fast migrating human IgG entity, while only gamma-G_1, gamma-G_2 and gamma-G_3 are represented among the electrophoretically slow migrating gamma-G molecules (Skvaril and Morell, 1970).

C. Allotypes

Genetically determined intraspecies antigenic differences among immunoglobulins were first observed in rabbits by Oudin (1956). While the class- and subclass-specific antigenic determinants are common to all individuals of a given species, the various allotypic markers are only present in a fraction of the species members.

In man two sets of allotypic markers, *Gm* and *InV*, have been identified. The *Gm* (genetic marker; Grubb, 1969) markers are exclusively located on the gamma chains (Franklin *et al.*, 1962) while the *InV* factors are properties of the kappa chains (Franklin *et al.*, 1962; Harboe *et al.*, 1962). Thus *Gm* types are only present within the IgG class while the *InV* factors are encountered in all immunoglobulins of the kappa light chain type. Twenty-three *Gm* factors have been identified (Grubb, 1969). Each individual may possess several of the *Gm* factors, but a particular IgG molecule carries only a single *Gm* determinant. Several *Gm* markers have been identified on the gamma-1 and gamma-3 chains, respectively, only one on gamma-2, and so far none on gamma-4 chains (Natvig *et al.*, 1967). *Gm*[1] and *Gm*[5] are mutually exclusive alleles in Caucasians (Grubb, 1969). However, in the Negro, *Gm*[1] and *Gm*[5] may occur together on the same IgG molecule (Steinberg *et al.*, 1960), and a similar observation was made with Gm^1 and Gm^4 in Chinese people (cf. Humphrey and White, 1970). Certain antibody specificities have been found to be restricted to particular Gm types (cf. Grubb, 1969).

Three InV factors, InV_1, InV_2, and InV_3, have been identified in man where InV_1 and InV_2 always are present together on the same kappa chain (cf. Humphrey and White, 1970). Sequence analyses have revealed that the distinction between InV_2 [$= InV$ (a+)] and InV_3 [$= InV$ (b+)] is due to the presence of either leucine or valine at position 191 (Easley and Putnam, 1966; Baglioni *et al.*, 1966). The InV factors are nonrandomly distributed among the IgG subclasses (cf. Grubb, 1969). Thus, Terry *et al.* (1965) found no IgG_2 and IgG_4 myeloma proteins carrying InV_1 or InV_3.

In human lambda chains arginine and lysine interchange at position 190 is the basis for Oz (−) and Oz (+) factors (Appella and Ein, 1967), which may occur together in the same individual (cf. Rowe, 1970).

D. Idiotypes

Idiotypes (idios = private) denote antigenic determinants that are unique to the individual. Kunkel *et al.* (1963) observed that several specifically purified human antibodies differed antigenically and were electrophoretically disperse. Similar observations were made in rabbits by Oudin and Michel (1963), and in 1966 Oudin coined the term *idiotypes*. The idiotypic determinants are located on the variable portion of the polypeptide chains (Hilschman *et al.*, 1969).

E. Antibody Specificity

It has been reported repeatedly that the light and heavy polypeptide chains both contribute to the antigen combining site (cf. Aalund, 1968) which is made up of the variable portions of the light and heavy polypeptide chains. Highly purified specific antibodies exhibit idiotypic specificities (Nisonoff *et al.*, 1969). The heavy polypeptide chains appear to play the predominant role for the function and specificity of the combining site (Franek and Nezlin, 1963; Lamm *et al.*, 1966). This is in agreement with affinity labeling studies by Singer and Doolittle (1966) who found heavy chain:light chain labeling ratios ranging from 1.3 to 2.5.

V. Immunoglobulin Heterogeneity

The extreme degree of heterogeneity of immunoglobulins has been emphasized by many investigators to be the most characteristic feature of this group of proteins. Thus, the scope of studying immunoglobulin heterogeneity was expressed by R. R. Porter and Press (1962) in the following statement: "The purification and fractionation of gamma globulins and antibodies is an unusual problem in that whatever criteria (biological, chemical, or physical) are applied, the products are still heterogeneous."

Each immunoglobulin class exhibits an extensive electrophoretic heterogeneity. However, monoclonal immunoglobulins, i.e., myeloma proteins, and highly purified antibodies with restricted specificity are electrophoretically rather homogeneous (Nussenzweig and Benacerraf, 1964).

The electrophoretic mobility is positively correlated with the sialic acid content of the molecule whereas the carbohydrate content seems not to be concerned with this (Fahey, 1962; Schultze, 1962; Oh and Sanders, 1966). The carbohydrate and sialic acid content of immunoglobulins are shown in Table I.

Antibodies of different specificities may have different electrophoretic mobilities (Nussenzweig and Benacerraf, 1964) and genetically determined electrophoretic differences among antibodies with the same specificity have been observed in mice (Fahey *et al.*, 1965).

Experiments in rabbits indicated a negative correlation between the electrical charge of the antigen and the charge of the antibodies (for references, see Nussenzweig and Green, 1971). Similar experiments in guinea pigs did not consistently demonstrate this type of charge relationship between antigen and antibodies (Nussenzweig and Green, 1971).

Studies on rabbit IgG antibodies to streptococcal carbohydrate revealed that antibody molecules with a distinct electrophoretic mobility had a characteristic individual antigenic specificity (Braun and Krause, 1968; Eichmann *et al.*, 1970). Furthermore, the electrophoretic mobility of the IgG antibody molecules was related to their antigen binding affinity which was decreasing with increasing negative charge (Eichmann and Greenblatt, 1971). The charge distribution was paralleled by the kappa chain subclass distribution of the molecules (Hood *et al.*, 1970).

The primary immune response generally follows a characteristic pattern with an early IgM antibody synthesis which is subsequently augmented by the synthesis of IgG antibodies. This pattern was first demonstrated in rabbits (Bauer and Stavitsky, 1961) and later in several mammalian and nonmammalian species (cf. Aalund, 1968). However, there are exceptions to this situation. Thus, rabbits responded exclusively with IgM antibodies against the O-antigen of *Salmonella typhosa* (Bauer *et al.*, 1963) and similar observations were made in cattle with anti-viral (Fernelius, 1966) and anti-protein (Hammer *et al.*, 1968) antibodies.

TABLE I

NOMENCLATURE AND MAIN CHARACTERISTICS OF THE HUMAN IMMUNOGLOBULINS

Class	Sub-class	Molecular weight[b]	Sedimentation coefficient (approx.)	Carbo-hydrate content, %[a]	Sensitivity to proteolytic enzymes[c]	Anti-body activity[b]	Serum concentra-tion, mg/ml	Relative distribu-tion in serum, %	Body content catab-olized per day, %	Synthetic rate, gm/day
IgG	IgG$_1$	150,000	7[b]	2.5	Intermediate sensitivity[i]	+	12.4[d]		3[a]	2.3[a]
	IgG$_2$				Most resistant[i]			65[d] 70[e]		
	IgG$_3$				Most sensitive[i]			23[d] 18[e]		
	IgG$_4$				Intermediate sensitivity[i]			8[d] 8[e]		
IgM		900,000	18-19[b]	5.0-10.0		++	1.2[d]	4[d] 3[e]	14[a]	0.4[a]
IgA	IgA$_1$ (Le)	150,000	7[i]; 11,4[g]: IgA with secretory piece	5.0-10.0	Most resistant[f]	++	2.8[d]	93.4[h]	12[a]	2.7[a]
	IgA$_2$ (He)				Most sensitive[f]					
IgD		150,000	7[i]	—		?	<0.001– 0.014[b]	6.6[h]	—	0.03[g]
IgE		190,000?	8[i]	10.5		+	0.0001– 0.0007[c]		—	—

[a] Fahey (1965).
[b] Humphrey and White (1970).
[c] Johansson et al. (1968).
[d] Kabat (1968).
[e] Natvig et al. (1967).
[f] Shuster (1971).
[g] Tomasi (1968).
[h] Vaerman et al. (1968).
[i] Virella and Parkhouse (1971).
[j] Weir (1967).

It must be emphasized that the threshold of sensitivity for detection of *Salmonella typhimurium* antibodies by macroscopic agglutination ranges from 1.0 to 5.0 μg and 25.0 to 50.0 μg antibody protein for IgM and IgG, respectively (Robbins *et al.*, 1965). Immunoglobulin M is 120 times more potent than IgG in sensitizing bacteria for complement dependent kill, and 500 to 1000 times as efficient as IgG as an opsonin (Robbins *et al.*, 1965). This may be the reason for the few reports (Freeman and Stavitsky, 1965; Wei and Stavitsky, 1967) on the simultaneous appearance of IgM and IgG antibodies after the primary antigenic stimulation.

Immunoglobulins may differ in their ability to elicit second stage reactions, i.e., reactions (precipitation, agglutination, hemolysis, complement fixation, bacteriolysis, opsonization, viral neutralization, and anaphylaxis) occurring as a consequence of the combining of antigen and antibody. Antibodies with the same specificity but belonging to different immunoglobulin classes may have the ability to elicit different second stage reactions or they may show quantitative differences for one particular secondary reaction. The functional role of antibodies is markedly influenced by their molecular characteristics and these are independent of antigen-binding activity (Fahey *et al.*, 1964a). Furthermore, antibody specificity and physicochemical homogeneity are not equivalent properties (Fahey, 1962).

The metabolic rate differs among immunoglobulin classes as may be seen in Table I for the human. The animal species with the highest general metabolic rates have the most rapid rates of immunoglobulin metabolism (Dixon *et al.*, 1952; Fahey and Robinson, 1963). IgA and IgM are metabolized at substantially higher rates than IgG in a variety of mammalian species (cf. Aalund, 1968). Experiments in mice (Fahey and Robinson, 1963), man (Solomon *et al.*, 1963), cattle (Nansen, 1970), and the horse (Nansen and Riising, 1972) have demonstrated a negative correlation between the metabolic rate of IgG and the serum level of this class, and the metabolism of the IgG subclasses in mice was nonselectively influenced by the total serum IgG level (Fahey and Sell, 1965). The factors controlling the metabolism of IgA and IgM are independent of the factors controlling the IgG metabolism (Fahey and Sell, 1965). Normal catabolic rates were found in hypogammaglobulinemic germfree guinea pigs (Sell, 1964).

The homocytotropic antibodies in man (reagins) have been demonstrated to reside in the IgE entity (Ishizaka *et al.*, 1966) which was characterized physicochemically by Johansson *et al.* (1968) after encountering a case of IgE myelomatosis.

IgA is quantitatively the predominant immunoglobulin of external secretions from man and a variety of other mammalian species (Vaerman, 1970). Reports on discrepancies between local and systemic immunity started to appear 50 years ago (cf. Tomasi and Bienenstock, 1968). Thus, protection against infections has been shown in many cases to be closely related to the antibody content of external secretions and to be more or less independent from the serum antibody level.

The secretory IgA has a sedimentation coefficient of 11 S and consists of two 7 S IgA monomer units and a so-called transport or secretory piece with an S value of 3.5 (Small *et al.*, 1969). The secretory piece is synthesized locally and is antigenically distinguishable from the 7 S IgA units (cf. Tomasi and Bienstock, 1968). *In vitro* experiments revealed that only the polymeric forms of human IgA combined with free secretory piece which could also be bound to 25 to 30 S IgM, but not to 19 S IgM, IgG, or IgD (Radl *et al.*, 1971).

VI. Genetic Control of Immune Responsiveness

The role of genetic factors involved in antigen recognition and antibody synthesis has been well documented experimentally (see Biozzi *et al.*, 1969). These authors have reported extensive studies on the selection of high and low antibody responders in mice to sheep erythrocytes. The selection was operative for both the primary and secondary response and for both IgG and IgM antibodies.

The selection was operative also for antigens unrelated to the antigen used as the basis of selection. The high responder line had a significantly higher immunoglobulin serum level than the low responder line (Biozzi *et al.*, 1970).

VII. Ruminant Immunoglobulins

A. IMMUNOGLOBULIN CLASSES AND SUBCLASSES

IgG, IgA, and IgM have been identified in ox, goat, and sheep and have been demonstrated to be antigenically cross-reactive with the Fc class specific determinants of the homologous human entities (Relyveld *et al.*, 1959; Richards and Marrack, 1963; Silverstein *et al.*, 1963b; Aalund *et al.*, 1965a,b; Murphy *et al.*, 1965; Aalund, 1968; Pan *et al.*, 1968; Curtain, 1969; Givol and Hurwitz, 1969; Gray *et al.*, 1969; Heimer *et al.*, 1969; Vaerman, 1970). The IgG of these species include at least two subclasses, IgG_1 and IgG_2, which are antigenically distinguishable on the basis of their Fc determinants (Milstein and Feinstein, 1968). Colostral and serum IgG_1 were indistinguishable by "fingerprint" analyses (Milstein and Feinstein, 1968). In sheep the IgG_1 entity has recently been shown to comprise at least two antigenic subclasses (Curtain, 1969). A third IgG entity with an electrophoretic mobility intermediary between that of IgG_2 and IgG_1 has also been encountered in sheep (Aalund *et al.*, 1965a).

1. Immunoglobulin G Subclasses

The physiochemical and biological parameters (Table II) correspond to the analogous human data. Hammer *et al.* (1968) have presented suggestive evidence for the presence of a 19 S IgG entity in bovine colostrum. IgG_1 and IgG_2 are metabolically distinguishable in the goat and ox where the metabolic rate for IgG_1 is significantly higher than for IgG_2 (Aalund, 1968; Nansen, 1970). Colostral and serum IgG_1 were metabolized at identical rates in the goat (Aalund, 1968). In sheep the metabolic rates for the two IgG entities do not differ significantly (Nansen and Aalund, 1972).

IgG_1 is quantitatively the predominant immunoglobulin in ruminant colostrum (Carroll, 1961; Murphy *et al.*, 1964; Pierce and Feinstein, 1965; Aalund, 1968; Sullivan *et al.*, 1969; Mach and Pahud, 1971). The colostrum immunoglobulins are derived directly from the serum (Askonas *et al.*, 1954; Blakemore and Garner, 1956; Larson and Gillespie, 1957; Garner and Crawley, 1958; Dixon *et al.*, 1961).

Mackenzie and Lascelles (1968) in experiments with ^{131}I-labeled IgG demonstrated a substantial serum-lacteal secretion IgG transfer in lactating sheep and the selective IgG_1 transfer pattern of the colostral phase apparently continued into lactation. During phases of mastitis there was a sharp rise in the serum to milk transfer of albumin and IgG_2 and only a moderate increase in the IgG_1 transfer (Mackenzie and Lascelles, 1968). In the bovine (Carroll, 1961) and the ovine (Mackenzie, 1968) noncolostral secretion, the $IgG_2:IgG_1$ ratio is comparable to the ratio in serum.

Curtain *et al.* (1971) have suggested that the vast majority of IgG_1 of mucous secretions from the gut and the respiratory tract in cattle is locally synthesized while IgG_2, which is present in only low concentrations in these secretions, is mainly derived from the plasma. There appears to be some selectivity of IgG_1 over IgG_2 in the diffusion from plasma into the secretions.

2. Immunoglobulin A

IgA has been identified in the serum and external secretions of ox, goat, and sheep (Mach *et al.*, 1969; Lascelles and McDowell, 1970; Morein, 1970; Pahud and Mach, 1970; Pedersen, 1970; P. Porter and

TABLE II

PHYSICOCHEMICAL AND BIOLOGICAL PARAMETERS OF RUMINANT IMMUNOGLOBULINS

Species Class Subclass	Mol. wt.[b]	Sedimentation coefficient	Carbohydrate content, in % of protein[b]	Hexose content, glucose equivalents in % of protein[a]	Serum conc., gm/100 ml	Fractional catabolic rate, %/day	Plasma disappearance half life, days
Sheep							
IgG₁		7[a]		1.53		10.2–15.5[f]	8.6–12.2[f]
IgG₂		7[a]		1.39		8.5–16.0[f]	7.8–14.8[f]
Colostral IgG₁							
IgM		18[a]		1.24			
Goat							
IgG₁				1.22			9.5–16.5[a]
IgG₂				1.02			15.5–30.5[a]
Colostral IgG₁							
IgM				1.10			11.0–13.0[a]
Ox							
IgG₁	163,000	7[d]	2–4	1.23	0.73[e]	14.1[e]	7.9[e]
IgG₂	150,000	7[d]	2–4	1.37	0.66[e]	6.6[e]	17.6[e]
Colostral IgG₁							
IgM	900,000	18[d]	12	1.34			
Secretory IgA		11[c]	8–9				

[a] Aalund (1970).
[b] Butler (1970).
[c] Morein (1970).
[d] Murphy et al. (1965).
[e] Nansen (1970).
[f] Nansen and Aalund (1972).

Noakes, 1970; Vaerman, 1970; Mach and Pahud, 1971; Pedersen *et al.*, 1971). In these species IgA is, quantitatively, the predominant immuno-globulin in external secretions other than colostrum (P. Porter and Noakes, 1970; Mach and Pahud, 1971). The selective abundance of IgA in external secretions over the concentration in serum may almost serve as a second order criterion in the characterization of this entity (Vaerman, 1970). Immunoglobulin A is present in relatively higher concentration in goat milk than in sheep milk (Vaerman, 1970). In bovine milk, glycoprotein-a, which was originally isolated from this secretion by Groves and Gordon (1967), occurs both free and bound to IgA (Butler *et al.*, 1968) and it may be equivalent of secretory piece in man and several animal species (Butler, 1970). Large amounts of glycoprotein-a may be synthesized by the mammary gland (Butler *et al.*, 1971). It has recently been demonstrated by Mach (1970) that human and bovine free secretory piece readily associate with secretory IgA of a broad variety of mammalian species.

3. Immunoglobulin M

IgM of the ruminant species is antigenically cross-reactive with human IgM (Mehta and Tomasi, 1969) and shares the physicochemical charac-teristics of human IgM (Aalund *et al.*, 1965a; Murphy *et al.*, 1965; Hammer *et al.*, 1968).

B. ALLOTYPES OF RUMINANT IMMUNOGLOBULINS

Immunoglobulin allotypes have been identified in the bovine species (Blakeslee, *et al.* 1971). Three markers A_1, A_2, and B_1 were identified. A_1 is located on the Fc portion of IgG_2 heavy chains, while B_1 resides on the light chains and hence is encountered in both IgG, IgA, and IgM molecules. The molecular localization of A_2 has not yet been determined. The genes controlling these markers were found to be autosomal dominants inherited independently. The genes for A_1 and A_2 may be alleles. The A_1 marker showed a high frequency in several breeds but occurred in a low frequency in the Hereford breed. The B_1 marker was uniformly infrequent or absent in the breeds examined (Blakeslee, 1970). The antisera used in these studies were obtained by isoimmuniza-tion. However, spontaneous occurring isoantibodies against allotypic de-terminants have been found in young pigs (Rasmussen, 1965; Nielsen, 1972) and should be expected also in young calves lacking one or several of the dam's allotype genes, since the immune system of the newborn calf will be exposed to intact maternal immunoglobulins after ingestion of colostrum (Andersen, 1972, personal communication).

C. DEVELOPMENT OF IMMUNOLOGICAL COMPETENCE IN RUMINANTS

1. Fetal Responsiveness

Immunological competence is developed early in the ruminant fetus. Homograft rejection was observed in the ovine fetus grafted between 80–117 days of gestation (Schinckel and Ferguson, 1953). Similar results were obtained by Silverstein *et al.* (1964) with orthotopic skin homografts applied to the fetal lamb at any time after the seventy-seventh day of gestation. The grafts did not stimulate the fetus to synthesize circulating antibodies against the grafts (Silverstein *et al.*, 1963a).

Antibodies against *Leptospira saxkoebing* were synthesized in bovine fetuses experimentally infected as early as the 132rd day of gestation (Fennestad and Borg-Petersen, 1962). Silverstein *et al.* (1963b) found marked differences in the antigenicity of a variety of antigens administered intramuscularly to the fetal lamb at different ages of gestation. Antibacteriophage antibodies were detected in a serum sample drawn six days after the inoculation of antigen at 60 days of gestation and anti-ferritin antibodies occurred 10 days after an injection at 70 days of gestation. Antibodies to ovalbumin were not detectable until 33 days after an injection at 90 days of gestation. None of the fetuses responded to diphtheria toxoid, *Salmonella typhosa*, or live BCG mycobacteria. The authors suggest that immunological maturation may be a relatively slow and stepwise procedure. Following the antigenic stimulus the fetal serum IgM level was uniformly increased while an increased IgG synthesis was noticed only after administration of complete Freund adjuvant (Silverstein *et al.*, 1963c). The fetal lamb exhibited the classical pattern of the primary antibody response, comprising an early IgM antibody synthesis which was subsequently augmented by the synthesis of IgG antibodies (Silverstein *et al.*, 1966; Osburn and Hoskins, 1969).

Brucella ovis antibodies and an elevated immunoglobulin level were demonstrated in the serum from fetal lambs of *Brucella* infected ewes (Osburn and Kennedy, 1966).

It should be recalled that the first recorded example of spontaneous occurring immunological tolerance was the blood group mosaicism of dizygotic bovine twins that had interchanged erythrocytes *in utero* via vascular anastomosis (Owen, 1945).

2. Maternally Derived Immunoglobulins

Since there is no transplacental passage of maternal immunoglobulin to the ruminant fetus, acquisition of this depends heavily on the passive immunity attained via ingestion of colostrum. Klaus *et al.* (1969) have reported the mean serum concentration of IgG and IgM in prenursing calves to be 1.2 mg/ml and 0.1 mg/ml, respectively. IgM and IgG are absorbed nonselectively from the intestine of the calf (Klaus *et al.*, 1969) and the sheep (Halliday, 1965a,b). Heterologous ungulate antibodies are also readily absorbed from the gut of newborn ruminants (Mason *et al.*, 1930; Comline *et al.*, 1951).

In the calf there is a complete lack of correlation between the immunoglobulin concentration of colostrum and the concentration in serum of the suckling calf (Klaus *et al.*, 1969). The IgM level of the cow's serum is not significantly different from the IgM colostral concentration, while the IgG level of colostrum is significantly ($P = 0.05$) higher than the serum level (Klaus *et al.*, 1969). Upon ingestion of colostrum the immunoglobulin reaches its maximum serum concentration in the calf approximately 24 hours later and then gradually declines (Klaus *et al.*, 1969). Although the gut is permeable for the intact immunoglobulin molecules during the first 36 hours of life, calves fed colostrum during the first 6 hours of life attain a significantly higher serum immunoglobulin concentration than calves ingesting colostrum at later hours (Selman *et al.*, 1970, 1971). This is consonant with findings by Kruse (1970b) that for the age interval of 2–20 hours a linear relationship exists between the absorption coefficient for immunoglobulin and the age of the first colostrum feeding. A significant positive correlation was observed (Kruse, 1970b) between the immunoglobulin serum concentration in the calf and the amount of immunoglobulin ingested. The immunoglobulin serum level of the calf is therefore markedly influenced by the type of husbandry under which it is maintained (Smith *et al.*, 1967; Selman *et al.*, 1971).

The colostral yield of immunoglobulin may vary significantly between different breeds of cattle (Kruse, 1970a). A failure of newborn ruminants to achieve normal serum concentrations of immunoglobulin during the early hours of life may result in substantial losses due to lack of protection against contagious diseases in cattle (Fey, 1968; Hurvell and Fey, 1970; McEwan *et al.*, 1970; Penhale *et al.*, 1970) and sheep (Halliday, 1965a,b). The converse may exist in that neonatal immunohemolytic anemia in calves on the basis of colostral transfer of maternal antierythrocyte antibodies has been reported in herds vaccinated with an anaplasmosis vaccine of bovine blood origin (Dennis *et al.*, 1970).

3. Effect of Maternal Immunoglobulin on Neonatal Antibody Synthesis

The maternal antibodies transferred to the newborn ruminants may have an inhibitory effect on the induction of antibody synthesis. Graves (1963) reported a complete lack of antibody synthesis in colostrum fed calves vaccinated with foot-and-mouth disease virus at 3 weeks of age. The ingested colostrum contained neutralizing antibodies to the foot-and-mouth disease virus. Revaccination of the calves was not successful until the passively acquired antibody titer had reached a low level. Similar observations have been made with mycoplasma vaccines against contagious bovine pleuropneumonia (Stone, 1970).

4. Hypogammaglobulinemias

Based on immunoelectrophoretic studies, the serum IgM level has been reported (Trainin *et al.*, 1968) to be extremely reduced or completely absent in leukotic cattle. Agamma-2-globulinemia has been found to occur in 1% (Mansa, 1965) to 2% (Nansen, 1970) of cattle of the Red Danish Milkbreed while approximately 15% of this breed of cattle had depressed serum levels of IgG_2 (Mansa, 1965). The frequency of agamma-2-globulinemia among the bovine patients at the large-animal clinic of the Royal Veterinary and Agricultural University in Copenhagen, Denmark, was 5 out of 29 cattle examined (Nansen, 1970). A significantly reduced fractional catabolic rate for IgG_2 was found in cattle lacking this entity (Nansen, 1970).

5. Thymectomy and Thymic Hypoplasia

Neonatal, i.e., 1–12 days of age, thymectomy of calves did not influence the serum immunoglobulin level and the calves were immunologically competent in regard to formation of antibodies to tetanus toxoid while only one calf responded to ovalbumin (Carroll *et al.*, 1970). A lethal autosomal recessive trait for thymus hypoplasia has been identified in Black Pied Danish cattle of Friesian descent (Andresen *et al.*, 1970). The immunological implications of this defect are currently under investigation. The calves appear clinically normal until 3–4 weeks of age when exanthemas start to develop and are accompanied by *Alopecia areata*. Nervous signs in the form of spasms of the hind legs is a constant finding. The affected calves invariably die at $1\frac{1}{2}$ to 4 months of age.

D. ANTIBODY HETEROGENEITY

Antibody heterogeneity has been studied in experimental listeriosis and anaplasmosis in sheep and cattle. In experimental listeriosis, IgG antibodies to the serotype 4b were exclusively encountered by macroscopic agglutination in situations where the animals had been exposed to this organism (Aalund *et al.*, 1966). In the bovine the well-known sequential synthesis of IgM and IgG was observed in animals experimentally infected with *Anaplasma marginale* (Murphy *et al.*, 1966b). During the phase of antibody synthesis a moderate hyper-IgM-globulinemia was observed in these cattle (Murphy *et al.*, 1966a). This situation is similar to the increased serum IgM level in patients infected with *Trypanosoma gambiense* (Mattern *et al.*, 1961; Mattern, 1962), and in rabbits experimentally infected with *Trypanosoma equiperdum* (Mattern *et al.*, 1963).

The change from IgM to IgG in the primary response has been reported in cattle injected with foot-and-mouth disease virus (Cowan, 1966) and in sheep inoculated with diphtheria and tetanus toxoids (Locke and Segre, 1965).

Normal IgG from ox and sheep reacts only weakly with staphylococcal protein A while normal IgG from man, dog, and swine has a high affinity for this protein (Lind *et al.*, 1970). Protein A binds to the Fc fragment of IgG (Mansa *et al.*, 1968). In ox and sheep the ability of IgG to combine with protein A resides almost exclusively in the IgG_2 entity (Lind *et al.*, 1970).

E. ANTIBODIES AT MUCOSAL SURFACES

1. Mammary Gland

Convincing evidence for local antibody production in lactating ovine mammary glands infused with the antigens *Salmonella typhi* and *Brucella abortus* during the phase of involution and/or nonlactation has been presented by Outteridge *et al.* (1965) and Lascelles *et al.* (1966). Infusion of antigen into the lactating gland did not produce an antibody concentration in the milk greater than that found in the plasma (Outteridge *et al.*, 1965). It was hypothesized that the failure of the lactating gland to respond may be due to loss of the antigen to the milk thus preventing the immunogen from reaching the immunocompetent cells (Outteridge *et al.*, 1965). The concentration of ^{131}I-labeled IgG in the efferent lymph from ovine mammary glands increased during experimental mastitis and there was a slow rise in the whey $[^{131}I]$IgG concentration which did not reach its peak until at least 24 hours after induction of the mastitis (Mackenzie *et al.*, 1966). Following intramammary infection of nonlactating (dry) sheep with *Brucella abortus* the majority of the antibody activity in plasma was associated with IgM and IgG_1, very little with IgG_2 or an entity provisionally identified as IgA (Outteridge *et al.*, 1968). All antibody activity in the whey was confined to IgM, IgG_1, and a further immunoglobulin entity that apparently was distinct from IgM and IgG.

2. Nasal, Cervical, and Vaginal Mucosae

In ruminant external secretions, other than lacteal secretions, the antibody activity has been demonstrated to reside to a great extent in the

IgA entity. In bovine nasal secretions the antibody activity to para-influ-
enze-3 virus in naturally infected as well as parenterally vaccinated
animals was found to belong almost exclusively to the IgA class (Morein,
1970). The antibody titers of the nasal secretions were significantly
higher in the naturally infected than in the parenterally vaccinated group
(Morein, 1970). In the cervicovaginal secretions of *Vibrio fetus* infected
heifers, Wilkie *et al.* (1971) found the agglutinating antibody activity
exclusively in the IgA class. Similar experiments utilizing immunofluorescent immunoglobulin differentiation revealed an almost equal
distribution of the antibodies among IgA, IgG_1, and IgM while no
activity was detected among IgG_2 (Pedersen *et al.*, 1971).

3. Digestive Tract

Recently Curtain and Anderson (1971) in immunocytochemical
studies found no immunoglobulin-containing cells in the abomasal mucosa of parasite-free sheep while the mucosae of the jejunum and the
ileum of these sheep and of parasitized (infected with *Ostertagia, Trichostrongylus,* and *Nematodirus* spp.) sheep contained IgG_1, IgG_{1A}
and IgA producing cells. Large numbers of IgG_1 and IgG_{1A} synthesizing
cells were found in the abomasomal mucosa of parasitized sheep. In
the cow IgA was the principal immunoglobulin synthesized by the ileum,
duodenum, colon, lungs, nasal mucosa, oral pharynx, and the parotid,
lacrimal, and thymus glands (P. Porter and Noakes, 1970; Butler *et
al.*, 1971; Mach and Pahud, 1971).

Spontaneous homocytotropic antibody activity has been reported in
sheep (Pan *et al.*, 1968) and cattle (Campbell, 1970; Krogh and Hasselager, 1970). In sheep this activity was suggested as being associated
with an, as yet, unidentified immunoglobulin class, possibly analogous
to human IgE (Pan *et al.*, 1968). Reaginic antibodies in sheep to *Ostertagia* infection were demonstrated by Hogarth-Scott (1969) and the
homologous passive cutaneous anaphylactic reaction could be blocked
by antibodies to the IgG_1 subclass, IgG_A, as identified by Curtain (1969).
Thus the IgG_A fraction may also contain the reaginic antibodies of sheep
(Curtain and Anderson, 1971).

VIII. Immunoglobulins of the Pig

A. IMMUNOGLOBULIN CLASSES AND SUBCLASSES

The pertinent data obtained on porcine immunoglobulins, up to 1967,
have been compiled by Brummerstedt-Hansen (1967). He, in extensive
immunoelectrophoretic studies on porcine serum proteins, designated
the immunoglobulin preciptin arcs $gamma_x$, $gamma_y$, and $gamma_z$,

which correspond morphologically to the arcs of IgG_2, IgG_1, and IgM of the ruminant immunoelectropherograms. The sedimentation coefficient for both $gamma_x$ and $gamma_y$ is 6.7 S and for $gamma_z$ 18.0 S (Franek *et al.*, 1961). Karlsson (1966) tentatively applied the names IgG, IgM, and IgA to the immunoelectrophoretic preciptin arcs of porcine immunoglobulins and the immunoglobulin of the first peak from Sephadex G-200 fractionation of porcine serum has been designated IgM by Metzger and Fougereau (1967b). Rejnek *et al.* (1966), in radioimmunoelectrophoretic studies of porcine serum from animals vaccinated with tetanus toxoid, demonstrated antibody activity in entities which may correspond to human IgG_1, IgG_2, IgG_3, IgM, and IgA. Electrophoretically fast and slow migrating porcine IgG, IgG_1, and IgG_2, respectively, both have the molecular weight 160,000 and a sedimentation coefficient of 7 S (Metzger and Fougereau, 1967a). While the immunochemical parameters of porcine IgG and IgM are comparable to the corresponding human entities, antigenic cross-reactivity with human class-specific IgG and IgM determinants remains to be established. However, class-specific determinants common to human and porcine IgA have been demonstrated by Vaerman and Heremans (1970). Pig serum IgA is present in two forms sedimenting at the rates of 10 S and 7 S, respectively (Vaerman and Heremans, 1970).

B. ANTIBODIES AT MUCOSAL SURFACES

Of colostral immunoglobulins, 80% are IgG (P. Porter *et al.*, 1970) and IgG_1 is quantitatively the main immunoglobulin of porcine colostral immunoglobulins (Rejnek *et al.*, 1966), though IgA is also a significant component of colostrum (P. Porter, 1969; Richardson and Kelleher, 1970; Vaerman *et al.*, 1970). After 2–3 days of lactation IgG and IgM fall to approximately 10% of the concentration observed in colostrum. However, the drop in the IgA concentration is only two- to threefold and thus it becomes the predominant immunoglobulin of porcine mature milk, to some extent being synthesized locally (P. Porter *et al.*, 1970).

Secretion of IgA via the porcine renal tubules has been demonstrated by P. Porter and Allen (1969) who also identified IgA in porcine saliva and intestinal secretions. Porcine secretory IgA has a sedimentation coefficient of 11 S (P. Porter and Allen, 1969; Richardson and Kelleher, 1970; Vaerman *et al.*, 1970).

C. ALLOTYPES

The allotypes of porcine immunoglobulins are determined by two codominant autosomal alleles, $G\ 1^a$ and $G\ 1^b$ expressing three phenotypes, G 1 $(a+b-)$, G 1 $(a+b+)$ and G 1 $(a-b+)$ (Rasmussen, 1965). Spontaneously occurring isoantibodies to the allotypic factors have been identified in 4-month-old pigs (Rasmussen, 1965, Nielsen, 1972), and the synthesis of these isoantibodies may be due to the neonatal absorption of ingested maternal immunoglobulins (Andersen,1972).

D. DEVELOPMENT OF IMMUNOLOGICAL COMPETENCE IN SWINE

1. Neonatal Response

The virtually agammaglobulinemic condition of newborn pigs was reported by Rook et al. (1951), Moustgaard and Hojgaard Olsen (1953), and Kim et al. (1966a). Sterzl et al. (1960), Segre and Kaeberle (1962a,b), and Martinson (1970) encountered the presence of low concentrations of immunoglobulins in newborn, colostrum-deprived pigs. There have also been reports (e.g., Myers and Segre, 1963) on transplacental immunoglobulin transfer in the pig. However, the reliability of such observations has been challenged by Kim et al. (1966a) who refer to reports on the defectiveness of the porcine placental barrier during infection with hog cholera virus and with antigens containing endotoxins.

Newborn, germfree and colostrum-deprived pigs were immunologically competent to respond to *Actinophage* and antigenic competition was recorded (Kim et al., 1966b). Thus, the antibody response was depressed when the phage was administered together with other antigens. Furthermore, the results indicated that "immunologically virgin" animals responded significantly better to an antigenic stimulus than piglets that had been exposed to antigens or immunoglobulins prior to immunization. During the primary response of the germfree piglets, a sequence of 19 S IgG and 7 S IgG antibody synthesis was observed (Kim et al., 1966b). The 19 S IgG was an electrophoretically fast migrating type and fused with the IgG_2 in the immunoelectropherogram (Kim et al., 1966b). The porcine 19 S IgG is antigenically distinguishable from IgM but has approximately the same molecular weight (Kim et al., 1968).

The newborn pig depends almost entirely on the antibodies obtained from ingestion of colostrum in its early defense against contagious diseases. Most reports describe a nonselective absorption of protein molecules from the intestine of the newborn pig (cf. Payne and Marsh, 1962). However, heterologous immunoglobulins appear to be absorbed less efficiently than their homologous counterparts (Pierce and Smith, 1967), and there are also data illustrating heterogeneity in the absorption of homologous antibodies of different specificities (Sharpe, 1965).

Colostral IgG and IgM antibodies to *Escherichia coli* were readily absorbed by the piglet, which did not acquire the colostral IgA antibody activity (P. Porter, 1969). Up to a certain maximum level, the amount of bovine IgG absorbed from the gut of the newborn pig increased with increasing amounts of ingested IgG (Pierce and Smith, 1967), though some of the ingested IgG became partly degraded prior to the absorption (Pierce and Smith, 1967). The immunoglobulin serum concentration of the neonatal pig reaches its maximum approximately 24 hours after ingestion of colostrum and this is followed by a steady decrease for 5–6 weeks (Karlsson, 1966; Martinsson, 1970). At this time the rate of immunoglobulin synthesis of the young pig supersedes the catabolic rate and the serum concentration starts to increase (Martinsson, 1970). Martinsson (1970) observed a pronounced protective effect against infection with *Escherichia coli* when specific antibody was given to newborn pigs by the oral and intraperitoneal route. To ensure that an entire litter of newborn pigs is subject to the colostral transfer of antibodies, it has been recommended that suckling be postponed until the total litter has been born (Bourne, 1969; Wilson and Svendsen, 1971; Svendsen and Wilson, 1971). Such protocol will avoid the situation where the piglets born first deplete the amount of colostral immunoglobulins available for the pigs born toward the end of the farrowing.

The ingestion of colostrum by the newborn piglet augments its capability to synthesize antibodies (Hoerlein, 1957; Segre and Kaeberle, 1962a,b). This effect does not entirely seem to depend on passively transferred antibodies (Segre and Kaeberle, 1962a,b), since, on the contrary, antibody synthesis may be depressed as a result of colostrally transferred antibodies (Hoerlein, 1957).

Colostrally acquired isoantibodies to the erythrocytes of the newborn piglet may cause hemolytic disease (Andresen *et al.*, 1965; Meyer *et al.*, 1969). Isoimmune thrombocytopenic purpura has been recognized in Norway, Sweden, and England (cf. Nansen *et al.*, 1970). Recently this syndrome was encountered in Denmark (Nansen *et al.*, 1970).

IX. Conclusion

The present review has been focused primarily on the humoral aspects of the ruminant and porcine immune system. The pertinent data have been examined comparatively with the relevant human information. This serves to illustrate the phylogeny of the immune system and the common ancestry of the immunoglobulins (Hood *et al.*, 1967). The antigenic cross-reactivity of the ungulate immunoglobulins with the comparable human entities has rationalized the application of the human terminology to these proteins.

The field of local immunity is attracting increasing interest. The local synthesis of antibodies has been found to be highly significant in the protection against contagious diseases and such observations will have significant bearing on the evaluation of the route of vaccination to be selected in order to achieve maximum protection.

There is at present only little information available on the cellular immunity of ruminants and swine, although the tuberculin skin test has been used extensively for diagnostic purposes in these animals. Recently studies on the inhibition of migration of peripheral bovine leukocytes have been initiated to examine the possible application of this test for the diagnosis of Johne's disease (Aalund *et al.*, 1970) and infections with other *Mycobacteria*. The test may also prove useful in the diagnosis of liver fluke (Nansen and Aalund, 1972) and other parasitic infections.

References

Aalund, O. (1968). "Heterogeneity of Ruminant Immunoglobulins." Munksgaard, Copenhagen.

Aalund, O., Osebold, J. W., and Murphy, F. A. (1965a). *Arch. Biochem. Biophys.* **109**, 142.

Aalund, O., Rendel, J., and Freedland, R. A. (1965b). *Biochim. Biophys. Acta* **110**, 113.

Aalund, O., Osebold, J. W., Murphy, F. A., and Dicapua, R. A. (1966). *J. Immunol.* **97**, 150.

Aalund, O., Hoerlein, A. B., and Adler, H. C. (1970). *Acta Vet. Scand.* **11**, 331.

Andresen, E., Preston, K. S., Ramsey, F. K., and Baker, L. N. (1965). *Amer. J. Vet. Res.* **26**, 303.

Andresen, E., Flagstad, T., Basse, A., and Brummerstedt, E. (1970). *Nord. Veterinaermed.* **22**, 473.

Appella, E., and Ein, D. (1967). *Proc. Nat. Acad. Sci. U.S.* **57**, 1449.

Askonas, B. A., Campbell, P. N., Humphrey, J. H., and Work, T. S. (1954). *Biochem. J.* **56**, 597.

Baglioni, C., Alescio Zonta, L., and Cioli, D. (1966). *Science* **152**, 1517.

Bauer, D. C., and Stavitsky, A. B. (1961). *Proc. Nat. Acad. Sci. U.S.* **47**, 1667.

Bauer, D. C., Mathiess, M. J., and Stavitsky, A. B. (1963). *J. Exp. Med.* **117**, 889.

Bence-Jones, H. (1847). *Lancet* **2**, 88.

Biozzi, G., Stiffel, C., Mouton, D., Bouthillier, Y., and Decreuse Fond, C. (1969). *Protides. Biol. Fluids, Proc. Colloq.* **17**, 161.

Biozzi, G., Asofsky, R., Lieberman, R., Stiffel, C., Mouton, D., and Benacerraf, B. (1970). *J. Exp. Med.* **132**, 752.

Blakemore, F., and Garner, R. J. (1956). *J. Comp. Pathol.* **66**, 287.

Blakeslee, D., Rapacz, J., and Butler, J. E. (1971). *J. Dairy Sci.* **54**, 1320.

Bordet, J. (1898). *Ann. Inst. Pasteur, Paris* **12**, 688.

Bourne, F. J. (1969). *Vet. Rec.* **84**, 607.

Brambell, F. W. R., Hemmings, W. A., and Oakley, C. L. (1959). *Proc. Roy. Soc., Ser. B* **150**, 312.

Brambell, F. W. R., Hemmings, W. A., Oakley, C. L., and Porter, R. R. (1960). *Proc. Roy. Soc., Ser. B* **151**, 478.

Braun, D. G., and Krause, R. M. (1968). *J. Exp. Med.* **128**, 969.

Brummerstedt-Hansen, E. (1967). "The Serum Proteins of the Pig." Munksgaard, Copenhagen.

Buchner, H. (1893). *Arch. Hyg. Bakteriol.* **17**, 112.

Butler, J. E. (1970). *J. Dairy Sci.* **52**, 1895.

Butler, J. E., Coulson, E. J., and Groves, M. L. (1968). *Fed. Proc., Fed. Amer. Soc. Exp. Biol.* **27**, 617 (Abstr. No. 2256).

Butler, J. E., Maxwell, C. F., Hylton, M. B., Kiddy, C. A., Coulson, E. J., and Asofsky, R. (1971). *Fed. Proc., Fed. Amer. Soc. Exp. Biol.* **30**, 243 (Abstr. No. 285).

Campbell, S. G. (1970). *Cornell Vet.* **60**, 684.

Carroll, E. J. (1961). *J. Dairy Sci.* **44**, 2194.

Carroll, E. J., Theilen, G. H., and Leighton, R. L. (1970). *Amer. J. Vet. Res.* **29**, 67.

Chesebro, B., Bloth, B., and Svehag, S.-E. (1968). *J. Exp. Med.* **127**, 399..

Cohen, S. (1965). *Immunology* **8**, 1.

Comline, R. S., Roberts, H. E., and Titchen, D. A. (1951). *Nature (London)* **167**, 561.

Cowan, K. M. (1966). *Amer. J. Vet. Res.* **27**, 1217.

Curtain, C. C. (1969). *Immunology* **16**, 373.

Curtain, C. C., and Anderson, N. (1971). *Clin. Exp. Immunol.* **8**, 151.

Curtain, C. C., Clark, B. L., and Dufty, J. H. (1971). *Clin. Exp. Immunol.* **8**, 335.

Dennis, R. A., O'Hara, P. J., Young, M. F., and Dorris, K. D. (1970). *J. Amer. Vet. Med. Ass.* **156**, 1861.

Dixon, F. J., Talmage, D. W., Maurer, P. H., and Deich-Miller, M. (1952). *J. Exp. Med.* **96**, 313.

Dixon, F. J., Weigle, W. O., and Vazquez, J. J. (1961). *Lab. Invest.* **10**, 216.

Doolittle, R. F., and Astrin, K. H. (1967). *Science* **156**, 1755.

Easley, C. W., and Putnam, F. W. (1966). *J. Biol. Chem.* **241**, 3671.

Edelman, G. M. (1959). *J. Amer. Chem. Soc.* **81**, 3155.

Edelman, G. M., and Poulik, M. D. (1961). *J. Exp. Med.* **113**, 861.

Ehrlich, P. (1897). *Fortschr. Med.* **15**, 41.

Ehrlich, P. (1900). *Proc. Roy. Soc., Ser. B* **66**, 424.

Eichmann, K., and Greenblatt, J. (1971). *J. Exp. Med.* **133**, 424.

Eichmann, K., Braun, D. G., Feizi, T., and Krause, R. M. (1970). *J. Exp. Med.* **131**, 1169.

Eisen, H. N., Little, J. R., Osterland, C. K., and Simms, E. S. (1967). *Cold Spring Harbor Symp. Quant. Biol.* **32**, 75.

Fahey, J. L. (1962). *Advan. Immunol.* **2**, 41.

Fahey, J. L. (1963a). *J. Immunol.* **91**, 438.

Fahey, J. L. (1963b). *J. Immunol.* **91**, 448.
Fahey, J. L. (1965). *J. Amer. Med. Ass.* **194**, 255.
Fahey, J. L., and Robinson, A. G. (1963). *J. Exp. Med.* **118**, 845.
Fahey, J. L., and Sell, S. (1965). *J. Exp. Med.* **122**, 41.
Fahey, J. L., Wunderlich, J., and Mishell, R. (1964a). *J. Exp. Med.* **120**, 223.
Fahey, J. L., Wunderlich, J., and Mishell, R. (1964b). *J. Exp. Med.* **120**, 243.
Fahey, J. L., Barth, W., and Ovary, Z. (1965). *J. Immunol.* **94**, 819.
Feinstein, D., and Franklin, E. C. (1966). *Nature (London)* **212**, 1496.
Fennestad, K. L., and Borg-Petersen, C. (1962). *J. Infec. Dis.* **110**, 63.
Fernelius, A. L. (1966). *J. Immunol.* **96**, 488.
Fey, H. (1968). *Bull. Schweiz. Akad. Med. Wiss.* **24**, 390.
Fleischman, J. B., Pain, R. H., and Porter, R. R. (1962). *Arch. Biochem. Biophys.,* *Suppl.* **1**, 174.
Fleischman, J. B., Porter, R. R., and Press, E. M. (1963). *Biochem. J.* **88**, 220.
Franek, F., and Nezlin, R. S. (1963). *Folia Microbiol. (Prague)* **8**, 128.
Franek, F., Riha, I., and Sterzl, J. (1961). *Nature (London)* **189**, 1020.
Franklin, E. C., and Stanworth, D. R. (1961). *J. Exp. Med.* **114**, 521.
Franklin, E. C., Fudenberg, H. H., Meltzer, M., and Stanworth, D. R. (1962). *Proc. Nat. Acad. Sci. U.S.* **48**, 914.
Freeman, M. J., and Stavitsky, A. B. (1965). *J. Immunol.* **95**, 981.
Garner, R. J., and Crawley, W. (1958). *J. Comp. Pathol.* **68**, 112.
Givol, D., and Hurwitz, E. (1969). *Biochem. J.* **115**, 371.
Graves, J. H. (1963). *J. Immunol.* **91**, 251.
Gray, G. D., Mickelson, M. M., and Crim, J. A. (1969). *Immunochemistry* **6**, 641.
Grey, H. M., and Kunkel, H. G. (1964). *J. Exp. Med.* **120**, 253.
Groves, M. L., and Gordon, W. G. (1967). *Biochemistry* **6**, 2388.
Grubb, R. (1969). *Protides Biol. Fluids, Proc. Colloq.* **17**, 107.
Halliday, R. (1965a). *J. Immunol.* **95**, 510.
Halliday, R. (1965b). *Nature (London)* **205**, 614.
Hammer, D. K., Kickhofen, B., and Henning, G. (1968). *Eur. J. Biochem.* **6**, 443.
Harboe, M., Osterland, C. K., Mannik, M., and Kunkel, H. G. (1962). *J. Exp. Med.* **116**, 719.
Harboe, M., Deverill, J., and Godal, H. C. (1965). *Scand. J. Haematol.* **2**, 137.
Hartley, P. (1951). *Proc. Roy. Soc., Ser. B* **138**, 499.
Heimer, R., Clark, L. G., and Maurer, P. H. (1969). *Arch. Biochem. Biophys.* **131**, 9.
Heremans, J. F. (1959). *Clin. Chim. Acta* **4**, 639.
Hill, R. L., Delaney, R., Lebovitz, H. E., and Fellows, R. E., Jr. (1966). *Proc. Roy. Soc., Ser. B* **166**, 159.
Hilschmann, N., Ponstingl, H., Baczko, K., Braun, D., Hess, M., Suter, L., Bernikol, H. U., and Watanabe, S. (1969). *Protides Biol. Fluids, Proc. Colloq.* **17**, 53.
Hoerlein, A. B. (1957). *J. Immunol.* **78**, 112.
Hogarth-Scott, R. S. (1969). *Immunology* **16**, 543.
Hood, L., Gray, W. R., Sanders, B. G., and Dreyer, W. J. (1967). *Cold Spring Harbor Symp. Quant. Biol.* **32**, 133.
Hood, L., Eichmann, K., Lackland, H., Krause, R. M., and Ohm, J. (1970). *Nature (London)* **228**, 1040.
Humphrey, J. H., and White, R. G. (1970). "Immunology for the Students of Medicine," 3rd ed., Blackwell, Oxford.

Hurvell, B., and Fey, H. (1970). *Acta Vet. Scand.* 11, 341.
Ishizaka, K., Ishizaka, T., and Hornbrook, M. M. (1966). *J. Immunol.* 97, 75.
Jerne, N. (1967). *Cold Spring Harbor Symp. Quant. Biol.* 32, 591.
Jerne, N. (1968). Lecture at Danish Society of Immunology and Allergology.
Johansson, S. G. O., Bennich, H., and Wide, L. (1968). *Immunology* 14, 265.
Kabat, E. A. (1968). "Structural Concepts in Immunology and Immunochemistry." Holt, New York.
Karlsson, B. W. (1966). *Acta Pathol. Microbiol. Scand.* 67, 237.
Kim, Y. B., Bradley, S. G., and Watson, D. W. (1966a). *J. Immunol.* 97, 52.
Kim, Y. B., Bradley, S. G., and Watson, D. W. (1966b). *J. Immunol.* 97, 189.
Kim, Y. B., Bradley, S. G., and Watson, D. W. (1968). *J. Immunol.* 101, 224.
Klaus, G. G. B., Bennett, A., and Jones, E. W. (1969). *Immunology* 16, 293.
Knight, K. L., Roelofs, M. J., and Haurowitz, F. (1967). *Biochim. Biophys. Acta* 133, 333.
Köhler, H., Shimizu, A., Paul, C., and Putnam, F. W. (1970). *Science* 169, 56.
Korngold, L., and Lipari, R. (1956a). *Cancer* 9, 183.
Korngold, L., and Lipari, R. (1956b). *Cancer* 9, 262.
Krogh, P., and Hasselager, E. (1970). *Nord. Veterinaermed.* 22, 141.
Kruse, V. (1970a). *Anim. Prod.* 12, 619.
Kruse, V. (1970b). *Anim. Prod.* 12, 627.
Kunkel, H. G., and Prendergast, R. A. (1966). *Proc. Soc. Exp. Biol. Med.* 122, 910.
Kunkel, H. G., Mannik, M., and Williams, R. C. (1963). *Science* 140, 1218.
Lamm, M. E., Nussenzweig, V., and Benacerraf, B. (1966). *Immunology* 10, 309.
Larson, B. L., and Gillespie, D. C. (1957). *J. Biol. Chem.* 227, 565.
Lascelles, A. K., and McDowell, G. H. (1970). *Immunology* 19, 613.
Lascelles, A. K., Outteridge, P. M., and Mackenzie, D. D. S. (1966). *Aust. J. Exp. Biol. Med. Sci.* 44, 169.
Laurell, C. B., and Snigurowicz, J. (1967). *Scand. J. Haematol.* 4, 46.
Lind, I., Live, I., and Mansa, B. (1970). *Acta Pathol. Microbiol. Scand., Sect. B* 78, 673.
Locke, R. F., and Segre, D. (1965). *J. Immunol.* 95, 480.
McEwan, A. D., Fisher, E. W., and Selman, I. E. (1970). *J. Comp. Pathol.* 80, 259.
Mach, J.-P. (1970). *Nature (London)* 228, 1278.
Mach, J.-P., and Pahud, J. J. (1971). *J. Immunol.* 106, 552.
Mach, J.-P., Pahud, J. J., and Isliker, H. (1969). *Nature (London)* 223, 952.
Mackenzie, D. D. S. (1968). *Aust. J. Exp. Biol. Med. Sci.* 46, 273.
Mackenzie, D. D. S., and Lascelles, A. K. (1968). *Aust. J. Exp. Biol. Med. Sci.* 46, 285.
Mackenzie, D. D. S., Outteridge, P. M., and Lascelles, A. K. (1966). *Aust. J. Exp. Biol. Med. Sci.* 44, 181.
Mannik, M., and Kunkel, H. G. (1962). *J. Exp. Med.* 116, 859.
Mannik, M., and Kunkel, H. G. (1963). *J. Exp. Med.* 118, 817.
Mansa, B. (1965). *Acta Pathol. Microbiol. Scand.* 63, 153.
Mansa, B., Kjems, E., and Lind, I. (1968). *Abstr. Commun., Int. Congr. Microbiol. Stand., 11th, 1968.*
Martinsson, K. (1970). "Immunoglobulin Therapy in Piglets." Thesis, The Veterinary College, Stockholm.
Mason, J. H., Dalling, T., and Gordon, W. S. (1930). *J. Pathol. Bacteriol.* 33, 783.
Mattern, P. (1962). *Ann. Inst. Pasteur, Paris* 102, 64.
Mattern, P., Masseyev, R., Michel, R., and Peretti, P. (1961). *Ann. Inst. Pasteur, Paris* 101, 382.

Mattern, P., Duret, J., and Pautrizel, M. R. (1963). *C. R. Acad. Sci.* **256**, 820.

Mehta, P. D., and Tomasi, T. B., Jr. (1969). *Fed. Proc., Fed. Amer. Soc. Exp. Biol.* **28**, 820 (Abstr. No. 3131).

Metzger, J. J., and Fougereau, M. (1967a). *C. R. Acad. Sci.* **265**, 724.

Metzger, J. J., and Fougereau, M. (1967b). *World Vet. Congr., Commun., 18th,* Vol. 2, p. 784.

Meyer, R. C., Rasmussen, B. A., and Simon, J. (1969). *J. Amer. Vet. Med. Ass.* **154**, 531.

Migita, S., and Putnam, F. W. (1963). *J. Exp. Med.* **117**, 81.

Milstein, C. P., and Feinstein, A. (1968). *Biochem. J.* **107**, 559.

Morein, B. (1970). *Int. Arch. Allergy Appl. Immunol.* **39**, 403.

Moustgaard, J., and Hojgaard Olsen, N. (1953). *Aarsberetn. Inst. Sterilitetsfor., Copenhagen,* p. 142.

Murphy, F. A., Aalund, O., Osebold, J. W., and Carroll, E. J. (1964). *Arch. Biochem. Biophys.* **108**, 230.

Murphy, F. A., Osebold, J. W., and Aalund, O. (1965). *Arch. Biochem. Biophys.* **112**, 126.

Murphy, F. A., Osebold, J. W., and Aalund, O. (1966a). *Amer. J. Vet. Res.* **119**, 971.

Murphy, F. A., Osebold, J. W., and Aalund, O. (1966b). *J. Infec. Dis.* **116**, 99.

Myers, W. L., and Segre, D. (1963). *J. Immunol.* **91**, 697.

Nansen, P. (1970). "Metabolism of Bovine Immunoglobulin G." Munksgaard, Copenhagen.

Nansen, P., and Riising, H. J. (1971). *Acta Vet. Scand.* **12**, 445.

Nansen, P., Nielsen, K., and Nielsen, R. (1970). *Nord. Veterinaermed.* **22**, 1.

Natvig, J. B., Kunkel, H. G., and Litwin, S. D. (1967). *Cold Spring Harbor Symp. Quant. Biol.* **32**, 173.

Nielsen, P. B. (1972). *Acta Vet. Scand.* **13**, 143.

Nisonoff, A., Wissler, F. C., Lipman, L. N., and Woernley, D. L. (1960). *Arch. Biochem. Biophys.* **89**, 230.

Nisonoff, A., Markus, G., and Wissler, F. C. (1961). *Nature (London)* **189**, 293.

Nisonoff, A., Hopper, J. E., MacDonald, A. B., and Daugharty, H. (1969). *Protides Biol. Fluids, Proc. Colloq.* **17**, 155.

Nussenzweig, V., and Benacerraf, B. (1964). *J. Exp. Med.* **119**, 409.

Nussenzweig, V., and Benacerraf, B. (1966). *J. Exp. Med.* **124**, 805.

Nussenzweig, V., and Green, I. (1971). *J. Immunol.* **106**, 1089.

Oh, Y. H., and Sanders, B. E. (1966). *Life Sci.* **5**, 827.

Osburn, B. I., and Hoskins, R. K. (1969). *J. Infec. Dis.* **119**, 267.

Osburn, B. I., and Kennedy, P. C. (1966). *Pathol. Vet.* **3**, 110.

Oudin, J. (1956). *C. R. Acad. Sci.* **242**, 2606.

Oudin, J. (1966). *Proc. Roy. Soc., Ser. B* **166**, 207.

Oudin, J., and Michel, M. (1963). *C. R. Acad. Sci.* **257**, 805.

Outteridge, P. M., Rock, J. D., and Lascelles, A. K. (1965). *Aust. J. Exp. Biol. Med. Sci.* **43**, 265.

Outteridge, P. M., Mackenzie, D. D. S., and Lascelles, A. K. (1968). *Arch. Biochem. Biophys.* **126**, 105.

Owen, R. D. (1945). *Science* **102**, 400.

Pahud, J. J., and Mach, J.-P. (1970). *Immunochemistry* **7**, 679.

Pan, I. C., Kaplan, A. M., Morter, R. L., and Freeman, M. F. (1968). *Proc. Soc. Exp. Biol. Med.* **129**, 867.

Payne, L. C., and Marsh, C. L. (1962). *J. Nutr.* **76**, 151.

Pedersen, K. B. (1970). "Infectious Bovine Keratoconjunctivitis." Thesis, Royal Vet. and Agric. Univ., Copenhagen.

Pedersen, K. B., Aalund, O., Nansen, P., and Adler, H. C. (1971). *Acta Vet. Scand.* **12**, 303.

Penhale, W. J., Christie, G., McEwan, A. D., Fisher, E. W., and Selman, I. E. (1970). *Brit. Vet. J.* **126**, 30.

Peterman, M. L. (1946). *J. Amer. Chem. Soc.* **68**, 106.

Pierce, A. E., and Feinstein, A. (1965). *Immunology* **8**, 106.

Pierce, A. E., and Smith, M. W. (1967). *J. Physiol. (London)* **190**, 1.

Porter, P. (1969). *Immunology* **17**, 617.

Porter, P., and Allen, W. D. (1969). *Immunology* **17**, 789.

Porter, P., and Noakes, D. E. (1970). *Biochim. Biophys. Acta* **214**, 107.

Porter, P., Noakes, D. E., and Allen, W. D. (1970). *Immunology* **18**, 245.

Porter, R. R. (1950). *Biochem. J.* **46**, 479.

Porter, R. R. (1958). *Nature (London)* **182**, 670.

Porter, R. R. (1959). *Biochem. J.* **73**, 119.

Porter, R. R. (1962). *In* "The Basic Problems in Neoplastic Disease" (A. Gellhorn and E. Hirschberg, eds.), Columbia Univ. Press, New York.

Porter, R. R. (1963). *Brit. Med. Bull.* **19**, 197.

Porter, R. R., and Press, E. M. (1962). *Annu. Rev. Biochem.* **31**, 625.

Putnam, F. W., and Köhler, H. (1969). *Naturwissenschaften* **56**, 439.

Putnam, F. W., Titani, K., Wikler, M., and Shinoda, T. (1967). *Cold Spring Harbor Symp. Quant. Biol.* **32**, 9.

Radl, J., Klein, F., van den Berg, P., de Bruyn, A. M., and Hijmans, W. (1971). *Immunology* **20**, 843.

Rasmusen, B. A. (1965). *Science* **148**, 1742.

Rejnek, J., Kostka, J., and Travnicek, J. (1966). *Folia Microbiol. (Prague)* **11**, 173.

Relyveld, E. H., van Triet, A. J., and Raynaud, M. (1959). *Antonie van Leeuwenhoek; J. Microbiol. Serol.* **25**, 369.

Richards, C. B., and Marrack, J. R. (1963). *Protides Biol. Fluids, Proc. Colloq.* **10**, 154.

Richardson, A. K., and Kelleher, P. C. (1970). *Biochim. Biophys. Acta* **214**, 117.

Robbins, J. B., Kenny, K., and Suter, E. (1965). *J. Exp. Med.* **122**, 385.

Rook, J. A. F., Moustgaard, J., and Jakobsen, P. E. (1951). *Kgl. Vet.-Landbohoejsk., Arsskr.* p. 81.

Rowe, D. S. (1970). *Nature (London)* **228**, 509.

Schinckel, P. G., and Ferguson, K. A. (1953). *Aust. J. Biol. Sci.* **6**, 533.

Schultze, H. E. (1962). *Arch. Biochem. Biophys., Suppl.* **1**, 290.

Segre, D., and Kaeberle, M. L. (1962a). *J. Immunol.* **89**, 782.

Segre, D., and Kaeberle, M. L. (1962b). *J. Immunol.* **89**, 790.

Seligmann, M., Mihaesco, C., and Meshaka, G. (1966). *Science* **154**, 790.

Sell, S. (1964). *J. Immunol.* **92**, 559.

Selman, I. E., McEwan, A. D., and Fisher, E. W. (1970). *J. Comp. Pathol.* **80**, 419.

Selman, I. E., de la Fuente, G. H., Fisher, E. W., and McEwan, A. D. (1971). *Vet. Rec.* **88**, 460.

Sharpe, H. B. A. (1965). *Res. Vet. Sci.* **6**, 490.

Shuster, J. (1971). *Immunochemistry* **8**, 405.

Silverstein, A. M., Prendergast, R. A., and Kraner, K. L. (1963a). *Science* **142**, 1172.

Silverstein, A. M., Uhr, J. W., and Kraner, K. L. (1963b). *J. Exp. Med.* **117,** 799.

Silverstein, A. M., Thorbecke, G. J., Kraner, K. L., and Lukes, R. J. (1963c). *J. Immunol.* **91,** 384.

Silverstein, A. M., Prendergast, R. A., and Kraner, K. L. (1964) .*J. Exp. Med.* **119,** 955.

Silverstein, A. M., Parshall, C. J., and Uhr, J. W. (1966). *Science* **154,** 1675.

Singer, S. J., and Doolittle, R. F. (1966). *Science* **153,** 13.

Skvaril, F., and Morell, A. (1970). *J. Immunol.* **104,** 1310.

Small, P. A., Curry, J. H., and Waldman, R. H. (1969). *In* "The Secretory Immunologic System" (D. H. Dayton, Jr. *et al.,* eds.), p. 13. Nat. Inst. Child Health Hum. Develop., Washington, D.C.

Smith, H. W., O'Neil, J. A., and Simmons, E. J. (1967). *Vet. Rec.* **80,** 664.

Solomon, A., Waldman, T. A., and Fahley, J. L. (1963). *J. Lab. Clin. Med.* **62,** 1.

Spiegelberg, H. L., and Weigle, W. O. (1965a). *J. Exp. Med.* **121,** 323.

Spiegelberg, H. L., and Weigle, W. O. (1965b). *J. Immunol.* **95,** 1034.

Steinberg, A. G., Stauffer, R., and Boyer, S. H. (1960). *Nature (London)* **188,** 169.

Sterzl, J., Kostka, J., Riha, I., and Mandel, L. (1960). *Pol. Microbiol.* **5,** 29.

Stone, S. S. (1970). *Immunology* **18,** 369.

Sullivan, A. L., Prendergast, R. A., Antunes, L. J., Silverstein, A. M., and Tomasi, T. B. (1969). *J. Immunol.* **103,** 334.

Svendsen, J., and Wilson, M. R. (1971). *Amer. J. Vet. Res.* **32,** 899.

Taranta, A., and Franklin, E. C. (1961). *Science* **134,** 1981.

Tchistovitch, T. (1899). *Ann. Inst. Pasteur., Paris* **13,** 406.

Terry, W. D., Fahey, L., and Steinberg, A. G. (1965). *J. Exp. Med.* **122,** 1087.

Tiselius, A. (1937). *Biochem. J.* **31,** 1464.

Tiselius, A., and Kabat, E. A. (1939). *J. Exp. Med.* **69,** 119.

Titani, K., Wikler, M., and Putnam, F. W. (1967). *Science* **155,** 828.

Todd, C. W., Walz, M. A., and Osterland, C. K. (1967). *Proc. Soc. Exp. Biol. Med.* **126,** 383.

Tomasi, T. B., Jr., (1968). *N. Engl. J. Med.* **279,** 1327.

Tomasi, T. B., Jr., and Bienenstock, J. (1968). *Advan. Immunol.* **9,** 1.

Trainin, Z., Nobel, T. A., Klopper, U., and Neumann, F. (1968). *Quart. Isr. Vet. Med. Ass.* **25,** 187.

Vaerman, J.-P. (1970). "Studies on IgA Immunoglobulins in Man and Animals." Thesis, Univ. of Louvain, Belgium.

Vaerman, J.-P., and Heremans, J. F. (1966). *Science* **153,** 647.

Vaerman, J.-P., and Heremans, J. F. (1970). *Int. Arch. Allergy Appl. Immunol.* **38,** 561.

Vaerman, J.-P., Heremans, J. F., and Laurell, C.-B. (1968). *Immunology* **14,** 425.

Vaerman, J.-P., Arbuckle, J. B., and Heremans, J. F. (1970). *Int. Arch. Allergy Appl. Immunol.* **39,** 323.

Virella, G., and Parkhouse, M. E. (1971). *Immunochemistry* **8,** 243.

Virella, G., Howard, A., and Cherrington, J. (1970). *Clin. Exp. Immunol.* **7,** 671.

von Behring, E. A., and Kitasato, S. (1890). *Deut. Med. Wochenschr.* **16,** 1113.

Wang, A. C., Pink, J. R. L., Fudenberg, H. H., and Ohms, J. (1970). *Proc. Nat. Acad. Sci. U.S.* **66,** 657.

Wei, W. M., and Stavitsky, A. B. (1967). *Immunology* **12,** 431.

Weir, D. M. (1967). "Experimental Immunochemistry." Blackwell, Oxford.

Wikler, M., Köhler, H., Shinoda, T., and Putnam, F. W. (1969). *Science* **163**, 75.

Wilkie, B. N., Duncan, J. R., and Winter, A. J. (1971). *J. Dairy Sci.* **54**, 1334.

Wilson, M. R., and Svendsen, J. (1971). *Amer. J. Vet. Res.* **32**, 891.

Yamada, H., Yamada, A., and Hollander, V. P. (1970). *J. Immunol.* **104**, 251.

Yount, W. J., Hong, R., Seligmann, M., Good, R., and Kunkel, H. G. (1970). *J. Clin. Invest.* **49**, 1957.

2 IMMUNE RESPONSE OF THE FOWL

W. T. WEBER

I. Introduction

As a result of studies conducted by numerous investigators during the past 10 years, it is now well established that the avian bursa of Fabricius and thymus play a crucial role in the full development of immunological competence in the chicken. In this species, the immune mechanism is uniquely expressed in that the bursa of Fabricius is responsible for development of humoral antibody-producing capability, whereas the thymus primarily influences immune reactivity assigned to cell-mediated immunity (CMI) or delayed hypersensitivity.

It is the purpose of this chapter to review our present state of knowledge regarding the function of the bursa and thymus by emphasizing work performed during the past 5 years. Extensive reviews have covered earlier accomplishments in considerable detail (Warner and Szenberg, 1964a; Warner, 1967).

II. Embryological Development of the Bursa of Fabricius and the Thymus

The primordia of the bursa and the thymus are first discernible on the fourth or fifth day of embryonic development (Romanoff, 1960). Lymphocytopoiesis is recognized first in the thymus between days 7–11 (Ackerman and Knouff, 1964) and is followed by lymphopoiesis in the bursa between days 12–15 of incubation (Meyer *et al.*, 1959; Ackerman and Knouff, 1959; Ackerman, 1962). As recently shown with the sex chromosome marker technique, the majority of the developing lymphoid cell population in the embryonic bursa as well as in the thymus arises from blood-born progenitor cells of yolk sac origin (Moore and Owen, 1966, 1967). The epithelial rudiments of the thymus and bursa probably furnish an inductive environment for development of bursal and thymic lymphocytes, respectively. The bursa and thymus reach their maximum size at approximately 1–2 months of life. Thereafter the bursa, unlike the thymus, undergoes a gradual but total involution that is completed around 20 weeks (Glick, 1956, 1960). The thymus persists throughout life as multiple atrophic lobes that fluctuate considerably in their cellular composition, but for much of the time lack a distinct cortex (Hohn, 1956). As determined by *in vitro* uptake of tritiated thymidine the bursa contains the largest population of DNA synthesizing lymphocytes (20–30%), followed by the thymus (3–9%) and spleen (2–6%) in that order (Warner, 1965; Weber, 1967).

III. The Function of the Bursa in the Immune System of the Chick

A. EFFECT OF BURSECTOMY ON IMMUNOGLOBULIN PRODUCTION AND HUMORAL ANTIBODY RESPONSE

When the bursa, a discrete lymphoepithelial organ attached to the hindgut, is removed early in life or its development is suppressed, definite deficiencies in humoral antibody production and serum immunoglobulin levels develop. The extent of these deficiencies depends primarily on the time the organ is removed and on the technique of removal. Early experiments employing surgical bursectomy at the time of hatching, or suppression of bursal development through administration of testosterone in the embryo, did demonstrate a marked reduction or elimination of antibody production in many chicks in response to a primary injection of a variety of antigens (Glick *et al.*, 1956; Mueller *et al.*, 1960; Warner *et al.*, 1962, 1969; Graetzer *et al.*, 1963; Isaković *et al.*, 1963; Warner and Szenberg, 1964b). A striking reduction in serum levels of IgG generally correlated well with these observations, but it was also noted that some hormonally bursectomized chickens incapable of producing detectable antibody still had considerable amounts of gamma globulin in their serum (Carey and Warner, 1964; Pierce *et al.*, 1966). Subsequent studies showed that the levels of IgM were not consistently decreased and sometimes even increased following hormonal or surgical bursectomy (Ortega and Der, 1964; Cooper *et al.*, 1966a, 1969; Claflin *et al.*, 1966; Warner *et al.*, 1969; Lerner *et al.*, 1970), and that considerable recovery in antibody producing capabilities could occur following repeated injections of antigen (Janković and Isaković, 1966; Pierce *et al.*, 1966; Warner *et al.*, 1969). The desired state of agammaglobulinemia coupled with complete failure of antibody production to repeated antigenic challenges was accomplished in only about 40% of the animals even when surgical bursectomy at the time of hatching was followed by total body irradiation (Cooper *et al.*, 1966a). In one laboratory, surgical bursectomy followed by X-irradiation failed to produce an agammaglobulinemic state and all birds formed some antibody, especially after a second antigen injection (Rose and Orlans,

1968). Hormonal *in ovo* bursectomy alone can result in agammaglobulinemia, but again in only 40–50% of treated chicks (Warner *et al.*, 1969).
Recently, the combined use of hormonal *in ovo* bursectomy and repeated
administration of the immunosuppressive drug cyclophosphamide during
the first few days after hatching has been reported to result in agammaglobulinemia in more than 90% of chicks (Lerman and Weidanz, 1969;
Weidanz, 1970, personal communication). These observations have essentially been confirmed (Weber, 1972) and at the present time the
combined use of testosterone and cyclophosphamide is the best available
model to consistently induce an agammaglobulinemic state. Repeated
administration of cyclosphosphamide alone in the newly hatched period
will also result in severe hypogammaglobulinemia and is accompanied
in most chicks by failure of antibody responsiveness to repeated antigen
administration (Lerman and Weidanz, 1970; Linna, 1970). The most
effective dose schedule is, however, accompanied by a high mortality, and
for this reason this procedure is probably not the method of choice.

B. Histological Changes Following Bursectomy

The degree of hypo- or agammaglobulinemia achieved through the
above mentioned experimental methods is reflected in the cellular composition of the spleen and other lymphoid tissue. In general, the number
of plasma cells in the spleen and cecal tonsils are reduced to a varying
degree (Szenberg and Warner, 1962; Isaković and Janković, 1964;
Cooper *et al.*, 1966a, 1969; Warner *et al.*, 1969) and are occasionally
entirely absent, more likely so when hormonal or surgical bursectomy
is followed by cyclophosphamide treatment (Glick, 1971) or by whole
body X-irradiation (Cooper *et al.*, 1969). The number of discrete germinal follicles in the spleen and cecal tonsils is similarly reduced and
their reduction appears to correlate also with the degree of immunological depression (Cooper *et al.*, 1966a, 1969; Warner *et al.*, 1969; Glick,
1971). It should be pointed out here that the methods for numerical
evaluation of germinal follicles, and particularly plasma cells, have been
relatively crude and results have generally been based on observations
of a few sections of the tissue in question. Nevertheless, because of
the definite influence of bursectomy on the plasma cell lineage in peripheral tissue as well as on germinal follicles, both have been characterized
as bursa-dependent structures (Szenberg and Warner, 1962; Cooper *et
al.*, 1966a). The possible participation of the thymus in germinal follicle
development has not been completely ruled out (Warner, 1967). Peripheral blood lymphocytes were reported to be present in normal numbers

in hormonally bursectomized (Warner *et al.*, 1962) and surgically bursectomized chickens (Long and Pierce, 1963). Glick and Sato (1964), on the other hand, reported a slight but significant decrease in the absolute number of lymphocytes in surgically bursectomized chickens, with fewer small than medium-sized lymphocytes at certain postbursectomy stages.

C. ONTOGENY OF IMMUNOGLOBULIN SYNTHESIS

Thorbecke *et al.* (1968) demonstrated that the bursa of Fabricius is the first site of IgM globulin synthesis in the developing chicken. Bursal tissue of 18-day embryos and from newly hatched chickens incorporated ^{14}C-labeled amino acids into IgM globulin, whereas this was not observed in spleen tissue until 7 days after hatching. Fluorescent antibody staining also indicated that immunoglobulin synthesis was primarily associated with medullary cells of most of the bursal follicles. In both bursa and spleen, IgM synthesis preceded IgG synthesis. This is in agreement with observations in mature immunized chickens where IgM antibodies are also formed prior to IgG antibodies (Benedict *et al.*, 1963).

Using purified antibodies to μ, γ, and light chains labeled with fluorochromes, Kincade and Cooper (1971) demonstrated cells containing μ and light chains in lymphoid follicles of the bursa of 14-day-old embryos. IgG containing cells were initially observed in bursal follicles at 21 days of incubation. This developmental sequence of immunoglobulin containing cells within the bursa was recapitulated approximately 1 week later in the spleen, cecal tonsils, and thymus.

Expansion of IgM and IgG containing cells began in the spleen on the third and eighth days, respectively, after hatching. Analysis of single cell suspensions revealed a considerable proportion (13/20) of single bursal cells containing heavy chains of both IgM and IgG, whereas spleen cells rarely contained both classes of immunoglobulins (1/25). This suggested a developmental switch from IgM to IgG occurring within the bursa of Fabricius. The same group of investigators recently strengthened this view by reporting that treatment of 13 day embryos with purified goat antibodies to IgM resulted in elimination of IgM containing cells from the bursa of 16 and 19 day embryos. When anti-IgM treatment *in ovo* was combined with bursectomy at hatching, suppression of not only IgM, but also of IgG production resulted. Experimental birds so treated failed to produce circulating immunoglobulins and lacked plasma cells and germinal centers at 10 weeks of age. When, on the other hand, anti-IgM treatment was instituted *after* bursectomy at hatching, chicks produced little IgM but normal amounts of IgG. The mechanism suggested here is that destruction occurred of those IgM-producing cells that had already seeded from the bursa to the peripheral lymphoid tissue prior to bursectomy, leaving IgG-producing cells intact and in the majority. The effect of embryonic administration of antibodies to IgM on subsequent IgG synthesis is interpreted to indicate that IgG-synthesizing cells are derived exclusively from cells that previously synthesized IgM. That this switch may occur only in the bursa and does not occur in the peripheral tissues is suggested by the observation that some bursectomized chickens having supernormal levels of IgM never repair their drastically low levels of IgG, even after prolonged periods (Kincade *et al.*, 1970).

The view of a possibly exclusive bursal origin of peripheral lymphoid cells bearing surface immunoglobulins has recently been expanded still further. Kincade *et al.* (1971) reported that with fluorescein-labeled antibodies to heavy chain determinants no cells staining for IgM or IgG could be detected in leukocyte preparations from peripheral blood or in lymphocyte populations of spleen, cecal tonsils, or thymus from agammaglobulinemic chicks. In contrast, approximately 35–40% of peripheral blood leukocytes stained for immunoglobulin determinants with approximately equal division (17–20%) for IgM or IgG determinants, and many were found in spleen, cecal tonsils, thymus, and bursa of normal chickens. In line with these observations, Rabellino and Grey (1971) also reported a decrease in the number of surface immunoglobulin carrying lymphocytes in blood and spleen of bursectomized chickens using fluoresceinated rabbit anti-chicken 7 S immunoglobulin. Their findings were less absolute than those of Kincade *et al.* (1971), possibly because of admitted incomplete surgical bursectomies, but there may be additional reasons. The conflicting results on the presence (Kincade *et al.*, 1971) or absence (Rabellino and Grey, 1971) of lymphocytes in the thymus of normal chickens carrying immunoglobulin receptors need to be resolved and independent confirmation on the absoluteness of failure to detect cells carrying surface immunoglobulins in various lymphoid tissues of agammaglobulinemic chickens is needed. Earlier, Alm and Peterson (1969) had reported that splenic lymphocytes of bursectomized irradiated chickens showed less stimulation of DNA synthesis when cultured with rabbit anti-chicken IgG, which would tend to support the findings made by Kincade *et al.* (1971).

Those experiments indicating that the bursa is the first organ in which immunoglobulin synthesis can be detected also correlate with the recent finding by Dwyer and Warner (1971) showing the presence of antigen binding cells in 14–15 day embryonic bursa well before significant numbers appear in spleen or thymus. In these experiments, cells that label with the ^{125}I-tagged antigen monomeric flagellin obtained from *Salmonella adelaide* are considered to have immunoglobulin surface receptors which combine specifically with the antigen. Some of the labeled cells in the bursa may however be cells of monocyte-macrophage type that have cytophilically bound, maternally derived immunoglobulin.

D. Transfer of Bursal Cells to Bursectomized Chicks

One approach to demonstrate that the bursa contains the source of potential immunologically competent cells, destined to humoral antibody production, is to study the effects on immunoglobulin and antibody production following transplantation of dispersed bursal lymphocytes to bursectomized chicks. Using an inbred strain of chicks, Gilmour *et al.* (1970) transferred bursal cells of 4-week-old donors intraperitoneally to hormonally bursectomized, X-irradiated, 3-day-old chicks and challenged them immediately by the same route with *Brucella abortus* and sheep erythrocyte antigens. Significant agglutinin titers were demonstrable 1 week later to *B. abortus*. Bursa cells were found incapable however of transferring a primary response to sheep erythrocytes unless 6–10-week-old bursa cell donors were employed and antigen challenge delayed until 5 days after cell transfer. These experiments nevertheless demonstrated that bursa cells could themselves transfer antibody formation, although it is not clear whether the cells developed this competence only after transfer to the host or were already competent within the donor bursa. This remains an interesting question in view of earlier reports that antibody production could not be demonstrated in the bursa itself following systemic administration of antigen (Dent and Good, 1965). Other efforts in demonstrating the *in vivo* functional potential of bursal cells have centered on the sequential course of antibody and immunoglobulin production in agammaglobulinemic chicks following transfer of sex chromsomally marked bursal cells, which allows actual demonstration of dividing donor cells in various lymphoid and hematopoietic tissues of the recipient (Weber and Weidanz, 1970; Weber, 1972). These studies showed that a primary response of transferred bursal cells to *B. abortus* as well as to sheep erythrocytes depends on the route of cell and antigen transfer. Thus, intravenously transferred bursal cells were nearly as capable of producing humoral antibody to sheep erythrocytes as to *B. abortus*. After intraperitoneal transfer of cells and antigen however an antibody response only to *B. abortus* and not to sheep erythrocytes could be elicited, a finding confirming that

TABLE I

ANTIBODY RESPONSE TO *Brucella abortus* AND SHEEP RED BLOOD CELLS (SRBC) IN TESTOSTERONE AND CYCLOPHOSPHAMIDE TREATED CHICKS FOLLOWING INTRAVENOUS OR INTRAPERITONEAL BURSAL LYMPHOCYTE TRANSFER AT 4 WEEKS OF AGE

Number of brusa cells transferred[a]	Antigen SRBC+B. abortus[c]	Brucella abortus								SRBC							
		No. recipients responding/no. injected				Mean log$_2$ titer of responders				No. recipients responding/no. injected				Mean log$_2$ titer of responders			
		Week 1	4	7	10	Week 1	4	7	10	Week 1	4	7	10	Week 1	4	7	10
1×10^8 i.v.	+, i.v.	14/18 (78%)	6/10 (60%)	3/3 (100%)	0/2 (0%)	5.1 (2–8)	8 (6–9)	7.6 (6–9)	0	12/18 (67%)	7/10 (70%)	3/3 (100%)	0/2 (0%)	3.7	6.1	6.6	0
1×10^8 i.v.	No antigen	0/7	0/3	0/1	—	0	0	0	—	0/7	0/3	0/1	—	0	0	0	—
1×10^8 i.v.[b]	+, i.v.	0/4	0/3	0/1	—	0	0	0	—	0/4	0/3	0/1	—	0	0	0	—
1×10^8 i.p.	+, i.p.	4/4	1/3	—	—	5.2	5	—	—	0/4	0/3	—	—	0	0	—	—
No cells	+, i.p.	0/4	0/1	—	—	0	0	—	—	0/4	0/1	—	—	0	0	—	—
No cells	+, i.v.	0/4	0/1	—	—	0	0	—	—	0/4	0/1	—	—	0	0	—	—

[a] Transfer of bursal cells of 4-week-old normal donors, made 24–36 hours following whole body exposure to 500R X-irradiation.
[b] Cell recipients not X-irradiated.
[c] First antigen inoculation within 2 hours of cell transfer.

of Gilmour *et al.* (1970) (Table I). It was also shown that antibody and IgM and IgG immunoglobulin production continued in repeatedly antigen challenged bursa cell recipients for as long as 8 weeks. A reversion to an agammaglobulinemic state coupled with lack of antibody production eventually followed in the recipients, and this reversion coincided with a disappearance of dividing donor bursa cells. During the course of the experiments it was furthermore demonstrated that the population of transferred bursal cells initially expanded two- to tenfold following antigen administration and that successful bursa cell transfer to 4-week-old agammaglobulinemic chicks could only be achieved after exposure of hosts to X-irradiation (Table I). Since chicks were of a highly inbred strain and histocompatible at the major B locus, the effect of X-irradiaton was most likely due to suppression and elimination of a large proportion of dividing host stem cells in spleen and bone marrow and not due to suppression of a host cellular immune response against any weak histoincompatibility antigens that may have been present on the transferred cells. Necessary elimination of host stem cell compartments prior to transfer of isogeneic cells has also been demonstrated in inbred mice (Takada *et al.*, 1971). Successfully transplanted bursal cells proliferated primarily in the spleen and bone marrow, but only very few (<2%) dividing donor cells have been found in the thymus. Histological examination of spleens and cecal tonsils of chicks, temporarily "reconstituted" by transferred bursal cells revealed the presence of considerable numbers of plasma cells, that were not seen in agammaglobulinemic chicks. Several small periarteriolar accumulations of pyroninophilic cells were found in the spleens of antigen-stimulated and unstimulated bursal cell recipients, but the discrete, well bordered follicles seen in spleens of normal chicks were not encountered even though chicks had been examined at various intervals after immunization (Weber, 1972). These latter "bursa-dependent" follicles had earlier been reported to develop after intraperitoneal autologous bursa cell transfer into newly hatched, bursectomized and irradiated chicks (Cooper *et al.*, 1966b). Some of the conclusions drawn from these earlier cell transfer experiments should be reexamined, since it is recognized today that a large proportion (50–60%) of surgically bursectomized, irradiated chicks failed to achieve an agammaglobulinemic state (Cooper *et al.*, 1966a; Rose and Orlans, 1968) and retained the potential to form small numbers of plasma cells and germinal follicles even without the transfer of any competent cells. The precise influence of the bursa or the direct participation of bursal cells in the formation of discrete germinal follicles remains unsolved. It is apparent from our studies that humoral antibody responses to *B. abortus* and to sheep erythrocytes, and IgM as well as IgG production can be accomplished by transferred bursal cells without the formation of discrete germinal follicles in the spleen.

E. Effect of Bursectomy on the Recovery from Tolerance

The influence of the bursa on recovery from immunological tolerance has only received scant attention. In a very recent report Peterson *et al.* (1971) induced tolerance to BSA in newly hatched, sublethally X-irradiated chickens by repeated intraabdominal injections of massive doses of BSA. Two days after cessation of the tolerance inducing regimen, spleens of BSA-injected chickens contained significantly fewer cells forming antibody to BSA than did spleens of control animals. Recovery from tolerance in normal chicks was gradual but complete by 72 days after cessation of tolerance induction. Surgical bursectomy, performed 3 days after BSA injections were stopped, significantly delayed recovery from tolerance. Impaired responses to BSA were still detected 94 days after bursectomy. This suggests that bursa-derived, potential antibody-producing cells can be made tolerant and that recovery from tolerance to this antigen may be dependent on the bursa for a source of new, immunocompetent cells. However, the thymus also may be involved in the recovery from tolerance as indicated by Chaperon (1965) who found that chicks made tolerant to BSA during embryonic life recovered at a slower rate after thymectomy than did control animals. It is not clear whether delay in recovery here was due to loss of thymus-dependent cells or due to an indirect effect of thymectomy on the bursa, e.g., a temporary bursal lymphoid cell depletion as a result of stress. The role of the thymus and the bursa in the recovery from tolerance obviously is not yet clearly defined and deserves more experimentation.

F. Effect of Bursectomy on Transplantation Immunity and Delayed Hypersensitivity

It is evident from the preceding discussion that bursal lymphocytes can serve as precursors to humoral antibody-producing cells. There is equally convincing evidence that the bursa and bursal lymphocytes are not involved in cell-mediated or delayed hypersensitivity-type of reactions. Bursectomized chicks with normal thymus glands are no less capable of rejecting skin homografts than are normal chickens (Warner *et al.*, 1962; Aspinall *et al.*, 1963). Similarly, delayed hypersensitivity reactions, e.g., experimental allergic encephalomyelitis and thyroiditis could be elicited in surgically bursectomized chickens (Janković and Isvaneski, 1963; Janković *et al.*, 1963). Because of the now known ability of a considerable number of bursectomized chicks to recover in their antibody-producing capabilities (Section III,A), these experiments were not conclusive in ruling out that circulating antibody was not involved in hypersensitivity reactions in chickens. Warner *et al.* (1971) therefore reinvestigated this problem in selected birds found to be agammaglobulinemic following only hormonal bursectomy, and demonstrated that a normal, delayed hypersensitivity reaction could be elicited in chickens that were incapable of a detectable circulating antibody response and that failed to synthesize serum immunoglobulins. Furthermore, the reactions fulfilled most criteria applied to this form of immune response in mammals, namely, delayed onset of response, lymphocytic infiltration at the test site, carrier specificity, and *in vitro* inhibition of macrophage migration. An important criterion, the cellular transfer of the delayed hypersensitivity reaction with lymphoid cells could not be demonstrated, however, possibly because rejection of cells resulted after transfer to an outbred strain of birds, or because too few sensitized cells were transferred in these experiments.

G. Cellular Immune Potential of Bursal Cells

Other evidence supporting the cellular immune incompetence of bursal lymphocytes was presented by Cain *et al.* (1968) who could not elicit significant splenomegaly when bursal cells were intravenously injected into allogeneic chick embryos. Similarly, following the inoculation of bursal cells onto the choriallantoic membrane of allogeneic chick embryos, essentially no pock formation resulted (Warner, 1965). Occasionally observed slight degrees of splenomegaly or development of a few pocks on the CAM after bursal cell inoculation could well have been due to a small number of competent peripheral blood lymphocytes contaminating an otherwise incompetent bursal cell population. In these attempted GVHR's with bursal cells, it would still seem important, however, to demonstrate the presence of or the proliferation of donor bursal cells in the absence of developing lesions on the CAM or in the spleen, because the failure to initiate a reaction could have been due to exceptionally poor viability of bursal cells under these conditions. As is presented in more detail below (Section IV,B), cell-mediated immunity is related in the chick, as well as in mammals, to the thymus and thymus-derived lymphocytes. One property of a proportion of mammalian (Schwarz, 1965; Weber, 1966; Claman, 1966) and avian thymus cells (Weber, 1967) is their ability to respond *in vitro* to PHA with significant proliferation. It is of interest here that bursal lymphocytes do not respond *in vitro* to PHA with significant DNA (Weber, 1967;

Van Alten *et al.,* 1969; Weber and Eichholtz, 1971) or protein synthesis, a finding further supporting the concept that bursal lymphocytes are functionally different from thymus cells.

H. FUNCTION OF THE BURSA IN BACTERIAL, VIRAL, AND PARASITIC DISEASES

The bursa of Fabricius clearly influences humoral antibody-producing capabilities in later life and one would therefore expect that in the absence of the bursa, resistance to viral, bacterial, fungal, and perhaps some parasitic infections might be decidedly decreased. Unfortunately most studies designed to answer such questions employed bursectomy procedures that are strongly suspect under present knowledge to have been incomplete and that must have allowed at least some immunoglobulin and antibody production to occur which obviously clouds the interpretation of results. Nevertheless, it was reported that fatal cases of leptospirosis as well as long-lasting leptospiral carrier states were more frequent in surgically bursectomized chickens than in controls after infection with virulent *Leptospira icterohaemorrhagiae.* However, antibody levels eventually rose to normal levels recalling the above stated suspicion (Kemenes and Pethes, 1963). Chickens surgically bursectomized at 2 weeks of age were reported to be 5 times less resistant to challenge with live *S. typhimurium* than were control chickens (Chang *et al.,* 1957). When surgically bursectomized, X-irradiated chicks were infected with *Mycobacterium avium,* the structure of the developing lesion and the survival of chicks was not significantly altered from that in normal animals (Cheville and Richards, 1971). Neonatal thymectomy also had no effect. Bursectomy had no significant influence on the development of Newcastle disease (Kono *et al.,* 1969) or on the course of a fungal (Candida albicans) infection (Fujiwara *et al.,* 1970), but it did potentiate avian encephalomyelitis (Cheville, 1970). Resistance to avian coccidiosis (*Eimeria tenella*) has been tested in normal and bursectomized chickens by giving an oral dose of sporulated oocysts followed by a challenging dose with a larger number of oocysts. Bursectomized chicks did not show a clearly decreased resistance (Long and Pierce, 1963). Longenecker *et al.* (1966) studied plasmodial infections in hormonally or surgically bursectomized chicks. They found higher parasitemias after i.v. infection with 100×10^6 *Plasmodium* lophurae organisms in bursectomized animals. Active, acquired immunity to *Plasmodium* did develop, however, as evidenced by the fact that bursectomized chicks could not be reinfected even with high doses of *Plasmodium* organisms. When chicks were bursectomized at 18 days of age, parasitemias did not differ significantly from controls, suggesting a slight effect of bursectomy when performed at 1 day of age. It would be of considerable interest to re-examine bacterial, viral, and parasitic infections in known agammaglobu-linemic chicks to more clearly establish the course of these infections in the absence of any humoral antibody formation.

I. FUNCTION OF THE BURSA IN AUTOIMMUNE AND NEOPLASTIC DISEASES

Although additional autoimmune diseases are likely to be recognized in the chicken, only autoimmune thyroiditis, a spontaneously occurring hereditary disease in white Leghorn chickens of the obese strain (OS), has been characterized and has received considerable attention in the past few years (Cole *et al.*, 1968; Witebsky *et al.*, 1969; Wick *et al.*, 1970a,b). The disease is phenotypically expressed by clinical symptoms of hypothyroidism, obesity, long silky feathers, and poor laying ability (Van Tienhoven and Cole, 1962; Cole, 1966). The characteristic histo-logical feature is the infiltration of thyroid glands by large and small lymphocytes and the appearance of large numbers of plasma cells, as well as germinal centers (Kite *et al.*, 1969). Neonatal and *in ovo* bursec-tomy have lowered the frequency and severity of the disease in OS chickens, and this inhibitory effect, in general, was paralleled by a lack of demonstrable precipitating and hemagglutinating serum antibodies directed against thyroglobulin (Wick *et al.*, 1970a). Neonatal thymec-tomy, on the other hand, resulted in a striking increase in the incidence and severity of chronic thyroiditis and thyroglobulin antibodies were detected in the majority of these animals (Wick *et al.*, 1970b). The latter finding has led these investigators to suggest a possible controlling function of the intact chick thymus over the "self recognition mecha-nism," a concept that had been originally postulated by Burnet (1962). Additional studies suggest that other organs in addition to the thyroid may occasionally be involved in the disease process and precipitating antibodies to extracts of liver and kidney have been reported (Wick, 1970). The convincing characterization of these as autoantibodies, di-rected against the respective organs, awaits additional work.

With regard to the influence of the bursa on development of neoplastic diseases in the chicken, only lymphoid leukosis and Marek's disease (MD) have received considerable experimentation. Lymphoid leukosis, or visceral lymphomatosis has been reported to be preventable by bur-sectomy (Peterson *et al.*, 1964; 1966; Cooper *et al.*, 1968). The neoplastic changes first appear within bursal follicles and, because the disease is preventable by bursectomy, it has been suggested that the spread of the neoplasm is due to metastasis of virally transformed cells from the bursa (Peterson et al., 1964, 1966). However, it is equally conceivable that the virus has a predilection for bursal lymphocytes but can infect bursa-dependent cells in the peripheral lymphoid tissue as well as those in the bursa. More controversial reports exist on the effect of bursectomy on the development of Marek's disease. The most recent and best documented study by Payne and Rennie (1970) showed that surgical bursectomy of 1-day-old chicks with or without total body irradiation did not influence the mortality from Marek's disease induced by HPRS-16 strain of virus. The development of MD in chicks with varying degrees of well documented impairment of the bursal lymphoid system, including some chickens that lacked antibodies, immunoglobulins, germinal follicles, and plasma cells, suggests that bursa and bursa-dependent lymphoid tissue were not essential in the pathogenesis of the disease. An earlier study by Kenyon et al. (1969) supports these findings, whereas Foster and Moll (1968) reported a decreased incidence of MD and Morris et al. (1969) reported an increased incidence of MD following bursectomy. Some of the differences in the results could be due to differences in the strain of virus, the type of inoculum, or the strain of chick used. Varying degrees of immunological suppression in bursectomized chicks could also have been responsible for the discrepant results obtained by different investigators.

J. Effect of Bursectomy on the Reticuloendothelial and Hematopoietic System

Several studies have indicated that the development of the macrophage system in the chicken following bursectomy is not significantly altered. Surgically bursectomized chickens were fully competent in phagocytizing carbon particles or S. aureus (Glick et al., 1964). Cooper et al. (1966a) were similarly unable to find any impairment of clearance of colloidal gold or hemocyanin tagged with an isotope in surgically bursectomized, irradiated chickens. However, if the influence of the bursa on the macrophage system should be one of extreme sensitivity, then one could argue that previously employed bursectomy procedures may not have been sufficiently complete to reveal such an effect. Also, there is thus far no information whether the intracellular handling of antigen in agammaglobulinemic chickens differs from that in normal animals.

It was recently reported that anemia commonly occurs in bursectomized irradiated chickens, as compared to control irradiated chickens. The hematocrit (Ht) and hemoglobin (Hb) values, the rbc counts, and MCHC were significantly depressed in bursectomized irradiated chickens and significantly fewer mature red blood cells were found in the bone marrow of anemic birds. The anemia was however not further defined as a hemolytic, aregenerative, or other type. Viral and bacterial infection were mentioned in consideration of possible causes and a humoral or cellular influence of the bursa on the hematopoietic regulatory system was suggested (Alm and Peterson, 1971).

K. MECHANISM OF BURSAL FUNCTION

The evidence presented above strongly favors the view that the bursa is an anatomical site where immigrant, undifferentiated stem cells of yolksac origin initially serve as precursors of a developing lymphocyte population that begins to differentiate into immunoglobulin producing cells late in embryonic life and continues to do so in the posthatching period. The epithelial component of the bursa may somehow serve as an inducing microenvironment during this entire phase, possibly through release of a locally active humoral factor, but evidence for this is lacking. Available data further suggest that in the bursa, cells producing IgG develop perhaps exclusively from cells that previously synthesized IgM as a normal event of differentiation to the plasma cell line. A switch by cells from IgM to IgG synthesis in peripheral tissues is believed to be a rare occurrence. As discussed by Kincade *et al.* (1970), antibody variability as well as class heterogeneity may be generated within the bursa. Once seeded from the bursa, cells may be irrevocably committed to the production of a single class and specificity of antibody. The bursa may therefore have a critical role in directing genetic events by which antibody heterogeneity is generated. Still undetermined is whether uncommitted stem cells continue to enter the bursa in the posthatching period, perhaps from bone marrow, for subsequent differentiation into immunocompetent cells, or whether bursal cell proliferation in the posthatching period is self-sustaining, without additional cell influx. The failure of the locally irradiated and lymphocyte-depleted bursa to repopulate with lymphoid cells suggests that stem cells no longer enter the bursa in the posthatching period, but radiation induced damage to the cellular microenvironment could be another explanation for failure of lymphocyte repopulation by cell influx (Weber and Weidanz, 1969). In the observed failure of lymphoid repopulation following cyclophosphamide-induced bursal cell depletion in the immediate posthatching period, similar considerations have been advanced (Glick, 1971). Direct evidence, obtained with localized infusion of [³H]thymidine into bursal tissue followed by analysis of splenic tissue for radioactivity, suggests migration of cells from the bursa to peripheral lymphoid tissue (Woods and Linna, 1965). Other work involving transplantation of bursal tissue to bursectomized chicks (Janković and Leskowitz, 1965) or implantation of bursal tissue in Millipore chambers (St. Pierre and Ackerman, 1965) suggested in addition a possible humoral factor in the development of humoral antibody-producing capability in the chicken. These experiments have not been confirmed (Dent *et al.*, 1968) and to date only additional evidence further discounting a bursa-derived humoral factor has been published (Thompson and Cooper, 1971).

Very little is known about the possibly continued functions of the bursa in young adult chickens. The bursa begins to involute at approximately 6–8 weeks of age, the exact time depending on the strain of chick under study, and has essentially disappeared as a discrete structure by 20 weeks of age. It would be of interest to know if a bursa undergoing involution could be called into a temporary regenerative phase following destruction of the mature and fully developed humoral antibody-producing cell lineage in the peripheral lymphoid tissues.

IV. The Function of the Thymus in the Immune System of the Chick

A. Histological Effects of Thymectomy

The thymus in the chicken appears to be almost exclusively concerned in reactions assigned to cell-mediated and transplantation immunity, placing this organ in direct functional opposition to the bursa of Fabricius. Thymectomy causes a marked reduction in the levels of peripheral blood small lymphocytes (Warner and Szenberg, 1962), especially when thymectomy is followed by X-irradiation (Cooper *et al.*, 1966a). This is accompanied by a reduction of small lymphocytes in the spleen and cecal tonsils, leaving the number of plasma cells and germinal follicles in these locations largely unaffected (Janković and Isaković, 1964; Cooper *et al.*, 1966a). Janković and Isaković (1964) also reported a lymphocytic depletion in the bursa following thymectomy, with replacement of small lymphocytes in many follicles by cells with deeply basophilic cytoplasm. The significance of this observation is not established, but this effect on the bursa could be due to a generalized postthymectomy stress since Glick (1967) reported that cortisone can induce a temporary bursal lymphocyte depletion.

B. The Thymus in Transplantation Immunity and Cellular Immune Competence of Thymus Cells

Prolongation of the skin homograft rejection time occurs following neonatal thymectomy (Warner and Szenberg, 1962; Aspinall *et al.*, 1963; Ruth *et al.*, 1964; Meyer and Aspinall, 1964), and appears to be more evident when skin grafts are applied within a few weeks after thymec-tomy (Warner and Szenberg, 1962, 1964b). That the thymus and its derived lymphocyte population are involved in transplantation immunity has also been convincingly shown with the chorioallantoic pock assay. The CAM assay determines the competence of a given cell population to react against histocompatibility antigens of the allogenic chick embryo and to produce lesions or pocks on the CAM. When blood and splenic lymphocytes of hormonally bursectomized chickens were tested, the number of pocks produced did not differ significantly from those pro-duced by blood and splenic lymphocytes of intact chicks (Warner *et al.*, 1962). It was later shown that thymus cells themselves could produce pocks on the CAM of allogeneic embryos and the results indicated that the competent cell population was derived primarily from the medulla, rather than the cortex of the thymus (Warner, 1964). Cain *et al.* (1968) similarly demonstrated that thymus cells were capable of inducing a GVHR in allogeneic embryos. More recently, *in vitro* studies demon-strated that chick medullary thymus cells but not cortical cells can re-spond with proliferation when mixed in culture with allogeneic thymus cells, and, on a numerical basis, medullary thymus cells were nearly as competent to respond against foreign histocompatibility antigens than were spleen cells (Weber, 1970). In line with these observations is the ability of chick thymus cells to respond with DNA synthesis to phyto-hemaglutinin as compared to the inability of bursal cells (Weber, 1967; Section III,G). Neonatal thymectomy, but not bursectomy, reduced the ability of peripheral blood lymphocytes (Greaves *et al.*, 1968) or splenic lymphocytes (Meuwissen *et al.*, 1969) to respond to PHA.

C. The Thymus and Cell-Mediated Immunity

Whereas allergic encephalomyelitis and thyroiditis can be experimen-tally induced with great uniformity in normal and bursectomized chickens, the occurrence of these experimentally induced diseases is markedly reduced in thymectomized chickens (Janković and Isvaneski, 1963). Similarly, the intensity of delayed wattle reactions to thyroid extract, tuberculin, and spinal cord lipid is reduced in thymectomized chicks (Janković and Isvaneski, 1963; Janković *et al.*, 1965). Cooper *et al.* (1966a) found that the development of delayed hypersensitivity to diphtheria toxoid occurred in only 2/14 thymectomized irradiated chickens in contrast to 100% of controls giving a positive response. The failure of thymectomy to yield clearcut evidence of suppression of cell-mediated immune reactions as compared to suppression of humoral anti-body-producing capability after the more critical bursectomy procedures

is probably due to the extreme difficulty of achieving complete thymec-
tomies in neonatal chicks. It is also known that the thymus develops
slightly earlier than the bursa, and it is therefore conceivable that
peripheralization of some thymus-dependent cells occurred already prior
to thymectomy in the neonatal period (Warner and Szenberg, 1964a).

D. THE THYMUS AND HUMORAL ANTIBODY FORMATION

The influence of the thymus and participation of thymus cells in
humoral antibody production is still controversial, and because of the
difficulties of achieving effective depletion of thymus-derived cells, this
is likely to remain an unfinished chapter in the foreseeable future.
Normal levels of antibody to human gamma globulin (Warner and Szenberg, 1962) and to human red blood cells (Isaković et al., 1963) were
evoked in chickens that had been surgically thymectomized at hatching.
Graetzer et al. (1963) studied the response of thymectomized chickens
to bovine serum albumin and found an essentially normal response in
94% of the chickens, but 6% of the birds failed to form detectable levels
of antibody. A reduction in the mean titer of antibody to B. abortus
and to BSA in thymectomized chickens was reported by Cooper et
al. (1965). However, this reduction in the mean titer was mainly due
to several birds that failed to make any response at all, and those
chickens that did respond made essentially normal levels of antibody.
More recent experiments have demonstrated that a cell population exists
in the chick thymus that is potentially capable of producing antibody.
When thymus fragments of adult donors, hyperimmunized with human
O red blood cells were transferred to the chorioallantoic membrane
of 12 day embryos, 87% of chicks had detectable levels of anti-O hemagglutinins 7 days after hatching, whereas none were found at this time
in chicks sham grafted in ovo, or grafted with freeze-thawed thymus
tissue (Janković and Isaković, 1968). Gilmour et al. (1970) were able
to transfer a response to sheep erythrocytes as well as to B. abortus
following intraperitoneal injection of thymus cells of preimmunized
4-week-old donors to hormonally bursectomized, irradiated chicks. Without preimmunization, the intraperitoneally injected thymus cells of
10-week-old donors also produced good levels of antibody to B. abortus
in 6/7 bursectomized, irradiated chicks that had been challenged i.p.
with antigen. In contrast, thymus cells of 4-week-old donors produced
a response to B. abortus in only 2/8 chicks, and a primary response
to sheep erythrocytes by intraperitoneally transferred thymus cells from
4- or 10-week-old donors was detectable in only 1/22 and 2/15 chicks,
respectively. These experiments indicate that the ability of a thymus

cell population to transfer an antibody response depends not only on the age of the cell donor, but also on the type of antigen used and whether or not donors were preimmunized. Other factors such as route of cell and antigen transfer probably also play a role (Section III,D). It is conceivable, although not yet convincingly shown, that these thymus-residing cells potentially capable of producing humoral antibody to several antigens are immigrant bursa-derived cells that are localized primarily in the medulla of the thymus. It is of interest that to date no clearcut evidence of cell cooperation between thymus and bursal cells in humoral antibody production has been reported (Gilmour *et al.*, 1970).

E. *In Vivo* Effects of Anti-lymphocyte Antibody

Recent reports suggest that antisera directed against bursa and thymus cells respectively may be useful in further delineating the functional differences of these two organs and lymphocytes derived from them. Janković *et al.* (1970a) studied the *in vivo* effects of repeatedly administered rabbit anti-bursa globulin (ABG) in 4-week-old chicks and recorded suppression of antibody to BGG, a moderate decrease in the number of germinal centers and plasma cells in the spleen but no significant histological effects in the thymus, bursa, cecal tonsils, Peyer's patches, and lymphoid masses of the gut. Experimentally induced allergic encephalomyelitis was not suppressed by ABG. All of the *in vivo* effects were elicited only when ABG and guinea pig complement were simultaneously administered, and some were not restricted to ABG. In fact, a more severe suppression of antibody response to BGG was observed when anti-thymus globulin (ATG) was similarly employed, and lymphocytopenia was observed after injection of ATG, ABG, and normal rabbit globulin. Following ATG administration, suppression of allergic encephalomyelitis and a moderate depletion of small lymphocytes in the spleen were noted. These results indicate nonspecificity of the ATG and ABG, and this is supported by additional *in vitro* experiments. Thus, assays by means of absorption, leukoagglutination, cytotoxicity tests, and passive hemagglutination revealed equally good reactions of ABG and ATG with both thymus and bursal cells (Janković *et al.*, 1970b). When chick embryos received 10 daily injections of ATG or ABG into the chorioallantoic cavity between the seventh and tenth week of incubation, high mortality (75–80%) resulted when either preparation was used in the presence of guinea pig complement. ABG caused a marked reduction in the number of bursal follicles and a diffuse granulocytic infiltration of the bursal folds. However, ATG produced similar, though slightly less severe changes in the bursa and, in addition, loss of recognizable follicular structure of the splenic white pulp. No changes were observed in the thymus after ATG and ABG injections.

In contrast to the above anti-lymphocyte preparations with largely nonspecific effects, Potworowski et al. (1971) reported highly specific bursa and thymus cell antisera. He obtained almost complete inhibition of hemolytic plaque formation when spleen cell preparations of immunized normal chickens were incubated in vitro with bursa-specific antisera, while incubation with thymus antisera had virtually no inhibiting effect. Separate antigenic specificities for thymus and bursa cells do appear to exist (Forget et al., 1971), but it remains to be seen if the specificity of the antisera obtained by some investigators can be independently observed by others. Some of the reported differences in the specificities of the antisera may be largely due to the age of the cell donors, the purity of the cell population, the use of intact versus lyophylized cells used for immunization, selection of species for immunization, types of cells used for cross absorption, and as yet undefined factors.

Acknowledgment

Work reported in this paper was supported by Public Health Service Grant AM 11693 from the Institute of Arthritis and Metabolic Diseases.

References

Ackerman, G. A. (1962). J. Cell Biol. 13, 127.
Ackerman, G. A., and Knouff, R. A. (1959). Amer. J. Anat. 104, 163.
Ackerman, G. A., and Knouff, R. A. (1964). Anat. Rec. 149, 191.
Alm, G. V., and Peterson, R. D. A. (1969). J. Exp. Med. 129, 1247.
Alm, G. V., and Peterson, R. D. A. (1971). Nature (London) 229, 201.
Aspinall, R. L., Meyer, R. K., Graetzer, M. A., and Wolfe, H. R. (1963). J. Immunol. 90, 872.
Benedict, A. A., Brown, R. J., and Hersh, R. T. (1963). J. Immunol. 90, 399.
Burnet, F. M. (1962). Brit. Med. J. 2, 807.
Cain, W. A., Cooper, M. D., and Good, R. A. (1968). Nature (London) 217, 87.
Carey, J., and Warner, N. L. (1964). Nature (London) 203, 198.
Chang, T. S., Rheins, M. S., and Winter, A. R. (1957). Poultry Sci. 36, 735.
Chaperon, E. (1965). Ph.D. Thesis, University of Wisconsin, Madison.
Cheville, N. F. (1970). Amer. J. Pathol. 58, 105.
Cheville, N. F., and Richards, W. D. (1971). Amer. J. Pathol. 64, 97.
Claflin, A. J., Smithies, O., and Meyer, R. K. (1966). J. Immunol. 97, 693.
Claman, H. N. (1966). Proc. Soc. Exp. Biol. Med. 121, 236.
Cole, R. K. (1966). Genetics 53, 1020.
Cole, R. K., Kite, J. H., and Witebsky, E. (1968). Science 160, 1357.

Cooper, M. D., Peterson, R. D. A., and Good, R. A. (1965). *Nature* (*London*) **205**, 143.

Cooper, M. D., Peterson, R. D. A., South, M., and Good, R. A. (1966a). *J. Exp. Med.* **123**, 75.

Cooper, M. D., Schwartz, M. M., and Good, R. A. (1966b). *Science* **151**, 471.

Cooper, M. D., Payne, L. N., Dent, P. B., Burmester, B. R., and Good, R. A. (1968). *J. Nat. Cancer Inst.* **41**, 373.

Cooper, M. D., Cain, W. A., Van Alten, P. J., and Good, R. A. (1969). *Int. Arch. Allergy Appl. Immunol.* **35**, 242.

Dent, P. B., and Good, R. A. (1965). *Nature* (*London*) **207**, 491.

Dent, P. B., Perey, D. Y. E., Cooper, M. D., and Good, R. A. (1968). *J. Immunol.* **101**, 799.

Dwyer, J. M., and Warner, N. L. (1971). *Nature* (*London*) **229**, 210.

Forget, A., Potworowski, E. F., Richer, G., and Borduas, A. G. (1970). *Immunology* **19**, 465.

Foster, A. G., and Moll, T. (1968). *Amer. J. Vet. Res.* **29**, 1831.

Fujiwara, A., Landau, J. W., and Newcomer, V. D. (1970). *Sabouradia* **8**, 9.

Gilmour, D. G., Theis, G. A., and Thorbecke, G. J. (1970). *J. Exp. Med.* **132**, 134.

Glick, B. (1956). *Poultry Sci.* **35**, 843.

Glick, B. (1960). *Poultry Sci.* **39**, 130.

Glick, B. (1967). *J. Immunol.* **98**, 1076.

Glick, B. (1971). *Transplantation* **11**, 433.

Glick, B., and Sato, K. (1964). *Amer. J. Physiol.* **207**, 1371.

Glick, B., Chang, T. S., and Japp, R. C. (1956). *Poultry Sci.* **35**, 224.

Glick, B., Sato, K., and Cohenour, F. (1964). *J. Reticuloendothel. Soc.* **1**, 442.

Graetzer, M. A., Wolfe, H. R., Aspinall, R. L., and Meyer, R. K. (1963). *J. Immunol.* **90**, 878.

Greaves, M. F., Roitt, I. M., and Rose, M. E. (1968). *Nature* (*London*) **220**, 293.

Hohn, E. O. (1956). *Can. J. Biochem. Physiol.* **34**, 90.

Isaković, K., and Janković, B. D. (1964). *Int. Arch. Allergy Appl. Immunol.* **24**, 296.

Isaković, K., Janković, B. D., Popesković, L., and Milosević, D. (1963). *Nature* (*London*) **200**, 273.

Janković, B. D., and Isaković, K. (1964). *Int. Arch. Allergy Appl. Immunol.* **24**, 278.

Janković, B. D., and Isaković, K. (1966). *Nature* (*London*) **211**, 202.

Janković, B. D., and Isaković, K. (1968). *Experientia* **24**, 1272.

Janković, B. D., and Isvaneski, M. (1963). *Int. Arch. Allergy Appl. Immunol.* **23**, 188.

Janković, B. D., and Leskowitz, S. (1965). *Proc. Soc. Exp. Biol. Med.* **118**, 1164.

Janković, B. D., Isvaneski, M., Milosević, D., and Popesković, L. (1963). *Nature* (*London*) **198**, 298.

Janković, B. D., Isvaneski, M., Popesković, L., and Mitrović, K. (1965). *Int. Arch. Allergy Appl. Immunol.* **26**, 18.

Janković, B. D., Isaković, K., Petrović, S., and Vujić, D. (1970a). *Clin. Exp. Immunol.* **7**, 693.

Janković, B. D., Isaković, K., Petrović, S., Vujić, D., and Horvat, J. (1970b). *Clin. Exp. Immunol.* **7**, 709.

Kemenes, F., and Pethes, G. (1963). *Z. Immunitaets- Allergieforsch.* **125**, 446.

Kenyon, A. J., Sevoian, M., and Horwitz, M. (1969). *Avian Dis.* **13**, 585.

Kincade, P. W., and Cooper, M. D. (1971). *J. Immunol.* **106**, 371.

Kincade, P. W., Lawton, A. R., Bockman, D. E., and Cooper, M. D. (1970). *Proc. Nat. Acad. Sci. U.S.* **67**, 1918.

Kincade, P. W., Lawton, A. R., and Cooper, M. D. (1971). *J. Immunol.* **106**, 1421.

Kite, J. H., Wick, G., Twarog, B., and Witebsky, E. (1969). *J. Immunol.* **103**, 1331.

Kono, R., Akao, Y., Sasagawa, A., and Nomura, Y. (1969). *Jap. J. Med. Sci. Biol.* **22**, 235.

Lerman, S. P., and Weidanz, W. P. (1969). *Bacteriol. Proc.* p. 91 (abstr.).

Lerman, S. P., and Weidanz, W. P. (1970). *J. Immunol.* **105**, 614.

Lerner, K., McDuffie, F. C., and Glick, B. (1970). *Fed. Proc., Fed. Amer. Soc. Exp. Biol.* **29**, 770.

Linna, T. J. (1970). *Fed. Proc., Fed. Amer. Soc. Exp. Biol.* **29**, 825.

Long, P. L., and Pierce, A. E. (1963). *Nature (London)* **200**, 426.

Longenecker, B. M., Breitenbach, R. P., and Farmer, J. N. (1966). *J. Nat. Cancer Inst.* **97**, 594.

Meuwissen, H. J., Van Alten, P. J., Cooper, M. D., and Good, R. A. (1969). *In* "Proceedings of the Third Leukocyte Culture Conference" (W. O. Rieke, ed.), p. 227. Appleton, New York.

Meyer, R. K., and Aspinall, R. L. (1964). *In* "The Thymus in Immunobiology" (R. A. Good and A. E. Gabrielsen, eds.), p. 376. Harper (Hoeber), New York.

Meyer, R. K., Rao, M. A., and Aspinall, R. L. (1959). *Endocrinology* **64**, 890.

Moore, M. A. S., and Owen, J. J. T. (1966). *Develop. Biol.* **14**, 40.

Moore, M. A. S., and Owen, J. J. T. (1967). *J. Exp. Med.* **126**, 723.

Morris, J. R., Jerome, F. N., and Reinhart, B. S. (1969). *Poultry Sci.* **48**, 1513.

Mueller, A. P., Wolfe, H. R., and Meyer, R. K. (1960). *J. Immunol.* **85**, 172.

Ortega, L. G., and Der, B. K. (1964). *Fed. Proc., Fed. Amer. Soc. Exp. Biol.* **23**, 546.

Payne, L. N., and Rennie, M. (1970). *J. Nat. Cancer Inst.* **45**, 387.

Peterson, R. D. A., Burmester, B. R., Frederickson, T. N., Purchase, H. G., and Good, R. A. (1964). *J. Nat. Cancer Inst.* **32**, 1343.

Peterson, R. D. A., Purchase, H. G., Burmester, B. R., Cooper, M. D., and Good, R. A. (1966). *J. Nat. Cancer Inst.* **36**, 585.

Peterson, R. D. A., Alm, G. V., and Michalek, S. (1971). *J. Immunol.* **106**, 1609.

Pierce, A. E.; Chubb, R. C., and Long, P. L. (1966). *Immunology* **10**, 321.

Potworowski, E. F., Richer, G., Borduas, A., and Forget, A. (1971). *J. Immunol.* **106**, 1416.

Rabellino, E., and Grey, H. M. (1971). *J. Immunol.* **106**, 1418.

Romanoff, A. L. (1960). *In* "The Avian Embryo," pp. 1305. Macmillan, New York.

Rose, M. E., and Orlans, E. (1968). *Nature (London)* **217**, 231.

Ruth, R. F., Allen, C. P., and Wolfe, H. R. (1964). *In* "The Thymus in Immunobiology" (R. A. Good and A. E. Gabrielsen, eds.), p. 183. Harper (Hoeber), New York.

St. Pierre, R. L., and Ackerman, G. A. (1965). *Science* **137**, 1307.

Schwarz, M. R. (1965). *Anat. Rec.* **151**, 414 (abstr.).

Szenberg, A., and Warner, N. L. (1962). *Nature (London)* **194**, 147.

Takada, A., Takada, Y., and Abrus, L. (1971). *Proc. Soc. Exp. Biol.* **136**, 222.

Thompson, J. H., and Cooper, M. D. (1971). *Transplantation* 11, 71.

Thorbecke, G. J., Warner, N. L., Hochwald, G. M., and Ohanion, S. H. (1968). *Immunology* 15, 123.

Van Alten, P. J., Good, R. A., and Meuwissen, H. J. (1969). *Int. Arch. Allergy Appl. Immunol.* 35, 381.

Van Tienhoven, A., and Cole, R. K. (1962). *Anat. Rec.* 142, 111.

Warner, N. L. (1964). *Aust. J. Exp. Biol. Med. Sci.* 42, 401.

Warner, N. L. (1965). *Aust. J. Exp. Biol. Med. Sci.* 43, 439.

Warner, N. L. (1967). *Folia Biol. (Prague)* 13, 1–17.

Warner, N. L., and Szenberg, A. (1962). *Nature (London)* 196, 784.

Warner, N. L., and Szenberg, A. (1964a). *Annu. Rev. Microbiol.* 18, 253.

Warner, N. L., and Szenberg, A. (1964b). *In* "The Thymus in Immunobiology" (R. A. Good and A. E. Gabrielsen, eds.), p. 395. Harper (Hoeber), New York.

Warner, N. L., Szenberg, A., and Burnet, F. (1962). *Aust. J. Exp. Biol. Med. Sci.* 40, 373.

Warner, N. L., Uhr, J. W., Thorbecke, G. J., and Ovary, Z. (1969). *J. Immunol.* 103, 1317.

Warner, N. L., Ovary, Z., and Kantor, F. S. (1971). *Int. Arch. Allergy Appl. Immunol.* 40, 719.

Weber, W. T. (1966). *J. Cell. Physiol.* 68, 117.

Weber, W. T. (1967). *Exp. Cell Res.* 46, 464.

Weber, W. T. (1970). *Clin. Exp. Immunol.* 6, 919.

Weber, W. T. (1972). *Cell. Immunol.* (in press).

Weber, W. T., and Eichholtz, D. (1971). *J. Reticuloendothel. Soc.* 9, 53.

Weber, W. T., and Weidanz, W. P. (1969). *J. Immunol.* 103, 537.

Weber, W. T., and Weidanz, W. P. (1970). *Reticuloendothel. Soc. Meet., 7th, 1970.* p. 50.

Wick, G. (1970). *Clin. Exp. Immunol.* 7, 187.

Wick, G., Kite, J. H., Cole, R. K., and Witebsky, E. (1970a). *J. Immunol.* 104, 45.

Wick, G., Kite, J. H., and Witebsky, E. (1970b). *J. Immunol.* 104, 54.

Witebsky, E., Kite, J. H., Wick, G., and Cole, R. K. (1969). *J. Immunol.* 103, 708.

Woods, R., and Linna, T. J. (1965). *Acta Pathol. Microbiol. Scand.* 64, 470.

3 CELL-MEDIATED IMMUNITY RESPONSES IN PARASITIC INFECTIONS

E. J. L. SOULSBY

I. Introduction

This review comes at a time of rapid progress in cellular immunity. It is a time when the traditional boundaries between immunity mediated by lymphoid cells and immunity mediated by antibody are indistinct and, indeed, may be untenable. Recent advances in the field of "cell-mediated immunity" have introduced, for example, the concepts of soluble nonantibody mediators of cellular events, such mediators being the by-products of immunologically specific reactions (lymphokines— Dumonde *et al.*, 1969). The role of the T cell (thymus-dependent lymphocyte) in this process is well recognized. However, it is also well established that interactions between T cells and B cells (bursa- or bone marrow-derived cells) are essential processes in several immune responses (J. F. A. P. Miller *et al.*, 1971).

In the complex immune systems that attend many, if not all, parasitic infections it is especially difficult to separate the component parts of the immune response. It would seem that the most appropriate approach in this review would be a consideration of studies dealing with lymphoid cell responsiveness in parasitic infections, regardless of the end result of such a response. This approach, because of the necessity of abbreviated treatment of the facts, may result in a less than acceptable proportionate impression of the situation. This is considered preferrable to an approach in which only mechanisms ascribable to "cell-mediated immunity" or delayed hypersensitivity are considered. The danger of the latter approach is that the existence of one or more parameters of "cell-mediated immunity" in an infection may lead to a conclusion that this is the sole mechanism that operates. The need for caution in the interpretation of immunological events in parasitic infections has been emphasized previously (Soulsby, 1970).

As far as can be determined, there have been no studies using specific reagents to antigenic markers of T and B cells to determine the origin of lymphoid cells that contribute to immune reactions in parasitic infections. The delineation of lymphoid cell populations based upon their antigenic characteristics will contribute very substantially to an understanding of the immune response to parasitism.

II. Cell-Mediated Immunity Responses—General

Cell-mediated immunity has been defined as immunity mediated primarily by lymphoid cells rather than by humoral antibody. It is transferable by lymphoid cells but not by serum.

Cell-mediated immunity responses require T cell activation, probably via recognition units, or receptors, on their surface and these most likely are immunoglobulin molecules or fragments of such. The evidence for this is discussed by J. F. A. P. Miller *et al.* (1971).

The specific activation of sensitized T cells results in the production of soluble, nonantibody, mediators that serve as nonspecific effectors of the immune event. These have been termed "lymphokines" by Dumonde *et al.* (1969). Dumonde and Maini (1971) have listed some eleven soluble factors generated by antigen-specific lymphocyte activation. Of these, the most familiar are the following.

A. Lymphocyte Mitogenic Factor (Lymphocyte Blastogenic Factor) (Wolstencroft and Dumonde, 1970)

This is responsible for the enhancement of lymphocyte DNA synthesis and blastogenesis of both sensitized lymphocytes and nonsensitized lymphocytes. Spitler and Lawrence (1969) have shown that the blastogenesis of lymphocytes by this material is proportional to the degree of antigenic stimulation that occurs in the donor cells as measured by radioactive thymidine incorporation. Exposure of normal lymphocytes to the supernatants from cultures of activated sensitized lymphocytes for 1 hour or less will cause mitogenesis (Caron and Poutala, 1969). There is, at present, a dearth of knowledge about the nature of the mitogenic factor; however, its relationship to cellular happenings in cell-mediated immunity lesions is significant. When in pathological states, there is an inability to mount a delayed hypersensitivity response as in miliary tuberculosis, Hodgkin's disease, and chronic lymphocytic leukemia, a markedly reduced blastogenic effect is evident (Melnick, 1971).

B. Macrophage Migration Inhibition Factor (MIF) (David, 1966; Bloom and Bennett, 1970)

This is responsible for the *in vitro* inhibition of migration of peritoneal cavity macrophages from capillary tubes. It has been reported also (Soborg, 1969) that this factor will result in the inhibition of migration of polymorphonuclear leukocytes. MIF is a nondialyzable and heat stable substance produced by lymphocytes cultured in the presence of a specific sensitizing antigen. It is elaborated within 6 hours of contact between cells and antigen but production may continue for as long as 4 days. Its production is inhibited by inhibitors of RNA and protein synthesis. MIF has a molecular weight of 50,000 to 75,000 and an electrophoretic mobility in the range of alpha globulins. However, dissociation of MIF from the antigen that induced it have proved difficult. Some MIF preparations from which antigen has been partially removed are enhanced by the further addition of antigen while definite antigen dependence of MIF has been demonstrated by Amos and Lachmann (1970).

C. Lymphotoxin (Lymphocytotoxic Factor, Cytopathic Factor)

This lymphokine causes cytotoxicity of target cells and also "innocent bystander" cells (Kolb and Granger, 1968; Ruddle and Waksman, 1967, 1968). A cytolytic effect can be produced by nonsensitized lymphoid cells stimulated by the nonspecific mitogen PHA or by antibody to immunoglobulin or its subcomponents (Granger and Williams, 1968). In both cases the cytotoxic effect can be measured on target cells, such as L-cells, by morphological alterations or the release of isotopic markers such as ^{51}Cr.

D. Inflammatory Factor (Dumonde et al., 1969)

This, when injected intradermally, causes the accumulation of cells which characterize delayed hypersensitive responses. The reaction, which can be assessed by an assay of the accumulation of isotopically labeled albumin or red cells into a lesion, is probably a primary effector substance in cell-mediated immunity reactions, since it is via the inflammatory response that a lesion is rendered patent to other elements of the immune system.

E. Significance of the Lymphokines in Immunity

Further information on the soluble mediators of cellular immunity and their interrelationships is given by Dumonde and Maini (1971). These authors have proposed a concept that integrates the lymphokines into the immunological phenomena associated with both cell-mediated and antibody-mediated immunity. They suggest that the lymphokines, in various combinations, mediate allergic inflammation and immune surveillance and facilitate antibody production, and that these are the product of different subpopulations of sensitized lymphocytes. They envisage that one mediator system may exist and function in the absence of another type of mediator system, but in all the lymphokines are substances which "amplify and regulate" the responses of populations of lymphoid cells to specific antigens.

Many of the mechanisms of cell-mediated immunity have been elucidated with regard to transplantation immunity, autoimmunity, contact sensitivity, and tuberculin-induced hypersensitivity. It is not too difficult to envisage the capability of mononuclear cells to destroy tissue and organ allografts, especially when tissues can be infiltrated by these cells following vascularization. With protozoal infections it is possible to envisage that intracellular, or even extracellular parasites, may be the targets of sensitized lymphocytes or their lymphokines. However, with helminths, which are not subject to vascularization nor are readily affected by cytotoxic systems, different criteria must be developed to assess damage by the immune response. It will be important in the future to establish *in vitro* criteria for such reactions.

III. Cell-Mediated Immunity in Protozoal Infections

A. LEISHMANIASIS

As obligate intracellular parasites of macrophages, the *Leishmania* species are prime candidates for the study of cell-mediated immunity mechanisms in protozoal infections. Three principal types of disease are recognized, cutaneous (*Leishmania tropica*), mucocutaneous (*Leishmania braziliensis*), and visceral (*Leishmania donovani*). Various subtypes of these are also recognized which may be due to variations in the virulence of the organism, the capacity of the vector to transmit, or the immunological competence of the host, either acting individually or in unison. In a recent review of immunological phenomena in leishmaniasis, Turk and Bryceson (1971) consider the infection as a spectral disease. With cutaneous leishmaniasis, one polar form consists of the disseminated cutaneous leishmaniases (DCL) of Venezuela and Ethiopia and the other polar form is lupoid leishmaniasis. The former is characterized by a lack of cell-mediated immunity and the latter by its exaggeration (Bryceson, 1970). Between these polar forms lie the majority of the cutaneous leishmaniases which occur clinically as discrete lesions that heal and result in immunity to reinfection. Turk and Bryceson (1971) consider kala azar to be a polar disease, being the visceral equivalent of DCL.

In cutaneous leishmaniasis, recovery from infection usually occurs and is followed by prolonged immunity. Following infection with promastigotes transmitted by the sandfly, amastigotes multiply in the local macrophages of the skin. Over the subsequent weeks a tissue response involving the accumulation of macrophages, lymphocytes, plasma cells, giant cells, and fibroblasts occurs. There is no generalization and no apparent change in the white blood count or serum proteins (Adler, 1963). With the accumulation of lymphocytes, macrophage proliferation ceases, the population declines, parasites decrease in numbers, and finally the lesion disappears. A delayed skin reaction develops within 6 weeks of the initial infection and persists thereafter following spontaneous cure. The existence of a delayed skin reaction is not an indication of immunity since it occurs before immunity to reinfection is established. Nevertheless, progression towards immunity is indicated by it and Dostrowsky *et al.* (1952) have shown that the current status of the original lesion (isophasic reaction) is produced on superinfection. Accelerated lesions are seen on reinfection of persons who have undergone spontaneous cure, ulceration occurring within a few days and resolution taking place quickly. Antibodies are not detectable in cutaneous leishmaniasis though Adler (1963) has remarked that the methods used for this may not be adequate to detect them. However, in experimental infections of the guinea pig with its parasite *Leishmania enriettii* immediate hypersensitivity skin reactions have been demonstrated at the time of the resolution of the lesion or at challenge (Bryceson *et al.*, 1970; Blewett, 1972) though antibodies related to this reaction (e.g., IgG_1 and IgE) cannot be detected in the serum by homologous passive cutaneous anaphylaxis (PCA) tests. Turk and Bryceson (1971) report unpublished studies in which antibody was detected by indirect immunofluorescence techniques in the serum of guinea pigs infected with *L. enriettii,* these being coincident with the development of lesions. The use of anti-guinea pig IgG_2 antisera suggested this antibody occurred in the γ_2 fraction and this would explain the absence of homocytotropic antibody activity in the serum as assessed by the PCA technique.

Leishmania enriettii in the guinea pig provides a useful animal model for the study of human cutaneous leishmaniasis. Evidence points to the fact that cell-mediated immunity mechanisms are the major components of the immune response. A single cutaneous lesion (e.g., on the dorsal aspect of the ear) ulcerates in 4–6 weeks after infection, resolves in 8–12 weeks, and is followed by long-lasting, if not permanent, immunity to reinfection (von Kretschmar, 1965; Blewett, 1972). Various *in vivo* and *in vitro* correlates of cell-mediated immunity have been demonstrated in the infection. Thus, Bryceson *et al.* (1970) and Blewett *et al.* (1971) have demonstrated delayed dermal hypersensitivity, antigen-induced lymphocyte transformation, and the inhibition of peritoneal macrophage migration by antigen. Supernatants from cultures of antigen-stimulated lymphocytes induced mitogenesis in other lymphocytes and caused the inhibition of migration of normal macrophages. Blewett (1972) demonstrated that the MIF was eluted from a Sephadex G-200 column in the albumin region and that no MIF activity occurred in the elution peaks that would normally contain immunoglobulins.

The role of lymphoid cells in the mediation of the curative process in cutaneous leishmaniasis might be anticipated in view of what is known about cell-mediated immunity mechanisms and the progression of events in cutaneous leishmaniasis. However, more direct and positive evidence for lymphocytes being the putative cells and for their production of lymphotoxin was presented by Bray and Bryceson (1968) and Bryceson *et al.* (1970). Using preauricular lymph nodes from guinea pigs recovered from *L. enriettii* infection, they demonstrated that immune lymphocytes, as opposed to normal lymphocytes, caused total destruction of a monolayer of amastigote infected macrophages within 24 hours. Parasitized macrophages were preferentially destroyed. However, lymph node cells from normal animals also affected monolayers of infected macrophage, but, in addition, they also had a comparable effect on noninfected monolayers. The specificity of this reaction has still to be determined, especially since lymph node cells from animals injected with Freund's complete adjuvant showed similar effects to the immune lymphoid cells.

It would be interesting to know whether in this system "innocent bystander cells" are destroyed when lymphocytes exert their cytotoxic effect. This might occur if cells in the lesion became coated with antigen after the destruction of parasite-infected macrophages. In this respect, Bryceson *et al.* (1970) have shown that macrophages passively coated with antigen suffer the same fate as infected cells in the presence of immune lymphocytes.

How amastigotes are destroyed in the healing process is unknown. They may be released from the macrophage and be lysed by local antibody, and an antibody of the γ_2 type would serve this function. An alternate mechanism might be for them to be taken up by other macrophages which have become activated as a result of the cell-mediated reaction possibly by a "macrophage activating factor" similar to that described by Barnet *et al.* (1968). An enhanced uptake of amasitgotes of *L. enriettii* by macrophages from immune animals has been demonstrated (Bryceson *et al.*, 1970), but there is no firm evidence that this is associated with an increased ability to destroy the organisms. Still a further possibility might be that newly infected macrophages rapidly become targets for sensitized lymphocytes or the cytotoxic lymphokine they produce. The efficacy of this mechanism, which would systematically destroy the sanctuary of the amastigote, would depend on how rapidly the macrophage expresses parasite antigens on its surface after invasion.

Delayed hypersensitivity has been transferred to normal guinea pigs by peritoneal cavity cells or lymph node cells from guinea pigs infected with *L. enriettii* or from animals immunized with promastigote antigen in Freund's complete adjuvant (Bryceson *et al.*, 1970). Successful transfer was also reported by Boysia (1968) using lymph node cells of guinea pigs sensitized to *L. donovani*, though, here also, sensitivity was induced by the injection of promastigotes in Freund's complete adjuvant.

In view of the ability to transfer delayed hypersentitivity to tuberculin in man with lymphoid cells (Landsteiner and Chase, 1942; Chase, 1945) or with a cell extract (Lawrence, 1969) it might be expected that delayed sensitivity to cutaneous leishmaniasis in man could be transferred in this manner. However, Adler and Nelkin (1965) were unable to do this with peripheral white cells or whole blood from a donor highly sensitive to the Montenegro reaction. Similarly, Bray and Bryceson (1965) failed to do this with cells from man and monkeys infected with *L. mexicana* and *L. braziliensis*. In the case of *L. braziliensis* it is interesting to note that Tremonti and Walton (1970) have demonstrated transformation of human peripheral lymphocytes by specific antigen, which indicates the potential of such cells to produce lymphokines, of which "transfer factor" is one.

The role of cell-mediated immunity in visceral leishmaniasis is less clear. Delayed dermal sensitivity occurs in cured cases of visceral leishmaniasis and in some recovered cases of kala azar a local skin lesion (post-kala azar leishmanoid) is seen. This sequel to visceral leishmaniasis is common in India and Kenya. It is seen within a year, or years, of cure of the visceral disease and occurs in the form of chronic lesions on the skin, face, limbs, or most of the body. The lesions are heavily infiltrated with macrophages, but there is a paucity of lymphocytes and such lesions rarely ulcerate (Maegraith, 1966).

There is massive involvement of the lymphoid macrophage system in visceral leishmaniasis, but the cell-mediated immunity response of the host is absent. There is a marked increase in serum gamma globulin and specific antibodies occur, but there is not necessarily a relationship between the two. Dumonde and Maini (1971) suggest that in visceral leishmaniasis the inflammatory and surveillance functions of the lymphokine systems of cell-mediated immunity are decreased, whereas the adjuvant function is increased in that it enhances antibody production and promotes autoimmune responses and the production of nonspecific immunoglobulin synthesis. They identify lymph node activation factor, mitogenic factor, and macrophage activating factor as the lymphokines responsible for this.

The absence of lymphocytic infiltration in post-kala azar dermal leishmanoid and in the diffuse cutaneous leishmaniases strongly suggests that the immune mechanisms regulating lymphoid cell activation, accumulation, and expression are seriously compromised. An analysis of these entities and the development of an experimental model for their study should go a long way toward an understanding of the whole spectrum of leishmanial infections. With the increased application of *in vitro* and *in vivo* techniques for the study of cell-mediated immunity, it should be possible to quantitate many of the immune reactions to leishmaniasis.

B. TOXOPLASMOSIS

Studies of the immune response to toxoplasmosis have been somewhat overshadowed by the efforts to develop serodiagnostic tests for the infection. The role of circulating antibody in resistance to toxoplasmosis has yet to be resolved and there is increasing information that antibody is not solely responsible for immunity. Thus Huldt (1966) reported that living parasites were necessary for the development of an adequate protective immunity in rodents and animals immunized with killed *Toxoplasma* organisms succumbed to challenge infections despite high levels of circulating antibody. Delayed hypersensitivity responses occur late in the course of human infection and a positive delayed skin reaction indicates a chronic form of the disease.

Correlates of cell-mediated immunity have been demonstrated in *Toxoplasma gondii* infection. For example, Frenkel (1948) reported dermal hypersensitivity in infected humans, monkeys, and guinea pigs and Tremonti and Walton (1970) have demonstrated antigen-induced lymphocyte blast transformation in culture and the inhibition of migration of peritoneal macrophages (MIF) from infected guinea pigs. Similarly Krahenbuhl et al. (1971) reported positive delayed skin tests in *Toxoplasma* infected guinea pig and the inhibition of macrophage migration. These reactions were evident as early as 1 week after infection. Earlier studies by Huldt (1967) had demonstrated antigen-induced blastogenesis of lymphocytes of the peripheral blood, spleen, and various lymph nodes of rabbits infected with *T. gondii* 7-9 weeks previously.

Further evidence that immunity to the parasite depends on cellular factors was presented by Frenkel (1967). These studies followed the demonstration by Vischer and Suter (1954) that immunity to *Toxoplasma* infection was mediated by macrophages and immune serum.

On the other hand, Frenkel demonstrated transfer of immunity by spleen and lymph node cells and a closely related form, *Besnoitia jellisoni*, showed similar requirements, though immunity to the two was species-specific. Immune serum showed a slight protective effect when transferred passively, but Frenkel considered this had little to do with successful transfer of immunity. Immunity was successfully transferred by cells in an isogeneic system, whereas in an allogeneic system appropriate conditioning of the recipients (total body irradiation) was necessary to avoid the rejection of the transferred cells. No cross-immunity was observed by Frenkel in his study of the cellular immune response to *B. jellisoni* and *T. gondii*. Both spleen and lymph node cells successfully transferred specific immunity to *Besnoitia* and *Toxoplasma;* however, *Besnoitia*-immune cells protected only against *Besnoitia* infections and *Toxoplasma*-immune cells against *Toxoplasma*. Furthermore, a bacterial infection (BCG) did not immunize against *B. jellisoni*.

However, in their studies of immunity to *Toxoplasma*, Ruskin and Remington (1968a) showed that immunity induced by *Toxoplasma* also induced resistance to the intracellular bacterium *Listeria monocytogenes*, to *Brucella melitensis* (Ruskin and Remington, 1968b), and to *Salmonella typhimurium*. Ruskin and Remington (1968b), and Remington and Merrigan (1969) further demonstrated that mice infected with *B. jellisoni* were able to resist a challenge infection of the above bacteria, as well as *Toxoplasma* and *B. jellisoni*. In initial studies, resistance to *Toxoplasma* was not demonstrated in mice immune to *Listeria;* however, later these authors found, using a less virulent strain of *Toxoplasma*, that *Listeria* organisms could induce immunity to the protozoan.

Additional evidence that intracellular organisms, such as bacteria and protozoa, can induce cross-resistance to each other is provided by subsequent work by Gentry and Remington (1971). Mice given a lethal dose of *Cryptococcus neoformans* showed decreased mortality, or increased survival before death, compared with controls when they were infected with *Besnoitia* or *Toxoplasma*. Such resistance was evident for as long as 20 months with certain strains of *Toxoplasma*. A comparable situation occurred in mice infected with *Listeria*. However, with the latter the resistance was evanescent unless restimulation occurred with live bacteria.

The present evidence indicates that "activated macrophages" are the effector mechanism for the resistance to the parasite. Mediating mechanisms dependent on circulating antibodies, such as enhanced reticuloendothelial clearance, do not appear to play a part since there is lack of enhanced clearance of intravenously administered carbon particles in *Besnoitia*-infected mice (Ruskin *et al.*, 1968).

C. Role of "Cellular Immunity" in Intracellular Parasitism

The situation described above (Section III,B) is reminiscent of the immune responses that occur with facultative intracellular bacterial forms such as *Listeria, Salmonella, Brucella*, etc. Extensive studies by Mackaness (1962) have shown that mice surviving an infection with *L. monocytogenes* are highly resistant to reinfection and show delayed dermal sensitivity to antigens of this bacterium. Mackaness and Blanden (1967) have demonstrated that this resistance is mediated by "activated macrophages," such cells showing increased synthesis of hydrolytic enzymes and liposomal granules. These macrophages, though capable of the destruction of intracellular bacteria, are incapable of transferring resistance to normal animals (Miki and Mackaness, 1964). Thus they function solely as a terminal cell in the effector limb of the immune response and their role is limited to their capacity to kill phagocytized organisms (Mackaness, 1969). Whether this function is associated with the macrophage activating factor described by Barnet *et al.* (1968), and which produces an enhancement of phagocytic capacity of cultured macrophages, requires to be demonstrated. Resistance to *L. monocytogenes* and the associated state of delayed hypersensitivity in the infection can be transferred with lymphoid cells from immune donors (Mackaness, 1969), whereas neither can be transferred with immune serum. North (1969) has shown that a required event for the passive transfer of immunity by lymphoid cells is that the mitotic potential of the recipient's cells must be intact. Thus, an active division of macrophages immediately precedes the onset of effective antimicrobial immunity and X-irradiated recipients of immune lymphoid cell fail to acquire protection. Recently North (1970a,b) has shown that though a marked proliferative response occurs in the macrophages of the liver and the peritoneal cavity, it is most likely that the fixed macrophages contribute minimally to the antibacterial immunity. Rather, the bactericidal activity derives from circulating monocytes which are being constantly produced by cell division and which accumulate at the sites of bacterial infection. A 15-hour pulse of vinblastine, given before infective foci are populated by activated macrophages, will inhibit the development of cellular immunity. An important finding in this work is that division of the Küppfer cells of the liver is irrelevant to the acquisition of immunity. The necessity for antigen–lymphoid cell contact in the activation of macrophages has been pointed out by Mackaness (1969) and it is possible that this contact results in the liberation of soluble effector substances, recognized in other situations as lymphokines.

Once macrophages are activated, their effector capacity to destroy intracellular organisms is nonspecific. As indicated previously, animals immunized to one of several intracellular organisms demonstrate immunity to the others (Mackaness, 1967). The specificity of the system lies in the need for specific antigen to trigger hypersensitive lymphoid cells. Thus, heterologous protection is initiated only after a recipient animal for sensitized cells has received a challenge of bacteria to which the donor cells were committed.

Since cellular immunity is mediated by lymphoid cells and other delayed hypersensitivity and cell-mediated immunity phenomena are similarly mediated, the question arises whether comparable populations of lymphoid cells can, when appropriately stimulated, produce soluble mediators with the same nonspecific effect against intracellular organisms. Work by Blanden (1969) shows that macrophages of mice undergoing a graft-versus-host reaction will show increased resistance to *Listeria* and *Salmonella*. A contrary opinion is expressed by Goihman-Yahr *et al.* (1969) who have shown that guinea pigs undergoing delayed hypersensitivity to tuberculin, contact dermatitis, and the graft-versus-host reaction failed to show any increased bactericidal response. These authors suggest that cellular immunity to bacterial organisms is restricted to such. However, this would seem to be an unduly restricted view of the situation since there has been a clear demonstration that the mechanism operates between intracellular protozoan and bacterial infections (see above). Additional evidence for this is the report by Adler (1954) that *Leishmania* infection of hamsters confers protection against *Plasmodium berghei* and one by Konopka *et al.* (1961) indicating that cross protection occurs between *Leishmania* and *Mycobacteria* species. Indeed, it is likely that resistance depending on macrophage activation extends to systems other than bacteria and protozoa. For example, Lunde and Gelderman (1971) reported a reciprocal resistance between chronic *Besnoitia jellisoni* infection and a congenital viral induced leukemia of AKR mice.

There are indications that comparable mechanisms may operate in helminth infections. Thus the growth of Walker sarcoma in rats infected with *Nippostrongylus brasiliensis* was either enhanced or suppressed according to timing of the infection in relation to the tumor growth. Rats infected five days before tumor implantation showed complete inhibition of the tumor growth (Keller *et al.*, 1971).

Further studies of this phenomenon by Keller and Jones (1971) have shown that activated peritoneal macrophages from donor rats infected with *N. brasiliensis* (or peptone-injected rats) engulf and destroy Walker tumor cells *in vitro*. Radio-sensitive cells in recipients of lymph node cells from helminth infected donors appear to be necessary for the response which can be inhibited by an IgG_2 component of antiserum of *N. brasiliensis*-infected rats.

Additional studies on the factors that mediate macrophage activation are clearly indicated since the phenomenon appears to occur in a wide range of intracellular and extracellular infections. For example, Ralston and Elberg (1969) have reported a macrophage ingestion promoting factor and Patterson and Youmans (1970) a low molecular weight serum factor(s) which facilitates the reduction in numbers of intracellular organisms (e.g., *M. tuberculosis*) by peritoneal macrophages when lymphocytic stimulation occurs. A factor possibly comparable to this has been recognized by Ralston and Elberg (1971). The substance appeared in the fourth protein peak of Sephadex G-200 fractionation and it promoted macrophage ingestion of *Brucella*. The relationship of this to the factor of Barnet *et al.* (1968), which when released from lymph node cells of immunized rabbits will induce erythrocyte phagocytosis of normal rabbit macrophages, has yet to be determined.

D. Interferon in Toxoplasmosis

The role of interferon and interferon producers in toxoplasmosis has been studied by Remington and Merrigan (1968). The production of interferon or interferonlike substances is associated with the antigenic stimulation of lymphoid cells and compounds associated with this family of substances are regarded as mediators of cellular immunity. Freshman *et al.* (1966) reported that interferon was detectable in serum and peritoneal fluid of mice infected with the Rh strain of *Toxoplasma* and it was characterized as being comparable to virus induced interferon. An interesting point was that the ability to stimulate interferon activity was correlated with the virulence of the *Toxoplasma* organism; thus, antiviral protection appeared more promptly with the Rh strain of *Toxoplasma* than with a less virulent form. Remington and Merrigan (1968) have shown that interferon will protect *in vitro* cultures from destruction by *Toxoplasma*. Interferon inducers, such as poly-IC and pyran, will induce resistance to *Toxoplasma in vivo* in mice (Remington and Merrigan, 1970). Clearly, the role of interferon and comparable substances in intracellular protozoan parasitic infections is a subject for more investigation.

E. Malaria

Early studies of avian malaria (Taliaferro, 1967) emphasized the role of cellular immunity in the protective mechanisms (phagocytosis by macrophages). A striking hyperplasia of the reticuloendothelial macrophages occurs, especially of those in the liver and spleen, though the specificity of this response is open to question and it has been suggested that it may be a nonspecific response to particular matter (MacCallum, 1969a,b). Hypertrophy of lymphoid organs occurs and the response here has been quantitated by Taliaferro and Taliaferro (1955) for *Plasmodium gallinaceum* and *Plasmodium lophurae*. In the spleen, "lymphatic nodules" increase as the parasitemia declines either on an initial or a super infection. This splenic response is also seen in mammalian malaria. This, and other evidence, would indicate that humoral factors play an important role in the protective mechanisms (Briggs *et al.,* 1966). The role of thymus-derived lymphocytes in the immune response to malaria is illustrated by experiments showing that neonatal thymectomy impairs the immune response. Thus, Stechschulte (1969a) has reported that neonatal thymectomy of rats reduced the protective immune response to *Plasmodium berghei*. Similar results have been reported by I. N. Brown *et al.* (1968) for *P. berghei* in rats and Longenecker and Breitenbach (1969) observed that bursectomy and thymectomy of chickens reduced the immune response to *P. lophurae*. Stechschulte (1969a) found that the failure of immune response in thymectomy was not due to a decreased phagocytic activity or antibody production, as measured by carbon clearance and various serological tests. In a further study, he (Stechschulte, 1969b) demonstrated that thoracic duct lymphocytes had less protective effect than lymphoid cells from lymph nodes and spleen in the transfer of protection of immunity to *P. berghei* in rats.

Investigations on the comparative ability of lymphoid cells and serum to transfer immunity in mice to *P. berghei* infection were conducted by Phillips (1970). Protection against homologous challenge with *P. berghei* was transferred both with serum and with cells but more effectively with the latter. Spleen cells, those of a peritoneal exudate, and a mixture of lymph node, thymus, and bone marrow cells were all effective. In some cases, serum from rats was nonprotective while their cells were protective. The reliance on living cells was indicated by the fact that disintegration of immune cells destroyed their ability to protect. In one experiment, splenectomy of the recipient of cells reduced the effectiveness of the transfer. Possibly this might be due to the role of the spleen as a site of phagocytosis, or alternatively, the transferred cells might concentrate in the spleen. Both factors may be important in this situation. Such evidence as the above would suggest that cell-mediated immunity mechanisms are less concerned in malarial infection than humoral antibodies. Additional evidence for this is provided by the studies of Barker and Powers (1971). They reported that treatment of *P. berghei*-infected mice with anti-lymphocyte serum (ALS) produced a delayed recovery from the malarial infection which was associated with a marked delay in the antibody response to the infection. Nevertheless, these authors caution that ALS treatment can suppress several immune mechanisms which have been shown to be associated with recovery from *P. berghei* infection.

The present evidence that thymus-dependent cells are not solely concerned with cell-mediated immunity mechanisms indicates that manipulations that deprive the body of T cells are no longer adequate criteria for the existence of cell-mediated immunity in an infection, especially where antibody responses are known to be an important part of the immune response to the infection. A summary of the evidence for the segregation of lymphoid cells into thymus-dependent and thymus-independent groups is presented by Parrott and de Sousa (1971). Germinal centers are in the main located in thymus-independent areas of lymph nodes and spleen and occur in neonatally thymectomized mice, and this would suggest that they are composed mainly of cells of bone marrow origin (B cells). However, recent work by Gutman and Weissman (1971) has demonstrated that some blastoid cells in germinal centers are of thymus origin and thus, presumably, susceptible to manipulations that affect T cells.

However, Phillips *et al.* (1970), who investigated the occurrence of cell-mediated immunity responses in *Plasmodium knowlesi* in monkeys, found that animals sensitized with schizont-infected cells in Freund's complete adjuvant survived challenge with homologous *P. knowlesi*. They considered that, in view of the ability of Freund's complete adjuvant to induce cell-mediated immunity, mechanisms other than humoral antibodies might be concerned in the immune response to this parasite. There was evidence of delayed-type skin hypersensitivity in Freund's. complete adjuvant sensitized monkeys and lymphocytes from the spleen and lymph nodes of such animals were responsive to antigen in culture as judged by the uptake of tritiated thymidine. Phillips *et al.* (1970) considered that these *in vivo* and *in vitro* correlates of delayed hypersensitivity suggested a role for CMI in the infection, though not necessarily a critical role in the protective mechanism.

One of the *in vitro* correlates of cell-mediated immunity studied by Phillips *et al.* (1970) was the cytotoxic effect of spleen cells from Freund's complete adjuvant-schizont infected cell sensitized animals or from chronically infected animals on parasitized cells. No specific cytotoxic effect was seen in this situation.

The clinical severity of malarial infection has, from time to time, been ascribed to autoimmune mechanism. Such mechanisms may have a cellular immunity basis and Dumonde and Maini (1971) have suggested that the "adjuvant" effect of the lymphokine mediators may be concerned. It is of interest, therefore, to note that Sheagren and Monaco (1969) reported a reduced severity of *P. berghei* infection in mice when the animals were given anit-lymphocyte serum (ALS). They considered that the ALS treatment suppressed phagocytic mechanisms and autoimmunity. The suppression of phagocytic potential in this work, however, might be explained also by the work of Pisano *et al.* (1969) who demonstrated a depression of phagocytic activity of the reticuloendothelial system by ALS, this being associated in particular with an injurious effect of ALS on the Küpffer cells of the liver.

Increasing attention is being paid to the role of the macrophage and its phagocytic capabilities in malaria. For example, in *P. knowlesi* infection, K. N. Brown *et al.* (1970) have shown in chronically infected animals that schizont-infected erythrocytes are specifically opsonized by serum and the opsonized schizont-infected cells are ingested by macrophages grown in monolayers. This effect is variant specific and the authors suggested it may be a way by which successive antigenic variant organisms in malarial infections are selectively destroyed.

F. Immunosuppression in Malaria

The immunosuppressive action of malaria has received increasing attention recently. Greenwood (1968) has suggested that the low incidence of autoimmune disease in some parts of the tropics may be related to the multiple parasitic infections that occur. Studies in mice infected with *Plasmodium berghei yoelii* showed that spontaneous autoimmune disease in two strains of mice was suppressed (Greenwood and Voller, 1970). Salaman *et al.* (1969) reported that mice infected with *P. berghei* showed a markedly diminished response to sheep erythrocytes during the phase of malaria parasitemia. This has been confirmed by Barker (1971) who found a complete suppression of the antibody response to sheep erythrocytes, but not to bacteriophage $\Phi_\chi 174$, in *Plasmodium berghei yoelii* infected Balb/C mice. He considered this to be due to an impairment of the processing of large particulate antigens or to a depletion of the population of lymphoid cells sensitive to sheep RBC's.

In further studies of the influence of *P. berghei yoelii* on humoral and cellular responses of mice, Greenwood *et al.* (1971a) found that the maximal degree of immunosuppression coincided with the period of maximal parasitemia. This resulted in a greatly reduced antibody response and a reduction in the number of plaque forming cells in the spleens of infected mice. The antibody response to human gamma globulin, but not to keyhole limpet hemocyanin, was also markedly reduced.

However, cell-mediated immunity reactions to skin grafts and contact hypersensitivity were not impaired during the infection and spleen cells from malaria-infected mice responded normally to phytohemagglutinin. The authors concluded that the suppression of the immune response to sheep erythrocytes and other antigens was related to a disturbance of macrophage function and the inductive phase of the immune response produced by the malaria infection. Spleen cells from malaria infected mice were able to reconstitute the ability of lethally irradiated mice to respond to sheep erythrocytes to the level of about one-half as effectively as spleens from normal mice.

Additional studies of this phenomenon by Greenwood *et al.* (1971b) led them to conclude that the immune defect lay in the depletion of the lymphoid cells responsible for the transport of immune complexes into the germinal centers. They noted that such cells are not part of the thymus-dependent population. This would explain why cell-mediated immunity processes appear to remain intact in malaria infected mice.

However, Salaman (1970) has commented that immune depression by viral and protozoal infections may, among other things, facilitate proliferation and metastasis of neoplastic cells. In this respect, studies of the relationship between malaria infection and malignant tumors suggest that cell-mediated immunity mechanisms may be affected by malaria infection. Jerusalem (1968) and Jerusalem *et al.* (1971) have shown that *P. berghei* infection of Swiss mice was associated with a greater incidence of nonleukemic malignant lymphomas than noninfected mice. The percentage of mice showing lymphomas was directly related to the severity of *P. berghei* infection. The liver was involved in 33% of mice immune to *P. berghei* whereas in normal mice liver involvement did not occur. These authors question whether malaria infection "conditioned" the lymphopoetic and reticuloendothelial system to malignant change induced by some carcinogenic virus in the infected animals. In view of the immune suppressive effects of malaria infection (see above) it is possible that it also suppresses the immune surveillance mechanism of the body. The lymphoma nodules of Swiss mice resembled the malignant lymphoma of Burkitt's tumor of African children. In a review of the etiology of Brukitt's lymphoma, Burkitt (1959) concluded there was an association between chronic malaria and the lymphoma, and he suggested that tumor formation resulted from the interaction of virus and a reticuloendothelial system altered by chronic heavy malarial infection. Further studies of the situation by Kafuko and Burkitt (1970) confirmed the relationship of the lymphoma to the endemcity of malaria though they were unable to decide whether the malaria-induced changes in the lymphoreticular system lowered the immune surveillance mechanisms to malignant transformation or whether they acted as a "co-carcinogen."

G. Interferon in Malaria

Some inducers of interferon and interferon itself have been shown to induce a degree of protection against trophozoite and sporozoite induced malaria (Schultz *et al.*, 1968; Jahiel *et al.*, 1968). Further studies of this phenomenon by Jahiel *et al.* (1969) showed that the highest degree of protection was achieved when Newcastle disease virus (NDV) or statolon was injected 16–24 hours after an injection of *P. berghei* sporozoites. The serum interferon inducing capabilities of NDV and statolon were related to their protection inducing effect against sporozoite infection. Injection of these interferon producers 10 hours before or 48 hours after sporozoite infection produced partial protection. The lowest level of protection was found when these interferon producers were used against an infection with the erythrocytic forms of *P. berghei*. Consequently, it was concluded that the stage most susceptible to interferon was that of preerythrocytic development.

H. Coccidiosis

Though there are numerous reports of the failure to associate immunity to coccidia with humoral antibody, there are few or no reports which unequivocally incriminate cell-mediated immunity mechanisms as factors in the response (see Rose, Chapter 14). Studies by Heydorn (1970) and Rommel and Heydorn (1970) with *Eimeria nieschulzi* in an inbred strain of rats showed that transfer of lymphocytes from the mesenteric lymph nodes of immune animals to recipients produced a highly significant reduction in oocyst output on challenge. It is of interest that lymphocytes from the Peyer's patches failed to transfer immunity. Using ALS, Rommel (1970) reported a suppression of development of immunity in pigs to *Eimeria scabra* but no effect on immunity already established to this parasite. An increase in *in vitro* phagocytosis of sporocysts of *Eimeria tenella* by macrophages from the blood of infected chickens has been reported by Patton (1970). This effect was noted 10 days after infection; the peak phagocytic activity occurred between 12–19 days after infection, and it then declined to normal levels by 27 days.

A minor role for humoral antibody in immunity to coccidia is suggested by the results of Long and Pierce (1963) and Pierce and Long (1965) who showed there was no suppression of immunity in chickens in which the bursa of Fabricius had been suppressed by *in ovo* treatment with testosterone. Splenectomy has been shown to have little or no effect on immunity to *Eimeria tenella* in chickens (Rose, 1968a). She (Rose, 1968b) notes that bursectomy may not completely inhibit humoral antibody formation and indeed there is sufficient evidence to indicate that an antibody response may occur to a secondary antigenic stimulus in bursaless chickens (Rose and Orlans, 1968). Gamma globulin production has been demonstrated in bursectomized chickens (Pierce *et al.*, 1966) while Isaković and Janković (1967) have found that germinal centers and plasma cell formation may occur with the production of both 7 S and 19 S antibody on hyperimmunization of birds that have been bursectomized.

Complete thymectomy is difficult to achieve in the chick in that thymus-derived cells may be seeded to the body before hatching and thus studies on thymectomy and its relationship to immunity to *E. tenella* have produced equivocal results. Pierce and Long (1965) fail to eliminate immunity to *E. tenella* by thymectomy and Rose (1968b) failed to modify immunity to *Eimeria maxima* and *Eimeria brunetti* by thymectomy or bursectomy combined with whole body irradiation. Birds, which as a result of this treatment were weak on nonreactors to *Mycobacterium avium*, became resistant to the parasites and this included those which, on retrospective examination, possessed no residual thymus tissue. Rose (1968a) has reported failure to modify the immunity to *Eimeria* species with antilymphocyte serum and she also failed to obtain unequivocal results in the adoptive transfer of immunity to these parasites with peripheral blood leukocytes, spleen, cecal tonsil, and peritoneal exudate cells. In view of these findings, the report by Rose (1971) that protective antibodies occur in the circulation is of significance. Their duration is limited, however, and they appear from about day 14 to day 21 after a single infection.

I. Trypanosomiasis

Almost no work has been done on the role of cellular immune mechanisms in trypanosome infections. However, studies of *Trypanosoma theileri* infection of cattle have provided an opportunity to examine the contribution of persistent *T. theileria* infection to lymphopoiesis, lymphocytosis, and possibly leukosis (leukemia) in these animals. In a survey of *T. theileri* infection in a leukosis herd and a leukosis-free herd there was a marked difference in the infection rate between the two (Hare *et al.*, 1970). Examination of the *in vitro* stimulating effect of *T. theileri* antigen on peripheral blood leukocytes (Hare and Soulsby,

1969) showed there was no relationship between the responses of lymphocytes to antigen and trypanosome levels or antibody production. There was a negative correlation between levels of lymphocyte response to antigen and lymphocytosis and a positive correlation between trypanosome infection and lymphocytosis. Such a finding could be explained on the basis that there was an immunological defect in the lymphocytes.

J. Theileriasis

The immune mechanisms to *Theileria parva* infection in cattle have yet to be elucidated. This is a highly fatal disease; the main pathogenic mechanism of which appears to be lymphocytolysis (Jarrett *et al.*, 1968). Recovered animals are solidly immune (Wilde, 1967). Barnett (1965) has expressed the opinion that immunity to *T. parva* is mediated by lymphoid cells and he (Barnett,1968) reported a failure to produce convincing evidence of protection when immune serum or globulin fractions were given to clinical cases of *T. parva*. Splenectomy has no effect on *T. parva* immunity though with other *Theileria* spp. infections it has (see Ristic, 1970) and *in vitro* studies on the effects of serum or lymphoid cells from immune animals on the multiplication of *T. parva* propagated in tissue culture showed no significant difference in control compared with immune systems (Hulliger *et al.*, 1965). Recent studies by Moulton *et al.* (1971) have shown that *T. parva* infection of a cell is a potent stimulus for lymphoblast formation. Spleen cultures from infected animals were reported to transform from macrophages to reticulum cells to lymphoblasts which showed nearly 100% infection. Since many of the body lymphocytes may be infected with *T. parva*, it would be of great interest to know whether this infection compromises the immune response of the animal to other antigens and infections.

IV. Cell-Mediated Immunity in Helminth Infections

Of the helminth infections that have received intensive study for cell-mediated immunity responses perhaps *Trichinella spiralis*, *Trichostrongylus colubriformis*, and the *Schistosoma* species infections are the best known. There is no evidence in any of these infections, nor indeed in any helminth infection, that cell-mediated immunity mechanisms are the sole mediators of immunity. On the contrary, many immune phenomena occur in helminth infections and the study of them is especially difficult because of the necessity to work with *in vivo* systems.

A. Trichinosis

In reviews of the immune response to *T. spiralis* infection Larsh (1963, 1967) has concluded that the expulsion of adult *T. spiralis* worms from the intestine was mediated by an acute inflammatory response which could be suppressed by cortisone or whole body irradiation.

A major advance in the study of immunity to *T. spiralis* infection was made when Larsh and his colleagues demonstrated the passive transfer of immunity with lymphoid cells, especially by oil-induced peritoneal exudate cells (Larsh *et al.*, 1964a,b). Synegeneic recipients of exudate cells from immune donors failed to produce antibodies as assessed by hemagglutination, flocculation, and fluorescent antibody techniques. This success was confirmed and extended by the use of spleen cells from artificially sensitized donors (Larsh *et al.*, 1969). Such cells were able to confer immunity to recipients when they were challenged 7, 14, or 21 days after cell transfer, but not after 1 or 3 days (Larsh *et al.*, 1970a). If the cells were killed by a freeze-thawing technique, they failed to confer immunity upon recipients, whereas living spleen cells from comparable donors did (Larsh *et al.*, 1970b). The latter result would indicate that the transfer of "super antigen" by macrophages in the preparation was not concerned in the transfer of immunity.

That antigens of *T. spiralis* can produce delayed hypersensitivity responses has been demonstrated by Kim (1966). Skin tests of the delayed type occurred 7 days after the injection of an acid soluble protein fraction or a crude saline extract of the parasite in Freund's complete adjuvant (FCA) into the footpad of guinea pigs. No humoral antibody was detected by passive cutaneous anaphylaxis and the delayed skin hypersensitivity could be transferred by lymph node cells (Kim *et al.*, 1967a). However, by 14 days some of the donors of such cells showed Arthus-type reactions and by 21–28 days, all donors showed this type of reaction. Animals that had received lymph node cells during the period of delayed hypersensitivity of the donors also developed an antibody response, but this occurred only after challenge skin tests (Kim *et al.*, 1967b). Jamuar *et al.* (1968) and Kim *et al.* (1971) reported *in vivo* and *in vitro* transformation of lymph node cells of guinea pigs given footpad injections of *T. spiralis* antigen in FCA and a further *in vitro* correlate of delayed hypersensitivity to *T. spiralis* antigen sensitization was reported by Cypess *et al.* (1971) who demonstrated the inhibition of macrophage migration with spleen cells of mice sensitized by footpad injections of *T. spiralis* antigen in FCA.

The readily demonstrable presence of humoral antibodies in *T. spiralis* infection and the accumulation of antibody-containing cells of different immunoglobulin types in the infection (Crandall *et al.*, 1967) indicates that substantial clarification of the situation in this infection is still required. For example, the work of Kim and colleagues might indicate that the initial response to *T. spiralis* antigens given in FCA is of the Jones-Mote type (Jones and Mote, 1934) which in many circumstances is a prelude to humoral antibody production.

Larsh (1967) has suggested that the soluble factors of cell-mediated immunity may be operative in mediating the inflammatory response in the anterior bowel in *T. spiralis* infection. This would be in line with the inflammatory function of the lymphokine mediators as suggested by Dumonde and Maini (1971). However, a more direct relationship of antibody to lymphoid cell reactivity may exist. Thus a role for antigen–antibody complexes in cell-mediated immunity responses has been suggested by Block-Shtacher *et al.* (1968) in that antigen–antibody-complement aggregates can stimulate blastogenesis of previously "uncommitted" lymphoid cells. Such cells, as well as stimulated "committed" lymphoid cells, may, through the release of leukotactic factor (Ward and David, 1969), play a part in the further accumulation of circulating, nonsensitized, mononuclear cells at the site of parasitism. Other chemotactic responses are undoubtedly important and that for eosinophils is of particular interest. This factor, described by Cohen and Ward (1971) is a soluble mediator released from specific antigen stimulated lymphocytes of delayed hypersensitive guinea pigs. It will react with immune complexes *in vitro* to generate a factor which is chemotactic for eosinophils. As noted by the authors, this factor is unique since previously described chemotactic factors for other cells required either immune complexes or soluble lymphokines from lymphocyte culture, but not both. Cohen and Ward (1971) found that the eosinophil chemotactic factor was specific in that the immune complexes which would be activated by the lymphokine had to contain the same antigen as that used to activate the lymphocyte cultures. These authors demonstrated that this factor, though generated in an *in vitro* system, also possessed *in vivo* activity. They predicted that elicitation of a delayed reaction with immune complexes, rather than by antigen alone, should evoke an eosinophil response.

The studies of Cohen and Ward (1971) have relevance to the findings of Basten *et al.* (1970) and Basten and Beeson (1970) who found in *T. spiralis* infection of rats, that procedures such as thymectomy, antilymphocyte serum treatment, and thoracic duct drainage caused a reduction in the eosinophil response. These results suggested that thymus-derived cells are concerned in the evolution of eosinophilia. The marked eosinophilia that occurs in intestinal helminth infections, and in *T.*

spiralis infection in particular, clearly requires further investigation along these lines.

Evidence of immunosuppression by *T. spiralis* infection was produced by Svet-Moldavsky *et al.* (1970). Allogeneic skin grafts survived longer in *T. spiralis*-infected mice. Thus rejection began at 10.7 days in normal mice compared with 24.5 days in infected mice. Second set reactions were also suppressed, skin allografts persisting twice as long in infected mice than in normal animals. A direct immunosuppressive effect of the secretions of the parasite is suggested as an explanation. It is interesting to note in this context that *T. spiralis* infection stimulates high levels of homocytotropic antibodies in mice (IgG$_1$ and IgE) (see Sadun, Chapter 4) and that there is evidence that atopic patients (with elevated levels of IgE), compared with the rest of the population, show a lower incidence of malignant tumors (Fisherman, 1960; Mackay, 1966). While the relationship may be fortuitous, the immune mechanisms operating against skin allografts and tumors are of the cell-mediated type.

B. Trichostrongylosis

Extensive studies by Dineen and co-workers on the immune response of the guinea pig to *Trichostrongylus colubriformis* have added substantially to an understanding of the immune mechanisms to intestinal nematodes in general. Signal progress was made when Wagland and Dineen (1965) demonstrated the transfer of protective immunity to the parasite in guinea pigs with mesenteric lymph node cells but not with immune serum. Spleen and other lymph node cells were not as effective as those from mesenteric lymph nodes but still could transfer immunity. Subsequently, Dineen and Wagland (1966a) showed that the susceptible developmental stages of the infection in the guinea pig was the fourth larval stage, the fifth and adult stages being insusceptible to the immunity transferred by cells. Cells transferred within 24–48 hours of the development of the fourth larval stage effectively inhibited this stage. Syngeneic transfer was successful, whereas immune allogeneic cells failed to transfer immunity (Dineen *et al.*, 1968). These authors (Dineen *et al.*, 1968) also showed that ^{51}Cr-labeled immune lymphoid cells from mesenteric lymph nodes and Peyer's patches preferentially accumulated in the infected small intestine. A difference in this accumulation between infected and noninfected animals was evident as early as 6 hours after cell transfer, the maximal difference being noted between 16–24 hours. Preferential accumulation was not evident when nonimmune ^{51}Cr cells were injected. It was considered that the transferred cells came into close contact with the parasite in the epithelium of the bowel and underwent "allergic death" at the site of the infection. However, whether the labeled immune cells specifically homed to the site of the infection or reached there in a random manner has yet to be determined. More recent studies by Dineen and Adams (1971) have shown that mesenteric lymphatic duct drainage of thymus-derived cells renders guinea pigs incapable of mounting an immune response to *T. colubriformis* infection. This provides further evidence for the role of CMI in this infection.

Unpublished studies by Dobson and Soulsby (1971) (see also Dobson, Chapter 7) on the responsiveness of lymphoid cells from local and distant lymphoid centers in *T. colubriformis* infection in the guinea pig have shown that a marked blastogenesis of lymphoid cells occurs in these sites and, furthermore, there is a rapid acquisition of specific responsiveness to antigen as assessed by the incorporation of radio-labeled thymidine in culture. Such results would confirm the previous work of Dineen and co-workers which indicates that thymus-derived cells are concerned in the immune response to *T. colubriformis* in guinea pigs. It is to be remembered, however, that immunity to *T. colubriformis* in the guinea pig can be transferred with immune serum (Connan, 1966) though the time relationships when this is possible as compared to when it is possible with cells are different. The situation does, however, raise the question of the relationship of thymus-derived cells to antibody production. In the case of *Nippostrongylus brasiliensis* infection in the rat, Ogilvie and Jones (1967) (and see below) have shown that reagin formation in the rat is thymus-dependent and a close relationship between immunoglobulins, such as IgA and IgE, and the responsiveness of small lymphocytes has been noted by Ammann *et al.* (1969) and Brostoff and Roitt (1969). Reaginic antibodies have been detected in *T. colubriformis* infection in the guinea pig by Dobson and Soulsby (1971) and work is now required to determine the relationships, at the site of parasitism, among cells passively transferred in an isologous situation, those that show mitogenesis in the presence of antigen, and those that produce reaginic antibodies (or IgA immunoglobulins).

C. Haemonchosis

The cellular aspects of the immune response to *Haemonchus contortus* infection in sheep has been touched on by Dineen and Wagland (1966b). They demonstrated that sheep under constant antigenic insult from sensitizing infections with the parasite entered a phase of immunological exhaustion that was associated with the depletion of germinal follicles in the cortex of the local lymphoid centers. The relation of this response to antigen-induced suppression (antigenic competition) has yet to be determined. Experimentally, this is demonstrable by the sequential administration of two non-cross-reacting antigens and is associated with a relative deficiency of a thymus-derived cell population created by a disproportionately marked proliferation of nonthymus derived cellular elements (Eidinger and Ackerman, 1971).

Antigen induced responsiveness of peripheral blood lymphocytes has been demonstrated by Chen (1971) in sheep infected with *H. contortus*. Responsiveness is acquired following infection and is well established in adult sheep. In lambs, however, the response is of less magnitude and the adult level is not reached until several weeks of age. The relationship of this to the immune unresponsiveness of lambs to *H. contortus* reported by Manton *et al.* (1962) is at present unclear.

Chen (1971) has also shown that the lymphokine MIF is produced in cultures of antigen-stimulated peripheral lymphocytes, that this is eluted from a Sephadex G-200 column in the albumin region and that the capacity of peripheral cells to produce it is related to the time of a challenge infection. Of particular interest is her demonstration of a reduction in lymphoid cell responsiveness at the periparturient period in *H. contortus*-infected sheep; the relationship of this to the post parturient rise in fecal egg count is clearly an area for further investigation.

There is, thus, increasing evidence that thymus dependent cells may be concerned with the immune response to *H. contortus*. Whether they function as antigen sensitive cells in the initiation of humoral antibodies (such as those that mediate the self-cure reaction) or in true CMI responses has yet to be determined. One report (Scott *et al.*, 1971) indicates the successful transfer of immunity to sheep by allogeneic mesenteric lymph node cell suspensions. This somewhat unusual result, if confirmed, would lend a new dimension to studies of immunity to *H. contortus*.

D. Nippostrongylosis

In studies with *Nippostrongylus brasiliensis*, Hunter and Leigh (1961) were unsuccessful in transferring immunity to the parasite by lymphoid cells, though they demonstrated adoptive immunity with a control immunoglobulin producing system. Attempts by Kassai and Szepes (1970) to transfer immunity by spleen and lymph node cells to isologous recipients were unsuccessful though these authors claimed successful transfer of tolerance to the parasite with cells from tolerant donors. On the other hand, Ogilvie and Jones (1968) were able to transfer immunity passively with lymphoid cells from immune isologous rats. However, the protection was transferred in only about 30% of the experiments and this was comparable to the situation with the transfer of immune serum. In view of their (Ogilvie and Jones, 1968) inability to demonstrate delayed cellular mechanisms in N. *brasiliensis* infection, they concluded that the protection induced by the transferred lymphoid cells was due to antibody produced by them. Suppression of the immune response of mice to N. *brasiliensis* with anti-lymphocyte serum was reported by Kassai *et al.* (1968), while that in rats to the same parasite was suppressed by the use of rabbit anti-rat peritoneal cavity cell serum (Hogarth-Scott and Bingley, 1971). These results add strength to the conclusion that immunity to N. *brasiliensis* is thymus-dependent but mediated by antibodies (Ogilvie and Jones, 1971) since the various manipulations mentioned above can be explained on the basis that T cells are affected.

Few studies of *in vitro* correlates of CMI have been reported for N. *brasiliensis* infection. However Malczewski *et al.* (1970) observed inhibition of the migration of cells from spleen fragments of infected rats, cultured in the presence of antigen. Antigen concentrations of 3 mg/ml of medium but not 0.1 or 2 mg/ml, caused inhibition of migration of cells from spleen fragments of rats infected 10 days previously. The relationship of this to the MIF reaction was not determined.

The intriguing effects of N. *brasiliensis* infection on the growth of Walker sarcoma in rats and a syngeneic adenosarcoma in mice (Keller *et al.*, 1971) have been referred to briefly above (Section III,C). Mice infected with N. *brasiliensis* larvae 7 days before, simultaneously with, or 7 days after inoculation of syngeneic adenocarcinoma tumor cells showed suppression of tumor growth or tumor cells failed to grow at all. Treatment of mice with ALS had no effect on the growth of tumors in uninfected mice but it suppressed the inhibitory effect of the helminth infection on tumor growth. Experiments with rats infected with the parasite and Walker sarcoma cells showed that when the helminth infection was given 5 days before the tumor cells were given, tumor growth was completely inhibited but infections created 10 to 30 days before tumor inoculation caused enhancement of tumor growth. Serum from rats infected for 10 to 30 days also caused enhancement of tumor growth. The authors considered that the enhancement of the Walker sarcoma was due to shared antigens between the tumor and the parasite and a type of antibody response that differed in some way from the response that occurred to these antigens earlier in the helminth infection. In the case of the mammary adenocarcinoma of mice, Keller *et al.* (1971) considered the effect was due to a stimulus of the thymus-dependent cells, possibly increasing the cell-mediated immunity responses. Further work on the *N. brasiliensis*–Walker carcinoma system in rats by Keller and Jones (1971) has already been mentioned. This showed that at the time of suppression of tumor cell growth (5 days) activated macrophages rapidly engulfed and destroyed the tumor cells. Furthermore, an IgG_2 fraction of helminth immune serum inhibited this effect which Keller and Jones believe to be analogous to the activated macrophage phenomenon of Mackaness (1969) rather than due to antigen relatedness.

E. ASCARIASIS

Interactions between the larvae of *Ascaris suum* and antigen-stimulated peripheral leukocytes of rabbits has been reported by Soulsby (1968). Such cells adhere to the antibody sensitized cuticle of *A. suum* larvae, the adhesion being complement-independent and the cells possess staining properties and ultrastructure comparable to the "large pyroninophilic cells" seen in skin homograft rejection sites and in the lymph nodes draining an area of contact sensitivity (Morseth and Soulsby, 1969).

Further studies on the lymphoid cell response in *A. suum* infection in guinea pigs (Soulsby, 1972) indicate that much of the response to this parasite is local. For example, peripheral lymphocyte responsiveness to antigen (as assessed by the uptake of tritiated thymidine) is acquired 8–10 days after infection whereas antigen responsiveness of cells in the lymphoid centers draining infected organs (e.g., hepatic lymph node, mediastinal lymph node) is acquired much sooner after infection. An example of this is given in Fig. 1. It is of interest that the antigen responsiveness of the lymph node cells follows the course of the helminth infection, in that the hepatic lymph node is the first to respond and this is followed by the mediastinal lymph node response. A similar situation is seen on a challenge infection of a previously sensitized animal. Again, the local lymphoid centers are highly responsive and the sequence of the response follows the migratory pattern of the parasite (Fig. 2).

A further parameter of cell-mediated immunity, inhibition of macrophage migration (MIF) is positive in *A. suum* infection of guinea pigs. Peritoneal cavity cells of infected animals show inhibition of migration about 10 days after infection. Of special interest is the apparent specificity of the response. For example, antigens prepared from third-stage larvae cause inhibition, whereas antigens prepared from the "metabolic products" of third-stage larvae, from adult worms, or from "moulting fluid" when third stage larvae metamorphose to fourth stage larvae are less reactive or not reactive at all.

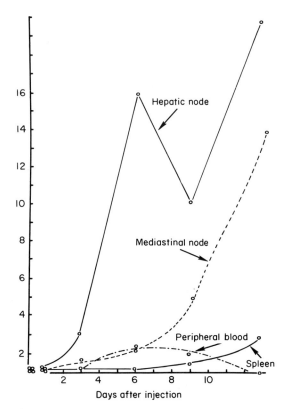

Fig. 1. Example of the *in vitro* responsiveness of guinea pig peripheral lymphocytes, spleen cells, and regional lymph node cells to *A. suum* antigen. Ordinate: ratio of uptake of tritiated thymidine (dpm/10^6 cells) in antigen-stimulated cultures to uptake in control cultures. Abscissa: days after infection. Guinea pigs were infected with 7500 artificially hatched second stage larvae of *A. suum* via the mesenteric vein on day 0. Each point is the mean for two animals.

F. Cell-Mediated Immunity Reactions in Other Nematode Infections

A number of other studies, covering a range of parasitic nematode infections indicate that CMI mechanisms or thymus-dependent cell reactions are not uncommon in helminth infections.

For example, Herd (1969), in a study of the effect of horse anti-sheep thymocyte serum (ATS) on the development of *Chabertia ovina* and anaphylactic antibody to this parasite in lambs, found that ATS had no effect on a primary infection of *C. ovina* but it did suppress resistance and anaphylactic antibody in a secondary infection. Herd considered

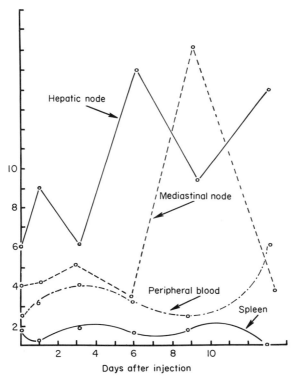

Fig. 2. Example of the *in vitro* responsiveness of immune guinea pig peripheral blood lymphocytes, spleen cells, and regional lymph node cells to *A. suum* antigen. Ordinate: ratio of uptake of tritiated thymidine ($dpm/10^6$ cells) in antigen stimulated cultures to uptake in control cultures. Abscissa: days after infection. Guinea pigs were previously immunized by several subcutaneous injections of infective eggs of *A. suum*. They were then challenged with 7500 artificially hatched second stage larvae of *A. suum* via the mesenteric vein on day 0. Each point is the mean for two animals.

this to indicate that anaphylactic antibody synthesis was possibly linked to CMI and at least partly under thymic control in the sheep.

In studies of the dog hookworm, *Ancylostoma caninum*, T. A. Miller (1967) transferred immunity by mesenteric lymph node cells from vaccinated animals. However, successful comparable transfer could be done with serum alone or with serum and lymphoid cells, which would suggest an antibody basis for the protection in this infection.

In studies of the immune response of the chicken to the tracheal nematode *Syngamus trachea* Varga (1971) experienced the same difficulty as workers in the field of coccidiosis in obtaining unequivocal results on the effect of bursectomy and thymectomy on this infection. Neither neonatal surgical bursectomy nor thymectomy altered the immune response of chickens to *S. trachea* infection.

G. Schistosomiasis

The present evidence would suggest that immunity to schistosomes is mediated by humoral factors (Smithers, 1968; Smithers *et al.*, 1969). For example, schistosomes grown in mice and transferred to the mesenteric veins of monkeys immunized against mouse liver cells, spleen cells, or erythrocytes are rapidly killed by an antibody-mediated immunological reaction directed against the tegument of the worms. In addition the humoral basis of the wide range of serological and immunodiagnostic tests in schistosome infection (Kagan, 1966) would further suggest that humoral antibody is the principal mechanism concerned in the response. Nevertheless, Warren *et al.* (1967) have shown that cell-mediated immunity mechanisms are concerned in schistosomiasis, particularly in the formation of granuloma around schistosome eggs.

In original studies of the schistosome egg pseudotubercle von Lichtenberg (1962) showed in mice that the intravenous injection of S. *mansoni* eggs, derived from infected mouse liver, caused granulomatous pseudotubercles in the lungs comparable to the natural occurring lesion. The peak size of granuloma was reached in 16–32 days after injection of eggs and thereafter it slowly resolved. Antigen diffused from the egg for at least 24 hours following injection and, using fluorescent antibody techniques, it was shown that it was taken up by the granuloma cells. Both live and dead eggs caused pseudotubercle formation while isolated miracidia and isolated egg shells did not produce the characteristic lesion. Mice that had been sensitized intraperitoneally with S. *mansoni* eggs showed an accelerated secondary granulomatous response (von Lichtenberg, 1967). and this was specific in that no cross-sensitization occurred between A. *suum* and S. *mansoni* eggs (Warren *et al.*, 1967). Further evidence of specificity was provided by Warren and Domingo (1970) who found there was little cross-reactivity between eggs of S. *mansoni, S. haematobium*, and S. *japonicum*. Furthermore, it was found in infected mice that pseudotubercle formation in the lungs was augmented and accelerated only when adult parasites produced eggs (Domingo and Warren, 1968a). The specificity of the reaction, including the stage specificity, is in keeping with the specificity expected of delayed sensitization mechanisms. As an example of this, mice exposed to irradiated cercariae, those with unisexual infections and those injected with killed 4-week-old worms behaved as unsensitized animals.

Warren and co-workers extended their studies of granuloma formation to schistosome eggs by demonstrating that the sensitization is transferable by cells and not by serum (Warren *et al.*, 1967) and that granuloma formation is inhibited by neonatal thymectomy of mice (Domingo and Warren, 1967) and by the use of anti-lymphocyte serum (Domingo and Warren, 1968b). On the other hand, situations in which the humoral antibody response is compromised, such as total body X-irradiation of mice (Perrotto and Warren, 1969) or mice infected with advanced Friend virus leukemia (Warren, 1969) had no effect on granuloma formation. On the other hand, the granulomatous lesion is much reduced in SJL/J mice with a reticulum cell sarcoma, an entity resembling Hodgkin's disease of man in which delayed sensitivity mechanisms are impaired (Warren, 1969).

Boros and Warren (1970) have isolated an antigen from schistosome eggs which in small quantities will sensitize mice to granuloma formation around eggs embolized into the lungs. The material was secreted by intact eggs and was present in high concentrations in fluid released at the time of hatching. The substance was capable of sensitizing mice to delayed type reactions and did not induce detectable antibody formation in such circumstances. It also elicited delayed reactions on foot pad injections of previously sensitized mice and when adsorbed into bentonite particles and embolized into the lungs, it produced granuloma formation of the delayed type. Von Lichtenberg *et al.* (1971) similarly have studied the response of mice to bentonite particles coated with the egg antigen and have observed an anamnestic granulomatous response to it in sensitized animals.

Footpad immunization of guinea pigs with 65 gamma of the schistosome egg antigen in Freund's complete adjuvant resulted in the acquisition of a MIF response by peritoneal cavity cells 3 days later and delayed skin reactivity and granuloma formation by 6 days. *In vivo* granuloma formation paralleled skin reactivity (Boros *et al.*, 1971). Colley (1971) has also shown that this egg antigen will cause blastogenesis of lymph node cells of mice infected with *S. mansoni*, whereas cells from normal mice are not stimulated by it. Whether the blastogenic effect of the egg antigen is a unique property compared to other antigens from schistosomes is not known. If this were to be the case, then exquisitely specific mechanisms would pertain in this complex host-parasite sytsem.

Further studies of the granuloma producing and sensitizing materials of *S. mansoni* eggs were carried out by Smith *et al.* (1971). For example, egg lipids contained significant quantities of phospholipids and lysophosphatides. Lysophosphatides are known to be cytotoxic and bentonite particles coated with these materials cause granulomata in both normal and sensitized mice, whereas the soluble egg antigen of S. *mansoni* eggs produces granulomata only in sensitized mice. Lysophosphatides thus may play a part in the early granulomatous response to S. *mansoni* eggs, the specific sensitization reaction occurring later to antigens produced by the egg.

H. FASCIOLIASIS

Passive transfer of immunity with lymphoid cells has been reported in *Fasciola hepatica* infection of mice by Lang *et al.* (1967) and of rats by Corba *et al.* (1971). In the former case, oil-induced peritoneal cavity exudate cells of infected mice were injected into isologous mice which were then each challenged with two metacercariae 21 days later. The cell recipients showed a statistically significant difference in worm development (10 "immunized mice" had 8 parasites and 8 control mice had 12 parasites). In the latter study, striking evidence of transfer of protection was obtained. Cells from the spleen and the mesenteric hepatic lymph nodes of *F. hepatica*-infected rats transferred syngeneically produced protection against challenge of the order of 60–100%. A minimal period of 8 weeks after infection was required for cells to acquire this capability. Serum failed to confer any significant protection. These authors (Corba *et al.*, 1971) also studied cell transfer of resistance to *F. hepatica* in a pair of monozygous twin calves. Here again, a substantial degree of protection was transferred whereas none was transmitted with serum.

These results are of interest when considered along with previous studies by Sinclair on the pathogenesis and resistance mechanisms to *F. hepatica* in sheep. Thus, Sinclair (1968) demonstrated accelerated development and enhanced pathogenicity of the parasite in lambs given daily injections of corticosteroid. He considered that suppression of the tissue response due to the anti-inflammatory action of the corticosteroid allowed unrestricted parasite development. This may be a valid interpretation since Claman *et al.* (1971) consider the main cytolytic action of corticosteroids to be on "immunologically irrelevant" cells especially the bone marrow-derived mononuclear cell in CMI reactions. Further studies (Sinclair, 1970a) indicated that the effect produced by corticosteroids given at the time of initial infection might extend into the phase of reinfection. Thus, though there was evidence of acquired resistance in lambs so treated, parasites matured earlier and were larger than those in a similar group of lambs not given corticosteroids on initial infection. Sinclair (1970b) also reported on the effect of splenectomy on the development of a primary infection with *F. hepatica* in sheep.

He reported a higher worm burden and a more severe clinical disease in splenectomized animals and concluded that the modification of the immune response to the parasite was based on effects other than the suppression of circulating antibody response such as absence or delay of the usual cellular reaction.

V. Cell-Mediated Immunity in Arthropod Infestations

Extensive studies of dermal sensitization to the cat flea (*Ctenocephalides felis felis*) have shown that a phase of delayed hypersensitivity occurs in the induction period. Benjamini *et al.* (1961) have described the sequence of reactions in sensitization of the guinea pig. A stage of nonobservable reaction (induction period) which lasts for approximately 4 days is followed by a stage of delayed skin reaction which lasts for approximately another 5–9 days. The reaction is characterized by an intense monocytic infiltration of the dermis accompanied by mononuclear invasion. Subsequently, there is a stage when immediate and delayed reactions coexist. This appears approximately 9 days following initial exposure and lasts for about 60 days. A stage of immediate hypersensitivity only follows, about 2 months after initial exposure; this lasts for about 1 month and ultimately a stage of nonreactivity occurs. This may begin at approximately 3 months following initial exposure and may last for half a year or longer. Transition from one stage to the next is gradual and not clear cut. Benjamini *et al.* (1960) have shown that the oral secretion of the cat flea is the material responsible for these reactions. It is a low molecular weight substance, stable to heat and acid hydrolysis (Benjamini, 1966), and is considered to be hapten (Michaeli *et al.*, 1965b) which will induce sensitivity when combined with Freund's complete adjuvant (Benjamini *et al.*, 1963). In natural sensitization it induces sensitization when irreversibly associated with skin collagen (Michaeli *et al.*, 1965a).

Similar reactions occur during the acquisition of sensitivity to *Phlebotomus* (Theodor, 1935) and *Aedes* (Mellanby, 1946). Passive transfer of mosquito bite delayed skin sensitivity to guinea pigs with leukocytes from sensitized animals has been reported by Allen and West (1966) and it is of interest that this was achieved in an allogeneic system.

VI. Conclusion

Parasitic infections offer a complex array of host–parasite relationships. As might be expected, the immune phenomena associated with them is equally complex and it is clear that the whole range of cellular immunity phenomena can and does occur. The analysis and the assessment of the proportionate role these phenomena play in protective immunity will require extensive work, tempered with cautious interpretation. However, the outlook is good for a meaningful understanding of the immune responses and it is to be hoped that this will lead to the development of immunizing agents that are so urgently needed for these infections.

Acknowledgments

Some of the work reported in this review was supported by USPHS Research Grant AI-06262 and USPHS Research Training Grant AI-00302.

References

Adler, S. (1954). *Trans. Roy. Soc. Trop. Med. Hyg.* **48**, 341.
Adler, S. (1963). *In* "Immunity to Protozoa" (P. C. C. Garnham, A. E. Pierce, and I. Roitt, eds.), p. 235. Blackwell, Oxford.
Adler, S., and Nelkin, D. (1965). *Trans. Roy. Soc. Trop. Med. Hyg.* **59**, 59.
Allen, J. R., and West, A. S. (1966). *Proc. Int. Congr. Parasitol., 1st, 1964* Vol. 2, p. 1091.
Amman, A. J., Cain, W. A., Ishizaka, K., Hong, R., and Good, R. A. (1969). *N. Engl. J. Med.* **281**, 469.
Amos, H., and Lachmann, P. J. (1970). *Immunology* **18**, 415.
Barker, L. R. (1971). *J. Infec. Dis.* **123**, 99.
Barker, L. R., and Powers, K. G. (1971). *Nature (London)* **229**, 429.
Barnet, K., Pekarek, J., and Johanovsky, J. (1968). *Experientia* **24**, 298.
Barnett, S. F. (1965). *Proc. Int. Congr. Protozool., 2nd, 1965* p. 36.
Barnett, S. F. (1968). *In* "Infectious Blood Diseases of Man and Animals" (D. Weinman, and M. Ristic, eds.), Vol. 2, p. 269. Academic Press, New York.
Basten, A., and Beeson, P. B. (1970). *J. Exp. Med.* **131**, 1288.
Basten, A., Boyer, M. H., and Beeson, P. B. (1970). *J. Exp. Med.* **131**, 1271.
Benjamini, E. (1966). *Proc. Int. Congr. Parasitol., 1st, 1964* Vol. 2, p. 1090.
Benjamini, E., Feingold, B. F., and Kartman, L. (1960). *Exp. Parasitol.* **10**, 214.
Benjamini, E., Feingold, B. F., and Kartman, L. (1961). *Proc. Soc. Exp. Biol. Med.* **108**, 700.
Benjamini, E., Feingold, B. F., Young, J. D., Kartman, L., and Shimizu, M. (1963). *Exp. Parasitol.* **13**, 143.
Blanden, R. V. (1969). *Transplantation* **7**, 484.
Blewett, T. M. (1972). To be published.
Blewett, T. M., Kadivar, D. M., and Soulsby, E. J. L. (1971). *Amer. J. Trop. Med. Hyg.* **20**, 546.
Block-Shtacher, N., Hirschorn, K., and Uhr, J. W. (1968). *Clin. Exp. Immunol.* **3**, 889.
Bloom, B. R., and Bennett, B. (1970). *Ann. N.Y. Acad. Sci.* **169**, 258.
Boros, D. V., and Warren, K. S. (1970). *J. Exp. Med.* **132**, 488.

Boros, D. V., and Schwartz, H. J., Warren, K. S., and Seabury, L. R. (1971). *Fed. Proc., Fed. Amer. Soc. Exp. Biol.* **30**, 351.

Boysia, F. T. (1968). Ph.D. Thesis, Graduate School, Rutgers University, New Brunswick, New Jersey (University Microfilms, Ann Arbor, Michigan).

Bray, R. S., and Bryceson, A. D. M. (1965). *Trans. Roy. Soc. Trop. Med. Hyg.* **59**, 535.

Bray, R. S., and Bryceson, A. D. M. (1968). *Lancet* **2**, 898.

Briggs, N. T., Wellde, B. T., and Sadun, E. H. (1966). *Mil. Med.* **131**, Suppl., 1243.

Brostoff, J., and Roitt, I. M. (1969). *Lancet* **2**, 1269.

Brown, I. N., Allison, A. C., and Taylor, R. B. (1968). *Nature (London)* **219**, 292.

Brown, K. N., Brown, I. N., and Phillips, R. S. (1970). *J. Parasitol.* **56**, Sect. 11, 37.

Bryceson, A. D. M. (1970). *Trans. Roy. Soc. Trop. Med. Hyg.* **64**, 369.

Bryceson, A. D. M., Bray, R. S., Wolstencroft, R. A., and Dumonde, D. C. (1970). *Clin. Exp. Immunol.* **7**, 301.

Burkitt, D. P. (1969). *J. Nat. Canc. Inst.* **42**, 19.

Caron, G. A., and Poutala, S. (1969). *Nature (London)* **221**, 470.

Chase, M. W. (1945). *Proc. Soc. Exp. Biol. Med.* **59**, 134.

Chen, P. (1971). Unpublished results.

Claman, H. N., Levine, M. A., and Cohen, J. J. (1971). *In* "Cell Interactions and Receptor Antibodies in Immune Responses" (O. Makela, A. Cross, and T. U. Kosunen, eds.), p. 333. Academic Press, New York.

Cohen, S., and Ward, P. A. (1971). *J. Exp. Med.* **133**, 133.

Colley, D. G. (1971). *J. Immunol.* **107**, 1477.

Connan, R. M. (1966). Cited by Ogilvie and Jones (1968).

Corba, J., Armour, J., Roberts, R. J., and Urquhart, G. M. (1971). *Res. Vet. Sci.* **12**, 292.

Crandall, R. B., Cebra, J. J., and Crandall, C. A. (1967). *Immunology* **12**, 147.

Cypess, R., Larsh, J. E., Jr., and Pegram, C. (1971). *J. Parasitol.* **57**, 103.

David, J. R. (1966). *Proc. Nat. Acad. Sci. U.S.* **56**, 72.

Dineen, J. K., and Adams, D. B. (1971). *Immunology* **20**, 109.

Dineen, J. K., and Wagland, B. M. (1966a). *Immunology* **11**, 47.

Dineen, J. K., and Wagland, B. M. (1966b). *Parasitology* **56**, 665.

Dineen, J. K., Ronai, P. M., and Wagland, B. M. (1968). *Immunology* **15**, 671.

Dobson, C., and Soulsby, E. J. L. (1971). Unpublished studies.

Domingo, E. O., and Warren, K. S. (1967). *Amer. J. Pathol.* **51**, 757.

Domingo, E. O., and Warren, K. S. (1968a). *Amer. J. Pathol.* **52**, 369.

Domingo, E. O., and Warren, K. S. (1968b). *Amer. J. Pathol.* **52**, 613.

Dostrowsky, A., Sagher, F., and Zuckerman, A. (1952). *Arch. Dermatol. Syph.* **66**, 665.

Dumonde, D. C., and Maini, R. D. (1971). *Clin. Allergy* **1**, 123.

Dumonde, D. C., Wolstencroft, R. A., Panayi, G. S., Matthew, M., Morley, J., and Howson, W. T. (1969). *Nature (London)* **224**, 38.

Eidinger, D., and Ackerman, A. (1971). *J. Exp. Med.* **133**, 1061.

Fisherman, E. W. (1960). *J. Allergy* **31**, 74.

Frenkel, J. K. (1948). *Proc. Soc. Exp. Biol. Med.* **68**, 634.

Frenkel, J. K. (1967). *J. Immunol.* **98**, 1309.

Freshman, M., Merrigan, T. C., Remington, J. S., and Brownlee, I. (1966). *Proc. Soc. Exp. Biol. Med.* **123**, 862.

Gentry, L. O., and Remington, J. S. (1971). *J. Infec. Dis.* **123,** 22.

Goihman-Yahr, M., Raffel, S., and Ferroresi, R. W. (1969). *J. Bacteriol.* **100,** 635.

Granger, G. A., and Williams, T. W. (1968). *Nature (London)* **218,** 1253.

Greenwood, B. M. (1968). *Lancet* **2,** 380.

Greenwood, B. M., and Voller, A. (1970). *Clin. Exp. Immunol.* **8,** 805.

Greenwood, B. M., Playfair, J. H. L., and Torrigiani, G. (1971a). *Clin. Exp. Immunol.* **8,** 467.

Greenwood, B. M., Brown, J. C., de Jesus, D. G., and Holborow, E. J. (1971b). *Clin. Exp. Immunol.* **9,** 345.

Gutman, G., and Weissman, I. L. (1971). *Advan. Exp. Med. Biol.* **12,** 595.

Hare, W. C. D., and Soulsby, E. J. L. (1969). *J. Parasitol.* **55,** 973.

Hare, W. C. D., Soulsby, E. J. L., and Abt, D. A. (1970). *In* "Comparative Leukemia Research 1969" (R. M. Dutcher, ed.), p. 504. Karger, Basel.

Herd, R. P. (1969). *Aust. Vet. J.* **45,** 595.

Heydorn, A. O. (1970). Vet. Med. Dissertation, Free Univ., Berlin.

Hogarth-Scott, R. S., and Bingley, J. B. (1971). *Immunology* **21,** 87.

Huldt, G. (1966). *Acta Pathol. Microbiol. Scand.* **68,** 605.

Huldt, G. (1967). *Acta Pathol. Microbiol. Scand.* **70,** 129.

Hulliger, L., Brown, C. G. D., and Wilde, J. K. H. (1965). *Proc. Int. Congr. Protozool., 2nd, 1965* p. 37.

Hunter, G. C., and Leigh, L. C. (1961). *Parasitology* **51,** 357.

Isaković, K. B., and Janković, B. D. (1967). "Germinal Centers in Immune Responses" (H. Cottier *et al.,* eds.), p. 379. Springer-Verlag, Berlin and New York.

Jahiel, R., Nussenzweig, R. S., Vanderberg, J., and Vilček, J. (1968). *Nature (London)* **220,** 710.

Jahiel, R., Nussenzweig, R. S., Vilček, J., and Vanderberg, J. (1969). *Amer. J. Trop. Med. Hyg.* **18,** 823.

Jamuar, M. P., Kim, C. W., and Hamilton, L. D. (1968). *J. Immunol.* **100,** 329.

Jarrett, W. F. H., Crighton, G. W., and Pirie, H. M. (1968). *In* "Reaction of the Host to Parasitism" (E. J. L. Soulsby, ed.), p. 280. Elwert, Marburg, Germany.

Jerusalem, C. (1968). *Z. Tropenmed. Parasitol.* **19,** 94.

Jerusalem, C., Jap, P., and Eling, W. (1971). *Advan. Exp. Med. Biol.* **15,** 391.

Jones, T. D., and Mote, J. R. (1934). *N. Engl. J. Med.* **210,** 120.

Kafuko, G. W., and Burkitt, D. P. (1970). *Int. J. Cancer* **6,** 1.

Kagan, I. G. (1966). *In* "The Biology of Parasites" (E. J. L. Soulsby, ed.), p. 277. Academic Press, New York.

Kassai, T., and Szepes, G. (1970). *Acta Vet. Acad. Sci. Hung.* **20,** 207.

Kassai, T., Szepes, G., Réthy, L., and Tóth, G. (1968). *Nature (London)* **218,** 1055.

Keller, R., and Jones, V. E. (1971). *Lancet* **2,** 847.

Keller, R., Ogilvie, B. M., and Simpson, E. (1971). *Lancet* **1,** 678.

Kim, C. W. (1966). *J. Infec. Dis.* **116,** 208.

Kim, C. W., Savel, H., and Hamilton, L. D. (1967a). *J. Immunol.* **99,** 1150.

Kim, C. W., Jamuar, M. P., and Hamilton, L. D. (1967b). *J. Immunol.* **99,** 1156.

Kim, C. W., Jamuar, M. P., and Hamilton, L. D. (1971). *J. Immunol.* **107,** 1382.

Kolb, W. P., and Granger, G. A. (1968). *Proc. Nat. Acad. Sci. U.S.* **61,** 1250.

Konopka, E. A., Goble, F. C., and Lewis, L. (1961). *Bacteriol. Proc.* **61,** 134.

Krahenbuhl, J. L., Blazkovec, A. A., and Lysenko, M. G. (1971). *Infec. Immunity* **3**, 260.

Landsteiner, K., and Chase, M. W. (1942). *Proc. Soc. Exp. Biol. Med.* **49**, 688.

Lang, B. Z., Larsh, J. E., Jr., Weatherly, N. F., and Goulson, H. T. (1967). *J. Parasitol.* **53**, 208.

Larsh, J. E., Jr. (1963). *Advan. Parasitol.* **1**, 347.

Larsh, J. E., Jr. (1967). *Amer. J. Trop. Med. Hyg.* **16**, 735.

Larsh, J. E., Jr., Goulson, H. T., and Weatherly, N. F. (1964a). *J. Elisha Mitchell. Sci. Soc.* **80**, 133.

Larsh, J. E., Jr., Goulson, H. T., and Weatherly, N. F. (1964b). *J. Parasitol.* **50**, 496.

Larsh, J. E., Jr., Goulson, H. T., Weatherly, N. F., and Chaffee, E. F. (1969). *J. Parasitol.* **55**, 726.

Larsh, J. E., Jr., Goulson, H. T., Weatherly, N. F., and Chaffee, E. F. (1970a). *J. Parasitol.* **56**, 978.

Larsh, J. E., Jr., Goulson, H. T., Weatherly, N. F., and Chaffee, E. F. (1970b). *J. Parasitol.* **56**, 1206.

Lawrence, H. S. (1969). *Advan. Immunol.* **11**, 195.

Long, P. L., and Pierce, A. E. (1963). *Nature (London)* **200**, 526.

Longenecker, B. M., and Breitenbach, R. P. (1969). *Amer. J. Trop. Med. Hyg.* **18**, 360.

Lunde, M. N., and Gelderman, A. H. (1971). *J. Nat. Cancer Inst.* **47**, 485.

MacCallum, D. K. (1969a). *J. Reticuloendothel. Soc.* **6**, 232.

MacCallum, D. K. (1969b). *J. Reticuloendothel. Soc.* **6**, 253.

Mackaness, G. B. (1962). *J. Exp. Med.* **116**, 381.

Mackaness, G. B. (1967). *Brit. Med. Bull.* **23**, 52.

Mackaness, G. B. (1969). *J. Exp. Med.* **129**, 973.

Mackaness, G. B., and Blanden, R. V. (1967). *Progr. Allergy* **11**, 1.

Mackay, W. D. (1966). *Brit. J. Cancer* **20**, 424.

Maegraith, B. (1966). *In* "Spezielle pathologische Anatomie," Vol. 5, p. 379. Springer-Verlag, Berlin and New York.

Malczewski, A., Zaleska-Rutczyńska, Z., Skopińska, E., and Ostrowski, K. (1970). *Bull. Acad. Pol. Sci.* **18**, 637.

Manton, V. J. A., Peacock, R., Poynter, D., Silverman, P. H., and Terry, R. J. (1962). *Res. Vet. Sci.* **3**, 308.

Mellanby, K. (1946). *Nature (London)* **158**, 554.

Melnick, H. D. (1971). *Ann. Allergy* **29**, 195.

Michaeli, D., Benjamini, E., de Buren, F. P., Larrivee, D. H., and Feingold, B. F. (1965a). *J. Immunol.* **95**, 162.

Michaeli, D., Benjamini, E., Young, J. D., and Feingold, B. F. (1965b). *Proc. Int. Congr. Entomol., 12th, 1964* Vol. 12, p. 832.

Miki, K., and Mackaness, G. B. (1964). *J. Exp. Med.* **120**, 93.

Miller, J. F. A. P., Basten, A., Sprent, J., and Cheers, C. (1971). *Cell. Immunol.* **2**, 469.

Miller, T. A. (1967). *Immunology* **12**, 231.

Morseth, D. J., and Soulsby, E. J. L. (1969). *J. Parsitol.* **55**, 22.

Moulton, J. E., Krauss, H. H., and Malmquist, W. A. (1971). *Lab. Invest.* **24**, 187.

North, R. J. (1969). *J. Exp. Med.* **130**, 315.

North, R. J. (1970a). *J. Exp. Med.* **132**, 521.
North, R. J. (1970b). *J. Exp. Med.* **132**, 535.
Ogilvie, B. M., and Jones, V. E. (1967). *Parsitology* **57**, 335.
Ogilvie, B. M., and Jones, V. E. (1968). *Parasitology* **58**, 939.
Ogilvie, B. M., and Jones, V. E. (1971). *Exp. Parasitol.* **29**, 138.
Parrot, D. M. V., and de Sousa, M. (1971). *Clin. Exp. Immunol.* **8**, 663.
Patterson, R. J., and Youmans, G. P. (1970). *Infec. Immunity* **1**, 600.
Patton, W. H. (1970). *J. Parasitol.* **56**, Sect. II, 260.
Perrotto, J. L., and Warren, K. S. (1969). *Amer. J. Pathol.* **56**, 279.
Phillips, R. S. (1970). *Exp. Parasitol.* **27**, 479.
Phillips, R. S., Wolstencroft, R. A., Brown, I. N., Brown, K. N., and Dumonde,
    D. C. (1970). *Exp. Parsitol.* **28**, 339.
Pierce, A. E., and Long, P. L. (1965). *Immunology* **9**, 427.
Pierce, A. E., Chubb, R. C., and Long, P. L. (1966). *Immunology* **10**, 321.
Pisano, J. C., Patterson, J. T., and Di Luzio, N. R. (1969). *Proc. Soc. Exp. Biol.
    Med.* **132**, 517.
Ralson, D. J., and Elberg, S. S. (1969). *J. Reticuloendothel. Soc.* **6**, 109.
Ralson, D. J., and Elberg, S. S. (1971). *J. Infec. Dis.* **123**, 507.
Remington, J. S., and Merigan, T. C. (1968). *Science* **161**, 804.
Remington, J. S., and Merigan, T. C. (1969). *Proc. Soc. Exp. Biol. Med.* **131**,
    1184.
Remington, J. S., and Merigan, T. C. (1970). *Nature (London)* **226**, 361.
Ristic, M. (1970). *In* "Immunity to Parasitic Animals" (G. J. Jackson, R. Herman,
    and I. Singer, eds.), Vol. 2, p. 831. Appleton, New York.
Rommel, M. (1970). *J. Parasitol.* **56**, Sect. II, 846.
Rommel, M., and Heydorn, A. O. (1970). *Z. Parasitenk.* **36**, 242.
Rose, M. E. (1968a). *Parasitology* **58**, 481.
Rose, M. E. (1968b). *In* "Immunity to Parasites" (A. E. R. Taylor, ed.), p. 43.
    Blackwell, Oxford.
Rose, M. E. (1971). *Parsitology* **62**, 11.
Rose, M. E., and Orlans, E. (1968). *Nature (London)* **217**, 231.
Ruddle, N. W., and Waksman, B. H. (1967). *Science* **157**, 1060.
Ruddle, N. W., and Waksman, B. H. (1968). *J. Exp. Med.* **128**, 1255.
Ruskin, J., and Remington, J. S. (1968a). *Science* **160**, 72.
Ruskin, J., and Remington, J. S. (1968b). *Antimicrob. Ag. Chemother.* p. 474.
Ruskin, J., McIntosh, J., and Remington, J. S. (1968). *J. Immunol.* **103**, 252.
Salaman, M. H. (1970). *Proc. Roy. Soc. Med.* **63**, 11.
Salaman, M. H., Wedderburn, N., and Bruce-Chwatt, J. L. (1969). *J. Gen. Microbiol.*
    59, 383.
Schultz, W. W., Huang, K. Y., and Gordon, F. B. (1968). *Nature (London)*
    220, 709.
Scott, H. L., Silverman, P. H., Mansfield, M. E., and Levine, H. S. (1971). *Amer.
    J. Vet. Res.* **32**, 249.
Sheagren, J. N., and Monaco, A. P. (1969). *Science* **164**, 1423.
Sinclair, K. B. (1968). *Brit. Vet. J.* **124**, 133.
Sinclair, K. B. (1970a). *Res. Vet. Sci.* **11**, 209.
Sinclair, K. B. (1970b). *Brit. Vet. J.* **126**, 15.
Smith, T. M., von Lichtenberg, F., and Lucia, H. L. (1971). *J. Infec. Dis.* **123**, 629.
Smithers, S. R. (1968). *In* "Immunity to Parasites" (A. E. R. Taylor, ed.), p.
    55. Blackwell, Oxford.

Smithers, S. R., Terry, R. J., and Hockley, D. J. (1969). *Proc. Roy. Soc.* 171, 483.
Soborg, M. (1969). *Acta Med. Scand.* 185, 221.
Soulsby, E. J. L. (1968). *In* "Reaction of the Host to Parasitism" (E. J. L. Soulsby, ed.), p. 211. Elwert, Marburg, Germany.
Soulsby, E. J. L. (1970). *J. Parasitol.* 56, Sect. II, 534.
Soulsby, E. J. L. (1972). To be published.
Spitler, L. E., and Lawrence, H. S. (1969). *J. Immunol.* 103, 1072.
Stechschulte, D. J. (1969a). *Proc. Soc. Exp. Biol. Med.* 131, 748.
Stechschulte, D. J. (1969b). *Mil. Med.* 134, Spec. Issue, 1147.
Svet-Moldavsky, G. T., Shaghijan, G. S., Chernyakhovskaya, I. Y., Mkheidze, D. M., Litovchenko, T. A., Ozeretskovskaya, N. N., and Kadaghidze, Z. G. (1970). *Transplantation* 9, 69.
Taliaferro, W. H. (1967). *Pan Amer. Health Organ. Sci. Publ.* 150, Washington, D.C.
Taliaferro, W. H., and Taliaferro, L. G. (1955). *J. Infec. Dis.* 97, 99.
Theodor, O. (1935). *Trans. Roy. Soc. Trop. Med. Hyg.* 29, 273.
Tremonti, L., and Walton, B. C. (1970). *Amer. J. Trop. Med. Hyg.* 19, 49.
Turk, J. L., and Bryceson, A. D. M. (1971). *Advan. Immunol.* 13, 209.
Varga, I. (1971). *Acta Vet. (Budapest)* 21, 107.
Vischer, W. A., and Suter, E. (1954). *Proc. Soc. Exp. Biol. Med.* 86, 413.
von Kretschmar, W. (1965). *Z. Tropenmed. Parasitol.* 16, 277.
von Lichtenberg, F. (1962). *Amer. J. Pathol.* 41, 711.
von Lichtenberg, F. (1967). *Pan Amer. Health Organ. Sci. Publ.* 150, Washington, D.C.
von Lichtenberg, F., Smith, T. M., Lucia, H. L., and Doughty, B. L. (1971). *Nature (London)* 229, 199.
Wagland, B. M., and Dineen, J. K. (1965). *Aust. J. Exp. Biol. Med.* 43, 429.
Ward, P. A., and David, J. R. (1969). *Fed. Proc., Fed. Amer. Soc. Exp. Biol.* 28, 630.
Warren, K. S. (1969). *Amer. J. Pathol.* 56, 293.
Warren, K. S., and Domingo, E. O. (1970). *Exp. Parasitol.* 27, 60.
Warren, K. S., Domingo, E. O., and Cowan, R. B. (1967). *Amer. J. Pathol.* 51, 735.
Wilde, J. K. H. (1967). *Advan. Vet. Sci.* 11, 207.
Wolstencroft, R. A., and Dumonde, D. C. (1970). *Immunology* 18, 599.

4 HOMOCYTOTROPIC ANTIBODY RESPONSE TO PARASITIC INFECTIONS

ELVIO H. SADUN

I. Introduction

Numerous parasitological articles are currently devoted to problems related to immunity. Although Erlich (1907) and Sergent and Sergent (1918) have already established some of the roles of acquired immunity in trypanosomiasis and malaria, up to the second quarter of the century most parasitologists were reluctant to recognize that immunity plays an important role in parasitic infections. This reluctance was a result of the paucity of immunological knowledge in general and of the unique complexities of life cycles, size, and metabolic requirements of animal parasites (Taliaferro, 1967). Taliaferro (1929) in his classic publication on the immunology of parasitic infections has pointed out that the large size and accessibility of parasites provide a great advantage in immunological investigations. Because of their size, parasites can be observed *in vivo* in relation to the host reaction and are a convenient source of large quantities of antigens for analysis and purification. However, the size and complexity of parasites also confront immunologists with a baffling array of antigens, some of which are stage specific and others which are common to other parasites or to antigens of the host (Capron, 1970).

In the past decade there has been an explosion of information pertaining to immunology in general, and the study of parasitic diseases has felt its impact. Numerous publications which have appeared recently describe the development of immunodiagnostic techniques, and evaluate them under field conditions (Bruce-Chwatt, 1970). Some of these publications point out the complexities of parasitic antigens (Capron, 1970), others deal with identification and purification of parasitic antigens (Korach and Benex, 1966a,b; Sadun *et al.*, 1965; Sawada *et al.*, 1965; Taillez and Korach, 1970), and still others explore factors which on one hand may be important in host resistance and on the other in the production of diseases through allergic or hypersensitivity mechanisms (Bier, 1967; Garnham *et al.*, 1963; Soulsby, 1967; Taylor, 1968; Zvaifler, 1970).

A summary of information available on homocytotropic antibodies in parasitic infections is much more meaningful if viewed from a perspective of the potential achievements of these studies rather than on past accomplishments. Yet, this review is particularly appropriate at this time, since in recent years there has been a considerable increase in the number of investigators interested in homocytotropic antibodies in parasitic infections and new findings are being reported at a rapid pace.

Hypersensitivity is an acquired state which develops as a result of exposure to some external harmful antigenic agent. Based on the time scales with which the reactions occur, hypersensitivity is divided into immediate-type and delayed-type. This actually reflects fundamental differences in mechanisms. The immediate-type reactions are those which are mediated by serum antibodies and whose first manifestations occur within minutes of the contact of antigen with antibody. Delayed-type hypersensitivity reactions appear to be independent of serum antibodies and dependent upon sensitized cells. They differ from immediate-type reactions in at least the following respects: (1) the intradermal injection of antigen into a previously exposed animal initiates a slowly evolving, indurated, and erythematous reaction which reaches a peak within 48 hours and wanes slowly during the following weeks; (2) the serum of a sensitized subject does not confer passive sensitivity to a nonsensitized recipient; and (3) lymphoid cells from a reactive donor confer passive sensitization to a normal subject.

In this discussion of immediate hypersensitivity only minimal consideration will be given to the diagnostic and protective aspects to be derived. These, and the effector mechanisms of immediate hypersensitivity, will be discussed authoritatively by Dr. Barbaro and Dr. Murray.

This review is not intended to be all inclusive and the list of individual studies published on immediate hypersensitivity in parasitic infections is somewhat incomplete. Although for reasons of greater familiarity undue emphasis may have been placed on investigations with which the author and his collaborators have been directly involved, this should by no means be construed as a suggestion that these studies are of greater significance than others which might have been omitted or mentioned only briefly. It is hoped that even though this report discloses some wide gaps in our present knowledge of the immediate hypersensitivity of parasitic infections, it will serve the purpose of stimulating further collaborative research between parasitologists and immunologists and will lead to the development of more fruitful approaches to these problems in terms of immunological concepts. Although increased emphasis on research in this area is badly needed, we are no longer at a stage where "There was the Door to which I found no Key; There was the Veil through which I might not see. ("Rubaiyat" of Omar Khayyam, XXXII, translation by Edward Fitzgerald). If this review will stimulate additional immunologists to take up problems directly or indirectly related to parasitic diseases, it will have served its purpose.

II. Reactions Mediated by Anaphylactic Antibodies

Antibodies to parasites and their products are easily demonstrated in the blood of infected humans or animals. This is not surprising when one considers the complex structure of the invading organisms, the various stages of this life cycle, and their many secretions and metabolic products which may serve as antigens. Moreover, many parasites may harbor a diverse array of cells in various stages of development and decay and may be contaminated by the products of these cells. This mosaic of antigens in various parasites stimulates the production of a remarkable multitude of antibodies which are found in different immunoglobulin classes.

Nearly 80 years ago, when antibodies were demonstrated by toxin neutralization, agglutination, precipitation, and hemolysis, immunologists believed that the antibodies responsible for each manifestation were different from one to another. However, the idea was reversed by several findings which indicated that the same antibody molecules could be responsible for different immunological reactions.

The unitarian theory, i.e., one and the same antibody being responsible for different immunological manifestations, has been accepted for a long time despite the heterogeneity of antibodies with respect to physico-chemical properties. In addition to 7 S gamma globulin, 19 S antibody was detected in 1939. Twenty years later, a third type of gamma globulin which is antigenically related but distinct for 7 S and 19 S gamma globulin was found by immunoelectrophoresis. It is now established that biological properties of antibodies differ depending on immuno-globulin classes and subclasses, and that the functions of the antibodies are based on certain structures in the Fc portion of the molecules (Ishizaka, 1971). Five main classes of antibodies (IgG, IgA, IgE, IgM, and IgD) have been described in man, and similar classes are gradually being characterized in other animals. Detailed descriptions of the im-munoglobulins and their properties have been presented in several recent reviews (Cohen and Milstein, 1967; Rowe, 1968; J. F. A. P. Miller, 1968). It may be pertinent here to indicate that, (a) the antibodies involved in the conventional serologic tests (Precipitin, fluorescent anti-body, agglutination, and complement fixation tests) belong mostly to the IgG and IgM classes of immunoglobulins, the latter being the most primitive immunoglobulin both ontogenetically and phylogenetically (Good and Papermaster, 1964); (b) IgA, although present in serum, predominates in many mucous secretions (Tomasi and Bienenstock, 1968); and (c) IgE, found in serum in minute amounts, is produced primarily in tissues adjacent to mucous surfaces (Ishizaka *et al.*, 1969). The only identified function of the IgE immunoglobulins is in the media-tion of immediate hypersensitivity reactions such as local and systemic anaphylaxis. One type of homocytotropic (reaginic) antibody resides in this fraction.

The term homocytotropic antibody was introduced by Becker and Austen (1966) to describe a unique function of an immunoglobulin, i.e., the capacity to attach to certain target cells of the same species so that subsequent contact with antigen leads to the noncytotoxic release of pharmacological mediators of anaphylaxis from that cell. Tissue or cells with homocytotropic antibodies fixed to the surface are referred to as sensitized. Two types of homocytotropic antibodies have been described; one fixes to the skin for a relatively brief period (2–6 hours) after intradermal injection for optimal antigen-induced local increase in vascular permeability as measured by the extravasation of the dye. This antibody has an electrophoretic mobility of gamma-1, a sedimentation coefficient of 7 S and the capacity to fix to tissue and bind antigen, and withstands heating at 56°C for 4 hours or reduction and alkylation. The second antibody, referred to as skin-sensitizing or reaginic antibody, is associated with the IgE immunoglobulin class (Ishizaka *et al.*, 1966). It is capable of fixing to skin after intradermal injection for days or weeks and continues to elicit antigen-induced vascular permeability. This antibody has the electrophoretic mobility of a fast gamma globulin, a sedimentation coefficient of approximately 8 S, is heat labile, and is susceptible to inactivation by reduction and alkylating agents. Human homocytotropic (reaginic) antibody is capable of sensitizing tissues of monkeys and chimpanzees, but not those of other animals. In humans the only homocytotropic antibodies described so far are reaginic and belong to the immunoglobulin class IgE. In lower animals (mouse, rat guinea pig, and rabbit) both reaginlike homocytotropic antibodies and other nonreaginic (heat stable 7 S) homocytotropic antibodies have been reported. The human reaginic antibody was found in the serum after development of hypersensitivity to various antigens and appeared to mediate immediate skin reactivity, the Prausnitz-Küstner (PK) reaction, certain systemic reactions, and *in vitro* antigen induced release of histamine from actively or passively sensitized leukocytes (Osler, 1963).

Sensitized tissues, following antigen challenge *in vivo* or *in vitro*, release one or more of the following pharmacologically active substances (mediators): histamine (Humphrey and Jaques, 1955; Van Arsdel *et al.*, 1958), serotonin (Zucker, 1959; Benditt and Wong, 1957; Benditt *et al.*, 1955), kinins (Greenbaum and Kim, 1967), slow reacting substance (Orange *et al.*, 1968), lysosomal enzymes (Treadwell, 1969), and eosinophilic chemotactic factor (Kay *et al.*, 1971). The sources of these substances (target cells or substrate) vary in different species, but have usually been attributed to neutrophilic leukocytes, mast cells, enterochromaffin cells, basophils, platelets, macrophages, and eosinophils. The release of pharmacologically active substances produces a series of rapid, explosive, and evanescent reactions which vary in different animals depending on the shock organs for that species. The role of these substances in the host–parasite relationship has not been defined.

Cutaneous anaphylaxis, a clinical manifestation of mediator release, can be elicited by the intradermal injection of antigen into a sensitized individual or animal or through intradermal injection of antibody into the skin of a normal animal with subsequent antigen challenge injected intravenously. The latter is referred to as passive cutaneous anaphylaxis (PCA). A blue dye (Evans or pontamine blue) which is injected intravenously prior to or at the time of antigen challenge binds to plasma proteins and is a convenient indication of the increased vascular permeability occurring 5–10 minutes after antigen interaction with homocytotropic antibody. Benaceraff *et al.* (1963), White and coworkers (1963), Mota (1964a,b), and Mota and Peixoto (1966) have shown that the various antibodies produced by a given species differ greatly in the kinds of anaphylactic reactions which they can mediate.

The term "cytophilic" has been used to describe immunoglobulins which have a special tendency to become attached to the surface of certain cells, not by virtue of their antibody combining sites, but of some other configurational property of the molecule. When these attach to cells of the same or closely related species (usually those of the class IgE) they are referred to as homocytotropic; when instead they attach to cells of unrelated species (those of other immunoglobulin classes) they are termed heterocytotropic.

III. Allergic Response of the Host

A. PROTOZOAN INFECTIONS

Although delayed hypersensitivity has been demonstrated or postulated for a variety of protozoan infections such as leishmaniasis, trypanosomiasis (Bryceson *et al.*, 1970), toxoplasmosis (Frenkel, 1948), and amebiasis (Maddison *et al.*, 1968), the antigens of parasitic protozoa are in general relatively ineffective in stimulating immediate hypersensitivity.

Suggestive evidence of homocytotropic (reaginic) antibodies being stimulated by a protozoan has been presented in *Trichomonas foetus* infections in cattle. The immune reaction to this parasite is localized in the uterus and according to Robertson (1963), anaphylactic reactions may follow repeated sensitization. Since no precise information is available as to the immunoglobulin class to which this anaphylactic antibody belongs, further studies with modern immunochemical techniques are warranted.

Infection with African trypanosomiasis produces the liberation of short chain peptides with kininlike activity in mice, rats, rabbits, and cattle (Goodwin and Richards, 1960; Boreham, 1968, 1970; Goodwin, 1971). The release of kinin is associated with antigen reaction and has been responsible for changes in vascular permeability that lead to some of the abnormalities occurring in diseased animals. Seed and Gam (1966) postulated that host tissue antigens released by hypersensitivity induced cell destruction are responsible for an autoimmune condition which plays an important role in the pathogenesis of trypanosomiasis. Monkeys and guinea pigs infected with *T. cruzi* (Rey-Calero, 1967), the agent of American trypanosomiasis, developed cytophilic antibodies. The antibodies detected in the skin of guinea pigs were 7 S and those detected in monkeys were defined as "beta-2A." The latter were sensitive to mercaptoethanol and were tentatively designated as reaginic antibodies.

Two types of cytophilic antibodies in sera from patients infected with *Leishmania braziliensis* were detected. The antibodies fixed in the skin of guinea pigs were of the 7 S type and those in the monkey were "beta-2A." He postulated that these antibodies are responsible for the symptomatology of this infection. However, the presence of homocytotropic antibodies has not been demonstrated in this leishmaniasis even though it has been stated: "It is likely that vascular damage and kinin release may be related to the allergic reactions that occur when antibodies are formed to successive antigenic variants of the parasite" (Goodwin, 1971).

The anoxemia-induced tissue damage in malaria also has been attributed to the release of pharmacologically active substances (Tella and Maegraith, 1962, 1963; Desowitz and Pavanand, 1967; L. H. Miller and Chongsuphajaisiddhi, 1968). Furthermore, a pharmacologically active agent, presumably histamine, has been demonstrated in the blood of monkeys infected with malaria (Maegraith and Onabanjo, 1970). It has been postulated that a similar factor may be responsible for plasma leakage and hemoconcentration in *P. falciparum* infections (Jervis *et al.*, 1972). However, mediator release can also occur by nonimmunological mechanisms.

Immediate and delayed hypersensitivity to *Entameba histolytica* was observed in patients hospitalized with severe amebiasis and in asymptomatic individuals (Maddison *et al.*, 1968). The authors could not detect homocytotropic antibodies in monkeys which received sera from these patients, although passive cutaneous anaphylactic reactions in guinea pigs were obtained. Immediate hypersensitivity was observed more frequently in invasive clinical amebiasis, whereas delayed hypersensitivity was more common in the asymptomatic group.

Alimentary hypersensitivity induced by *Giardia lamblia* infection has been reported (Halstead and Sadun, 1965). Biopsy of the duodenum showed marked eosinophilic infiltration of the lamina propria. Since the syndrome with *Giardia* infection was concomitant with ingestion of meat of mammalian origin, it was postulated that meat might provide the appropriate environment for maximal liberation of parasite excretory allergens or that parasite metabolic products may serve as haptens, with the allergy being a result of the degradation products of the mammalian muscle. Another possibility was that *Giardia* infection induces a tissue sensitization in which there is an allergy to one or more components of the diet.

Therefore, it is concluded that homocytotropic (reaginic) antibodies in protozoan infections have not been convincingly demonstrated as of the present time. However, one must consider the possibility that failure of detection might be due to the scarcity of proper antigens and not necessarily to the absence of these antibodies.

B. Helminthic Infections (Fig. 1)

Contrary to the findings with protozoan infections, there is no problem in demonstrating homocytotropic antibodies in the blood of humans or animals infected with helminths. In fact, most parasitic worm infections elicit an immediate-type of hypersensitivity and the development of high titer reaginic antibodies. This may be aided by the uniquely complex helminth life cycles which permit intimate contact with the

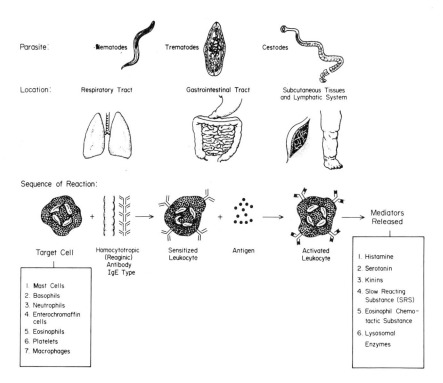

Fig. 1. Immediate hypersensitivity in parasitic diseases.

mucosae of the respiratory or gastrointestinal systems at some stage during the migration of the parasite within the mammalian host.

The nearly universal capability of helminthiases to stimulate the immediate-type of hypersensitivity has been used widely in immunodiagnosis for more than half a century. Intradermal tests of the histamine type have been described for the presumptive diagnosis of such human infections as ascariasis (Rackemann and Stevens, 1927), creeping eruption (Beaver *et al.*, 1952), dracontiasis (Fairley and Liston, 1924), enterobias (Grubel, 1924), filariasis (Taliaferro and Hoffman, 1930; Culbertson *et al.*, 1944; Hoffman and Vargas, 1931; Bozicevich *et al.*, 1947), strongyloidiasis (Fulleborn, 1924, 1926), hookworm infection (Sawada *et al.*, 1954), trichinosis (Bachman, 1928), diphyllobothriasis (Brunner, 1928), echinococcosis (Magath, 1921; Rackemann and Stevens, 1927; Casoni, 1912), taeniasis (Brunner, 1928; Ramsdell, 1927), paragonimiasis (Sadun *et al.*, 1959a, 1960), clonorchiasis (Sadun *et al.*, 1959b), and schistosomiasis (Fairley and Williams, 1927; Guerra *et al.*, 1945; Mayer and Pifano, 1945; Bozicevich and Hoyem, 1947; Sadun *et al.*, 1959b; Pellegrino *et al.*, 1968; Pellegrino, 1958). These intradermal reactions, although very useful for diagnosing helminthic infections, do not necessarily provide precise information on the presence, time course development, or role of reaginic antibodies in parasitic infections.

Many helminthic infections cause various manifestations of immediate hypersensitivity such as eosinophilia, edema, dermatitis, asthma, acute diarrheas, and in some cases anaphylactic shock, but most of the efforts designed to detect, define immunochemically, and classify homocytotropic antibodies are directed toward only a relatively few infections. In some of these efforts, reaginlike antibodies with characteristics similar or identical to those of human IgE immunoglobulin class (Zvaifler and Robinson, 1969) have been defined (Table I), whereas in others the antibodies that induce the allergic response to parasites have not been clearly defined or have been ascribed to IgA or IgG immunoglobulin classes.

In addition to being important inducers of homocytotropic antibody, helminths have long been known for their unique ability to evoke eosinophilia (Soulsby, 1967). This is of particular interest since eosinophilia appears characteristically in many instances of allergy. An increase in the number of eosinophils, either local or general, usually is associated with local hypersensitivity reactions. This enhancement in number is so commonly associated with hypersensitivity reactions of the immediate type, that according to Raffel (1953) abnormal numbers of eosinophils in any disease of unknown etiology should suggest the probability of an allergic component. More recently Samter and Alexander (1965)

TABLE I

Helminths and Hosts in Which Reaginlike Antibodies with Characteristics
Similar to Those of Human IgE Immunoglobulin Have Been Demonstrated

Helminth	Host	References
Ascaris lumbricoides	Man	Weiszer *et al.*, 1968; Parish, 1969
	Rhesus	Ishizaka *et al.*, 1969; Malley *et al.*, 1968
	Dog	Patterson *et al.*, 1969
	Guinea pig	Dobson *et al.*, 1971
	Rat	Strejan and Campbell, 1968; Tada *et al.*, 1971
Toxocara spp.	Man	Hogarth-Scott, 1967a, 1969
Nippostrongylus brasiliensis	Rat	Ogilvie, 1964; Wilson & Bloch, 1968; Jones *et al.*, 1970
Trichinella spiralis	Man	Zvaifler *et al.*, 1966; Williams *et al.*, 1972
	Rabbit	Sadun *et al.*, 1968
	Guinea pig	Catty, 1969
	Rat	Williams *et al.*, 1970
	Mouse	Sadun *et al.*, 1968; Mota and Wong, 1968
Schistosoma spp.	Man	Sadun *et al.*, 1966; Sadun and Gore, 1970; Williams *et al.*, 1971
	Chimpanzee	Sadun *et al*, 1966, 1970; Williams *et al.*, 1971
	Rhesus	Sadun *et al.*, 1966; Ogilvie *et al.*, 1966; Hsu and Hsu, 1966; Sadun and Gore, 1970; Williams *et al.*, 1971
	Cercopithecus	Sadun and Gore, 1970
	Rabbit	Zvaifler *et al.*, 1966, 1967; Schoenbechler and Sadun, 1968; Sadun and Gore, 1970; Williams *et al.*, 1971
	Guinea pig	Sadun and Gore, 1970
	Rat	Ogilvie *et al.*, 1966
Dirofilaria uniformis	Rabbit	Sadun *et al.*, 1967
Amphicaeum robertsi	Rat	Dobson, 1968
Ostertagia spp.	Sheep	Hogarth-Scott, 1969
Nematospiroides dubius	Mouse	Panter, 1969

called attention to the fact that eosinophils participate conspicuously in allergic reactions, and he noted the particular effectiveness of a derivative of *Ascaris* worms in the induction of eosinophilia.

High levels of circulating eosinophils are usually observed in those helminthic infections in which the association of the parasite with the host tissues is the closest. Examples of this are seen in eosinophilic meningitis due to infection in man of *Angiostrongylus cantonensis,* a worm which normally inhabits the pulmonary arteries of rats (Rosen *et al.,* 1961). Loeffler's syndrome or pulmonary eosinophilia is another complication of helminthiases (Manson-Bahr, 1960). The symptoms produced include spasmodic bronchitis and bronchial asthma accompanied by massive leukocytosis most of which is eosinophilic. This may be caused by a passage to the lungs of parasites of man such as *A. lumbricoides* or by nonhuman parasites such as *Toxocara canis* or *T. cati.* Tropical eosinophilia or eosinophilic lung is also a respiratory tract condition which is associated with elevated eosinophil numbers. The fact that the signs associated with this condition frequently subside after administration of antifilarial drugs suggests that tropical eosinophilia might be a form of filariasis. Infection with larvae of *Brugia malayi* of monkey origin or *B. phangi* of feline origin produced the classical symptoms of the disease which were terminated by treatment with antifilarial drugs (Buckley, 1958). This led to the belief that the disease was due to infection with nonhuman filarial parasites. Lung biopsies performed on patients with tropical eosinophilia showed eosinophilic foci surrounding the generating microfilariae (Webb *et al.,* 1960; Danaraj *et al.,* 1966). Therefore, tropical eosinophilia or eosinophilic lung has been ascribed to filarial worms that become established in a normal host and produce an unusual degree of hypersensitivity. On that basis this disease has been defined as an immediate hypersensitivity reaction. As pointed out by Andrews (1962) however, it is important to remember that while eosinophilia is commonly associated with immediate hypersensitivity, this dyscrasia may also be a prominent sign in a number of other disorders which thus far have not been identified with certainty as having hypersensitivity components. In his presidential address to the American Society of Parasitologists, he lamented that "little is known about the actual incidence of allergic morbidity and mortality due to hypersensitivity to helminth parasites." Although information on these aspects is accumulating rapidly, major gaps in our knowledge still exist.

1. Ascaris and Related Nematodes

Many descriptions of toxic effects following the administration of *Ascaris* extracts to animals have appeared in the literature. Symptoms resembling those of anaphylactic shock occur after intravenous injection of *Ascaris* tissues. Similarly, digestive disturbances and degenerative changes have been observed following oral administration of *Ascaris* body fluid (Sakaguchi, 1928; Read, 1931; Herrick and Emery, 1929). *Ascaris* extracts caused an increase in tonus and in the rate of contraction in the isolated intestine of several species of mammals and produced vomiting and diarrhea. An aqueous extract of *Ascaris lumbricoides* and *Parascaris equorum* was toxic to horses, guinea pigs, dogs, and rabbits but not to mice and rats. Weinberg and Julien (1911, 1913) found that the body fluid of *P. equorum* when instilled into the eyes of horses caused acute conjunctivitis and edema of the eyelids. These results were probably manifestations of immediate hypersensitivity, although they might have been due to toxic products. However, evidence of hypersensitivity produced by tissues and fluids of *Ascaris* has been presented in infected individuals (Coventry and Taliaferro, 1928) in laboratory workers who frequently handle worms (LeRoy, 1910; Rackemann and Stevens, 1927; T. L. Jones and Kingscote, 1935) and in animals experimentally sensitized (Coventry, 1929). Even minute amounts of volatile substances from *A. lumbricoides* are sufficient to induce phenomena of immediate hypersensitivity. The mere odor of fluids from *A. lumbricoides* may be sufficient to bring about severe symptoms (Goldschmidt, 1910), and laboratory coats worn while handling this nematode may induce allergic rhinitis in a sensitive person (T. L. Jones and Kingscote, 1935). Sensitization to *Ascaris* protein was also observed after infection with other nematodes. The fact that antibodies are involved in the mechanism of *Ascaris* allergy was demonstrated by transferring sensitivity by means of the PK reaction in humans (Brunner, 1934; Tezner, 1934) and in dogs (Brunner *et al.*, 1944). Oliver-Gonzalez (1946) reported that guinea pigs injected intraperitoneally with the serum from rabbits immunized with whole worm material developed anaphylactic symptoms when challenged with *Ascaris* intestine, blood, or body fluids but not when challenged with cuticle, muscle, or egg or sperm homogenates of the worm. Sprent (1949) was able to demonstrate that homogenates of body fluid, intestine, cuticle, muscle, and ovary of *A. lumbricoides* from the pig failed to produce symptoms of shock when injected intravenously into mice, rabbits, and guinea pigs, provided that no previous sensitization had occurred. However, these substances were shown to cause active anaphylactic sensitization of the guinea pig to the same antigen, skin sensitivity and precipitins in rabbits, and skin reactions in persons sensitized to *Ascaris*. Guinea pigs infected with the larvae of *A. lumbricoides, P. equorum, Trichinella spiralis,* and *Paraspidodera* spp. were found to be hypersensitive to *Ascaris* body fluid. Guinea pigs infected with *A. lumbricoides* manifested anaphylactic shock when injected intravenously with extracts prepared from *A. columnaris, Toxascaris leonina,* and *Phytoloptera maillaris* but not by extracts prepared from *Trichinella spiralis* nor by those from three cestodes and a trematode (Sprent, 1950, 1951). The changes in the histamine content and the mechanisms of the shock induced by anaphylaxislike reactions produced by *Ascaris* have been studied by Rocha e Silva and Grana (1946a,b).

The first indication that homocytotropic (reaginic) antibodies were involved in *Ascaris* hypersensitivity was provided by Weiszer *et al.* (1968). They demonstrated cutaneous reactivity by skin testing and passively transferred it to the skin of monkeys. The antibody activity was lost after heating at 56°C and was found to reside in the same fraction of a Sephadex G-200 eluate as the human reaginic sera. Normal rhesus monkeys were also shown to produce reaginic antibodies when injected with *Ascaris* crude extracts or with an electrophoretically isolated *Ascaris* fraction (Malley *et al.*, 1968). Ishizaka *et al.* (1969) showed that monkeys immunized with *Ascaris* extract possessed detectable amounts of a serum protein that cross-reacted with antisera specific for human IgE. The physicochemical properties of this monkey protein such as electrophoretic mobility, molecular size, and behavior on column chromatography also resembled those of human IgE. The sedimentation velocity of the monkey protein was likewise comparable with that of human IgE and significantly faster than that of IgG. They concluded that this monkey protein represents a distinct immunoglobulin class corresponding to human IgE and that IgE formation may be stimulated by parasitic infections. Strejan and Campbell (1968) sensitized rats with crude *Ascaris* extracts as well as with chromatographically isolated fractions. They found that when these fractions were administered with killed *B. pertusis* organisms as adjuvants, they elicited homocytotropic antibodies in relatively high titers. They called attention to the fact that *Ascaris* extracts are much more important inducers of homocytotropic antibodies than standard protein antigens such as ovalbumin or bovine serum albumin. The histamine releasing capacity of one fraction was not inhibited by specific rabbit anti-rhesus immunoglobulins (IgA, IgG, IgM). This suggested that the histamine release factor which they identified as an immunoglobulin may be an IgE-like antibody. Booth and his co-workers (1970) identified in dogs an antibody which can transfer sensitivity to *Ascaris* and which is analogous to human IgE immunoglobulin. Winsor (1971) observed that sensitization of guinea pigs to *A. lumbricoides* antigen can be elicited not only by infection and by parenteral injection of crude antigens from adult worms, but also by exposure to air passed over whole *Ascaris*. When tested by the PK test, guinea pig sera reacted to an *Ascaris* fraction believed to be the allergen described by Hogarth-Scott (1968). He observed that the airborne antigens from hemolymph reacted with sera from sensitized guinea pigs as well as with human reaginic sera, and concluded that the active allergen is present in the worm hemolymph and metabolites. A homocytotropic (reaginic) antibody which reaches high titers during *Ascaris* infections in guinea pigs was reported by Dobson *et al.* (1971). This antibody was considered analogous to human IgE antibody and differs from other guinea pig anaphylactic antibodies by virtue of its greater molecular weight, its sensitivity to heat and mercaptoethanol, and by its ability to sensitize homologous skin sites for prolonged periods of time and to remain active at high dilutions. Further studies (Dobson *et al.*, 1972) revealed that the reaginic activity was not absorbed by rabbit anti-guinea pig IgM and IgG, but was absorbed by rabbit anti-guinea pig IgE antisera. An 8 S and an 11 S component were detected by sucrose sedimentation of guinea pig IgE. The 11 S reaginic fraction had a greater skin sensitizing activity than the 8 S component. They could not exclude the possibility that a distinct reaginic antibody other than 8 S IgE is present in guinea pigs. The reaginic activity in a canine reaginic antiserum against *Ascaris* antigen was studied by Patterson *et al.* (1969) who concluded that because of similarities of the characteristics of the canine and human reagin, the canine immunoglobulin with reaginic activity should be considered the IgE equivalent. The IgG, IgA, and IgM antibodies to *A. lumbricoides* antigen were measured in the sera of normal and allergic persons by Parish (1969), who suggested that reagins are not necessarily confined to a single class of immunoglobulins. Further work on the heterogenicity of IgE has confirmed these observations (Reid, 1970).

Homocytotropic antibody formation against dinitrophenylated *Ascaris* extracts was selectively suppressed in rats by the passive administration of homologous antibody against the same antigen. The suppression was preferentially directed to the homocytotropic antibody response while the hemagglutinating antibody formation was unaffected. The results indicate the presence of a "feedback" regulation in the homocytotropic antibody response (Tada and Okumura, 1971). Whole body X-irradiation greatly suppressed the production of IgG antibody and resulted in a defective humoral feed back regulation (Tada *et al.*, 1971). Homocytotropic antibody formation was greatly enhanced and prolonged by splenectomy and thymectomy in adult rats. However, in contrast to adult thymectomy, neonatal thymectomy caused a loss of the ability to produce homocytotropic antibodies to the dinitrophenylated *Ascaris* extracts (Okumura and Tada, 1971).

Specific homocytotropic (reaginic) antibody measured by passive cutaneous anaphylactic tests in baboons and monkeys was detectable in the sera of patients with proven visceral larva migrans (Hogarth-Scott, 1967a; Hogarth-Scott *et al.*, 1969). These patients had 10–15 times the normal level of IgE as determined by the radioimmunosorbent test.

Johannson *et al.* (1970) found that whereas bacterial and viral infections are of minor importance in raising IgE levels, parasitic infections gave rise to high IgE concentrations in individuals without atopic manifestations. Very high IgE levels were found in an unselected group of Ethiopian children (Johannson *et al.*, 1968) who had on the average about 20 times as high IgE levels as healthy Swedish children of the same age. When children were selected for *Ascaris* infection, a mean IgE level 28 times higher than that of the Swedish children was found.

2. *Nippostrongylus braziliensis*

In 1964 Ogilvie reported that rats infected with *N. brasiliensis* developed a skin-sensitizing antibody in the third week after an initial infection. This antibody persisted for many months even in the absence of subsequent reinfection. However, after a second infection, there was an abrupt rise in antibody titer. This skin-sensitizing antibody had many of the properties of human reagin. It was heat labile and persisted in the skin so as to produce a PCA reaction after a latent period of 72 hours. It produced passive cutaneous anaphylaxis in the skin of the rat but did not sensitize the skin of other species. Rats vaccinated with fresh extracts of adult worms with Freund's complete adjuvant produced precipitating antibodies indistinguishable in gel diffusion tests from those produced by repeatedly infected rats. However, vaccinated animals did not produce reagins but contained blocking antibodies which when incubated with antigen *in vitro* prevented the PCA reaction (Ogilvie, 1964, 1967). Reagin production following initial infection was delayed in neonatally thymectomized rats and in immunologically immature newborn rats, and further there was a reduced anamnestic response after reinfection. Conversely, splenectomy in adult rats had no effect on the level of reaginic antibodies (Ogilvie and Jones, 1967). Reagins could not be detected in young rats suckled by immune mothers, although they were found in the milk and the sera of the mothers (V. E. Jones and Ogilvie, 1967a).

Attempts were made to characterize physicochemically the homocytotropic antibody developing in the rat following infection with *N. brasiliensis* (R. J. Wilson and Bloch, 1968; V. E. Jones *et al.*, 1970; Giertz *et al.*, 1970) and to define the antigen which combined with the rat homocytotropic antibody. The rat reaginic antibodies to *N. brasiliensis* were shown to be intermediate in molecular size between 7 S and 19 S globulins and migrated with fast immunoglobulins but could not be related to either IgG or IgA rat immunoglobulins. The same serum fractions which gave homologous passive cutaneous anaphylaxis also produced systemic anaphylaxis. The antigenic material for both the homologous PCA and systemic anaphylaxis seem to be a protein with a molecular weight of approximately 12,000 to 17,000 (V. E. Jones and Ogilvie, 1967b).

Washed peritoneal mast cells obtained from actively infected rats or normal mast cells passively sensitized *in vitro* with serum from infected rats released histamine upon contact with worm antigen (Wilson and Bloch, 1968). Degranulation of mast cells occurred at the site of PCA reactions. Both the PCA and mast cell disruption were maximal 5 minutes after antigen challenge in the rat reagin system. However, the skin reaction was not primarily dependent on or associated with mast cell disruption, since it was possible to induce skin reaction when the mast cells had been disrupted by other means and, conversely, skin reactions could be obtained without significant mast cell disruption (Goose and Blair, 1969). The appearance and course of sensitization of rat peritoneal mast cells and pleural cells was followed by measuring antigen induced release of histamine *in vitro*. Two peaks of sensitivity were detected. The first was observed approximately 1 month after initial infection and soon after a second infection, the second peak was seen after a fourth infection. These results were similar to those obtained in the investigation of systemic anaphylaxis *in vivo* with *N. brasiliensis* by Keller (1970).

3. *Trichinella spiralis*

Infection with *T. spiralis* elicits an immediate-type hypersensitivity demonstrable by *in vitro* and *in vivo* immunological techniques. Allergic manifestations such as muscle pain, fever, skin rashes, edema, and eosinophilia usually accompany heavy infections with this parasite. Most of these characteristic signs reach their peak between the twelfth and twentieth day following infection (Gould, 1945) and tend to subside at the time when the larvae achieve maximal growth. These symptoms could be related to irritation and mechanical damage due to migration of the larvae. The eosinophilia precedes the development of serological reactions or positive skin reactions. However, the presence of eosinophils in the initial invasion of striated muscle fibers and in the muscle walls of the arterioles often accompanied by inflammatory changes resembling those seen in periartheritis nodosa or serum sickness suggest an allergic or immune reaction (Rose, 1965).

Allergic sensitization has been demonstrated in experimentally infected guinea pigs (Sharp and Olson, 1962) and mice (Briggs, 1963, 1966). Intravenous or intracardial injection of antigens into *T. spiralis* infected animals produced generalized anaphylactic reactions and frequently death. Such sensitivity was demonstrable soon after infection and persisted for many months, possibly for the life of the host. Sensitization of individual tissues was also shown by: (1) *in vitro* exposure of intestinal tissues from infected guinea pigs to somatic and metabolic antigens of *Trichinella,* and in some cases heterologous worm antigens, which resulted in muscular contractions and (2) exposure of subcutaneous mast cells of mice to similar antigens which produced cell disruption with release of granular contents. However, mast cell disruption was not produced with antigens from other worms. Such sensitivity of intestinal and subcutaneous tissues could be passively transferred to normal animals by injections of serum containing anti-*Trichinella* antibodies from homologous hosts. Antiserum from rabbits only poorly sensitized mouse subcutaneous tissues. Although some of these studies are suggestive of reactions elicited by reaginic antibodies, it is not possible to determine with certainty whether gamma E antibodies are involved in them.

T. spiralis infection has recently been shown to elicit the formation of homocytotropic antibodies in man (Zvaifler *et al.,* 1966), mice (Sadun *et al.,* 1968; Mota and Wong, 1968; Mota *et al.,* 1969a,b), guinea pigs (Catty, 1969), and rabbits (Sadun *et al.,* 1968). PCA activity in rabbits was detected as early as 2 weeks after feeding the infected larvae; it did not reach its peak until 18 weeks later and was still present 38 weeks after infection. The instability of mouse and rabbit PCA antibody after heating or reduction and alkylation contrasted with the failure of such treatment to alter the activity of fluorescent antibodies. Electrophoretically faster immunoglobulins contained PCA activity, but did not contain detectable fluorescent antibodies. Cross-reacting reaginlike antibodies were detected between *T. spiralis* and *Dirofilaria uniformis* (Sadun *et al.,* 1968).

Mice produced two homocytotropic antibodies following infection with *T. spiralis.* A heat-resistant antibody responsible for PCA reactions induced after a short sensitization period (2–4 hours), and a heat labile antibody responsible for PCA reactions induced after 72 hours. Both antibodies appeared in the circulation 5 weeks after infection and reached the highest levels in the ninth week. Later, the antibody which induced PCA reactions with a latency of 72 hours disappeared from the serum in some animals whereas the antibody having a 4 hour latency remained. In animals subjected to repeated reinfections, the reaginlike antibody either decreased or disappeared from the serum. On the other hand, the antibody with a 2 hour latency increased. Absorption of mouse antisera with a highly specific rabbit anti-mouse 7 S gamma-1, completely removed the 2 hour PCA activity of mouse antiserum without changing its ability to induce PCA reactions after 72 hours (Mota and

Wong, 1968). The two homocytotropic antibodies detected in serum of mice following infection with *T. spiralis* could be distinguished by their biological and chromatographic behavior.

Immunization with larval extracts of *T. spiralis* led to the appearance of both (2 and 72 hours) antibodies in the serum, with similar properties to those obtained in the course of infection. Although a second dose of antigen resulted in increases in the levels of both antibodies, further injections resulted in a high level of the antibody with a 2 hour latency and the disappearance of the reaginlike antibody (Mota and Wong, 1968). The two homocytotropic antibodies could also be separated by biological screening (Mota *et al.*, 1969b). Antisera collected 8 days after single antigenic stimulation demonstrate both homologous and rat heterologous PCA activity. Heating of these early antisera resulted in complete inactivation of heterologous PCA activity and almost complete inactivation of homologous PCA activity, thus suggesting that the rat heterologous antibody was due to mouse reaginic antibody. These results were strengthened by those obtained following serum absorption. Absorption of these same sera with rabbit anti-mouse gamma-1, caused no change in homologous or heterologous PCA activity, indicating that the PCA activity of the very early antisera was due to mouse reaginic antibody. Early mouse antiserum was found to be very efficient in passive sensitization of rat mast cells and heating at 56°C resulted in the complete loss of this capability (Mota *et al.*, 1969a). The main reason for using a closely related heterologous system such as the rat is that, of the homocytotropic antibodies present in mice, only the reaginlike IgE and not the gamma-1 is detected. Moreover, a shorter latent period is observed.

Homocytotropic (reaginic) antibodies in guinea pigs infected with *T. spiralis* were demonstrated by Catty (1969). He observed PCA activity in the 7 S region at 17 hours after intradermal injection and reaginlike antibodies which were detectable after a latent period of 7 days. The reaginlike antibodies resided in an electrophoretically faster region, had a sedimentation rate greater than 7 S, and were highly sensitive to heat. This long-term sensitizing antibody with biological and physicochemical properties analogous to the human reagin could be demonstrated in the serum of guinea pigs infected with *T. spiralis* but not in those immunized with a worm extract.

A radioactive iodine labeled microprecipitin (RAMP) assay was developed for measuring the binding of antigen by antibody. In both naturally infected humans and experimentally infected animals reaginic antibodies could be detected by PCA after a latent period of 72 hours. Heating or reduction and alkylation of the immune sera destroyed or markedly reduced the *T. spiralis* antibody reactions in the RAMP assay. The results indicate that the RAMP assay can reliably measure activity due to antibodies primarily of the immunoglobulin E class and can be used as a means of demonstrating binding of antigen by reaginic antibody in trichinosis (Williams *et al.*, 1971).

4. *Schistosoma* spp.

Allergic manifestations in man occur as a result of infection with all three species of human schistosomes. In persons previously exposed to infection, cercarial penetration is frequently followed by urticaria, asthmatic attacks, subcutaneous edema, leukocytosis, and eosinophilia. A second clinically recognizable phase beginning 1 month after exposure to infection and usually coincidental with the onset of egg laying of the worms consists of anorexia, fever, headache, and weight loss. This has been known in Japan as "Katayama fever." It has been generally acknowledged that these two clinical phases of schistosomiasis are due to immediate hypersensitivity phenomena, although until recently no definite proof has been obtained to that effect. When cercariae of non-human species penetrate the skin, a dermatitis termed "swimmer's itch" often develops which consists primarily of pruritic papules (Cort, 1928). Evidence that swimmer's itch is a sensitization phenomenon was provided by McFarlane (1949) and Olivier (1949). Whereas primary exposure to cercariae was followed in some subjects by no visible reaction, repeated exposures brought a reaction usually seen immediately after penetration and followed within several hours by the development of large papules accompanied by erythema, edema, and pruritis. Secondary reactions revealed edema and massive round cell invasion of the dermis and epidermis (McFarlane, 1949). A similar condition has been observed in Sardinia following repeated exposures by man to cercariae of *S. bovis* (Biocca, 1960; Sadun and Biocca, 1962). A form of swimmer's itch has long been recognized in Japan as "Kabure" (Cort, 1950). This is also apparently produced by nonhuman schistosome cercariae. The wheal and flair type reaction involved in swimmer's itch has been ascribed to local anaphylaxis and can be relieved by the use of antihistamines (McFarlane, 1949).

The second phase of schistosomiasis "Katayama fever" is more systemic in character. In addition to fever and eosinophilia, there is usually splenomegaly, generalized lymphadenopathy, urticaria, and often diarrhea or dysentery (Billings *et al.*, 1946; Ching, 1958; Diaz-Rivera *et al.*, 1956; Liu *et al.*, 1958). Congested spleens with large numbers of histocytes and eosinophils were seen by Bogliolo in man (1958) and by Fairley (1919) in experimentally infected monkeys. The latter also observed swollen kidney glomeruli which had been infiltrated by neutrophils and eosinophils.

Homocytotropic reaginlike antibodies in schistosomiasis were reported recently in rats and monkeys (Ogilvie *et al.*, 1966), rabbits (Zvaifler *et al.*, 1966, 1967), human patients (Sadun *et al.*, 1966), chimpanzees (Sadun and Gore, 1970; Sadun *et al.*, 1966, 1970; von Lichtenberg *et al.*, 1972), and in rhesus monkeys infected repeatedly with irradiated cercariae of *S. japonicum* (Hsu and Hsu, 1966). These reactions are mediated by antibodies which differ from the conventional 7 S immunoglobulins.

The immunological response of people, chimpanzees, rhesus and *Cercopithecus* monkeys, rabbits, guinea pigs, and mice was recently studied by Sadun and Gore (1970). Antibodies detected by fluorescent and flocculating techniques were heat stable, were not sensitive to mercaptoethanol, and were eluted from Sephadex G-200 in the IgG fraction. Antibodies detected by anaphylactic reactions were destroyed by heating, were inactivated by mercaptoethanol reduction and alkylation, had a faster electrophoretic mobility than IgG, and were eluted from Sephadex G-200 after IgM and before IgG. There was a suggestive correlation between the natural resistance of these animals to infection with *S. mansoni* and the presence of reaginlike antibody in the blood of these animals. Rabbits and rats which are highly resistant to this infection developed high titers of PCA antibody. Conversely, mice, which have little or no resistance to schistosomiasis, did not show reaginlike antibody even though they were capable of making this kind of antibody when challenged with *T. spiralis*. The results for humans, chimpanzees, and rhesus monkeys were intermediate between these two extremes. This admittedly circumstantial evidence of a possible protective role of reaginic antibodies is further supported by the fact that rabbits which are highly susceptible to schistosomiasis japonica develop only relatively low titers of reaginic antibodies to this infection.

The observation by Zvaifler and his co-workers (1967) that a homocytotropic reaginic antibody is produced in rabbits infected with *S. mansoni* led to a study designed to determine if infection "sensitized" platelets and leukocytes for *in vitro* histamine release following the addition of *S. mansoni* antigen in the absence of rabbit plasma. Histamine release was detected from rabbits regardless of whether or not passive cutaneous anaphylactic antibodies were produced in the infected animals. A pure platelet suspension from sensitized rabbits did not release histamine when challenged with antigen. Histamine release did occur, however, in the presence of whole washed blood when similarly challenged. It is now believed that basophilic leukocytes, sensitized with homocytotropic antibody, release a factor (PAF) which induces histamine release from platelets.

A radioactive microprecipitin (RAMP) assay using iodinated (^{125}I) extracts of *S. mansoni* cercariae as antigen was used in testing sera from schistosomiasis patients and from experimentally infected chimpanzees, monkeys, rabbits, and mice (Williams *et al.*, 1971). Like the PCA test with a 72-hour latent period, this test reacted in all species except in mice. Antibodies detected by this test were thermolabile and their reactivity could be prevented by mercaptoethanol reduction and alkylation. A striking similarity was observed with the time course development of homocytotropic antibodies and antibodies detected by the RAMP assay. Both reactions could be inhibited by absorption with goat anti-rabbit gamma E serum but not with anti-rabbit gamma G serum.

5. Filarial Worms

The many different species of *Filaria* which affect man produce a wide variety of clinical signs, a number of which appear to be attributable to immediate hypersensitivity. The widespread occurrence of tropical eosinophilia and its probable filarial etiology have been discussed previously. Profound allergic reactions associated with infection with a nematode related to filarial worms, *Dracunculus medinensis*, are well-known. These are particularly evident at the time of the sudden release into the host's system of toxic by-products of the gravid female worms. In addition to local cutaneous lesions, there are pronounced systemic prodromes consisting of erythemia and urticarial rash with intense pruritis, nausea, vomiting, diarrhea, severe dyspnea, and giddiness (Faust *et al.*, 1970). Anaphylactic shock following the accidental breaking of the worms during surgical removal has also been reported. Some of the clinical manifestations of filariasis can be relieved by injecting *Dirofilaria immitis* antigen (Beye *et al.*, 1956). Temporary swellings commonly observed in *Loa loa* infections following the migration of the worms in the subcutaneous tissue have been interpreted as being hypersensitivity reactions. Allergic symptoms occurring in onchocerciasis have also been described. The sera from a high proportion of American military personnel evacuated from the South Pacific with suspected *Wuchereria* infection gave positive PK tests with filarial antigens (Hodge *et al.*, 1945.). Serum from persons with other filarial infections such as *Acanthocheilonema perstans*, *Loa loa*, and *Onchocerca volvulus* also produced positive PK reactions (Goodman *et al.*, 1945; Lippelt and Mohr, 1938). In general, all filarial infections are associated with eosinophilia.

Rabbits infected with *Dirofilaria uniformis* produced homocytotropic (reaginic) antibodies detectable by passive cutaneous anaphylactic reactions after a 60–72 hour latent period. This antibody was found to be different from the IgG class of rabbit immunoglobulin, had a faster electrophoretic mobility than gamma G globulin and was eluted in Sephadex G-200 after gamma M and before gamma G globulin. It was largely destroyed by heating or by reduction and alkylation. Serum fractions which contained the major amount of IgG immunoglobulin and all of the detectable fluorescent antibody activity did not react in the PCA test. Conversely, electrophoretically faster immunoglobulins which contained passive cutaneous anaphylactic activity showed no fluorescent antibody titer (Sadun *et al.*, 1967).

6. Other Helminths

Dobson (1968) compared various immunoglobulin responses of rats to a nematode infection with *Amplicaecum robertsi* and demonstrated serum PCA activity after 6 days of infection. The PK titers rapidly rose to a peak at the end of the first month and then decreased to extinction before the third month of infection. The antibodies responsible for these reactions were heat labile and disappeared after being heated at 60°C for 1 hour.

Skin reactions were provoked by a saline extract of *Ostertagia* in sheep (Hogarth-Scott, 1969). The ability to provoke a PCA reaction in the sera of sheep was greatest just after the "self-cure" phenomenon had taken place. Several skin-tested animals showed signs of severe general anaphylaxis following administration of the allergen, manifested by prostration, copious salivation, cyanosis, dyspnea, defecation, and urination. However, most of the animals recovered within half an hour. The author concluded that the homocytotropic antibody detected in sheep in response to *Ostertagia* infection has properties similar to the antibody which occurs in other mammalian species in contact with nematode allergens and is probably analogous to human IgE. However, he pointed out that the successful detection *in vitro* of this antibody will depend on the isolation of an ovine gamma E analog, and that the present lack of information available on sheep myeloma proteins renders this possibility somewhat remote. Subsequent investigations (Hogarth-Scott *et al.*, 1969) revealed the presence of reaginic antibodies in the sera of infected sheep by means of Evans blue dye and a ^{131}I-radiolabeled technique. The author concluded that this homocytotropic antibody is probably associated with the "self cure" reaction.

The sera of mice immune to *Nematospiroides dubius* contain homocytotropic antibodies which can be detected by immunoelectrophoresis and by passive cutaneous anaphylaxis (Panter, 1969). Immune mice

are subject to anaphylactic shock and the intestine of such mice partici-
pates strongly in the reaction. The author concluded that a state of
immediate hypersensitivity is involved in the immunity of mice to *N.
dubius* and he suggested that in immune mice a fresh intake of larvae
initiates an anaphylactic reaction which prevents a large proportion of
the larvae from becoming established.

Homocytotropic antibodies were detected in several other animals
infected with various helminths. However, it is not clear whether or
not these are true reaginic antibodies of the IgE immunoglobulin class.
Some of these antibodies have not been immunochemically defined, and
others, such as those resulting from *Ostertagia* and *Trichostrongylus*
infections in sheep, have been shown to be related to the subclass IgG_{1a}
(Curtain and Anderson, 1971). Homocytotropic antibodies were also
demonstrated in the intestinal mucous of sheep infected with *Oesophagostomum columbianum* by means of the cutaneous anaphylactic test
(Dobson, 1966). Homologous PCA tests in guinea pigs revealed the
production of skin sensitizing antibody by *Metastrongylus* spp. infection
(Barratt and Herbert, 1970). However, it could not be determined
whether or not two types of anaphylactic antibodies were present
as suggested earlier (Colquhoun and Brocklehurst, 1965). Injection of
antigen into the skin of sensitized rats led to mast cell degranulation
in those which were infected with *Strongyloides ratti* (Goldgraber and
Lewert, 1965).

Hookworm infection in endemic areas is characterized frequently by
a persistent asthmatic cough. Rabbits infected with *Ancylostoma* develop
antibodies which produce a PK reaction in uninfected recipients of the
homologous species (Harada, 1962). As quoted by Winsor (1971), Ball
and Bartlett (1969) studied the time-course development of antibodies
detectable by the PK tests with sera from hookworm patients. They
reported that the PK tests became positive within 4 weeks after infection,
reached the maximum titer 3 months later and were no longer detectable
after 1 year.

7. Potentiated Reaginic Responses in Helminthiases

Recently it was shown that *N. brasiliensis* infections may influence
reagin-producing systems in rats and that this influence is not specific
for reagins against *N. brasiliensis* antigens, but can influence the existing
production of reagins against other antigens (Orr and Blair, 1969). The
potentiated response was found to occur only in those animals given
antigen before the helminthic infection. The authors concluded that
a factor may be present in the helminthic infections which stimulates
the reagin-producing system and which under normal conditions results

in a high titer of homocytotropic antibodies against the parasite. However, if the reagin system is already producing antibodies against the given antigen, the helminthic infection potentiates the reagin production against that antigen. Maximal PCA titers against egg albumin were obtained when rats were infected with *N. brasiliensis* 10 days after immunization. Results from experiments with sensitized peritoneal mast cells from these animals indicated that histamine release on challenge with egg albumin was maximal within 3 weeks, whereas challenge with worm extract released histamine maximally between 4 and 5 weeks. Homocytotropic antibodies against the antigen as demonstrated by PCA were not obtained when DNP–BGG was substituted for egg albumin in this system (Smith *et al.*, 1971).

Similar mechanisms of potentiation may be involved in producing allergic manifestations to many allergens in individuals infected with helminths. A significant association, as yet unconfirmed, was observed by Tullis (1970) between bronchial asthma and intestinal parasites. He postulated that the acquisition of an allergy to an antigen may depend on exposure to the antigen at some stage of infection by one or more helminth parasites.

IV. Summary and Conclusions

It is obvious from this review that different types of antibodies are produced following parasitic infections. These can react with antigen within tissue spaces such as in the conventional antibodies which belong to the immunoglobulin classes IgG, IgA, and IgM, or the antibodies may become fixed to tissues. The latter, known as reagins in humans, belong to the immunoglobulin group IgE and are thought to be responsible for the different manifestations and IH of anaphylaxis. Since reagins adhere strongly to tissues, they are often called tissue-sensitizing antibodies. Whereas conventional antibodies can be detected in the serum by standard *in vitro* procedures such as precipitation, agglutination, complement fixation, and immunofluorescence, reagins can best be detected *in vivo* by passive or direct cutaneous anaphylaxis. In lower animals antibodies other than reagins can produce anaphylaxis in other homologous and heterologous species and can be detected by passive cutaneous anaphylaxis, but only after a very short latent period. Those antibodies which produce anaphylaxis in the homologous species are also referred to as homocytotropic antibodies. They can easily be differentiated from reagins by the fact that in addition to their short latent period they are heat stable, cannot be destroyed by mercaptoethanol reduction and alkylation, and have a different electrophoretic mobility than that of IgE. *In vitro* tests for reaginic activity are now in the process of being developed.

Although homocytotropic antibodies and cutaneous anaphylaxis have been reported in many protozoan and helminthic infections, reaginic antibodies have been demonstrated only in those parasitic infections which are due to helminths (Table I). Anaphylactic phenomena are caused by the antigen–antibody reaction activating a series of enzymes leading to the release of certain pharmacological agents such as histamine, serotonin, slow reacting substance, kinins, and eosinophilic chemotactic factor which produce local or systemic anaphylaxis. Cutaneous urticaria and the formation of wheal and flare lesions in the skin are anaphylactic phenomena usually ascribed to homocytotropic antibodies. However, nonimmune reactions such as trauma or cold can also release pharmacological agents. Therefore, the numerous observations of kinin release, urticaria, and wheal and flare lesions in the skin in the course of protozoan infections are not necessarily immunological phenomena and may be mistakenly interpreted as demonstrating the presence of reaginic antibodies.

The eosinophiles are closely associated with helminthic infections and anaphylactic reactions. However, their exact role is still controversial. As reported by Vaughn (1953) an association between eosinophils and allergic states has been known since 1898 and the attraction of eosinophils to sites of parasite infections has been reported since the beginning of the century. There is no doubt that infiltration of the tissues with eosinophils is a common denominator of many anaphylactic reactions and that most helminthic infections are generally associated with eosinophilia. Eosinophils are attracted by antigen–antibody complexes and have been shown to phagocytose these complexes. However, eosinophils may also be found in the skin in urticaria reactions regardless of whether these reactions have an immunological or pharmacological basis. This would suggest that the eosinophils are attracted by concentrations of mediators, and that they are potentially capable of causing histamine release from mast cells. Although release of histamine and other mediators, as well as hypersecretion of mucous are phenomena associated with allergic response, the role which eosinophils may play in accentuating allergic reactions or in protecting against allergy has not been clarified. The intradermal injection of histamine into young horses has been shown to cause an accumulation of eosinophils at the site of the developing wheal (Turk, 1969). Moreover, equine eosinophils have been shown to inactivate histamine and serotonin both *in vivo* and *in vitro* (Archer, 1968).

Since the earliest observation of a virtual disappearance of eosinophils from the blood of persons following injection of ACTH (Thorn *et al.*, 1948), dramatic variations in the level of eosinophils have been reported following injections of cortisone or cortisone and atropine (Sundell, 1958). Further experiments showed that the pituitary and adrenal glands were necessary for maintenance of a normal level of eosinophils in the small intestine. Hypophysectomy or adrenalectomy resulted in the increased eosinophil levels in the gut which could be counteracted by cortisone injections. In experimental trichinosis it has been shown that the release of histamine and not serotonin is associated with eosinophilia (Ismail and Tanner, 1969). The association between histamine and eosinophils is still not clear even though it is known that mast cells contain most of the histamine of the body (Riley, 1950) and that basophiles contain most of the histamine in the human blood (Sampson and Archer, 1967). The accumulation of eosinophils in the peripheral blood can be inhibited by antihistaminic drugs.

In general, eosinophilia could be considered as the earliest evidence of antibody induced sensitivity in helminth infections. Experimentally, eosinophilia is frequently followed by sensitivity of the mediator-releasing tissues and by demonstrable anaphylactic reactions to worm extracts (Olson and Schulz, 1963). Eventually, circulating homocytotropic reaginic antibodies can be detected by PCA in a percentage of the infected animals. *In vitro* tests such as antigen induced histamine release and radioactive microprecipitin assays appear to be considerably more sensitive than PCA for detecting reaginic antibodies. This sequence of events which can be postulated primarily on the basis of separate experiments conducted in laboratory animals may parallel the succession of occurrences observed in man and lower animals following natural infections with helminth parasites. In these, one often observes eosinophilia, followed by changes in the numbers of mast cells and platelets, increases in serum levels of pharmacologically active substances, and cutaneous anaphylaxis.

What is the reason for the development of high titer homocytotropic (reaginic) antibodies frequently resulting from helminthic infections? The explanation cannot be found in the continuous release of antigen or in the specific location of the parasite (Ogilvie, 1967). All evidence accumulated so far indicates that production of large amounts of reaginic antibodies are obtained only when an actual infection takes place. Conversely, immunization with helminth extracts frequently results in failure of eliciting reagins or at best only produces reagins at an extremely low titer. It has also been demonstrated *in vitro* (R. T. M. Wilson, 1967) that the antigens involved in stimulation of reaginic antibodies are released by the living helminths. This contrasts with the production of high levels of homocytotropic (nonreaginic) antibodies by artificial immunization with a variety of parasite antigens.

The reason helminthic infections stimulate reagins and eosinophils so efficiently still remains a matter of speculation. Recently, however, evidence has been provided that at least one helminth species possesses some kind of adjuvant effect on the production of reagin containing immunoglobulins (Orr and Blair, 1969). These results, which were obtained in rats infected with *N. brasiliensis,* must be extended to other helminthiases and other hosts before suggesting that helminths stimulate nonspecifically the proliferation of reagin-producing cells. Further studies have indicated that the reaginic adjuvant effect of helminthic infections is not observable if DNP–BGG has been used as sensitizing antigen. Therefore, the observed potentiation may not necessarily be a general phenomenon, but may be restricted to specific antigens and, possibly, to only some host–parasite relationships.

Only suggestive evidence has been obtained thus far on the possible relationship between homocytotropic (reaginic) antibodies and the protective mechanisms of the host. Some aspects of this subject will be reviewed by Murray.

It is obvious from this review that the very large amount of information accumulated in recent years on the development of homocytotropic antibodies in parasitic infections has only succeeded to "push the demon one step further." Much additional experimental evidence is required before the various pieces of the jigsaw puzzle can be made to fit together into a clear coherent picture, but herein lies both the lure and challenge for future parasitologists and immunologists. "Knowledge is proud that he has learned so much; wisdom is humble that he knows no more" (William Cowper, The Task, verses 94, 95).

Acknowledgments

I wish to express my appreciation to Dr. D. J. Stechschulte, Robert B. Brigham Hospital, Boston, Massachusetts, and Dr. J. Barbaro, Walter Reed Army Institute of Research, Washington, D.C., for their suggestions and constructive criticisms. Thanks are also due to the Department of Medical Audio-Visual Services, Walter Reed Army Institute of Research, for their valuable assistance in preparing the figure.

References

Andrews, J. M. (1962). *J. Parasitol.* **48**, 3.
Archer, G. T. (1968). *Bibl. Haematol.* **29**, Part 1, 71.
Bachman, G. W. (1928). *J. Prev. Med.* **2**, 169; for final rep., see *ibid.*, p. 513.

Ball, P. A., and Bartlett, A. (1969). *Trans. Roy. Soc. Trop. Med. Hyg.* **63**, 362.

Barratt, M. E., and Herbert, I. V. (1970). *Immunology* **18**, 23.

Beaver, P. C., Snyder, C. H., Carrera, G. M., Dent, J. H., and Lafferty, J. W. (1952). *Pediatrics* **9**, 7.

Becker, E. L., and Austen, K. F. (1966). "Anaphylaxis. Textbook of Immunopathology," Vol. 1. Grune & Stratton, New York.

Benacerraf, B., Ovary, Z., Bloch, K. J., and Franklin, E. C. (1963). *J. Exp. Med.* **117**, 937.

Benditt, E. P., and Wong, R. L. (1957). *J. Exp. Med.* **105**, 509.

Benditt, E. P., Wong, R. L., Arase, M., and Roeper, E. (1955). *Proc. Soc. Exp. Biol. Med.* **90**, 303.

Beye, H. K., Mille, R., Thorris, G., and Tapu, J. (1956). *Amer. J. Hyg.* **64**, 23.

Bier, O. (1967). *Pan Amer. Health Organ., Sci. Publ.* **150**.

Billings, F. T., Winkenwerder, W. L., and Hunninen, A. V. (1946). *Bull. Johns Hopkins Hosp.* **78**, 21.

Biocca, E. (1960). *Parasitologia* **2**, 47.

Bogliolo, L. (1958). "Subsidios para o conhecimento da Forma Hepato-Explenica e da Forma Toxemica da Esquistossomose Mansonica." Serv. Nac. Educ. Sanit. Min. Sauda, Rio de Janeiro, Brasil.

Booth, B. H., Patterson, R., and Talbot, C. A. (1970). *J. Lab. Clin. Med.* **26**, 181.

Boreham, P. F. L. (1968). *Brit. J. Pharmacol. Chemother.* **32**, 493.

Boreham, P. F. L. (1970). *Trans. Roy. Soc. Trop. Med. Hyg.* **64**, 394.

Bozicevich, J., and Hoyem, H. M. (1947). *Nat. Inst. Health Bull.* **189**, 199.

Bozicevich, J., Donovan, A., Mazzotti, L., Diaz, A. F., and Padilla, E. (1947). *Amer. J. Trop. Med.* **27**, 51.

Briggs, N. T. (1963). *Ann. N.Y. Acad. Sci.* **113**, 456.

Briggs, N. T. (1966). *Amer. J. Trop. Med. Hyg.* **15**, 919.

Bruce-Chwatt, L. J. (1970). *J. Parasitol.* **56**, Sect. II, 552.

Brunner, M. (1928). *J. Immunol.* **15**, 83.

Brunner, M. (1934). *J. Allergy* **5**, 257.

Brunner, M., Altman, I., and Bowman, K. (1944). *J. Allergy* **15**, 2.

Bryceson, A. D. M., Bray, R. S., Wolstencroft, R. A., and Dumonde, D. C. (1970). *Clin. Exp. Immunol.* **7**, 301.

Buckley, J. J. C. (1958). *East Afr. Med. J.* **35**, 493.

Capron, A. R. (1970). *J. Parasitol.* **56**, Sect. II, 515.

Casoni, T. (1912). *Folia Clin., Chim. Microsc.* **4**, 5.

Catty, D. (1969). *Monogr. Allergy* **5**, 1.

Ching, W. (1958). *Chin. Med. J.* **76**, 1.

Cohen, S., and Milstein, C. (1967). *Advan. Immunol.* **7**, 1.

Colquhoun, D., and Brocklehurst, W. E. (1965). *Immunology* **9**, 591.

Cort, W. W. (1928). *J. Amer. Med. Ass.* **90**, 1027.

Cort, W. W. (1950). *Amer. J. Hyg.* **52**, 251.

Coventry, F. A. (1929). *J. Prev. Med.* **3**, 43.

Coventry, F. A., and Taliaferro, W. H. (1928). *J. Prev. Med.* **2**, 272.

Culbertson, J. T., Rose, H. M., and Demarest, C. R. (1944). *Amer. J. Hyg.* **39**, 152.

Curtain, C. C., and Anderson, N. (1971). *Clin. Exp. Immunol.* **8**, 151.

Danaraj, T. J., Pacheco, G., Shanmugarantnam, K., and Beaver, P. C. (1966). *Amer. J. Trop. Med. Hyg.* **15**, 183.

Desowitz, R. S., and Pavanand, K. (1967). *Amer. J. Trop. Med. Parasitol.* **61**, 128.

Diaz-Rivera, A. A., Machand, E. J., Gonzalez, O., and Torregrosa, M. V. (1956). *Amer. J. Med.* **21**, 918.

Dobson, C. (1966). *Aust. J. Biol. Sci.* **19**, 339.

Dobson, C. (1968). *Aust. J. Exp. Biol. Med. Sci.* **46**, 319.

Dobson, C., Morseth, D. J., and Soulsby, E. J. L. (1971). *J. Immunol.* **106**, 128.

Dobson, C., Rockey, J. H., and Soulsby, E. J. L. (1971). *J. Immunol.* **107**, 1431.

Erlich, P. (1907). *Berlin. Klin. Wochenschr.* **44**, 233, 280, 310, and 341.

Fairley, N. H. (1919). *J. Pathol. Bacteriol.* **23**, 289.

Fairley, N. H., and Liston, W. G. (1924). *Indian Med. Gaz.* **50**, 377.

Fairley, N. H., and Williams, F. E. (1927). *Med. J. Aust.* **11**, 811.

Faust, E. C., Russell, P. F., and Jung, R. C. (1970). "Clinical Parasitology." Lea & Febiger, Philadelphia, Pennsylvania.

Frenkel, J. K. (1948). *Proc. Soc. Exp. Biol. Med.* **68**, 634.

Fulleborn, F. (1924). *Klin. Wochenschr.* **4**, 709.

Fulleborn, F. (1926). *Arch. Schiffs- Trop.-Hyg.* **30**, 732.

Garnham, P. C. C., Pierce, A. E., and Roitt, I., eds. (1963). "Immunity to Protozoa." Blackwell, Oxford.

Giertz, H., Glanzmann, C., and Keller, R. (1970). *Int. Arch. Allergy Appl. Immunol.* **38**, 413.

Goldgraber, M. B., and Lewert, R. M. (1965). *J. Parasitol.* **51**, 169.

Goldschmidt, R. (1910). *Muenchen. Med. Wochenschr.* **57**, 1991.

Good, R. A., and Papermaster, B. W. (1964). *Advan. Immunol.* **4**, 1.

Goodman, A. A., Weinberger, E. M., Lippincott, S. W., Marble, A., and Wright, W. H. (1945). *Ann. Intern. Med.* **23**, 823.

Goodwin, L. G. (1971). *Trans. Roy. Soc. Trop. Med. Hyg.* **65**, 82.

Goodwin, L. G., and Richards, W. H. G. (1960). *Brit. J. Pharmacol. Chemother.* **15**, 152.

Goose, J., and Blair, A. M. (1969). *Immunology* **16**, 749.

Gould, S. E. (1945). "Trichinosis." Thomas, Springfield, Illinois.

Greenbaum, L. M., and Kim, K. S. (1967). *Brit. J. Pharmacol. Chemother.* **29**, 238.

Grubel, E. (1924). *Dermatol. Wochenschr.* **79**, 1182.

Guerra, P., Mayer, M., and DiPrisco, J. (1945). *Rev. Sanid. Assistencia Soc.* **10**, 51.

Halstead, S. B., and Sadun, E. H. (1965). *Ann. Int. Med.* **62**, 564.

Harada, Y. (1962). *Yonago Acta Med.* **2**, 109.

Herrick, C. A., and Emery, F. E. (1929). *J. Pharmacol.* **35**, 129.

Hodge, I. G., Denhoff, E., and Van der Veer, J. B. (1945). *Amer. J. Med. Sci.* **210**, 207.

Hoffman, C. C., and Vargas, K. (1931). *Salubridad* **2**, 121.

Hogarth-Scott, R. S. (1967a). *Immunology* **13**, 535.

Hogarth-Scott, R. S. (1967b). *Int. Arch. Allergy* **32**, 201.

Hogarth-Scott, R. S. (1968). *Parasitology* **58**, 221.

Hogarth-Scott, R. S. (1969). *Immunology* **16**, 543.

Hogarth-Scott, R. S., Johannson, S. G. O., and Bennich, H. (1969). *Clin. Exp. Immunol.* **5**, 619.

Hsu, H. F., and Hsu, S. Y. L. (1966). *Z. Tropenmed. Parasitol.* **17**, 166.

Humphrey, J. H., and Jaques, R. (1955). *J. Physiol. (London)* **128**, 9.

Ishizaka, K. (1971). "Biological Functions of the Different Classes of Immunoglobulins." First International Congress of Immunology, Washington, D.C.

Ishizaka, K., Ishizaka, T., and Hornbrook, M. (1966). *J. Immunol.* **97**, 75.

Ishizaka, K., Ishizaka, T., and Tada, T. (1969). *J. Immunol.* **103**, 445.

Ismail, M. M., and Tanner, C. E. (1969). *Wiad. Parazytol.* **15**, Nos. 5–6.

Jervis, H. R., Sprinz, H., Johnson, A. J., and Wellde, B. T. (1972). *Amer. J. Trop. Med. Hyg.* **21**, 272.

Johannson, S. G. O., Mellbin, T., and Vahlquist, B. (1968). *Lancet* **1**, 1118.

Johannson, S. G. O., Bennich, H., Berg, T., and Hogman, E. (1970). *Clin. Exp. Immunol.* **6**, 43.

Jones, T. L., and Kingscote, A. A. (1935). *Amer. J. Hyg.* **22**, 406.

Jones, V. E., and Ogilvie, B. M. (1967a). *Int. Arch. Allergy Appl. Immunol.* **31**, 490.

Jones, V. E., and Ogilvie, B. M. (1967b). *Immunology* **12**, 583.

Jones, V. E., Edwards, A. J., and Ogilvie, B. M. (1970). *Immunology* **18**, 621.

Kay, A. B., Stechschulte, D. J., and Austen, K. F. (1971). *J. Exp. Med.* **133**, 602.

Keller, R. (1970). *Int. Arch. Allergy Appl. Immunol.* **38**, 305.

Korach, S., and Benex, J. (1966a). *Exp. Parasitol.* **19**, 193.

Korach, S., and Benex, J. (1966b). *Exp. Parasitol.* **19**, 199.

LeRoy, A. (1910). *Arch. Int. Physiol.* **9**, 276.

Lippelt, H., and Mohr, W. (1938). *Klin. Wochenschr.* **17**, 1684.

Liu, J., Cheng, W., Huang, M., Pan, J., Chiang, S., Hsu, C., Hsu, P., and Tang, C. (1958). *Chin. Med. J.* **76**, 229.

McFarlane, W. V. (1949). *Amer. J. Hyg.* **50**, 152.

Maddison, S. E., Kagan, I. G., and Elsdon-Dew, R. (1968). *Amer. J. Trop. Med.* **17**, 650.

Maegraith, B. G., and Onabanjo, A. O. (1970). *Brit. J. Pharmacol.* **39**, 755.

Magath, T. B. (1921). *Med. Clin. N. Amer.* **5**, 549.

Malley, A., Amkraut, A. A., Strejan, G., and Campbell, D. H. (1968). *J. Immunol.* **101**, 292.

Manson-Bahr, P. H. (1960). "Tropical Diseases: A Manual of the Diseases of Warm Climates," 15th ed. Cassell, London.

Mayer, M., and Pifano, F. (1945). *Rev. Sanid. Assistencia Soc.* **10**, 3.

Miller, J. F. A. P. (1968). *In* "Clinical Aspects of Immunology" (P. G. H. Gell and R. R. A. Coombs, eds.), 2nd ed., p. 289. Blackwell, Oxford.

Miller, L. H., Chongsuphajaisiddhi, T., and Kanakakorn, K. (1968). *Ann. Trop. Med. Parasitol.* **62**, 218.

Mota, I. (1964a). *Immunology* **7**, 681.

Mota, I. (1964b). *Immunology* **7**, 700.

Mota, I., and Peixoto, J. M. (1966). *186th Annu. Meet. Brazil. Soc. Advan. Sci., 1966.*

Mota, I., and Wong, D. (1968). *Life Sci.* **7**, 1289.

Mota, I., Sadun, E. H., and Gore, R. W. (1969a). *Exp. Parasitol.* **24**, 251.

Mota, I., Sadun, E. H., Bradshaw, R. M., and Gore, R. W. (1969b). *Immunology* **16**, 71.

Ogilvie, B. M. (1964). *Nature (London)* **204**, 91.

Ogilvie, B. M. (1967). *Immunology* **12**, 113.

Ogilvie, B. M., and Jones, V. E. (1967). *Parasitology* **57**, 335.

Ogilvie, B. M., Smithers, S. R., and Terry, R. J. (1966). *Nature (London)* **209**, 1221.

Okumura, K., and Tada, T. (1971). *J. Immunol.* **106**, 1019.

Oliver-Gonzalez, J. (1946). *J. Infec. Dis.* **78**, 232.

Olivier, L. (1949). *Amer. J. Hyg.* **49**, 290.

Olson, L. J., and Schulz, C. W. (1963). *Ann. N.Y. Acad. Sci.* **113**, 440.

Orange, R. P., Valentine, M. D., and Austen, K. F. (1968). *J. Exp. Med.* **127**, 767.

Orr, T. S., and Blair, A. M. (1969). *Life Sci.* **8**, 1073.

Osler, A. G. (1963). *Amer. J. Hyg., Monogr. Ser.* **22**, 1.

Panter, H. C. (1969). *J. Parasitol.* **55**, 38.

Parish, W. E. (1969). *Int. Arch. Allergy Appl. Immunol.* **36**, 245.

Patterson, R., Roberts, M., and Pruzansky, J. J. (1969). *J. Immunol.* **102**, 466.

Pellegrino, J. (1958). *Bull. WHO* **18**, 945.

Pellegrino, J., Borda, C. E., and Valetti, J. A. (1968). *Rev. Inst. Med. Trop. Sao Paulo* **10**, 277.

Rackemann, F. M., and Stevens, A. H. (1927). *J. Immunol.* **13**, 389.

Raffel, S. (1953). "Immunity-Hypersensitivity-Serology." Appleton, New York.

Ramsdell, S. G. (1927). *J. Parasitol.* **14**, 102.

Read, H. (1931). *Arch. Schiffs- Trop.-Hyg.* **35**, 227.

Reid, R. T. (1970). *J. Immunol.* **104**, 935.

Rey-Calero, J. (1967). *Med. Trop. (Madrid)* **43**, 245.

Riley, J. F. (1950). "The Mast Cells." Livingston, Edinburgh.

Robertson, M. (1963). *In* "Immunity to Protoza" (P. C. C. Garnham, A. E. Pierce, and I. Roitt, eds.), p. 336. Blackwell, Oxford.

Rocha e Silva, M., and Grana, A. (1946a). *Arch. Surg. (Chicago)* **52**, 523.

Rocha e Silva, M., and Grana, A. (1946b). *Arch. Surg. (Chicago)* **52**, 713.

Rose, B. (1965). *In* "Immunological Diseases" (M. Samter, ed.), p. 470. Little, Brown, Boston, Massachusetts.

Rosen, L., Laigret, J., and Bories, S. (1961). *Amer. J. Hyg.* **74**, 26.

Rowe, D. S. (1968). *In* "Clinical Aspects of Immunology" (P. G. H. Gell and R. R. A. Coombs, eds.), 2nd ed., p. 369. Blackwell, Oxford.

Sadun, E. H., and Biocca, E. (1962). *Bull. WHO* **27**, 810.

Sadun, E. H., and Gore, R. W. (1970). *Exp. Parasitol.* **28**, 435.

Sadun, E. H., Buck, A. A., and Walton, B. C. (1959a). *Mil. Med.* **124**, 187.

Sadun, E. H., Walton, B. C., Buck, A. A., and Lee, B. K. (1959b). *J. Parasitol.* **45**, 129.

Sadun, E. H., Buck, A. A., and Walton, B. C. (1960). *Amer. J. Trop. Med. Hyg.* **9**, 562.

Sadun, E. H., Schoenbechler, M. J., and Bentz, M. (1965). *Amer. J. Trop. Med. Hyg.* **14**, 977.

Sadun, E. H., von Lichtenberg, F., Hickman, R. L., Bruce, J. T., Smith, J. H., and Schoenbechler, M. J. (1966). *Amer. J. Trop. Med. Hyg.* **15**, 496.

Sadun, E. H., Duxbury, R. E., Gore, R. W., and Stechschulte, D. J. (1967). *J. Infec. Dis.* **117**, 317.

Sadun, E. H., Mota, I., and Gore, R. W. (1968). *J. Parasitol.* **54**, 814.

Sadun, E. H., von Lichtenberg, F., Cheever, A. W., and Erickson, D. G. (1970). *Amer. J. Trop. Med. Hyg.* **19**, 258.

Sakaguchi, T. (1928). *Arch. Schiffs- Trop.-Hyg.* **32**, 517.

Sampson, D., and Archer, G. T. (1967). *Blood* **29**, 722.

Samter, M., and Alexander, H. L. (1965). "Immunological Diseases." Little, Brown, Boston, Massachusetts.

Sawada, T., Suzuki, I., Oka, T., and Sano, M. (1954). *Gumma J. Med. Sci.* **4**, 29.

Sawada, T., Takei, K., Williams, J. E., and Moose, J. W. (1965). *Exp. Parasitol.* **17**, 340.

Schoenbechler, M. J., and Sadun, E. H. (1968). *Proc. Soc. Exp. Biol. Med.* **127**, 601.

Seed, J. R., and Gam, A. A. (1966). *J. Parasitol.* **52**, 1134.

Sergent, Ed., and Sergent, Et. (1918). *Ann. Inst. Pasteur, Paris* **32**, 382.

Sharp, A. D., and Olson, L. J. (1962). *J. Parasitol.* **48**, 362.

Smith, S. A., Petillo, J., Hwang, A., and Adams, B. (1971). *Fed. Proc., Fed. Amer. Soc. Exp. Biol.* **30**, 411.

Soulsby, E. J. L. (1967). *Pan Amer. Health Organ.* **150**, 66.

Sprent, J. F. A. (1949). *J. Infec. Dis.* **84**, 221.

Sprent, J. F. A. (1950). *J. Infec. Dis.* **86**, 146.

Sprent, J. F. A. (1951). *J. Infec. Dis.* **88**, 168.

Strejan, G., and Campbell, D. H. (1968). *J. Immunol.* **101**, 628.

Sundell, B. (1958). *Acta Endocrinol. (Copenhagen)* **28**, Suppl. 39.

Tada, T., and Okumura, K. (1971). *J. Immunol.* **106**, 1002.

Tada, T., Taniguchi, M., and Okumura, K. (1971). *J. Immunol.* **106**, 1012.

Taillez, R., and Korach, S. (1970). *Ann. Inst. Pasteur, Paris* **118**, 61.

Taliaferro, W. H. (1929). "The Immunology of Parasitic Infections." Century, New York.

Taliaferro, W. H. (1967). *Pan Amer. Health Organ., Sci. Publ.* **150**, 3.

Taliaferro, W. H., and Hoffman, W. A. (1930). *J. Prev. Med.* **4**, 261.

Taylor, A. E. R., ed. (1968). "Immunity to Parasites." Blackwell, Oxford.

Tella, A., and Maegraith, B. G. (1962). *Trans. Roy. Soc. Trop. Med. Hyg.* **56**, 6.

Tella, A., and Maegraith, B. G. (1963). *Trans. Roy. Soc. Trop. Med. Hyg.* **57**, 1.

Tezner, O. (1934). *Arch. Dermatol.* **70**, 293.

Thorn, G. W., Forsham, P. H., Prunty, F. T., and Hills, A. G. (1948). *J. Amer. Med. Ass.* **137**, 1005.

Tomasi, T. B., and Bienenstock, J. (1968). *Advan. Immunol.* **9**, 1.

Treadwell, P. E. (1969). *J. Reticuloendothel. Soc.* **6**, 354.

Tullis, D. C. H. (1970). *N. Eng. J. Med.* **282**, 370.

Turk, J. L. (1969). "Immunology in Clinical Medicine." Heinemann, London.

Van Arsdel, P. P., Middleton, E., Sherman, W. B., and Buchwald, H. (1958). *J. Allergy* **29**, 429.

Vaughn, J. (1953). *Blood* **8**, 1.

von Lichtenberg, F., Sadun, E. H., Cheever, A. W., Erickson, D. G., Johnson, A. J., and Boyce, H. W. (1971). *Amer. J. Trop. Med. Hyg.* **20**, 850.

Webb, J. K. G., Job, C. K., and Bault, E. W. (1960). *Lancet* **1**, 835.

Weinberg, M., and Julien, A. (1911). *C. R. Soc. Biol.* **70**, 337.

Weinberg, M., and Julien, A. (1913). *C. R. Soc. Biol.* **72**, 1162.

Weiszer, I., Patterson, R., and Pruzansky, J. J. (1968). *J. Allergy* **41**, 14.

White, R. G., Jenkins, G. C., and Wilkinson, P. C. (1963). *Int. Arch. Allergy Appl. Immunol.* **22**, 156.

Williams, J. S., Sadun, E. H., and Gore, R. W. (1971). *J. Parasitol.* **57**, 220.

Williams, J. S., Gore, R. W., and Sadun, E. H. (1972). *Exp. Parasitol.* **31**, 299.

Wilson, R. J., and Bloch, K. J. (1968). *J. Immunol.* **100**, 622.

Wilson, R. J. M. (1967). *Immunology* **18**, 621.

Winsor, E. L. (1971). Dissertation, Tulane University, New Orleans, Louisiana.

Zucker, M. G. (1959). *Progr. Hematol.* **2**, 206.

Zvaifler, N. J. (1970). *In* "Resistance to Infectious Diseases," (R. H. Dunlop and H. W. Moon, eds.) p. 277. Modern Press, Saskatoon, Canada.

Zvaifler, N. J., and Robinson, J. O. (1969). *J. Exp. Med.* **130**, 907.

Zvaifler, N. J., Sadun, E. H., and Becker, E. L. (1966). *Clin. Res.* **14**, 336.

Zvaifler, N. J., Sadun, E. W., Becker, E. L., and Schoenbechler, M. J. (1967). *Exp. Parasitol.* **20**, 278.

5 IMMEDIATE HYPERSENSITIVITY EFFECTOR MECHANISMS

I. *In Vitro* Reactions

JOHN F. BARBARO

I. Introduction

This review will be primarily concerned with the immediate-type hypersensitivity reactions. The topics discussed will be restricted to essentially those dealing with reactions that can be experimentally determined *in vitro*, although there will be occasions when *in vivo* reactions will be briefly discussed. It is divided into two parts. The first, deals with the various immunological mechanisms with particular emphasis on mediators formed and released during an immediate type hypersensitivity reaction. The second part will attempt to relate these mechanisms, where applicable, to parasitic infections, particularly in relation to the various cells involved and their possible interactions.

The hypersensitivity reactions have been divided into two types, the immediate-type and the delayed-type (cell-mediated). The immediate type includes all those reactions that are the result of various kinds of antibodies found in the circulation and body fluids. This hypersensitive state can be transferred to normal animals by an appropriate antiserum. In contrast, the delayed-type reactions are not dependent upon circulating antibodies and the hypersensitive state can be accomplished, in general, only by the transfer of lymphoid cells. The nature of the specific recognition sites for the delayed-type reactions are essentially unknown, although it is felt that these recognition factors are antibodies similar to those found in the circulation. However, presently none of the circulating antibodies has been demonstrated to be responsible for the delayed-type reactions. The cell-mediated reactions of the delayed-type response will not be discussed as these reactions will be reviewed by others.

II. Immunological Mechanisms in Immediate Hypersensitivity

A. COMPONENTS OF IMMUNOLOGICAL REACTIONS

An immunological reaction, be it beneficial or detrimental to the host, involves primarily two main components—antibody and antigen. Accompanying the interaction of antigen with antibody are many auxillary components such as complement, various cell types and as a consequence in many situations the participation of various chemical mediators.

1. Antibodies

There are five known classes of immunoglobulins within all the animal species, each possessing similar as well as distinct chemical structures that are unique for each class (Cohen and Milstein, 1967; Edelman and Gall, 1969). These various classes and subclasses of immunoglobulins all possess a single property in common, namely their immunological specificity, i.e., their ability to react preferentially with the immunogen responsible for their production. Although this characteristic of specificity is of considerable importance, the diverse biological properties of these various immunoglobulins are usually responsible for the damage observed as a consequence of antigen–antibody combination. These biological properties include the ability to activate complement, the capacity to fix to cells or tissue, the preparation of particles for phagocytosis, and the ability to cross the placental membrane (Franklin and Frangione, 1969).

Much of what will follow depends upon these biological properties which lead to various manifestations of the immediate-type reactions particularly through the actions of pharmacological mediators that are released from various cells. One property that has direct relevance is the ability of antibody to sensitize various cells and tissues. The ability of antibodies to sensitize cells of the same species, or closely related species has been termed homocytotropic while those antibodies that lack this capacity but are capable of sensitizing foreign species are called heterocytotropic (Becker and Austen, 1966; Austen and Becker, 1966).

The homocytotropic antibodies are divided into two types. The first type are those antibodies that are characterized by heat and sulfhydryl lability, firm binding to cells, and which are usually present in low concentrations in serum. This type of homocytotropic antibody in man has been demonstrated to belong to the IgE class of immunoglobulins (K. Ishizaka *et al.*, 1966). Many, if not all, animal species (Dobson *et al.*, 1971; K. Ishizaka *et al.*, 1969; Levine *et al.*, 1971; Mota and Peixoto, 1966; Stechschulte *et al.*, 1970; Zvaifler and Becker, 1966) possess an immunoglobulin with these properties and these have been called IgE-like antibodies. Present evidence supports the conclusion that these IgE-like antibodies in various animal species are homologous to the IgE of humans (K. Ishizaka *et al.*, 1969; Kanyerezi *et al.*, 1971; Perelmutter and Khera, 1970; Zvaifler and Robinson, 1969).

Many species of animals infected with a variety of helminths elicit IgE antibodies. The formation of IgE antibodies, as stated by Ogilvie and Jones (1969), appears to be a general phenomenon in helminth-infected animals. The production of IgE immunoglobulin is extensively reviewed by Dr. Sadun (Chapter 4). Of interest, from an immunological standpoint, is the demonstration by Orr and Blair (1969) of a potentiation of IgE response to an unrelated protein antigen by a subsequent parasitic infection. This stimulating property of a parasitic infection may lead to a better understanding of the conditions which results in IgE production.

The second type of homocytotropic antibodies are characterized by heat and sulfhydryl resistance, are weakly bound to cells, and are usually present in relatively high concentrations in serum. These belong to the IgG class of immunoglobulins and are examples of this type of homocytotropic antibody: guinea pig IgG₁ (Ovary *et al.*, 1963); rat IgGa (Morse *et al.*, 1968); rabbit IgG (Henson and Cochrane, 1969); and mouse IgG₁ (Vaz and Ovary, 1968). A comparable heat stable IgG₁ antibody has not been demonstrated in humans but its existence is quite probable (Reid *et al.*, 1966).

Although the IgE and IgG homocytotropic antibodies differ in many properties, they are remarkably similar in their ability to manifest an immediate-type reaction through the release of various chemical reactions.

The group of antibodies that are termed heterocytotropic antibodies belong to the IgG class of immunoglobulins and in the guinea pig and mouse are referred to as gamma-2 antibodies. They are heat stable, sulfhydryl resistant, and migrate slowly electrophoretically. They are usually capable of fixing complement and although incapable of sensitizing their own species, they possess the ability to sensitize foreign species, as is evident by passive cutaneous anaphylaxis (Ovary, 1958).

2. Antigens

Antigens can be considered from two viewpoints. First, is their capacity, as immunogens, to elicit the formation of specific antibodies. In parasitic infections there is a multiplicity of antigens, heterophilic as well as specific (Soulsby, 1962, 1963), continually evolved during infection. The parasite infected host is constantly being sensitized with immunogens or haptens conjugated to host proteins that develop during various larval stages, from secretory and excretory products (Soulsby, 1963) as well as altered host proteins or cells (Oliver-Gonzalez, 1953). The ever changing pattern of antigenic stimulation results in a constant flux of immunological reactivity, which is further complicated by the continual presence of antigenic material.

It is of interest that the production of IgE antibody in helminth infected animals depends primarily on the presence of living parasites (Ogilvie, 1964). The reason for this requirement is not clear. However, the recent observations that small quantities of immunogen, as well as proper adjuvant, elicit a better IgE antibody response in guinea pigs (Levine *et al.*, 1971) and mice (Levine and Vaz, 1970) than large amounts of antigen may offer a possible explanation. The potentiated IgE response may be the consequence of the release of small quantities of appropriate antigen, along with a "factor" (Orr and Blair, 1969) contributed by the parasite *in vivo*.

The second aspect of the function of antigen, which is more germane to this section is: How does the reaction between cell-bound antibody and antigen initiate the release of pharmacologically active agents from target cells?

Henney and Stanworth (1966) demonstrated that antigen–antibody combination resulted in exposure of new antigenic determinants on immunoglobulin molecules. As shown by K. Ishizaka and Ishizaka (1968) these structural changes that occur with IgE globulin, either specifically combined with antigen or nonspecifically aggregated, caused increased capillary permeability in human skin. It is postulated that the mechanisms whereby pharmacological agents are released is through the exposure or production of cell-reactive sites on the antibody molecule which in contact with the cell surface initiates the necessary series of enzymatic reactions (Stanworth, 1970).

B. Classification of Immediate-Type Hypersensitivity Reactions

The classification of immediate-type reactions, as proposed by Becker (1971) can be seen in Fig. 1. The basis for this system of classification into various categories is whether or not chemical mediators are released. With this in mind, the various immediate-type reactions are divided into direct reactions and indirect reactions. The direct reactions are those that are manifested by the damage resulting from direct action of antigen–antibody on cells or noncellular substances. Although it is recognized that in various parasitic infections this type of reaction does occur, particularly with regard to the fixation of parasitic antigens to various host cells as well as the aggregation of antigen–antibody resulting in damage to cells in the vicinity, these reactions will not be discussed.

The indirect reactions are those reactions that are caused by the formation and release of various chemical mediators as a consequence of an antigen–antibody reaction. This class of immediate-type reactions is subdivided according to the nature of the mediators produced, either pharmacological mediators or macromolecular mediators. The former are termed anaphylactic-type reactions and it is these reactions only that will be discussed in detail.

The anaphylactic-type reactions are further divided into three types: (1) those reactions which result as a consequence of antigen combining with antibody fixed to cells; (2) those reactions in which antibody reacts with cell fixed antigen; and (3) those reactions in which mediators are formed or released by aggregates of antigen–antibody without the direct intervention of cells.

C. Pharmacological Mediators Released during Anaehylactic-Type Reactions

The combination of antigen with specific cell-bound antibody initiates a series of enzymatic steps leading to the release of various pharmaco-

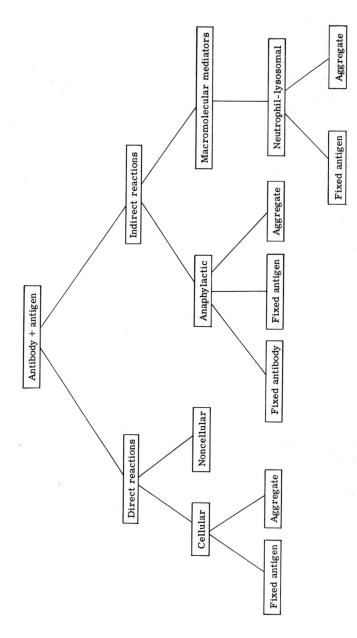

Fig. 1. Classification of immediate-type hypersensitivity reactions. Derived from Becker (1971).

logical mediators from sensitized cells or noncellular substances (Mongar and Schild, 1957; Austen and Brocklehurst, 1961; Becker and Austen, 1964). These pharmacological agents, notably vasoactive amines (histamine and serotonin), slow reacting substance of anaphylaxis SRS-A) and kinins, cause increased vascular permeability, and/or smooth muscle contraction (Orange and Austen, 1969a; Ratnoff, 1969). Eosinophil chemotactic factor of anaphylaxis (ECF-A), a recently described mediator (Kay et al., 1971a,b), merits inclusion among these agents for reasons discussed later.

There are a variety of *in vitro* models of anaphylactic-type reactions that demonstrate the release of chemical mediators from target cells. The *in vitro* cell systems principally used are human leukocytes (Osler et al., 1968), rabbit platelets (Schoenbechler and Sadun, 1968; Henson, 1970; Barbaro and Zvaifler, 1966; Siraganian and Osler, 1971a), mast cell of rats (Morse et al., 1968; Orange et al., 1970) and of mice (Prouvost-Danon et al., 1968), and lung tissue of guinea pig (Austen and Brocklehurst, 1961; Becker and Austen, 1964), monkey (T. Ishizaka et al., 1970) and human (Kay et al., 1971b; Assem and Schild, 1969).

Generally the investigations in each of these systems have been concerned primarily with the release of histamine, although recent emphasis has been directed towards other mediators, notably SRS-A.

1. Histamine

The histamine in mammals is primarily contained in the granules of tissue mast cells where it is associated with a heparin–protein complex (Uvnas, 1964). The immunological release of histamine from this bond involves the interaction of cell-bound immunoglobulins IgE, IgG$_1$, or IgGa with antigen. Passive sensitization of normal cells with antisera containing either of these immunoglobulins (Osler et al., 1968; Colwell et al., 1971; Orange et al., 1970) confirms that these immunoglobulins are cell-bound. Further evidence of the involvement of cell-bound immunoglobulins as well as the class of immunoglobulins is obtained with anti-immunoglobulin serum (Lichtenstein et al., 1970; T. Ishizaka et al., 1969). Furthermore, the mechanism of histamine release from human leukocytes by anti-IgE appears to be identical to the antigen-mediated response (Lichtenstein et al., 1970). A correlation between histamine release and the production of homocytotropic antibodies has been demonstrated with rabbit platelets (Barbaro and Zvaifler, 1966), rat lung tissue (Strejan and Campbell, 1968), monkey lung tissue (Malley et al., 1968), and peritoneal mouse mast cells (Prouvost-Danon et al., 1968).

The release of histamine and other pharmacological agents from various *in vitro* systems appears to be a secretory process rather than a cytotoxic reaction as evident by vital dye studies (Johnson and Moran, 1969), by the selective release of only amines without release of cytoplasmic enzymes (Henson, 1969), and by the absence of an efflux of potassium (Lichtenstein, 1968).

Evidence that the release of histamine involves the activation of cell-bound esterases by antigen–antibody combination was initially demonstrated by Brocklehurst (1959) and Austen and Brocklehurst (1961) and was subsequently extended by Becker (1968). He has also suggested that all the various forms of noncytotoxic histamine release, and probably the release of other pharmacological agents involve the activation of a serine esterase. In addition, recent studies indicate that cyclic adenosine 3',5'-monophosphate (cAMP) system is involved in the release of certain mediators (Lichtenstein, 1969; Koopman *et al.*, 1970; T. Ishizaka *et al.*, 1971).

2. Slow Reacting Substance of Anaphylaxis (SRS-A)

The term slow reacting substance of anaphylaxis is a descriptive one designating those substances formed and released as a result of an antigen–antibody reaction which cause a slow, sustained contraction of only certain isolated smooth muscle preparations (Orange and Austen, 1969a). Its chemical composition is not known and it is distinguished from other chemical mediators by bioassay with selective pharmacological antagonists.

The immunological mechanisms for the formation and release of SRS-A has been studied in various species, with particular reference to the immunoglobulins and cellular elements involved. Both the heat-stable homocytotropic antibodies IgGa of the rat (Morse *et al.*, 1968), IgG$_1$ of the guinea pig (Stechschulte *et al.*, 1967) and the heat labile homocytotropic antibodies IgE of the rat (Orange *et al.*, 1970) and IgE of humans (T. Ishizaka *et al.*, 1970) are capable of mediating the release of SRS-A.

The cellular requirements for the formation of SRS-A have been studied in detail only with the rat system. It appears that the cellular requirement depends primarily on the immunoglobulins used for sensitization as well as the influence of competing globulins. The formation and release of SRS-A mediated by IgE globulins demonstrates a definite requirement for mast cells and requires neither participation of circulating neutrophils nor an intact complement system (Orange *et al.*, 1970). However, antiserum containing IgGa in addition to nonspecific gamma globulin, demonstrates an essential prerequisite for neutrophils and complement (Orange *et al.*, 1968). In contrast, when purified IgGa is used for sensitization, the cellular requirement for the formation and release of SRS-A involves both neutrophils and mast cells (Orange and Austen, 1971). This latter requirement for mast cells occurs only when competition with nonspecific gamma globulin is minimal. These differences in the requirement of the cellular elements are probably a reflection of the nature of the antigen–antibody reaction involved.

3. Kinin

The kinins are a group of pharmacologically active polypeptides with vascular permeability, vasodilation, smooth muscle contractility, and pain producing properties (Lewis, 1963; Epstein *et al.*, 1969). Although these polypeptides are generally believed to be formed in plasma from the action of a variety of enzymes called kallikreins derived from prekallikreins on a variety of alpha globulin plasma substrates, kininogens (Ratnoff, 1969), recent evidence indicates that kinin formation may involve a single kallikrein on a single kininogen (Wuepper *et al.*, 1970). The generation of kinins in plasma is, generally, thought to be initiated by the activation of Hageman factor (Webster, 1969). The activation of this factor is accomplished with surface contact and with a variety of biological materials (Ratnoff, 1969) and possibly, although not proven conclusively, by immune aggregates (Movat *et al.*, 1969; Eisen and Smith, 1970) or soluble complexes (Epstein *et al.*, 1969). Therefore, whenever the kinin cascade is activated it is essential to determine whether the activation is the result of an immunological reaction or secondary to nonspecific tissue injury.

There is evidence in a number of different animal species—dog (Beraldo, 1950), guinea pigs (Jonasson and Becker, 1966), rabbits, and rats (Brocklehurst and Lahiri, 1962)—that kinins are formed during an anaphylactic reaction.

Immune aggregates formed with rabbit or guinea pig IgG antibody, either IgG$_1$ or IgG$_2$ (Movat *et al.*, 1969), as well as soluble immune complexes formed by the interaction of IgM rheumatoid factor with human IgG (Epstein *et al.*, 1969) have been shown to generate kinin formation. The formation of kinins is an example of an anaphylactic-type reaction that is derived entirely from soluble substrates by the aggregation of antigen–antibody reaction without the intervention of cells directly.

4. Eosinophilic Chemotactic Factor of Anaphylaxis (ECF-A)

Kay *et al.* (1971a), described a factor released, along with histamine and SRS-A, from sensitized guinea pig lung by antigen that was specifically chemtoactic for eosinophil leukocytes (ECF-A). This factor could be differentiated from other pharmacologic mediators of anaphylaxis. The release of ECF-A could be accomplished by IgG_1 antibody in contrast to IgG_2 and was independent of the complement system. A similar factor has been obtained from human lung passively sensitized with IgE immunoglobulin (Kay *et al.*, 1971b). The inclusion of the ECF-A as a chemical mediator of anaphylaxis is on the basis of its low molecular weight (500–1000) and its release under identical conditions as other pharmacological mediators.

The importance of this factor can not be fully appreciated at this time primarily because of our ignorance as to the function of the eosinophil leukocytes. The association of eosinophils with allergic reactions and parasitic infections is well documented but their role in these reactions is largely unknown.

III. Cellular Relationships in Immediate Hypersensitivity

This section will deal primarily with cells involved in the immediate-type response with particular reference to parasitic infections and is not intended to be an exhaustive review of the literature, but rather a speculative discussion of the interrelationships of cells involved in the immediate-type response. It is hoped that this approach will act as an impetus for discussion and a stimulus of further experimentation involving the interaction of cells in the immediate-type response.

The cells to be discussed can be divided into two types: target cells and trigger cells. Target cells are those affected by antigen–antibody reaction either through the reaction of fixed antibody with antigen or by the subsequent interaction with another cell type. These cells can also be referred to as mediator cells, i.e., those cells capable of releasing various pharmacological mediators.

Trigger cells, also called effector cells, are those cells which as a consequence of an antigen–antibody reaction affect other cells, namely target cells.

It should be noted that these designations of target and trigger cells are functional descriptions and that a particular cell can act as a target cell under certain conditions and under different circumstances be considered a trigger cell.

A. Lymphocytes

The lymphocytes have primarily been considered as cells involved in the delayed-type reactions, however, there are indications that these cells have a function or role to play in the immediate-type response. The immunological response involving both delayed-type and immediate-type responses is especially evident in parasitic infections. Parasitic growth usually involves a series of different developmental stages with an array of different antigenic components that may function or evoke both types of responses either simultaneously or in series. Further, the necessity of different cell types in an immunological response has only recently been appreciated. A large body of evidence has been obtained recently that clearly demonstrates the need for cooperation between thymic derived lymphocytes and bone marrow cells for antibody synthesis (Talmage *et al.*, 1970; Abdou and Richter, 1970).

Presently, there is only a limited number of situations that demonstrate association of lymphocytes with immediate-type responses. The clearest example of the involvement of lymphocytes with immediate-type responses is with eosinophils. Eosinophilia is characteristic of an immediate-type response that is also observed in parasitic infections. Although the chemotaxis of these cells was indicated in these states, it has only recently been clearly demonstrated. The experiments of Kay *et al.* (1971a,b) established the requirement of homocytotropic antibodies, guinea pig IgG_1 and human IgE, for the generation of eosinophil chemotactic factor from guinea pig and human lung, respectively. This eosinophil chemotactic factor of anaphylaxis has been shown not to be dependent upon complement as are most other leukocyte chemotactic factors (Ward *et al.*, 1965), and the suggested source of this factor is probably the mast cell (Kay, 1970).

Eosinophils have been demonstrated to accumulate in draining lymph nodes immediately after antigenic stimulation (Litt, 1964; Cohen *et al.*, 1966). Further, Arnason and Waksman (1963) obtained infiltration of eosinophils when sites of a delayed-type reaction were retested. These studies indicated that the generation of chemotaxis for eosinophils appeared to depend upon antibody, antigen, and lymphoid cells. Cohen and Ward (1971) were able to demonstrate eosinophil chemotactic factor only when sensitized lymphocytes were reacted with antigen in conjunction with immune complexes provided the immune complex contained the same antigen as that used to activate the lymphocytes. Neither the immune complex nor the antigen activated lymphocytes alone were capable of generating eosinophil chemotaxis.

The elegant experiments of Basten *et al.* (1970) and Basten and Beeson (1970) on the mechanism of eosinophilia in *Trichinella*-infected rats strongly suggest the involvement of lymphocytes in the generation of eosinophilotaxis. Their findings demonstrated that the large lymphocytes from the thoracic duct, and not lymphocytes from the thymus, spleen, or lymph nodes, are responsible for the eosinophilia observed in these rats. Furthermore, it was shown that the lymphocytes produced a diffusible factor which affected the bone marrow cells. Although the precise nature of this "factor" was not determined it was suggested to be some form of antibody such as homocytotropic antibody.

The blast transformation of peripheral lymphocytes is generally considered a correlate of the delayed-type response (Mills, 1966; Oppenheim et al., 1967). However, lymphocytes from patients exhibiting immediate-type responses were also capable of blastogenesis regardless if a delayed-type response existed or not (Girard et al., 1967; Fellner et al., 1967). Greaves and Roitt (1969) demonstrated both blast-cell formation and IgE antibody production with peripheral lymphocytes from atopic patients on the addition of specific allergen. Interestingly, the detection of IgE antibody on some of the peripheral lymphocytes was not demonstrable until the cells were activated with antigen, which suggests that the lymphocytes were not passive carriers of IgE antibody but the antigen induced a specific anamnestic response involving antibody synthesis. Brostoff and Roitt (1969) have postulated that sensitized thymus-derived cells cooperate in the production of IgE antibody by the bone marrow cells. The evidence for this hypothesis was based on the demonstration of lymphocyte transformation, and delayed skin reactions when the immediate-type response was inhibited.

Similar conclusions concerning the cooperative action of thymus-derived lymphocytes for the production of IgE antibodies were suggested by Ogilvie and Jones (1967) and Wilson et al. (1967) from their studies on Nippostrongylus brasiliensis infections on neonatal thymectomized rats. In neonatal thymectomized rats, the IgE antibody production following initial infection was delayed and a reduced anamnestic response was obtained on rechallenge. Okumura and Tada (1971) in neonatally thymectomized rats demonstrated a similar requirement for thymus-derived lymphocytes for the initiation of homocytotropic antibody with DNP–Ascaris antigen. In addition, they also demonstrated that adult thymectomy followed by immunization resulted in an enhanced and sustained homocytotropic antibody production. These results, and those of the effect of X-irradiation (Tada et al., 1971) were interpreted as suggestive of the "regulatory" role of thymus-derived lymphocytes for the production of homocytotropic antibody.

Schoenbechler and Sadun (1968) using rabbits infected with Schistosoma mansoni were unable to obtain histamine release from a pure suspension of platelets unless leukocytes were present. The requirement of leukocytes from Schistosoma-infected rabbits for histamine release from platelets suggested a cooperative action between leukocytes and platelets. These results were confirmed and extended to demonstrate that neither peritoneal neutrophils nor peritoneal monocytes were involved, whereas a "pure" suspension of lymphocyte was effective in causing platelet histamine release (Schoenbechler and Barbaro, 1968).

Although the investigation of Henson (1970) using purified protein antigens was essentially in agreement with these results, there were notable exceptions; namely, a soluble factor was produced and the cell type was found to be a mononuclear cell. Recent results reported by Siraganian and Osler (1971b) and Henson and Benveniste (1971) were unable to establish the involvement of lymphoid cells in this cooperative reaction and indications, which will be discussed later, appear to implicate the basophil. Whether lymphocytes from parasite-infected animals are truly involved in a cooperative reaction with platelets or merely an experimental artifact remains to be established.

There are several notable differences that separate the cooperative reaction observed in parasite-infected animals and those immunized with purified proteins. All rabbits infected with *S. mansoni* exhibit the leukocyte-dependent histamine release whether or not the animals produce detectable homocytotropic antibody. Furthermore, the animals retain this capacity more than 3 years. On the other hand rabbits immunized with purified proteins demonstrate a leukocyte-dependent reaction, which is demonstrable for a relatively short time unless the animals are restimulated. This correlates with the percentage producing homocytotropic antibody. It should also be noted that continual restimulation by antigen results in a decreased leukocyte-dependent release with protein antigens (Siraganian and Osler, 1971a). It is difficult at this time to determine if these differences between parasite-infected animals and protein-immunized animals are indicative of an enchanced stimulation of IgE antibody by the helminth infections or the "sensitization" of long-lived cells such as thymic lymphocytes.

Although inconclusive, the results of the cellular involvement of lymphocytes in eosinophilia, their possible interaction with platelets, as well as their role in the production and regulation of IgE antibody, do suggest that lymphocytes have a function in the immediate-type hypersensitivity reaction.

B. EOSINOPHILS

In general the physiology of eosinophils resembles that of neutrophils, i.e., both are produced in bone marrow, spend a short time in the circulation, and then pass into the tissue. The granules of both neutrophils and eosinophils are lysosomelike structures; however, the eosinophils unlike the neutrophils contain large amounts of peroxidase. The relationship between eosinophils and pharmacological agents, particularly with regard to histamine is somewhat contradictory. There have been claims that these cells contain histamine; however, opposing views have also been reported (Hirsch, 1965). The results of Orange and Austen (1969b) appear to indicate that eosinophils do not form or release SRS-A in rat peritoneal cavity. The presence of exudates consisting predominantly of eosinophils results in a reduction of SRS-A release. It was not determined if this was an effect of this cell on antibody, on the antigen–antibody complexes, or on the release of SRS-A. There have been numerous reports that eosinophils inactivate histamine (Kovacs, 1950; Broome and Archer, 1961) and demonstrations that eosinophil extracts are capable of antagonizing serotonin and bradykinin (R. K. Archer and Broome, 1963).

The eosinophilia that is usually associated with parasitic infections, allergic diseases, and following an anaphylactic reaction is well documented. The *in vitro* adhesion of eosinophils on the surface of various parasitic helminths has been adequately described. Dobson (1968) studying the hematological changes induced in rats by *Amplicaeum robertsi* larvae reported marked peripheral eosinophilia associated with infection. The investigation of G. T. Archer (1969), using antigen–antibody precipitates prepared with extracts of *A. robertsi* or *Ascaris suum,* demonstrated chemotaxis of rat eosinophils. The chemotaxis was slower or lost when heated normal serum was substituted for fresh serum. Soulsby (1963) demonstrated the attraction of eosinophils and monocytes with marked pyroninophilic cytoplasma to *A. suum* larvae pretreated with immune serum and showed this reaction was independent of complement. Higashi and Chowdhury (1970) were unable to demonstrate significant *in vitro* adhesion of eosinophils to *Wuchereria bancrofti* larvae unless immune serum was present during the incubation of larvae and eosinophils and the reaction was shown to be complement-dependent.

It is apparent that adhesions of eosinophils in the cited examples demonstrate a definite requirement for an antigen–antibody reaction with either preformed aggregates or complexes formed in the presence of eosinophils. The necessity of heat labile components in some and not in others is probably a reflection of the class of immunoglobulins involved. Litt (1962) suggested that the mechanism of eosinophilia involved first the production of antibody which becomes localized at tissue sites and second the union of antigen and antibody. The recent results of Kay *et al.* (1971a) substantiate and extend this suggestion by the demonstration of the production of an eosinophil chemotactic factor.

There are numerous instances of the association of eosinophils and mast cells with helminth infections. Wells (1962) demonstrated that tissue eosinophilia was associated with increased mast cells in rats infected with *Nippostrongylus brasiliensis*. Fernex and his co-workers (Fernex and Bezes, 1962; Fernex and Fernex, 1962; Fernex and Sarasin, 1962) have observed a relationship between mast cells and eosinophils with helminth infections. They noted an increase in mast cells in the skin of mice or man infected with *Schistosoma mansoni*, *Hymenolepsi nana*, or *Wuchereria bancrofti*. G. T. Archer and McGovern (1968) reported mast cell disruption with the subsequent appearance of a new mast cell population in rats developing eosinophilia after infection with *A. robertsi*.

This association between eosinophils and mast cells can be viewed as the result of an immediate-type response. The mast cell containing homocytotropic antibody is disrupted and degranulated upon reaction with antigen. Concomitant with the decrease in mast cells is the elaboration of eosinophil chemotactic factor which is evident by the accumulation of eosinophils around degranulated mast cells and the presence of ingested granules in the eosinophils (Welsh and Geer, 1959). Mann (1969) suggests that the eosinophil leukocyte selectively phagocytizes mast cell granules and offers several possibilities for this specificity. First, the eosinophil may be acting as an antihistaminic cell, phagocytizing granules to minimize the histamine shock. Second, the eosinophil removes excessive mast cell granules and may provide the stimulus for a new population of mast cells.

The investigations cited concerning eosinophils indicate that they play a secondary role in the immediate-type response. Their appearance is the consequence of an antigen–antibody reaction and they apparently do not affect other cells. However, unless the precise function of these cells is known, it is difficult to evaluate if, indeed, they can act as trigger cells in the immediate-type responses.

C. Mast Cells

Mast cells are widely distributed throughout the body, particularly around small blood vessels and in organs rich in connective tissue. The high content of pharmacological agents and their ability to bind antibody or complexes make these cells suitable for the study of immediate-type responses.

The dynamic changes in mast cell population and the role of mast cells that occur during parasitic infections will be discussed in detail by others, particularly in relation to theories of immunity. The *in vitro* studies concerned with mast cells has centered around the production of IgE-like antibody and the release of amines from mast cells as indicative of the production of homocytotropic antibody. The reactivity of mast cells correlates directly with the demonstration of homocytotropic antibody as determined by passive cutaneous anaphylaxis (Malley *et al.*, 1968; Strejan and Campbell, 1968). Generally, homocytotropic antibody, as determined by release of histamine from sensitized mast cells, can be detected during a primary infection prior to the appearance of homocytotropic antibody in serum (Wilson and Bloch, 1968; Smith *et al.*, 1971). These results suggest that initial amounts of homocytotropic antibody produced are rapidly absorbed to mast cells and detectable in serum only when there is an excess. However, it should be mentioned that antigen-induced histamine release from peritoneal mast cells decreases despite the continual presence of homocytotropic antibody (Wilson and Bloch, 1968) or by subsequent reinfections (Keller, 1970). Of interest in this regard is the finding of Keller that after a primary infection the antigen-induced histamine release from pleural cavity mast cells was similar to that obtained from peritoneal mast cells. However, after several reinfections the antigen-induced histamine release from pleural cavity mast cells was decidedly higher than from cells obtained from the peritoneal cavity of the same group of animals. The decrease of antigen-induced histamine release observed after primary infection and the greater sensitivity of pleural cavity mast cells in contrast to peritoneal mast cells after the reinfection, may indicate a heterogeneity of homocytotropic antibodies with different affinities for different mast cells.

The examples cited establish that, in general, mast cells can be viewed as primarily mediator cells, releasing their stores of pharmacological agents. However, if the elaboration of eosinophil chemotactic factor is derived from mast cells, as the evidence seems to indicate, then the mast cell acts as a trigger cell for the increased eosinopoiesis seen in immediate-type responses.

D. BASOPHILS

The blood basophil and tissue mast cells are similar in structure and chemical characteristics and tend to respond to various stimuli in a similar manner. It is reasonable to assume that the blood basophil represents the circulating form of the tissue mast cell (Selye, 1965), and similarly, can be considered primarily a mediator cell. The reason for discussing the basophil separately from the mast cell stems from recent work that indicates that it may act as the effector cell in the leukocyte-dependent histamine release from rabbit platelets (Henson and Benveniste, 1971; Siraganian and Osler, 1971b).

K. Ishizaka *et al.* (1970) have presented evidence that the human basophil fixes IgE antibody, with release of its content of histamine by challenge with specific antigen or anti-IgE antibody (T. Ishizaka *et al.*, 1969; Lichtenstein *et al.*, 1970). In addition to the release of histamine, the basophil releases a soluble factor which reacts with normal rabbit platelets causing the release of platelet histamine (Siraganian and Osler, 1971a; Henson and Benveniste, 1971). The soluble factor, or platelet-activating factor (Henson and Benveniste, 1971), is capable of binding to blood cellular elements and can only be demonstrated in the fluid phase by the incorporation of serum albumin to Tyrode's buffer. Initially, Barbaro and Schoenbechler (1970) were unable to demonstrate the production of soluble factor with leukocytes from *Schistosoma mansoni*-infected rabbits; however, they did not discount its existence. More recent results (Barbaro and Schoenbechler, 1971, unpublished data) using Tyrode's buffer fortified with bovine serum albumin have demonstrated the elaboration of platelet-activating factor with leukocytes from *S. mansoni*-infected rabbits. The possibility now exists that the initial report of Schoenbechler and Barbaro (1968), that the lymphocyte was the cell causing histamine release from platelets, may have been due to the binding of platelet-activating factor to lymphocytes. Whether the leukocyte-dependent histamine reaction is dependent upon lymphocytes or basophils or both requires further work.

E. Platelets

Although there have been numerous reports of platelets acting as target cells in the immediate-type response, few of them pertain to parasitic infections. The *in vitro* system most studied involves rabbit platelets primarily because of their high content of histamine in contrast to platelets from other mammals.

The studies of Schoenbechler and Sadun (1968), subsequently confirmed by Schoenbechler and Barbaro (1968), established that platelets from *S. mansoni*-infected rabbits were not sensitized with homocytotropic antibody and the antigen-induced release of histamine required the presence of leukocytes from infected rabbits. Although most of the experiments involved rabbits infected with *S. mansoni*, similar results could be obtained with *Trichinella spiralis* (Colwell *et al.*, 1971), *Dirofilaria immitis* (Barbaro and Schoenbechler, 1971, unpublished data), and most likely all helminthic infections producing homocytotropic antibody.

The antigen-induced histamine release can be detected in all rabbits regardless of the presence or absence of circulating homocytotropic antibody (Schoenbechler and Sadun, 1968). Histamine release, generally, occurred before the appearance of homocytotropic antibody in serum, similar to the rat mast cell system. In contrast to the rat mast cells, the release of histamine from platelets did not decrease but remained through the life of the animals.

The electron microscopic study of the interaction of normal rabbit platelets with leukocytes from *S. mansoni*-infected rabbits demonstrated the close association of platelets and lymphocytes (Aikawa *et al.*, 1971). Of particular interest was the formation of platelet pseudopods and the interdigitation with leukocytes with the concomitant decrease in platelet granular inclusions. No evidence of platelet lysis was observed which is in keeping with the evidence from mast cells and human leukocytes that the release of histamine is a secretory process.

IV. Closing Remarks

The problems associated with the study of immediate-type hypersensitivity in parasitic infections is rendered difficult by the number and complexity of the antigens involved. The parasites, as well as the altered host tissue, constitute a whole array of antigens which vary both qualitatively and quantitatively as the parasites develop within the host. The complexity of antigens is concomitantly manifested in the complexity of the antibodies produced towards these antigens. This complexity can be a cause for despair when attempting to unravel the immunological mechanisms of the immediate-type response. However, with the recent advances in our knowledge of the various immunoglobulins and with the development of newer techniques of separation and purification of both antigens and antibodies, this area of research has been made both challenging and rewarding.

There are many questions to be answered concerning the immediate hypersensitivity reaction in parasitic infections. The most notable is the apparent inability of parasitic protozoa to stimulate the production of homocytotropic antibody, whereas helminthic infections are extremely effective in this regard. The ability to produce large quantities of homocytotropic antibody, a property of the living worm, causes enhanced production of homocytotropic antibody to unrelated proteins and leads one to ask how the potentiation is accomplished. Undoubtedly, through the effective separation and purification of helminthic antigens, it should be possible to establish if this "adjuvant" effect is the result of the chemical structure of certain antigens or the more basic biological relationship between parasite and host. The need for investigation concerning the relationship between allergies and helminth infections is evident from the conflicting observations. On the one hand there appears to be a relationship between helminthic infections and the incidence of asthma, suggesting potentiation of the allergic response by helminths. On the other hand the incidence of atopic diseases, as hay fever and eczema, are rare in parasitic endemic areas, suggesting suppression of the allergic response.

The question of the role played by immediate-type hypersensitivity, or more specifically of IgE antibody, in theories of immunity has been the subject of a number of investigations in recent years and has been discussed by others. These theories of immunity to certain parasitic diseases, if proved correct, are perhaps the only example of the biological justification of immediate-type hypersensitivity reactions as a beneficial, rather than injurious, response.

The interaction of various cells is an intriguing and much neglected area of research in immediate-type reactions. Only recently has the importance of cellular interactions been appreciated. It is hoped that this discussion of some of these cellular interactions will serve as a stimulus for more probing research in this area. Hopefully the dichotomy that now exists between immediate- and delayed-type hypersensitivity reactions will be resolved into a unified concept of immunology.

Undoubtedly, the techniques and principles of immunology have been a great advantage as applied to parasitologic problems. However, it must be remembered that scientific knowledge is a "two-way street," and that parasitologic techniques have and continue to be a useful tool for the study of basic immunological mechanisms. It is hoped that this mutually benefiting relationship between the two disciplines will be as productive in the future as it has been in the past.

Acknowledgments

I wish to sincerely thank Dr. E. L. Becker (1971) for permitting me the opportunity to read a preprint of "Nature and classification of immediate-type allergic reactions" and allowing the use of his system of classification prior to publication. In addition, I wish to express my gratitude to him, Dr. E. H. Sadun, and Dr. D. T. O. Wong for their constructive criticism of this review.

References

Abdou, N. I., and Richter, M. (1970). *Advan. Immunol.* **12**, 202.
Aikawa, M., Schoenbechler, M. J., Barbaro, J. F., and Sadun, E. H. (1971). *Amer. J. Pathol.* **63**, 85.

Archer, G. T. (1969). *Pathology* **1**, 133.
Archer, G. T., and McGovern, V. J. (1968). *J. Pathol. Bacteriol.* **95**, 217.
Archer, R. K., and Broome, J. (1963). *Nature (London)* **198**, 893.
Arnason, B. G., and Waksman, B. H. (1963). *Lab. Invest.* **12**, 737.
Assem, E. S. K., and Schild, H. O. (1969). *Nature (London)* **224**, 1028.
Austen, K. F., and Becker, E. L. (1966). *J. Exp. Med.* **124**, 397.
Austen, K. F., and Brocklehurst, W. E. (1961). *J. Exp. Med.* **113**, 521.
Barbaro, J. F., and Schoenbechler, M. J. (1970). *J. Immunol.* **104**, 1124.
Barbaro, J. F., and Zvaifler, N. J. (1966). *Proc. Soc. Exp. Biol. Med.* **122**, 1245.
Basten, A., and Beeson, P. B. (1970). *J. Exp. Med.* **131**, 1288.
Basten, A., Boyer, M. H., and Beeson, P. B. (1970). *J. Exp. Med.* **131**, 1271.
Becker, E. L. (1959). *In* "Mechanisms of Hypersensitivity" (J. H. Shaffer, G. A. LoGrippo, and M. W. Chase, eds.), p. 312. Little, Brown, Boston, Massachusetts.
Becker, E. L. (1968). *In* "Biochemistry of the Acute Allergic Reactions" (K. F. Austen and E. L. Becker, eds.), pp. 199–213. Davis, Philadelphia, Pennsylvania.
Becker, E. L. (1971). *Advan. Immunol.* **13**, 267.
Becker, E. L., and Austen, K. F. (1964). *J. Exp. Med.* **120**, 491.
Becker, E. L., and Austen, K. F. (1966). *J. Exp. Med.* **124**, 379.
Beraldo, W. T. (1950). *Amer. J. Physiol.* **163**, 283.
Brocklehurst, W. E. (1959). Quoted in Becker (1959).
Brocklehurst, W. E., and Lahiri, S. C. (1962). *J. Physiol. (London)* **160**, 15.
Broome, J., and Archer, R. K. (1961). *Nature (London)* **193**, 446.
Brostoff, J., and Roitt, I. M. (1969). *Lancet* **2**, 1269.
Cohen, S., and Milstein, C. (1967). *Advan. Immunol.* **7**, 1.
Cohen, S., and Ward, P. A. (1971). *J. Exp. Med.* **133**, 133.
Cohen, S., Vassalli, P., Benacerraf, B., and McCluskey, R. T. (1966). *Lab. Invest.* **15**, 1143.
Colwell, E. J., Ortaldo, J. R., Schoenbechler, M. J., Barbaro, J. F., and Fife, E. H., Jr. (1971). *Exp. Parasitol.* **29**, 263.
Colwell, E. J., Ortaldo, J. R., Schoenbechler, M. J., and Barbaro, J. F. (1971). *Int. Arch. Allergy Appl. Immunol.* **41**, 754.
Dobson, C. (1968). *Aust. J. Biol. Sci.* **21**, 341.
Dobson, C., Morseth, D. J., and Soulsby, E. J. L. (1971). *J. Immunol.* **106**, 128.
Edelman, G. M., and Gall, W. E. (1969). *Annu. Rev. Biochem.* **38**, 415.
Eisen, V., and Smith, H. G. (1970). *Brit. J. Exp. Pathol.* **51**, 328.
Epstein, W. V., Tan, M., and Melman, K. L. (1969). *Ann. N.Y. Acad. Sci.* **168**, 173.
Fellner, M. J., Baer, R. L., Ripps, C. J., and Hirschhorn, K. (1967). *Nature (London)* **216**, 803.
Fernex, M., and Bezes, H. (1962). *Acta Trop.* **19**, 252.
Fernex, M., and Fernex, P. (1962). *Acta Trop.* **19**, 248.
Fernex, M., and Sarasin, R. (1962). *Acta Trop.* **19**, 258.
Franklin, E. C., and Frangione, B. (1969). *Annu. Rev. Med.* **20**, 155.
Girard, J. P., Rose, N. R., Kunz, M. L., Kobayashi, S., and Arbesman, C. E. (1967). *J. Allergy* **39**, 65.
Greaves, M. F., and Roitt, I. M. (1969). *Lancet* **1**, 803.
Henney, C. S., and Stanworth, D. R. (1966). *Nature (London)* **210**, 1071.
Henson, P. M. (1969). *Fed. Proc., Fed. Amer. Soc. Exp. Biol.* **28**, 1721.
Henson, P. M. (1970). *J. Exp. Med.* **131**, 287.
Henson, P. M., and Benveniste, J. (1971). *In* "Biochemistry of the Acute Allergic Reactions" (K. F. Austen and E. L. Becker, eds.), pp. 111–123. Davis, Philadelphia, Pennsylvania.

Henson, P. M., and Cochrane, C. G. (1969). *J. Exp. Med.* **129**, 153.

Higashi, G. I., and Chowdhury, A. B. (1970). *Immunology* **19**, 65.

Hirsch, J. G. (1965). *In* "The Inflammatory Process" (B. W. Zweifach, L. Grant, and R. F. McCluskey, eds.), pp. 245–280. Academic Press, New York.

Ishizaka, K., and Ishizaka, T. (1968). *J. Allergy* **42**, 330.

Ishizaka, K., Ishizaka, T., and Hornbrook, M. M. (1966). *J. Immunol.* **97**, 75.

Ishizaka, K., Ishizaka, T., and Tada, T. (1969). *J. Immunol.* **103**, 445.

Ishizaka, K., Tomioka, H., and Ishizaka, T. (1970). *J. Immunol.* **105**, 1459.

Ishizaka, T., Ishizaka, K., Johannsson, S. G. O., and Bennich, H. (1969). *J. Immunol.* **102**, 884.

Ishizaka, T., Ishizaka, K., Orange, R. P., and Austen, K. F. (1970). *J. Immunol.* **104**, 335.

Ishizaka, T., Ishizaka, K., Orange, R. P., and Austen, K. F. (1971). *J. Immunol.* **106**, 1267.

Johnson, A. R., and Moran, N. C. (1969). *Fed. Proc., Fed. Amer. Soc. Exp. Biol.* **28**, 1716.

Jonasson, O., and Becker, E. L. (1966). *J. Exp. Med.* **123**, 509.

Kanyerezi, B., Jaton, J. C., and Bloch, K. J. (1971). *J. Immunol.* **106**, 1411.

Kay, A. B. (1970). *Clin. Exp. Immunol.* **6**, 75.

Kay, A. B., Stechschulte, D. J., and Austen, K. F. (1971a). *J. Exp. Med.* **133**, 602.

Kay, A. B., Stechschulte, D. J., Kaplan, A. P., and Austen, K. F. (1971b). *Fed. Proc., Fed. Amer. Soc. Exp. Biol.* **30**, 682.

Keller, R. (1970). *Int. Arch. Allergy Appl. Immunol.* **38**, 305.

Koopman, W. J., Orange, R. P., and Austen, K. F. (1970). *J. Immunol.* **105**, 1096.

Kovacs, B. A. (1950). *Experientia* **6**, 349.

Levine, B. B., and Vaz, N. M. (1970). *Int. Arch. Allergy Appl. Immunol.* **39**, 156.

Levine, B. B., Chang, H., and Vaz, N. M. (1971). *J. Immunol.* **106**, 29.

Lewis, G. P. (1963). *Ann. N.Y. Acad. Sci.* **104**, 236.

Lichtenstein, L. M. (1968). *In* "Biochemistry of the Acute Allergic Reactions" (K. F. Austen and E. L. Becker, eds.), p. 153. Davis, Philadelphia, Pennsylvania.

Lichtenstein, L. M. (1969). *In* "Cellular and Humoral Mechanisms in Anaphylaxis and Allergy" (H. Z. Movat, ed.), pp. 176–178. Karger, Basel.

Lichtenstein, L. M., Levy, D. A., and Ishizaka, K. (1970). *Immunology* **19**, 831.

Litt, M. (1962). *J. Allergy* **33**, 532.

Litt, M. (1964). *Ann. N.Y. Acad. Sci.* **116**, 964.

Malley, A., Amkraut, A. A., Strejan, G., and Campbell, D. H. (1968). *J. Immunol.* **101**, 292.

Mann, P. R. (1969). *J. Pathol.* **98**, 183.

Mills, J. A. (1966). *J. Immunol.* **97**, 239.

Mongar, J. L., and Schild, H. O. (1957). *J. Physiol.* (*London*) **135**, 301.

Morse, H. C., Bloch, K. J., and Austen, K. F. (1968). *J. Immunol.* **101**, 658.

Mota, I., and Peixoto, J. M. (1966). *Life Sci.* **5**, 1723.

Movat, H. Z., Treloar, M. P., DiLorenzo, N. L., Robertson, J. W., and Sender, H. B. (1969). *In* "Cellular and Humoral Mechanisms in Anaphylaxis and Allergy" (H. Z. Movat, ed.), pp. 215–223. Karger, Basel.

Ogilvie, B. M. (1964). *Nature* (*London*) **204**, 91.

Ogilvie, B. M., and Jones, V. E. (1967). *Parasitology* **57**, 335.

Ogilvie, B. M., and Jones, V. E. (1969). *In* "Cellular and Humoral Mechanisms in Anaphylaxis and Allergy" (H. Z. Movat, ed.), p. 13. Karger, Basel.

Okumura, K., and Tada, T. (1971). *J. Immunol.* **106,** 1019.

Oliver-Gonzalez, J. (1953). *Proc. Soc. Exp. Biol. Med.* **84,** 520.

Oppenheim, J. J., Wolstencroft, R. A., and Gell, P. G. H. (1967). *Immunology* **12,** 89.

Orange, R. P., and Austen, K. F. (1969a). *Advan. Immunol.* **10,** 105.

Orange, R. P., and Austen, K. F. (1969b). *In* "Cellular and Humoral Mechanisms in Anaphylaxis and Allergy" (H. Z. Movat, ed.), p. 196. Karger, Basel.

Orange, R. P., and Austen, K. F. (1971). *Hosp. Pract.* **6,** 79.

Orange, R. P., Valentine, M. D., and Austen, K. F. (1968). *J. Exp. Med.* **127,** 767.

Orange, R. P., Stechschulte, D. J., and Austen, K. F. (1970). *J. Immunol.* **105,** 1087.

Orr, T. S. C., and Blair, A. M. J. N. (1969). *Life Sci.* **8,** 1073.

Osler, A. G., Lichtenstein, L. M., and Levy, D. A. (1968). *Advan. Immunol.* **8,** 183.

Ovary, Z. (1958). *Progr. Allergy* **5,** 459.

Ovary, Z., Benacerraf, B., and Bloch, K. J. (1963). *J. Exp. Med.* **117,** 951.

Perelmutter, L., and Khera, K. (1970). *Int. Arch. Allergy Appl. Immunol.* **39,** 27.

Prouvost-Danon, A., Peixoto, J. M., and Javierre, M. Q. (1968). *Immunology* **15,** 271.

Ratnoff, O. D. (1969). *Advan. Immunol.* **10,** 145.

Reid, R. T., Minden, P., and Farr, R. S. (1966). *J. Exp. Med.* **123,** 845.

Schoenbechler, M. J., and Barbaro, J. F. (1968). *Proc. Nat. Acad. Sci. U.S.* **60,** 1247.

Schoenbechler, M. J., and Sadun, E. H. (1968). *Proc. Soc. Exp. Biol. Med.* **127,** 601.

Seyle, H. (1965). *In* "The Mast Cells," p. 331. Butterworth, London.

Siraganian, R. P., and Osler, A. G. (1971a). *J. Immunol.* **106,** 1244.

Siraganian, R. P., and Osler, A. G. (1971b). *J. Immunol.* **106,** 1252.

Smith, S. R., Petillo, J., Hwang, A., and Adams, B. (1971). *Fed. Proc., Fed. Amer. Soc. Exp. Biol.* **30,** 411.

Soulsby, E. J. L. (1962). *Advan. Immunol.* **2,** 265.

Soulsby, E. J. L. (1963). *Ann. N.Y. Acad. Sci.* **113,** 492.

Stanworth, D. R. (1970). *Clin. Exp. Immunol.* **6,** 1.

Stechschulte, D. J., Austen, K. F., and Bloch, K. J. (1967). *J. Exp. Med.* **125,** 127.

Stechschulte, D. J., Orange, R. P., and Austen, K. F. (1970). *J. Immunol.* **105,** 1082.

Strejan, G., and Campbell, D. H. (1968). *J. Immunol.* **101,** 628.

Tada, T., Taniguchi, M., and Okumura, K. (1971). *J. Immunol.* **106,** 1012.

Talmage, D. W.., Radovich, J., and Hemmingsen, H. (1970). *Advan. Immunol.* **12,** 271.

Uvnas, B. (1964). *Ann. N.Y. Acad. Sci.* **116,** 880.

Vaz, N. M., and Ovary, Z. (1968). *J. Immunol.* **100,** 1014.

Ward, P. A., Cochrane, C. G., and Muller-Eberhard, H. J. (1965). *J. Exp. Med.* **122,** 327.

Webster, M. E. (1969). *In* "Cellular and Humoral Mechanisms in Anaphylaxis and Allergy" (H. Z. Movat, ed.), p. 207. Karger, Basel.

Wells, P. D. (1962). *Exp. Parasitol.* **12,** 82.

Welsh, R. A., and Geer, J. C. (1959). *Amer. J. Pathol.* **35,** 103.

Wilson, R. J. M., and Bloch, K. J. (1968). *J. Immunol.* **100**, 622.
Wilson, R. J. M., Jones, V. E., and Leskowitz, S. (1967). *Nature* (*London*) **213**, 398.
Wuepper, K. D., Tucker, E. S., and Cochrane, C. G. (1970). *J. Immunol.* **105**, 1307.
Zvaifler, N. J., and Becker, E. L. (1966). *J. Exp. Med.* **123**, 935.
Zvaifler, N. J., and Robinson, J. O. (1969). *J. Exp. Med.* **130**, 907.

⑥ IMMEDIATE HYPERSENSITIVITY EFFECTOR MECHANISMS

II. *In Vivo* Reactions

MAX MURRAY

I. Introduction

In recent years intensive immunopathological studies of mucous membranes have been made and there has been increasing interest in the role of local immunity in defense mechanisms. The identification of IgA and IgE as locally produced antibodies has led to considerable speculation as to their immunological function and the manner in which they effect a maximal protective response, i.e., the method and route by which anti-organism antibodies are released and pass across the epithelial sheet to their target sites.

In certain systems, it would appear from observations on the effects of immunological reactions that there is probably a sudden release of antibody into the lumen of say, the intestine. Parasitic systems in particular offer an excellent model for studying the immunological apparatus of mucous membranes. The progress of the infection and the immunological effects can be measured directly and accurately as the parasites usually remain localized in the lumen and do not multiply within the body. Also the site of reaction can be identified easily because of the size of the worms.

The model system we employ is *Nippostrongylus brasiliensis* infection in the hooded Lister rat. This has the advantage that a large number of animals can be used and that *N. brasiliensis* is a potent antigen. In interpretation of results, the breed of rat used should be borne in mind as there is evidence to indicate that various strains of rats can respond differently to parasitic infection (Corba *et al.*, 1972).

Following subcutaneous inoculation into adult rats, *N. brasiliensis* larvae travel via the lungs to the small intestine where by day 3–4 they establish a stable adult worm population. At this time the majority of parasites which lie intertwined between intestinal villi are concentrated in a 4–5 cm area of the jejunum about 20 cm from the pylorus. The host's immune response to the presence of worms can be judged by two markers. The first is a drop in worm egg output which occurs 24–48 hours prior to the onset of worm expulsion (Fig. 1). The second is worm loss which occurs in two phases. The initial phase begins around day 10 after inoculation when there is a slow loss of worms; the subsequent phase starts at day 12 or 13, is exponential, and proceeds at a faster rate (Murray *et al.*, 1971a). The slope of the line showing the kinetics of the worm population can be taken as a measure of the immune status of the host; second and third infections show an increased speed of expulsion (E. E. E. Jarrett *et al.*, 1968a).

With the onset of the rapid phase of worm expulsion, the area of maximal worm concentration becomes markedly edematous and congested. The intestinal mucosa above and below this site is only moderately affected. Following expulsion from this area, the parasites which do not die move away mainly in a posterior direction, and another intense localized reaction occurs at the next site of worm concentration.

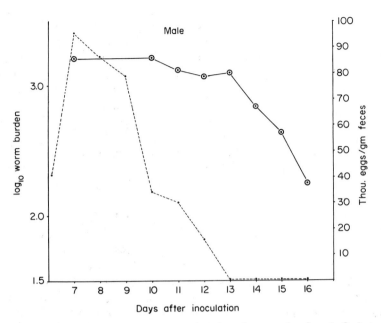

Fig. 1. Kinetics of worm egg output (- - -) and worm burden (-⊙-) in rats infected with 3000 *N. brasiliensis*.

During the period of worm loss these reactions are found at intervals along the small intestine as far as the ileum. The consistency of initial worm localization in a 4–5 cm area approximately 20 cm from the pylorus, allows the exact sequence of cytological events associated with the presence and expulsion of parasites to be followed throughout the infection. Therefore the criticism of Ogilvie and Jones (1971), that because the parasites do not remain in the same location cellular changes cannot be followed sequentially, is not valid.

Thus *N. brasiliensis* infection in the rat offers an excellent model system for studying immunological mechanisms at mucous surfaces because (1) the host's immune response can be measured by worm egg output and the time of onset and the rate of worm expulsion; and (2) the constant initial localization of the majority of the adult worm population in a 4–5 cm area of the jejunum facilitates the detailed study of the nature of the changes associated with worm loss.

II. Hypersensitivity Mechanisms in Parasitic Disease

Helminth infections have long been known to be associated with induction of hypersensitivity in man and positive Prausnitz-Küstner tests have been demonstrated in a number of parasitic infections, thus providing evidence of the immediate nature of the hypersensitivity state (Andrews, 1962). Such reactions are usually regarded as being harmful to the host but evidence has accumulated over a number of years that immediate hypersensitivity mechanisms may play a part in specific immune protective responses at local mucous surfaces. Stewart (1953), studying the expulsion of gastrointestinal nematodes by sheep, found that there was a rapid rise in blood histamine, that the wall of the target organ became edematous, and that, in some cases, the administration of antihistaminics blocked the expulsion of adult worms. He suggested that the local reaction produced an environment unfavorable to the survival of the parasites.

Further work, using heterologous anaphylactic shock, indicated that immediate hypersensitivity reactions might be involved. First Mulligan *et al.* (1965) and then Neilson (1969) demonstrated that when adult *Nippostrongylus* worms were transplanted into susceptible rats, they were subsequently expelled by an immune reaction. The time of onset of the expulsion of the infection could be shortened by passively transferred hyperimmune serum (Mulligan *et al.*, 1965; Ogilvie and Jones, 1968; Neilson, 1969). The system was further developed by Barth *et al.* (1966) who pretreated recipient rats with *Bordetella pertussis*-adjuvanted ovalbumin. When worms were transplanted into such animals which had also received hyperimmune serum the administration of the shocking dose of ovalbumin caused an acceleration of worm loss when compared to identical animals which were not shocked and which were shocked but were not given antiserum. This work suggested that gut anaphylaxis—the intestine is the shock organ in the rat (Sanyal and West, 1958; Kabat and Mayer, 1961)—could cause an increased outpouring of antibody, i.e., enhanced antibody release was caused by an immediate-type hypersensitivity reaction or was mast cell-mediated.

III. The Mast Cell in Intestinal Immunological Reactions— *Nippostrongylus brasiliensis* in the Rat

A. CHARACTERISTICS OF THE INTESTINAL MAST CELL

Mast cells in the rat intestinal lamina propria have been the subject of conflicting reports. Some workers have found very few or no mast cells in this tissue (Mota *et al.*, 1956; Whur, 1966) while others have shown that there is a high density (Lindholm, 1960; Wells, 1962). Enerback (1966a), H. R. P. Miller *et al.* (1967), and Murray *et al.*

(1968) found that their demonstration depended on the method of fixation.

Mast cells are distinguished by a number of salient characteristics.

1. Their granules contain the cationic vasoactive compounds, 5-hydroxytryptamine (5-HT) and histamine (Enerback, 1966b; H. R. P. Miller *et al.*, 1967; Murray *et al.*, 1968; Hakanson *et al.*, 1967). These are bound electrostatically to a complex of a polyanionic polymer (sulfated acid mucopolysaccharide) and a highly basic polycationic protein (Spicer, 1963; Benditt and Lagunoff, 1964; W. F. H. Jarrett *et al.*, 1967a; H. R. P. Miller *et al.*, 1967; Murray *et al.*, 1968) which consists at least in part of specific proteases (Darzynkiewicz and Barnard, 1967; Budd *et al.*, 1967). Histochemical studies have shown that there is a lower degree of sulfation of acid mucopolysaccharide in subepithelial intestinal mast cells than in connective tissue mast cells (Murray *et al.*, 1968; H. R. P. Miller, 1970). Combs *et al.* (1965) found that in the rat connective tissue mast cell, cell maturation is accompanied by increasing degrees of sulfation. Subepithelial intestinal mast cells may therefore represent an immature cell population or perhaps another type of mast cell.

2. Mast cell discharge involves granules and/or their contents being extruded into the surrounding tissue spaces. The extrusion of whole granules is usually regarded as the most common method of discharge, but it in fact depends on the nature of the stimulus, e.g., 48/80, the potent connective tissue mast cell lytic agent, causes mast cell granule damage and extrusion, whereas antigen–antibody reaction applied directly to the mast cell results in loss of granule contents but no extrusion (Kruger *et al.*, 1970). The latter method of discharge has been shown to be the origin of that enigmatic cell the globule leukocyte. Despite the striking morphology of this cell, until a few years ago its origin was unknown and function uncertain. The globule leukocyte is found within epithelia and characteristically contains large globules or granules. It occurs in many species and is particularly prominent in parasitic infections (Fig. 2, Murray *et al.*, 1968). Some workers considered that the globule leukocyte originated from immunoglobulin-producing cells and postulated that its function was to carry antibody into the intestinal lumen (Dobson, 1966; Whur and Gracie, 1967; Whur and Johnston, 1967). However, immunofluorescence studies demonstrated that these cells do not contain immunoglobulin (Whur and White, 1970) and detailed quantitative (W. F. H. Jarrett *et al.*, 1967b; H. R. P. Miller and Jarrett, 1971) cytochemical and ultrastructural data (Murray *et al.*, 1968; H. R. P., Miller, 1971a) are now available which show that there is progressive transformation of mast cells to globule leukocytes during

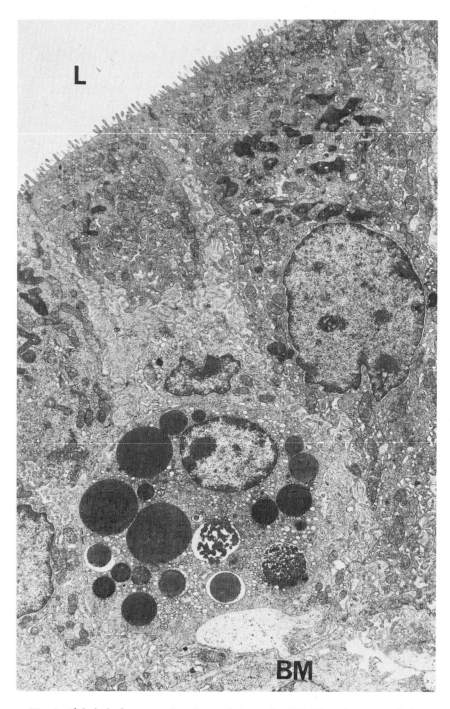

Fig. 2. Globule leukocyte within the epithelium of gallbladder of parasitized sheep. The cytoplasm is packed with large membrane-bound granules. L, lumen; BM, basement membrane. ×5000. Reproduced from Murray *et al.* (1968) by courtesy of the editor of *Lab. Invest.*

the amine discharge reaction. The fact that globule leukocytes are mast cells which are discharging or have discharged some or all of their granule content must be taken into consideration in any study of cellular population kinetics at mucous surfaces.

3. The cell membrane of the mast cell has an affinity for globulin molecules (Tigelaar *et al.*, 1971) and a particularly strong and long-lasting attraction for IgE (Ishizaka and Ishizaka, 1970), hence the name homocytotropic, mast cell-sensitizing, or reaginic antibody (see Section V,A,2).

B. INTESTINAL MAST CELL DURING PARASITIC INFECTION

Taliaferro and Sarles (1939) reported that the population of "connective tissue basophils," thought at that time to be different from mast cells, in the intestinal mucosa of the rat increased during the course of infection with the nematode *N. brasiliensis*, while Wells (1962) found that following worm loss intestinal mast cells and histamine levels in the bowel increased. The number of globule leukocytes also increased during the period of worm expulsion (Whur, 1966).

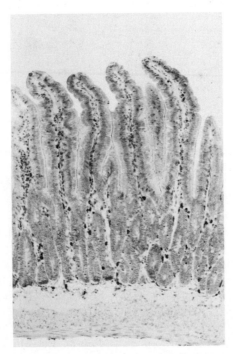

Fig. 3. Intestinal mucosa of normal parasite-free rat containing 10–12 mast cells/villus crypt unit. Astra blue/safranin. ×110.

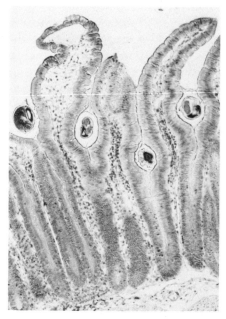

Fig. 4. Intestinal mucosa of rat 7 days after inoculation with 3000 *N. brasiliensis.* Mast cells have largely disappeared from the lamina propria and parasites are lying between the villi. Astra blue/safranin. ×110.

A series of detailed quantitative studies have now been made of the intestinal mast cell population during primary infection (W. F. H. Jarrett *et al.,* 1967b; H. R. P. Miller and Jarrett, 1971; Murray *et al.,* 1971a,b). In the latter two studies, samples were constantly taken from the jejunum at a point approximately 20 cm from the pylorus, the site of maximal worm concentration. Mast cell-globule leukocytes were quantitated on a villus–crypt structural unit basis as described by H. R. P. Miller and Jarrett (1971) and Murray *et al.* (1971a). This was found to give more reliable results than quantitation on an area unit basis.

Major changes occur in the intestinal mast cell population of the rat during infection with *N. brasiliensis.* In the normal young adult rat there are about 10–12 mast cells per villus–crypt unit (Fig. 3). Shortly after the young adult worms reach the intestine there is marked degranulation (Fig. 4) and destruction of mast cells (H. R. P. Miller, 1970). It has been shown that the worms secrete a degranulator (E. E. E. Jarrett *et al.,* 1969; Murray, 1972). Such a substance has been isolated and characterized as a polypeptide of MW 2000–3000 in *Ascaris* (Uvnas and Wold, 1967). This in *Nippostrongylus* may be part of the worm's feeding mechanism. Carbon black injected at this stage shows a vascular leakage from the postcapillary venules and there is marked edema and engorgement of the villi. Injection of Evan's blue demonstrates the areas of albumin leak. These events occur specifically at sites of worm location.

Until about day 10 of the infection there is almost complete disappearance of demonstrable mast cells. About this time a large number of mononuclear cells ultrastructurally indistinguishable from hemocytoblasts or lymphoblasts appear in the lamina propria. These have a round or oval nucleus with a large nucleolus and margination of chromatin; cytoplasm is fairly abundant and is packed with polyribosomes (Fig. 6, H. R. P. Miller, 1971b). They undergo mitosis (Fig. 7) and progressively differentiate into mast cells acquiring membrane-bound granules which contain all the constituents of mast cell granules including 5-HT (H. R. P. Miller, 1970). Following this there is an exponential rise in intestinal mast cells (Fig. 5 and Fig. 8, H. R. P. Miller and Jarrett, 1971). The cause of this rise is not known. It is not dependent on the continuing presence of the parasite. In an experiment in which

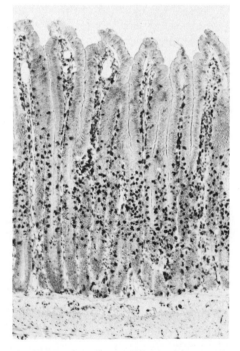

Fig. 5. Intestinal mucosa of rat 14 days after inoculation with 3000 *N. brasiliensis.* There is an intense mast cell reaction in the lamina propria and large numbers are migrating into the epithelial sheet, i.e., transforming to globule leukocytes. Astra blue/safranin. ×110.

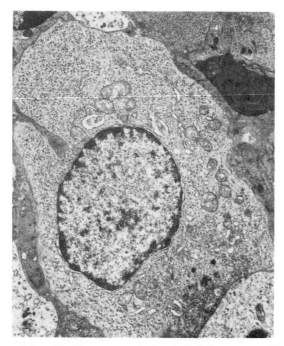

Fig. 6. A mastoblast showing numerous ribosomal aggregates. ×6000. Reproduced from H. R. P. Miller (1971b) by courtesy of the editor of *Lab. Invest.*

groups of infected rats were treated with an anthelmintic, it was found that if the worms were removed by day 7, a subsequent mast cell rise still took place (Murray *et al.*, 1971b).

The source of these mast cell precursors which populate the intestinal lamina propria has yet to be determined although much evidence is now available which suggests that they might be lymphoid in origin. Thus Ginsburg (1963) and Ginsburg and Sachs (1963) described mast cell differentiation in normal mouse thymic lymphoid cells grown on embryonic fibroblast monolayers; spleen cultures similarly prepared showed no such differentiation. Similarly, Csaba and Barath (1970) reported the transformation of lymphoid cells into mast cells in tissue culture; they found that thymic lymphoid cells and small peritoneal lymphocytes rather than cells from lymph nodes were involved. Burnett (1965) found large numbers of mast cells accumulating in thymuses of NZB mice; he proposed that mast cells, like plasma cells, are specialized executive derivatives of the lymphoid series and transformation into one or the other depends on the nature of the stimulus. Antigenic stimulation can produce an increase in mast cell population in rat lymph nodes (J. J. Miller and Coles, 1968). *In vitro* studies by Ginsburg and

Lagunoff (1967) have shown that when cells from lymph nodes or thoracic duct of mice hyperimmunized with protein antigens are cultured on embryonic fibroblast monolayers in the presence of antigen, numerous clones of mast cells appear particularly in the vicinity of large lymphoid cells; in unimmunized cultures or cultures lacking antigen, phagocytic histiocytes appear. Another possibly significant finding is that of S. J. Morse and Bray (1969) who demonstrated that *Bordetella pertussis,* a potent adjuvant for reagin-mediated systems, possesses a lymphocyte-stimulating factor.

Thus the possibility might be envisaged that helminths produce factors which stimulate the production not only of plasma cells but also of "mastoblasts." These cells may be thymic dependent and, like the large lymphocytes of the thoracic duct, home on the gut lamina propria (Griscelli *et al.,* 1969) and differentiate into mast cells. The isolation and characterization of this mastoblast-stimulating factor would be of considerable importance in the study of the role of the mast cell in immune responses.

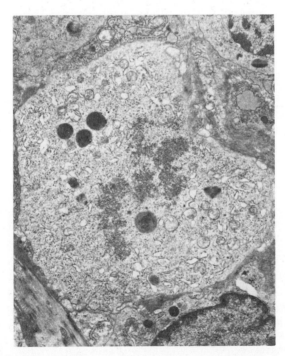

Fig. 7. Maturing mast cell in mitosis. Note the electron-dense membrane-bound granules in the cytoplasm which is packed with polyribosomes. ×6000. Reproduced from H. R. P. Miller (1971b) by courtesy of the editor of *Lab. Invest.*

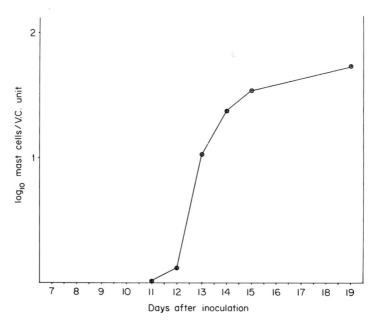

Fig. 8. Changes in the intestinal mast cell population in rats infected with 3000 *N. brasiliensis.*

Possibly related to this is the finding of Greaves and Roitt (1969) who, using immunofluorescence, demonstrated that allergen, in this case a pollen extract, could cause blast transformation of peripheral blood lymphocytes from atopic human donors and the differentiation of IgE-producing plasma cells (see Section III,C). Immunoglobulins of other classes, IgG, IgA, IgM, and IgD were not found.

C. MODE OF MAST CELL DISCHARGE

While the exponential rise of intestinal mast cells is taking place, a corresponding increase in the amount of 5-HT in the intestinal wall at the site of maximal worm concentration can be demonstrated by spectrofluorometry whether the worms are removed or not (Fig. 9, Murray *et al.*, 1971b). During this period, if worms are present, a marked release of amines from mast cells can be demonstrated by histochemistry and mast cell discharge is also seen on electron microscopy (Fig. 10) (H. R. P. Miller *et al.*, 1967; Murray *et al.*, 1968; W. F. H. Jarrett *et al.*, 1970; H. R. P. Miller, 1971a). It is at this stage that there is marked transformation of mast cells into globule leukocytes (W. F. H. Jarrett *et al.*, 1967b; H. R. P. Miller and Jarrett, 1971).

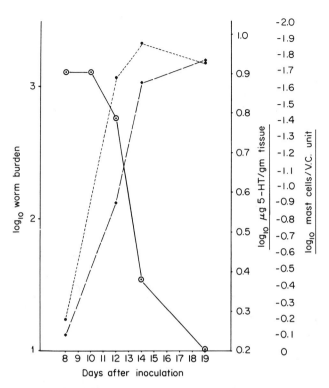

Fig. 9. Worm kinetics (⊙), 5-HT levels (●) and intestinal mast cell population (♦) in rats infected with 3000 *N. brasiliensis*. Associated with worm expulsion, there is a marked increase in mast cells and a corresponding rise in 5-HT levels in the bowel wall. Reproduced from Murray *et al.* (1971b) by courtesy of the editor of *Int. Arch. Allergy Appl. Immunol.*

It has been shown that mast cell discharge in the intestinal lamina propria only takes place if worms are present (Murray *et al.*, 1971b); if worms are removed by drug treatment, discharge does not occur. It is known that *Nippostrongylus* worms produce at least two factors capable of causing mast cell discharge, a degranulator (see Section III,B) and an allergen, e.g., Urquhart *et al.* (1965) found the bowel wall of rats infected with *N. brasiliensis* to be sensitive to the administration of *Nippostrongylus* antigen and proposed that a local anaphylactic reaction might play a part in worm expulsion. It has been shown that *Nippostrongylus* worms produce an allergen, MW 12,000–17,000 (Jones and Ogilvie, 1967; R. J. M. Wilson, 1967; Hogarth-Scott, 1967) and Ogilvie (1964, 1967) has demonstrated reaginlike antibodies in the serum of rats infected with *N. brasiliensis*. R. J. M. Wilson and Bloch (1967)

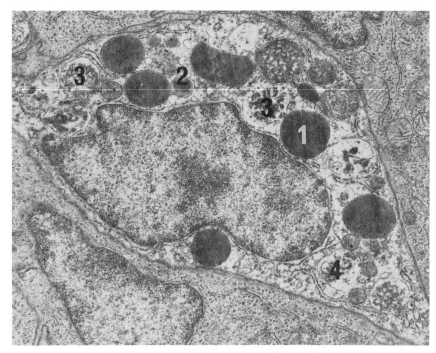

Fig. 10. Discharging mast cell lying between epithelial cells, i.e., a globule leuko-cyte. Unit membranes invest homogenous electron-dense granules (1). Other granules have small rims of less electron-dense matrix (2). Some granules contain moth eaten or paracrystalline structures surrounded by disrupted unit membranes (3). Others contain only paracrystalline structures and have virtually lost their unit membranes (4). ×12,000.

detected reagin-sensitized peritoneal mast cells as early as the tenth day of a primary infection. The appearance of these antibodies at this time makes it tempting to suggest that at least some of the extensive mast cell discharge reaction which is occurring at this time is caused by an allergen–reagin-mediated system. This suggestion is further supported by the results of Tada and Ishizaka (1970) who found that in the human most IgE (homocytotropic or reaginic antibody) is produced by plasma cells in the lamina propria of mucous membranes (see Section V,A,2). At the present however, the action of the mast cell-degranulating factor cannot be excluded.

D. Consequences of Mast Cell Discharge

The foregoing results show that the onset of worm expulsion is related to the rise in the number of intestinal mast cells and to the discharge of their vasoactive compounds. Since it appeared that release of vasoactive amines might be responsible for increased permeability of the intestinal mucosa, Murray *et al.* (1971a) examined this possibility quantitatively with polyvinylpyrrolidone labeled with iodine ([¹³¹I]PVP) and with the electron microscope using the tracer enzyme horseradish peroxidase (HPO). It was found that during the phase of worm loss, i.e., from days 11–16 in a primary infection, the permeability of the bowel wall to macromolecules did increase. On day 14, however, there was a very sharp rise in permeability which coincided with the onset of the rapid phase of worm expulsion (Fig. 11).

At this time, the epithelial cells, blood vessels, and cells in the lamina propria are markedly damaged (Fig. 12; H. R. P. Miller, 1970). When HPO is given, it is found leaving the microcirculation via fenestrae, open cell junctions (Fig. 13), and damaged endothelial cells. It passes between epithelial cells into the lumen of the intestine via open cell junctions or zonulae occludentes (Fig. 14); it is also found within epithelial cells. In the normal rat intestine HPO passes up to but not beyond

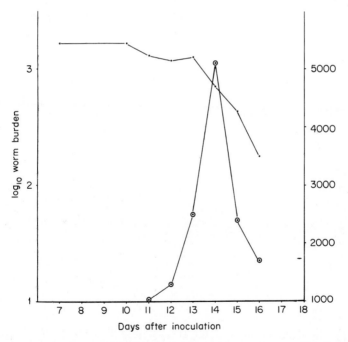

Fig. 11. Leak of plasma ([¹³¹I]PVP) into the intestine of rats infected with 3000 *N. brasiliensis*. ⊙, calculated plasma in intestinal contents. ●, kinetics of worm burden from Fig. 1. Reproduced from Murray *et al.* (1971a) by courtesy of the editor of *Immunology*.

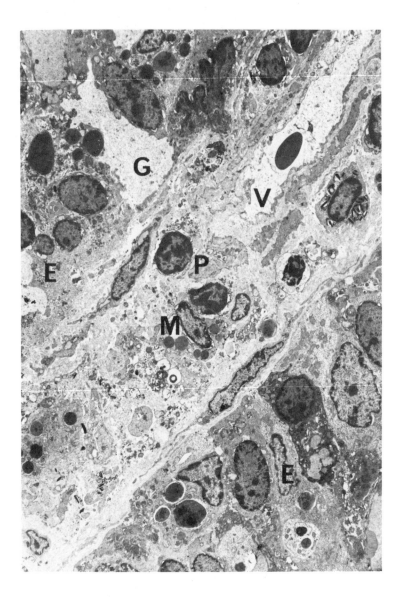

Fig. 12. Markedly damaged intestinal mucosa of parasitized rat 14 days after inoculation. There is a gap (G) in the epithelium (E). Mast cells (M) are disrupted and there are several cells in the lamina propria undergoing lysis. P possibly represents a disrupted plasma cell. The endothelium of a postcapillary venule is fragmented (V). ×3000.

the zonulae occludentes (Fig. 15). The zonula occludens represents a complete seal around the juxtaluminal segments of the lateral plasma-lemmata of epithelial cells and in the normal mucosa it is generally accepted that it acts as a barrier to the egress of· macromolecules (Farquhar and Palade, 1963; Hampton and Rosario, 1967; Hugon and Borgers, 1968; Murray et al., 1969; Murray, 1970).

Similar structural changes have been found in other protein-losing enteropathies such as ostertagiasis and fascioliasis (Murray, 1969; Murray et al., 1969, 1970) in which enhanced permeability has been demonstrated and quantitated with macromolecules labeled with radioactive isotopes (Halliday et al., 1968; Dargie et al., 1968). While the structural changes found in nippostrongylosis, ostertagiasis, and fascioliasis are similar, their genesis is probably different. In *Nippostrongylus*-infected rats the "leak" lesion is possibly mast cell-mediated whereas in ostertagiasis and fascioliasis there would appear to be some basic structural defect.

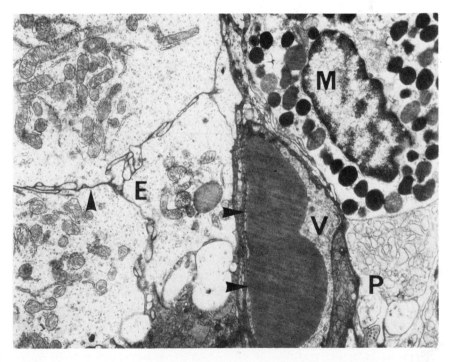

Fig. 13. Intestinal mucosa of parasitized rat 14 days after inoculation. HPO (arrows) is leaking from a postcapillary venule (V) via fenestrae into the lamina propria and epithelial cells (E). Note the close apposition of the mast cell (M), the plasma cell (P), the postcapillary venule, and the epithelium. ×8000. Reproduced from Murray et al. (1971a) by courtesy of the editor of *Immunology*.

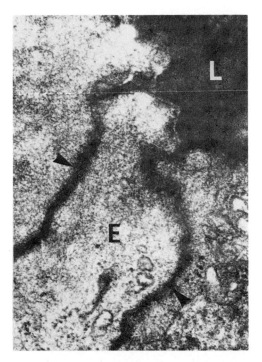

Fig. 14. Intestinal mucosa of parasitized rat 14 days after inoculation. HPO (arrows) lies between separated epithelial cells (E) and in the lumen (L) of the gut. ×45,000. Reproduced from Murray *et al.* (1971a) by courtesy of the editor of *Immunology.*

It is known that in fetal tissues junctional complexes between epithelial cells take some time before becoming fully formed (Trelstad *et al.*, 1966; Dunn, 1967). Also, studying a number of different cancers Martinez-Palomo (1970) found that intercellular tight junctions, i.e., zonulae occludentes, were lacking between malignant epithelial cells. Murray (1969) proposed that a similar situation might exist in ostertagiasis and fascioliasis, namely that the zonulae occludentes between immature rapidly dividing cells lining the hyperplastic parasitized mucosa have not had time to become fully differentiated and form a complete seal.

It would seem reasonable to conclude that in these parasitic infections and possibly many other conditions in which enhanced mucosal permeability has been quantitated with macromolecules labeled with radioactive isotopes, the morphological basis of this lesion is an opening up of an intercellular pathway in the epithelial sheet.

We propose that in *Nippostrongylus*-infected rats the intercellular pathway as demonstrated in Fig. 13 represents a route for the rapid translocation of circulating or locally produced anti-worm antibody across the mucous membrane and believe that this reaction is mediated by intestinal mast cell discharge.

It is also possible that the mast cell discharge reaction is responsible for the extensive damage to cells in the intestinal lamina propria which is known to occur during the period of worm expulsion. The damaged cells include plasma cells (Fig. 12) and it may be that in this way large amounts of locally produced antibody are released.

The mechanism involved in the severe mucosal damage is not fully understood. It would appear that vasoactive amines must play some role in this reaction, e.g., it has been shown by Majno et al., (1969) that histamine and 5-HT cause endothelial cell contraction and the formation of intercellular gaps. It may be that amines can act in a similar way on epithelial cells. A note of caution should be interposed here; there may well be other pharmacological mediators involved in this process apart from vasoactive amines, e.g., mast cell granules may be

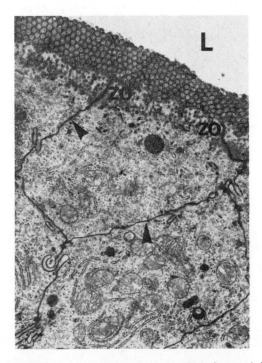

Fig. 15. Intestinal mucosa of a parasite-free rat. HPO (arrows) lies between the epithelial cells up to the level of, but not beyond, the zonula occludens (ZO). L, lumen. ×9000. Reproduced from Murray *et al.* (1971a) by courtesy of the editor of *Immunology*.

releasing the proteolytic enzymes they contain (Darzynkiewicz and Barnard, 1967; Budd *et al.,* 1967). Also it has been shown that allergen–reagin-mediated mast cell discharge releases slow reacting substance (SRS-A) as well as histamine (Orange *et al.,* 1970).

Ogilvie and Jones (1971) quoting the results of Ogilvie (1967) and W. F. H. Jarrett *et al.* (1967b) doubted the importance of mast cells in intestinal anaphylaxis because Ogilvie (1967) was able to induce intestinal shock in rats 6–8 days after a primary infection, at a time when according to W. F. H. Jarrett *et al.* (1967b) no intestinal mast cells are present. In fact it was only in the selected areas of worm concentration that W. F. H. Jarrett *et al.* (1967b) found few or no mast cells; the remaining 85–90 cm of the small intestine does contain mast cells.

In a series of experiments using the system of transferring normal adult worms (i.e., worms not damaged by antibody) and damaged adult worms (i.e., worms damaged by antibody) directly into the small intestine of uninfected rats via laparotomy, Jones and Ogilvie (1971) objected to the leak lesion hypothesis and concluded that two steps were required to expel worms. It was suggested that the first step involved the action of antibodies on the worms which were then irreversibly damaged showing the loss of isoenzyme production (Edwards *et al.,* 1971) and severe structural damage (Ogilvie and Hockley, 1968). The second step was unknown but appeared to be an irradiation sensitive step. They found that damaged worms when transplanted into normal rats were expelled whereas normal worms were not, indicating the normal worms were able to live and feed normally but damaged worms could not. When damaged worms were transferred into irradiated rats their results showed that these worms were only partially expelled and it was concluded that irradiation destroyed the second factor required for expulsion; it was suggested that this factor might be amines released from subepithelial mast cells. If this is the case, it is possible that the release of proteolytic enzymes and SRS-A from mast cells, as well as vasoactive amines, which are known to be inactivated very rapidly, would very quickly gain access to the worms via the permeable mucosa and might have the same destructive effect on worms as they apparently have on the mucosa (Fig. 12). However, Jones and Ogilvie (1971) made no morphological studies of the intestine at this time and care should be taken before extrapolating results obtained from this highly artificial system involving total body irradiation, intraperitoneal inoculation of hyperimmune serum, and transfer of irreversibly damaged worms directly into the intestine via laparotomy, to the situation in naturally infected rats.

Although the finding that damaged worms can survive in irradiated but not in normal rats is an intriguing one, it is not necessary to postulate a second step. It may be that irreversibly damaged worms with the loss of isoenzymes and possibly the ability to feed, die rapidly when transferred into normal rats, but when transferred into the slightly "leaky" intestine of irradiated rats, are able to survive for a longer period in this plasma-enriched environment.

When hyperimmune serum was given to irradiated rats infected with either normal or previously damaged worms, unlike the controls, it apparently made no significant difference (Jones and Ogilvie, 1971) although the large standard deviations quoted might indicate that the antibody was having some effect. These workers claimed that this experiment should have mimicked the leak lesion, described by Murray *et al.* (1971a) in natural primary infections and by Barth *et al.* (1966) in rats subjected to heterologous anaphylactic shock, and refuted the "leak lesion" hypothesis. While it is generally accepted that total body irradiation can induce intestinal damage (Schmidt, 1968), the results of Jones and Ogilvie (1971) have shown that the half-life of ^{131}I-labeled rat 7 S γ_2 was only marginally reduced in irradiated rats. Murray *et al.* (1972a) studied the effect of total body irradiation (550 R) on the intestinal permeability of rats over a period of 3 weeks. Using [^{125}I]PVP it was found that there was little increased leakage of plasma into the gut of such rats, whereas in rats subjected to heterologous anaphylactic shock, there was a significant increase. Therefore, total body irradiation "mimics" neither the macromolecular leak produced by anaphylactic shock nor the massive leak lesion which occurs in naturally infected rats (Fig. 11). A possible explanation for Jones and Ogilvie's (1971) failure to accomplish protection in irradiated rats is that the protective antibody given was being eluted into the enlarged extravascular pool created by the generalized vascular leak which would be caused by total body irradiation. It is then possible that antibody was not reaching the parasites in the intestine in sufficient quantities to be of protective value; it is widely accepted that in the adult worm transfer system large quantities of antibody are required for protection. Jones and Ogilvie's (1971) results, therefore, in no way negate the importance of increased mucosal permeability in the mechanism of worm expulsion.

E. Inhibition of Mast Cell Activity

The effect of specific inhibitors of vasoactive amines lends strong support to the importance of the mast cell discharge reaction in worm expulsion. Urquhart *et al.* (1965) and Sharp and Jarrett (1968) in nippostrongylosis and Campbell *et al.* (1963) in trichinosis, found that specific antagonists of amines could partially inhibit worm loss. Work by Murray *et al.* (1971c) has confirmed and enlarged upon these studies. They found that specific inhibitors of histamine and 5-HT do not prevent the initial slow phase of worm loss, but stop the onset of the rapid phase of worm expulsion (Fig. 16). These results could be interpreted as showing that inhibitors of histamine and 5-HT do not inhibit small amounts of anti-worm antibody initiating the first phase of worm loss, but prevent the rapid phase of worm loss, indicating that this phase must be mediated, at least to some extent, by histamine and 5-HT. The inhibitors do not stop the fall in worm egg production which always precedes worm loss, another indication that the availability of anti-worm antibody is not stopped at this time by inhibitors of histamine and 5-HT. These drugs do not prevent the increase in the number of mast cells or their discharge but do inhibit the effects of their release of amines; the villar edema seen in untreated rats during this phase was not observed in treated rats.

Keller (1970) found that the potent connective tissue mast cell depletor 48/80 administered daily from days 9–19 reduced worm loss. He

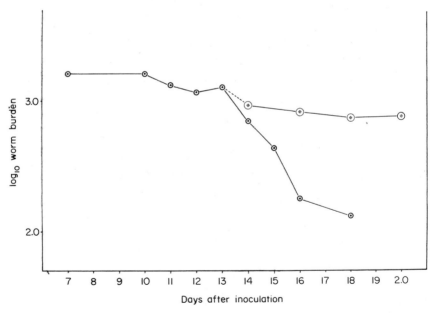

Fig. 16. Worm burden in rats inoculated with 3000 *N. brasiliensis* and treated with histamine and 5-HT inhibitors from day 8 (⊛). The kinetics of the worm burden of a primary infection are inserted from Fig. 1 (○). Reproduced from Murray *et al.* (1971b) by courtesy of the editor of *Exp. Parasitol.*

concluded that if biogenic amines were important in worm expulsion, treatment with 48/80 should have accelerated worm loss and not reduced it. The most likely explanation for his results, however, is that by continuous daily treatment with the 48/80 the intestinal mucosa was depleted of biogenic amines and hence the effector mechanism for antibody translocation was not fully functional.

Inhibition of worm expulsion and intestinal mast cell expansion can be produced by total body irradiation (Murray *et al.*, 1972a) and by cytostatic drugs such as cyclophosphamide. This drug also prevents drop in worm egg output and depresses serum reaginic antibody response. These results were obtained whether drug treatment was started at the time of infection or just prior to the onset of worm expulsion (Murray *et al.*, 1972b). Also, antilymphocytic serum and neonatal thymectomy have been shown to have some effect, if variable, in delaying the immune response as judged by worm loss and worm egg production (Ogilvie and Jones, 1967; Kassai *et al.*, 1968; Jones and Ogilvie, 1971). Rabbit anti-rat peritoneal cell serum significantly depressed the immune response to *N. brasiliensis* as judged by fecal egg counts and also interfered with the passive cutaneous anaphylaxis test (Hogarth-Scott and Bingley, 1971). It was concluded that this antiserum was active against pharmacologically active cells including mast cells, and that by prolonging *Nippostrongylus* infection the importance of such cells in this intestinal immunological reaction was demonstrated. Recently, Urquhart *et al.* (1972) found that trypanosome infections in rats had an apparent immunosuppressive effect when such animals were challenged with *N. brasiliensis;* worm expulsion was delayed and the intestinal mast cell as well as the reaginic and protective antibody response was suppressed.

Ogilvie (1965) and Urquhart *et al.* (1965) found that cortisone could suppress worm expulsion and Luffau and Urquhart (unpublished results) were able to arrest the process after it had started by administration of this drug. Cortisone has several modes of action, and Urquhart *et al.* (1965) concluded that the effect of cortisone occurred so rapidly that its role in interfering with worm expulsion could not involve a suppression of antibody production. W. F. H. Jarrett *et al.* (1967b) found that administration of cortisone suppressed the mast cell response in *Nippostrongylus* infections in the rat. Correspondingly, Murray *et al.* (1971a) showed that increased mucosal permeability did not occur in cortisone-treated rats. In this respect, it would appear that stress can play a significant role in worm expulsion; we have found that in rats subjected to repeated anesthesia during the period of worm expulsion, worm loss is considerably reduced and that there is a corresponding depression of the mast cell response (unpublished data).

Certain hormones can delay worm expulsion, e.g., Connan (1970) showed that lactation and possibly prolactin reduced worm loss in rats infected with *N. brasiliensis*. Also, Waddell *et al.* (1971) found that sex hormones probably played a significant role in the onset of worm expulsion (see Section IV).

IV. The Influence of Sex on Intestinal Immunological Reactions

The sex of the host has been shown to be involved in a number of parasitic infections, a situation reviewed by Dobson (1961a,b) who found that male mice (1961a) and male rats (1961b) were more susceptible to infection with *Nematosporoides dubius* than females. However, work in our laboratory (Murray *et al.*, 1971a,b; Waddell *et al.*, 1971) found that the sex of rats infected with *N. brasiliensis* had no significant effect on susceptibility to infection, but influenced the time of onset and rate of worm expulsion. As stated previously, a striking temporal relationship exists between the onset of worm expulsion, the rise in intestinal mast cells and increased macromolecular leakage into

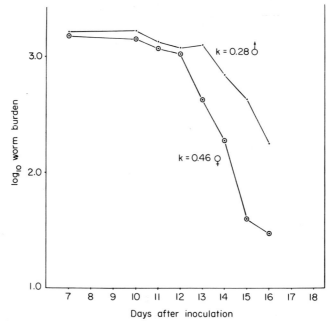

Fig. 17. Kinetics of worm burden in male and female rats inoculated with 3000 *N. brasiliensis*.

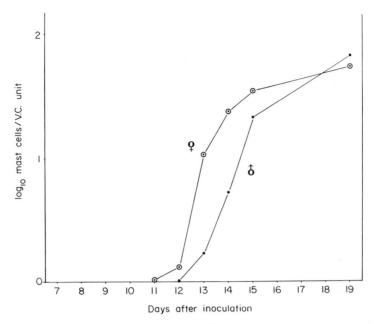

Fig. 18. Changes in the intestinal mast cell population in male and female rats infected with 3000 *N. brasiliensis.*

the gut (see Section III,D). Murray *et al.* (1971a) found that female rats effect the rapid phase of worm expulsion at least 1 day earlier and 1.5 times faster than males (Fig. 17) and there is a corresponding difference in the timing of mast cell rise (Fig. 18) and peak of macromolecular leak between the sexes. This evidence further suggests that these three circumstances are related. It would appear that sex hormones, androgens in particular, play a significant role in this process as it has been shown that worm loss commences at the same time and proceeds at approximately the same speed in castrated males as in intact females (Waddell *et al.*, 1971).

V. Immunoglobulins in Intestinal Immunological Reactions

In parallel to the exponential increase in subepithelial intestinal mast cells in nippostrongylosis, there is also a striking increase in plasma cells. The types of immunoglobulin being produced by these cells have yet to be determined, but their possible nature can be suggested from work in other systems, e.g., in the human, each of the known immunoglobulin heavy chains has been demonstrated in the cytoplasm of lymphoid cells in the gastrointestinal tract (Kraft and Kirsner, 1971).

A. Location of Antibody-Producing Plasma Cells

1. IgA

Numerous reports have shown that in a variety of species, including the rat (Nash *et al.*, 1969; Bistany and Tomasi, 1970), IgA is the predominant immunoglobulin in external secretions at mucous surfaces and that it is the major immunoglobulin being produced by plasma cells in the adjacent lamina propria (Crabbé *et al.*, 1965, 1968; Crabbé and Heremanns, 1966; Crandall *et al.*, 1967; Bull *et al.*, 1971; Haakenstad and Coe, 1971). There is now considerable evidence that locally produced IgA is a protective antibody and constitutes a major line of defence at mucous-lined surfaces (see reviews by Tomasi *et al.*, 1965; Tomasi, 1967, 1970; Bellanti, 1968; Collins-Williams *et al.*, 1969; Smith, 1969; D. I. Wilson and Williams, 1969; Johnson, 1970), e.g., Keller and Dwyer (1968) have shown that resistance to poliovirus infection following vaccination is related to the level of coproantibody and not to the level circulating antibody. They established that this was a virus-neutralizing antibody and that it was IgA. Likewise, lack of IgA predisposes to infection (Ammann *et al.*, 1969; Schlegel *et al.*, 1970).

The secreted IgA is an 11 S dimer, MW 380,000 consisting of 2 serum IgA-like subunits of MW 170,000, linked to a nonimmunoglobulin polypeptide termed the secretory piece or component (Tomasi and Calvanico, 1968). It has been suggested that this configuration is responsible for the resistance of the molecule to proteolysis and that in this way it can operate more effectively at mucous surfaces (Tomasi, 1970).

Little is known about the mode of antibody translocation across mucous surfaces. Tourville *et al.* (1969), in immunofluorescence studies, proposed that the secretory piece might be involved in this mechanism. They found 7 S IgA in the local plasma cells and lying between epithelial cells and demonstrated secretory piece only in apical cytoplasm of epithelial cells, although Rossen *et al.* (1968) provided conflicting evidence when they demonstrated the secretory piece in plasma cells in the lamina propria. Tourville *et al.* (1969) proposed that IgA leaves the plasma cells, passes across the basement membrane and between epithelial cells up to but not beyond the zonulae occludentes; here it is picked up by the secretory piece which is possibly synthesized by the epithelial cells and passes intracellularly to the apical cytoplasm and the lumen. While this route may be operative normally, the intercellular route, described earlier, (see Section III,D and Fig. 14) would seem a more likely one in conditions of enhanced antibody leakage.

2. IgE

The discovery of the identity of the IgE with homocytotropic, reaginic or mast cell-sensitizing antibody (see review by Ishizaka and Ishizaka, 1970) has raised questions as to its immunological function. IgE is a heat labile 8 S γ_1-glycoprotein, MW 200,000 (Bennich *et al.*, 1968; Ishizaka and Ishizaka, 1970; Stechschulte *et al.*, 1970; Kanyerezi *et al.*, 1971) which is manufactured mainly by plasma cells in the tonsils, adenoids, gastrointestinal lamina propria, mesenteric lymph nodes, upper respiratory tract, and bronchopulmonary lymph nodes; very few IgE-producing plasma cells are found in the peripheral lymph nodes or spleen (Tada and Ishizaka, 1970).

The immunological function of IgE has not been obvious since most of the reactions in which it is known to participate have been harmful rather than helpful to the host. Nematode parasites offer an excellent opportunity to study IgE as most are recognized as potent allergens and producers of reagins (E. E. E. Jarrett and Urquhart, 1971). It would appear that reaginic activity per se has no direct protective effect, e.g., Jones *et al.* (1970) found that in *Nippostrongylus*-infected rats, passive protection could be achieved by hyperimmune serum devoid of reagin. The major property of IgE is its affinity for the mast cell membrane and there, in contact with allergen, vasoactive amines and SRS-A are released (Orange *et al.*, 1970). The release of such substances at mucous surfaces is believed to be responsible for creating enhanced permeability and it has been proposed that such a situation facilitates rapid translocation of anti-worm or protective antibody (see Section III,D). The existence of an allergen–reaginic antibody (IgE)–mast cell axis in the intestinal mucosa of *Nippostrongylus*-infected rats makes it tempting to speculate that IgE has a specific protective role, and not a harmful one, as part of a mucosal effector mechanism or unit for rapid antibody release (see Section III,C).

Another antibody exists in the rat capable of mast cell discharge and histamine release; this is a heat stable subclass of IgG, termed IgGa. This antibody is also capable of SRS-A release, but as yet has not been identified in *Nippostrongylus*-infected rats (H. C. Morse *et al.*, 1969).

3. IgG

IgG is the major protective immunoglobulin class found in the sera of rats infected with *N. brasiliensis* (V. E. Jones *et al.*, 1970). This antibody has been demonstrated in the serum around day 20 of a primary infection and in animals subjected to repeated infections the level in the serum is even higher (Mulligan *et al.*, 1965). IgG, therefore, would appear to have a major role in active immune processes in nippostrongylosis and possibly most so in animals subjected to reinfection.

4. IgM

IgM, like IgG, is manufactured mainly in the regional lymph nodes and in the spleen. Its structure appears to be particularly adapted for protective activity against microbes and large antigens which have a repeated antigenic motif on their surface, although IgM has been shown to have some protective value against *N. brasiliensis* worms (V. E. Jones *et al.*, 1970).

Evidence is now available which suggests that in some way the production of IgA and IgE is linked and dissociable from the production of IgG and IgM. Both IgA and IgE are manufactured largely at mucous surfaces (see Sections V,A,1 and 2) and like IgA, IgE-reagin activity is found in external secretions (Ishizaka and Newcomb, 1970). Some studies now indicate that the production of both these immunoglobulin classes might be to some extent thymus dependent. Homocytotropic antibody formation in the rat is markedly depressed by neonatal thymectomy (Ogilvie and Jones, 1967; Okumura and Tada, 1971). Similarly, in neonatally thymectomized rats, mice, and rabbits, serum IgA antibody response is significantly reduced with little effect on IgG and IgM (Arnason *et al.*, 1964a,b; Clough *et al.*, 1971). Cremer *et al.* (1966) reported that rats infected with Moloney virus, a leukemogenic virus which multiplies in the thymus gland, have subnormal serum IgA levels. Absence of serum and secretory IgA has been reported in a child with thymic dysplasia suffering from mucocutaneous candidiasis and chronic pulmonary disease (Schlegel *et al.*, 1970). No examination was made of IgE levels in any of the above studies. Studying the immunopathology of ataxia telangiectasia, a condition in humans with congenital thymic deficiency and increased susceptibility to sinopulmonary infections, Ammann *et al.* (1969) found a deficiency of both IgA and IgE and concluded that there was an intimate relationship between these immunoglobulin classes whereas there was little association of either IgG or IgM with IgE and IgA. In the same way, the development of IgE during childhood seems to resemble most closely that of IgA rather than IgG or IgM (Berg and Johannson, 1969).

B. Intestinal Antibody-Producing Plasma Cells during Parasitic Infection

In disease processes there are few detailed kinetic studies of the response of immunoglobulin-producing plasma cells in the lamina propria of mucous surfaces. Such data would be useful in interpreting the roles of various immunoglobulin classes in local immune responses. In *Nippostrongylus*-infected rats there is an expansion of subepithelial plasma cells in parallel to the exponential expansion of subepithelial mast cells prior to the onset of worm expulsion (see Section III,B). This increase in plasma cells has yet to be quantitated and the nature of immunoglobulins being produced determined. Crandall *et al.* (1967) found that in *Trichinella*-infected rabbits there was a relative increase in IgM containing plasma cells in the intestine early in the infection followed by an increase in IgG late in infection and also in reinfection. The number of IgA-containing plasma cells remained uniformly high during the course of infection. No examination was made for IgE. It has been shown by Curtain and Anderson (1971) that in sheep parasitized with gastrointestinal nematodes there is a marked increase in the number of IgG_1 and IgG_{1a} producing plasma cells; IgG_{1a} fraction in sheep is thought to carry reaginic activity and IgG_1 is considered a major exocrine immunoglobulin in the ruminant in addition to IgA.

While much work remains to be done in determining immunoglobulin function at mucous surfaces, studies done in a variety of diseases in a number of species would suggest that both IgA and IgG have major protective roles, the latter possibly being more important in hyperimmune states, while the function of IgE maybe as part of an effector unit to facilitate protective antibody, i.e., IgA and IgG, translocation.

VI. Immunological Unresponsiveness in Baby Rats

In a series of experiments, E. E. E. Jarrett and associates (1966, 1967, 1968b, 1969; Jarrett and Urquhart, 1969; Jarrett, 1971) demonstrated a degree of immunological unresponsiveness in hooded Lister baby rats up to 6 or 7 weeks of age. She found that worm expulsion commenced later and proceeded more slowly in babies than in adult rats and that a stable threshold level of around 200 worms was left as compared with 40 in adults. As in adults worm loss was preceded by a drop in worm egg output. When infective doses of 500 *N. brasiliensis* larvae or less were given, a stable population of around 200 worms was established and was not lost, i.e., worm expulsion only occurred if more than 200 worms were present in the intestine. These infected rats were apparently immunologically competent producing both reaginic and protective antibodies, demonstrable in passive protection tests, and an increase in intestinal mast cell population (E. E. E. Jarrett *et al.*, 1969). Murray *et al.* (1972c) found that, as in adult rats, baby female rats started to expel their worm burden 1 or 2 days before baby male rats. Correspondingly there was an expansion of the subepithelial intestinal mast cell population coinciding with the onset of worm expulsion and this occurred a day or so earlier in female baby rats, suggesting again that these events are related. In addition, the appearance of reaginic antibodies was slower in baby males than in baby female rats.

Ogilvie and Jones (1971), objecting to the importance of intestinal anaphylaxis and the involvement of mast cells and reagins, stated that if these factors are important in worm expulsion it is surprising that they are found in neonatally infected rats because worms are not expelled from these animals. In fact, using infective doses of greater than 500, E. E. E. Jarrett and her colleagues and Murray *et al.* (1972c) have shown that worms are expelled, albeit at a slower rate and commencing a day or so later.

What explanation can be offered for this phenomenon in baby rats? In adult rats infected with *N. brasiliensis* we have proposed that worm expulsion is mediated by an effector unit or mechanism consisting of an allergen-reaginic antibody–mast cell axis which allows translocation of anti-worm antibody. If this is the case a similar pattern of events probably occurs in baby rats. E. E. E. Jarrett (1971) postulated that, because baby rats produced protective antibodies, reaginic antibodies, and an increase in intestinal mast cells, it was more likely to be a qualitative rather than a purely quantitative deficiency in response. Could it be that while effector units are being produced in infected baby rats they are not available in sufficient quantity or concentration to be completely efficient, e.g., x number of effector units may be required to kill one parasite?

We have observed that in baby rats, the worm population is scattered over a wider area than in adults. It may be that in baby rats the antigenic stimulus from the worms is not as great because it is not localized as in adults and so the host's ability to provide a sufficient number of effector units at the site of worm localization is more limited. A similar situation may exist in adult rats subjected to low level infections of *N. brasiliensis:* Jenkins and Phillipson (1971) found that such rats are unable to achieve an effective immune response.

On the other hand, baby rats may not be able to respond as efficiently as adult rats on a quantitative basis, i.e., they are not able to provide a sufficient number of effector units. It is known that there are fewer intestinal mast cells in normal baby rats than in adult rats (5 mast cells/villus crypt unit compared with 10 to 12/villus crypt unit—Murray *et al.,* 1972c). It may be that although there is an increase in mast cells in the parasitized intestinal mucosa of baby rats these might not be sufficient. So far such data are not available to confirm this. Murray *et al.* (1972c) have shown that by day 19 of infection the level of intestinal mast cells is significantly lower than that reported in adult rats on the same day of infection by Murray *et al.* (1971a); however, in these experiments a lower infective dose was given to the baby rats and Urquhart *et al.* (1972) have found that the level of the intestinal mast cell response depends on the infective dose. Similarly the work of E. E. E. Jarrett *et al.* (1969) does not allow conclusions to be made. She found no significant difference between the expanded intestinal mast cell population of adult and baby rats inoculated with the same dose of larvae. However, in this study tissue samples from adults were not selected from the site of maximal worm concentration and this would account for the fact that the level of mast cells found was lower than that reported by Murray *et al.* (1971a) in similarly infected adult rats.

If a certain concentration of antibody is required to kill a parasite which is lying intertwined between numerous villi over a considerable area, and if for either of the above reasons, an insufficient number of effector units is available, antibody translocation, although it is taking place, might not be localized at high enough concentration around the worm to kill it and to produce an efficient expulsive phase; this may also account for the 200-worm threshold level seen in baby rats.

VII. Conclusions

In studying possible immunological mechanisms at intestinal mucous surfaces of *Nippostrongylus*-infected rats a number of new factors have come to light.

1. Under the stimulation of a worm infection, hemocytoblast- or lymphoblastlike cells appear in the intestinal lamina propria and differentiate into mast cells which proliferate exponentially. Paralleling this there is an expansion in the subepithelial plasma cell population.

2. In the presence of worms (which produce both a mast cell degranulator and an allergen) these mast cells discharge mediators of mucosal permeability reactions. The relative importance of these two systems has yet to be evaluated but it is highly likely that at least some of the extensive mast cell discharge is mediated by an allergen-reaginic antibody system.

3. A marked leak occurs in the small blood vessels of the villi and also between epithelial cells allowing the egress of macromolecules into the lumen. This has been shown quantitatively, using macromolecules

labeled with radioactive isotopes and morphologically by electron microscopy using tracer enzymes.

4. A striking temporal relationship exists between the rise in number and discharge of intestinal mast cells, the onset of worm expulsion and the increased macromolecular leak into the gut. The fact that female rats effect worm expulsion sooner and at a faster rate than males and that there is a corresponding difference in the timing of the mast cell rise and the peak of macromolecular leak between the sexes further suggests that there is a relationship between these events.

5. This reaction is notable for the production of globule leukocytes (or discharged mast cells). These cells have been found in the epithelia of many species, including the human, e.g., an increase in subepithelial mast cells and globule leukocytes occurs in the abomasa of cattle infected with *Ostertagia ostertagi* and of sheep infected with *Ostertagia circumcincta* and these events are associated with an exponential loss of adult worms (Murray *et al.*, 1970; Armour *et al.*, 1966). It is possible that this mast cell-associated leak mechanism may be a general phenomenon at mucous surfaces and be involved in many infections.

6. Immunological effector mechanisms at mucous surfaces would appear to be the summation of the interaction of a variety of immunological events. The following model is proposed for enhanced antibody release and translocation across the epithelial sheet. Stimuli or a stimulus from the worms cause the synchronous development and cooperation of new populations of mast cells and also new populations of plasma cells producing at least three classes of immunoglobulin, IgE, IgA, and IgG. The pharmacological mediators in the mast cells are released by an allergen-reaginic antibody-mediated system; this is proposed as the specific function of locally produced IgE at mucous surfaces. These mediators then create an intercellular pathway across the mucous membrane and also cause disruption of plasma cells with subsequent release of anti-worm antibody. This serves to deliver increased amounts of locally produced (IgA) and or systemically produced (IgG) anti-worm antibody to sites specifically occupied by the worm, thereby effecting a maximal protective response.

References

Ammann, A. J., Cain, W. A., Ishizaka, K., Hong, R., and Good, R. A. (1969). *N. Engl. J. Med.* **281**, 469.
Andrews, J. M. (1962). *J. Parasitol.* **48**, 3.
Armour, J., Jarrett, W. F. H., and Jennings, F. W. (1966). *Amer. J. Vet. Res.* **27**, 1267.

Arnason, B. G., de Vaux St-Cyr, C., and Relyveld, E. H. (1964a). *Int. Arch. Allergy Appl. Immunol.* 25, 206.

Arnason, B. G., de Vaux St-Cyr, C., and Shaffner, J. B. (1964b). *J. Immunol.* 93, 915.

Barth, E. E. E., Jarrett, W. F. H., and Urquhart, G. M. (1966). *Immunology* 10, 459.

Bellanti, J. A. (1968). *Amer. J. Dis. Child.* 115, 239.

Benditt, E. P., and Lagunoff, D. (1964). *Progr. Allergy* 8, 195.

Bennich, H. H., Ishizaka, K., Johannson, S. G. O., Rowe, D. S., Stanworth, D. R., and Terry, W. D. (1968). *Immunology* 15, 323.

Berg, T., and Johannson, S. G. O. (1969). *Acta Paediat. Scand.* 58, 513.

Bistany, T. S., and Tomasi, T. B. (1970). *Immunochemistry* 7, 453.

Budd, G. C., Darzynkiewicz, Z., and Barnard, E. A. (1967). *Nature (London)* 213, 1202.

Bull, D. M., Bienenstock, J., and Tomasi, T. B. (1971). *Gastroenterology* 60, 370.

Burnett, F. M. (1965). *J. Pathol. Bacteriol.* 89, 271.

Campbell, W. C., Hartman, R. K., and Cuckler, A. C. (1963). *Exp. Parasitol.* 14, 23.

Clough, J. D., Mims, L. H., and Strober, W. (1971). *J. Immunol.* 106, 1624.

Collins-Williams, C., Lamenza, C., and Nizami, R. (1969). *Ann. Allergy* 27, 225.

Combs, J. W., Lagunoff, D., and Benditt, E. P. (1965). *J. Cell Biol.* 25, 577.

Connan, R. M. (1970). *Parasitology* 61, 27.

Corba, J. C., Armour, J., Dargie, J. D., and Urquhart, G. M. (1972). In preparation.

Crabbé, P. A., and Heremanns, J. F. (1966). *Gastroenterology* 51, 305.

Crabbé, P. A., Carbonara, A. O., and Heremans, J. F. (1965). *Lab. Invest.* 14, 235.

Crabbé, P. A., Bazin, H., Eyssen, H., and Heremans, J. F. (1968). *Int. Arch. Allergy Appl. Immunol.* 34, 362.

Crandall, R. B., Cebra, J. J., and Crandall, C. A. (1967). *Immunology* 12, 147.

Cremer, N. E., Taylor, D. O. N., and Hagens, S. J. (1966). *J. Immunol.* 96, 495.

Csaba, G., and Barath, P. (1970). *Acta Biol. Acad. Sci. Hung.* 21, 421.

Curtain, C. C., and Anderson, N. (1971). *Clin. Exp. Immunol.* 8, 151.

Dargie, J. D., Holmes, P. H., MacLean, J. M., and Mulligan, W. (1968). *J. Comp. Pathol.* 78, 101.

Darzynkiewicz, Z., and Barnard, E. A. (1967). *Nature (London)* 213, 1198.

Dobson, C. (1961a). *Parasitology* 51, 173.

Dobson, C. (1961b). *Parasitology* 51, 499.

Dobson, C. (1966). *Aust. J. Agr. Res.* 17, 955.

Dunn, J. S. (1967). *J. Anat.* 101, 57.

Edwards, A. J., Burt, J. S., and Ogilvie, B. M. (1971). *Parasitology* 62, 339.

Enerback, L. (1966a). *Acta Pathol. Microbiol. Scand.* 66, 289.

Enerback, L. (1966b). *Acta Pathol. Microbiol. Scand.* 66, 365.

Farquhar, M. G., and Palade, G. E. (1963). *J. Cell Biol.* 17, 375.

Ginsburg, H. (1963). *Ann. N.Y. Acad. Sci.* 103, 20.

Ginsburg, H., and Lagunoff, D. (1967). *J. Cell Biol.* 35, 685.

Ginsburg, H., and Sachs, L. (1963). *J. Nat. Cancer Inst.* 31, 1.

Greaves, M. F., and Roitt, I. M. (1969). *Lancet* 1, 803.

Griscelli, C., Vassali, P., and McCluskey, R. T. (1969). *J. Exp. Med.* 130, 1427.

Haakenstad, A. O., and Coe, J. E. (1971). *J. Immunol.* 106, 1026.

Hakanson, R., Owman, C., and Sjobert, N. O. (1967). *Life Sci.* 6, 2535.

Halliday, G. J., Mulligan, W., and Dalton, R. G. (1968). *Res. Vet. Sci.* 9, 224.

Hampton, J. C., and Rosario, B. (1967). *Anat. Rec.* 159, 159.

Hogarth-Scott, R. S. (1967). *Immunology* 13, 535.

Hogarth-Scott, R. S., and Bingley, J. B. (1971). *Immunology* 21, 87.

Hugon, J. S., and Borgers, M. (1968). *J. Histochem. Biochem.* 16, 229.

Ishizaka, K., and Ishizaka, T. (1970). *Ann. Allergy* 28, 189.

Ishizaka, K., and Newcomb, R. W. (1970). *J. Allergy* 46, 197.

Jarrett, E. E. E. (1971). *Clin. Exp. Immunol.* 8, 141.

Jarrett, E. E. E., and Urquhart, G. M. (1969). *Exp. Parasitol.* 25, 245.

Jarrett, E. E. E., and Urquhart, G. M. (1971). *Int. Rev. Trop. Med.* 4, 53.

Jarrett, E. E. E., Jarrett, W. F. H., and Urquhart, G. M. (1966). *Nature (London)* 211, 1310.

Jarrett, E. E. E., Jarrett, W. F. H., and Urquhart, G. M. (1967). *In* "Reaction of the Host to Parasitism" (E. J. L. Soulsby, ed.), pp. 242–249. Elwert, Marburg, Germany.

Jarrett, E. E. E., Jarrett, W. F. H., and Urquhart, G. M. (1968a). *Parasitology* 58, 625.

Jarrett, E. E. E., Jarrett, W. F. H., and Urquhart, G. M. (1968b). *Exp. Parasitol.* 23, 151.

Jarrett, E. E. E., Urquhart, G. M., and Douthwaite, R. M. (1969). *Exp. Parasitol.* 24, 270.

Jarrett, W. F. H., Miller, H. R. P., and Murray, M. (1967a). *Vet. Rec.* 80, 505.

Jarrett, W. F. H., Jarrett, E. E. E., Miller, H. R. P., and Urquhart, G. M. (1967b). *In* "Reaction of the Host to Parasitism" (E. J. L. Soulsby, ed.), pp. 191–198. Elwert, Marburg, Germany.

Jarrett, W. F. H., Miller, H. R. P. and Murray, M. (1970). *In* "Resistance to Infectious Disease" (R. H. Dunlop and H. W. Moon, eds.), pp. 287–297. Saskatoon Modern Press.

Jenkins, D. C., and Phillipson, R. F. (1971). *Parasitology* 62, 457.

Johnson, J. S. (1970). *J. Infec. Dis.* 121, Suppl., 115.

Jones, V. E., and Ogilvie, B. M. (1967). *Immunology* 12, 583.

Jones, V. E., and Ogilvie, B. M. (1971). *Immunology* 20, 549.

Jones, V. E., Edwards, A. J., and Ogilvie, B. M. (1970). *Immunology* 18, 621.

Kabat, E. A., and Mayer, M. M. (1961). *In* "Experimental Immunochemistry," 2nd ed., p. 287. Thomas, Springfield, Illinois.

Kanyerezi, B., Jaton, J. C., and Bloch, K. J. (1971). *J. Immunol.* 106, 1411.

Kassai, T., Szepes, G., Rethy, L., and Toth, G. (1968). *Nature (London)* 218, 1055.

Keller, R. (1970). *Clin. Exp. Immunol.* 6, 207.

Keller, R., and Dwyer, J. M. (1968). *J. Immunol.* 101, 192.

Kraft, S. C., and Kirsner, J. B. (1971). *Gastroenterology* 60, 922.

Kruger, P. G., Diamant, B., and Scholander, L. (1970). *Exp. Cell Res.* 63, 101.

Lindholm, S. (1960). *Acta Pathol. Microbiol. Scand.* 48, 328.

Martinez-Palomo, A. (1970). *Lab. Invest.* 22, 605.

Majno, G., Shea, S. M., and Leventhal, M. (1969). *J. Cell Biol.* 42, 647.

Miller, H. R. P. (1970). Ph.D. Thesis, University of Glasgow, Glasgow.

Miller, H. R. P. (1971a). *Lab. Invest.* 24, 348.

Miller, H. R. P. (1971b). *Lab. Invest.* 24, 339.

Miller, H. R. P., and Jarrett, W. F. H. (1971). *Immunology* 20, 277.

Miller, H. R. P., Murray, M., and Jarrett, W. F. H. (1967). *In* "Reaction of the Host to Parasitism" (E. J. L. Soulsby, ed.), pp. 198–210. Elwert, Marburg, Germany.

Miller, J. J., and Coles, L. J. (1968). *Nature (London)* 217, 263.

Morse, H. C., Austen, K. F., and Bloch, K. J. (1969). *J. Immunol.* 102, 327.

Morse, S. J., and Bray, K. K. (1969). *J. Exp. Med.* 129, 523.

Mota, I., Ferri, A. G., and Yoneda, S. (1956). *Quart. J. Microsc. Sci.* 97, 251.

Mulligan, W., Urquhart, G. M., Jennings, F. W., and Neilson, J. T. M. (1965). *Exp. Parasitol.* 16, 341.

Murray, M. (1969). *Gastroenterology* 56, 763.

Murray, M. (1970). *Res. Vet. Sci.* 11, 411.

Murray, M., Miller, H. R. P., and Jarrett, W. F. H. (1968). *Lab. Invest.* 19, 222.

Murray, M. (1972). Unpublished data.

Murray, M., Jarrett, W. F. H., Jennings, F. W., and Miller, H. R. P. (1969). *In* "Pathology of Parasitic Disease" (S. M. Gaafar, ed.), p. 197. Purdue Univ. Studies, Lafayette, Indiana.

Murray, M., Jennings, F. W., and Armour, J. (1970). *Res. Vet. Sci.* 11, 417.

Murray, M., Jarrett, W. F. H., and Jennings, F. W. (1971a). *Immunology* 21, 17.

Murray, M., Miller, H. R. P., Sanford, J., and Jarrett, W. F. H. (1971b). *Int. Arch. Allergy Appl. Immunol.* 40, 236.

Murray, M., Smith, W. D., Waddell, A. H., and Jarrett, W. F. H. (1971c). *Exp. Parasitol.* 30, 58.

Murray, M., Weir, E. C., and Jennings, F. W. (1972a). In preparation.

Murray, M., Higginson, G., and Jarrett, W. F. H. (1972b). In preparation.

Murray, M., Hamil, D. J., Duncan, I. D., Waddell, A. H., and Jarrett, W. F. H. (1972c). In preparation.

Nash, D. R., Vaerman, J. P., Bazin, H., and Heremans, J. F. (1969). *J. Immunol.* 103, 145.

Neilson, J. T. M. (1969). *J. Parasitol.* 55, 346.

Ogilvie, B. M. (1964). *Nature (London)* 204, 91.

Ogilvie, B. M. (1965). *Parasitology* 55, 723.

Ogilvie, B. M. (1967). *Immunology* 12, 113.

Ogilvie, B. M., and Hockley, D. J. (1968). *J. Parasitol.* 54, 1073.

Ogilvie, B. M., and Jones, V. E. (1967). *Parasitology* 57, 335.

Ogilvie, B. M., and Jones, V. E. (1968). *Parsitology* 58, 939.

Ogilvie, B. M., and Jones, V. E. (1971). *Exp. Parasitol.* 29, 138.

Okumura, K., and Tada, T. (1971). *J. Immunol.* 106, 1019.

Orange, R. P., Stechschulte, D. J., and Austen, K. F. (1970). *J. Immunol.* 105, 1087.

Rossen, R. D., Morgan, C., Hsu, K. C., Butler, W. T., and Rose, H. M. (1968). *J. Immunol.* 100, 706.

Sanyal, R. K., and West, G. B. (1958). *J. Physiol. (London)* 142, 571.

Schlegel, R. J., Bernier, G. M., Bellanti, J. A., Maybee, D. A., Osborne, G. B., Stewart, J. L., Pearlsman, D. S., Quelette, J., and Biehusen, F. C. (1970). *Pediatrics* 45, 926.

Schmidt, R. L. (1968). *J. Okla. State Med. Ass.* 61, 450.

Sharp, N. C. C., and Jarrett, W. F. H. (1968). *Nature (London)* 218, 1161.

Smith, R. T. (1969). *Pediatrics* 43, 317.

Spicer, S. S. (1963). *Ann. N.Y. Acad. Sci.* 103, 322.

Stechschulte, D. J., Orange, R. P., and Austen, K. F.. (1970). *J. Immunol.* **105**, 1082.

Stewart, D. F. (1953). *Aust. J. Agr. Res.* **4**, 100.

Tada, T., and Ishizaka, K. (1970). *J. Immunol.* **104**, 377.

Taliaferro, W. H., and Sarles, M. P. (1939). *J. Infec. Dis.* **64**, 157.

Tigelaar, R. E., Nelson, M. V., and Ovary, Z. (1971). *J. Immunol.* **106**, 661.

Tomasi, T. B. (1967). *Hosp. Pract.* **7**, 26.

Tomasi, T. B. (1970). *Ann. Rev. Med.* **21**, 281.

Tomasi, T. B., and Calvanico, N. (1968). *Fed. Proc., Fed. Amer. Soc. Exp. Biol.* **27**, 617 (Abstr.).

Tomasi, T. B., Tan, E. M., Solomon, A., and Prendergast, R. A. (1965). *J. Exp. Med.* **121**, 101.

Tourville, D. R., Adler, R. H., Bienenstock, J., and Tomasi, T. B. (1969). *J. Exp. Med.* **129**, 411.

Trelstad, R. J., Revel, J. P., and Hay, E. D. (1966). *J. Cell Biol.* **31**, C6–C10.

Urquhart, G. M., Mulligan, W., Eadie, R. M., and Jennings, F. W. (1965). *Exp. Parasitol.* **17**, 210.

Urquhart, G. M., Jennings, F. W., and Murray, M. (1972). In preparation.

Uvnas, B., and Wold, J. K. (1967). *Acta Physiol. Scand.* **70**, 269.

Waddell, A. H., Jarrett, W. F. H., and Murray, M. (1971). *Res. Vet. Sci.* **12**, 396.

Wells, WP. D. (1962). *Exp. Parasitol.* **12**, 82.

Whur, P. (1966). *J. Comp. Pathol.* **76**, 57.

Whur, P., and Gracie, M. (1967). *Experientia* **23**, 655.

Whur, P., and Johnston, H. S. (1967). *J. Pathol. Bacteriol.* **93**, 81.

Whur, P., and White, R. (1970). *Int. Arch. Allergy Appl. Immunol.* **38**, 185.

Wilson, D. I., and Williams, R. C. (1969). *J. Clin. Invest.* **48**, 2409.

Wilson, R. J. M. (1967). *J. Parasitol.* **53**, 752.

Wilson, R. J. M., and Bloch, K. J. (1967). *J. Immunol.* **100**, 622.

7 IMMUNE RESPONSE TO GASTROINTESTINAL HELMINTHS

COLIN DOBSON

I. Introduction

The preparation of this review comes at a time when the concept of local immunity as expressed by Besredka (1927) and later developed by Burrows (see Burrows, 1963) for the gastrointestinal tract and by Fazekas de St. Groth (1950), and his co-workers (Fazekas de St. Groth and Donnelley 1950; Fazekas de St. Groth and White, 1958) for the respiratory system is being revitalized by recent discoveries concerning the secretory immunological system (Tomasi and Bienenstock, 1968). The suggestion that local immunity probably plays a role in the protection of the gut against metazoan parasites is also of long standing

(Chandler, 1932; Ackert *et al.*, 1939; Sprent, 1962), but here again it is only recently that evidence concerning these reactions has accumulated.

While it is plausible to explain the immunological damage and expulsion of worms from the gut in terms of the secretory immunological system, it is also evident that the protective responses of the host can be more complex. They may depend as well on mobilization of the cellular and humoral elements of resistance from outside the alimentary tract, as on local immune reactions, since many intestinal parasites enjoy varying degrees of invasiveness and migration through the somatic tissues of the host.

In view of the recent publication of a number of stimulating reviews concerning immunity to parasitic infections (Gemmell and Soulsby, 1968; Sprent, 1969; Desowitz, 1970; Ogilvie, 1970; Ogilvie and Jones, 1971; Soulsby, 1970) and the congruent nature of the other articles in this book, I intend to restrict my discussion only to certain aspects of the immune response to gastrointestinal parasites, namely, the characteristics of the secretory immunological system and its relationship to parasitic infections, cellular responses to parasitism, protection, and some evolutionary aspects of the host–parasite relationship in the gut.

II. The Secretory Immunological System

The hypothesis of the secretory immunological system stemmed dually from the early recognition that the mucosal surfaces were capable of local resistance to infection and from the description of Heremans *et al.* (1959) of the IgA class of immunoglobulins. Subsequently it was found that many external secretions bathing mucosal surfaces contained a predominance of IgA (Hanson, 1961) which was not only quantitatively greater than the serum levels but also differed physically and chemically from serum IgA. Secretory IgA was shown to be an association of two 7 S IgA molecules with a secretory piece which together had a sedimentation coefficient of 11 S (Cebra and Small, 1967; Tomasi and Czerwinski, 1968). Furthermore, these findings were related to the observation that the majority of antibody-containing cells within the tissues of the mucosal surface produced IgA (Tomasi *et al.*, 1965).

The role of secretory antibodies in resistance to viral and bacterial infections of the mucosae has been established (Chanock, 1969; Ogra, 1969; Cluff, 1969), but the situation with regard to the parasitic metazoa of the gastrointestinal tract is not so clearly understood. Nevertheless, it has been known for many years that intestinal secretions have a parasiticidal or inhibitory effect on the growth of helminths (Frick and Ackert, 1948). It has also been shown that the secretory activity of the gut increases following infections with these parasites (Ackert *et al.*, 1939; Mathies, 1962; Wells, 1963), and in some instances specific antibodies have been demonstrated in these secretions. Douvres (1962) obtained immune precipitates around cultured *Oesophagostomum radiatum* larvae after they were bathed in intestinal extracts from infected cattle. Similarly Dobson (1966a) detected hemagglutinating antibodies in mucosal extracts and exudates from sheep infected with *Oesophagostomum columbianum*. Weinmann (1963) also related the resistance of mice infected with *Hymenolepis nana* to antibodies in the intestine. However in none of these cases was the class of immunoglobulin identified nor was the protective capacity of the antibodies assessed, although Dobson (1967) showed that the presence of antibody in mucus specifically enhanced the natural ability of intestinal mucus from infected sheep to inhibit the respiration of the third-stage larvae of *O. columbianum*. Moreover Matsumori (1941, 1943) showed that while the intraperitoneal injection of serum from rats, heavily infected with *Nippostrongylus brasiliensis*, transferred immunity to this worm in normal rats, the injection of intestinal extracts from these donors had a much greater passive immunizing effect. In addition the local intestinal immunity was stronger using extracts from the upper and lower portions of the intestine than for those from the middle.

The existence of antibodies against helminths at the gut surface suggests that IgA immunoglobulin may be particularly important in the protection of the host against intestinal parasitic infections. However the evidence so far would rather indicate that this was not the case. R. B. Crandall *et al.* (1967) found that the IgA-producing cells were not increased in numbers in the intestinal mucosa of rabbits following infections with *Trichinella spiralis;* only IgG antibodies were detected in gut extracts although IgA was also present in these preparations. Moreover, while Jones *et al.* (1970) found IgA in some serum fractions which protected rats passively against *Nippostrongylus brasiliensis* adults, both IgM and IgG immunoglobulins were present in the same fractions. Thus, as Ogilvie (1970) pointed out, there is no evidence as yet for or against the involvement of IgA in the protection of the host against helminth parasites.

In contrast to the paucity of information concerning the effectiveness of the IgA immunoglobulin system in resistance to helminths there is an increasing body of evidence which implicates IgE immunoglobulins in these reactions. Studies, notably by Austen, Ishizaka, Stanworth, and their colleagues, have shown that IgE plays an important role in the development of many allergic conditions associated with the mucosae (Orange *et al.,* 1970; Ishizaka and Ishizaka, 1970; Stanworth, 1970). Moreover IgE or reaginic antibody formation has been identified following an impressive number of helminth infections in man, rats, mice, primates, dogs, and guinea pigs (see Ogilvie and Jones, 1969; Catty, 1969; Dobson *et al.,* 1971a; Williams and Pérez-Esandi, 1971; Moss, 1971). In only three cases, other than in man, however, has this reaginic antibody activity specifically been associated with the IgE class of immunoglobulins, namely, in dogs (Schwartzman *et al.,* 1971), rats (Stechshulte *et al.,* 1970; Kanyerezei *et al.,* 1971), and guinea pigs (Dobson *et al.,* 1971b).

Immunoglobulin E is a very minor component of the serum proteins which nevertheless is a powerful mediator of anaphylactic reactions. Structurally IgE resembles other immunoglobulins comprising two heavy and two light chains (Bennich and Johansson, 1968). The major immunological property of IgE is its capacity to elicit Prausnitz-Küstner reactions in normal homologous recipients. This function is related to the ability of the antibody to fix to cells (Lichtenstein and Osler, 1964; Ishizaka *et al.,* 1969). Studies of the distribution of IgE-forming plasma cells show that these cells predominate at mucosal surfaces and in the lymph nodes regional to these tissues (Tada and Ishizaka, 1970). IgE formed at these local sites may be secreted, but unlike IgA it lacks a secretory piece. Indeed it has been suggested that IgE secreted in this way is largely wasted and that its main reactions occur within the tissues; in fact efficient IgE-mediated allergic reactions only take place if the antibody has been fixed to cells prior to its reaction with allergen (Ishizaka *et al.,* 1969).

Reaginic antibody formation appears to be a universal phenomenon following trematode, nematode (see Ogilvie and Jones, 1971), and cestode (Williams and Pérez-Esandi, 1971) infections in mammals. Levels of reaginic antibody formation following these infections are usually so high that cells away from the local intestinal site of infection, particularly those from the spleen, peritoneum, and lymph nodes *in vivo*, as well as fragments from these organs *in vitro* will produce reaginic antibodies (Ogilvie and Jones, 1968; Wilson, 1967). The formation of so much reaginic antibody is possibly related to the worms having an adjuvant effect on IgE or reaginic antibody formation. Orr and Blair (1969) demonstrated that *Nippostrongylus brasiliensis* infections increased the reaginic antibody response of rats to other unrelated antigens. Johansson *et al.* (1968) also showed that the total level of IgE in children from areas endemic for *Ascaris* infections was 25 times greater than the normal human level. De Vos-Cloetens *et al.* (1971)

showed that antigen induced the proliferation of a cell population, only part of which secretes specific antibodies, and the remainder synthesize immunoglobulins which do not react with the antigen but are in some way specifically related to it. Another possible factor in the production of high levels of reaginic antibody or IgE is the local stimulation of mucosae containing large numbers of IgE-producing plasma cells. This could account for the early rise in the primary reaginic or IgE antibody titers recognized following some infections with helminth parasites (Mota *et al.*, 1969; Dobson *et al.*, 1971a).

To paraphrase a recent comment by Hong *et al.* (1969), the search for a beneficial activity of IgE seems to fulfill more of an emotional or teleological need. Nevertheless the persistence of any body system is a compelling argument for the survival advantage of the system. The formation of high levels of reaginic antibodies following so many metazoan parasite infections is indeed a compelling reason for rationalizing the anaphylactic reactions mediated by these antibodies with the protection of the host against invasion of the mucosae by parasites. However, it is evident that IgE reactions alone cannot, as yet, be unequivocally identified in this context with regard to the parasitic metazoa. It has been suggested that the anaphylactic reactions accompanying "self-cure" (Stewart, 1950a,b,c, 1953, 1955) in gastrointestinal nematode infections involve reaginic antibodies at the intestinal surface (Ogilvie, 1964). In some cases it has been demonstrated that anaphylactic reactions provoked with nonhelminth antigens will either accelerate the expulsion of adult worms (Stewart, 1953) or prevent the establishment of the infective larvae (Panter, 1969). These effects are not universal since Barth *et al.* (1966) showed that anaphylaxis would only accelerate the expulsion of *N. brasiliensis* from rats if immune serum was also passively transfered to these animals. Ogilvie (1970) concluded that anaphylactic antibodies were not vital to worm expulsion but could speed elimination. However, Hogarth-Scott and Bingley (1971) reported that rabbit anti-rat peritoneal cell serum significantly suppressed the immune response of rats to *N. brasiliensis* and that the infection could be prolonged by such an antiserum. They suggested that homocytotropic reaginic antibody–allergen-mediated reactions were important in the immune expulsion of this worm. This conclusion is in tandem with the findings of W. F. H. Jarrett and his co-workers, that amine release from mast cells, synchronously produced in response to parasitic infections, by allergen-reaginic antibody reactions, creates a pathway between the cells of the intestinal mucosa for the leakage of protective antibodies (W. F. H. Jarrett *et al.*, 1970; Murray *et al.*, 1969, 1971). In fact they demonstrated a striking temporal relationship between the increase in mast cell numbers, the onset of worm expulsion, and macromolecular leakage into the gut (Murray *et al.*, 1971). Ishizaka *et al.* (1969) also suggested, that the probable role of IgE antibody–antigen reactions in the protection of the mucosal surface against infection is by changing the permeability so that serum immunoglobulins may leak into the area and contribute to the protection. Whatever the precise role of IgE is in this respect, the clinical data of Hong *et al.* (1969) concerning IgE-deficiency diseases in man indicated that this antibody system has survival advantage in the protection of mucosal surfaces from infectious and antigenic onslaught.

III. Cellular Aspects of Immunity

Immunologically the gastrointestinal tract maintains a functional identity with the peripheral lymphoid system, particularly the mesenteric lymph nodes and spleen, by experiencing an antigenic challenge and contributing to the overall immune response. In addition, the central lymphoid tissue, which is the area of primary lymphopoiesis and determines the immunological competence of the individual, stems from the embryonic gut. Current immunological thought holds that the lymphoid system comprises a dynamic group of cells, the functions of which are served by a number of morphologically identical but functionally heterogeneous lymphocytes. Thus the probability arises that an immune response can be similarly expressed by multiple rather than single cell systems (Abdou and Richter, 1970). At present it is recognized that at least two distinct lymphocyte populations are required for the initiation of an antibody response and there are indications that memory and transforming lymphocytes, which are sensitive to the initial antigen insult, are thymus-derived, while antibody-forming cells are derived from the bone marrow (Davies *et al.*, 1966, 1967; Mitchell and Miller, 1968; J. F. A. P. Miller and Mitchell, 1968, 1969; Nossal *et al.*, 1968). Furthermore, lymphocyte transformations to specific antigens *in vitro* have been variously interpreted as either an expression of cell-mediated immunity (CMI) (Mills, 1966; Oppenheim *et al.*, 1967) or as the *in vitro* counterpart of immunological memory (Dutton, 1967).

Cell-mediated immune responses have been reported for a number of helminth infections (see Soulsby, 1970), but they are best known for *Trichinella spiralis*, *Trichostrongylus colubriformis*, and *Schistosoma* spp. in laboratory animals. While CMI mechanisms are increasingly incriminated in the protective immune responses of mammals to helminth infections, much clarification is still needed concerning the role of sensitized lymphocytes, in view of the range of immunoglobulins and the array of other immunological phenomena which are produced against metazoan parasites. In no instance so far can CMI be recognized as the sole mediator of protective immunity against helminth parasites.

Larsh (1963) interpreted the cellular reactions which occur in the small intestine of mice infected with *Trichinella spiralis* as evidence for the expulsion of the adult worms by an acute inflammation. Later he found that whole body X-irradiation and treatment with cortisone suppressed the expulsion of the worms (Larsh, 1967). This immunity was transferable to normal recipients with lymph node cells and particularly peritoneal exudate cells from sensitized mice (Larsh *et al.*, 1964a,b). The recipients of the exudate cells did not produce detectable antibody; furthermore, cells from nonimmune donors failed to transfer immunity to recipient mice. Antigens from *T. spiralis* can also produce delayed hypersensitivity responses without the production of detectable anaphylactic antibody. However, animals which had received prolonged sensitizations with these antigens eventually demonstrated immediate hypersensitivity reactions of the Arthus-type (Kim, 1966; Kim *et al.*, 1967a,b). Nevertheless, cutaneous delayed hypersensitivity reactivity could be transfered with lymph node cells from sensitized animals; moreover, lymphocytes from guinea pigs injected with *T. spiralis* antigens were capable of transformation (Jamaur *et al.*, 1968).

R. B. Crandall *et al.* (1967) readily demonstrated humoral and intestinal antibodies against *T. spiralis* and the accumulation of antibody-producing cells at the site of infection. The predominance of antibody was found in the IgG class of immunoglobulins which may suggest that the inflammation, interpreted by Larsh (1963) as a CMI response could equally have a mechanism initiated by an antibody–antigen reaction.

Trichostrongylus colubriformis, a sheep intestinal nematode, has been established in guinea pigs which then acquired immunity to subsequent infections (Herlich *et al.*, 1956; Gordon *et al.*, 1960). The studies of Dineen and his co-workers indicated that the mechanism of protective immunity in guinea pigs to this parasite was mediated by lymphocytes in a manner analogous to transplantation immunity and delayed hypersensitivity (Dineen *et al.*, 1968a,b). This conclusion was based on their earlier findings that a single injection of immune serum failed to confer immunity while the transfer of sensitized mesenteric lymph node cells to nonimmune syngeneic recipients induced protection (Wagland and Dineen, 1965; Dineen and Wagland, 1966). However, Connan (1965) also showed that the passive transfer of immune serum does confer protective immunity on guinea pigs to *T. colubriformis*.

One important aspect of Dineen's work was the demonstration of the local nature of the host response. Dineen and Wagland (1966) showed that while immune spleen cells conferred protection on virgin guinea pigs, immune mesenteric lymph node cells were much more effective. By labeling immune lymphocytes from the mesenteric lymph nodes and Peyer's patches of infected guinea pigs with ^{51}Cr, Dineen *et al.* (1968b) were able to show the preferential accumulation of these cells in the infected small intestine. The labeled cells came into intimate contact with the parasite in the gut epithelium and underwent "allergic death" at the site of infection. Dineen and Wagland (1966) had earlier shown that the susceptible stage of the infection in guinea pigs was the fourth larval stage; cells transferred within 24–48 hours prior to the occurrence of this stage were effective in initiating the protective immune response. This work amplified the results of Herlich *et al.* (1956).

Dobson and Soulsby (1972) have recently studied the kinetics of the lymphocyte reactions in guinea pigs during primary and multiple infections with *T. colubriformis* using the uptake of tritiated thymidine *in vivo* and *in vitro* as an index of lymphoid activity. The induction of the immune response was rapid; blastogenesis in the Peyer's patches increased markedly during the first day of infection and continued to increase until the tenth day. During this time the lymphocyte response disseminated into the infected lamina propria and to the local mesenteric lymph nodes. In both these areas the peak response occurred 6 days after infection, but it never surpassed that in the Peyer's patches. These observations lead to the conclusion that immunogenesis began in the Peyer's patches and that further recruitment of lymphocytes from the mesenteric lymph nodes rapidly augmented these lymphopoietic changes. It is also possible that the increased numbers of lymphoblasts in the lamina propria represented local areas of mitosis, but the relatively short duration of these responses rather suggests that they were migrations of transforming cells which mature and mount the initial protective response in the infected intestine.

The local nature of these reactions was further exemplified by the demonstration that the peak of lymphoblast formation in the mesenteric lymph nodes of the lower small intestine occurred later than that in the anterior region. Furthermore, there was no evidence of increased lymphocyte activity in either the lymphoid patches of the cecum or in the inguinal lymph nodes. The recruitment of further lymphocytes from the mesenteric lymph nodes of the lower small intestine coincided with the movement of adult *T. colubriformis* down the intestine, which has been shown to commence about the tenth day after infection (Herlich *et al.*, 1956; Sturroch, 1963; Herlich, 1966; Connan, 1966). The responses in the lower small intestine may represent, on the one hand a further dissemination of the initial response from the anteriad regions of the intestine, or on the other, lymphocyte transformations to new antigenic stimuli from later stages in the development of the worm.

At the time that the lymphoblast populations were increasing along the infected gut there was a sharp decline in the number of lymphoblasts counted in the spleen, which returned to normal at the time of the peak lymphoblast responses in the anterior small intestine. Furthermore large numbers of lymphocytes capable of nonspecific *in vitro* transformation in response to phytohemagglutinin, appeared in the circulation 5 days after infection and had disappeared 3 days later. These results suggest that the spleen exports cells capable of a mitogenic response, shortly after the infection becomes established, which then converge on the infected gut and adjacent lymphoid tissue where they augment the population of cells capable of responding to the parasite. Sandberg (1970) reported a similar egress of lymphocytes from the spleen in guinea pigs injected with sheep erythrocytes. Despite the early and possibly nonspecific role of the spleen in immunogenesis it was obvious that the spleen became specifically involved later in the infection because after 11 days infection the lymphoblast population increased above that in noninfected guinea pigs. Moreover, Dineen and Wagland (1966) have demonstrated that spleen cells transferred from immune guinea pigs confer protection on nonimmune recipients.

During primary infections, lymphocytes capable of *in vitro* transformation to *T. colubriformis* antigen increased in the circulation between the second and fifth days after infection. This response was transient and disappeared by the twelfth day. At this time immune elimination of the adult worms was advanced. Later the transformation level of the peripheral lymphocytes increased to its maximal level by day 15 and then declined to a low, but persistent number of transforming cells by 30 days after infection. The responses of immune animals were different in that the lymphocyte transformations first declined during the initial week of the challenge infection, returning to normal by the fifteenth day. The extent of this reaction was proportional to the number of previous infections the guinea pigs had experienced. Similarly the rapid increase in the lymphocyte transformations after the fifteenth day of infection was also proportional to the previous experience the host had had of the parasite.

Lymphocyte transformations to specific antigens *in vitro* have been variously interpreted as an expression of CMI or the *in vitro* counterpart of immunological memory. Weber (1967) and Weber and Eichholtz (1971) have shown that the cells responsible for transformation were derived from or dependent on the thymus. Recently Dineen and Adams (1971) found that the cells responsible for initiating the rejection of *T. colubriformis* from guinea pigs were thymus-dependent, recirculating, and long-lived.

The drain of specifically sensitized transforming lymphocytes from the circulation at the time of the protective immune response in the infected gut of guinea pigs may reflect the involvement of these cells in this response. Furthermore the rapid increase in transforming lymphocytes in the circulation after this time may represent the dispersal phase of the overall immune response. It is generally assumed that the circulation of transforming lymphocytes is crucial to the distribution of specifically sensitized lymphocytes and the commitment to a specific anamnestic response (Daniels and Weigle, 1968; Jacobson and Thorbecke, 1969).

The information from the work of Dineen and his co-workers strongly suggested the importance of CMI in the immune responses of guinea pigs to *T. colubriformis* infections. However the existence of high titers of IgE and hemagglutinating antibodies during these infections (Connan, 1966; Dobson and Soulsby, 1972) also supports the involvement of antibodies in the protection of the host, particularly since positive cutaneous delayed hypersensitivity reactions to *T. colubriformis* antigens could not be demonstrated until after the immune elimination of the worm had commenced. Strong immediate hypersensitivity reactions of both the anaphylactic- and Arthus-type could be shown as early as 5 days after infection. Nevertheless, these results may merely reflect the paucity of sensitized lymphocytes in the circulation before this time. Thymus-derived or thymus-dependent lymphocytes are important in the initiation and maintenance of protective immunity against intestinal nematodes in guinea pigs. Ogilvie and Jones (1967) have demonstrated that reaginic antibody formation was dependent on the presence of the thymus during *N. brasiliensis* infections in rats. They later concluded (Ogilvie and Jones, 1971) from this work and the studies of Orr and Blair (1969) that *N. brasiliensis* had a massive stimulatory effect on thymus-dependent immunity in rats. Herd (1969) also showed that antithymocyte serum depressed the protective immune responses of sheep to *Chabertia ovina* and suggested that, although immunity was probably related to the formation of anaphylactic antibodies, the synthesis of this antibody was linked in some way with CMI and that it was partly under thymic control. Dineen and Adams (1971) and Dobson and Soulsby (1972) have both implicated thymic cells in the local responses of guinea pigs to gastrointestinal nematode infections. These findings are reinforced by the experiments of Bienenstock and Dolezel (1971) who found that the Peyer's patches in hamsters did not produce antibody-producing cells normally *in vivo* when stimulated by bovine serum albumin. Thus the normal lymphocyte population of the Peyer's patches may be predominantly of thymic rather than bone marrow type lymphocytes.

Protective immunity to gastrointestinal parasites appears to be intimately linked with an initial local response of thymus-derived cells which rapidly disseminate into the regional lymph nodes and lamina propria. The disseminative phase of the response may either be linked with the expression of a CMI response which directly affects the parasite, or alternatively, it may be associated with the stimulation of reaginic antibody formation within the gut and the initiation of extraintestinal antibody responses, which play an important part in the local anaphylactic reactions of "self-cure."

The induction of the immune response against gastrointestinal parasites is associated with the local macrophage–lymphocyte system of cells, but immune damage and elimination of these parasites coincides with dramatic increases in the nonlymphoid elements of the reticuloendothelial system. The classical studies of Taliaferro and Sarles (1939) showed that the reaction of rats to *N. brasiliensis* was a mixed inflammation which involved eosinophil leukocytes and mast cells as well as macrophages and lymphocytes.

Eosinophilia is characteristic of most parasitic infections (see Hirsch, 1965) and although the eosinophil leukocyte resembles neutrophil leukocytes in many respects, they behave differently in response to infection, antigenic challenge, and adrenal steroid administration, and have a propensity to accumulate in the skin and at mucosal surfaces. Many factors have been suggested as mediating eosinophilia (Kline *et al.*, 1932; Archer, 1963; Sampter *et al.*, 1953; Parish and Coombs, 1968), however Litt (1964) found that eosinophil leukocytes migrated actively to sites of antibody–antigen reaction. Parish (1969) and Kay (1970a) showed that this accumulation preferentially occurred at sites containing IgG_1 antibodies in guinea pigs, although Kay (1970a) did not discount the involvement of other anaphylactic immunoglobulins. Dobson and Soulsby (1971, unpublished) have shown that eosinophil leukocytes will accumulate in IgE induced cutaneous anaphylactic reactions in guinea pigs.

Kay (1970b) found that eosinophil leukocyte migration was stimulated by a chemotactic factor (ECF-C) released from serum by antibody–antigen complexes which was dependent on complement for its action. Later Kay *et al.* (1971) found that anaphylactic reactions in sensitized guinea pig lung released another chemotactic factor (ECF-A) which was independent of complement in its action and which accompanied the release of histamine and SRS-A.

Basten *et al.* (1970) studied the pathogenesis of eosinophilia in rats infected with *T. spiralis* and concluded that it was an immunological phenomena. They found that immunologically competent lymphocytes participated in the events leading to an increased eosinophil leukocyte production (Basten and Beeson, 1970). Neonatal thymectomy and thoracic duct drainage of lymphocytes together with antilymphocyte serum treatment decreased these responses. Furthermore, the eosinophil leukocyte response was transferred by sensitized lymphocytes either in suspension or contained within a Millipore chamber (Basten and Beeson, 1970).

Eosinophil leukocytes thus migrate toward and are involved in type 1 immediate hypersensitivity reactions (Coombs and Gell, 1964) which are variously mediated by IgG_1 and IgE antibodies. It is interesting to speculate that eosinophilia is involved in the implementation and moderation of the immunological reactions of thymus-dependent cells and IgE antibodies, both of which appear to be closely associated with the development of CMI phenomena and protection in parasitic infections.

Ammann *et al.* (1969) revealed an intimate relationship between IgA and IgE deficiencies in people with ataxia-telangiectasia which was associated with an abnormal thymus and deficient delayed hypersensitivity responses (Peterson *et al.*, 1966) but not with other immunoglobulins. They interpreted these observations as evidence for an important link between the production of IgA with that of IgE and the development of CMI which was dissociated from IgG and IgM. Brostoff and Roitt (1969) also showed a relationship between IgE production and CMI responsiveness in patients suffering from summer hay fever.

The subject of mast cells and helminth infections at mucosal surfaces has been the source of a considerable recent literature because these cells are involved in the immune expulsion of parasites. Mast cells in mammals are the main effector cells which release histamine, serotonin, and SRS-A following the reactions of allergens with IgG_1 and IgE fixed to their cell surface. Stanworth (1970) suggested that the release of vasoactive amines from mast cells was dependent on an allosteric conformative change which occurs in the cell-fixed antibody when it reacts with allergen, which is transmitted to the cell surface triggering off the chain of energy-dependent enzyme reactions which culminate in the release of histamine. Stanworth's system suggests that two antibody molecules are necessary for the reaction to occur. This may explain why 11 S IgE dimers in guinea pigs have considerably more Prausnitz-Küstner activity than 8 S IgE monomeric antibodies (Dobson *et al.*, 1972). Orange *et al.* (1970) found that the release of histamine and SRS-A from rat mast cells by homologous IgE–allergen reactions did not require polymorphonuclear leukocytes or an intact complement system, thus differing from the polymorphonuclear leukocyte- and complement-dependent pathway of SRS-A release mediated by IgG_a antibodies. These studies may indicate that the anaphylactic expulsion of worms from the gut may have multiple pathways initiated by different classes of immunoglobulins.

IV. Protection

Immunity is the sum of all factors which prevent the establishment or continuation of an infection. Thus in part it is reflected by the degree of suitability of each host species for any particular parasite and the immunity may be complete when the host is completely unsuitable or partial if there is a degree of compatibility between the host and parasite. In this latter situation the host is usually capable of expressing antagonistic reactions which further restrict the life expectancy of the parasite. Sprent (1969) recently analyzed the importance of suitability factors in immunity to metazoan parasites and consequently the present discussion is restricted to the antagonistic adaptive immune mechanisms involved in protecting the host against gastrointestinal parasitism.

The antagonistic responses of the host and their effects on the population dynamics of parasites are complex for they affect parasites of different developmental stages, each with complex host associations, and involve hosts of different phylogenetic positions undergoing similar development. Protective immunity is probably related to the accessibility to the host of antigens which have an important part to play in the biology of the parasite. Soulsby (1962) described these substances as functional antigens which were only associated with the living parasite because the living parasite, in an unaltered or attenuated form, must be present in the host to produce a satisfactory immunity. Immunity produced in this manner may range from inhibition of larval establishment through retarded growth and development and reduced fecundity to complete elimination of the infection. Furthermore, in order to produce the full spectrum of these effects the immunological mechanisms must be continuously active.

Recent work on protective immunity to helminth parasites has largely been concentrated on the immune expulsion of the adult stages from the infected host. However earlier work demonstrated that antagonistic protective mechanisms were operative from the moment the infective stage of the parasite entered the host.

Stirewalt (1963) categorized the secretions of larval helminths as either developmental, including those materials involved in hatching, exsheathment, and the formation of cysts and membranes, or invasive secretions, which comprised lytic, enzymatic, adhesive, and protective larval products. From the work of Sarles and Taliaferro (1936), Sprent (1951), and Thorson (1954), it was concluded that the excretions and secretions of the larval stages were a major source of antigens which stimulated protective immunity. Otto (1940), Mauss (1940), and Thorson (1954) showed that larval nematodes immersed in immune serum were less infective than normal larvae. Washing the larvae after immersion in immune serum failed to reduce the deleterious effects of the antiserum. Taliaferro and Sarles (1942) also found that the passive transfer of immune serum slowed larval development. Later Thorson (1953) demonstrated that antiserum inhibited the lipase activity of *N. brasiliensis* larvae. Lewert (1958) suggested that the speed and relative success of larval stages penetrating the tissues of the host was influenced by the immune state of the host. Chandler (1932, 1935) had earlier stated that this was due to specific anti-enzyme antibodies acting against the penetration enzymes. Thorson (1953, 1956), Lewert *et al.* (1959), and C. L. Lee and Lewert (1960) have amply demonstrated these anti-penetration enzyme reactions using a variety of helminth parasites. Thus the initial protection of the host involves the reduction of the invasive potential of the infective larval stage. Subsequently death of established larvae within the tissues of the immune host may also be a contributing factor in protection. The early work of Sarles and Taliaferro (1936), Sarles (1938), and later by Jackson (1960) showed that the body orifices of larval nematodes were frequently blocked by immune precipitates and suggested that these immobilized the parasite allowing further immunological attack from the host. However, experiments involving X-irradiated third-stage larval. *N. brasiliensis* indicated that the immunogenic potential of this developmental stage was low (Prochazka and Mulligan, 1965) and thus, apart from the secretion of penetration enzymes, their contribution towards the induction of the protective immune response may also be low. This poor immunogenicity may be related to the failure of exsheathed third-stage nematode larvae to feed (Sommerville, 1964). Thus the larva's main functional significance in development is probably migration within the host prepatory to a growth phase during the fourth larval stage. Sprent (1963) reached this conclusion with respect to second-stage ascaridoid larvae. Nevertheless, physiological changes do occur during these early developmental stages of nematodes which may reflect their responses to immunological reactions. There is evidence for a change from an oxidative to a fermentative metabolism once the infective larva assumes the parasitic mode of life which would account for the observations that, although immune sera inhibit the respiration rates of some preparasitic nematode larvae (Schwabe, 1957; Dobson, 1967), the respiration of the parasitic third-stage larva may not be affected (Schwabe, 1957).

The invasive potential of infective nematode larvae may thus be reduced in immune hosts. Similar conclusions can be reached concerning cestode (Gemmell and Soulsby, 1968) and trematode larvae (Weinstein, 1967). Immunity to the preencystment stages of cestodes has been shown to be a major protective mechanism of the host. This immunity appears to be localized in the gut. Leonard and Leonard (1941) considered that the initial immune response occurred at the intestinal level with a second phase of immunity in the tissues against the metacestode stage. Froyd and Round (1960) were able to bypass the intestinal phase of immunity in cattle immune to oral challenge with *Taenia saginata* by parenteral injection of artificially activated embryos. Gemmell (1962) also suggested that the intestinal mucosa was an effective barrier not only in acquired immunity but also in innate resistance to some species of cestodes.

As yet there is no unequivocal evidence that demonstrates the nature and site of the immune reactions against cestode larvae. However the humoral basis for protective immunity to several species has been shown by the transfer of serum from immune donors to noninfected recipients (H. M. Miller and Gardiner, 1934; Kerr, 1935; Campbell, 1938a,b,c; Leonard and Leonard, 1941; Di Conza, 1969). Di Conza (1969) found that the active serum factors were associated with the 7 S IgG immunoglobulin fractions of *Hymenolepis nana*-infected mouse serum. He did not discount the possibility of locally produced IgA contributing to the protective immunity because of the rapidity with which acquired immunity developed after oral challenge (Hearin, 1941; Weinmann, 1958; Heyneman, 1962) and the fact that intestinal mucosal extracts had a greater antiparasitic effect against *H. nana* than serum from immune mice (Weinmann, 1966). Weinmann (1966) and Di Conza (1969) both suggested that the hexocanth was the source of the immunogens, possibly from the penetration glands, which induced the early local response in the intestine, and that failure of the larvae to establish in immune hosts was caused by the direct action of antibody affecting the physiology of the larva.

In addition to the direct effects of the protective immune response on larvae, the subsequent establishment of the parasite may also be changed, which is reflected in abnormalities in their ecology in immune hosts. The distribution of *Ostertagia* larvae in the abomasal mucosa of sheep after primary infection is mainly in the prepyloric region (Sommerville, 1954; Dunsmore, 1965). In immune animals the fundic zone is more heavily parasitized than the pyloric region (Dunsmore, 1965). This suggests a local immune response inhibiting larval penetration at their normal site. Dobson (1966b) also attributed the progressive movement of *Oesophagostomum columbianum* larval penetration down the small intestine of sheep following second and third infections to the inhibitory effects of antibodies on the activities of the third-stage larvae. Similar effects have also been reported for the adult stages of gastrointestinal nematodes (Larsh *et al.*, 1952; Brambell, 1965).

A major effect of helminth immunity is retardation of worm growth and development. In many cases growth is completely arrested and usually this occurs about the time of developmental change (see Michel, 1968). Many factors contribute to arrested development, but the removal of the adult worm burden is often sufficient to reactivate the larvae. Among nematodes different species are arrested at different stages in their life cycle. *Trichostrongylus retortaeformis* is inhibited at the late third-stage; *Haemonchus*, *Ostertagia*, *Nematodirus*, and *Oesophagostomun* spp. at the fourth-stage; and *Dictyocaulus viviparus* at the early fifth-stage (Michel, 1952a; Dineen *et al.*, 1965; Sommerville, 1954; Gibson, 1959; Veglia, 1923; Taylor and Michel, 1953). The mechanisms involved in arrested development are poorly understood, but it is possible that a threshold level of antigenic information from larval and adult parasites is constantly required to maintain the larvae in a quiescent state (Dineen, 1963a,b; Donald *et al.*, 1964). If the adult population is eliminated, then the threshold will no longer be maintained and the larvae would then recommence their development. Michel (1952b) found evidence for such a response with *T. retortaeformis* in rabbits, although this situation does not hold true for all host–parasite relationships demonstrating arrested larval development (Michel, 1963).

There is clear evidence that the egg production of some nematodes may be inhibited because of an immunological reaction. Chandler (1936) and Ogilvie (1965) noted that *N. brasiliensis* adults in immune rats rapidly stopped producing eggs and that when these worms were transferred to nonimmune hosts egg production was renewed.

The action of protective immunity against the adult parasite in the gastrointestinal tract is invariably viewed as an expulsion of the worm population. However, more subtle changes in the feeding, metabolism, behavior, and reproduction of the parasite may also occur. The term "self-cure" was introduced by Stoll (1929) to describe the spontaneous loss of adult *Haemonchus contortus* from grazing sheep. Stewart (1950a,b,c, 1953, 1955) attributed this loss of worms to immediate hypersensitivity reactions in the gut and Soulsby and Stewart (1959) found that substances liberated during the third-ecdysis of larval *H. contortus* were the allergens which initiated the reaction. Michel (1952b) described similar reactions in rabbits infected with *T. retortaeformis* and spontaneous elimination of adult parasites without the intake of a second dose of infective larvae has been shown for *N. brasiliensis* in rats (Chandler, 1936). *N. brasiliensis* infections in rats have been the most intensively studied model for immunity to gastrointestinal parasites in recent years. Immunity can be induced by very small infections, it is long-lived, thymus-dependent, and is antibody-mediated (Ogilvie and Jones, 1971). The present view is that worm expulsion is governed by a two-step immunological mechanism which involves both the damage of worms by antibody and the initiation of anaphylactic inflammation in the gut by worm allergens which precipitates worm expulsion (Urquhart *et al.*, 1965; Barth *et al.*, 1966; E. E. E. Jarrett *et al.*, 1968; Murray *et al.*, 1969; Ogilvie and Jones, 1971).

Immunological damage to worms may become manifest as developmental, morphological, behavioral, and reproductive abnormalities shift the dynamics of the host-parasite relationship in favor of the host. One of the earliest and perhaps still most satisfying explanations for the direct actions of immunity against parasites is the anti-enzyme hypothesis of Chandler (1932, 1935). The work of Thorson (1963), Schwabe (1957), and Dusanic (1966) has shown that specific antibody will inhibit enzyme activities of nematodes. Tran Van Ky *et al.* (1967) identified the antigens of *Schistosoma mansoni* as enzymes following their reactions with precipitating antibodies produced in rabbits. Enzymes have been identified in the esophogeal and exodigestive glands of *N. brasiliensis* which may be important in the protective responses of rats to this parasite (D. L. Lee, 1970; Edwards *et al.*, 1971; Sanderson and Ogilvie, 1971). Sanderson and Ogilvie (1971) found that acetylcholinesterase levels increased sharply in worms as rats became immune. Moreover the levels of three isoenzymes associated with this enzyme decreased in worms damaged by immunity but were vastly increased in parasites which had adapted to the immune response. Rhodes *et al.* (1965) injected *Ascaris suum* malic dehydrogenase into guinea pigs which produced both enzyme inhibiting and precipitating antibodies and were resistant to oral challenge with this worm.

The influence of immunity on the biology of the parasite may be manifest in morphological changes. Michel (1967) reported that an increased proportion of *Ostertagia ostertagi* females failed to develop vulva flaps in immune calves. Keith (1967) also showed that immunity in cattle affects the structure of the spicules in *Cooperia* spp. The permanent immunological damage of the parasite may involve cellular changes as well as the formation of gross morphological abnormalities. Taliaferro and Sarles (1939) noted that *N. brasiliensis* from immune hosts were vacuolated and had distended guts. D. L. Lee (1969) showed that the first immunological damage preceding depression of egg production in *N. brasiliensis* took place in the gut of the worms. Damaged gut cells lost their ribosomes and became vacuolated. Towards the end of the infection lipid droplets appeared in the hypodermis, muscles, excretory glands, and reproductive system; spermatozoa were resorbed in males and egg production ceased in females. Ogilvie and Hockley (1968) showed that the structural damage was not repaired when the worms were transplanted in nonimmune hosts.

The behavior of helminths may change following immunological damage. Brambell (1965) found that, when the majority of adult *N. brasiliensis* were expelled from rats, the residual population moved from its preferred locus in the jejunum before the onset of immunity into the duodenum.

The immunological mechanism of worm expulsion from the gastrointestinal tract is the sum of the direct effects of antibody and sensitized cells on the parasite disturbing its normal physiology and the anaphylactic reactions in the mucosal tissues induced by the allergens of the parasite (see Ogilvie and Jones, 1971). In addition it has also been suggested that immunologically damaged worms may secrete substances which directly influence mast cells to release vasoactive amines (Uvnäs and Wold, 1967; Keller, 1971). Antibody may reach parasites in the intestine through traumatic lesions produced by the worms in the mucosal surface or by macromolecular leakage induced by local IgE anaphylactic reactions. At this juncture all the evidence points to IgG immunoglobulins being the main protective antibodies. Jones *et al.* (1970) showed that rat 7 S γ_1-globulins contained most protective antibodies against *N. brasiliensis*, but some were also found in the 7 S γ_2-globulins. Di Conza (1969) demonstrated that 7 S IgG immunoglobulins were important in the resistance of mice to *Hymenolepis nana*. Dobson (1967) found that hemagglutinating antibodies were only found in mucosal exudates from sheep when *O. columbianum* were present in gut lumen, but high levels of antibody were detected in the mucosal tissues of immune sheep even in the absence of an adult worm infection. These antibodies also induced heterocytotropic PCA reactions which suggests that they belong in a 7 S IgG class of immunoglobulin.

Several authors have found that sensitized lymphocytes make an important contribution to the elimination of parasites from the gut, however the mechanisms whereby these CMI reactions affect parasites are poorly understood. Nevertheless, Larsh (1967) hypothesized that pharamacologically active substances, such as lymph node permeability factor

(Schild and Willougby, 1967), may operate in the inflammatory responses in *T. spiralis* infections by increasing vascular permeability and attracting leukocytes. Soulsby (1970) suggested that several other effector substances, which have been distinguished following antigenic stimulation of lymphocytes involved in CMI, may also be concerned in the mediation of these responses against parasites, such as macrophage inhibition factor (Bloom and Bennett, 1970), mitogenic factor (Dumonde *et al.*, 1967), and transfer factor (Lawrence and Valentine, 1970). One possible mechanism for the damage of worms by these systems may be through the release of lymphotoxin (Ruddle and Waksman, 1968).

V. Immunity and the Evolution of Host–Parasite Relationships

Sprent (1959) in his stimulating essay "Parasitism Immunity and Evolution" proposed that host–parasite interactions evolve by a process of reciprocal adaptation where invading organisms survive because of a series of adaptations to the host, which, in turn, responds by modifying its defense mechanisms. In formulating this hypothesis Sprent emphasized not only the basic role of natural selection but also the premise, for all lasting interspecific interactions, that evolution progresses from disoperation towards toleration between the interacting individuals. He used the term "adaptation tolerance" for the evolved association.

In pursuing the mechanisms underlying adaptation tolerance Sprent (1969) proposed two possible pathways leading to specific unresponsiveness of the host. The first was reduction of antigen stimulation by the parasite. This has also attracted the attention of Damian (1962, 1964), Jenkin (1963), Dineen (1963a,b), Schad (1966), and Zabriskie (1967). The second was specific unresponsiveness despite the presence of antigens. Here the development of adaptation tolerance relies on the selection of hosts which have immunological defects and cannot respond to particular antigens, thus resulting in the evolution of immunologically host–parasite associations; or possibly through the initiation of immunological tolerance early in life of the host (Urquhart, 1970).

Current thought on the relationship between the specific aspects of immunity and the evolution of the host–parasite relationship has since developed along two lines. First, as already outlined, is the evolution of systems by either the host or parasite leading to a state of immunological inertness. Second is the development of systems where the parasite masks itself in some way with host components to prevent the induction of harmful immune responses or avoid them (Smithers and Terry, 1965; Soulsby, 1969; Capron, 1970). While these ideas have considerable merit no one would deny that the most striking examples of tolerance and intolerance between host and parasite exist because of factors usually categorized as innate immunity. This passive antagonistic state occurs in individual hosts that have never had previous contact with particular infections and may range from complete unsuitability to a state of resistance so low that all individual hosts will be infected.

A. Parasite Adaptations and Passive Host Antagonism

There is considerable evidence to show that passive antagonism against infection is related to the genetic structure of the host population and is greatly influenced by the reproductive and aging physiology of the host (Sandground, 1929; Lewert, 1958). Investigations in fields other than parasitology support these hypotheses since it has been shown that the reproductive hormones affect the nature of the intercellular ground substance as well as changing the activity of the reticuloendothelial system (Asboe-Hansen, 1958; Kao and McGavack, 1959; Nicol and Bilbey, 1958) that, in turn, influences the invasive and survival potential of parasitic larvae.

The evolutionary significance of these findings may lie either in the development of efficient mechanisms of larval penetration and establishment, or in life cycle patterns which avoid the need to cross the penetration barriers of the host. However, one other interesting relationship may be the development of seasonal rhythms in the population dynamics of the parasite so that their life patterns are synchronized with the reproduction of their hosts. Parasitic populations showing annual rhythms are particularly evident in temperate climates and in geographical areas where extremes of climate occur for periods of the year. Obviously one of the main reasons for these fluctuations in the parasitic fauna of these regions is the seasonal variation in temperature (Dogiel, 1958). Nevertheless, synchronous reproductive patterns of parasites with those of their hosts also occur for physiological reasons. The adaptive merits of this synchrony are twofold; first, it ensures an increase in the parasitic population at the time when the host congregates to mate, and second, it facilitates transmission of the parasite progeny to the next generation of the host. Two main pathways of evolution appear to have been followed. On the one hand, synchronization of the parasite population so that the main reproductive effort coincides with host mating and reproduction, and, on the other, alterations of the parasitic life cycle to synchronize it with parturition and lactation and toward elimination of a free-living stage in the life cycle.

Seasonal fluctuations in parasitic fauna have been reported for a wide variety of hosts and usually the greatest number of species, each with their greatest population density, occurs during the breeding season of the host (Stunkard, 1955; Lees, 1962; Smyth, 1966; Schad, 1963; Dunsmore, 1965). The basic mechanism underlying this synchrony is not fully understood but it is known that the reproductive cycles of birds and mammals are triggered by changes in the photoperiod and ambient temperature which result in a complex alteration of the endocrinological balance of the animals. This in turn changes their behavior, attracts the opposite sex, induces mating, and maintains the resulting progeny or pregnancy. Studies with the various endocrines involved in these processes show that those parasites which synchronize their reproduction with that of the host are affected by these hormones. In most cases a hypothalamic-adenohyphysis gonad adrenal response has been alluded to as the sequence of stimuli initiating the changes in the biology of the parasite.

Among helminths the most convincing evidence for synchrony has been obtained from studies of the polystomes of amphibians (Thurston, 1964). A more complex phenomenon, but one with a similar end point, is the "spring-rise" in fecal nematode eggs in ewes. Many reasons have been suggested to explain this rise but the most interesting are those proposed by Dunsmore (1966) and Gibbs (1968) who suggested that the basic means of overwintering among the strongyles of sheep in temperate climates is by quiescent larva lodged in the tissues of the host. In spring these larvae are stimulated by the reproductive processes of the host and begin their maturation. The onset of lactation in the parturient ewe induces a further massive production of parasitic ova to coincide with lambing. There is no information concerning the mechanisms whereby the parasite is triggered to recommence its development, but the work of Davey (1964, 1966) on the neurosecretory system of *Ascaris* may mean that the neurosecretory mechanism of the quiescent larvae are stimulated by the reproductive activity of the host. While these studies explain the recommencement of development of these larvae, they offer no solution to why they should become quiescent in the first place. The studies of Itagaki (1928) are interesting in this context since he found that when *Ascaridia galli* developed in unfavorable free-living conditions their subsequent development in chickens was prolonged by the occurrence of a histotropic phase. More recently Anderson *et al.* (1965a,b) showed that the development of large numbers of *Ostertagia ostertagii* picked up by cattle in autumn was inhibited even in susceptible calves. Michel *et al.* (1965) and Parfitt and Sinclair (1967) found that unfavorable culture conditions for the free-living stages of *Dictyocaulus viviparous* could be related to arrested development of these larvae in cattle. Thus the onset of unfavorable climatic conditions affecting the development of larvae could be the instigator of the quiescent overwintering stage in the life cycle; possibly for similar reasons which induce diapause in insects.

Adaptations involving changes in parasitic life cycle patterns in order to coordinate the transmission of the infective stage with the breeding of the host without the necessity for a free-living phase have occurred among hookworms and ascaridoid nematodes. Only in two cases, however, has this pattern of development been shown to be the exclusive mode of transmission, namely, in *Uncinaria lucasi* in fur seals (Olsen and Lyons, 1965) and *Toxocara vitulorum* in cattle (Warren, 1969). Transuterine and mammary migrations of *T. canis* and *Ancylostoma caninum* larvae to the fetus and neonate also occur but this is not the only life cycle pattern despite the frequency with which it happens. Olsen and Lyons (1965) considered the unique nature of the life cycle of *U. lucasi* to be related to the evolution of the seal and was an adaptation of a terrestrial life cycle to cope with the marine phase of its host's life which spans half the year. Sprent (1962), when discussing the evolution of ascaridoid nematodes, stated that they appear to have aspired to reach the top of the food chain, progressively gaining hosts on the way, so that the majority parasitize the dominant predators. Subsequently there occurred a loss of hosts as a form of adaptation in those species parasitizing noncarnivorous animals. On this basis some members of the genus *Toxocara* are among the most highly evolved ascaridoids since they have only one host. *T. canis* has evolved towards transfer of the second-stage larva from the mother across the placenta to the liver of the fetus, with the return of part of this infection to the mother by third-stage larvae from the newborn pups (Sprent, 1958). This evolutionary tendency has gone further with *T. vitulorum* in cattle where transmission of larvae to the newborn calf appears to be solely transmammary (Warren, 1969).

B. Parasitic Adaptations and Active Host Antagonism

One interesting feature of host–parasite relationships, particularly among vertebrate hosts, is the ability of natural populations of parasites to exist and reproduce in the face of an active immune response from the host. From studies on both invertebrate and vertebrate hosts it is evident that when a parasite enters an unusual host it is more rapidly recognized and more intensely reacted to than in its usual host. Recognition of the relative foreignness of the parasite thus lies at the heart of the evolution of the adaptively tolerant host–parasite association. However, have parasites, which are tolerated by their hosts, developed a genetic pattern which allows them to mimic their host's proteins during synthesis of their own potentially antigenic components? Or, on the other hand, does recognition depend on the parasite failing to maintain an optimal life pattern, because the host is unusual, and then cannot combat the deleterious effects of the host's immune responses? These questions cannot, as yet, be answered, but avoidance of recognition by the parasite originated before the evolution of the adaptive immune system because invertebrate–parasite associations demonstrate it as efficiently as their vertebrate counterparts.

Antigen parity between the host and parasite has been the most frequent theme used to analyze the evolutionary adaptations of parasites to the immune reactions of the host (Sprent, 1959, 1969; Rowley and Jenkin, 1962; Jenkin, 1963; Zabriskie, 1967). Dineen (1963a,b) chose the term "fitness antigens" for those parasite antigens which most closely corresponded to host components. He envisaged host–parasite associations in which a degree of immunological interaction occurred but where the stimulus initiating these reactions was kept below a threshold level. However, the difficulty of distinguishing host components from parasitic antigens mimicking those of the host frustrates accurate analysis of these hypotheses. Williams and Soulsby (1970) commenting on the differences of opinion concerning host antigenic determinants in parasites (Sprent, 1969; Capron *et al.*, 1965, 1968; Capron and Lefebvre-Bonnange, 1970) stated that satisfactory answers would come when the parasites could be cultured in the absence of host material.

The incorporation of host components into the structure of parasites has recently been suggested as an evolutionary adaptation to parasitism (Smithers *et al.*, 1969; Soulsby, 1969; Capron, 1970). Smithers *et al.* (1969) have obtained convincing evidence of antigen masking among schistosomes in mammals. They proposed the term "concomitant immunity" for this phenomenon and suggested that adult *Schistosoma mansoni* incorporate host antigens into their own structure conceivably to disguise their own antigens and so prevent rejection by an immune response they themselves engendered. They detected mouse components within the tegument of schistosomes grown in mice and showed these parasites adapted when transferred to monkeys by losing the mouse substances and probably exchanged them for monkey components. Adult worms could thus protect themselves and endure immune reactions that killed immature parasites. Capron *et al.* (1965) and Damian (1967) have also detected host antigens in the tissues of schistosomes.

Soulsby (1969) put forward a similar view to explain certain immune reactions to nematodes in mammals. He suggested that blood group antigens masked nematodes by reacting with hemagglutinins which en-

dowed the parasite with a protective coat of host globulins. Those hosts
which did not react to the blood group substances presumably recognized the parasite as "self."

There is much evidence suggesting that this system may exist. Splitter
et al. (1967) found that host serum components were so closely associated with *Trypanosoma theileri* that repeated washings failed to remove them. Coombs *et al.* (1965) reported that serum factors, possibly
globulins, adsorbed to the surface of free-living nematodes (*Turbatrix
aceti*). Hogarth-Scott (1968) demonstrated the adsorption of IgA, IgM,
and IgG from normal human serum to the cuticle of a variety of ascaridoid infective larvae and to *N. brasiliensis* and *T. aceti*. He concluded
that these were reactions with antigenic determinants commonly found
in nature. Similar findings have been reported by C. A. Crandall and
Arean (1967) and Soulsby (1969) for *Ascaris suum* larvae. There is
no evidence that the reaction of antibody with blood group or heterophile antigens adversely affects the progress of parasitic infections
(Soulsby and Coombs, 1959). Soulsby (1969) looked upon the reactions
of antibody with heterophile antigens as having a beneficial rather than
harmful effect on the parasite because they could sterochemically mask
those antigens which produced harmful reactions. He further concluded
that antigen released at the time of molting or at other times of physiological change would not be masked and may represent the antigens
inducing protective immunity in the host. The work of Capron (1970)
suggests that the coating of worms with antibody may have a facilitatory
effect on the development of some nematode larvae. He showed that
rats normally overcame infections with *Dipetolenema viteae* third-stage
larvae, but if these larvae were transferred together with serum from
immune rats a normal microfilaremia developed. He suggested that
the antigenic stimulus of the worms caused the formation of enhancing
antibodies; a situation analogous to the immunological enhancement
of tumors.

Sprent (1969) also proposed that hosts with immunological defects
could be selected for during the development of adaptive tolerance,
possibly through the existence of an immunological blind spot in the
induction mechanism of the immune system. He envisaged a situation
similar to the failure of mammals to process certain synthetic antigens,
which in turn may be similar to the immunological paralysis which
develops following the treatment of mammals with pneumococcal polysaccharide antigens (Kearney and Halliday, 1970). He also considered
that the direct suppression of immune reactions by parasite toxins could
occur. Urquhart (1970) in considering the possible significance of immunological unresponsiveness of the host to parasitic infections suggested three possible ways in which it could arise: first, by the develop-

ment of immunological tolerance to parasitic antigens; second, through the passive transfer of significant amounts of antibody in the young host suppressing further immunological activity, and third, through the masking of parasite antigens. In conclusion, Urquhart (1970) stated that the significance of immunological unresponsiveness was not readily demonstrable. However, the prolongation of the survival of certain cestode and nematode infections in young animals may be related to a reduction of the immunological performance of these hosts (Penfold and Penfold, 1937; Urquhart, 1961; Soulsby, 1965; W. F. H. Jarrett *et al.*, 1961, 1970).

C. Immunity and Interspecific Competition among Parasites

Competition between organisms is a potent factor in animal life which results, in part, in the evolution of space and time separations between these organisms in order to avoid the disoperative effects of the phenomenon. Pavlovski (1937) defined the arena in which competing parasitic organisms congregated as the "parasitocoenosis" and Dogiel (1958) commented that some members of the parasitocoenosis may exert antibiotic effects on other members. Hairston *et al.* (1960) stated that active competition may take the form of mutual habitat exclusion but more commonly it resulted in niche diversification. Schad (1966) further analyzed the relationships between competition and the regulation of parasite populations and concluded that nonreciprocal cross-immunity between different populations of parasites was important in niche diversification. Antigenic similarities frequently occur among parasite species and he suggested that if the host response elicited by one species is potent against another, natural selection would favour genotypes that permitted the expression of this antigenicity. Competetive effects may be exerted in this manner by causing the immunological expulsion of the parasite population possessing the cross-reacting antigen. For example, Stewart (1953) showed that the "self-cure" reaction of sheep against *Haemonchus contortus* can inadvertently cause the removal of *Trichostrongylus colubriformis* as well.

D. Conclusion

Any hypothesis concerning the evolutionary adaptation of parasites to the antagonistic responses of the host must account for both the elimination of the debilitatory effects of these reactions and the possible synergic effects they may also have on maintaining a balanced host–parasite relationship. The masking hypotheses are attractive in both respects and also account for the great adaptive plasticity of metazoan parasites. Haley (1962), from his studies of *N. brasiliensis* in different hosts, commented that parasite populations in nature have a remarkable ability to adapt to new hosts. Moreover, those immune mechanisms which have been suggested by Schad (1966) as controlling niche diversification could still operate because masked parasites would still liberate antigens which stimulate the immune response while remaining protected against the reactions they thus engender. Masking may also account for the development of adaptation tolerance among invertebrate hosts. For example, some mollusks are only capable of recognizing their normal parasites as foreign when these move from their usual niche and parasitize a different organ (Cheng, 1967).

There is, nevertheless, little doubt that the basic success of parasites is due to much more fundamental reasons than their adaptation of the immune responses of the host. Such factors as their ability to locate, enter into, and feed on the host, together with their resistance to temperature changes and the digestive enzymes within their environment, are important in this respect.

References

Abdou, N. I., and Richter, M. (1970). *Advan. Immunol.* 12, 201.

Ackert, J. E., Edgar, S. A., and Frick, L. P. (1939). *Trans. Amer. Microsc. Soc.* 58, 81.

Ammann, A. J., Cain, W. A., Ishizaka, K., Hong, R., and Good, R. A. (1969). *N. Engl. J. Med.* 281, 469.

Anderson, N., Armour, J., Jennings, F. W., Ritchie, J. S. D., and Urquhart, G. M. (1965a). *Vet. Rec.* 77, 146.

Anderson, N., Armour, J., Jarrett, W. F. H., Jennings, F. W., Ritchie, J. S. D., and Urquhart, G. M. (1965b). *Vet. Rec.* 77, 1196.

Archer, R. K. (1963). "The Eosinophil Leucocytes." Blackwell, Oxford.

Asboe-Hansen, G. (1958). *Physiol. Rev.* 38, 446.

Barth, E. E. E., Jarrett, W. F. H., and Urquhart, G. M. (1966). *Immunology* 10, 459.

Basten, A., and Beeson, P. B. (1970). *J. Exp. Med.* 131, 1288.

Basten, A., Boyer, M. G., and Beeson, P. B. (1970). *J. Exp. Med.* 131, 1271.

Bennich, H., and Johansson, S. G. O. (1968). *Gamma Globulins, Proc. Nobel Symp., 3rd, 1967* p. 199.

Besredka, A. (1927). "Local Immunization." Williams & Wilkins, Baltimore, Maryland.

Bienenstock, J., and Dolezel, J. (1971). *J. Immunol.* 106, 938.

Bloom, B. R., and Bennett, B. (1970). *Ann. N.Y. Acad. Sci.* 196, 258.

Brambell, M. R. (1965). *Parasitology* 55, 313.

Brostoff, J., and Roitt, I. M. (1969). *Lancet* 2, 1269.

Burrows, W. (1963). "Textbook of Microbiology," 18th ed. Saunders, Philadelphia, Pennsylvania.

Campbell, D. H. (1938a). *J. Immunol.* 35, 195.

Campbell, D. H. (1938b). *J. Immunol.* 35, 205.

Campbell, D. H. (1938c). *J. Immunol.* 35, 465.
Capron, A. (1970). *J. Parasitol.* 56, No. 4, Sect. II, Part 3, 515–521.
Capron, A., and Lefebvre-Bonnange, M. N. (1970). *Int. J. Parasitol.* 1, 515.
Capron, A., Biguet, J., Rose, F., and Vernes, A. (1965). *Ann. Inst. Pasteur, Paris* 109, 798.
Capron, A., Biguet, J., Vernes, A., and Afchain, D. (1968). *Pathol. Biol.* 16, 121.
Catty, D. (1969). *Monogr. Allergy* 5.
Cebra, J. J., and Small, P. A., Jr. (1967). *Biochemistry* 6, 503.
Chandler, A. C. (1932). *J. Parasitol.* 18, 135.
Chandler, A. C. (1935). *Amer. J. Hyg.* 22, 157.
Chandler, A. C. (1936). *Amer. J. Hyg.* 23, 46.
Chanock, R. M. (1969). *In* "The Secretory Immunologic System" (D. H. Dayton, Jr. *et al.*, eds.), pp. 83–92. Nat. Inst. Child Health Hum. Develop., Washington, D.C.
Cheng, T. C. (1967). *Advan. Mar. Biol.* 5, 1.
Cluff, L. E. (1969). *In* "The Secretory Immunologic System" (D. H. Dayton, Jr. *et al.*, eds.), pp. 479–484. Nat. Inst. Child Health Hum. Develop., Washington, D.C.
Connan, R. M. (1965). Cited by Ogilvie and Jones (1968).
Connan, R. M. (1966). *Parasitology* 56, 521.
Coombs, R. R. A., and Gell, P. G. H. (1964). *In* "Clinical Aspects of Immunology" (P. G. H. Gell, and R. R. A. Coombs, eds.); pp. 317–337. Blackwell, Oxford.
Coombs, R. R. A., Pout, D. D., and Soulsby, E. J. L. (1965). *Exp. Parasitol.* 16, 311.
Crandall, C. A., and Arean, V. M. (1967). *J. Parasitol.* 53, 105.
Crandall, R. B., Cebra, J. J., and Crandall, C. A. (1967). *Immunology* 12, 147.
Damian, R. T. (1962). *J. Parasitol.* 48, 16.
Damian, R. T. (1964). *Amer. Natur.* 98, 129.
Damian, R. T. (1967). *J. Parasitol.* 53, 60.
Daniels, J. C., and Weigle, W. O. (1968). *J. Immunol.* 101, 1230.
Davey, K. G. (1964). *Can. J. Zool.* 42, 731.
Davey, K. G. (1966). *Amer. Zool.* 6, 243.
Davies, A. J. S., Leuchars, E., Wallis, V., and Koller, P. C. (1966). *Transplantation* 4, 438.
Davies, A. J. S., Leuchars, E., Wallis, V., Marchant, R., and Elliott, E. V. (1967). *Transplantation* 5, 222.
Desowitz, R. S. (1970). *J. Parasitol.* 56, No. 4, Sect. II, Part 3, 521–525.
De Vos-Cloetens, C., Minsart-Paleriaux, V., and Urbain-Vansanten, G. (1971). *Immunology* 20, 955.
Di Conza, J. J. (1969). *Exp. Parasitol.* 25, 368.
Dineen, J. K. (1963a). *Nature (London)* 197, 268.
Dineen, J. K. (1963b). *Nature (London)* 197, 471.
Dineen, J. K., and Adams, D. B. (1971). *Immunology* 20, 109.
Dineen, J. K., and Wagland, B. M. (1966). *Immunology* 11, 47.
Dineen, J. K., Donald, A. D., Wagland, B. M., and Offner, J. (1965). *Parasitology* 55, 515.
Dineen, J. K., Ronai, P. M., and Wagland, B. M. (1968a). *Immunology* 15, 335.
Dineen, J. K., Ronai, P. M., and Wagland, B. M. (1968b). *Immunology* 15, 671.
Dobson, C. (1966a). *Aust. J. Agr. Res.* 17, 779.
Dobson, C. (1966b). *Aust. J. Agr. Res.* 17, 765.
Dobson, C. (1967). *Parasitology* 57, 201.

Dobson, C., and Soulsby, E. J. L. (1972). *Exp. Parasitol.* In preparation.

Dobson, C., Morseth, D. J., and Soulsby, E. J. L. (1971a). *J. Immunol.* **106**, 128.

Dobson, C., Rockey, J. H., and Soulsby, E. J. L. (1972b). *J. Immunol.* **107**, 1431.

Dogiel, V. A. (1958). In "Parasitology of Fishes" (V. A. Dogiel, G. K. Petrushevski, and Y. U. Polyanski, eds.), pp. 1–47. Leningrad University Press. (Translated by Z. Kabata, Oliver & Boyd, Edinburgh, 1961.)

Donald, A. D., Dineen, J. K., Turner, J. H., and Wagland, B. M. (1964). *Parasitology* **54**, 527.

Douvres, F. W. (1962). *J. Parasitol.* **48**, 852.

Dumonde, D. C., Howson, W. T., and Wolstencroft, R. A. (1967). In "Mechanisms of Inflammation Induced by Immune Reactions" (P. A. Miescher and P. Graber, eds.), pp. 263–278. Grune & Stratton, New York.

Dunsmore, J. D. (1965). *J. Helminthol.* **39**, 159.

Dunsmore, J. D. (1966). *J. Helminthol.* **40**, 39.

Dusanic, D. G. (1966). *Exp. Parasitol.* **19**, 310.

Dutton, R. W. (1967). *Advan. Immunol.* **6**, 253.

Edwards, A. J., Burt, J. S., and Ogilvie, B. M. (1971). *Parasitology* **62**, 339.

Fazekas de St. Groth, S. (1950). *Lancet* **1**, 1101.

Fazekas de St. Groth, S., and Donnelley, M. (1950). *Aust. J. Exp. Biol. Med. Sci.* **28**, 61.

Fazekas de St. Groth, S., and White, D. O. (1958). *J. Hyg.* **56**, 151.

Frick, L. P., and Ackert, J. E. (1948). *J. Parasitol.* **34**, 192.

Froyd, G., and Round, M. C. (1960). *Res. Vet. Sci.* **1**, 275.

Gemmell, M. A. (1962). *Nature (London)* **194**, 701.

Gemmell, M. A., and Soulsby, E. J. L. (1968). *Bull. WHO* **39**, 45.

Gibbs, H. C. (1968). In "Reaction of the Host to Parasitism" (E. J. L. Soulsby, ed.), pp. 160–173. Elwert, Marburg, Germany.

Gibson, T. E. (1959). *Brit. Vet. J.* **115**, 120.

Gordon, H. McL., Mulligan, W., and Reinecke, R. K. (1960). *Aust. Vet. J.* **36**, 466.

Hairston, N. G., Smith, F. E., and Slobodkin, L. B. (1960). *Amer. Natur.* **94**, 421.

Haley, J. A. (1962). *J. Parasitol.* **48**, 671.

Hanson, L. A. (1961). *Int. Arch. Allergy Appl. Immunol.* **18**, 241.

Hearin, J. T. (1941). *Amer. J. Hyg.* **33**, 71.

Herd, R. P. (1969). *Aust. Vet. J.* **45**, 595.

Heremans, J. F., Heremans, M. T., and Schultze, H. E. (1959). *Clin. Chim. Acta* **4**, 96.

⊢Herlich, H. (1966). *J. Parasitol.* **52**, 871.

Herlich, H., Douvres, F. W., and Isenstein, R. S. (1956). *Proc. Helminthol. Soc. Wash., D.C.* **23**, 104.

Heyneman, D. (1962). *J. Immunol.* **88**, 217.

Hirsch, J. G. (1965). In "The Inflammatory Process" (B. W. Zweifach, L. Grant, and R. T. McCluskey, eds.), p. 266. Academic Press, New York.

Hogarth-Scott, R. S. (1968). *Parasitology* **58**, 221.

Hogarth-Scott, R. S., and Bingley, J. B. (1971). *Immunology* **21**, 87.

Hong, R., Ammann, A. J., Cain, W. A., and Good, R. A. (1969). In "The Secretory Immunologic System" (D. H. Dayton, Jr. *et al.*, eds.), pp. 433–445. Nat. Inst. Child Health Hum. Develop., Washington, D.C.

Ishizaka, K., and Ishizaka, T. (1970). *Clin. Exp. Immunol.* **6**, 25.

Ishizaka, K., Ishizaka, T., Tada, T., and Newcomb, R. W. (1969). In "The Secretory

Immunologic System" (D. H. Dayton, Jr. *et al.*, eds.), pp. 71–80. Nat. Inst. Child Health Hum. Develop., Washington, D.C.

Itagaki, S. (1928). *World's Poultry Congr., Rep. Proc. 3rd, 1927.* p. 339.

Jackson, G. J. (1960). *J. Infec. Dis.* 106, 20.

Jacobson, E. B., and Thorbecke, G. J. (1969). *J. Exp. Med.* 130, 287.

Jamaur, M. P., Kim, C. W., and Hamilton, L. D. (1968). *J. Immunol.* 100, 329.

Jarrett, E. E. E., Jarrett, W. F. H., and Urquhart, G. M. (1968). *Exp. Parasitol.* 23, 151.

Jarrett, E. E. E., Urquhart, G. M., and Douthwaite, R. M. (1969). *Exp. Parasitol.* 24, 270.

Jarrett, W. F. H., Jennings, F. W., McIntyre, W. I. M., Mulligan, W., and Sharp, N. C. C. (1961). *Amer. J. Vet. Res.* 22, 186.

Jarrett, W. F. H., Miller, H. R. P., and Murray, M. (1970). *In* "Resistance to Infectious Diseases" (R. H. Dunlop and H. W. Moon, eds.), pp. 287–297. Univ. of Saskatchewan, Canada.

Jenkin, C. R. (1963). *Advan. Immunol.* 3, 351.

Johansson, S. G. O., Mellbin, T., and Vahlquist, B. (1968). *Lancet* 1, 1118.

Jones, V. E., Edwards, A. J., and Ogilvie, B. M. (1970). *Immunology* 18, 621.

Kanyerezei, B., Jaton, J. C., and Block, K. J. (1971). *J. Immunol.* 106, 1411.

Kao, K. Y. T., and McGavack, T. H. (1959). *Proc. Soc. Exp. Biol. Med.* 101, 153.

Kay, A. B. (1970a). *Clin. Exp. Immunol.* 6, 75.

Kay, A. B. (1970b). *Clin. Exp. Immunol.* 7, 723.

Kay, A. B., Stechshulte, D. J., and Austen, K. F. (1971). *J. Exp. Med.* 133, 602.

Kearney, R., and Halliday, W. J. (1970). *Aust. J. Exp. Biol. Med. Sci.* 48, 215.

Keith, R. K. (1967). *Vet. Rec.* 81, 209.

Keller, R. (1971). Cited by Ogilvie and Jones (1971).

Kerr, K. B. (1935). *J. Parasitol.* 21, 124.

Kim, C. W. (1966). *J. Infec. Dis.* 116, 208.

Kim, C. W., Sanel, H., and Hamilton, L. D. (1967a). *J. Immunol.* 99, 1150.

Kim, C. W., Jamaur, M. P., and Hamilton, L. D. (1967b). *J. Immunol.* 99, 1156.

Kline, B. S., Cohen, M. B., and Rudolph, S. A. (1932). *J. Allergy* 3, 531.

Larsh, J. E., Jr. (1963). *Advan. Parasitol.* 1, 213.

Larsh, J. E., Jr. (1967). *Amer. J. Trop. Med. Hyg.* 16, 123.

Larsh, J. E., Jr., Gilchrist, H. B., and Greenberg, B. G. (1952). *J. Elisha Mitchell Sci. Soc.* 68, 1.

Larsh, J. E., Jr., Goulson, H. T., and Weatherly, N. F. (1964a). *J. Elisha Mitchell Sci. Soc.* 80, 133.

Larsh, J. E., Jr., Goulson, H. T., and Weatherly, N. F. (1964b). *J. Parasitol.* 50, 496.

Lawrence, H. S., and Valentine, F. T. (1970). *Ann. N.Y. Acad. Sci.* 169, 269.

Lee, C. L., and Lewert, R. M. (1960). *J. Infec. Dis.* 106, 69.

Lee, D. L. (1969). *Parasitology* 59, 29

Lee, D. L. (1970). *Tissue Cell* 2, 225.

Lees, E. (1962). *Parasitology* 52, 95.

Leonard, A. B., and Leonard, A. E. (1941). *J. Parasitol.* 27, 375.

Lewert, R. M. (1958). *Rice Inst. Pam.* 45, 97.

Lewert, R. M., Lee, C. L., Mandlowitz, S., and Dusanic, K. G. (1959). *J. Infec. Dis.* 105, 180.

Lichtenstein, L. M., and Osler, A. G. (1964). *J. Exp. Med.* **120**, 507.

Litt, M. (1964). *Ann. N.Y. Acad. Sci.* **116**, 964.

Mathies, A. W. (1962). *J. Parasitol.* **48**, 244.

Matsumori, M. (1941). *Keio Igaku* **21**, 67.

Matsumori, M. (1943). *Keio Igaku* **23**, 137.

Mauss, E. A. (1940). *Amer. J. Hyg.* **32**, 80.

Michel, J. F. (1952a). *Nature (London)* **169**, 933.

Michel, J. F. (1952b). *Nature (London)* **169**, 881.

Michel, J. F. (1963). *Parasitology* **53**, 63.

Michel, J. F. (1967). *Nature (London)* **215**, 520.

Michel, J. F. (1968). In "Immunity to Parasites" (A. E. R. Taylor, ed.), pp. 67–89. Blackwell, Oxford.

Michel, J. F., MacKenzie, A., Bracewell, C. D., Cornwell, R. L., Elliot, J., Herbert, C. N., Holman, H. H., and Sinclair, I. J. B. (1965). *Res. Vet. Sci.* **6**, 344.

Miller, H. M., Jr., and Gardiner, M. L. (1934). *Amer. J. Hyg.* **20**, 424.

Miller, J. F. A. P., and Mitchell, G. F. (1968). *J. Exp. Med.* **128**, 801.

Miller, J. F. A. P., and Mitchell, G. F. (1969). *Transplant. Rev.* **1**, 3.

Mills, J. A. (1966). *J. Immunol.* **97**, 239.

Mitchell, G. F., and Miller, J. F. A. P. (1968). *J. Exp. Med.* **128**, 821.

Moss, G. D. (1971). *Parasitology* **62**, 285.

Mota, I., Sadun, E. H., Bradshaw, R. M., and Gore, R. W. (1969). *Immunology* **16**, 71.

Murray, M., Jennings, F. W., Jarrett, W. F. H., and Miller, H. R. P. (1969). In "Pathology of Parasitic Diseases" (S. M. Gaafar, ed.), pp. 197–208. Purdue Univ. Studies, Lafayette, Indiana.

Murray, M., Jarrett, W. F. H., and Jennings, F. W. (1971). *Immunology* **21**, 17.

Nicol, J., and Bilbey, D. L'. (1958). In "Reticuloendothelial Structure and Function" (J. H. Heller, ed.), pp. 301–320. Ronald, New York.

Nossal, G. J. V., Cunningham, A., Mitchell, G. F., and Miller, J. F. A. P. (1968) *J. Exp. Med.* **128**, 839.

Ogilvie, B. M. (1964). *Nature (London)* **204**, 91.

Ogilvie, B. M. (1965). *Parasitology* **55**, 325.

Ogilvie, B. M. (1970). *J. Parasitol.* **56**, No. 4, Sect. II, Part 3, 525–534.

Ogilvie, B. M., and Hockley, D. J. (1968). *J. Parasitol.* **54**, 1073.

Ogilvie, B. M., and Jones, V. E. (1967). *Parasitology* **57**, 335.

Ogilvie, B. M., and Jones, V. E. (1968). *Parasitology* **58**, 939.

Ogilvie, B. M., and Jones, V. E. (1969). In "Cellular and Humoral Mechanisms in Anaphylaxis and Allergy" (H. Z. Movat, ed.), pp. 13–22. Karger, Basel.

Ogilvie, B. M., and Jones, V. E. (1971). *Exp. Parasitol.* **29**, 138.

Ogra, P. L. (1969). In "The Secretory Immunologic System" (D. H. Dayton, Jr. *et al.*, eds.), pp. 259–279. Nat. Inst. Child Health Hum. Develop., Washington, D.C.

Olsen, O. W., and Lyons, E. T. (1965). *J. Parasitol.* **51**, 689.

Oppenheim, J. J., Wolstencroft, R. A., and Gell, P. G. H. (1967). *Immunology* **12**, 89.

Orange, R. P., Stechshulte, D. J., and Austen, K. F. (1970). *J. Immunol.* **105**, 1087.

Orr, T. S. C., and Blair, A. M. J. N. (1969). *Life Sci.* **8**, 1073.

Otto, G. F. (1940). *Amer. J. Hyg.* **31**, 23.

Panter, H. C. (1969). *J. Parasitol.* **55**, 38.

Parfitt, J. W., and Sinclair, W. B. (1967). *Res. Vet. Sci.* 8, 6.

Parish, W. E. (1969). *Brit. J. Dermatol.* **81**, Suppl. 3, 28.

Parish, W. E., and Coombs, R. R. A. (1968). *Brit. J. Haematol.* **14**, 425.

Pavlovski, E. N. (1937). *Izr. Akad. Nauk SSSR Ser. Biol.* **4**, 1385.

Penfold, W. J., and Penfold, H. B. (1937). *J. Helminthol.* **15**, 37.

Peterson, R. D. A., Cooper, M. D., and Good, R. A. (1966). *Amer. J. Med.* **41**, 342.

Prochazka, Z. D., and Mulligan, W. (1965). *Exp. Parasitol.* **17**, 51.

Rhodes, M. B., Nayak, D. P., Kelley, G. W., Jr., and Marsh, C. L. (1965). *Exp. Parsitol.* **16**, 373.

Rowley, D., and Jenkin, C. R. (1962). *Nature (London)* **193**, 151.

Ruddle, N. W., and Waksman, B. H. (1968). *J. Exp. Med.* **128**, 1267.

Sampter, M., Kofoed, M. A., and Piper, W. (1953). *Blood* 8, 1078.

Sandberg, G. (1970). *Acta Pathol. Microbiol. Scand.* **78**, 277.

Sanderson, B. E., and Ogilvie, B. M. (1971). *Parasitology* **62**, 367.

Sandground, J. H. (1929). *Parasitology* **21**, 227.

Sarles, M. P. (1938). *J. Infec. Dis.* **42**, 337.

Sarles, M. P., and Taliaferro, W. H. (1936). *J. Infec. Dis.* **39**, 207.

Schad, G. A. (1963). *Nature (London)* **198**, 404.

Schad, G. A. (1966). *Amer. Natur.* **100**, 359.

Schild, H. O., and Willoughby, D. A. (1967). *Brit. Med. Bull.* **23**, 46.

Schwabe, C. W. (1957). *Amer. J. Hyg.* **65**, 338.

Schwartzman, R. M., Rockey, J. H., and Halliwell, R. E. (1971). *Clin. Exp. Immunol.* **9**, 549.

Smithers, S. R., and Terry, R. J. (1965). *Parasitology* **55**, 701.

Smithers, S. R., Terry, R. J., and Hockley, D. J. (1969). *Proc. Roy. Soc., Ser. B* **171**, 483.

Smyth, J. D. (1966). "The Physiology of Trematodes." Oliver & Boyd, Edinburgh.

Sommerville, R. I. (1954). *Aust. J. Agr. Res.* **5**, 130.

Sommerville, R. I. (1964). *Nature (London)* **202**, 316.

Soulsby, E. J. L. (1962). *Advan. Immunol.* **2**, 265.

Soulsby, E. J. L. (1965). "Textbook of Veterinary Clinical Parasitology," Vol. I. Blackwell, Oxford.

Soulsby, E. J. L. (1969). *In* "Pathology of Parasitic Disease" (S. M. Gaafar, ed.), pp. 243–257. Purdue Univ. Studies, Lafayette, Indiana.

Soulsby, E. J. L. (1970). *J. Parasitol.* **56**, No. 4, Sect. II, Part 3, 534–547.

Soulsby, E. J. L., and Coombs, R. R. A. (1959). *Parasitology* **49**, 505.

Soulsby, E. J. L., and Stewart, D. F. (1959). *Aust. J. Agr. Res.* **11**, 595.

Splitter, E. J., Soulsby, E. J. L., Williams, J. F., and Jeska, E. L. (1967). *Exp. Parasitol.* **20**, 160.

Sprent, J. F. A. (1951). *J. Infec. Dis.* **88**, 168.

Sprent, J. F. A. (1958). *Parasitology* **48**, 184.

Sprent, J. F. A. (1959). *In* "The Evolution of Living Organisms" (G. S. Leeper, ed.), pp. 149–165. Melbourne Univ. Press, Melbourne.

Sprent, J. F. A. (1962). *J. Parasitol.* **48**, 818.

Sprent, J. F. A. (1963). *Parasitology* **53**, 7.

Sprent, J. F. A. (1969). *In* "Immunity to Parasitic Animals" (G. J. Jackson, R. Herman, and I. Singer, eds.), Vol. 1, pp. 1–62. Appleton, New York.

Stanworth, D. R. (1970). *Clin. Exp. Immunol.* **6**, 1.

Stechschulte, D. J., Orange, R. P., and Austen, K. F. (1970). *J. Immunol.* **105**, 1082.

Stewart, D. F. (1950a). *Aust. J. Agr. Res.* 1, 285.
Stewart, D. F. (1950b). *Aust. J. Agr. Res.* 1, 301.
Stewart, D. F. (1950c). *Aust. J. Agr. Res.* 1, 413.
Stewart, D. F. (1953). *Aust. J. Agr. Res.* 4, 100.
Stewart, D. F. (1955). *Nature (London)* 176, 1273.
Stirewalt, M. A. (1963). *Ann. N.Y. Acad. Sci.* 113, 36.
Stoll, N. R. (1929). *Amer. J. Hyg.* 10, 384.
Stunkard, H. W. (1955). *J. Parasitol.* 41, 35.
Sturroch, R. F. (1963). *Parasitology* 53, 189.
Tada, T., and Ishizaka, K. (1970). *J. Immunol.* 104, 377.
Taliaferro, W. H., and Sarles, M. P. (1939). *J. Infec. Dis.* 64, 137.
Taliaferro, W. H., and Sarles, M. P. (1942). *J. Infec. Dis.* 71, 69.
Taylor, E. L., and Michel, J. F. (1953). *J. Helminthol.* 27, 199.
Thorson, R. E. (1953). *Amer. J. Hyg.* 58, 1.
Thorson, R. E. (1954). *Exp. Parasitol.* 3, 9.
Thorson, R. E. (1956). *J. Parasitol.* 42, 21.
Thorson, R. E. (1963). *Exp. Parasitol.* 13, 3.
Thurston, J. P. (1964). *Parasitology* 54, 441.
Tomasi, T. B., and Bienenstock, J. (1968). *Advan. Immunol.* 9, 1.
Tomasi, T. B., and Czerwinski, D. S. (1968). In "Immunologic Deficiency Diseases in Man" (D. Bergsma and R. A. Good, eds.), Vol. IV, No. 1, p. 270. National Foundation, March of Dimes, New York.
Tomasi, T. B., Tan, E. M., Solomon, A., and Prendergast, R. A. (1965). *J. Exp. Med.* 121, 101.
Tran Van Ky, P., Vaucelle, T., Capron, A., and Biguet, J. (1967). *Ann. Inst. Pasteur, Paris* 112, 763.
Urquhart, G. M. (1961). *J. Parasitol.* 47, 857.
Urquhart, G. M. (1970). *J. Parasitol.* 56, No. 4, Sect. II, Part 3, 547–551.
Urquhart, G. M, Mulligan, W., Eadie, R. M., and Jennings, F. W. (1965). *Exp. Parasitol.* 17, 210.
Uvnäs, B., and Wold, J. K. (1967). *Acta Physiol. Scand.* 70, 269.
Veglia, F. (1923). *Rep. Dir. Vet. Res. Union S. Afr.* 9–10, 811.
Wagland, B. M., and Dineen, J. K. (1965). *Aust. J. Exp. Biol. Med. Sci.* 43, 429.
Warren, E. G. (1969). *Aust. Vet. J.* 45, 388.
Weber, W. T. (1967). *Exp. Cell Res.* 46, 464.
Weber, W. T., and Eichholtz, D. (1971). *J. Reticuloendothel. Soc.* 9, 53.
Weinmann, C. J. (1958). *J. Parasitol.* 44, 16.
Weinmann, C. J. (1963). *Proc. Int. Congr. Zool., 16th, 1963* Vol. 1, p. 135.
Weinmann, C. J. (1966). In "The Biology of Parasites" (E. J. L. Soulsby, ed.), pp. 301–320. Academic Press, New York.
Weinstein, P. P. (1967). *Pan Amer Health Organ., Sci. Publ.* 150, 91–99.
Wells, P. D. (1963). *Exp. Parasitol.* 14, 15.
Williams, J. F., and Pérez-Esandi, M. V. (1971). *Immunology* 20, 451.
Williams, J. F., and Soulsby, E. J. L. (1970). *Exp. Parasitol.* 27, 150.
Wilson, R. J. M. (1967). *J. Parasitol.* 53, 752.
Zabriskie, J. B. (1967). *Advan. Immunol.* 7, 147.

⑧ IMMUNE RESPONSE TO TISSUE HELMINTHS

I. Nematodes

L. J. OLSON and N. N. IZZAT

I. Introduction

Tissue nematodes are those species whose adult forms are characteristically found in tissues other than those of the gastrointestinal (GI) tract. By this definition, tissue nematodes would include the filarial worms, guinea worms, some spirurids, lung worms, kidney worms, and several species of the capillarids and related nematodes. Of these groups, only the filarial and lung worms have received any significant amount of study in terms of immunity.

Tissue nematodes may also be defined to include the larva migrans types of infections. In the first type, larval nematodes invade the tissues of hosts other than those hosts in which the pathogen normally develops into an adult. In these infections, the larvae survive in tissues for extended periods of time and cause a disease unlike that associated with the parasite in its normal host. This type of larva migrans includes

223

a number of organisms which have been associated with the "cutaneous and visceral larva migrans" syndromes of man and animals, e.g., *Toxocara canis* larvae.

A second type of larva migrans, known for several species of GI nematodes, occurs in the parasite's normal host when some infective larvae fail to return to the gut following their characteristic tissue migration. These larvae persist in an infective state in deep tissue sites. A fascinating example of this type of larva migrans is transmammary passage of infective larvae to the newborn, a route of infection now known for several species of GI nematodes in domestic animals, e.g., *Ancylostoma caninum* (Stone and Peckham, 1970).

A third type of larva migrans has been reported for several species of GI nematodes in which larvae invade gut tissue of their normal host and enter a state of "arrested development." This state is reversible for reasons, possibly immunological, that are poorly understood, and hence these larvae eventually return to the gut to become adult worms (Michel, 1963; Soulsby, 1966).

In a fourth type of larva migrans, involving GI nematodes in abnormal hosts, the early pathogenesis of the infection approximates that in the normal host, but the full development of the parasite does not occur and the infection is aborted. This type is well documented in experimental work, and probably also occurs in nature. An example of this type is *Ascaris lumbricoides* or *A. suum* infection in the guinea pig where hatching and deep tissue migration into the liver and lungs together with some development occurs as in the normal host, but, following tracheal migration and return to the gut, the infection is aborted (Sprent, 1952). Investigations of this type have resulted in a good deal of basic information on nematode immunity, e.g., cellular reactions, which will be discussed elsewhere.

II. Filaria

The experimental work on immune responses to many of the filarial worms has been held back by the lack of suitable hosts. The chronicity of filarial infections leads one to predict that protective immunity must either develop slowly or be of a relatively low level of efficiency in terms of reducing worm burdens. The immunopathology associated with filarial infections may be the most significant aspect of the immune response to these nematodes.

The best studied of the filarial worms in terms of immunity is *Litomosoides carinii*, a parasite of the pleural and peritoneal cavities of the cotton rat. The extensive studies on this tissue nematode, particularily those of Bertram and Kershaw and their associates in Great Britain and of Scott and his associates in the U.S. have been reviewed by Bertram (1966). These studies have demonstrated that some immunity develops in cotton rats to reinfection; this resistance is expressed by retarded growth and development of worms as well as some reduction in worm burden (Macdonald and Scott, 1953). Retarded development and growth were also shown for challenging worms in cotton rats immunized by surgical transfer of postmigration stages of *L. carinii*, although resistance to challenge of these rats was less than that of rats immunized with infective larvae (Scott and Macdonald, 1958; Scott *et al.*, 1958).

These and other studies by Scott and associates indicate that immunity expressed as retarded growth has a greater effect on early third-stage larvae (i.e., tissue migration stage) than on later stages in the pleural cavity. Furthermore, early third-stage larvae are more immunogenic in this regard than later stages (Scott, 1959).

The response of an abnormal rodent host to *L. carinii* is of interest in that the responses, while qualitatively similar to that in cotton rats, are heightened. After primary infection, less larvae are able to complete their tissue migration to the pleural cavity of white rats. If tissue migration in the white rat is bypassed by surgical transfer of worms from the pleural cavity of the cotton rat, to the peritoneal cavity of white rats, these worms survive during the first month approximately as well as in their normal host. Thereafter, marked encapsulation and reduced survival of worms occurred in the white rat. Third-stage larvae appeared to be more susceptible after transfer than were the more advanced stages (Olson, 1959a).

The increased encapsulation in white rats does not appear to be correlated with a greater number of inflammatory cells per worm in the pleural cavity of white rats, nor with a difference in the types of these cells; eosinophils and lymphoid-macrophage cells were elevated in both hosts. Immunization of white rats by infection resulted in reduced worm burdens in the pleural cavity after challenge and increased encapsulation; cortisone blocked these immune responses. Encapsulated worms were sometimes alive (motile) but many were immobile and of doubtful viability. Eosinophils and lymphoid-macrophage cells were the prominent cell types in the capsule (Olson, 1959b).

Briggs (1963) has reported on the production of precipitating antibody in cotton and white rats repeatedly immunized by infection with *L. carinii*. The serological response was related to the size and frequency of immunizing doses. Briggs also showed that white rats treated with cortisone before infection, i.e., during the antibody-sensitive period, failed to develop detectable precipitating antibody. Cortisone treatment as above or at the time of infection did result in a marked survival of worms in white rats, although the growth and development of these worms was retarded as compared to that of control worms in cotton rats. Briggs' work suggests that precipitating antibody is of doubtful significance in terms of protection.

Work on *L. carinii* by workers in Delhi and Tokyo has extended these earlier studies. Ramakrishnan *et al.* (1962) reported an interesting condition in albino rats in which viable adult worms persisted after the period of microfilaremia, i.e., a latent state. Adult worms taken from rats in this latent state were surgically transplanted to uninfected rats who then developed a microfilaremia; an immune mechanism was postulated for the disappearance of circulating microfilarae in latent infections. Bagai and Subrahmanyam (1968) confirmed the above observation and found that passive immunization of infected rats with sera from rats in a latent state of infection, or sera from rabbits immunized by whole-worm homogenates did not affect the microfilaremias of these rats; according to these authors, both types of sera contained precipitating antibody to *L. carinii* in high titers. These and related experiments (also see Bagai and Subrahmanyam, 1970) led these workers to conclude that circulating antibodies do not protect against this infection and do not affect microfilarae or adult worms. Bagai and Subrahmanyam (1968) interpreted the development of a latent infection as resulting from a local immune reaction (cell-mediated immunity) to microfilariae. They found that the absence of microfilarae in peripheral blood during latent infection did not result from inhibition of microfilarial production by female worms in the pleural cavity.

In a later paper Bagai and Subrahmanyam (1970) reported that microfilarae in the thoracic cavity of rats with latent infection were found with lymphocytes, macrophages, eosinophils, and giant cells adhering to their surface; they reported immobilization of microfilarae by this cell adhesion and regarded this as a prelude to destruction of the microfilarae. They also considered the possibility that microfilariae, after entry into the blood, were destroyed in the lung, spleen, and other sites, but could obtain no histological evidence for such destruction in latent infections.

In the same paper (1970) Bagai and Subrahmanyam reported that rabbit antiserum to rat thymus cells, when added to *in vitro* preparations of microfilarae with cellular adhesion, caused release of these cells from the larvae. Furthermore, injection of this antiserum into the thoracic cavity of rats with latent infection was associated with the reappearance of a microfilaremia. Cortisone treatment and irradiation were also shown to induce microfilaremias in rats with latent infection. Conceivably, these studies on latent *L. carinii* infection will provide a model to explain occult or cryptic filariasis in man and animals.

Some characterization of the antigens of *L. carinii* and the antibodies to this worm has been done, although much remains. Studies of this nature on this and other filarial worms have for the most part been directed toward the practical goal of immunodiagnosis, an aspect of immunity that will be omitted here.

Ishii (1970) has shown that metabolites of *L. carinii* (adults) are antigenic on the basis of complement-fixation and indirect hemagglutination tests with sera from infected cotton rats. He reported that pleural fluid from infected rats was highly antigenic and lacked detectable antibody. The functional significance of these antigens in terms of protection or as allergens is not known. Bagai *et al.* (1968) have shown that adult *L. carinii*, as might be expected, are antigenically complex; twelve different antigens were identified in extracts by immunoelectrophoresis. Some of these antigens were shared with *Dirofilaria* and *Ascaris*, a finding which points out the chronic problem of cross-reactions for investigators seeking species-specific filarial antigens for diagnostic use (e.g., Tanaka *et al.*, 1970).

Fujita and Kobayashi (1969a) have provided some information on the antibody response of cotton rats to *L. carinii* infection. Rats were bled during a 2–51 week period after infection with approximately eighty larvae. A sequential appearance of 17 S (IgM) and 7 S (IgG) was noted. IgM was first detected at 6–7 weeks; titers were elevated through week 12 and then declined. A similar elevation in IgG titers occurred approximately at the time IgM titers started to decline. These workers (Fujita and Kobayashi, 1969b) also reported on the antibody response of cotton rats following surgical transplantation of adult *L. carinii* into the abdominal cavity. Thirty to fifty adult worms were given to each rat; blood was collected during a 5–91 day period. Sera were fractionated and tested for antibody. Earliest titers were recorded for 19 S at 10 days postinfection; the 7 S antibody response was slightly later but after day 18 was predominant, although some 19 S activity persisted until day 91. Two interesting observations on the above data were made by the authors: (1) the onset of antibody was markedly earlier in rats after infection via surgical transplant (10 days) as compared to rats infected by vector and third-stage larvae (6–7 weeks); (2) encapsulation of transplanted worms commenced at about the same time as detectable antibody.

While there are other experimental host–filarial worm systems in addition to the rat–*L. carinii* model, immune studies on these other systems have been limited, with the exception of the recent work on *Brugia malayi* in nonhuman primates and cats (e.g., Wong *et al.*, 1969; Ramachandran, 1970). A basic problem thus far in *Brugia* research has been the difficulty in obtaining quantitative data on worm burdens after challenge. In recent work, El Bihari and Ewert (1971) and Ewert (1971) have developed techniques of infection and recovery of *B. malayi* that should greatly reduce this problem.

III. Lung Worms

A considerable amount of research has been done on the immunity of lung worms, particularily *Dictyocaulus* in cattle. Among the interesting findings in this area of research was the report that a live attenuated vaccine would induce protection in cattle to challenge with *D. viviparus* (Jarrett *et al.*, 1960). The immune response to these pathogens will be discussed elsewhere and hence will be omitted here, except to point out the recent work with *Aelurostrangylus abstrusus*, a lung worm of cats, by Hamilton (1969) who showed that vaccination of cats with small numbers of live larvae leads to a high degree of protection to later infection, and offers a method of controlling the pneumonia associated with this infection in cats.

IV. Larva Migrans—*T. canis*

One of the problems in the experimental study of many of the larva migrans infections has been the lack of suitable laboratory models. For example, there are large gaps in our understanding of the skin disease of man caused by dog and cat hookworm larvae because of inadequate experimental hosts. Hence, the part played by immune reactions in these various host–parasite relationships is not known.

An exception to the problem of suitable laboratory hosts may be made in the case of larva migrans caused by second-stage *T. canis* larvae. This pathogen is well documented as an etiological agent of the visceral larva migrans (VLM) syndrome in man (hyperchronic eosinophilia, hepatomegaly, hypergamma globulinemia, pneumonitis, neurological disorders, ocular infection). The designation "visceral larva migrans" was proposed by Beaver and his associates in 1952 following their identification of the first human cases of this disease in man (review, Beaver, 1956). Chronic VLM, similar to that in man, has subsequently been shown for a variety of mammals following infection with *T. canis*.

This type of larva migrans, i.e., infection of paratenic hosts, may be far more common in man and domestic animals than present evidence shows. For example, on the basis of life cycles and experimental data there are several other species of nematodes that may eventually be shown to cause VLM in man in addition to *T. canis*, e.g., other ascarid larvae and the hookworm larvae of dogs, cats, and other mammals.

A frequent criterion of acquired immunity to nematodes is the ability of the host to reduce the worm burden following a challenge infection. Some data in this regard are available for *T. canis* infections. Lee (1960) reported that superinfected (test) mice harbored about 20% less larvae than challenge controls; however, Lee's challenge control mice that received a single dose equal to the divided doses given test mice suffered at 30% mortality. Hence, it is possible that natural rather than acquired resistance was being tested. Furthermore, as Lee points out, resistance did not correlate with the number of inoculations, i.e., mice given 2000 eggs in 5 or 6 doses harbored more larvae than those given 2000 in 3 or 4 doses. Lee noted that superinfection did influence the distribution of larvae in the body of the mouse with a greater number being recovered in the liver of test mice as compared to controls.

Olson (1962) reported that the worm burden of mice after reinfection with *T. canis* was less than that of control mice. Since group digests were done rather than individual mouse digests to recover larvae, statistical analysis was not possible. Olson (1962) also observed a higher proportion of *T. canis* larvae in the livers of these mice during a 14-day period after reinfection as compared to that for controls. This finding was regarded as evidence of a delayed migration through the liver.

Fernando (1968a) compared the resistance of rabbits given 2 immunizing doses of *T. canis* eggs prior to challenge to that of rabbits receiving only challenge. Fernando's data on worm burden are limited to liver and lung digests; hence, no information is available on total numbers of larvae in the body. Fernando observed that immunized rabbits at 20–43 days after challenge harbored less larvae in the lungs as compared to challenge controls; worm burdens of the livers of these two groups were not strikingly different. He concluded that acquired resistance was directed against larval migration to the lungs.

Fernando (1968a) also concluded that immunization by 2 oral doses of 1200 eggs prior to challenge with 100,000 eggs partially protected rabbits in terms of symptoms and survival following challenge. He also correlated resistance after challenge with increased antibody titers. It should be pointed out that higher titers would be expected in the immunized rabbits on the basis of a greater antigenic stimulus and that these circulating antibodies were not shown to be protective.

Izzat and Olson (1970) reported several experiments of a standard design in which mice were orally immunized during various schedules of sublethal infection prior to oral challenge with 3000 *T. canis* eggs and subsequent total body digests to measure worm burdens. Immunization schedules varied in terms of total numbers of infective eggs and schedule of administration. The results of these experiments showed some reduction in worm burdens after challenge in the mice given multiple immunizing doses (3×1000 eggs; 6×500); however, these differences were not statistically significant. In an attempt to obtain significant protection, the number of eggs in each multiple dose was increased (6×1000); this schedule of immunization resulted in a severe weight loss and a worm burden at autopsy equal to that of control mice. In a similarily designed experiment, Izzat and Olson (1970) also reported on the use of extracts of infective eggs and adult worms (soluble and particulate antigens) in the immunization of mice prior to challenge. Large amounts of these materials (total 4 mg dry weight/mouse) were given subcutaneously in divided doses with Freund's complete adjuvant prior to challenge by infection. Significantly less worms were found in these mice as compared to controls. An additional group of mice, similarily injected with an *Ascaris lumbricoides* adult extract, was found to harbor approximately the same burden of *T. canis* larvae after challenge as that of the control. This latter experiment suggests that protective antigens, not shared with *Ascaris*, are present within the body of infective *T. canis* larvae (and the body of adult *Toxocara*), but that significant amounts of these antigens are not released during an infection—at least during the period of infection in these experiments.

Analysis of serum proteins of mice during these experiments showed that all schedules of immunization (infection or injection of extracts) and challenge caused elevated total proteins, particularily the gamma globulins, and albumin levels dropped. No association could be made between these protein changes and protection. Further analysis of these sera with the indirect hemagglutination test revealed low titers that showed no correlation with immunization schedules or worm burdens. In this connection, Huntley *et al.* (1965) in studies of human cases of VLM reported no relationship between gamma globulin concentrations and duration of symptoms in these children. Furthermore, comparison of gamma globulin levels in patients with or without hepatomegaly did not yield any significant associations. They did get a correlation between the higher globulins concentrations and the presence of precipitating antibody.

Further analysis of the experiments reported by Izzat and Olson (1970) was done on the basis of weight changes. We have noted that a dose of 3000 eggs per mouse (120 to 150/gm body weight) results in weight loss during the next 7 days, which correlates with lung pathology. Data on weight showed that immunization by infection or injection of extracts did not prevent weight loss after challenge with 3000 eggs, although weight losses in the immunized groups were not as marked as that of challenged controls (Izzat and Olson, 1968, unpublished).

Another test of immunity is survival following challenge with doses that are lethal in the nonimmune animal. We (unpublished data) immunized two groups of mice with a single sublethal dose of 170 or 340 eggs/gm body weight (3500 and 7000 eggs/mouse). Twenty-four days later these mice and a control group were challenged with 700 eggs/gm (oral LD_{50} 560 eggs/gm). Deaths were recorded during a 20-day postchallenge period. Some evidence of protection was seen in that deaths were delayed in the immunized groups; however, by day 20 there were essentially no differences in the survival rate of immunized and·controls (20 and 10%, respectively).

The experiments above lead us to the conclusion that *T. canis* larvae do not elicit a strong immune response in terms of preventing reinfection and subsequent deep tissue invasion of these larvae. The observations on the long-term survival of these larvae in various hosts supports the concept of *T. canis* larvae as being weakly immunogenic [e.g., 6 months in mice (Sprent, 1953); 9 and 10 years in monkeys on the basis of liver biopsies (Beaver, 1966)]. In mice, larvae survive for several months in skeletal muscle, brain, and eye (Olson 1962; Olson *et al.*, 1970), and we (Olson and Petteway, 1972) are accumulating information that similar survival takes place in the spinal cord of mice. It may be significant that *T. canis* larvae do not develop beyond the infective second-stage in mice and certain other hosts; hence, no molt occurs, an event that has been associated with the release of antigen and protection against other nematodes (Soulsby, 1962).

Yet, infection with *T. canis* does result in circulating antibody which has been extensively investigated in terms of the immunodiagnosis of this infection (review, Ferguson and Olson, 1967). But the role of circulating antibody in mediating this disease is not clear. Olson (1960) and Hogarth-Scott (1966) have demonstrated that metabolic secretions of second-stage larvae react with sera from infected rabbits and suspected human sera to form precipitates around the mouth and other areas of the larvae. Larvae were also observed to lose motility in homologous antisera. Cross-reactions were noted when *T. canis* larvae were incubated in rabbit anti-*A. lumbricoides* sera. Presumably similar release of metabolic antigen occurs *in vivo*. The nature and functional significance of these precipitates are not known, although on the basis of information from other nematode–host systems these precipitates may represent an enzyme–antienzyme reaction (e.g., antibody to lactic dehydrogenase of *Trichinella spiralis,* Dusanic, 1966).

One of the signs of toxocariasis in children is a hypergamma globulinema with decreased albumin. The characterization of these globulins as to class and specificity is incomplete. Huntley *et al.* (1965) reported that part of the increased globulin in human VLM cases was IgM, but not IgA. Hogarth-Scott *et al.* (1969) reported that antibody of the IgM and IgG classes was formed against *T. canis.* Some evidence also exists that IgG isohemagglutinins develop in children following this infection (Huntley *et al.,* 1969). There is also some evidence of increased IgE in humans with VLM (Hogarth-Scott *et al.,* 1969). And possibly, some of this increase in globulin is not antibody to *T. canis* but rather is nonspecific as has been noted for other infections, e.g., schistosomiasis (Smithers, 1967). A heterophile sheep red cell agglutinin has been reported in children with VLM (Silver *et al.,* 1952); heterophile antibodies to *T. canis* have also been demonstrated experimentally in rabbits with this infection (Fernando, 1968b). The report of Huntley *et al.* (1966) on the high incidence of rheumatoid factor in children with a VLM syndrome is intriguing in terms of a possible transient autoimmune component of this disease.

The increased levels of IgE reported by Hogarth-Scott *et al.* (1969) in children with a diagnosis of VLM and the finding of reaginlike antibodies to *T. canis* in animals (Dobson *et al.,* 1967; Hogarth-Scott, 1967a) support the concept that allergic injury may play a role in toxocariasis as well as in other parasitic infections. The eosinophilia and allergic reactions experimentally associated with this infection (Olson and Schulz, 1963; Sharp and Olson, 1962; Ivey, 1965) may be evidence of IgE-target cell-toxocara antigen reactions leading to the release of vasoactive amines, slow reacting substance-anaphylaxis, and the activation of kinins. However, the role of complement-mediated release and activation of mediators should also be considered.

Studies on the nature of metabolic or somatic antigens of second-stage *T. canis* have not been reported, although some work has been done with somatic fractions of adult *Toxocara.* Jeska (1967, 1970) reported isolation and immunochemical analysis of genus-specific antigens from cuticle and ovarian tissue of adult *T. canis.* Hogarth-Scott (1967b) has reported a molecular weight range of 10,000–50,000 for the allergenic components of adult *T. canis.* Capron *et al.* (1968) found that adult *T. canis* share antigens with several species of mammals, including man.

A frequently observed tissue reaction to *T. canis* larvae (and certain other tissue helminths) is a granuloma, often containing epithelioid and giant cells and associated eosinophils, which suggests that cell-mediated immunity (CMI) may play a role in the disease process. The role of granulomas in terms of injury and destruction of *T. canis* larvae is not clear, but it is clear that such tissue changes and their sequelae in vital organs can to some degree impair the functioning of these organs, e.g., retina. Several investigators have observed morphologically intact larvae within tissue sections of granulomas, which suggests that these larvae are quite resistant to this reaction. There is also some histological evidence that *T. canis* larvae may break out of a granuloma (e.g., Aljeboori *et al.*, 1970). In experiments with pigs, Done *et al.* (1960) associated the onset of clinical nervous signs with the development in the brain of granuloma around dead (PAS negative) or static *T. canis* larvae; histopathological changes of adjacent brain tissue were noted. In this connection the data of Warren and Domingo and Cowan (see Warren and Domingo, 1970) on granuloma formation around schistosome eggs show that this tissue response is largely a manifestation of CMI.

References

Aljeboori, T. I., Stout, C., and Ivey, M. H. (1970). *Amer. J. Trop. Med. Hyg.* **19**, 815.

Bagai, R. C., and Subrahmanyam, D. (1968). *Amer. J. Trop. Med. Hyg.* **17**, 833.

Bagai, R. C., and Subrahmanyam, D. (1970). *Nature (London)* **228**, 682.

Bagai, R. C., Subrahmanyam, D., and Singh, V. B. (1968). *Indian J. Med. Res.* **56**, 1064.

Beaver, P. C. (1956). *Exp. Parasitol.* **5**, 587.

Beaver, P. C. (1966). *In* "The Biology of Parasites" (E. J. L. Soulsby, ed.), pp. 215–227. Academic Press, New York.

Bertram, D. S. (1966). *Advan. Parasitol.* **4**, 255–319.

Briggs, N. T. (1963). *J. Parasitol.* **49**, 255.

Capron, A., Biguet, J., Vernes, A., and Afchain, D. (1968). *Pathol. Biol.* **16**, 121.

Dobson, C., Campbell, R. W., and Webb, A. I. (1967). *J. Parasitol.* **53**, 209.

Done, J. T., Richardson, M. D., and Gibson, T. E. (1960). *Res. Vet. Sci.* **1**, 133.

Dusanic, D. G. (1966). *Exp. Parasitol.* **19**, 310.

El Bihari, S., and Ewert, A. (1971). *J. Parasitol.* **57**, 1170.

Ewert, A. (1971). *J. Parasitol.* **57**, 1039.

Ferguson, E. C., III, and Olson, L. J. (1967). *In* "International Ophthalmology Clinics" (D. M. Gordon, ed.), Vol. 7, pp. 583–603. Little, Brown, Boston, Massachusetts.

Fernando, S. T. (1968a). *Parasitology* **58**, 91.

Fernando, S. T. (1968b). *J. Comp. Pathol.* **78**, 323.

Fujita, K., and Kobayashi, J. (1969a). *Jap. J. Exp. Med.* **39**, 481.

Fujita, K., and Kobayashi, J. (1969b). *Jap. J. Exp. Med.* **39**, 585.

Hamilton, J. M. (1969). *J. Comp. Pathol.* **79**, 161.

Hogarth-Scott, R. S. (1966). *Immunology* **10**, 217.

Hogarth-Scott, R. S. (1967a). *Int. Arch. Allergy Appl. Immunol.* **32**, 201.

Hogarth-Scott, R. S. (1967b). *Immunology* **13**, 535.
Hogarth-Scott, R. S., Johansson, S. G. O., and Bennich, H. (1969). *Clin. Exp. Immunol.* **5**, 619.
Huntley, C. C., Costas, M. C., and Lyerly, A. (1965). *Pediatrics* **36**, 523.
Huntley, C. C., Costas, M. C., Williams, R. C., Lyerly, A. D., and Watson, R. G. (1966). *J. Amer. Med. Ass.* **197**, 124.
Huntley, C. C., Lyerly, A. D., and Patterson, M. V. (1969). *J. Amer. Med. Ass.* **208**, 1145.
Ishii, A. (1970). *Jap. J. Exp. Med.* **40**, 39.
Ivey, M. H. (1965). *Amer. J. Trop. Med. Hgy.* **14**, 1044.
Izzat, N. N., and Olson, L. J. (1970). *Can. J. Zool.* **48**, 1063.
Jarrett, W. F. H., Jennings, F. W., McIntyre, W. I. M., Mulligan, W., and Urquhart, G. M. (1960). *Immunology* **3**, 145.
Jeska, E. L. (1967). *J. Immunol.* **98**, 1290.
Jeska, E. L. (1970). *J. Parasitol.* **55**, 465.
Lee, H.-F. (1960). *J. Parasitol.* **46**, 583.
Macdonald, E. M., and Scott, J. A. (1953). *Exp. Parasitol.* **2**, 174.
Michel, J. F. (1963). *Parasitology* **53**, 63.
Olson, L. J. (1959a). *J. Parasitol.* **45**, 182.
Olson, L. J. (1959b). *J. Parasitol.* **45**, 519.
Olson, L. J. (1960). *Tex. Rep. Biol. Med.* **18**, 473.
Olson, L. J. (1962). *Tex. Rep. Biol. Med.* **20**, 651.
Olson, L. J., and Petteway, M. B. (1972). *J. Parasitol.* (in press).
Olson, L. J., and Schulz, C. W. (1963). *Ann. N.Y. Acad. Sci.* **113**, 440.
Olson, L. J., Izzat, N. N., Petteway, M. B., and Reinhart, J. A. (1970). *Amer. J. Trop. Med. Hyg.* **19**, 238.
Ramachandran, C. P. (1970). *Southeast Asian J. Trop. Med. Pub. Health* **1**, 78.
Ramakrishnan, S. P., Singh, D., and Krishnaswami, A. K. (1962). *Indian J. Malariol.* **16**, 263.
Scott, J. A. (1959). *An. Inst. Med. Trop. Lisbon* **16**, Supl. 6.
Scott, J. A., and Macdonald, E. M. (1958). *J. Parasitol.* **44**, 187.
Scott, J. A., Macdonald, E. M., and Olson, L. J. (1958). *Amer. J. Trop. Med. Hyg.* **7**, 70.
Sharp, A. D., and Olson, L. J. (1962). *J. Parasitol.* **48**, 362.
Silver, H. K., Henderson, P., and Contopoulos, A. (1952). *Amer. J. Dis. Child.* **83**, 649.
Smithers, S. R. (1967). *In* "Immunologic Aspects of Parasitic Infections," pp. 43–49. World Health Organ., Washington, D.C.
Soulsby, E. J. L. (1962). *Advan. Immunol.* **2**, 265–308.
Soulsby, E. J. L. (1966). *In* "The Biology of Parasites" (E. J. L. Soulsby, ed.), pp. 255–276. Academic Press, New York.
Sprent, J. F. A. (1952). *J. Infec. Dis.* **90**, 165.
Sprent, J. F. A. (1953). *J. Infec. Dis.* **92**, 114.
Stone, W. M., and Peckham, J. C. (1970). *Amer. J. Vet. Res.* **31**, 1693.
Tanaka, H., Fujita, K., Sasa, M., Tagawa, M., Naito, M., and Kurokawa, K. (1970). *Jap. J. Exp. Med.* **40**, 47.
Warren, K. S., and Domingo, E. O. (1970). *Exp. Parasitol.* **27**, 60.
Wong, M. M., Fredericks, J. H., and Ramachandran, C. P. (1969). *Bull. WHO* **40**, 493.

9 IMMUNE RESPONSE TO TISSUE PARASITES

II. Cestodes

M. A. GEMMELL and F. N. MACNAMARA

I. Introduction

Organisms of the class Cestoda have adapted to occupy a niche in relatively specific food chains. It is the embryonic hexacanth form which invades the tissues of the prey or intermediate host. Following invasion, a sequence of events occurs which leads to the reorganization and multiplication of specific cells in the oncosphere to form the metacestode complete with bladder or modification of it and larval scolex or scolices. The healthy metacestode (except for *Hymenolepis nana*) remains in this form until released into a nontissue environment in the predator or definitive host.

The immune response of the mammalian host following an antigenic stimulation by larval cestodes involves the production of an altered state which may (a) have no deleterious effect on the host or parasite; (b) result in a reaction which is directly beneficial or harmful to the parasite; and (c) result in a state of clinical hypersensitivity which may be harmful to the host and indirectly harmful or beneficial to the parasite. In considering specific mechanisms, reasonable discussion must be confined to those that are generally accepted, namely the inactivation or killing of the parasite by (d) humoral antibody with or without the cooperation of complement and other nonspecific mechanisms which are enhanced by specific mechanisms; (e) adverse effects due to an immediate or antibody-induced hypersensitivity; and (f) cell-mediated immunity with cytotoxic activity and effects consequence upon delayed-type hypersensitivity.

It is an *a priori* assumption that the antigenic macromolecules of the various parasitic cells and of their secretions can in appropriate systems induce an immunogenic (allergic) response. It cannot, however, be assumed that all of the potential antigens, many of which can be demonstrated (Kagan and Norman, 1963a; Kagan and Agosin, 1968), are automatically inducers of an immune response in the host or that they are necessarily subjected to an immune response which may have been induced by identical antigens from another parasite at another stage of development. It also cannot be assumed that, because a response is demonstrable against a certain stage in an immune animal, that stage during the immunization process was solely, or even in part, the generator of the response or was affected by it. Thus, it is necessary not only to determine which mechanism was operative in protecting the host, but also to define which developmental stage of the parasite produced antigens that initiated one or more of the various mechanisms. The problems of sifting the evidence are further complicated by the realization that an immune mechanism acting upon a parasite may have a delayed effect which may not be manifested until a later stage of development is reached by that parasite (Bertram, 1966; Lang, 1967; Gemmell *et al.*, 1968a).

Reviews on the pertinent literature indicate that strong immunity can be acquired and can be artificially induced (Weinmann, 1966, 1970; Gemmell and Soulsby, 1968). Owing to the complexity of the problems presented and because we believe that there are many as yet undemonstrated interactions associated with the numerous morphological structures and physiological processes, we have reviewed certain aspects of the developmental biology of vertebrate and invertebrate metacestodes before examining existing knowledge of the antigens produced by the different stages and the reactions mounted against them. Finally, the significance of immunity in limiting cestode populations is discussed in the light of that knowledge. Limitations of space restrict the review to the order Cyclophyllidea.

II. Mode of Infection and Cellular Reorganization

Comprehensive reviews have been given on ontogeny (Stunkard, 1962); on biology of life cycles (Smyth, 1963), biochemistry (Read and Simmons, 1963; von Brand, 1966), embryogenesis (Rybicka, 1966), cestode cuticle (Lee, 1966), postoncospheral differentiation (Voge, 1967a), physiology (Smyth, 1969a), and pathogenesis (Smyth and Heath, 1970). Specific reviews on *Echinococcus* spp. have been made with reference to biology (Smyth, 1964, 1969b; Lupascu and Panaitescu, 1968) and serodiagnosis (Kagan, 1968a; Kagan and Agosin, 1968).

A. The Hatching of the Egg in the Intestinal Lumen

Studies on the fine structure of the taeniid and hymenolepid-type egg demonstrate that complex layers surround the hexacanth embryo

(Inatomi, 1962; Morseth, 1965; Nieland, 1968; Pence, 1970). Whereas differences exist in the chemical requirements for hatching taeniid eggs, the events which occur are similar for all species studied. These include: (a) dissolution of the outer embryophoral membrane; (b) disaggregation of the embryophoral blocks and disintegration of the inner embryophoral membrane; (c) chemical activation of the hexacanth embryo; and (d) mechanical and possibly chemical disruption of the oncospheral membrane with release of the embryo (Isobé, 1922; Yoshino, 1933a; Bullock et al., 1934; Leonard and Leonard, 1941; Wantland, 1953; Silverman, 1954a,b; Berberian, 1957; Meyers, 1957; Jones et al., 1960; Meymerian, 1961; Huffman and Jones, 1962; Gönnert et al., 1967; Laws, 1968; Gönnert and Thomas, 1969; Gönnert, 1970). The chemical hatching requirements differ for the hymenolepids, but, allowing for differences in structure, the physical events which occur are similar (Isobé, 1926; Voge and Berntzen, 1961; Berntzen and Voge, 1962, 1965; Collings and Hutchins, 1965).

Apart from the disaggregation of the blocks of taeniid eggs, which have been shown to be a keratin (Johri, 1957; Morseth, 1966; Pence, 1967), and disorganization of the various membranes, a secretion(s) is expressed from epidermal glands. These glands may serve some common functions in vertebrates and invertebrates, since they have been described in the oncospheres of several genera (Reid, 1948; Millemann, 1955; Ogren, 1957, 1958a, 1959; Enigk and Sticinsky, 1957; Gallati, 1959; Sawada, 1960, 1961; Hickman, 1963; Pence, 1967) including taeniids (Silverman, 1954b; Silverman and Maneely, 1955; Bilques, 1968; Nieland, 1968) and hymenolepids (Reid, 1948; Ogren, 1955, 1958b, 1961; Hickman, 1964; Collin, 1969; Pence, 1970). Histochemical studies suggest that the secretion may be a mucopolysaccharide (Silverman and Maneely, 1955; Sawada, 1961), but ultrastructure studies show that two types of granules are present in the glands and that more than one secretion may be expressed (Collin, 1969; Pence, 1970).

B. The Process of Penetration

Penetration of the intestine represents the first stage of tissue parasitism. Yoshino (1933b) observed the penetration of the intestine of the pig by *Taenia solium*. H. T. Chen (1934) described the physical movements of *Dipylidium caninum* into the intestinal mucosa of *Ctenocephalides felis*. Penetration into the mammalian gut by *Taenia pisiformis* and *Taenia saginata* takes place within 10–40 minutes (Silverman and Maneely, 1955) and by *Taenia taeniaeformis* within 30 minutes (Banerjee and Singh, 1969). The oncospheres of *T. pisiformis, Taenia serialis, Echinococcus granulosus, Taenia ovis,* and *Taenia hydatigena* penetrate through the tips of the villi in the jejunal region of the rabbit and sheep appropriately and continue to migrate down the villus until a venule of sufficient size is reached (Heath, 1970a, 1971).

The role of the hooklets, which also appear to be in part a keratin (Morseth, 1966; Pence, 1967), in aiding penetration is not disputed. A chemical or physical role has been suggested for the secretion from the epidermal glands either by eroding the intestinal cells or by adhesive properties assisting the hooklets to obtain a firmer purchase or by a lubricating effect assisting the organism to squeeze between the epithelial cells (H. T. Chen, 1934; Reid, 1948; Ogren, 1955, 1957; Silverman and Maneely, 1955; Sawada, 1961; Barker, 1970). Lewart and Lee (1955) were unable to demonstrate changes in host glycoprotein during the penetration of *T. taeniaeformis* and Barker (1970) failed to detect any lytic effect during the penetration of *T. pisiformis.* Heath (1970a, 1971), on the other hand, also working with normal nonimmune rabbits, observed lysis of the columnar epithelium and parenchyma cells in juxtaposition to actively penetrating *T. pisiformis* and suggested that several enzymes assisted penetration and migration into the tissues.

C. PASSIVE TRANSLOCATION AND ACTIVE TRAVERSING OF TISSUES

Normally, *H. nana* develops in the intestinal wall of rodents, but since cysticercoids have been found in extraintestinal sites (Mahon, 1954) including lymph nodes (Price, 1930; Garkavi, 1956; Garkavi and Glebova, 1957; Astafiev, 1966a,b,c; Solonenko, 1969), these organisms are capable of translocation.

All taeniids develop in extraintestinal sites. Translocation of *T. granulosus* from the intestinal villus to the liver takes place via the portal system (Dew, 1925) and may for *T. pisiformis* occur within 40 minutes (Barker, 1970). Those organisms which develop in extrahepatic sites traverse this organ and in some cases also the lung to reach the appropriate site for postoncospheral differentiation. Direct translocation via lymph drainage has been postulated for *E. granulosus* to explain variations in the lung:liver ratios but the evidence is equivocal (Tenhaeff and Ferwerda, 1935; Dévé, 1942, 1949; Heath, 1970a, 1971).

D. POSTONCOSPHERAL REORGANIZATION

The initial posthexacanth stage of hymenolepids represents a time of synthetic activity and cell growth and the larva is formed from specific germinal cells within the oncosphere (Ogren, 1962, 1967, 1968a,b). The ultrastructure of the hatched oncosphere and its early reorganizing stages has been described by Collin (1968, 1969, 1970).

1. In Invertebrates

Of all the species with a tissue phase in invertebrates only *Hymenolepis nana* is also, in that phase, capable of parasitizing vertebrates. The pattern of cellular reorganization in the latter follows a similar course of events as in invertebrates (Hunninen, 1935a; Di Conza, 1968; Weinmann, 1968a). The gross cellular reorganization of the oncosphere has been described for a number of genera in invertebrates (Venard, 1938; Rendtorff, 1948; Freeman, 1952; Millemann, 1955; Gallati, 1959; Hickman, 1963) including the hymenolepids (Voge, 1956, 1960a; Voge and Heyneman, 1957; Rybicka, 1957; Rothman, 1957; Schiller, 1959; Ogren, 1962; Marshall, 1967). Although temperature affects the speed of reorganization (Voge, 1959a,b, 1961a,b; Voge and Turner, 1956; Voge and Heyneman, 1958), the events which occur include Stage 1, formation of a spherical ball of cells; Stage 2, formation of a central cavity; Stage 3, increased growth and reorganization into distinct regions; Stage 4, withdrawal of the scolex; Stage 5, completion of development (Voge and Heyneman, 1957). The outer layer of the mature cysticercoid in contact with the tissue is thin and surrounds the whole organism. The scolex contains the attachment organs and most of the nervous, excretory, and muscle systems of the adult and is retracted and thus separated from the host tissues by two thicknesses of the bladder wall (Voge, 1960b, 1961c, 1963a; Voge and Heyneman, 1960).

2. In Vertebrates

The cysticercus can be regarded as the archetypal form of taeniid metacestode. Little, however, is known of the mode of transformation of the oncosphere into a bladder in vertebrates. Slais (1966a–e, 1967, 1970), has given a detailed description of the formation of the scolex anlage of *T. solium, T. saginata, T. hydatigena,* and *Taenia crassiceps* and its mode of differentiation from specific cells in the mother bladder wall together with an account of aberrant forms of development.

Most of the studies on larval development have been concerned with the time taken for the organism to: (a) become visible to the naked eye; (b) migrate; (c) develop a scolex anlage; (d) develop hooks and suckers; (e) become infective to the definitive host; and (f) induce an inflammatory response. The species studied include *T. solium* (Yoshino, 1933b,c), *T. saginata* (McIntosh and Miller, 1960; Silverman and Hulland, 1961), *T. hydatigena* (Pullin, 1955; Sweatman and Plummer, 1957), *T. ovis* (Sweatman and Henshall, 1962), *T. pisiformis* (Crusz, 1948a,b; Potsueleva, 1953), *T. crassiceps* (Freeman, 1962, 1964; Bilques, 1969; Bilques and Freeman, 1969), and *Taenia twitchelli* (Rausch, 1959). Comparable studies have been made on the strobilocercus of *T. taeniaeformis* (Bullock and Curtis, 1924; Mlodianowska, 1931; Kan, 1933; Crusz, 1947, 1948a; Lewert and Lee, 1955; Hutchison, 1958; Orihara, 1962; Singh and Rao, 1969) and on the hydatid cyst of *E. granulosus* (Dévé, 1916; Dew, 1925, 1928; Webster and Camberon, 1961) and *E. multilocularis* (Rausch, 1954; Mankau, 1956a,b, 1957; Yamashita *et al.*, 1958; Yamashita, 1960; Ohbayashi, 1960; Webster and Cameron, 1961).

Depending on the species and host parasitized and the site of development, the reorganizing oncosphere together with the associated inflammatory response becomes visible to the naked eye within about 1 week. Active migration as manifested by the presence of tracks coincides with the formation of muscle tissue (Heath and Smyth, 1970) and begins after the early posthexacanth reorganization, but before the development of a scolex anlage. It is initiated within 1 week for *T. pisiformis* and *T. taeniaeformis* and 2 weeks in the case of *T. hydatigena, T. ovis, T. solium, T. saginata,* and *Taenia multiceps.* Since hooks have not developed at this stage, migration may be assisted by enzymatic action of the parasite. The significance of enzymatic activity during penetration and migration of tissue parasites has been reviewed by Lewert (1958), Lewert and Lee (1954, 1955), and Stirewalt (1963). A necrotizing effect on host tissues by *T. multiceps* has been suggested by Larsh *et al.* (1965).

Depending on the species, the scolex anlage begins to form between the third and fifth week, but full development may not occur until after the ninth week. The mature cysticercus has two histologically distinct regions comprising the bladder wall and an invaginated scolex (Logachev, 1959; Schiller, 1960). The former encloses the fluid and the latter contains hooks which have been shown to be keratin in part (Crusz, 1947, 1948a; Gallagher, 1964; Baron, 1968) together with other structures of the adult form (Rees, 1951; Voge, 1962, 1963b; Slais, 1966b, 1967, 1970). The outer layer of the cysticercus, strobilocercus, and coenurus in contact with the tissues of the host is a living membrane involved in the uptake of nutrients. Histochemical studies indicate that there is a complex enzyme system (Waitz, 1963; Bogitsh, 1967). Ultrastructure studies show that the surface of the tegument of the bladder is raised in microtriches. The plasma membrane which covers the surface of the tegument is continuous with the microtriches (Waitz, 1961;

Sidiqui, 1963; Race *et al.*, 1965; Baron, 1968). In almost all situations, a fibrous tissue capsule of host origin is laid down during the process of development and this is the point of contact between the host and the living cytoplasmic layer of the parasite. Within the cystic capsule, lymphocytes and other cells can frequently be detected (Race *et al.*, 1965; Sinclair, 1970), indicating that the tissue cyst wall does not form a barrier to the transfer of large molecules between the tissues and the bladder wall of the metacestode. The scolex of the cysticercus is invaginated and the scolex has only a single-layered bladder wall separating it from the tissues of the host.

The reorganization of the hydatid oncosphere includes vesiculization and brood capsule formation. The whole process may take 1 to 4 months for *E. multilocularis*, but more than 1 year for *E. granulosus*. Ultrastructure studies show that the germinal membrane is a thin-walled nucleated structure and is continuous with the brood capsule wall and the tegument of the protoscolices (Morseth, 1967; Sakamoto and Sugimura, 1969). The germinal layer is surrounded by a complex mucopolysaccharide laminated membrane (Kilejian *et al.*, 1962) which at least in *in vitro* culture originates from the germinal layer (Yamashita, 1960; Yamashita *et al.*, 1962; Smyth, 1962), although it may consist of both host and parasite material *in vivo* (Schwabe, 1959).

3. In Vitro

Monoxenic culture of the oncospheres of *H. diminuta* has been achieved (Graham and Berntzen, 1970). Successful axenic culture of *Mesocestoides* from oncosphere to mature tetrathyridium has also been demonstrated (Voge, 1967b; Voge and Seidel, 1968). Partial success has also been achieved in the culture of oncospheres of *E. granulosus*, *T. hydatigena*, *T. ovis*, *T. pisiformis*, and *T. multiceps* (Heath, 1970a; Heath and Smyth, 1970).

The specific stages of development of the taeniids include Stage 1, cell reorganization; Stage 2, cell multiplication; Stage 3, cavity formation; Stage 4, cytoplasmic reorganization and, for migratory species, formation of muscles; Stage 5, further cavity formation; Stage 6, further growth and, for migratory species, movement; Stage 7, differentiation of the scolex anlage with continued growth of the bladder. The first three stages represent Ogren's (1962) posthexacanth condition and are similar to those described by Voge and Heyneman (1957) in invertebrates. Subsequent histological reorganization represents the development of the mother bladder and the formation of the scolex anlage described by Slais (1970) in vertebrates.

E. Asexual Reproduction

Asexual reproduction is a characteristic of certain species. This may take place by polyembrony by endogenous budding of the protoscolex in special brood capsules (Dew, 1922) or directly from the cyst wall of the coenurus of *T. multiceps* (Clapham, 1940). Exogenous budding is a characteristic of *T. crassiceps* (Freeman, 1962), *T. twitchelli* (Rausch, 1959), and some other taeniids (Voge, 1954) and for the vesicular formation of *E. multilocularis* (Rausch, 1954; Ohbayashi, 1960) and sometimes for *T. multiceps* (Clapham, 1940; Yamashita *et al.*, 1957a; Voge and Berntzen, 1963). Fission appears to be a common method of propagation of *Mesocestoides corti* (Sprecht and Voge, 1965) and sometimes of *T. pisiformis in vivo* (Crusz, 1948b) and *in vitro* (Heath and Smyth, 1970).

In the case of *E. granulosus*, the protoscolex may revert into a bladder (daughter cyst) in the infected animal and will do so if serially transferred to a receptive rodent host such as the mouse (Dévé, 1933a,b, 1934a, 1935, 1946, 1949; Coutelen, 1936a,b; De Cooman, 1937; De Waale and De Cooman, 1938a,b; Coutelen *et al.*, 1939; Batham, 1957; Schwabe *et al.*, 1959, 1964, 1970; Yamashita *et al.*, 1960; Webster and Cameron, 1961; Sweatman *et al.*, 1963a; Sorice *et al.*, 1964; Schwabe and Yamashita, 1968; Pennoit-De Cooman and De Rycke, 1970; Heath, 1970a,b) or if grown in unsuitable media for strobilization *in vitro* (Dévé, 1926, 1928; Coutelen, 1927a,b; Sergeeva and Euranova, 1962; Smyth, 1962, 1967, 1968; Gurri, 1963; Schwabe *et al.*, 1963; Pauluzzi *et al.*, 1965; Smyth *et al.*, 1966; Benex, 1968a,b,c). The protoscolex of *E. multilocularis* may also revert under similar *in vivo* or *in vitro* conditions (Yamashita *et al.*, 1957b, 1960, 1962, 1963a; Lukashenko, 1960; Norman and Kagan, 1961; Webster and Cameron, 1961, 1963). In addition, the germinal membrane of this latter species can propagate in the absence of the protoscolices *in vitro* (Rausch and Jentoft, 1957; Lukashenko, 1964; Sakamoto and Kotani, 1967) and individual germinal cells will proliferate (Sakamoto *et al.*, 1967) and vesicles will continue vegetative propagation *in vivo* by serial transmission (Lubinsky, 1960a,b, 1967, 1968, 1969). Successful larval multiplication *in vitro* has been described for *Mesocestoides corti* (Voge and Coulombe, 1966) and for *T. crassiceps* (Robinson *et al.*, 1963; Voge, 1963c).

F. Longevity of Metacestodes

Metacestodes which propagate vegetatively can be transferred serially indefinitely. An original metacestode, however, having reached the infective stage can also survive *in vivo* for considerable periods. In the case of *E. granulosus* and *T. solium,* there is circumstantial medical evidence that these may survive for more than 30 years. Despite early conclusions (H. B. Penfold, 1937; W. J. Penfold and Penfold, 1937) to the contrary, experimental evidence for the survival of *T. saginata* in cattle for 2 years has been demonstrated (Dewhirst *et al.,* 1963; Froyd, 1964; Urquhart and Brocklesby, 1965; van den Heever, 1967). Age per se of cattle at an initial exposure to a large number of eggs was not found to influence the susceptibility to infection, but its effect on metacestode survival was not determined (Vegors and Lucker, 1971). It has, however, been suggested that light rather than heavy infections acquired early in life may persist (Urquhart and Brocklesby, 1965), and it seems likely that, under certain circumstances, *T. saginata* may survive for the lifetime of the host (Urquhart, 1961). Immunological factors which may be involved in survival of the metacestode are discussed in Section VII.

III. General Factors Associated with Early Deaths

Many workers studying the development, longevity, and histopathology of larval cestodes in previously uninfected vertebrates have emphasized that (a) the number of larvae which develop is not necessarily proportional to the number of eggs fed; (b) deaths occur throughout the period of development; (c) inflammatory reactions are excessive in juxtaposition to dead or dying organisms; and (d) abnormal morphogenesis of the bladder wall and failure to form a scolex anlage are common observations. In some respects, however, it seems that the rate of development may be related to the intensity of the inflammatory response (Silverman and Hulland, 1961).

A. Host Factors

Age, strain, and sex of rodents have been incrimated as possible causes for variations in the establishment and subsequent development of *T. taeniaeformis* (Greenfield, 1942; Curtis *et al.,* 1933; Campbell, 1939; Feng and Hoeppli, 1939; Fortuyn and Feng, 1940; Campbell and Melcher, 1940; Rohde, 1960; Dow and Jarrett, 1960; Shults and Andreeva, 1960; Orihara, 1962; Olivier, 1962a; Hinz, 1965). Similar observations have been made for *H. nana* (Hunninen, 1935b,c; Larsh, 1944a, 1946a, 1951) and for *Echinococcus* spp. (Schwabe *et al.,* 1959; Yamashita *et al.,* 1958, 1963b; Ohbayashi, 1960; Sorice *et al.,* 1964; Ohbayashi and Sakamoto, 1966).

A number of factors may reduce or enhance natural resistance to taeniids or hymenolepids including cortisone (Olivier, 1962b; Esch, 1964, 1967), endotoxins (Weinmann, 1965); thyroid extracts, protein deficient diet, anemia, alcohol, pregnancy, body temperatures or variations in intestinal emptying time (Larsh, 1943, 1944b, 1945, 1946b, 1947a,b, 1949, 1950a,b), and concurrent nematode infections (Larsh and Donaldson, 1944; Larsh and Campbell, 1952).

B. PARASITE FACTORS

Egg batches used may vary not only between worms, but also in different segments in the same worm (Silverman, 1954b; Hinz, 1962), as well as from anomalous worms (Esch and Murrell, 1968). Strains differ in their ability to invade and develop in a given normal host. This is well demonstrated by the "rat" and "mouse" strains of *H. nana* (Shorb, 1933; Larsh, 1944a). Smyth and Smyth (1964) have pointed out that *Echinococcus* has a mode of sexual and asexual reproduction that favors the expression of mutants. They suggest that *E. granulosus* and *E. multilocularis* represent two extreme points on a theoretical speciation scale and between these two extremes there exists a number of strains with morphological, physiological, and immunological characteristics tending towards one or other end of the scale. Certainly there is evidence that different strains of *Echinococcus* vary in their ability to infect and survive (Bacigalupo, 1933; Dévé, 1935, 1938; Coutelen *et al.*, 1939; Pennoit-De Cooman, 1940; Euzéby, 1962; Sweatman and Williams, 1963; Williams and Sweatman, 1963; Rausch, 1963, 1967, 1968; Rausch and Nelson, 1963; Verster, 1965; Dailey and Sweatman, 1965; Gill and Rao, 1967). Strain differences may well account for variations in hosts and predilection sites successfully parasitized by *T. multiceps* (Clapham, 1942; Esch and Self, 1965; Esch, 1967).

IV. Methodology in Measuring the Immune Response

A. HISTORICAL

Early experiments using *T. taeniaeformis*, *T. pisiformis*, or *H. nana* in small laboratory animals demonstrated that specific resistance with varying degrees of efficiency could (a) be acquired or artificially induced (Miller, 1930, 1931a,b,c, 1932a,b; Miller and Kerr, 1932; Miller and Massie, 1932; Kerr, 1934, 1935; Hunninen, 1935b, 1936; Campbell, 1936; Hearin, 1941; Larsh, 1944c); (b) be transferred via serum or from maternal sources (Miller, 1932c,d, 1934, 1935; Miller and Gardiner, 1932a,b, 1934; Kerr, 1934, 1935; Sima, 1937; Hearin, 1941; Larsh, 1942, 1944c); (c) be altered in effect in recipients by transferring serum from donors at different times during an infection (Campbell, 1938a,b,c); (d) be involved with an accelerated tissue response (Leonard, 1940); and (e) be varied by injecting oncospheres into the mesenteric vein, thereby bypassing an intestinal phase of immunity (Leonard and Leonard, 1941).

Subsequent to this promising early work with metacestodes of laboratory animals, attention was paid more to diagnostic serological techniques than to an analysis of immune mechanisms; and it is only in the past 15 years that there has been a resurgence of effort to understand the fundamental processes of protective immunity.

B. Theoretical Considerations

A number of developmental stages discussed in previous sections provides points of reference for studying the immune responses. Ideally, experiments should show (a) the presence and composition of the antigens which at least are subjected to and affected by an immune response; (b) evidence that the observed effects have been initiated at that specific stage and not at preceding stages of reorganization; (c) the origin of the antigens and the parasitic stage which liberated or exposed them; (d) evidence on tolerance induction in the host; (e) antigenic mutability of the parasite.

1. In Vitro

Cestode antigens in the past have been prepared from homogenates of strobilate, or larval tissue or fluids (Miller, 1930, 1931a,c, 1932a,b; Miller and Kerr, 1932; Dévé, 1927, 1933a, 1934b,c; Kerr, 1934, 1935; Campbell, 1936; Sima, 1937; Turner et al., 1937; Larsh, 1944c; Moya and Blood, 1964; Evranova and Yashina, 1966; Sorice et al., 1966a). The procedures used could not inter alia distinguish whether components resembling host proteins are adsorbed or synthesized by the parasites. The enumeration, separation, and differentiation of antigens has been greatly aided by immunodiffusion techniques and by the separation of protein fractions by column chromatography. The culture of the organism in invertebrates or in vitro, if this can be done in the absence of host protein, may provide the means for obtaining the important parasite components for identification.

Antibodies of the different classes IgG, IgA, IgM, and IgE with their distinctive properties have been differentiated in most experimental laboratory animals; thus, humoral antibodies will be increasingly described in terms of the class to which they belong (Kagan, 1968a,b; Kagan *et al.,* 1968; Moriarty, 1968; Di Conza, 1969). Since antibodies of these classes may be distinguished by their own inherent antigenicity, their presence may be detected by fluorochrome conjugated antibodies prepared against them. Hence, the attachment of antibodies of the different classes to sites on the reorganizing metacestode should now be demonstrable.

It can also be anticipated that the electron microscope will reveal details of damage done to the reorganizing oncosphere as well as to the metacestode, particularly with reference to any synergistic effect of complement. In addition, the *in vitro* demonstration of cell-mediated immunity employing techniques of lymphocytic transformation or macrophage migration inhibition is now sufficiently well advanced to warrant its use with cestode antigens.

2. *In Vivo*

In order to determine the stage of reorganization affected by an immune reaction, the exposure of the organism to that response must be made within defined time limits. This can be achieved by growing the organism in a host rendered immunologically incompetent before supplying the immune response (De Sa and Coleman, 1964; Friedberg *et al.,* 1967, 1970). Such a procedure is possible for serum transfer using heterogenic animals, but isogenic animals are required to study cell-mediated responses. In studies involving cell transfer designed to demonstrate the latter, preparations from spleens are far less satisfactory than those from lymph nodes, since splenic lymphocytes are much more likely to transform into immunoglobulin-producing plasma cells. Therefore, if splenic cells are used (Nemeth, 1970), observations on any subsequent antibody titers are even more essential if the experiment is to have any meaning (Blundell *et al.,* 1969).

C. Analysis of Data

An arithmetic normal distribution may be expected if the observed events are derived purely by chance and if any other factors involved are also influenced purely by chance and are independent of other events. If, however, the second or subsequent events are influenced in a multiplicative way by the previous events, then a logarithmic normal curve may be expected. In multiplication logarithms are added; therefore, the variances as logarithmic transformations can be added and the curves will remain log normal.

In describing their results, most authors usually provide information on the mean and standard deviation. Nevertheless, few have stated whether or not the distribution approaches one that is normal. This is disappointing not only because means and standard deviations per se have less meaning if applied to curves that are not normal, but also because the type of distribution may give reviewers a valuable guide as to the processes that might have led to that distribution (Cassie, 1954; Southwood, 1966; Sokal and Rohlf, 1969).

One of the simplest ways to determine whether a distribution is arithmetic or logarithmic normal is to plot the data on probability papers and to determine whether straight lines are observed on the arithmetic or logarithmic sheets. If the distribution is log normal, standard deviations and significances between means are best calculated on transformed figures. The comparison between the total larval counts in the treated and control groups is straight forward. However, where there are differences both in the number of larvae established and in the number surviving between the two groups, viable metacestode counts cannot be directly compared between the two groups. In this case, a modification of Abbott's (1925) formula may be used to describe percentage immunity. If the distribution is log normal a comparison of geometric means provides a convenient method for comparing survival rates.

V. Evidence for Affected and Effective Antigens

An analysis is given here of the experimental evidence for the presence of antigens at specific stages of development and their ability to induce an immune response against identical or other phases. The responses described are not necessarily lethal to one or any phase.

A. The Egg

1. Antigens Observed To Be Affected by Immune Responses

A diffuse granular deposition occurred within the eggs of *H. nana* and these clumped and had a reduced infectivity to mice following immersion *in vitro* in serum of rabbits immunized by injections of homogenates of adult *H. nana* (Heyneman and Welsh, 1959). Weinmann (1966) did not confirm the reduced infectivity using mouse serum. In addition, embryophoral blocks of *T. pisiformis* aggregated *in vitro* in the presence of serum from experimentally infected animals, but not in that inactivated by heating at 56°C for 30 minutes (Smyth, 1967). Blocks under the conditions of immune aggregation also attached to free oncospheres (Blundell-Hasell, 1971), Hence, the phenomenon may be one related to immune adherence by which the blocks attached to other antigen–antibody complexes.

2. Antigens Inducing Immune Responses

Only experiments employing killed or X-irradiated eggs can be considered here. Irradiated eggs of *T. taeniaeformis* induced resistance in rats (Dow *et al.*, 1962). Since immunity was not induced to *T. hydatigena* in sheep injected with 50,000 homologous eggs which had been killed by deep freezing (Gemmell, 1964a), the immunity induced by the irradiated eggs could have been due to antigens produced during the early reorganization of the oncospheres and not necessarily those present in the eggs at the time of ingestion. There is, therefore, no evidence that egg antigens per se are effective inducers of immunity. Nevertheless, the blocks are keratin, and keratins are known inducers of reaginic antibody (Berrens, 1970), particularly if inhaled. It is not known whether an intestinal allergy with an ensuing hypermotility could be mounted against the blocks or other discarded membranes (Fernex and Fernex, 1962), but, if so, it is possible that an alteration in gut motility could handicap the oncospheres before penetration (Larsh, 1947a). Egg antigens, therefore, cannot yet be excluded as the inducer of an immune response indirectly affecting the oncosphere.

B. THE ONCOSPHERE

1. Antigens Observed To Be Affected by Immune Responses

Silverman (1955) exposed the oncospheres of *T. pisiformis* and *T. saginata* to the serum of immunized animals and observed precipitates which could have been formed by antibody reacting with body secretions from the epidermal glands and from the surface of the oncospheres. Such reactions were confirmed by Blundell-Hasell (1971) employing immunofluorescent techniques. Heath (1970a) investigated the effect of complement on the immune reactions at a time when the oncospheres of *T. pisiformis* were being liberated from the egg. The oncospheres became paralyzed and did not secrete fluid from the epidermal glands. Subsequently in culture media they failed to reorganize in the presence of serum and degenerated in about 7 days.

What other antigens are affected before reorganization by an immune response still remain to be determined. Some of them appear to be identical or closely related to antigens occurring later in development, since antibodies which have been prepared by injecting experimental animals with homogenates of other larval stages appear to be lethal to oncospheres (Campbell, 1936; Weinmann, 1966). Freeman (1962) demonstrated that the implanted metacestodes of *T. crassiceps* were capable of inducing a response that was lethal to an egg-challenge infection. Such findings, however, have not been invariable (J. T. Chen, 1950).

2. Antigens Inducing Immune Responses

Killed oncospheres of *T. hydatigena* in numbers up to 50,000 failed to induce resistance in sheep (Gemmell, 1964a). This might be accounted for by the injection of too small a quantity of antigen. Against this conclusion is the evidence of the early onset of immunity in mice against *H. nana* (Hearin, 1941; Bailey, 1951; Weinmann, 1958; Heyneman, 1962, 1963; Astafiev, 1966c). This suggests that the oncospheres themselves may have been antigenic. However, owing to the rapid reorganization of this species, the antigenicity may have been produced during this stage as will be further discussed.

Rats develop some immunity against *T. taeniaeformis* 7 to 14 days after infection (Campbell, 1938a) and also acquire resistance to the same organism following the ingestion of irradiated eggs (Dow *et al.*, 1962). Oncospheres in the latter experiment did not complete their reorganization. Likewise, activated oncospheres of *T. hydatigena* injected into the muscles of lambs 7 days before the oral challenge developed slightly, but died before full reorganization (Gemmell *et al.*, 1968a). During this period they initiated an immune response which resulted in a significant degree of resistance to the challenge infection. Furthermore, injected activated oncospheres of *T. hydatigena* and *T. ovis* induced resistance even when they did not complete their reorganization (Gemmell, 1969a). It follows that these and other experiments suggest that living organisms or their metabolites may be essential for the induction of immunity. Thus, it seems that oncosphere survival, but not necessarily complete reorganization, is important in stimulating immunity. Evidence that some of the antigens may be metabolic products has been strengthened by experiments showing that oncospheres implanted in Millipore chambers or culture fluid in which *T. taeniaeformis* and *T. ovis* have been grown induced strong resistance to the homologous challenge infection in rats and sheep, respectively (Rickard and Bell, 1972a,b).

C. The Metacestode

1. Antigens Observed To Be Affected by Immune Responses

Precipitates have been observed *in vitro* when the protoscolex of *E. granulosus* was placed in immune serum (Shults and Ismagolova, 1962).

Fluorescent antibody tests have shown the conjugation of specific antibody with protoscolices of hydatid cysts (de Azevedo and Rombert, 1964; Pozzuoli *et al.*, 1965; Sorice *et al.*, 1966a,b). In addition, Fischman (1968) has successfully used protoscolices as antigens in a diagnostic fluorescent antibody test for human hydatidosis.

Blundell-Hasell (1971) observed, by the immune adherence of human red cells *in vitro*, the binding of antibody to the scolex and bladder surface of *T. pisiformis*. Furthermore, after exposure to antiserum for several hours, the tegument of the metacestode showed a "bubbling" effect similar to that observed on *T. taeniaeformis* by J. T. Chen (1950). This phenomenon has also been observed on the tails of beetle-derived cysticercoids of *H. nana* when they were exposed to immune sera (Heyneman and Welsh, 1959). At the same time, the rostellum with sessile suckers was everted. J. T. Chen (1950) found that the strobilocercus of *T. taeniaeformis* was killed *in vitro* by immune heat-inactivated rat serum. The controls, however, produced confusing results. The antibodies in the immune serum were not absorbed out by adding antigens from killed and desiccated larvae, but were absorbed by living organisms; a phenomenon suggesting that some of the antibodies were acting against excretory or secretory products (Campbell, 1938c). Perhaps, it cannot always be assumed that antibodies against metabolites have adverse effects on the parasites; and Ogilvie (1970) has suggested that they may be advantageous by causing the rapid removal of waste products.

2. Antigens Inducing Immune Responses

Kagan and Agosin (1968) have reviewed the evidence on the multiplicity of the antigens of *Echinococcus* spp. present in the fluid, cyst wall, and protoscolices. These data together with those of Benex (1970) indicate clearly that there are a very large number of potential antigens. The failure of dried products and the partial success of some fresh products (Turner *et al.*, 1937) to immunize against infection indicate the possible importance of labile antigens in protection. Hydatid fluid contains many antigens that react with immune serum from hosts infected by natural routes, but, since the crucial experiment of absorbing serum obtained from experimental animals immunized only against this fluid, with antigens from premetacestode stages has not been performed, it is not possible to conclude that under natural conditions the antibodies were formed in response to the fluid and not to the earlier stages of development. In sheep with long established infections, there is little correlation between the antibody titer and the occurrence of a visible infection (Blundell-Hasell, 1969). This finding is consistent with the view that there is little recurring antigenic stimulation from metacestodes.

VI. Evidence for Immunity *in Vivo* at Defined Phases of Development

In immune animals, the reduction in the number of dead and viable organisms from the expected at autopsy has been used as an index and termed "early" (Campbell, 1938a,b,c) or "preencystment" (Gemmell and Soulsby, 1968) immunity. Such an index must be regarded as an oversimplification of the events which occur, since it provides no information as to whether the lethal effect was directed against the egg, the oncosphere in the intestinal lumen, the oncosphere in the mucosa or in translocation, or the early posthexacanth phase in the tissues. Similarly, the differences from the expected in the proportions of dead and viable organisms observed at autopsy have been used as an index and termed "late" (Campbell, 1938a,b,c) or "postencystment" (Gemmell and Soulsby, 1968) immunity. Here again this index is also an oversimplification, since it provides no information on the lethal effects which were initiated during the earlier stages, but were not lethal until some later stage of development. It follows that in any critical review only those experiments which define the specific events can be used as evidence for an immune attack at a specific site and at a specific phase of development.

A. IMMUNITY TO THE ONCOSPHERE IN THE INTESTINAL LUMEN

Specific immunity against the egg as distinct from that against the oncosphere has not been distinguished. Histological examinations of hatched oncospheres injected into isolated intestinal loops provide evidence of lethal reactions against the oncosphere. Oncospheres of *H. nana* failed to penetrate naturally immunized mice (Bailey, 1951; Weinmann and Lee, 1964). Those of *E. granulosus* and to a lesser extent those of *T. hydatigena* and *T. ovis* made no attempt to penetrate the intestine of sheep artificially immunized against *E. granulosus* (Heath, 1970a) by the technique recorded in Gemmell (1966). This may be a humoral effect, since the immunity was induced by parenteral injection, and immunity can be transferred via serum or colostrum from artificially immunized donors to nonimmune recipients (Blundell *et al.*, 1968; Gemmell *et al.*, 1969). It is emphasized, however, that in these transfer studies antibodies could have acted on the oncospheres before or shortly after penetration of the intestinal mucosa.

The effects of digestion resistant IgA antibodies on hatching and penetration of the oncospheres in naturally immunized animals requires investigation. Such antibodies could be present in the intestinal lumen derived either from colostrum or from local plasma cells (Weinmann, 1966; Tomasi and Bienenstock, 1968). Although the evidence shows that colostrum from naturally infected and immune cattle and sheep does not provide protection against *T. saginata* and *T. hydratigena,* respectively (Urquhart, 1961; Gemmell *et al.,* 1969), it cannot be accepted from this that IgA antibodies have no protective role (Lascelles and McDowell, 1970). Indeed, the failure of splenectomy or neonatal thymectomy to influence acquired resistance of mice to *H. nana* (Weinmann, 1968b) provides good reason for further investigating the role of IgA on the hatching mechanisms and the events that occur before the oncosphere attempts to penetrate the intestinal villus.

B. Immunity to the Oncosphere in the Intestinal Mucosa

The reactions occurring during the few hours from the point of initial contact by the hooklets with the columnar cells to the passive translocation via venules cannot readily be studied with the taeniids, but information from *H. nana* may give equivalent evidence provided due account is taken not only of rapid reorganization but also of the rapid development of immunity by the host.

C. Immunity to the Oncosphere during Translocation

To differentiate early reactions in the lumen and intestinal wall from those occurring later, experiments should include the parenteral injection of organisms. Here, the evidence is conflicting. Leonard and Leonard (1941), Froyd and Round (1959, 1960), and Heath (1970a), by appropriate bypass experiments with either *T. pisiformis, T. saginata,* or *E. granulosus* in immune rabbits, cattle, or sheep, appropriately, were able to demonstrate the successful establishment but not necessarily long-term survival of the oncospheres in tissues. In contrast, Urquhart (1965) and Gemmell (unpublished) by equivalent bypass experiments were unable to establish *T. saginata* or *T. ovis* in naturally immune cattle and sheep, respectively. The degree of immunological destruction appears to be variable and may depend largely on the level of circulating antibody, although other factors may be operative (Leonard, 1940).

D. Immunity to the Reorganizing Oncosphere

Oral or parenteral infections have been used for examining lethal reactions during active migration and reorganization of the oncospheres.

This can be done provided absolute resistance has not been acquired or induced to an earlier phase of development. As previously pointed out, however, there is no way of telling whether under these circumstances the organism has already been crippled by a reaction against an earlier stage. Thus a measurement of the specific effects of immune serum given at specific times after infection provides a better index of reactions occurring during postoncospheral differentiation.

Campbell (1938a,b,c) transferred serum from rats immunized by a 28-day infection of *T. taeniaeformis* to previously unexposed recipients at various intervals before and after giving an oral challenge dose of eggs. Since the half-life of the immunoglobulin of rats is about 1 week or less (Waldmann and Strober, 1960) and the dose of serum given was only about 6 times that shown to have an appreciable effect, Campbell exposed the larvae *in vivo* to pulses of immunoglobulins of 2–3 weeks duration or less. He found that the immune serum induced a high mortality (50% versus 13% in the controls) to those larvae which became established, with the maximum effect when the immune serum was given about the time of the challenge. It seems that the maximum effect was obtained at a very early stage after their penetration, although some effect was also observed using serum 1 week after infection.

The experiments of Di Conza (1969) using the reorganizing stages of *H. nana* (Voge and Heyneman, 1957) demonstrated the effect of humoral (probably 7 S) antibodies. Heath (1970a) and others have shown that, during migration through the liver, reorganizing oncospheres of *T. pisiformis* may be surrounded by lymphocytes and that these accumulate in their wake. Oncospheres of *H. nana* injected subcutaneously into mice also appear to attract macrophages and lymphocytes (Di Conza, 1970). To what extent these phenomena represent cell-mediated sensitivity remains to be explored, but it will take very carefully contolled experiments to demonstrate cytotoxicity on the organisms during each phase of reorganization.

E. Immunity to the Metacestode at the Site of Predilection

The terms "late" or "postencystment" immunity imply an increase in the proportion of metacestodes becoming necrotic in immune animals compared with animals not previously immunized by infections or the transfer of a passive immunity. The terms do not necessarily imply that any process originated at the cyst stage. There is indeed yet very little conclusive evidence on immunological processes even during the late stages of postoncospheral differentiation. The difficulties to be overcome include: (a) the assessment of effects occurring at earlier stages; (b) the assessment, unless isogenic animals are used, of effects parallel to those of homograft rejection; and (c) where distinction between humoral and cell-mediated immunity is required, transfer of cells from one animal to another must exclude the transfer of antibody-producing cells, or the effect of antibody.

Experiments on the passive transfer of immunity to animals previously rendered immunologically deficient or incompetent by thymectomy, splenectomy, or X-irradiation have proved possible (Okamoto, 1970; Neas *et al.*, 1966; Friedberg *et al.*, 1970) although not invariable so (Weinmann, 1968b). Unfortunately, these experiments do not refer to the metacestode. Observations on secondary echinococcosis and the well-known dangers of seeding daughter cysts into the peritoneal cavities of patients undergoing operative procedures for the removal of *E. granulosus* indicate that, against this developmental stage at least, there may be little true immunity and what there is may be slow to develop (Orihara, 1969; Pauluzzi, 1969). An explanation, however, may be required for "sterile metacestodes." There is, however, some evidence that the metacestode of *T. saginata* and *T. hydatigena* may be killed by an immune response stimulated after their establishment (Leikina *et al.*, 1964; Gemmell, 1970). In each case, the metacestodes of the first infection died. The other evidence of immunological activity *in vivo* against them is histological. Where there is an appreciable fluid-filled space between the outer host cyst capsule and the parasitic bladder (*e.g.*, in *T. hydatigena*), the fluid contains a predominance of lymphocytes. Some of the lymphocytes were classified by Sinclair (1970) as large and were suggestive of undergoing transformation.

VII. Immunity and Host–Parasite Relationships

The very fact that the tissue phases of cestodes and the metacestode in particular can remain viable for relatively long periods in their host indicates that the parasite is able to avoid or resist immunological attack. There is no suggestion that the parasites can suppress nonspecifically the immune mechanisms of the host, nor that their growth is so rapid that like malignant tumors they can outstrip a specific immune response. The wall of fibrous tissue around the metacestode is usually too thin to suggest any restraint on the access of immune mechanisms. Even in the case of the thick-walled metacestode of *E. granulosus,* host albumens and immunoglobulins may be found to have reached the cyst fluid (Chordi and Kagan, 1965; Novoselska, 1964, 1965; Kagan, 1967; Kagan and Agosin, 1968). A phenomenon that Smyth (1969b) suggested may account for death of scolices and acephalic bladder forms. However, the presence or absence of scolices in the various bladder forms has not yet been defined.

Several mechanisms of resistance by helminths against attack have been suggested. These include: (a) hiding of the successfully adapted parasite behind a self-made mask of molecular mimicry of host tissue, so that the host does not recognize it as foreign (Sprent, 1959; Dineen, 1963a,b; Damian, 1964); (b) adsorption onto the parasite surface of host tissue material so that the parasite is not recognized as foreign (Smithers and Terry, 1967; Capron, 1970); (c) coating of the parasite by itself with an antigen that is expendable or useless in regard to its own survival, but by its presence and interaction with specific host immune reactions blocks further immunological attack; and (d) the induction in the host of a specific immunological tolerance for the parasite.

These possible mechanisms for metacestode survival are discussed subsequently.

A. MIMICRY

The formation of antigens resembling those of the host must be genetically determined on a hereditary basis since random mutation is unlikely to be an efficient method to promote survival of the species. Where a parasite is capable of becoming established in several hosts, either an antigen common to these diverse hosts must be formed or the parasite must be capable of forming different antigens to suit different hosts. In this last case, repression of the genes coding for the unwanted antigens and a derepression of those coding for the mimicking antigen must operate. Such a repression and derepression would have to operate on all those cells coming into contact with the immune response.

The method of mimicry which might be important with the metacestode and which has analogies among bacteria includes the formation of common antigens such as polysaccharides. In this respect, it may be noted that mucopolysaccharides form a major component of the bladder wall of *E. granulosus* (Fischman and Allen, 1967; Kagan and Agosin, 1968; Benex, 1970). Other similar substances which may be formed by cestodes are the P, I, and ABO antigens of blood cells (Cameron and Stavely, 1957; Dzierskowa-Borodej *et al.*, 1970; Novoselska, 1968; Raik *et al.*, 1970) as well as Forsmann and C antigens (Hacig *et al.*, 1959; Biguet *et al.*, 1965). Smyth (1969c) has reported that the hydatid organism also produces P substance *in vitro*. Just what role this type of antigen plays in protecting the organism and thereby permitting long-term survival remains to be determined.

B. Adsorption of Chemicals

Adsorption of chemicals onto the surface of cestodes has been observed by Lumsden *et al.* (1970), but the frequency with which host proteins are found in metacestode fluids suggests a high permeability of the bladder wall. Although albumin and other proteins are found in hydatid fluid, specific anti-parasite antibody is insufficient to inhibit either the use of the fluid as a passive antigen in diagnostic tests (Kagan and Norman, 1961, 1963a,b; Fischman and Allen, 1967; Kagan, 1968a; Abrantes and Avila, 1968) or the use of protoscolices in fluorescent antibody tests. It is, however, not yet clear whether host antigens, such as histocompatibility antigens, can be firmly adsorbed onto the bladder surface, or even onto protoscolices (Urquhart, 1970). The failure to transplant protoscolices of *E. granulosus* from one sheep to another (Heath, 1970a,b) suggests a highly specific immune reaction involving host antigens. This finding is, however, particularly difficult to interpret, since serial transfer of *E. multilocularis* from rodent to rodent is an accepted technique for continuous propagation.

C. Coating of the Parasite

The attachment of 7 S antibody to histocompatibility antigens, thereby blocking their susceptibility to cell-mediated immunity, has been advanced as one rather simplified explanation of immunological enhancement (of growth) of grafts (Nelson, 1962). In this model it has to be assumed that the antibodies have no destructive effect. Whether or not such a mechanism acts in regard to metacestodes is unknown.

However, Varela-Diaz *et al.* (1972) have postulated an analogous system to account for the survival of metacestodes involving two antibodies and two antigens in juxtaposition. One of the antibodies itself, while having a neutral effect on the parasite, may by steric hindrance block the action of a lethal antibody. The authors thus account for an observed enhancement of the survival of *T. ovis* in the presence of antibodies induced by *T. hydatigena* (Gemmell, 1969b).

Schad (1966) has speculated that interspecies competition between worms could lead to one species producing antigens similar to those of another species yet having no essential role for the first species. Any immune reaction mounted against the antigen was postulated to be deleterious to the second parasite but not the first. Gemmell (1969c) extended this to include the cestodes, and suggested that a shared antigen may have no functional significance in one phase of the life cycle in the intermediate host but may assume importance in another phase in the definitive host.

D. TOLERANCE

The induction of immunological tolerance is theoretically possible (Soulsby, 1962, 1963; Urquhart, 1970) and, in view of the similarity of host and parasite antigens, this may be a tolerance due to exposure to repeated very small doses of a weak antigen—low zone tolerance. The picture may be confused by a relative immunological incompetence observable in young animals (Ingram and Smith, 1965; Gemmell *et al.*, 1968b). In making deductions from infections, particularly those naturally acquired, care is needed in interpretation owing to the different results which may be obtained from large single doses or multiple lesser doses of eggs (Gemmell, 1969b). If it is accepted that experiments involving very young animals and others involving field infections are equivocal, then there is practically no evidence for immunological tolerance.

VIII. The Significance of Acquired Resistance and the Application of Immunization

The majority of metacestodes causing human health and or economic problems to agriculture occur within the family *Taenidae*. A number of reports confirm the importance of acquired resistance in limiting the population of *T. saginata* in cattle (W. J. Penfold *et al.*, 1936; H. B. Penfold, 1937; Peel, 1953, 1961; Urquhart, 1961; Froyd, 1964). Indeed, immunological control either by varying grazing practices (W. J. Penfold and Penfold, 1937) or by artificial immunization (Urquhart, 1961) has been suggested. It has also been shown that infections may occur early in postnatal life (Urquhart, 1961) but rarely *in utero* (McManus, 1960, 1963), and it has been suggested that calves infected early in postnatal life may develop tolerance to infection (Soulsby, 1962, 1963). These together with similar studies on the survival of metacestodes provide no critical information on the epizootiology, host–parasite relationships or the problems of vaccination in the field.

In this section, immunization in the laboratory is compared with that in the field, taking account of the epizootiology of cestode infections. The model used includes the sheep metacestodes *E. granulosus, T. hydatigena,* and *T. ovis.* This model is likely to provide comparable results for *T. saginata* and *T. solium;* although due to the adult stage parasitizing dogs in the former and man in the latter group, some differences in the epizootiology may be expected.

A. Immunization in the Laboratory

1. Acquired Immunity

Previously uninfected lambs have been shown to acquire a degree of resistance to superinfection from *T. hydatigena* and *E. granulosus* following the fixed feeding of a specified dose of homologous eggs (Sweatman, 1957; Sweatman *et al.*, 1963b). In addition, when nonimmune lambs of 3 months of age were fed eggs of *T. hydatigena* or *T. ovis* at a weekly rate of 10 or 100 eggs for 9 weeks, the number of organisms which developed was similar to that expected from a single dose of 10 or 100 eggs (Gemmell, 1969b). This implies that after one or two sensitizing egg doses, subsequent impinging infections may be rejected shortly before or after penetration of the tissues.

2. Artificially Induced Immunity

Previously uninfected lambs can be immunized artificially at 3 months of age against all three sheep metacestodes by a parenteral injection of homologous viable eggs or activated oncospheres and to a lesser extent heterologous oncospheres, but not by killed organisms or oncospheres of the rabbit metacestode *T. pisiformis* (Gemmell, 1964a, 1965a,b, 1966). In the case of *E. granulosus* most of the homologous challenge organisms do not appear to penetrate the intestinal mucosa of immunized lambs (Heath, 1970a). This lends support to the possibility that in immunized animals species-specific and interspecific responses may occur before and after penetration of the intestinal mucosa, respectively (Gemmell, 1962, 1964b, 1967).

For *T. hydatigena*, a period of 14 days must elapse between immunization and challenge infection before strong resistance can be induced (Gemmell *et al.*, 1968a), and the immunity is likely to be stronger when lambs are immunized at 8 weeks than when they are younger (Gemmell *et al.*, 1968b). A short-acting immunity can also be passively transferred via serum or colostrum from hyperimmunized ewes (Blundell-Hasell *et al.*, 1968; Gemmell *et al.*, 1969).

B. Natural Infection in the Field

The infection pressure is defined as the exponential k in the term $Y = 1 - e^{-kt}$ determining the infection prevalence (Y) in previously unexposed animals during time t. When this is strong, animals may ingest eggs within the first few days of life and, provided the source of infection is not removed, they will continue to do so indefinitely. This may give rise to an "epidemic-type" pattern of infection (see, for example, Schultz *et al.*, 1969). When, however, the infection pressure is weak either by virtue of a low egg production, for example from *E. granulosus* compared to that from *T. hydatigena* (Gemmell, 1961), or due to control measures such as those reported in the "Styx-Field Trial" (Gemmell, 1968), only a small proportion of the flock may have ingested eggs within the first few months of life. This may give rise to an "endemic-type" pattern for the prevalence rate. These two infection pressures provide different problems for vaccination. This may be further complicated by the presence of more than one species with similar antigens.

C. IMMUNIZATION IN THE FIELD

Among the more important practical questions requiring investigation are (a) Can a useful degree of immunity be induced before the host receives an initial infection? (b) Are very young lambs competent to recognize the whole range of larval cestode antigens? (c) Does early exposure to antigen affect the development of an immune response subsequently? (d) Does the acquisition of resistance following the repeated ingestion of eggs interfere with the immunizing properties of live organisms injected as antigen subsequently?

1. Under Conditions of a Strong Infection Pressure

In nonvaccinated lambs, the sequence of events which appears to occur under a strong infection pressure from *T. hydatigena*, for example, includes: (a) the ingestion of eggs almost from birth; and (b) the acquisition of absolute resistance and rejection of further impinging oncospheres with indefinite survival of those already established metacestodes (Gemmell, 1971).

Under these conditions, hyperimmunization of the ewe with viable organisms does not protect the lamb. In addition, immunization at 1 week does not prevent some development of oncospheres from eggs ingested from the pasture but may prevent their long-term survival as metacestodes in the same way as that observed in the laboratory (Gemmell *et al.*, 1968b). Here the evidence in both the field and laboratory suggests that there is a gradual acquisition of competence to the full range of larval antigens as observed in lambs for some bacterial antigens (Silverstein, 1964). Immunization at three months does not effect the survival of established metacestodes. In this case, it seems that the animals may already be so resistant that the injected homologous oncospheres may be destroyed prematurely before releasing the appropriate antigens associated with the death of metacestodes, as appeared to be the case in the laboratory (Gemmell *et al.*, 1968a).

2. Under Conditions of a Weak Infection Pressure

When few eggs are available, only a small proportion of the flock may have ingested eggs of *T. hydatigena* at 3 months of age, and, although some animals may harbor viable metacestodes, strong immunity may not have been acquired. In this situation, an injection of homologous viable organisms may prevent infection and superinfection, appropriately, and these as well as those of *T. ovis* may induce a retrospective lethal effect in lambs against already established *T. hydatigena* (Gemmell, 1970) in a similar way to that described for *T. saginata* in cattle by Leikina *et al.* (1964).

D. Correlation between Applied and Basic Problems

In any control program directed against echinococcosis or cysticercosis of domestic food animals, immunization as the sole means of control, to be successful, would have to prevent not only infection and reinfection, but also survival of any metacestodes in almost all animals.

This preliminary attempt to integrate the complex problems of developmental physiology, host–parasite relationships, and epizootiology, suggests that successful vaccination of the intermediate host with viable organisms may depend *inter alia* on the infection pressure, i.e., being less effective under a strong than a weak one. This is possible due to: (a) the gradual acquisition of competence to the full range of larval antigens; and (b) the premature rejection of homologous viable organisms injected as the antigen complex in animals with a strong acquired resistance. Although it appears likely that lambs may not recognize the full range of larval antigens until about 8 weeks of age, no evidence could be found indicating that immunization before that age induced tolerance or subsequently interfered with the development of acquired resistance.

It has yet to be determined whether oncospheres of a heterologous species or antigens obtained from axenically cultured organisms (Rickard and Bell, 1971a,b) can overcome the problems of premature rejection observed with homologous oncospheres in lambs with a strong acquired resistance, and thereby induce a response that is lethal to metacestodes successfully established *in situ* before vaccination. Here, the complete absence of data on the antigens (i.e., metabolic products or somatic antigens) associated with the death or survival of the reorganizing oncosphere or the mature metacestode limits speculation. In this regard, it also must be admitted that there is as yet very little laboratory evidence indicating that accumulating infections, however administered and with or without successful establishment, can induce in the host an effective lethal attack against other already established metacestodes.

To what extent the longevity of metacestodes is determined by exposure to immune responses is difficult to determine. The increasing proportion of necrotic organisms in older animals suggests an increase in the immune response or perhaps an alteration in the conformation of the antigens on the scolex or the bladder wall, but an equally possible explanation includes an exponential decline in the number of living organisms following an early exposure to an immune response. This explanation could also account for the phenomenon of dead and living metacestodes being found in juxtaposition. Whether genetic factors are involved remains to be confirmed, but the basic concepts of genetic similarities and differences in the conformation of antigens in the various tapeworm populations (Varela Diaz et al., 1972) may well need further clarification before the problems of vaccination can be more fully understood.

References

Abott, W. S. (1925). J. Econ. Entomol. 18, 265.
Abrantes, P., and Avila, R. (1968). Lancet 2, 432.
Astafiev, B. A. (1966a). Med. Parazitol. Parazit. Bolez. 35, 93.
Astafiev, B. A. (1966b). Med. Parazitol. Parazit. Bolez. 35, 149.
Astafiev, B. A. (1966c). Med. Parazitol. Parazit. Bolez. 35, 705.
Bacigalupo, J. (1933). C. R. Soc. Biol. 114, 390.
Bailey, W. S. (1951). J. Parasitol. 37, 440.
Banerjee, D., and Singh, K. S. (1969). Indian J. Anim. Sci. 39, 149.
Barker, I. K. (1970). Can. J. Zool. 48, 1329.
Baron, P. J. (1968). Parasitology 58, 497.
Batham, E. J. (1957). N. Z. Vet. J. 5, 74.
Benex, J. (1968a). Ann. Parsitol. Hum. Comp. 43, 561.
Benex, J. (1968b). Ann. Parasitol. Hum. Comp. 43, 573.
Benex, J. (1968c). Bull. Soc. Pathol. Exot. 61, 785.
Benex, J. (1970). Ann. Inst. Pasteur, Paris 118, 49.
Berberian, D. A. (1957). Annu. Rep. Orient Hosp., Beirut 10, 33–43.
Berntzen, A. K., and Voge, M. (1962). J. Parasitol. 48, 110.
Berntzen, A. K., and Voge, M. (1965). J. Parasitol. 51, 235.
Berrens, L. (1970). Progr. Allergy 14, 259.
Bertram, D. S. (1966). Advan. Parasitol. 4, 255.
Biguet, J., Rose, F., Capron, A., and Tran Van Ky, P. (1965). Rev. Immunol. 29, 5.
Bilques, F. M. (1968). Can. J. Zool. 46, 763.
Bilques, F. M. (1969). Aust. J. Zool. 17, 487.
Bilques, F. M., and Freeman, R. S. (1969). Can. J. Zool. 47, 251.

Blundell-Hasell, S. K. (1969). *Aust. Vet. J.* **45**, 334.
Blundell-Hasell, S. K. (1971). Ph.D. Thesis, University of Otago, Dunedin, New Zealand.
Blundell-Hasell, S. K., Gemmell, M. A., and Macnamara, F. N. (1968). *Exp. Parasitol.* **23**, 79.
Blundell, S. K., Gemmell, M. A., and McNamara, F. N. (1969). *Exp. Parasitol.* **24**, 291.
Bogitsh, B. J. (1967). *Exp. Parasitol.* **21**, 373.
Bullock, F. D., and Curtis, M. R. (1924). *J. Cancer Res.* **8**, 446.
Bullock, F. D., Dunning, W. F., and Curtis, M. R. (1934). *Amer. J. Cancer* **20**, 390.
Cameron, G. L., and Stavely, J. M. (1957). *Nature (London)* **179**, 147.
Campbell, D. H. (1936). *Amer. J. Hyg.* **23**, 104.
Campbell, D. H. (1938a). *J. Immunol.* **35**, 195.
Campbell, D. H. (1938b). *J. Immunol.* **35**, 205.
Campbell, D. H. (1938c). *J. Immunol.* **35**, 465.
Campbell, D. H. (1939). *Science* **89**, 415.
Campbell, D. H., and Melcher, L. R. (1940). *J. Infec. Dis.* **66**, 184.
Capron, A. R. (1970). *J. Parasitol.* **56**, 515.
Cassie, R. M. (1954). *Aust. J. Mar. Freshwater Res.* **5**, 513.
Chen, H. T. (1934). *Z. Parasitenk.* **6**, 603.
Chen, J. T. (1950). *J. Infec. Dis.* **86**, 205.
Chordi, A., and Kagan, I. G. (1965). *J. Parasitol.* **51**, 63.
Clapham, P. A. (1940). *J. Helminthol.* **18**, 45.
Clapham, P. A. (1942). *J. Helminthol.* **20**, 31.
Collin, W. K. (1968). *J. Parasitol.* **54**, 74.
Collin, W. K. (1969). *J. Parasitol.* **55**, 149.
Collin, W. K. (1970). *J. Parasitol.* **56**, 1159.
Collings, S. B., and Hutchins, C. P. (1965). *Exp. Parasitol.* **16**, 53.
Coutelen, F. (1927a). *Ann. Parsitol. Hum. Comp.* **5**, 1.
Coutelen, F. (1927b). *Ann. Parasitol. Hum. Comp.* **5**, 239.
Coutelen, F. (1936a). *C. R. Soc. Biol.* **121**, 730.
Coutelen, F. (1936b). *C. R. Soc. Biol.* **121**, 1266.
Coutelen, F., Lecroart, D., and Cochet, G. (1939). *Ann. Parasitol. Hum. Comp.* **17**, 4.
Crusz, H. (1947). *J. Parasitol.* **33**, 87.
Crusz, H. (1948a). *J. Helminthol.* **22**, 165.
Crusz, H. (1948b). *J. Helminthol.* **22**, 179.
Curtis, M. R., Dunning, W. F., and Bullock, F. D. (1933). *Amer. J. Cancer* **17**, 894.
Dailey, M. D., and Sweatman, G. K. (1965). *Ann. Trop. Med. Parasitol.* **59**, 463.
Damian, R. T. (1964). *Amer. Midl. Natur.* **98**, 129.
de Azevedo, J. F., and Rombert, P. C. (1964). *Rev. Inst. Med. Trop. Sao Paulo* **6**, 35.
De Cooman, E. (1937). *Naturrwetensch. Tijdschr. (Ghent)* **19**, 261.
De Sa, L. M., and Coleman, R. M. (1964). *J. Parasitol.* **50**, 20.
Dévé, F. (1916). *Arch. Med. Exp.* **28**, 113.
Dévé, F. (1926). *C. R. Soc. Biol.* **94**, 440.
Dévé, F. (1927). *C. R. Soc. Biol.* **97**, 1130.
Dévé, F. (1928). *C. R. Soc. Biol.* **98**, 1176.

Dévé, F. (1933a). C. R. Soc. Biol. 113, 1443.
Dévé, F. (1933b). C. R. Soc. Biol. 114, 455.
Dévé, F. (1934a). Arch. Int. Hydatid 1, 85.
Dévé, F. (1934b). C. R. Soc. Biol. 115, 954.
Dévé, F. (1934c). C. R. Soc. Biol. 115, 1025.
Dévé, F. (1935). C. R. Soc. Biol. 119, 351.
Dévé, F. (1938). C. R. Soc. Biol. 128, 340.
Dévé, F. (1942). C. R. Soc. Biol. 136, 647.
Dévé, F. (1946). "L'échinococcose secondaire." Masson, Paris.
Dévé, F. (1949). "L'échinococcose primitive (Maladie hydatique)." Masson, Paris.
Dew, H. R. (1922). Med. J. Aust. 2, 381.
Dew, H. R. (1925). Med. J. Aust. 1, 101.
Dew, H. R. (1928). "Hydatid Disease." Australasian Publ. Co. Ltd., Sydney.
De Waale, A., and De Cooman, E. (1938a). Ann. Parasitol. Hum. Comp. 16, 121.
De Waale, A., and De Cooman, E. (1938b). Vlaams Diergeneesk. Tijdschr. 7, 215.
Dewhirst, L. W., Cramer, J. D., and Pistor, W. J. (1963). J. Parsitol. 49, 297.
Di Conza, J. J. (1968). Z. Parasitenk. 31, 276.
Di Conza, J. J. (1969). Exp. Parasitol. 25, 368.
Di Conza, J. J. (1970). Exp. Parasitol. 28, 482.
Dineen, J. K. (1963a). Nature (London) 197, 268.
Dineen, J. K. (1963b). Nature (London) 197, 471.
Dow, C., and Jarrett, W. F. H. (1960). Exp. Parasitol. 10, 72.
Dow, C., Jarrett, W. F. H., Jennings, F. W., McIntyre, W. I. M., and Mulligan, W. (1962). Amer. J. Vet. Res. 23, 146.
Dzierskowa-Borodej, W., Seyfried, H., Nichols, M., Reid, M., and Marsh, W. C. (1970). Vox Sang. 18, 222.
Enigk, K., and Sticinsky, E. (1957). Z. Parasitenk. 18, 48.
Esch, G. W. (1964). J. Elisha Mitchell Sci. Soc. 80, 114.
Esch, G. W. (1967). Parasitology 57, 175.
Esch, G. W., and Murrell, K. D. (1968). J. Parasitol. 54, 181.
Esch, G. W., and Self, J. T. (1965). J. Parasitol. 51, 932.
Euzéby, J. (1962). Rev. Med. Vet. 113, 111.
Evranova, V. G., and Yashina, G. I. (1966). Uch. Zap. Kazan. Vet. Inst. 96, 215.
Feng, L. C., and Hoeppli, R. (1939). Chin. Med. J. 55, 45.
Fernex, M., and Fernex, P. (1962). Acta Trop. 19, 248.
Fischman, A. (1968). Bull. WHO 39, 39.
Fischman, A., and Allen, J. L. (1967). Aust. J. Exp. Biol. Med. Sci. 45, 221.
Fortuyn, A. B. D., and Feng, L. C. (1940). Peking Natur. Hist. Bull. 15, 139.
Freeman, R. S. (1952). J. Parasitol. 38, 111.
Freeman, R. S. (1962). Can. J. Zool. 40, 969.
Freeman, R. S. (1964). Can. J. Zool. 42, 367.
Friedberg, W., Neas, B. R., Faulkner, D. N., and Friedberg, M. H. (1967). J. Parasitol. 53, 895.
Friedberg, W., Cearly, J. E., Neas, B. R., Faulkner, D. N., and Coleman, R. L. (1970). Int. J. Radiat. Biol. 17, 449.
Froyd, G. (1964). Brit. Vet. J. 120, 205.
Froyd, G., and Round, M. C. (1959). Nature (London) 184, 1510.
Froyd, G., and Round, M. C. (1960). Res. Vet. Sci. 1, 275.

Gallagher, I. H. C. (1964). *Exp. Parasitol.* **15**, 110.
Gallati, W. W. (1959). *J. Parasitol.* **45**, 363.
Garkavi, B. L. (1956). *Dokl. Akad. Nauk SSSR* **111**, 240.
Garkavi, B. L., and Glebova, I. Y. (1957). *Zool. Zh.* **36**, 986.
Gemmell, M. A. (1961). *N. Z. Vet. J.* **9**, 40.
Gemmell, M. A. (1962). *Nature (London)* **194**, 701.
Gemmell, M. A. (1964a). *Immunology* **7**, 489.
Gemmell, M. A. (1964b). *Nature (London)* **204**, 705.
Gemmell, M. A. (1965a). *Immunology* **8**, 270.
Gemmell, M. A. (1965b). *Immunology* **8**, 281.
Gemmell, M. A. (1966). *Immunology* **11**, 325.
Gemmell, M. A. (1967). *Nature (London)* **213**, 500.
Gemmell, M. A. (1968). *Bull. WHO* **39**, 73.
Gemmell, M. A. (1969a). *Exp. Parasitol.* **26**, 58.
Gemmell, M. A. (1969b). *Aust. Vet. J.* **45**, 521.
Gemmell, M. A. (1969c). *Exp. Parasitol.* **26**, 67.
Gemmell, M. A. (1970). *Aust. Vet. J.* **46**, 366.
Gemmell, M. A., and Soulsby, E. J. L. (1968). *Bull. WHO* **39**, 57.
Gemmell, M. A., Blundell, S. K., and Macnamara, F. N. (1968a). *Exp. Parasitol.* **23**, 83.
Gemmell, M. A., Blundell, S. K., and Macnamara, F. N. (1968b). *Proc. Univ. Otago Med. Sch.* **46**, 4.
Gemmell, M. A., Blundell, S. K., and Macnamara, F. N. (1969). *Exp. Parasitol.* **26**, 52.
Gill, H. S., and Rao, B. V. (1967). *Parasitology* **57**, 695.
Gönnert, R. (1970). *J. Parasitol.* **56**, 559.
Gönnert, R., and Thomas, H. (1969). *Z. Tropenmed. Parasitol.* **32**, 237.
Gönnert, R., Meister, G., Strufe, R., and Webbe, G. (1967). *Z. Tropenmed. Parasitol.* **18**, 76.
Graham, J. J., and Berntzen, A. K. (1970). *J. Parasitol.* **56**, 1184.
Greenfield, S. H. (1942). *J. Parasitol.* **28**, 207.
Gurri, J. (1963). *An. Fac. Med., Univ. Repub., Montevideo* **48**, 372.
Hacig, A., Solomon, P., and Weinbach, R. (1959). *Arch. Roum. Pathol. Exp. Microbiol.* **18**, 611.
Hearin, J. T. (1941). *Amer. J. Hyg.* **33**, 71.
Heath, D. D. (1970a). Ph.D. Thesis, Australian National University, Canberra.
Heath, D. D. (1970b). *Parasitology* **60**, 449.
Heath, D. D. (1971). *Int. J. Parasitol.* **1**, 145.
Heath, D. D., and Smyth, J. D. (1970). *Parasitology* **61**, 329.
Heyneman, D. (1962). *J. Immunol.* **88**, 217.
Heyneman, D. (1963). *Ann. N.Y. Acad. Sci.* **113**, 114.
Heyneman, D., and Welsh, J. F. (1959). *Exp. Parasitol.* **8**, 119.
Hickman, J. L. (1963). *Pap. Proc. Roy. Soc. Tasmania* **97**, 81.
Hickman, J. L. (1964). *Pap. Proc. Roy. Soc. Tasmania* **98**, 73.
Hinz, E. (1962). *Z. Tropenmed. Parasitol.* **13**, 182.
Hinz, E. (1965). *Z. Tropenmed. Parasitol.* **16**, 322.
Huffman, J. L., and Jones, A. W. (1962). *Exp. Parasitol.* **12**, 120.
Hunninen, A. V. (1935a). *J. Parasitol.* **21**, 124.

Hunninen, A. V. (1935b). *Amer. J. Hyg.* **22**, 414.

Hunninen, A. V. (1935c). *J. Parasitol.* **21**, 312.

Hunninen, A. V. (1936). *J. Parasitol.* **22**, 84.

Hutchison, W. M. (1958). *J. Parasitol.* **44**, 574.

Inatomi, S. (1962). *Okyama Igakkai Zasshi* **74**, Suppl., 31.

Ingram, D. G., and Smith, A. N. (1965). *Can. Vet. J.* **6**, 194.

Isobé, M. (1922). *Trans. Jap. Pathol. Soc.* **12**, 41.

Isobé, M. (1926). *Acta Sch. Med. Univ. Kioto* **8**, 519.

Johri, L. N. (1957). *Parasitology* **47**, 21.

Jones, A. W., Segarra, J. M., and Wyant, K. D. (1960). *J. Parasitol.* **46**, 170.

Kagan, I. G. (1967). *Pan. Amer. Health Organ., Sci. Publ.* **150**, 25.

Kagan, I. G. (1968a). *Bull. WHO* **39**, 25.

Kagan, I. G. (1968b). *Amer. J. Trop. Med. Hyg.* **17**, 79.

Kagan, I. G., and Agosin, M. (1968). *Bull. WHO* **39**, 13.

Kagan, I. G., and Norman, L. (1961). *Amer. J. Trop. Med. Hyg.* **10**, 727.

Kagan, I. G., and Norman, L. (1963a). *Ann. N.Y. Acad. Sci.* **113**, 130.

Kagan, I. G., and Norman, L. (1963b). *Amer. J. Trop. Med. Hyg.* **12**, 346.

Kagan, I. G., Maddison, S. E., and Norman, L. (1968). *Amer. J. Trop. Med. Hyg.* **17**, 79.

Kan, K. (1933). *Keio Igaku* **13**, 753.

Kerr, K. B. (1934). *J. Parasitol.* **20**, 328.

Kerr, K. B. (1935). *Amer. J. Hyg.* **22**, 169.

Kilejian, A., Sauer, K., and Schwabe, C. W. (1962). *Exp. Parasitol.* **12**, 377.

Lang, B. Z. (1967). *J. Parasitol.* **53**, 21.

Larsh, J. E. (1942). *Amer. J. Hyg.* **36**, 187.

Larsh, J. E. (1943). *J. Parasitol.* **29**, 61.

Larsh, J. E. (1944a). *J. Parasitol.* **30**, 21.

Larsh, J. E. (1944b). *Amer. J. Hyg.* **39**, 133.

Larsh, J. E. (1944c). *Amer. J. Hyg.* **39**, 129.

Larsh, J. E. (1945). *J. Parasitol.* **31**, 291.

Larsh, J. E. (1946a). *J. Parasitol.* **32**, 477.

Larsh, J. E. (1946b). *J. Parasitol.* **32**, 61.

Larsh, J. E. (1947a). *J. Parasitol.* **33**, 79.

Larsh, J. E. (1947b). *J. Parasitol.* **33**, 339.

Larsh, J. E. (1949). *J. Parasitol.* **35**, 37.

Larsh, J. E. (1950a). *J. Parasitol.* **36**, 473.

Larsh, J. E. (1950b). *J. Parasitol.* **36**, 45.

Larsh, J. E. (1951). *J. Parasitol.* **37**, 343.

Larsh, J. E., and Campbell, D. H. (1952). *J. Parasitol.* **38**, 20.

Larsh, J. E., and Donaldson, A. S. (1944). *J. Parasitol.* **30**, 18.

Larsh, J. E., Race, G. J., and Esch, G. W. (1965). *J. Parasitol.* **51**, 45.

Lascelles, A. K., and McDowell, G. H. (1970). *Immunology* **19**, 613.

Laws, G. F. (1968). *Exp. Parasitol.* **23**, 1.

Lee, D. L. (1966). *Advan. Parasitol.* **4**, 187.

Leikina, E. S., Moskvin, S. N., Sokolovskaya, O. M., and Poletaeva, O. G. (1964). *Med. Parazitol. Parazit. Bolez.* **33**, 694.

Leonard, A. B. (1940). *Amer. J. Hyg.* **32**, 117.

Leonard, A. B., and Leonard, A. E. (1941). *J. Parasitol.* **27**, 375.

Lewert, R. M. (1958). *Rice Inst. Pam.* **14**, 97.

Lewert, R. M., and Lee, C. L. (1954). *J. Infec. Dis.* **95**, 13.

Lewert, R. M., and Lee, C. L. (1955). *J. Infec. Dis.* **97**, 177.

Logachev, E. D. (1959). *Dokl. Akad. Nauk SSSR* **125**, 1390.

Lubinsky, G. (1960a). *Can. J. Zool.* **38**, 149.

Lubinsky, G. (1960b). *Can. J. Zool.* **38**, 1117.

Lubinsky, G. (1967). *Can. J. Zool.* **45**, 175.

Lubinsky, G. (1968). *Can. J. Zool.* **46**, 29.

Lubinsky, G. (1969). *J. Parasitol.* **55**, 224.

Lukashenko, N. P. (1960). *Med. Parazitol. Parazit. Bolez.* **29**, 601.

Lukashenko, N. P. (1964). *Med. Parazitol. Parazit. Bolez.* **33**, 271.

Lumsden, R. D., Threadgold, L. T., Oaks, J. A., and Arme, C. (1970). *Parasitology* **60**, 185.

Lupascu, Gh., and Panaitescu, D. (1968). "Hidatidoza." Acad. Rep. Soc. Romania.

McIntosh, A., and Miller, D. (1960). *Amer. J. Vet. Res.* **21**, 169.

McManus, D. (1960). *Vet. Rec.* **72**, 847.

McManus, D. (1963). *Vet. Rec.* **75**, 697.

Mahon, J. (1954). *Proc. Zool. Soc. London* **124**, 527.

Mankau, S. K. (1956a). *Amer. J. Trop. Med. Hyg.* **5**, 872.

Mankau, S. K. (1956b). *Trans. Amer. Microsc. Soc.* **75**, 401.

Mankau, S. K. (1957). *J. Parasitol.* **43**, 153.

Marshall, A. G. (1967). *Parasitology* **57**, 419.

Meyers, H. F. (1957). *J. Parasitol.* **43**, 322.

Meymerian, E. (1961). *Amer. J. Trop. Med. Hyg.* **10**, 719.

Millemann, R. E. (1955). *J. Parasitol.* **41**, 424.

Miller, H. M. (1930). *Proc. Soc. Exp. Biol. Med.* **27**, 926.

Miller, H. M. (1931a). *J. Prev. Med.* **5**, 429.

Miller, H. M. (1931b). *J. Prev. Med.* **5**, 453.

Miller, H. M. (1931c). *Proc. Soc. Exp. Biol. Med.* **28**, 884.

Miller, H. M. (1932a). *J. Prev. Med.* **6**, 37.

Miller, H. M. (1932b). *Proc. Soc. Exp. Biol. Med.* **29**, 1125.

Miller, H. M. (1932c). *Proc. Soc. Exp. Biol. Med.* **29**, 1124.

Miller, H. M. (1932d). *Proc. Soc. Exp. Biol. Med.* **30**, 82.

Miller, H. M. (1934). *Amer. J. Hyg.* **19**, 270.

Miller, H. M. (1935). *Amer. J. Hyg.* **21**, 456.

Miller, H. M., and Gardiner, M. L. (1932a). *J. Prev. Med.* **6**, 479.

Miller, H. M., and Gardiner, M. L. (1932b). *Science* **75**, 270.

Miller, H. M., and Gardiner, M. L. (1934). *Amer. J. Hyg.* **20**, 424.

Miller, H. M., and Kerr, K. B. (1932). *Proc. Soc. Exp. Biol. Med.* **29**, 670.

Miller, H. M., and Massie, E. (1932). *J. Prev. Med.* **6**, 31.

Mlodzianowska, B. (1931). *Bull. Int. Acad. Pol. Sci., Nat. Zool.* No. 3/5, p. 475.

Moriarty, K. M. (1968). *J. Lab. Clin. Med.* **72**, 721.

Morseth, D. J. (1965). *Exp. Parasitol.* **16**, 207.

Morseth, D. J. (1966). *Exp. Parasitol.* **18**, 347.

Morseth, D. J. (1967). *J. Parasitol.* **53**, 312.

Moya, V., and Blood, B. D. (1964). *Bol. Chil. Parasitol.* **19**, 7.

Neas, B. R., Friedberg, W., and Self, J. T. (1966). *Int. J. Radiat. Biol.* **11**, 349.

Nelson, D. S. (1962). *Brit. J. Exp. Pathol.* **43**, 2.

Nemeth, I. (1970). *Acta. Vet. Hung.* **20**, 69.

Nieland, M. L. (1968). *J. Parasitol.* **54**, 957.

Norman, L., and Kagan, I. G. (1961). *J. Parasitol.* **47**, 870.

Novoselska, L. (1964). *C. R. Acad. Bulg. Sci.* **17**, 163.

Novoselska, L. (1965). *Nauch. Tr. Vissh. Med. Inst.*, *Sofia* 44, 1.
Novoselska, L. (1968). *Dokl. Bol. Akad. Nauk* 21, 79.
Ogilvie, B. M. (1970). *J. Parasitol.* 56, 525.
Ogren, R. E. (1955). *Proc. Pa. Acad. Sci.* 29, 258.
Ogren, R. E. (1957). *J. Parasitol.* 43, 505.
Ogren, R. E. (1958a). *J. Parasitol.* 44, 477.
Ogren, R. E. (1958b). *J. Parasitol.* 44, 44.
Ogren, R. E. (1959). *J. Parasitol.* 45, 575.
Ogren, R. E. (1961). *J. Parasitol.* 47, 197.
Ogren, R. E. (1962). *Exp. Parasitol.* 12, 1.
Ogren, R. E. (1967). *Trans. Amer. Microsc. Soc.* 86, 250.
Ogren, R. E. (1968a). *Trans. Amer. Microsc. Soc.* 87, 82.
Ogren, R. E. (1968b). *Trans. Amer. Microsc. Soc.* 87, 448.
Ohbayashi, M. (1960). *Jap. J. Vet. Res.* 18, 134.
Ohbayashi, M., and Sakamoto, T. (1966). *Jap. J. Vet. Res.* 14, 65.
Okamoto, K. (1970). *Exp. Parasitol.* 27, 28.
Olivier, L. (1962a). *J. Parasitol.* 48, 373.
Olivier, L. (1962b). *J. Parasitol.* 48, 758.
Orihara, M. (1962). *Jap. J. Vet. Res.* 10, 37.
Orihara, M. (1969). *Jap. J. Vet. Res.* 17, 121.
Pauluzzi, S. (1969). *Amer. J. Trop. Med. Hyg.* 18, 7.
Pauluzzi, S., Sorice, F., Castagnari, L., and Serra, P. (1965). *Ann. Sclavo* 7, 191.
Peel, C. (1953). *Vet. Rec.* 65, 244.
Peel, C. (1961). *J. Trop. Med. Hyg.* 64, 239.
Pence, D. B. (1967). *J. Parasitol.* 53, 1041.
Pence, D. B. (1970). *J. Parasitol.* 56, 84.
Penfold, H. B. (1937). *Med. J. Aust.* 1, 579.
Penfold, W. J., and Penfold, H. B. (1937). *J. Helminthol.* 15, 37.
Penfold, W. J., Penfold, H. B., and Phillips, M. (1936). *Med. J. Aust.* 1, 417.
Pennoit-De Cooman, E. (1940). *Vlaams Diergeneesk. Tijdschr.* 9, 107.
Pennoit-De Cooman, E., and De Rycke, P. H. (1970). *Z. Parasitenk.* 34, 362.
Potsueleva, V. A. (1953). *In* "Papers on Helminthology Presented to Academician K. I. Skryabin on his 75th Birthday," pp. 564–566. Izd. Akad. Nauk SSSR, Moscow.
Pozzuoli, R., Constanzi, G., Deiana, S., and Tamburini, G. (1965). *Riv. Parassitol.* 26, 85.
Price, E. W. (1930). *J. Parasitol.* 17, 57.
Pullin, J. W. (1955). *Can. J. Comp. Med.* 19, 17.
Race, G. J., Larsh, J. E., Esch, G. W., and Martin, J. H. (1965). *J. Parasitol.* 51, 364.
Raik, E., Hunter, E., and Warner, H. (1970). *Med. J. Aust.* 1, 1055.
Rausch, R. L. (1954). *J. Infec. Dis.* 94, 178.
Rausch, R. L. (1959). *J. Parasitol.* 45, 465.
Rausch, R. L. (1963). *In* "Thapar Commemoration Volume" (J. Dayal and K. S. Singh, eds.), pp. 233–246. Lucknow.
Rausch, R. L. (1967). *Ann. Parasitol. Hum. Comp.* 42, 19.
Rausch, R. L. (1968). *Bull. WHO* 39, 1.
Rausch, R. L., and Jentoft, V. L. (1957). *J. Parasitol.* 43, 1.
Rausch, R. L., and Nelson, G. S. (1963). *Ann. Trop. Med. Parasitol.* 57, 127.
Read, C. P., and Simmons, J. E. (1963). *Physiol. Rev.* 43, 263.

Rees, G. (1951). *Parasitology* **41**, 46.

Reid, W. M. (1948). *Trans. Amer. Microsc. Soc.* **67**, 177.

Rendtorff, R. C. (1948). *J. Parasitol.* **34**, 243.

Rickard, M., and Bell, K. (1971a). *J. Parasitol.* **57**, 571.

Rickard, M., and Bell, K. J. (1971b). *Res. Vet. Sci.* **12**, 401.

Robinson, D. L. H., Silverman, P. H., and Pearce, A. R. (1963). *Trans. Roy. Soc. Trop. Med. Hyg.* **57**, 238.

Rohde, K. (1960). *Tropenmed. Parasitol.* **11**, 43.

Rothman, A. H. (1957). *J. Parasitol.* **43**, 643.

Rybicka, K. (1957). *Acta. Parasitol. Pol.* **5**, 613.

Rybicka, K. (1966). *Advan. Parasitol.* **4**, 107.

Sakamoto, T., and Kotani, T. (1967). *Jap. J. Vet. Res.* **15**, 165.

Sakamoto, T., and Sugimura, M. (1969). *Jap. J. Vet. Res.* **17**, 67.

Sakamoto, T., Yamashita, J., and Ohbayashi, M. (1967). *Jap. J. Vet. Res.* **15**, 75.

Sawada, I. (1960). *Z. Parasitenk.* **20**, 350.

Sawada, I. (1961). *Exp. Parasitol.* **11**, 141.

Schad, G. A. (1966). *Amer. Midl. Natur.* **100**, 359.

Schiller, E. L. (1959). *Exp. Parasitol.* **8**, 91.

Schiller, E. L. (1960). *J. Parasitol.* **46**, 9.

Schultz, M. G., Halterman, L. G., Rich, A. B., and Martin, G. A. (1969). *J. Amer. Vet. Med. Ass.* **155**, 1708.

Schwabe, C. W. (1959). *Amer. J. Trop. Med. Hyg.* **8**, 20.

Schwabe, C. W., and Yamashita, J. (1968). *Bull. WHO* **39**, 126.

Schwabe, C. W., Schinazi, L. A., and Kilejian, A. (1959). *Amer. J. Trop. Med. Hyg.* **8**, 29.

Schwabe, C. W., Hadidian, L. and Koussa, M. (1963). *Amer. J. Trop. Med. Hyg.* **12**, 338.

Schwabe, C. W., Luttermoser, G. W., Koussa, M., and Ali, S. R. (1964). *J. Parasitol.* **50**, 260.

Schwabe, C. W., Kilejian, A., and Lainas, G. (1970). *J. Parasitol.* **56**, 80.

Sergeeva, P. A., and Euranova, V. G. (1962). *Uch. Zap. Kazan. Vet. Inst.* **89**, 145.

Shorb, D. A. (1933). *Amer. J. Hyg.* **18**, 74.

Shults, R. S., and Andreeva, N. K. (1960). *Tr. Inst. Zool., Akad. Nauk Kaz. SSR* **12**, 104.

Shults, R. S., and Ismagolova, R. G. (1962). *Vestn. Sel'skokhoz. Nauki* (*Alma-Ata*) **6**, 45.

Sidiqui, E. H. (1963). *Quart. J. Microsc. Sci.* **104**, 141.

Silverman, P. H. (1954a). *Ann. Trop. Med. Parasitol.* **48**, 207.

Silverman, P. H. (1954b). *Ann. Trop. Med. Parasitol.* **48**, 356.

Silverman, P. H. (1955). *Nature* (*London*) **176**, 598.

Silverman, P. H., and Hulland, T. J. (1961). *Res. Vet. Sci.* **2**, 248.

Silverman, P. H., and Maneely, R. B. (1955). *Ann. Trop. Med. Parasitol.* **49**, 326.

Silverstein, A. M. (1964). *Science* **144**, 1423.

Sima, I. (1937). *Allatorv. Lapok* **60**, 1.

Sinclair, E. B. (1970). Thesis for B.Sc. Hons., University of Otago, Dunedin, New Zealand.

Singh, B. B., and Rao, B. V. (1969). *Ceylon Vet. J.* **15**, 121.

Slais, J. (1966a). *Z. Parasitenk.* **27**, 25.

Slais, J. (1966b). *Folia Parasitol.* **13**, 73.

Slais, J. (1966c). *Anat. Anz.* **118**, 495.

Slais, J. (1966d). *Folia Parasitol.* **13**, 193.

Slais, J. (1966e). *Parasitology* **56**, 707.

Slais, J. (1967). *Folia Parasitol.* **14**, 27.

Slais, J. (1970). "The Morphology and Pathogenicity of the Bladder Worms *Cysticercus cellulosae* and *Cysticercus bovis.*" Publ. House Czech. Acad. Sci., Prague.

Smith, B. L. (1967). Thesis for Dip. Microbiol., University of Otago, Dunedin, New Zealand.

Smithers, S. R., and Terry, R. J. (1967). *Trans. Roy. Soc. Trop. Med. Hyg.* **61**, 517.

Smyth, J. D. (1962). *Parasitology* **52**, 441.

Smyth, J. D. (1963). *Commonw. Bur. Helminthol. (Gt. Brit.), Tech. Commun.* **34**, 1–38.

Smyth, J. D. (1964). *Advan. Parasitol.* **2**, 169.

Smyth, J. D. (1967). *Parasitology* **57**, 111.

Smyth, J. D. (1968). *Bull. WHO* **39**, 5.

Smyth, J. D. (1969a). "The Physiology of Cestoda." Oliver & Boyd, Edinburgh and London.

Smyth, J. D. (1969b). *Advan. Parasitol.* **7**, 327.

Smyth, J. D. (1969c). *Parasitology* **59**, 73.

Smyth, J. D., and Heath, D. D. (1970). *Helminthol. Abstr.* **39**, 1.

Smyth, J. D., and Smyth, M. M. (1964). *Parasitology* **54**, 493.

Smyth, J. D., Howkins, A. B., and Barton, M. (1966). *Nature (London)* **211**, 1374.

Sokal, R. R., and Rohlf, F. T. (1969). "Biometry." Freeman, San Francisco, California.

Solonenko, I. G. (1969). *Parazitologiya* **3**, 74.

Sorice, F., Pauluzzi, S., Castagnari, L., and Serra, P. (1964). *G. Mal. Infet. Parassit.* **10**, 563.

Sorice, F., Pauluzzi, S., Castagnari, L., and Serra, P. (1966a). *Boll. Ist. Sieroter. Milan.* **45**, 114.

Sorice, F., Castagnari, L., and Tolu, A. (1966b). *G. Mal. Infet. Parassit.* **18**, 192.

Soulsby, E. J. L. (1962). *Advan. Immunol.* **2**, 265.

Soulsby, E. J. L. (1963). *Proc. World Vet. Congr., 17th, 1962* Vol. 1, p. 761.

Southwood, T. R. E. (1966). "Ecological Methods." Methuen, London.

Specht, D., and Voge, M. (1965). *J. Parasitol.* **51**, 268.

Sprent, J. F. A. (1959). *In* "Evolution of Living Organisms," pp. 149–165. Melbourne Univ. Press, Melbourne.

Stirewalt, M. A. (1963). *Ann. N.Y. Acad. Sci.* **113**, 36.

Stunkard, H. W. (1940). *Amer. J. Trop. Med. Hyg.* **20**, 305.

Sweatman, G. K. (1957). *Can. J. Comp. Med.* **21**, 65.

Sweatman, G. K., and Henshall, T. C. (1962). *Can. J. Zool.* **40**, 1287.

Sweatman, G. K., and Plummer, P. J. G. (1957). *Can. J. Zool.* **35**, 93.

Sweatman, G. K., and Williams, R. J. (1963). *Parasitology* **53**, 339.

Sweatman, G. K., Robinson, R. G., and Manktelow, B. W. (1963a). *Amer. J. Trop. Med. Hyg.* **12**, 199.

Sweatman, G. K., Williams, R. J., Moriarty, K. M., and Henshall, T. C. (1963b). *Res. Vet. Sci.* **4**, 187.

Tenhaeff, C., and Ferwerda, S. F. (1935). *Tijdschr. Diergeneesk.* **62**, 79.

Tomasi, T. B., and Bienenstock, J. (1968). *Advan. Immunol.* **9**, 2.
Turner, E. L., Dennis, E. W., and Berberian, D. A. (1937). *J. Parasitol.* **23**, 43.
Urquhart, G. M. (1961). *J. Parasitol.* **47**, 857.
Urquhart, G. M. (1965). *J. Parasitol.* **51**, 544.
Urquhart, G. M. (1970). *J. Parasitol.* **56**, 547.
Urquhart, G. M., and Brocklesby, D. W. (1965). *J. Parasitol.* **51**, 349.
Van den Heever, L. W. (1967). *J. Parasitol.* **53**, 1168.
Varela-Diaz, V. M., Gemmell, M. A., and Williams, J. F. (1972). *Exp. Parasitol.* (in press).
Vegors, H. H., and Lucker, J. T. (1971). *Proc. Helminthol. Soc. Wash., D.C.* **38**, 122.
Venard, C. E. (1938). *Ann. N.Y. Acad. Sci.* **37**, 273.
Verster, A. J. M. (1965). *Onderstepoort J. Vet. Res.* **32**, 7.
Voge, M. (1954). *J. Parasitol.* **40**, 411.
Voge, M. (1956). *J. Parasitol.* **42**, 485.
Voge, M. (1959a). *J. Parasitol.* **45**, 175.
Voge, M. (1959b). *Exp. Parasitol.* **5**, 586.
Voge, M. (1960a). *J. Parasitol.* **46**, 717.
Voge, M. (1960b). *Proc. Helminthol. Soc. Wash., D.C.* **27**, 32.
Voge, M. (1961a). *J. Parasitol.* **47**, 189.
Voge, M. (1961b). *J. Parasitol.* **47**, 839.
Voge, M. (1961c). *Proc. Helminthol. Soc. Wash., D.C.* **28**, 1.
Voge, M. (1962). *Proc. Helminthol. Soc. Wash., D.C.* **29**, 62.
Voge, M. (1963a). *Proc. Helminthol. Soc. Wash., D.C.* **30**, 67.
Voge, M. (1963b). *J. Parasitol.* **49**, 85.
Voge, M. (1963c). *J. Parasitol.* **49**, 59.
Voge, M. (1967a). *Advan. Parasitol.* **5**, 247.
Voge, M. (1967b). *J. Parasitol.* **53**, 78.
Voge, M., and Berntzen, A. K. (1961). *J. Parasitol.* **47**, 813.
Voge, M., and Berntzen, A. K. (1963). *J. Parasitol.* **49**, 983.
Voge, M., and Coulombe, L. S. (1966). *Amer. J. Trop. Med. Hyg.* **15**, 902.
Voge, M., and Heyneman, D. (1957). *Univ. Calif., Berkeley, Pub. Zool.* **59**, 549.
Voge, M., and Heyneman, D. (1958). *J. Parasitol.* **44**, 249.
Voge, M., and Heyneman, D. (1960). *Proc. Helminthol. Soc. Wash., D.C.* **27**, 185.
Voge, M., and Seidel, J. S. (1968). *J. Parasitol.* **54**, 269.
Voge, M., and Turner, J. A. (1956). *Exp. Parasitol.* **5**, 580.
von Brand, T. (1966). "Biochemistry of Parasites." Academic Press, New York.
Waitz, J. A. (1961). *J. Parasitol.* **47**, 27.
Waitz, J. A. (1963). *J. Parasitol.* **49**, 73.
Waldmann, T. A., and Strober, W. (1960). *Progr. Allergy* **13**, 1.
Wantland, W. W. (1953). *J. Parasitol.* **39**, 667.
Webster, G. A., and Cameron, T. W. M. (1961). *Can. J. Zool.* **39**, 877.
Webster, G. A., and Cameron, T. W. M. (1963). *Can. J. Zool.* **41**, 185.
Weinmann, C. J. (1958). *J. Parasitol.* **44**, 16.
Weinmann, C. J. (1965). *J. Parasitol.* **51**, 560.
Weinmann, C. J. (1966). *In* "The Biology of Parasites" (E. J. L. Soulsby, ed.), pp. 301–320. Academic Press, New York.
Weinmann, C. J. (1968a). *J. Parasitol.* **55**, 1141.

Weinmann, C. J. (1968b). *Exp. Parasitol.* **22**, 68.
Weinmann, C. J. (1970). *In* "Immunity to Parasitic Animals" (G. J. Jackson, R. Herman, and I. Singer, eds.), Vol. 2, pp. 1021–1059. Appleton, New York.
Weinmann, C. J., and Lee, D. L. (1964). *J. Parasitol.* **50**, 17.
Williams, R. J., and Sweatman, G. K. (1963). *Parasitology* **53**, 391.
Yamashita, J. (1960). *Parasitologia* **2**, 399.
Yamashita, J., Ohbayashi, M., and Konno, S. (1957a). *Jap. J. Vet. Res.* **5**, 14.
Yamashita, J., Ohbayashi, M., and Konno, S. (1957b). *Jap. J. Vet. Res.* **5**, 197.
Yamashita, J., Ohbayashi, M., Kitamura, Y., Suzuki, K., and Okugi, M. (1958). *Jap. J. Vet. Res.* **6**, 135.
Yamashita, J., Ohbayashi, M., and Sakamoto, T. (1960). *Jap. J. Vet. Res.* **8**, 315.
Yamashita, J., Ohbayashi, M., Sakamoto, T., and Orihara, M. (1962). *Jap. J. Vet. Res.* **10**, 85.
Yamashita, J., Ohbayashi, M., and Doi, R. (1963a). *Jap. J. Vet. Res.* **11**, 55.
Yamashita, J., Ohbayashi, M., Sakamoto, T., Orihara, M., Suzuki, K., and Okugi, M. (1963b). *Jap. J. Vet. Res.* **11**, 50.
Yoshino, K. (1933a). *Taiwan Igakkai Zasshi* **32**, 139.
Yoshino, K. (1933b). *Taiwan Igakkai Zasshi* **32**, 91.
Yoshino, K. (1933c). *Taiwan Igakkai Zasshi* **32**, 103.

10 IMMUNE RESPONSE TO ARTHROPODS

S. M. GAAFAR

I. Introduction

The relationships between a host and the arthropods with which it is associated are complex and quite variable. The fleeting association between a host (e.g., man) with arthropod particles such as insect wings in the air is quite different from the true parasitism of myiasis or mange. In the former association, the host is exposed to nonliving biological fragments and in the latter it is exposed and must react to a mosaic of living and nonliving particles which may contain enzymes capable of reacting with the host's various tissues in which it is located or through which it is passing. Because of this variation in the nature of arthropod–host association, the reaction of the host is also variable and sometimes quite complex. Interest in arthropods as carriers and transmitters of disease and parasite organisms has long overshadowed the equally important and sometimes more important fact that these arthropods can produce pathological changes in their hosts without transmitting any organisms. The mechanisms and progression of these reactions in many instances are not completely understood and more investigations are needed.

The development of hypersensitivity and/or immunity in a host is dependent upon the availability of the antigenic materials of the arthropods to the immune component tissues and elements of that host. The responses of the host's tissues and fluids during the primary and subsequent exposures constitute the main points of interest in the present paper. Immunity is dealt with as the capacity of the host to protect itself against invasion of the arthropods or their products and also the manner in which the skin and other tissues dispose of these foreign materials.

II. The Skin and Mucous Membranes as a Natural Barrier

The skin constitutes the largest single tissue of the body and is the organ that is constantly being exposed to action by arthropods. The skin by its anatomical and histological structure also constitutes one of the main barriers against invasion of the body by pathogenic organisms including arthropods. Anatomically it is tough, resilient, and has a great capacity for expansion without losing much of its protective function. Histologically the keratinized layer is laminated and presents a very efficient primary barrier against the action of many physical and chemical factors in the environment, including many arthropods. The hair may also be useful in some instances by preventing many arthropods from coming in direct contact with the skin surface.

The epidermis with its several layers of epithelial cells in various stages of keratinization is another important part of the skin and adds to the efficiency of the skin as a barrier. The zona lucida, which is present in the epidermis of some species of animals, may impart even greater efficiency to the skin. The epithelial cells of the epidermis have the added strength of desmosomal attachments preventing all but the specialized organisms from gaining access to the skin layers underneath. The ability of epidermal cells to regenerate is remarkable and is useful in healing and covering any damaged areas underneath. The basement membrane underneath the malpighian cell layer is another barrier which may prevent seepage of many destructive fluids and organisms. The continuity of the basement membrane, however, is easily destroyed when there is exceptionally active proliferation of the malpighian cell layer.

The avascularity of the epidermis may possibly be an adaptive resistance factor. Only those arthropods that are able to penetrate the epidermal layers and reach the dermis are successful in obtaining a blood meal or depositing their products in a reactive part of the host's body. If this epidermal layer is thick and covered with thick layers of keratin, many arthropods are incapable of penetration.

The sebaceous and sweat glands in the skin may also be important factors in preventing penetration of many injurious organisms and arthropod materials to the deeper layers of the skin. The lipoidal nature of sebum and the electrolyte contents of sweat may act to neutralize and limit the spread of any foreign material deposited on the skin surface.

The mucous membranes lining the body openings, such as the nasal and buccal mucosa, generally possess characteristics designed to protect the internal organs from exposure to the action of various organisms including arthropods and their fragments. The presence of ciliated border in the epithelial cells, the production of mucus, and the secretion of immunologically active materials are all a part of this defense mechanism.

In summary, the epidermis and mucous membranes constitute the first line of defense or immunity against invading organisms, including arthropods. The various physiological and anatomical characteristics of the skin are important in this immune and defensive mechanism. These characteristics vary considerably and may be adaptive in nature. These characteristics should be considered whenever immunity against arthropod parasites is discussed.

III. Antigenicity of Arthropod Parasites

In a discussion of antigenicity of arthropod parasites, one should be familiar with the bionomies of the parasite in question, the exact method by which it gains access in the host, the products it releases, and the sequence in which these products become available to the host's tissues. It must also be understood that many arthropod products and somatic tissues are not antigenically available to the host until their death and fragmentation.

The biochemical and immunogenic properties of arthropod products such as bee venom, mosquito salivary extracts, and tick secretions have been the subject of several investigations (Benjamini *et al.*, 1963a,b; Gregson, 1970; Langlois *et al.*, 1965a,b; Voorhorst *et al.*, 1969; Bianchi and Chessa, 1970). Shulman (1967, 1968) and Shulman *et al.* (1962,

1963, 1964, 1966a,b) reviewed most of these biochemical and immunological characteristics, but more investigations are required to define
the composition of these products. Several fractions were isolated by
electrophoresis and tested for activity in experimental animals. Some
of these fractions were hemolytic and local irritant and others contained
enzymes such as phospholipase and hyaluronidase. Although similarities
in the constituents of the products were recognized, species variations
were identified (Shulman, 1968; Voorhorst *et al.*, 1969; Langlois, 1969).
In fleas, for example, the oral secretions contain various amino acids,
peptides, low molecular weight sugars, polyhydric alcohols, aldehydes,
phenols, phosphates, ketones, and other reducing and spreading substances. It was also indicated that these oral secretions are haptenic
in nature, and conjugation with dermal collagen is necessary to initiate
hypersensitive or immune reactions (Benjamini *et al.*, 1963a). The sensitizing activity of this oral secretion was found associated with the acid-
soluble as well as with the salt-soluble fraction of the skin collagen
(Benjamini *et al.*, 1963b).

The antigenic properties of tick secretions were shown by Gregson
(1970). These secretions contain an anticoagulant, hemolysins, cement
substances, and other fluid substances necrotizing in nature. Liquefying
enzymes, as well as a spreading agent, are presumed to be contained
in the oral secretion of the chigger mite *Trombicula* sp. because of
the action of these secretions when injected into the skin.

Fractionation of mosquito extracts was attempted by McKiel and
Clunie (1960) and Wilson and Clements (1965). Several components
were isolated in various degrees of purity but none was completely
pure. It is possible that the antigenic activity is associated with several
components of the oral secretion. Such components could be closely
related biochemically as well as antigenically.

It is interesting to note that differences in electrophoretic patterns
of protein extracts of arthropods increase according to taxonomic differences (Mastrilli *et al.*, 1970).

Histamine and similar derivatives have been isolated from many arthropod secretions as well as somatic tissue (Haberman, 1965; Hosen,
1970). Decarboxylases found in salivary secretions of some arthropods
could react with various polypeptides in the host to produce physiologically active amines (Chefurka, 1965).

The composition of the arthropod somatic tissue is quite variable
among the different species (Richards, 1951). This is also true with regards to the various stages in the life cycle of a certain species. Chitin
which is a high molecular weight polymer of anhydro-N-acetylglucos-
amine residues is present in the body wall and trachea of acari. Decom-

position of this compound is effected by chitinases which may be found in the host's tissues. Arthropodin, which is a water-soluble protein, and sclerotin, which is insoluble except in potassium hydroxide solutions, are also found in the integument of arthropods in various concentrations. Polyphenols, which are important in hardening and darkening of the integument, are also found in the arthropod cuticle.

Enzymes such as tyrosinase and phosphatase as well as melanin and nonmelanin pigments are also present in the integument.

The lipids contained in the arthropod exoskeleton are all waxes varying considerably in their physical properties. It is possible that these lipids act as an adjuvant in the reactions developing from invasion of some arthropods in the tissues of the host.

In general the arthropod cuticle varies from that of mammals in that the former is made up of polysaccharide framework with protein matrix, while the latter is made of collagen with polysaccharide matrix (Rudall, 1966).

The study of antigenicity of arthropod somatic tissues and products should not be confined to these constituents, but should also include the by-products resulting from the action of these chemicals on the host tissues. Essentially these conjugated or degraded proteins and polysaccharides have become foreign to the host and are regarded as such by its immunological system. Because the parasite may traverse several kinds of tissues during its cycle in the body of its host, one can expect many antigens that stimulate the immunologically active tissues. An example of this may be the invasion of cattle with *Hypoderma* sp. where the larvae penetrate the epidermal epithelial tissue, the dermal collagen, and the subcutaneous fibrous tissue, and pass between the peritoneal folds to the thoracic cavity where it must pass through some smooth muscle tissue to embed in the stratified squamous epithelium of the esophagus. This parasite must then pass to the skin on the back of the animal where it again must utilize enzymatic secretions as well as its larval mouth parts to puncture an opening and gain access to the outside. If the parasite does not follow the normal route and becomes lodged in other tissues such as the spinal cord or viscera, other antigens may be released as a result of this activity.

Despite the extensive and numerous investigations attempting to isolate arthropod antigens in chemically pure forms, none have so far been identified. It is possible that the mosaic character of these antigens and their close resemblance and integration with the host's tissues are the factors responsible for these difficulties. [For a more extensive review of the antigenic characteristics of arthropods, see Benjamini and Feingold (1970), Shulman (1968), and Frazier (1969).]

IV. Reaction of the Host

The association between an arthropod and its host results in reactions in both the arthropod and the host. The present discussion will deal with the reaction of the host. All of these reactions are probably initiated basically as protective mechanisms against the primary association and/or any further associations with the parasite in question or closely related parasites. Three general areas are of importance in such a relationship: (1) the skin or mucous membranes, (2) the regional lymph nodes, and (3) serum proteins, specifically immunoglobulins.

A. THE SKIN

1. The Epidermis

Although the epithelial cells of the basal cell layer possess the ability of being highly active, they are immunologically noncompetent. Mitosis usually progressing at a slow rate under normal conditions is stimulated by injury to adjoining cells, excessive erosion of the external layers, or in response to increased activity in the dermis below. As a result of this accelerated mitotic activity of the basal cell layer, the basement membrane may rupture, the number of nucleoli in each nucleus may increase, and the newly formed cells may become crowded in new rete pegs in the dermis. The number of cell layers of the epidermis may be increased. In such a reaction it is also observed that the rate of keratinization is increased, resulting in hyperkeratosis or parakeratosis. The intercellular spaces are increased in width and acanthosis of varying degrees becomes evident in chronic irritations such as chronic ectoparasitism. All of the above-mentioned changes are not only reactions but also intended to a greater or lesser extent to be protective to the host through its first line of defense.

2. The Dermis

This layer of the skin is even more reactive than the epidermis by virtue of its vascularity and fibroblastic nature. When arthropods or their by-products are introduced in this layer of the skin, typical inflammatory reactions are immediately instigated. Polymorphonuclear cells are summoned to the area within minutes as a result of tissue destruction. Edema and increased vascularity are intended for clearing of soluble toxic material. Monocytic or macrophage infiltration is aimed at removal of particulate matter, and fibroblastic proliferation is aimed at encapsulating the residue. The resulting granuloma or abscess is a defense mechanism which sometimes may become extensive and leads to clinical cutaneous lesions. The increased vascularity of the dermis caused by the inflammatory process leads to increased presence of nutrients available to the basal cell layer of the epidermis as well as stretching of the surface. These basal cell layers may react to this stimulus and the rate of mitosis may increase.

3. *The Hair Follicle and Appendages*

The increased activity in the dermis naturally will affect the hair follicle and its appendages. These structures may become directly or indirectly involved in augmenting the defensive status of the host. In one condition, demodicosis, the hair follicle epithelium layers attempt an increase in number aimed at containing the mites in the follicle. Often this is not accomplished because the mite colony between the inner and outer sheath is growing faster than the basal cells are proliferating. The proliferation of the sebaceous and sweat glands are sometimes noted in conditions of ectoparasitism. Their reactions may be regarded as indirect contributions to the total defense mechanism of the skin.

B. The Regional Lymph Nodes

The fate of the foreign material deposited by the arthropod parasite or these substances conjugated with the host's body constituents should be of utmost importance in the understanding of ectoparasitism. Of equal importance, however, are the local and regional lymph node reactions, since they are not only the second line of body defense, but they are also directly involved in the immunological and/or hypersensitive status of the host.

Enlargement and induration of the regional lymph nodes are usually observed following arthropod bites. This lymphadenitis is sometimes quite severe and at times has been mistaken for lymphoblastoma (A. G. Allen, 1967). Despite the obvious importance of the regional lymph nodes in the initiation of hypersensitive conditions and/or immune capacity of the host, there is a paucity of information on the kinetics of the lesions in these organs following cutaneous exposure to arthropods. It is speculated, however, that the general pattern of reaction is similar to that occurring in contact dermatitis and intradermal inoculation with biological substances. In contact dermatitis there is an initial increase in the size of the paracortical area accompanied by a rise in the number of large pyroninophilic cells. This increase lasts for the first 10 days following initial application of the contactant. Continued exposure to contact sensitizer, however, results in induration of the lymph node with a hyperplasia of the germinal centers (Oort and Turk, 1965; Turk and Stone, 1963). It was also indicated that most of the contact sensitizers are irritant haptenes (Medenica and Rostenberg, 1971) and usually conjugate with the skin proteins forming new antigenic proteins. The inoculation by an arthropod of its saliva or other products could well have a similar mechanism. The reaction of the draining lymph node to the intradermal injection of various chemicals and the resultant granulomas in these organs were studied by Gaafar and Turk (1970). It was found that the granulomas in the nodes were mainly composed of histiocytes passing through the afferent lymphatics following their phagocytic activity in the skin. There was little evidence that accumulation of histiocytes was a direct result of a reaction in the lymph node itself.

The kinetics of the reactions in both skin and the draining lymph nodes are basically dependent on the physical and chemical character of the materials applied and the fate of these materials. Soluble and solubilized materials are capable of being drained by the blood or lymph systems from the site of inoculation in the skin while particulate matter is engulfed by phagocytic cells, most of which are carried to the regional lymph nodes. The filtering capacity of the lymph node is at present somewhat controversial, but it is generally agreed that much of the particulate matter is retained there either in the macrophages or in the phagocytic reticular cells. Thus the lymph node can be regarded as an active part of the protective system of the body. In the lymph node the engulfed foreign particles in the macrophages are continually acted on by the enzymatic systems of the lysomes of these cells. The products of this lysing action contains several constituents identified as super antigen, lymph node permeability factor, and lymphokine and skin-reactive factor by various authors. The presence of the antigen and macrophages in the mileau of immune competent lymphocytes in the lymph nodes is prerequisite to development of immunological changes. In arthropod parasitisms the antigens of the salivary and other secretions and particulate material of the parasite somatic tissue may be found in the regional lymph nodes.

C. General Body Response

Despite all the obstacles and reactions of the skin and regional lymph nodes in attempting to limit the progress of the invasion by antigenic materials, exemplified by arthropod parasites and their products, some of this material escapes and the immunological systems are stimulated. This stimulation brings about several changes in various tissues as well as secretion of products intended to neutralize the presence of the antigenic materials. The production of immunoglobulins by the plasma cells is one of these attempts. The clinical manifestations observed in the host following repeated infestations with arthropods are partly caused by these attempted neutralizations. The mechanisms by which immunoglobulins are produced are not well understood. Precipitating as well as nonprecipitating classes of immunoglobulins have been associated with development of hypersensitivity and immunity to arthropod invasions of the host (J. R. Allen, 1966; Fox and Bayona, 1968; Rockwell and Johnson, 1952; Wilson and Clements, 1965; Michaeli and Goldfarb, 1968). It is not known, however, which of the various classes are directly involved in immunity or hypersensitivity. It is highly suspected that the skin reaction of sensitive hosts following exposure to arthropod infestation is due to the presence in the skin of reaginic antibodies recently designated immunoglobulin E (IgE). This is not conclusive evidence since other classes of immunoglobulins have been shown to sensitize the skin (Ovary, 1958). The role of IgE in body defenses has not been well elucidated (Good and Chol, 1971). The presence of IgE-like substances in some animal species has been demonstrated. Many of these animals exhibit allergic and immunological diseases similar to man and suffer from anaphylactic shocks caused by antigen–antibody reactions when exposed to arthropod invasions (Campbell, 1970; Aitken and Sanford, 1968; Lipzig and Schyus, 1967; Lawler, 1970; Walton, 1966; Eckert *et al.,* 1969). It is also known that many of these animals become immune or at least tolerant to subsequent invasions with the same and sometimes similar parasites. It is presumed that in these cases the immunologically competent tissues of the hosts have been highly mobilized. The ability of the skin to form granulomas around the invading arthropods is greatly enhanced. The circulating antibodies may combine with the secretory and excretory products of the arthropod, leading to a more severe inflammatory response following the second and third invasion, but eventually these reactions become less pronounced if more invasions are encountered. Brown (1969) indicated that this decreased reaction may be related to loss of precipitating antibodies.

The development of a state of unresponsiveness or immune tolerance is the ultimate goal toward which the host's immune system is striving. The exact mechanisms by which this is attained are not completely known. The reaction of the skin during the course of repeated invasions with arthropod parasites and their products was reported in a few arthropod–host relationships (Benjamini *et al.,* 1961; Gaafar, 1966). In flea bite dermatitis five stages of reaction have been reported, namely: (1) nonreaction for the first 4 days, (2) delayed reaction for the following

5 days, (3) immediate and delayed reaction during the following 9 days, (4) immediate reaction for 60 days, and (5) Nonreaction for a period of 90 days. The implication in this condition is that during days 5–14 postexposure cell-mediated immunity (CMI) or fixed antibodies are active while during days 15–60 only circulating antibodies are functioning. Whether or not similar stages develop in other arthropod invasions remains uninvestigated. Roberts (1968) indicated that cattle become resistant to infestations with *Boophilus microplus* 8 days past infestation after which each animal maintains a relatively constant number of ticks. Bell *et al.* (1966) showed that an intensive exposure to lice produces a stage of acquired resistance in mice. Such resistance was apparently specific since ixodid ticks fed on resistant mice. The period of nonreaction of the host may vary considerably between species of hosts and the invading arthropod or its antigenic products (Michaeli and Goldfarb, 1968; Brown, 1969). The exact mechanism of the development of unresponsiveness is as yet unexplained. Two theories are advanced (Lowney, 1971). One is a dual pathway theory where the tolergenic unchanged material, "nonactivated antigen," passes to the lymphoid cells and blocks the receptor sites, and the other is the single pathway theory where various levels of antigens would have a direct effect on the lymphocytes. Neither of these theories completely explains unresponsiveness of the skin.

Nelson and Bainborough (1963) and Tatchell (1969) indicated that the development of resistance may be related to restriction of available nutrients by constriction of blood vessels in the skin. This was shown in cases of sheep kid infestations as well as lice and tick infestations of cattle. Tatchell showed that ticks on nonimmune animals were larger than those on immune animals. Restriction of food also caused reduction in egg laying capacity of the tick. It was also proposed that toxic products forming of antigen–antibody complex may affect those parasites that obtain blood for feeding. Argasid ticks may feed normally on immune rabbits, but they die shortly afterwards. Roberts (1971), however, indicated that this toxic effect on the tick may not be an important factor at least in the larval stage. He showed that larvae of *B. microplus* feeding in chambers on cattle of varying degrees of resistance behave in similar fashion and that the survival of larvae removed from the host after feeding is not affected regardless of the degree of resistance of the host.

Use was made of the development of nonreaction to arthropod in maintaining cattle in tick infested areas of Australia. Breed variations in acquiring the resistance were observed (Riek, 1962). Purebred *Bos taurus* showed less ability to acquire the resistance than crossbreeds.

Some evidence was obtained that it may be possible to induce reduction of tick burden by repeated subcutaneous injection of 0.5 ml of 1:10 larval extracts of ticks. Among two populations of cattle varying in resistance to ticks, Wilkinsen (1962) recognized a difference in hair follicle depth which he attributed to difference in resistance.

Hyposensitization against flea bite dermatitis has been attempted with whole flea extracts and flea saliva. The best results were obtained by weekly subcutaneous or intradermal injection of the haptemic fraction of the flea saliva in a 1% solution of sodium alginate. A hyposensitive state was achieved following 3–4 injections and lasted on the average of 5–6 weeks (Michaeli and Goldfarb, 1968).

V. Summary

Immunity against arthropod parasites was discussed mostly on anatomical and physiological basis. The various barriers in the skin, lymph nodes, and serum immunoglobulins were considered. The reaction of the skin and lymph nodes during primary and subsequent infestations was pointed out as physiopathological means of protection of the host against further invasions with arthropod parasites of the same and possibly closely related species. It is apparent that the role of antibodies in the serum of parasitized or immune animals is not well understood. Immunoglobulins of the precipitating and nonprecipitating classes are apparently found in parasitized animals but no information is available on the types involved. Hyposensitization or nonreaction in resistant animals was discussed.

References

Aitken, M. M., and Sanford, J. (1968). *Vet. Rec.* **82**, 418.
Allen, A. G. (1967). "The Skin. A Clinicopathological Treatise," 2nd ed. Grune & Stratton, New York.
Allen, J. R. (1966). *Exp. Parasitol.* **19**, 132.
Bell, J. F., Clifford, C. M., Moore, G. J., and Raymond, G. (1966). *Exp. Parasitol.* **18**, 49.
Benjamini, E. B., and Feingold, B. F. (1970). *In* "Immunity to Parasitic Animals" (G. J. Jackson, R. Herman, and I. Singer, eds.), Vol. 2, p. 1061–1134. Appleton, New York.
Benjamini, E. B., Feingold, B. F., and Kartman, L. (1961). *Proc. Soc. Exp. Biol. Med.* **108**, 700.
Benjamini, E. B., Feingold, B. F., and Kartman, L. (1963a). *Exp. Parasitol.* **14**, 75.

Benjamini, E. B., Feingold, B. F., Young, J. D., Kartman, L., and Shimizu, M. (1963b). *Exp. Parasitol.* 13, 143.
Bianchi, U., and Chessa, G. (1970). *Rev. Parasitol.* 31, 299.
Brown, H. (1969). J. Allergy 44, 146.
Campbell, S. G. (1970). *Cornell Vet.* 60, 240.
Chefurka, W. (1965). *In* "The Physiology of Insecta" (M. Rockstein, ed.), Vol. 2, p. 684. Academic Press, New York.
Eckert, V. J., Gloor, H., Krabe, E., and Ruhm, W. (1969). *Schweiz. Arch. Tierheilk.* 3, 447.
Fox, I., and Bayona, I. G. (1968). *J. Parasitol.* 54, 1239.
Frazier, C. A. (1969). "Insect Allergy," p. 493. Green, St. Louis, Missouri.
Gaafar, S. M. (1966). *In* "The Biology of Parasites" (E. J. L. Soulsby, ed.), Vol. 1, p. 229. Academic Press, New York.
Gaafar, S. M., and Turk, J. L. (1970). *J. Pathol.* 100, 9.
Good, R. A., and Chol, Y. S. (1971). *N. Engl. J. Med.* 284, 552.
Gregson, J. D. (1970). *J. Parasitol.* 56, 1038.
Haberman, E. (1965). *Proc. 2nd Int. Pharmacol. Meet., 1963* Vol. 9, pp. 53–62.
Hosen, H. (1970). *Ann. Allergy* 28, 296.
Langlois, C. (1969). *Postgrad. Med.* 45, 190.
Langlois, C., Shulman, S., and Arbesman, C. E. (1965a). *J. Allergy* 36, 12.
Langlois, C., Shulman, S., and Arbesman, C. E. (1965b). *J. Allergy* 36, 109.
Lawler, D. C. (1970). *N. Z. Vet. J.* 18, 111.
Lipzig, V. J., and Schyus, M. (1967). *Tijdschr. Diergeneesk.* 92, 168.
Lowney, E. D. (1971). *J. Invest. Dermatol.* 54, 355.
McKiel, J. A., and Clunie, J. F. (1960). *Can. J. Zool.* 38, 478.
Mastrilli, M. L., Sacca, G., and Silano, V. (1970). *Rev. Parsitol.* 31, 215.
Medenica, M., and Rostenberg, A. (1971). *J. Invest. Dermatol.* 56, 259.
Michaeli, D., and Goldfarb, S. (1968). *Aust. Vet. J.* 44, 161.
Nelson, W. A., and Bainborough, A. R. (1963). *Exp. Parasitol.* 13, 118.
Oort, J., and Turk, J. L. (1965). *Brit. J. Exp. Pathol.* 46, 147.
Ovary, Z. (1958). *Progr. Allergy* 5, 459–508.
Richards, A. G. (1951). "The Integument of Arthropods." Univ. of Minnesota Press, Minneapolis.
Riek, R. F. (1962). *Aust. J. Agr. Res.* 13, 532.
Roberts, J. A. (1968). *J. Parasitol.* 54, 657.
Roberts, J. A. (1971). *J. Parastiol.* 57, 651.
Rockwell, E. M., and Johnson, P. (1952). *J. Invest. Dermatol.* 19, 137.
Rudall, K. M. (1966). *In* "Aspects of Insect Biochemistry" (T. W. Goodwin, ed.). pp. 83–92. Academic Press, New York.
Shulman, S. (1967). *Annu. Rev. Entomol.* 12, 323.
Shulman, S. (1968). *Progr. Allergy* 12, 246.
Shulman, S., Rapp, D., Bronson, P., and Arbesman, C. E. (1962). *J. Allergy* 33, 438.
Shulman, S., Bronson, P., and Arbesman, C. E. (1963). *J. Allergy* 34, 1.
Shulman, S., Langlois, C., and Arbesman, C. E. (1964). *J. Allergy* 35, 446.
Shulman, S., Langlois, C., Miller, J., and Arbesman, C. E. (1966a). *J. Allergy* 37, 350.
Shulman, S., Bigelsen, F., Lang, R., and Arbesman, C. E. (1966b). *J. Immunol.* 96, 29.
Tachell, R. J. (1969). *Parasitology* 59, 93.

Turk, J. L., and Stone, S. H. (1963). *In* "Cell-Bound Antibodies." (B. Amos and H. Koprowski, eds.), p. 51. Wistar Inst. Press, Philadelphia, Pennsylvania.

Voorhorst, R., Spieksma, F. T. M., and Varekamp, H. (1969). "House-dust Atropy and the House-dust Mite *Dermatophagoides pteronyssinus* (Tronessart 1897)" Staffers Sci. Publ., Leiden, The Netherlands.

Walton, G. S. (1966). *J. Small Anim. Pract.* **7,** 749.

Wilkinsen, P. R. (1962). *Aust. J. Agr. Res.* **13,** 974.

Wilson, A. B., and Clements, A. N. (1965). *Int. Arch. Allergy Appl. Immunol.* **26,** 294.

11 IMMUNE RESPONSE TO HEMOPROTOZOA

I. Trypanosomes

W. H. R. LUMSDEN

I. Introduction

It seems that some of the difficulties and misconceptions in the immunology of protozoal infections derive from the uncertainties of nomenclature. In the present treatment Humphrey and White (1970) and Herbert and Wilkinson (1971) are followed, so that terminology will conform as closely as possible to accepted immunological usage.

For the proper understanding of, or rather for the proper orientation of thought on, the immunology of trypanosome infections it is essential first to realize that *Trypanosoma* spp. are not all of broadly similar behavior in the vertebrate host as are, for example, members of the same bacterial or virus genus. They differ fundamentally in their development pattern, and consideration of the immunological response of the host must take this into account. For the purpose of the present discussion the species may be divided up as follows:

A. STERCORARIA

Trypanosoma spp. transmitted from host to host by infective forms occurring in the feces of insect vectors.

1. Group A

Trypanosoma spp. whose multiplication takes place in the lumen of blood vessels of the host, in the peripheral circulation, or in the capillaries of internal organs. The infection typically consists of an initial short multiplicative phase in which trypanosomes are abundant in the peripheral blood and a second longer phase in which multiplication is inhibited and small numbers of trypanosomes circulate peripherally. *Trypanosoma* species of this group are host-species-specific and generally nonpathogenic. Example: *Trypanosoma lewisi* of *Rattus rattus*.

2. Group B

Trypanosoma spp. whose multiplication takes place intracellularly in the vertebrate host, in muscle, macrophage, and other cells; small numbers of nondividing trypanosomes circulate peripherally. *Trypanosoma* spp. of this group are typically nonhost-species-specific and often pathogenic. Example: *Trypanosoma cruzi* of many mammalian species, pathogenic in man (Chagas' disease).

B. SALIVARIA

Trypanosoma spp. transmitted from host to host by infective forms occurring in the saliva or mouth parts of the insect vector. Multiplication of these species takes place in the lumen of the blood vessels of the host, perhaps importantly in some cases, in the capillaries of internal organs, and in tissue spaces, but not intracellularly. These species are not typically host-species-specific, and are often pathogenic. Examples: *Trypanosoma brucei brucei* of African antelopes and cattle, *T. b. gambiense* and *T. b. rhodesiense* causing sleeping sickness in man.

It will be logical to consider the evidence for humoral and for cell-mediated immunity, in turn, in each of these three characteristic categories.

II. Stercoraria—Group A, *Trypanosoma lewisi* and Allied Species

A. CHARACTERISTICS OF INFECTION

The phases of the infection are most sensitively followed by observing the coefficient of variation (CV) of the length of the organisms (D'Alesandro, 1970). During the initial phase of active multiplication, lasting up until about day 10 of the infection, the CV is about 25%. Thereafter it falls to 3–5%, the so-called adult population which persists in small numbers in the peripheral blood for weeks or months before finally being eliminated. The host, subsequently, is sterilely immune, probably for life (D'Alesandro, 1970).

B. NONSPECIFIC IMMUNITY

Firstly, it is to be noted that it is in relation to this group that nonspecific immune mechanisms are most conspicuous. The host-species specificity of the *Trypanosoma* spp. of this group has been mentioned above.

C. ACQUIRED SPECIFIC IMMUNITY

1. Humoral Immunity

The process of the infection is ascribed to the effects of humoral antibodies (D'Alesandro, 1970) of three different activities: (a) a trypanocidal antibody specific for division forms and responsible for the termination of that phase; (b) an antibody inhibiting parasite reproduction (ablastin) responsible for maintaining the "adult" population at low levels; and (c) a second trypanocidal antibody responsible for the termination of the infection by killing the adult forms. According to D'Alesandro (1970) the early trypanocidal antibody is IgG while the terminal one is IgM which is in a manner opposite to that expected for immune responses to new antigens. D'Alesandro points out that the two trypanocidal antibodies have different specificities the first killing division forms, but not adults. Thus the pattern is atypical only in the first response; the second response is classical.

D'Alesandro (1970), comparing these organisms with the salivarian organisms which (see below) characteristically produce a series of antigenic variants, considers that they are similar except that antigenic variation is limited to the production of only two antigenic types. As regards the mechanisms of destruction of organisms by the trypanocidal antibodies, these are likely to comprise agglutination, lysis, and phagocytosis (D'Alesandro, 1970).

The status of the reproduction-inhibition antigen, ablastin, is less clear. Its existence is postulated on the evidence that adult trypanosomes inoculated along with immune serum into normal animals do not reproduce but simply circulate in the blood at a constant level. In controls receiving normal serum, reproduction begins and the usual course of infection is followed. Similar effects can be demonstrated *in vitro* (D'Alesandro, 1970). Ablastin is, however, not absorbable from serum, nor are living organisms used for absorption inhibited from reproduction if inoculated into a new host. However, ablastin has qualities characteristic of antibodies. It is an IgG; its formation is suppressed by factors suppressing antibody formation, such as X-irradiation and splenectomy; and it is specific. The most puzzling feature with regard to the concept of ablastin is the failure to demonstrate absorption by homologous antigen. However, immune sera repeatedly absorbed with trypanosomes to remove all trypanocidal antibodies can be shown by immunoelectroabsorption still to provide thicker layers in reaction to antigen than do normal sera (D'Alesandro, 1970). D'Alesandro (1970) argues against other theories, ascribing the observed effects to reproduction of the parasite limited to internal organs, to enzyme effects, etc. As regards the mode of action of ablastin, he considers it likely that it acts on the cell surface affecting transport of metabolites across the cell membrane.

2. Cell-Mediated Immunity

D'Alesandro's (1970) exhaustive review of the immunology of this group of trypanosomes ascribes the effects solely to humoral immunity and does not advance any evidence that cell-mediated processes are involved.

III. Stercoraria—Group B, *Trypanosoma cruzi*

A. CHARACTERISTICS OF INFECTION

The typical picture of long term *T. cruzi* infection is of intracellular multiplication proceeding in tissue, mainly muscle, cells with release of nonmultiplying trypomastigote forms into the blood in small numbers. Miles (1971) points out that it is uncertain whether this long-term persistence of trypanosomes in the peripheral blood is due simply to continued release from the tissues, mimicry of host antigens by the parasite, or lack of effective humoral defence mechanisms.

B. Nonspecific Immunity

Nonspecific immune mechanisms are less evident in the case of *T. cruzi* and *T. cruzi*-like organisms. They are typically not host-species-specific, at least among mammal species. Sera of some mammal species will lyse epimastigote culture forms of *T. cruzi*, but not infective trypomastigote forms (Goble, 1970). Similarly, cultural forms inoculated into nonimmune animals are rapidly destroyed by macrophages, but blood stream trypomastigotes are only in part digested in macrophages; most develop into intracellular fission forms (Goble, 1970).

C. Acquired Specific Immunity

1. Humoral Immunity

Attempts to demonstrate humoral antibodies by agglutination and lytic tests have given inconsistent or contradictory results, perhaps because of lack of standardized antigens. Neutralization activity of antisera has not been investigated (Miles, 1971). However, humoral antibodies do occur as is evidenced by the effective use of complement-fixation, indirect hemagglutination, and indirect fluorescent antibody tests for diagnosis of the disease.

The protective significance of these humoral antibodies remains uncertain. Immune sera are ineffective against trypomastigote blood forms *in vitro*. Some workers have demonstrated passive transfer of protection, at least to the extent of delaying or depressing the infection; others failed to show any effect (Goble, 1970).

In contradistinction to the inconsistency of passive protection by serum is the transmission of immunity from mother to young demonstrated by several workers and thought to be milk transmitted (Miles, 1971). Miles, himself, found 13 of 17 mice, born from and suckled by mothers recovered from an acute phase infection 6–10 weeks before, resistant to 100 organism challenge. Also the mice showed fluorescent antibody titers of 64–256. Evidence was adduced to indicate that this resistance was indeed milk transmitted and not due to transmission of infection from the mothers to the young or by placental transfer. The clear demonstration of passive transfer of resistance by suckling deserves further study. Perhaps antibody in milk is in some special form, or perhaps cells or sensitizing factors are transferred as well as humoral antibodies.

2. Cell-Mediated Immunity

The difficulty of consistently showing protection by humoral antibodies has emphasized the likelihood that CMI is involved. Pizzi (1957) concludes that the defense mechanism is' essentially cellular but considers that antibodies may play a coadjuvant role. While this seems likely, especially as CMI mechanisms have been demonstrated in the case of another predominantly intracellular kinetoplastid flagellate, *Leishmania*, by Bray and Bryceson (1968), the details of the process in *T. cruzi* infections are still obscure. The section on cellular immune factors in Goble's (1970) recent review of immunity to *T. cruzi* states that "although normal sera of various animals contain substances which are lethal to the crithidial forms of *T. cruzi*, the main defense against the parasite seems to be phagocytosis by inflammatory macrophages, perhaps assisted by nonlytic or opsonin-like factors." Further discussion of the subject is limited to the actual process of phagocytosis and the effects of splenectomy, reticuloendothelial blockade, and anti-spleen serum, which were generally without marked effect on the course of the infection.

However, there is some recent evidence that cooperative CMI mechanisms are concerned. Seah (quoted in Miles, 1971) obtained delayed hypersensitivity type skin reactions in monkeys with a lyophilized antigen extract, but not satisfactorily in mice. Gonzalez Cappa *et al.* (1968), using antigens of *T. cruzi* prepared under pressure, succeeded in demonstrating delayed-type hypersensitivity with an intradermal test in guinea pigs. Seah (1970) has shown, with mouse peritoneal cells, comprising both lymphocytes and macrophages, that macrophage spreading was inhibited by *T. cruzi* antigen in mice immunized in various ways against *T. cruzi*. This has not, however, yet been shown to be dependent on the presence of the lymphocytes.

IV. Salivaria—*Trypanosoma brucei* and Related Species

A. CHARACTERISTICS OF INFECTIONS

Most of the attention in studies on salivarian trypanosomes has been devoted to the trypomastigote forms in the peripheral circulation. Goodwin (1971) has drawn attention to the equal or perhaps greater abundance of trypanosomes in the tissue spaces where they both multiply and are phagocytosed. Besides trypomastigotes in vessels and in tissue spaces, spherical forms, with or without flagella, have been described and controversy has arisen as to whether these are integrally involved in the cycle of development of the parasite in the host or are simply degenerative forms. Ormerod and Venkatesan (1971) have recently described amastigote forms in the choroid plexus of the lateral ventricles of rats infected with *T. brucei* strains from sleeping sickness cases in Botswana. They suggest that these forms constitute an "occult" phase in the cycle of development of the trypanosome in the mammal host. Ormerod (1971, personal communication) further suggests that the organisms in this position may be sheltered from antibody attack by blocking of, and stasis in, the vessels concerned, arteriovenous shunts between artery and vein.

It is characteristic of salivarian infections that they are periodic, waves of parasitemia succeeding each other at intervals of some few days. It is believed that each wave represents in its crescendo phase the multiplication of a population of a new antigenic type and that its diminuendo phase represents the destruction of this population by the antibody response of the host. Thus the persistence of the infection is due to the trypanosome population evading the immune response of the host by repeatedly changing its antigenic character. Morphological changes in the trypanosome population accompany the wave of the parasitemia; in the crescendo phase the organisms are mainly long and slender, in its diminuendo phase, short and stumpy.

B. Antigens of Salivarian Trypanosomes

The antigens present in salivarian trypanosomes may be classified in relation to this periodicity of parasitemia and successive appearances of different antigenic types. They may be classified (World Health Organization, 1969), on the basis of their liability to vary, into "stable" and "variant" antigens.

The stable antigens comprise those antigenic materials that are common to the same trypanosome species at different times of its cycle of development, and may be common to several populations of the same, or even of different, *Trypanosoma* spp. Such antigens probably include many of the "run-of-the-mill" antigenic components of the cells—enzymes, structural proteins, and so on. The variant antigens essentially characterize the populations composing each of the successive waves of parasitemia in a continuing infection.

C. Location of the Variant Antigens

From the antigenic type specificity of the direct agglutination test in *T. brucei* organisms it has been assumed that the variant antigens are manifested at the surface of the organism. They are also released into the ambient under certain conditions—the exoantigen of Weitz (1960). These phenomena are to be related to recently described aspects of the morphology of the organisms as follows.

Vickerman (1969) drew attention to the existence, as demonstrated by electron microscopy, of a compact, 15-nm thick, surface coat lying outside the 3-ply unit membrane which forms the boundary of the trypanosome cell. This coat occurred in blood stream forms and in the infective forms in the salivary glands of the insect vector, *Glossina* (tsetse fly), not in earlier developmental forms in the vector or in culture forms. In other words it was confined to forms existing or preparing to exist in the mammalian body. The coat was particularly well developed, compact, and dense in salivarian organisms in which antigenic variation was conspicuous; it was less dense and filamentous in *T. lewisi* in which species antigenic variation was of very minor degree. Further evidence that the variant antigens are located in the surface coat has been obtained from studies with ferritin-labeled antibodies (Vickerman and Luckins, 1969).

Wright *et al.* (1970) showed by phase contrast microscopy of trypanosomes suspended in a viscid medium, and by electron microscopy, that *Trypanosoma brucei* produced long filamentous streamers, up to 70 μm long, from its anterior and posterior extremities. These streamers called "filopodia," or preferably, "plasmanemes," were shown to have the same superficial structure as the trypanosome body, i.e., a unit membrane covered externally with a compact surface coat. These plasmanemes may be shed by the trypanosome into the ambient medium.

These observations together with the assumption that the surface coat is largely comparised of variant antigen are consistent with several other observed phenomena, e.g., (1) the shedding of variant antigen to the ambient—the exoantigen of Weitz (1960); (2) the absence of antigenic variant specificity in culture trypanosomes, which lack the surface coat; and (3) the failure to bind homologous antibody ferritin conjugate, of trypanosomes whose surface coat had been removed by washing (Vickerman, 1971).

D. Constitution of the Variant Antigens

Williamson and Brown (1964) and Brown and Williamson (1964) believed the principal precipitating antigen in *T. brucei* to be a 4 S unconjugated protein. Allsopp *et al.* (1971) have shown that the 4 S antigen of Williamson and Brown and the exoantigen of Weitz (1960) are largely identical and that this antigen is a major component of the surface coat.

Allsopp *et al.* (1971) have further established that the 4 S antigen is in fact a heterogeneous antigen of at least three components with a common antigenic determinant. Each of the components is a protein–carbohydrate complex. The presence of carbohydrate in the surface coat has been confirmed by Wright and Hales (1970) by cytochemical electron microscopy techniques.

E. Mechanisms Controlling Antigenic Variation

The mechanisms possibly mediating these antigenic changes are discussed by Vickerman (1971). Of the two possible mechanisms—genetic mutation, or switch to a new serotype by trypanosomes possessing a genotypic potentiality to produce the full range of variant antigens (with subsequent proliferation of the new serotype in each case)—Vickerman prefers the latter. He bases his preference mainly on Gray's (1965) demonstration that antigenic types appear in a predictable sequence and tend to revert to a constant basic antigen on cyclical transmission. Such predictability is unlikely to be accounted for by mutation.

Regarding the actual formation of the surface coat or its shedding and substitution by a new one, Vickerman (1971) points out that between the nucleus and the flagellar pocket the salivarian blood form trypanosome is provided with abundant granular endoplasmic reticulum for the synthesis of protein, and a well-developed system of tubules to convey the secreted protein to the flagellar pocket from which the protein could be distributed over the surface of the organism. And he suggests that a function of the plasmanemes might be to rid the organism of the coat of the old antigenic type.

Desowitz (1970) proposes another mechanism. He postulates that the trypanosome has little or no ability to alter the surface antigen endogenously, thus accounting for the reversion to a basic or common antigen during the initial days of an infection. Antibody elaborated against that antigen would act to alter the structure of the basic antigen, in the process exposing new determinant sites. The altered antigen would elicit new antibody, further modification, and so on, *ad infinitum*. Such a mechanism might account for the comparatively ordered sequence of antigenic types shown by Gray (1965).

F. Nonspecific Immunity

Although salivarian trypanosome species are less host-species-specific than are the *T. lewisi* and related organisms, there are certain well-defined nonspecific phenomena. For example, *Trypanosoma brucei*

brucei is distinguished from its morphologically identical "subspecies"
T. b. rhodesiense and *T. b. gambiense* by its incapability to infect man.
T. b. brucei strains when newly isolated are susceptible to human serum
while *T. b. gambiense* and *T. b. rhodesiense* strains are not (Desowitz,
1970). This difference has recently been exploited by Rickman and Robson (1970) to develop a test (the blood incubation infectivity test)
which seems likely to afford a useful laboratory tool for the differentiation of man-infecting from non-man-infecting strains. *Papio* spp. (baboons) are quite refractory to salivarian trypanosome infections while
the taxonomically closely related *Cercopithecus* spp. (monkeys) are susceptible. Normal *Sigmodon* (cotton rat) serum contains an antibody
which is active against rat-adapted *Trypanosoma vivax* but does not
affect other salivarian trypanosome spp. (Terry, 1957).

There are many other examples, but the mechanisms determining natural trypanocidal activity and host susceptibility or refractoriness are not
well understood. Desowitz (1963, 1970) has reviewed the effect of
chemical agents, dietary deficiencies, etc., on susceptibility to trypanosome infection and has pointed out similarities between properdin and
natural trypanocidal antibody.

G. Acquired Specific Immunity

1. Humoral Immunity

That antibodies are produced against the stable antigens of salivarian
trypanosomes is evidenced by immunofluorescence and complement fixation tests not being specific for particular antigenic types. The stable
antigens, however, do not appear to be involved in the development
of immunity of the host as cross immunity between different populations
of the same species, or different trypanosome species, is absent. Neither
is immunization with culture forms protective against inoculation with
blood forms.

The variant antigens, on the other hand, are associated with protective
immunity, but only against the homologous antigenic type. Recent experimentation on raising immunity to salivarian trypanosome infections
by means of vaccines has given more consistent results than earlier
work because greater control over the antigenic character and stability
of the materials used has been possible by their being viably preserved
at low temperatures (Cunningham *et al.*, 1963). Immunization has been
accomplished by the use of trypanosome suspensions inactivated by various means, with or without adjuvants and by the use of exoantigen
(summary in Lumsden, 1970). A formalinized vaccine (Herbert and
Lumsden, 1968), administered intravenously to mice, provided a simple

rapid method of assessing the results of simultaneous immunization against several different antigenic types. A mixed vaccine containing four antigenic types protected against challenge by all those four types; but no protection was shown on heterologous challenge.

Direct agglutination, lytic, and neutralization tests, like protective immunity, are mediated by the variant antigens (Lumsden, 1970).

One other characteristic of the humoral response to salivarian trypanosome infection must be discussed. This is the remarkable quantity of IgM produced in the serum and the cerebrospinal fluid of infected hosts. Because of various shortcomings in serological tests for infection, the estimation of IgM immunoglobulin has attracted much attention as a diagnostic tool (Mattern, 1962, 1968; Lumsden, 1966). Although rises in IgG occur also (Lumsden, 1970), the rises in IgM are much the more dramatic, amounting sometimes to 16 or more times normal levels.

The remarkable rise in IgM in salivarian trypanosome infections is customarily ascribed to the repeated stimulation of the host by each succeeding new antigenic type of the organism. This may well be generally true, but the IgM contains antibodies other than those to trypanosomal antigens. Houba and Allison (1966) and Houba *et al.* (1969) showed increases in heterophile antibodies as evidence by increases in agglutination titers to sheep erythrocytes, concurrent with the trypanosome infection. There were increases also in rheumatoid factor.

Although there has been much study of humoral responses to salivarian trypanosome infection and the conditions in which a solid immunity to a given antigenic type have been defined, at least in mice, the resistance, or adjustment, of hosts in the field is obscure. The knowledge that hosts could be immunized simply against single antigenic types has prompted studies directed to establish the "spectrum" and stability of antigenic types circulating in circumscribed field areas in Africa. The wide range of antigenic types found (Wilson, 1971, personal communication) discourages any idea of protection of animals by polyvalent vaccines.

Field situations, in which hosts survive repeated trypanosome infection, are related, in any case, not to a sterile immune state but to a state in which the parasitemia is controlled at low, nonpathogenic levels (Desowitz, 1970). The influence of classical immune mechanisms on limiting parasitemia in this way is uncertain and protection seems not necessarily related to serum antibody titers in any particular reaction. Some cattle breeds, such as N'Dama and Muturu, are more capable of adaptation than are others (Desowitz, 1970). Such adaptation, according to Desowitz, depends on the animals being born to an immune dam and being subject to trypanosome infection early in life.

2. Cell-Mediated Immunity

No evidence for CMI in salivarian trypanosome infections has been noticed.

V. Conclusion

Most of the work on the immunology of trypanosome infections, as is evidenced by the balance of the foregoing review, has been on the humoral aspects. Evidence of cell-mediated mechanisms is practically confined to the demonstration of delayed-type hypersensitivity and inhibition of macrophage spreading in *Trypanosoma cruzi* infections.

Brown (1970) has summarized the cell-mediated mechanisms likely to be operative and suggested how they might be investigated. He suggests two cell-mediated effects likely to have a destructive effect on cells bearing foreign antigens.

1. *Contact cytotoxicity* in which cells, probably mainly lymphocytes but perhaps also macrophages, can have a toxic action on target cells with which they are brought into contact. Lymphocytes may become cytotoxic by: being sensitized to target cell antigens; being sensitized to microbial antigens absorbed on target cells; being brought into contact with target cells in the presence of antibody reacting with the target cells; and by being sensitized with antigen *in vitro*.

2. *Macrophage activation* in which specifically activated lymphocytes in the presence of antigen secrete substances which inhibit macrophage migration and activate macrophages.

Brown further points out that more than one of these postulated responses may take place at the same time and that interpretation may be further complicated by antigenic variation on the part of the organism.

Brown (1970) concludes with suggestions for the investigation of cell-mediated protective mechanisms in protozoal infections—growth of parasites *in vitro* in tissue monolayers in the company of lymphoid cells, study of growth of parasites in normal and activated macrophages, etc. Certainly expansion of studies in CMI aspects of trypanosome infections is needed now to balance the previous concentration on humoral studies and to improve our understanding of the whole immune process.

References

Allsopp, B. A., Njogu, A. R., and Humphreys, K. C. (1971). *Exp. Parasitol.* 29, 271.

Bray, R. S., and Bryceson, A. D. M. (1968). *Lancet* 2, 898.

Brown, K. N. (1970). *J. Parasitol.* 56, 36.

Brown, K. N., and Williamson, J. (1964). *Exp. Parasitol.* 15, 69.

Cunningham, M. P., Lumsden, W. H. R., and Webber, W. A. F. (1963). *Exp. Parasitol.* 14, 280.

D'Alesandro, P. A. (1970). *In* "Immunity to Parasitic Animals" (G. J. Jackson, R. Herman, and I. Singer, eds.), Vol. 2, pp. 691–738. Appleton, New York.

Desowitz, R. S. (1963). *Ann. N.Y. Acad. Sci.* 113, 74.

Desowitz, R. S. (1970). *In* "Immunity to Parasitic Animals" (G. J. Jackson, R. Herman, and I. Singer, eds.), Vol. 2, pp. 551–596. Appleton, New York.

Goble, F. C. (1970). *In* "Immunity to Parasitic Animals" (G. J. Jackson, R. Herman, and I. Singer, eds.), Vol. 2, pp. 597–689. Appleton, New York.

Gonzalez Cappa, S. M., Schmunis, G. A., Traversa, O. C., Yanovsky, J. F., and Parodi, A. S. (1968). *Amer. J. Trop. Med. Hyg.* 17, 709.

Goodwin, L. G. (1971). *Trans. Roy. Soc. Trop. Med. Hyg.* 65, 82.

Gray, A. R. (1965). *J. Gen. Microbiol.* 41, 195.

Herbert, W. J., and Lumsden, W. H. R. (1968). *J. Med. Microbiol.* 1, 23.

Herbert, W. J., and Wilkinson, P. C. (1971). "A Dictionary of Immunology." Blackwell, Oxford.

Houba, V., and Allison, A. C. (1966). *Lancet* 1, 848.

Houba, V., Brown, K. N., and Allison, A. C. (1969). *Clin. Exp. Immunol.* 4, 113.

Humphrey, J. H., and White, R. G. (1970). "Immunology for Students of Medicine," 3rd ed. Blackwell, Oxford.

Lumsden, W. H. R. (1966). *Trans. Roy. Soc. Trop. Med. Hyg.* 60, 125.

Lumsden, W. H. R. (1970). *Advan. Parasitol.* 8, 227.

Mattern, P. (1962). *Int. Sci. Comm. Trypanosom. Res., 9th, 1962* pp. 377–385.

Mattern, P. (1968). *Bull. WHO* 38, 1.

Miles, M. (1971). Ph.D. Thesis, University of London.

Ormerod, W. E., and Venkatesan, S. (1971). *Trans. Roy. Soc. Trop. Med. Hyg.* 65, 14.

Pizzi, T. (1957). "Immunologia de la Enfermedad de Chagas." University of Chile, Santiago.

Rickman, L. R., and Robson, J. (1970). *Bull. WHO* 42, 911.

Seah, S. (1970). *Nature (London)* 225, 1256.

Terry, R. J. (1957). *Exp. Parasitol.* 6, 404.

Vickerman, K. (1969). *J. Cell. Sci.* 5, 163.

Vickerman, K. (1971). *In* "Ecology and Physiology of Parasites" (A. M. Fallis, ed.), p. 58. Univ. of Toronto Press, Toronto.

Vickerman, K., and Luckins, A. G. (1969). *Nature (London)* 224, 1125.

Weitz, B. (1960). *J. Gen. Microbiol.* 23, 589.

Williamson, J., and Brown, K. N. (1964). *Exp. Parasitol.* 15, 44.

World Health Organization (1969). *World Health Org., Tech. Rep. Ser.* 411.

Wright, K. A., and Hales, H. (1970). *J. Parasitol.* 56, 671.

Wright, K. A., Lumsden, W. H. R., and Hales, H. (1970). *J. Cell Sci.* 6, 285.

12 IMMUNE RESPONSE TO HEMOPROTOZOA

II. *Babesia* spp.

D. F. MAHONEY

I. Introduction

The genus *Babesia* (Starcovici, 1893) consists of a heterogenous group of protozoan parasites that infect the red blood cells of the vertebrate host and are transmitted by ixodid ticks. They were originally observed in cattle in eastern Europe by Babes (1888) but were not associated with infectious disease until Smith and Kilborne (1893) showed that *B. bigemina* was the etiological agent of Texas fever in the United States. Levine (1971) listed a total of 71 species in the genus but only 18 are found naturally in domestic animals. Of the latter, 6 species are found in cattle (*B. argentina,* * *B. Berbera, B. bigemina, B. bovis, B. divergens, B. major*), 3 in sheep (*B. foliata, B. motasi, B. ovis*), 2 in horses (*B. caballi, B. equi*), 2 in pigs (*B. perroncitoi, B. trautmanni*), 1 in goats (*B. taylori*), 3 in dogs (*B. canis, B. gibsoni, B. vogeli*), and 1 in cats (*B. felis*). In their respective hosts these species cause disease (babesiosis) characterized by fever, anemia, hemoglobinuria, jaundice, signs of cerebral involvement, and variable mortality. The genus is represented in most countries of the world, and babesiosis is a widespread problem in animal health. However, objective assessment of its economic importance on a global basis is difficult because of the many factors that determine its relative importance in different countries. These include the presence of other severe vector-borne protozoal infections, the species of *Babesia* present and the hosts involved, prevailing environmental conditions, and intensity of livestock management. The only generalization possible is the observation that problems with babesiosis are most serious among herd animals, e.g., cattle and sheep, where the combination of large numbers and seasonal fluctuation in vector populations predispose to the occurrence of severe outbreaks.

* Riek (1968) suggested that *B. argentina, B. bovis,* and *B. divergens* were synonyms.

These livestock industries were fortunate that a method of immunization against babesiosis was developed soon after the disease was recognized (Hunt, 1897), but although this relieved economic stress, it probably retarded the development of research work. The last decade or so has witnessed considerable intensification of interest in this field, not only in response to development of new techniques and the changing demands of animal industry, but also to the emergence of babesiosis as a zoonosis and to a recognition that it may provide a useful model for some problems in malaria. This review is intended to complement earlier papers on the subject (Neitz, 1956; Riek, 1963) by giving an account of recent advances in research on immunity to babesiosis with inclusion of work on biology of the parasites and on pathology of the disease that may be generally relevant to immunological problems.

II. Life Cycle

A. INVERTEBRATE HOST

The most comprehensive description of the invertebrate life cycle was given by Riek (1964, 1966) who followed transovarial development of *B. bigemina* and *B. argentina* in the one-host tick, *Boophilus microplus*. Similar patterns of development were observed by Holbrook *et al.* (1968a) for *B. caballi* in another one-host tick *Dermacentor nitens* and by Friedhoff (1969) for *B. ovis* in females and eggs of a two-host tick *Rhipicephalus bursa*. Initiation of the cycle from ingested erythrocytic parasites in the gut of the tick has not been clearly defined, but Riek (1968) postulated a sexual phase preceding the early club-shaped body (Fig. 1a) that undergoes multiple fission in the epithelial cells of the gut. This multiplication produces large numbers of vermicules which penetrate all tissues of the tick and repeat the multiplication cycle. Some invade the eggs and divide in the gut epithelium of the developing larva. After the larva feeds, vermicules enter cells of the salivary gland and grow into large bodies from which the small round and pear-shaped forms, infective for the vertebrate host, are derived. Shortt (1962) described transmission of *B. canis* from stage-to-stage in a three-host tick *Rhipicephalus sanguineus*, and the vermicule form passed from one stage of the tick to the next. Observations by Holbrook (1970) on *B. caballi* in *D. nitens* suggested that vermicules might also bypass the vertebrate host and directly infect the next generation of ticks. Although a similar mechanism of transmission has been suggested for *B. ovis* in *R. bursa* (Markov and Abramov, 1968), there was no evidence of carry-over of

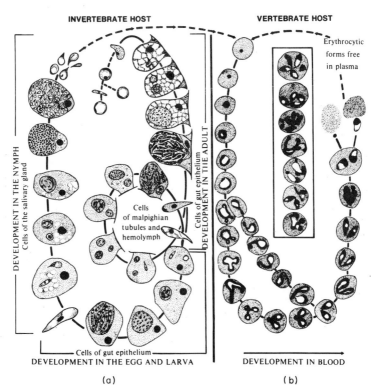

Fig. 1. (a) Life cycle of a large *Babesia* (*B. bigemina*) in the one-host tick *B. microplus* (from Riek, 1964) illustrating development of vermicules in the adult tick and in following generation larvae and nymphs. (b) Life cycle of a large *Babesia* (*B. caballi*) in erythrocytes of the vertebrate host (from Holbrook *et al.*, 1968b). Shows commencement of the cycle with the anaplasmoid form, enlargement to round form with cytoplasm and alternate methods of division into daughter cells. The last 4–5 stages represent reorientation of nuclear material within the parasite and extrusion of the nucleuslike body. Inset shows atypical forms that only arise from multiple infection of cells or from multiple division. The dotted lines represent areas in which knowledge of the cycle is incomplete.

B. bigemina in *B. microplus* (Riek, 1964; Callow, 1965). Figure 1a reproduced from Riek (1964) shows the developmental sequence of *B. bigemina* in *B. microplus*.

B. Vertebrate Host

After inoculation by the tick, *Babesia* pass directly into the bloodstream (Hoyte, 1961, 1965; Krylov, 1964) and infect the erythrocytes. They first become small rounded bodies that consist of a nucleus and little cytoplasm ("anaplasmoid" forms). These forms increase in size and finally reproduce by budding to form two, or exponential multiples of two, pyriform parasites that eventually separate, leave the cell, and presumably recommence the cycle (Fig. 1b). In severe infections, multiple invasion of erythrocytes may simulate schizogony (Ewing, 1965a). Both Riek (1964) and Holbrook *et al.* (1968b) described a small "nucleus" in *B. bigemina* and *B. caballi*, respectively, that was extruded from the blunt end of the pyriform body into the cytoplasm of the erythrocyte toward the end of the cycle. Histochemical studies by Ray (1938) and studies by Wright (1971) with the electron microscope have shown that this body is not composed of nuclear material and is therefore unlikely to be concerned with reproduction. Events that take place during the passage of parasites from one erythrocyte to another are poorly understood. Organisms similar to those in erythrocytes are frequently observed free in plasma, but the existence of forms with characteristics that set them apart from the latter has not been unequivocally demonstrated. Figure 1b, reproduced from Holbrook *et al.* (1968b), shows a typical development cycle (*B. caballi*) in erythrocytes together with some atypical forms that may occur as a result of multiple infection and/or multiple division.

The time required to complete the erythrocytic cycle has not received much attention. As *Babesia* are asynchronous, it is impossible to measure the cycle directly. However, in species that mostly produce a constant number of daughter cells per cycle, the rate of exponential increase in the blood has some significance provided the host population is uniformly susceptible. This condition was satisfied in mice infected with *B. rodhaini* (Bungener, 1967; Overdulve and Antonisse, 1970a,b), and a linear relationship was established between incubation period and logarithm of parasite dose. Multiplication rate in this host–*Babesia* system was thus defined by a constant, and effects of certain treatments on the organisms were measured precisely by observing variation of its value.

III. Babesiosis and Babesiasis

There are two states of infection in the vertebrate host, and following the definitions of Whitlock (1949) the terms "babesiosis" and "babesiasis" are used to designate them. The former represents the clinical disease—a transient state in which uncontrolled parasite multiplication either causes death or leads to a period of debility during which gradual recovery takes place. The latter represents the process of subclinical infection, observed in passively immune young animals and also in those recovered from a clinical attack. The parasites remain in the blood, but their number fluctuates around levels insufficient to cause illness. This state of dynamic equilibrium between the *Babesia* and the defenses of its host may be maintained even under the stress of repeated challenge. The division between the two manifestations of infection is not sharp, and particularly where mild cases are concerned, separation of one from the other is difficult.

A. BABESIOSIS

The clinical disease is characterized by signs of fever, anorexia, diarrhea, vomiting, anemia, hemoglobinuria, uremia, and jaundice. At the commencement of infection, parasites multiply rapidly in the blood for several days until their number reaches a peak. If the host survives, rapid reduction of the parasite population marks the onset of recovery. Although a great variety of clinical signs and post mortem changes have been observed, pathological processes are related to the following events.

1. Growth and multiplication of *Babesia* inside the host erythrocytes.

2. Intravascular destruction of erythrocytes by escaping parasites. This initiates the development of anemia which parallels the rise in level of parasitemia. However, total erythrocyte loss indicated by falls in red cell count and packed cell volume is usually higher than that accounted for by direct rupture of cells. Other mechanisms such as lysis and phagocytosis of normal and infected erythrocytes are also involved in the production of anemia (Neitz, 1938).

Reticulocytosis is observed even while *Babesia* are actively multiplying in blood (Karput, 1966; Dorner, 1967). This response shows that hemopoiesis is not retarded by infection and often results in early replenishment of erythrocytes during recovery. However, infections with some *Babesia*, e.g., *B. canis* in the dog, produce anemia that may persist for several weeks after parasites disappear from peripheral blood despite active hemopoiesis (Wright, 1971).

3. Release of parasite and host constituents from erythrocytes. Circulating antigens have been demonstrated and appear to be toxic for some hosts (K. H. Sibinovic *et al.*, 1967b). The reaction of specific antibody with such products may contribute to a condition of shock (Holbrook, 1965). Stress of damaged organs required to eliminate abnormal quantities of hemoglobin and triggering of intravascular coagulation, probably by phospholipids from the stroma of lysed erythrocytes (Mahoney and Goodger, 1969), are examples of physiological disturbance by host constituents.

4. Damage to internal organs caused by anoxia. This commences early in the disease particularly in liver and kidney and is the result of reduced blood flow through the organs due to shock probably initiated by a physiological mechanism (Maegraith *et al.*, 1957; Goodwin and Richards, 1960). Anoxia is increased by the later development of severe anemia and by the clumping and adherence of parasitized erythrocytes on the walls of capillaries. The latter phenomenon further impedes blood flow and is often marked in the brain where severe damage may occur from capillary blockage in *B. argentina* and occasionally in *B. canis* infections.

B. BABESIASIS

Studies of babesiasis have been mostly concerned with the maximum duration of subclinical infection, the subject of discussion in a following section. However, observations of dynamic situations in which cattle were exposed to continuous natural challenge with *B. argentina* and *B. bigemina* from the tick-infested environment showed that the frequency of detectable parasitemia in clinically normal animals increased sharply from birth until about 2 years of age and then declined (Mahoney, 1962a; Johnston, 1967). The general pattern was maintained in groups of cattle living under different environmental conditions, but the incidence of parasitemia was related to the rate of inoculation of infection by ticks (Fig. 2). This situation was caused by interaction

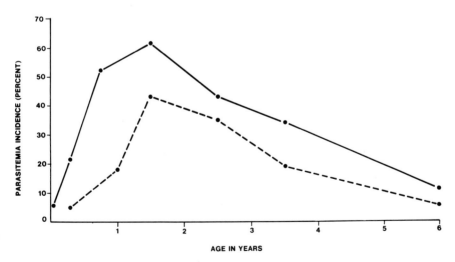

Fig. 2. The incidence of detectable parasitemia with *B. argentina* in various age groups in two herds of *B. taurus* cattle situated in different areas of eastern Australia. Analysis of these data showed that rate of inoculation of infection by ticks in Herd A (●——●) was more than twice that in Herd B (●- - -●) (Mahoney, 1969).

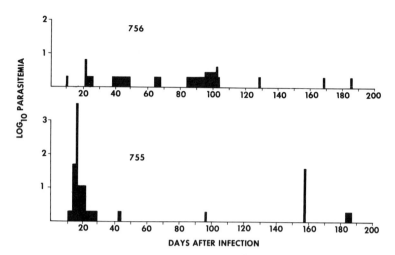

Fig. 3. The daily occurrence of detectable parasitemia measured as the number of organisms per cubic millimeter of blood in calves (*B. taurus*) after one tick-transmitted infection with *B. argentina* at 6 weeks of age. The calves were then maintained tick-free at the laboratory.

among a number of factors. First, after one naturally acquired infection, detectable parasitemia recurred at fairly regular intervals[*] (Fig. 3) continuing for several years in the absence of further transmission (Mahoney, 1969). Then the superposition of one infection upon another in each animal (superinfection) by natural transmission increased the frequency of detectable parasitemia and caused the rise in incidence. The decline of the curve shown in Fig. 2 appeared to represent a phenomenon of acquired immunity obviously superimposed on those mechanisms that prevented clinical disease. Only after the experience of repeated infection was the host finally able to depress the occurrence of parasite waves faster than they could be induced by superinfection, and evidence of strong immunity was apparent only in old age (Mahoney, 1962a).

IV. Nonspecific Factors

Innate immunity refers to factors that collectively render a host physiologically unsuitable for propagation of a parasite. It is distinguished

[*] Data from Ewing (1965b) indicate that cyclic variation in levels of *B. canis* parasitemia also occurs.

from natural immunity consisting of factors possessed by all animals that assist in the removal of invading organisms (Sprent, 1963). Because there is insufficient knowledge of the mechanisms involved, various non-specific factors known to influence host resistance to *Babesia* will be discussed under the general heading above.

A. HOST SPECIFICITY

Until recently, it seemed that innate immunity was the main factor determining host specificity of *Babesia* and cross-infections were readily explained on the basis of close phylogenetic relationship between hosts, e.g., transmission of *B. divergens*, *B. motasi*, and *B. ovis* to deer (Spindler *et al.*, 1958; Enigk *et al.*, 1964; Enigk and Friedhoff, 1962; Nilsson *et al.*, 1965), *B. canis* to the coyote (Ewing *et al.*, 1964), *B. equi* to zebra (Dennig, 1966a), and the wide distribution of *B. microtia* among wild rodents (Levine, 1971). However, cross-infections have occurred that are not readily explained in this way. Baby mice have been infected with *B. canis* (Dennig, 1959), horses with *B. bigemina* (Callow, 1965), man with *B. bovis*, *B. divergens*, and *B. microtia*, and splenectomized monkeys with *B. divergens* and *B. microtia* (Skrabalo and Deanovic, 1957; Scholtens *et al.*, 1968; Garnham *et al.*, 1969; Western *et al.*, 1970; Shortt and Blackie, 1965; Garnham and Voller, 1965). In man, all cases except one have occurred in splenectomized individuals. Splenectomy facilitates establishment of *Babesia* in unnatural hosts, and the activity of phagocytes may be as important in determining host specificity as physiological differences. Attempts to exploit these effects of splenectomy in developing experimental models of economically important parasites in laboratory animals have not been successful (Crowe and Pullen, 1968; Frerichs *et al.*, 1969c). However, further examination of mechanisms involved in host specificity seems desirable as it might lead to better understanding of natural immunity.

B. GENETIC FACTORS

Specific genetic factors that alter host susceptibility to babesiosis have not been detected in domestic animals. However, susceptibility of cattle varies in different genetic types. In Australia, *Bos indicus* cattle are more resistant than *B. taurus* to *B. argentina* infection (Daly and Hall, 1955), and a low incidence of babesiasis has been reported among these cattle in the field (Francis and Little, 1964; Francis, 1966; Johnston, 1967). The latter study was critical and in parallel surveys of comparable groups of *B. indicus* and *B. taurus* cattle a significant difference in incidence of *B. argentina* parasitemia was demonstrated. However, experience in Australia and also elsewhere (Dumag *et al.*, 1962; Schiffo and Lombardero, 1964; Davidson, 1969) has shown that babesiosis can be a serious disease in previously unexposed hybrid cattle, and in populations of predominantly crossbred animals the overall effect of breed factors in resistance requires further evaluation.

C. Age

In most diseases, natural immunity increases with age, but in babesiasis it was thought initially to be strongest in young animals. This was established mostly from observation of enzootic situations in which immunity is now known to be passively transferred from mother to offspring by antibodies. Pups and young rats and mice bred from unexposed mothers are highly susceptible to *B. canis* and *B. rodhaini*, respectively. Apart from one exception reported by Pipano (1969), recent comparison of infections with either *B. argentina, B. bigemina*, or *B. divergens* in nonimmune adult cattle and calves under 3 months of age failed to reveal differences in severity of the disease related to age (Hall, 1960; Lohr, 1969b; Brocklesby *et al.*, 1971). Nevertheless, Riek (1963) determined, on the basis of field and laboratory observations, that calves for nonimmune mothers exhibit significant resistance to *B. argentina* and *B. bigemina* 4–7 months after birth. This situation is anomalous because the weight of experimental evidence suggests that protection is passively acquired in the very young. However, natural resistance must be involved later in order to extend the period of protection beyond that possibly provided by maternal antibody. Thus the factors responsible for natural immunity might be inhibited or poorly developed in early life. A comparative study of the latter in different age groups and perhaps in colostrum-deprived and colostrum-fed animals is required to determine its role in resistance to babesiosis.

D. Miscellaneous Nonspecific Factors

Tests at our laboratory demonstrated that calves treated with small doses (1.25 μg/kg live weight) of *E. coli* lipopolysaccharide (Difco) immediately before infection with *B. argentina* were slightly more resistant than untreated animals possibly due to reticuloendothelial (RE) stimulation. Concurrent infections with other parasites may also induce nonspecific resistance to babesiosis although resistance derived from infections with organisms known to share antigen with the *Babesia* spp. would not necessarily rely on nonspecific factors, e.g., cross-immunization between *Plasmodium* and *Babesia* in rats and mice appears to be related to the presence of antigenically similar substances in the plasma of infected animals (H. W. Cox and Milar, 1968; F. E. G. Cox and Young, 1969). However, *Theileria mutans* does not cross-react serologically with *B. argentina* (Mahoney, 1962b), but we have consistently observed that splenectomized calves infected with this parasite showed increased resistance to *B. argentina* compared with *Theileria*-free animals. Such nonspecific effects were weak and their chief practical importance lay in the interference with experimental procedures. Evidence suggesting that the presence of *Babesia* is masked by *Theileria* infections has also been reported in Japan (Ishihara, 1968). Alteration of the erythrocytes may be concerned in this nonspecific resistance as well as RE stimulation.

V. Antigens of *Babesia* Parasites

A. Stages in the Life Cycle

The assumption that erythrocytic parasites produce the antigens responsible for induction of acquired immunity appears justified, mainly for the reason that, apart from those forms inoculated by the tick, other stages have not been demonstrated in the vertebrate host. The occurrence of superinfection in the field suggests that the infective forms are not strongly immunogenic. However, because of infrequent exposure under enzootic conditions (Mahoney, 1969), the quantity of such antigens presented to the host may remain below the level required to provoke an immune response. For this reason the stages in the tick should not be excluded from consideration as a possible source of antigen for immunization and quantitative aspects of host reaction to material from this source particularly warrants investigation.

B. Preparation of Parasite Suspensions

1. Growth of Organisms

As *in vitro* cultivation on a scale required for antigen production has not been achieved, parasites are grown in the blood of a living host which is usually splenectomized to increase susceptibility. In the species infecting domestic animals the selection of strains that have the ability to grow extensively in peripheral blood of the host is desirable. The organisms are transferred intravenously from one animal to the next while parasitemia is increasing, using a large volume of blood for each passage. Terminal parasitemia ranging from 20–50% of erythrocytes may be observed after a small number of passages, perhaps due to a cumulative effect from increases in total parasite number in each successive inoculum. In the cow, continuation of rapid passage of *B. bigemina* and *B. argentina* beyond 2–3 times does not result in further increases of the parasitemia (Mahoney, 1965).

Harvesting of intermediate stages of *Babesia* spp. from ticks is possible. Vermicule forms are numerous in ticks at certain times in the nonparasitic life of the vector. At our laboratory this stage of *B. argentina* has been collected by withdrawing hemolymph from the legs of heavily infected *B. microplus* females during oviposition. The forms infective for the host would be difficult to obtain from feeding ticks because only a small proportion of larval progeny become infected during transovarial transmission and moreover, the developmental period of *B. argentina* in salivary glands is short (Mahoney and Mirre, 1971).

2. Isolation of Parasitized Erythrocytes

The isolation of parasitized erythrocytes from infected blood is desirable for the preparation of antigen because, with the exception of *B. rodhaini*, parasitemia in the general circulation is usually less than 50%. In experiments with cattle parasites, methods that rely on possible variations in density between infected and noninfected cells appear to have failed although *B. canis-* and *B. caballi*-infected cells concentrate at the top of the packed cell mass during centrifugation of infected blood (Watkins, 1962; Hirsh *et al.*, 1969). Erythrocytes infected with *B. argentina* are more resistant to lysis by hypotonic salt solutions than those noninfected, and a method of separating parasitized erythrocytes from blood was based on this observation (Mahoney, 1967c). It was unsuitable for concentrating *B. bigemina*-infected erythrocytes.

3. Lysis of Erythrocytes and Release of Parasites

A number of methods have been described for release of intraerythrocytic parasites from host cells. These include lysis by saponin (Fulton, 1939; Spira and Zuckerman, 1962), by anti-erythrocyte serum and complement (Bowman *et al.*, 1960; Dennig, 1962), by pressure (D'Antonio *et al.*, 1966), and digestion of stroma with enzymes (Stauber and Walker, 1946). Investigation of the above methods for separation of *B. argentina* and *B. bigemina* from bovine erythrocytes has not been uniformly successful. The method of D'Antonio *et al.* (1966) freed some parasites from host cells, but examination of freshly prepared material by phase-contrast microscopy revealed a high proportion of parasites still entangled in erythrocyte membranes. However, even lysis with distilled water or hypotonic saline liberates a small proportion of the parasites and these were isolated by centrifugation through density gradients (Mahoney, 1967c). The yield however was small. Thus, in immunological studies of *Babesia* spp. most workers have commenced with parasitized erythrocytes or parasite–stroma mixtures simply prepared by centrifugation of infected blood previously lysed with hypotonic solutions or saponin.

C. Extraction of Antigen from *Babesia*

Parasite–stroma mixtures have been disintegrated by ultrasonic treatment, freeze-drying, freezing and thawing, and extracted with distilled water or buffered salt solutions (Schindler and Dennig, 1962b; Dennig, 1966b; Mahoney, 1964; Curnow and Curnow, 1967). These crude extracts consist of complex mixtures of material from the parasites and host erythrocytes in which the antigenic components are present in particulate and/or soluble forms. There are relatively few studies in which modern biochemical techniques have been applied to the problem of antigen purification. There is considerable scope for the application of such methods, not only in the improvement of diagnostic tests but also in the investigation of functional significance of parasite antigens in immunity. Ristic and Sibinovic (1964) obtained a precipitating antigen from horse blood infected with *B. caballi* and *B. equi* by precipitation from a crude extract with protamine sulfate. It was later purified by boiling (S. Sibinovic *et al.*, 1966) and found to be a carbohydrate with a sedimentation coefficient of 4 S. Goodger (1971) isolated serologically active fractions from bovine erythrocytes infected with *B. argentina* and *B. bigemina.* Supernatant material, usually discarded during preparation of parasite suspensions, was treated with DEAE-cellulose (equilibrated with 0.003 *M* sodium phosphate, pH 7.0). The bound protein recovered from the ion-exchanger was then passed through Sephadex G-200 and the void-volume fraction contained antigen. In addition, another antigen of large molecular size was extracted from parasite suspensions by sonic disintegration and fractionation of soluble material on Sephadex G-200. The two antigens did not cross-react and obviously originated in different parts of the infected red cell. Further purification of these antigens is required before characterization becomes meaningful. However a weak cross-reaction between material isolated from parasite–stroma mixtures and a component similarly extracted from normal bovine stroma indicated that this antigen resembled a host constituent. The soluble antigen isolated from the lysate of infected erythrocytes might be a metabolic product of the parasites.

D. Antigens in the Plasma of Infected Animals

During the acute phase of babesial infection, substances immunogenic for the host and derived from the parasites and/or as a result of host-parasite interaction circulate in the blood. They have been detected by serological reactions between infected plasma and specific antibodies present in the host after recovery, and by reactions in noninfected hosts after inoculation of plasma taken from other infected animals (K. H. Sibinovic *et al.*, 1965; Mahoney, 1966). Fractions of infected plasma that contain gamma globulins, beta globulins, and haptoglobin–hemoglobin complexes also contain these antigens (K. H. Sibinovic *et al.*, 1967a; Mahoney and Goodger, 1969; Goodger, 1970). Although some properties of such antigen-containing plasma fractions have been investigated and found to be different from those of comparable preparations from normal plasma, the antigenic substances themselves have not been isolated and characterized. Differences have been observed in the reactions of hosts to injection of plasma antigens obtained from various sources. K. H. Sibinovic *et al.* (1967b) found that those associated with *B. caballi* and *B. equi* infection in horses, *B. canis* infection in dogs, and *B. rodhaini* infection in rats have the following general effects: they (a) cause erythrocyte destruction soon after injection; (b) cross-react in serological tests with each other and with plasma antigens of some malaria parasites (H. W. Cox *et al.*, 1968); and (c) induce protection against homologous and heterologous *Babesia* spp. within the group.

Our studies have shown that the plasma antigens of *B. argentina* in cattle do not cause erythrocyte destruction after injection into noninfected calves, but that they stimulate the formation of antibodies and induce protection specific for *B. argentina*. Most of the antigen appeared to be bound to serum proteins in a serologically inactive form. In contrast, the infected plasma from other hosts must contain antigen that is free to combine with antibodies *in vitro* and with erythrocyte membranes *in vivo*. The nonspecific protection obtained after immunization with material from dogs and rats possibly resulted from the physical state of the antigen in their plasma. In addition to specific immunity, "free" antigen might also induce nonspecific resistance similar to that observed in malaria after treatment of the host with endotoxin or interferon inducers (Martin *et al.*, 1967; Jahiel *et al.*, 1968; Ludford *et al.*,

1969). The absence of this nonspecific effect after immunization of calves with material from other infected cattle might have been caused by changes in the antigen associated with binding to serum proteins.

E. THE VARIABLE ANTIGENS

A brief reference to pioneering work on antigenic variation of malaria parasites seems relevant to a discussion of this aspect of babesiasis. H. W. Cox (1959) showed that relapse strains of *P. berghei* in mice were immunologically different from the original population of parasites from which they arose, and he suggested that selection by the immune host resulted in the production of variants that caused relapses of parasitemia. Working with *P. knowlesi* in rhesus monkeys, K. N. Brown and Brown (1965) and I. N. Brown *et al.* (1968) showed that agglutinogens on the surface of schizont-infected red cells of a relapse parasitemia possessed different antigenic specificity from those on schizonts of other relapse populations in the same animal. Curnow (1968) also found strain-specific agglutinogens on the surface of bovine erythrocytes infected with *B. argentina* and suggested that the relapsing nature of *B. argentina* infection was the result of changes in these or similar antigens. He has since demonstrated (Curnow, 1971, personal communication) that, in individual animals infected with *B. argentina,* succeeding relapse populations of parasites are characterized by specific agglutinogens on the surface of infected erythrocytes. Phillips (1971a) found that rats immunized by infection with a particular population of *B. rodhaini* were less resistant to challenge with a relapse population from the rat that provided the original parasites for immunization than with parasites from the population used for immunization. These results suggested that variable antigens were concerned with protection against *B. rodhaini.*

The characterization of variable antigen awaits further study but some comment on its origin and location is possible at this stage. One location, of course, must be the surface of infected erythrocytes, but electron microscope studies (Wright, 1971) have not demonstrated anatomical connection between the parasite and host cell membrane. The origin of antigen at this site is thus obscure, but the apparent changes in the configuration of its determinant groups are probably controlled by the parasite. Circumstantial evidence suggests that this agglutinogen of infected cells is the antigen concerned in suppressing parasite relapses. However the two may not be identical. Variable antigens of *Trypanosoma rhodesiense,* for example, were fractionated into "protective" and "nonprotective" groups of which only the latter showed demonstrable reactions in gel diffusion tests (Seed, 1963).

VI. Acquired Immunity and the Presence of Infection

Acquired immunity to babesiosis has been traditionally regarded as coincident with the presence of infection and the difficulties involved in the determination of this presence have been blamed for misconception concerning the above relationship between the two states of the host (Sergent, 1963). However, in recent years the persistence of immunity to *Babesia* has been demonstrated for periods of up to $2\frac{1}{2}$ years after the loss of infection established with reasonable probability by subinoculation. The species involved were *B. divergens, B. argentina,* and *B. bigemina* in cattle (Davies *et al.,* 1958; Joyner and Davies, 1967; Callow, 1964, 1967, 1968; Mahoney, 1964), *B. caballi* in horses (Frerichs *et al.,* 1969a), and *B. canis* in dogs (Schindler *et al.,* 1970). With the exception of one dog infected with *B. canis,* immunity was demonstrated against homologous strains of parasite only. Callow found that residual immunity in cattle was ineffective against heterologous strains of *B. bigemina* and *B. argentina,* but, as he used mostly splenectomized animals, further work with nonsplenectomized animals is needed to confirm and extend the findings.

The presence of parasites might be essential for protection against heterologous strains of *Babesia,* and, as animals are often exposed to different strains under field conditions, the duration of infection is still relevant to the control of babesiosis. Many observations concerning the persistence of infection in the host have been made and for each species of *Babesia* the times reported have varied from several weeks to many years (Neitz, 1956; Riek, 1963). To recognize possible causes of such variation is probably as important as the details of the observations themselves. A number of factors should be considered.

1. The longevity of infection with each species has a characteristic range, e.g., in cattle Neitz (1969) reported that *B. bovis* generally persists for several years, whereas *B. bigemina* persists for less than 1 year.

2. Strains of parasite within each species may differ in ability to persist in the host.

3. Variation in reactions of breeds may occur in host species.

4. The criterion used to determine the presence of infection is not definitive. It depends on the subinoculation of blood and sensitivity of the test is related to the proportion of the donor's blood volume withdrawn and the minimum number of parasites required to infect the recipient. A negative result merely represents a certain probability that infection is not present.

5. Ability of a species or strain to produce antigenic variants might determine the duration of subclinical infection.

Babesiosis sometimes occurs after reinfection of nonsplenectomized animals known to be still carrying parasites from a previous infection. This has been demonstrated in *B. ovis* (Suleimanov, 1965) and *B. argentina* (Rogers, 1971a) infections by use of different strains for immunization and challenge. However, the reports of failure to break through immunity in this way (Raynaud, 1962; Johnston and Tammemagi, 1969) show that the occurrence of clinical disease after challenge of infected animals with heterologous strains is not general. In every enzootic area, a wide spectrum of variation probably exists both in the antigenic composition of parasites and in the ability of hosts to respond immunologically. At one end of this scale a combination of these factors causes disease and at the other only minor effects ensue. Until the mechanisms of immunity in babesiosis become clear, the outcome of cross-infection between strains must remain largely a matter of local experience.

Strain differences however are not the only basis for interpretation of apparent loss of immunity of infected animals under natural conditions. The following factors should also be considered.

1. Infection status of animals exposed may be doubtful. For example, natural exposure of calves to infected ticks is often infrequent (Mahoney, 1969) and protection by maternal antibodies and natural immunity may be lost before the first infection occurs.

2. Stress of the host by events such as starvation, concurrent disease, and change of environment. These may depress the immunological response and allow minor differences between strains or simply between successive antigenic variants to overwhelm body defenses. The rise in level of recurrent parasitemia after cortisone treatment (Callow and Parker, 1969) lends support to this suggestion.

VII. Cellular Factors in Immunity

A. Phagocytosis

Observations on phagocytosis in *Babesia* infections have been made infrequently and direct knowledge of the role of this type of cellular activity in immunity to *Babesia* is fragmentary. Most references to phagocytosis have been made in the context of histopathological studies, but the material examined has often been taken from acutely infected subjects, dead or sacrificed before acquired immunity could develop fully. There has been a tendency to accept the description of cellular events in malaria (Taliaferro and Cannon, 1936) as generally applicable to babesiosis. Although the available descriptions provide some justification for this attitude it is regrettable that more studies of phagocytosis in *Babesia* infections have not been undertaken. Its most important function might be the removal of infected erythrocytes from the circulation after the combination of antibodies with variable antigen on the erythrocyte surface, and through this mechanism the control of parasite multiplication, particularly in subclinically infected animals.

Most descriptions of phagocytic activity have concerned *B. canis* infection in dogs (Graham-Smith, 1905; Christophers, 1907; Schuberg and Reichenow, 1912; Neitz, 1938; Maegraith *et al.*, 1957), but some observations have been made in mice (*B. rodhaini*) (Paget *et al.*, 1962) and in cattle (*B. argentina*) (Karput, 1966; Rogers, 1971b). The cellular reactions described include mobilization of mesenchymal reserves with hyperplasia of reticuloendothelial elements in spleen, liver, and bone marrow. Phagocytosis of nonparasitized and parasitized erythrocytes by macrophages occurs in these organs and in the medulla of the lymph glands. There is depletion of lymphocytes of germinal centers in the latter organs and in the spleen at this time. These general changes are probably a part of the early manifestation of natural immunity, an immediate response of the RE system to substances liberated by parasites. The phagocytosis of infected and noninfected red cells might thus commence as a nonspecific reaction accompanying a rise in the general level of activity of those elements normally responsible for the removal of damaged and effete erythrocytes. As infection progresses, there is intensification of phagocytic activity particularly in the spleen, liver, and bone marrow, and plasma cells appear in these organs (Rogers, 1971b). In the blood, lymphocytosis may occur (Karput, 1966; Dorner, 1967), and monocytes and neutrophils ingest free parasites as well as infected and noninfected erythrocytes (Neitz, 1938). Production of specific opsonic antibody for parasites might be expected to accompany such changes.

Phagocytosis of normal and parasitized erythrocytes has been correlated experimentally with antibodies against the red cells. In rats infected with *B. rodhaini*, Schroeder *et al.* (1965, 1966) found that erythrophagocytosis was correlated with the presence of an agglutinin for trypsinized normal rat erythrocytes. Later work, however (H. W. Cox *et al.*, 1966), demonstrated the same agglutinin in some normal rats after repeated bleeding, an observation that cast some doubt on its functional significance. An opsonin for undamaged erythrocytes was also found during the same infection (Schroeder, 1966) by *in vitro* opsonic tests at 37°C. As prior absorption of serum with normal erythrocytes at 25°C was required for its demonstration the presence of an inhibitor for the opsonin was postulated. Suppression of the inhibitor *in vivo* was attributed to local conditions in organs where phagocytosis mostly occurs. Because of the obvious difficulty in demonstrating *in vivo* functional activity for this system its role must also be regarded as speculative. Adherence of antigens isolated from plasma of infected dogs and rats to normal red cells was demonstrated by K. H. Sibinovic *et al.* (1969). This suggested an immune mechanism for indiscriminate removal of erythrocytes in the above hosts during late stages of infection. The antibodies were lytic for antigen-sensitized cells *in vitro*, but opsonization might also occur in the infected animal.

B. ROLE OF THE SPLEEN

The role of the spleen in immunity to *Babesia* has not been clearly defined. The necessity for this organ may change according to the phase of infection and the combination of host and parasite. In mice, for example, removal of the spleen has little effect on the severity of initial infection with *B. rodhaini* although the operation increases susceptibility of most other hosts to their respective parasites. In general, the spleen is required for development of acquired immunity and its maintenance during the phase of subclinical infection. However in the cow, recurrence of clinical disease with *B. argentina* rarely occurs after splenectomy performed in the subclinical phase (Legg, 1935), and a significant percentage of animals even recover from postsplenectomy attacks with *B. bigemina* (Uilenberg, 1969). The immunological functions of the spleen depend on anatomy and position of the organ in addition to its phagocytic and antibody-forming activities, and the complex interplay of those factors involved in natural and acquired immunity to babesiosis has produced varying degrees of reliance on the organ in each host–parasite association.

In recent years studies directly concerned with splenic function in *B. rodhaini* infection of rats (Todorovic *et al.*, 1967; Phillips, 1969b) have found that important splenic activities were phagocytosis and its rapid formation of antibody to blood-borne antigens, a property originally described by Taliaferro (1955). Phagocytosis was mostly the province of the spleen in the early phase of infection, but other organs (i.e., liver, bone marrow) performed this function equally well at a later stage. The rapidity of the splenic antibody response, however, appeared to be critical not only for initial development of acquired immunity but also to deal with antigenic variation of the parasite during the subclinical phase. However, if this general interpretation of splenic function is to endure, some explanation should be offered for the behavior of *B. argentina* in splenectomized hosts because, although this parasite undergoes antigenic variation, splenectomy of subclinically infected animals is rarely followed by the recurrence of disease. The provision of some permanent protection by stimulation of extrasplenic sites with nonvariable parasite antigens might be a basis for reconciliation with the general hypothesis. Removal of the spleen might also reduce "selection pressure" on the parasite population and antigenic variation might not occur as frequently as it does in nonsplenectomized hosts.

C. Adoptive Transfer of Immunity

Roberts (1968) transferred immunity to *B. rodhaini* with spleen cells from immune rats. He considered that the functional elements were phagocytes and antibody-producing cells or perhaps small lymphocytes. For obvious reasons there have been no studies of this nature in large domestic animals. However, adoptive transfer experiments should be possible in pairs of dizygotic twin calves, most of which accept skin grafts from each other (Anderson *et al.*, 1951).

VIII. Humoral Factors in Acquired Immunity

A. Detection of Antibody

Interest in antibody formation to *Babesia* arose with recognition of the necessity for diagnostic tests that could reliably detect infection during the subclinical phase. Smear examination was obviously inadequate and the expense of subinoculation techniques often prohibitive. Serological methods gave promise of the sensitivity and economy that was required both for research and for practical control of the disease. Early workers in this field chose complement fixation (CF) probably because the technique was well established, sensitive, and suitable for use with crude antigens of either a soluble or particulate nature. In recent years, gel diffusion tests, indirect fluorescent antibody tests, and various types of passive agglutination tests have been developed in efforts to find the most sensitive and specific method of detecting and measuring antibody in the various host–*Babesia* associations in different parts of the world.

1. CF Test

Complement fixation is the technique most frequently used. First reported by Hirato *et al.* (1945) for detection of antibody in horses infected with *B. caballi*, it has since been employed in the diagnosis of infection with *B. bigemina, B. argentina, B. bovis* (Mahoney, 1962b, 1964; Denev and Kyurtov, 1967; Kyurtov and Denev, 1967), *B. canis* (Schindler and Dennig, 1962a,b), *B. equi* and *B. caballi* (Dennig, 1966b; Frerichs *et al.*, 1969a,b), and *B. ovis* (Kyurtov, 1967). All antigens were either parasite suspensions prepared from infected erythrocytes or crude extracts of this material usually particulate in nature. They may be preserved by freeze-drying (Stepanova *et al.*, 1969), but at our laboratory storage of freshly prepared material at $-70°C$ has been more satisfactory.

The specificity of CF tests for babesiosis is high. Only 1–2% false positive reactions occurred in noninfected cattle (Mahoney, 1967c), and cross-reaction between *B. argentina* and *B. bigemina* was weak and confined to a short period following the acute phase of infection. The reported pattern of CF antibody response after a single infection was similar in all host–parasite associations, although detectable antibody to each species may persist for different periods. The serum titer rises to a peak 2–3 weeks after infection and then gradually declines without recognition of the relapse parasitemia that often occurs. In cattle and sheep, CF antibody falls below detectable levels before infection is lost and *B. argentina* infection, for example, may be diagnosed with certainty for only 7 months and *B. bigemina* for 4 months after infection. Under natural conditions, calves show a poor antibody response to initial infection owing to inhibition by passively acquired maternal antibody, but superinfection then maintains antibody levels. In horses, CF antibodies to *B. caballi* were detectable throughout infection, and after recovery a few animals still gave positive reactions. Reinfection of CF negative horses produced a typical anamnestic response with significantly higher titers than originally recorded (Frerichs *et al.*, 1969a). The CF test might thus be more generally useful in studies of infection in horses than in ruminants because of greater sensitivity in detecting the presence of antibody in the former host. Nevertheless, in the control of bovine babesiosis, the CF test has been used to locate and eliminate foci of infection with *B. argentina* and *B. bigemina* in one part of Australia in which *B. microplus* is under eradication (Watts, 1969).

2. Indirect Fluorescent Antibody (IFA) Test

Reactions in the IFA test are highly specific for each species and continue for a long time after infection. With *B. bigemina*, antibodies have been detected for 18–24 months after single infection (Ross and Lohr, 1968) and with *B. argentina* for 13 months (Johnston and Tammemagi, 1969). In the latter study all animals carried parasites for the entire period and parallel CF tests were mostly negative at the end.

In studies of specificity, Madden and Holbrook (1968) found that *B. equi* antiserum does not react with *B. caballi* parasites, and Ludford (1969) observed only minor degrees of cross-reaction between *B. argentina, B. bigemina,* and *B. canis,* and none of the antisera reacted with *B. rodhaini.*

3. Agglutination Tests

Various types of agglutination tests have been used to diagnose infection in cattle and horses. Curnow and Curnow (1967) first used the passive hemagglutination (PHA) test (Boyden, 1951) for diagnosis of *B. argentina,* but their results were similar to those obtained with the CF test. Goodger (1971) purified soluble antigens of *B. argentina* and *B. bigemina* and observed a marked increase in sensitivity of the PHA test. Homologous reactions with *B. bigemina* antigen were weaker than those with *B. argentina* and further study of antigens of the former parasite is required. However, the PHA test for *B. argentina* antibody is well established at our laboratory and reactions persisted for 4 years in 21 out of 22 naturally infected cattle in the absence of reinfection. At the end of this period infection was demonstrated in all but one animal by subinoculation. Lohr and Ross (1969) adapted the capillary tube agglutination test (Ristic, 1962) for detection of antibodies to *B. bigemina* and positive reactions were obtained after the cattle lost infection. The pattern of antibody response was similar to that obtained with the CF test, except that titers persisted for a longer time. The heat-stable polysaccharide antigen extracted from *B. caballi* (Ristic and Sibinovic, 1964) has also been used in bentonite agglutination (BA) and PHA tests (S. Sibinovic *et al.,* 1969). Again the pattern of antibody response characterized by maximum titers immediately after infection and then a gradual decline was observed in carrier horses after a single infection. The sensitivity of these tests appeared similar to that reported for complement fixation.

4. Gel Diffusion Test

Precipitin reactions in gel were obtained with the polysaccharide antigen and *B. caballi* antiserum (Ristic and Sibinovic, 1964). The test gave similar results in diagnosis of infection to the BA and PHA tests (S. Sibinovic *et al.,* 1969).

B. Antibody Classes

F. E. G. Cox and Turner (1970) found IgM and IgG antibodies, detectable by IFA test, in mice soon after infection with *B. microtia,*

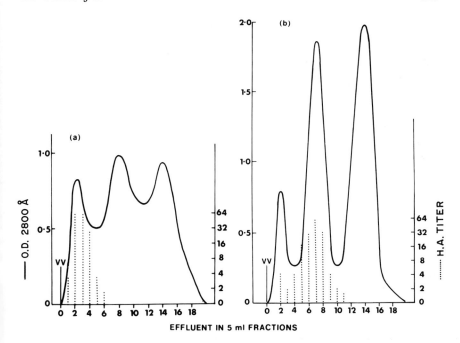

Fig. 4. Shows the distribution of antibody detectable by passive hemagglutination test, in Sephadex G-200 fractions of serum taken from calf No. 615 (a) 3 weeks after *B. argentina* infection and (b) 6 months later. The animal was maintained tick-free at the laboratory during the period. Solid line, O.D. 2800Å; dotted line, H.A. titer; VV, void volume.

but evidence of a shift from IgM to IgG synthesis was not observed. However, at our laboratory we have made a preliminary study of the antibody classes concerned with the response of cattle to the hemagglutinating antigens of *B. argentina,* and our findings suggested that the "normal" shift in antibody synthesis occurred. Fig. 4 shows the distribution of hemagglutinating activity in fractions of early and late antiserum obtained by filtration on Sephadex G-200 columns. The sera were taken from the same animal 3 weeks (Fig. 4a) and 6 months (Fig. 4b) after a single infection. Relative purity of the PHA antigen probably helped to obtain the evidence for sequential production of the two antibody classes in this infection.

C. Levels of Detectable Antibody during Infection

The period in which antibodies are detectable depends on the sensitivity of the serological method used and perhaps the antigenic relationship between host and infecting parasites. Regardless of species, host, or method of detection, the quantity of circulating antibody measured by titration of serum reaches an early peak and gradually declines while infection continues. The parasites are always present in the blood even though their number fluctuates, exposing the host to a continuous antigenic stimulus, but the apparent concentration of antibody falls. The early peak may be an artifact coinciding with the change from IgM to IgG production but with continued immunization by parasites, the affinity of IgG antibodies for antigen should increase (Wallace et al., 1950) and compensate for the earlier effect. If the decline in detectable antibody concentration is real, several possible explanations may be considered:

1. Variation of parasite antigen during infection. The antigen–antibody systems involved in the reactions obtained with diagnostic CF, PHA, and IFA tests are mainly species-specific. Variation is therefore unlikely to affect the antibody patterns detectable with such antigens.

2. Partial immunological tolerance may result from prolonged exposure of the host to parasite antigen (Dresser, 1962). However, superinfection should exacerbate this condition, but in fact it prevents the decline in titer (Mahoney, 1964).

3. Species-specific constituents of the parasite might be relatively weak antigens that have to be present in high concentration for host stimulation. Resulting formation of detectable antibody during subclinical infection would be minimal or perhaps intermittent and unable to maintain a constant level in competition with absorption by ever-present circulating antigen.

D. PROTECTION BY ANTIBODIES

Detection of species-specific antibodies may indicate immunity in the host but only in so far as it usually represents the presence of infection. The concentration of these antibodies often falls below detectable levels before immunity wanes (Mahoney, 1964; Schindler et al., 1970; Frerichs et al., 1969a) and correlation of such levels in serum with protection by passive transfer test has failed (Mahoney, 1967a; Phillips, 1969a). In vitro tests designed to detect protective antibody would assist the study of immunity to babesiosis, but so far only the work on opsonins for erythrocytes (Schroeder, 1966) and agglutinins for infected erythrocytes (Curnow, 1968) represent an approach in this direction.

Evidence that antibodies were concerned with protection against Babesia was first provided by Hall (1960, 1963) who demonstrated passive transfer of immunity to B. argentina from mother to offspring, presumably by antibody in colostrum. Since then, a number of workers have demonstrated passive transfer of immunity to *B. rodhaini* (Matson, 1964; Ludford, 1967; Phillips, 1969a) and to *B. argentina* (Mahoney, 1967a) with serum from infected animals. In both host–parasite systems, protection was manifest by a delay in the onset of parasitemia if antiserum was administered at the time of infection, but was enhanced when serum administration was delayed for several days until parasites were detected in the peripheral blood. With *B. argentina,* protective activity of antiserum was increased by superinfection of donors. However, there was no cross-protection in passive transfer tests between two strains of *B. argentina* isolated from widely separated areas in Australia (Fig. 5) even though infection with one strain conferred active protection against the other.

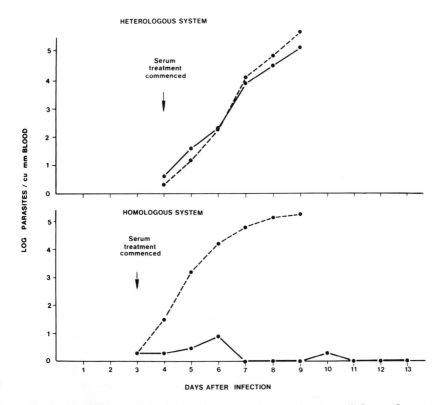

Fig. 5. Mean $\log_{10}$ parasitemia with *B. argentina* in groups of four calves in passive transfer experiments. Heterologous system = "L" strain infection vs treatment with "G" strain antiserum. Homologous system = "G" strain infection vs "G" strain antiserum. Treated (●——●); control (● - - - ●).

The protective antibodies in serum, demonstrable by a passive transfer test, appear to be part of the variable immune system, and the reasons for this interpretation of available data are summarized as follows.

1. The delay in the development of infection after early treatment with antiserum is reminiscent of that observed in similar experiments with *P. berghei* shown to be associated with antigenic change in the parasite population after exposure to antibody (Wellde *et al.*, 1966).

2. Protection in cattle is strain-specific, not only in passive transfer tests but in protection of calves by colostrum as well (Hall *et al.*, 1968).

3. Protective activity of *B. argentina* antiserum was markedly increased by superinfection of the donor. Superinfection exposes the individual animal to a large number of variant populations in a short time and its serum then becomes a comprehensive "information bank" consisting of antibodies which represent most of the possible antigenic determinants produced by a particular strain. This would protect the recipient against most variants of a strain in contrast to the limited "information" contained by serum obtained shortly after one infection. Cross-protection between strains in passive transfer tests should therefore depend on the degree of overlapping in the spectrum of antigenic determinants possessed by each.

E. THE NATURE OF PROTECTION

Antibodies against normal and damaged red cell membranes in babesial infections have been discussed in Section VII. If they promote indiscriminant phagocytosis of erythrocytes, perhaps they may indirectly help the host resist infection, although such a mechanism would be inefficient and unlikely to be of major importance in controlling parasite multiplication. However, the effectiveness of antibodies specifically against those erythrocytes that contain the infecting dose of organisms has been demonstrated in experimental models of *B. rodhaini* infection. Ludford (1967) showed that mice were protected from infection with infected rat erythrocytes by antiserum against normal rat red cells. Thus antigen–antibody systems that promote removal of infected erythrocytes should be protective although in this particular model host antigen could have been absorbed to the parasite and the latter killed by the antihost reaction taking place on its surface (McHardy, 1967). Antibody to- a plasma antigen of *B. canis* and *B. rodhaini* showed apparent parasiticidal activity *in vitro* (K. H. Sibinovic *et al.*, 1969). It caused agglutination and lysis of infected cells and loss of infectivity after incubation for 1 hour at 37°C. Although immunization with this antigen protected dogs and rats, death of parasites observed *in vitro* could have been an artifact produced nonspecifically by lysis of host erythrocytes (Moulder, 1962).

In experiments at our laboratory, *B. argentina*-infected erythrocytes did not lose infectivity for splenectomized calves after incubation with antiserum that protected cattle in passive transfer tests. In addition, lysis of the infected erythrocytes with sheep antiserum and complement prior to their treatment with immune serum did not alter their infectivity. In another experiment, calves were immunized with normal erythrocytes from one donor calf and were later inoculated with *B. argentina*-infected blood from this donor. The presence of antibodies to the erythrocytes that contained the infecting *Babesia* did not alter the subsequent course of infection in these calves. *In vitro* exposure of *B. argentina* to antibodies failed to affect infectivity of the organisms probably because protective antibodies had a low affinity for antigen and this resulted in immediate dissociation of complexes after inoculation of the treated parasitized cells. In passive transfer tests, dissociation would be inhibited by the high concentration of antibodies in the recipient animal. Unlike the antibodies in mice and rats, antibodies in cattle against red cells of the inoculum were not protective. However, there could be a difference between cattle and mice in the way sensitized red cells are removed from the circulation. In some circumstances antibody-coated red cells are merely sequestered and not destroyed (Swisher, 1965). If this happened to the infected red cells in cattle, the *Babesia* would have been able to multiply. There was no suggestion that *B. argentina* adsorbed host red cell antigens thereby rendering the parasite susceptible to the action of antibodies to such tissues.

F. ENHANCEMENT OF INFECTION BY ANTIBODIES

Enhancement of infection with *B. rodhaini* after treatment with immune serum was first observed by Ludford (1967). It was not a constant feature of his passive transfer experiments but similar findings were also observed in the same host–parasite system by Roberts (1968). The latter author suggested that different types of antibody, antagonistic in action and produced in different proportion, might be involved. Further studies of the phenomenon are imperative particularly with regard to its mechanism, possibility of interference with development and maintenance of acquired immunity, and occurrence in other *Babesia* infections. Enhancement should be considered in relation to the failure of passive transfer tests for *B. argentina* in cattle. However, as this has been correlated with the use of heterologous strains for infection of passively immunized animals, difference in antigenic type between populations of parasites has probably been the chief cause of failure in this system.

X. Immunization against Babesiosis

A. LIVING PARASITES

1. Blood Transmission

The oldest form of immunization against babesiosis consists of transmitting the disease to susceptible animals simply by inoculation of infected blood (Hunt, 1897). Babesiacidal drugs to control the resulting disease were introduced later (Nuttall and Graham-Smith, 1908), and these procedures are still being applied up to the present day (Kolabskii *et al.*, 1961; Tunkel *et al.*, 1961; Nugera and Fernando, 1963; Gasanov, 1965; Dalgleish, 1965; Bazurto, 1967; Lohr, 1969a). The problems of immunization mainly affect herd animals, particularly cattle, and owing to the nature of babesiasis, the reliability of vaccination with blood from subclinically infected donors has always caused concern (Tsur, 1961; Kemron *et al.*, 1964; Callow and Tammemagi, 1967). Attenuation of *B. argentina* by continued passage through splenectomized calves allowed Callow and Mellors (1966) to use large numbers of organisms per dose, and standardization of vaccination procedures for cattle in Australia has been achieved. Using this technique, infection is reliable but only mild disease that rarely requires treatment ensues. There appears to be no reason why similar principles could not be applied to the commercial production of vaccine for other economically important species of parasite.

There are still a number of risks attending the use of the blood vaccine. One is transmission of other diseases and in recent years attention has been drawn to the spread of bovine leukosis by this means (Hugoson *et al.*, 1968). Also in situations where repeated vaccination with attenuated organisms was necessary to maintain immunity of cattle in the absence of natural challenge, concurrent immunization with heterologous blood-group antigens caused hemolytic disease in newborn calves (Dimmock and Bell, 1970; Langford *et al.*, 1971).

2. Irradiated Parasites

Damage to malaria parasites and trypanosomes by ionizing radiation occurs in two stages. There is suspension of growth and multiplication in dose ranges up to about 20 krad. Between about 20 and 100 krad the organisms remain alive, unable to multiply but metabolically active (Halberstaedter, 1938; Ceithaml and Evans, 1946). These properties have been exploited in immunization against these parasites (Corradetti, *et al.*, 1966; Wellde and Sadun, 1967; Duxbury and Sadun, 1969). Preliminary studies have been reported with irradiated *Babesia*. Duranov (1968) found that 15 krad suspended growth of *B. ovis*, but the parasites were not immunogenic. However, Phillips (1970, 1971b) inoculated mice and rats with *B. rodhaini*-infected erythrocytes irradiated with 40 and 80 krad and found that subsequent immunity against challenge with homologous parasites was more effective than that induced by an equivalent number of killed organisms. Metabolic antigens may thus have been produced, but the high dose of parasites apparently required to immunize small laboratory animals raised little hope of practical application at present.

3. Use of Prophylactic Drugs

The use of depot-forming prophylactic drugs to protect cattle against the clinical effects of infection with *B. divergens* and *B. argentina* but allowing the development of immunity has been investigated by Ryley (1964), Callow and McGregor (1969), and Newton and O'Sullivan (1969). Drug treatment is combined with immunization by infected blood, or by natural transmission, although in the latter event some knowledge of infection rates of ticks in the environment is desirable to ensure that animals receive infection within the period of drug protection. Toxicity of the quinuronium compounds used has delayed practical application of the method, but another chemoprophylactic agent, 3, 3'-bis(2-imidazolin-2-yl) carbanilide dihydrochloride (imidocarb), gave encouraging results in field trials (Callow and McGregor, 1970; Roy-Smith, 1971).

B. Use of Antigenic Preparations

The characterization of antigens found in the plasma of animals infected with *Babesia* was discussed in Section V. Even though much effort has gone toward purification, these substances have not been isolated entirely free of serum protein, and information on their nature has been derived from observations on serological reactions and on immunogenic activity of fractions of infected plasma in susceptible hosts. Antigens in the serum of dogs infected with *B. canis*, rats infected with *B. rodhaini*, and, to a lesser degree, horses infected with *B. caballi* confer protection on all three hosts against homologous and heterologous parasites within the group (K. H. Sibinovic *et al.*, 1967a,b). Serological cross-reaction between serum antigens established their relationship, but there is still a possibility that enhancement of natural immunity by unrelated factors in the material may contribute to the protection observed. Effects of this type could be very short-lived and the duration and complete species range of protection by this material must be determined in order to provide a basis of its evaluation in prophylactic immunization against other economically important *Babesia* spp.

Resistance was induced in susceptible mice and cattle by immunization with killed *B. rodhaini* and *B. argentina*, respectively (Phillips, 1967; Mahoney, 1967b). The material used consisted of parasite–stroma suspensions or parasitized erythrocytes, mixed with adjuvant and inoculated subcutaneously. Protection was not complete, and in nonspelenectomized animals, amounted to abrogation of clinical signs without prevention of infection. The effect lasted for about 3 months. Studies of *B. argentina* have been extended at our laboratory in order to assess the importance of antigenic variation in immunization of cattle with nonviable material. For practical control of the disease, species-specific protection is obviously required, and evidence of such activity in antigens contained by infected plasma and by parasites was sought.

Two strains of *B. argentina* designated "G" and "L" in which antigenic differences had been demonstrated by passive transfer tests were used in the experiments. The antigenic material consisted of freeze-dried parasite–stroma suspensions and freeze-dried plasma from infected animals. Groups of calves were immunized with antigen prepared from one strain, splenectomized, and then challenged with parasites that possessed one of the following relationships with the material used for immunization.

Heterologous: organisms of the other strain.
Homologous: organisms of the same strain but not of the same variant
               population.
Isologous: organisms from the same variant population, preserved in 10%
               dimethylsulfoxide at −70° at the time the corresponding
               antigen was prepared.

The results of the experiments are summarized in Fig. 6. After immunization with killed parasites, there was protection against homologous challenge characterized by a delay in the occurrence of detectable parasitemia and by cessation of parasite multiplication about the level of 10^4 organisms/cu mm of blood and then recovery 15–16 days after infection (Fig. 6a). Control calves died at 10 days. Comparison of homologous with heterologous challenge (Fig. 6a) showed no measurable protection against the heterologous parasites. There was protection against

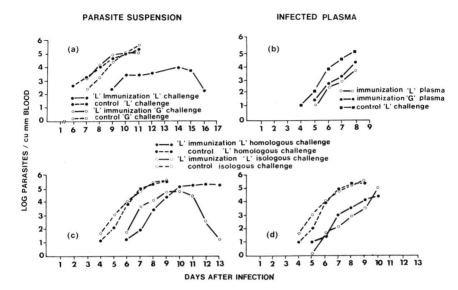

Fig. 6. Mean $\log_{10}$ parasitemia in groups of calves immunized with *B. argentina* antigen obtained from parasites (a,c) and infected plasma (b,d) and challenged with various strains of the organism. Eight calves were used in experiments (a), (c), and (d) and eighteen in experiment (b).

isologous challenge (Fig. 6c) with earlier recovery of the calves than that following homologous challenge. The groups immunized with plasma antigen showed equal protection regardless of the antigenic types used for challenge inoculation (Figs. 6b,d). In each experiment with plasma antigens there was a delay of about a day in the appearance of parasites in peripheral blood, the multiplication of which then paralleled that in the controls and immunized calves invariably died 1 or 2 days after the controls.

Although killed parasites gave a high degree of protection against homologous challenge, species-specific protection was obtained only with plasma antigen. It was slight and was related to an unknown event early in the process of infection. This gave only partial protection in our experimental model, and was overwhelmed by the time parasitemia reached detectable levels. This pattern of infection again suggests variation of antigen by the parasite, but the species-specific nature of the phenomenon is difficult to reconcile with this hypothesis. An alternative might be that it represented an immune response against a metabolite elaborated by the parasite. This system might be inefficient at controlling multiplication with the result that it soon became blocked by excess antigen.

Variable antigens appeared to be concerned with protection in experiments with killed parasites because the rate of recovery of immunized calves was directly related to the degree of matching between antigens of parasites used for immunization and challenge. The reason why killed parasites induced strain-specific protection only is not clear. However, parasite–stroma suspensions did not contain the soluble contents of parasitized cells because the latter products were removed during lysis and washing. This discarded material may have contained antigens similar to those demonstrated in plasma, and the use of parasitized erythrocytes for immunization might induce immunity against heterologous strains.

XI. Immunopathology

A. Destruction of Erythrocytes

It is well established that the destruction of erythrocytes occurs in babesial infection and anemia is well in excess of that caused by emerging parasites. In some infections, e.g., *B. argentina* and *B. bigemina*, this phenomenon closely parallels the development of parasitemia, but in others, e.g., *B. canis*, red cell destruction may continue for some time after the decline in parasitemia. *Babesia* spp. are not unique in this regard. A similar phenomenon occurs in malaria, and a variety of mechanisms involving autoimmune phenomena, production of lysins and toxins, and hyperactivity of RE elements, have been suggested (Laser, 1948; Zuckerman, 1964, 1966; Dixon, 1966; Zuckerman *et al.*, 1969). The antigenic substances demonstrated in *B. canis*- and *B. rodhaini*-infected plasma by K. H. Sibinovic *et al.* (1969) have been discussed in Section VIII. Because of adsorption to normal erythrocytes they cause anemia in these infections. With *B. argentina*, however, there was no evidence that infected plasma contained similar material as we could not detect excessive erythrocyte destruction with ^{51}Cr-labeled autologous red cells during prolonged immunization of normal cattle with plasma antigen. During *B. argentina* infections, antibodies to normal haptoglobin–hemoglobin (Hp–Hb) complexes arise and also to a protein extracted from normal bovine erythrocytes (Goodger, 1970, 1971). We have been able to stimulate the former by injecting purified Hp–Hb complexes in adjuvant without producing any effect on the hematological picture of the animals or alteration of susceptibility to babesial infection. Similar work with the red cell protein has not yet been performed. We have also induced production of agglutinins for trypsinized normal erythrocytes in cattle merely by injection of Freund's complete adjuvant, a procedure that did not disturb packed cell volume readings or again influence the course of subsequent *B. argentina* infection. It has thus been easy to demonstrate autoimmune-like phenomena associated with *B. argentina* but difficult to suggest any role in pathogenesis on the basis of artificial production of similar conditions in normal animals. The function of antibodies implicated in production of kidney damage in *B. rodhaini* infections (Iturri and Cox, 1969) might also be examined in this way.

B. EFFECT OF CIRCULATING ANTIGEN

Shock appears to be a major factor in the cause of death from babesiosis (Maegraith *et al.*, 1957). The general effects of circulating antigen–antibody complexes are well-known and Holbrook (1965) suggested that a condition similar to anaphylaxis occurred in horses infected with *B. caballi* and *B. equi* after antibody production occurred. The pathological processes, however, commence early in the course of infection before specific antibody has time to appear, and the biological activity of substances liberated from parasites or by the activity of parasites has to be considered in relation to pathological processes associated with babesiosis. Goodwin and Richards (1960) isolated biologically active peptides from blood and urine of mice infected with *B. rodhaini*, and the role of similar substances in the pathogenesis of malaria has been demonstrated by Onabanjo and Maegraith (1970a,b,c). These inflammatory products of host origin could be released by either direct or indirect action of parasite material. In *B. argentina*-infected plasma for example, parasite antigen was found in large complexes composed of serum proteins in which γ-globulin was present (Mahoney and Goodger, 1969). Nonspecific aggregation of γ-globulin could initiate complement fixation and the production of anaphlatoxin (Muller-Eberhard, 1968). This effect would be immediate, not requiring time for specific antibody formation.

XII. Discussion

An understanding of the disease processes that accompany infection is relevant to all aspects of immunity because it helps to define the problem with which host defenses must contend. Babesiosis commences with mechanical destruction of erythrocytes by emerging parasites that release metabolic products of mixed origin. Normal erythrocytes are also destroyed. No single explanation for this is entirely satisfactory, and perhaps many of the suggested factors such as autoimmunity, toxic and antigenic activity of parasite products adsorbed to cell membranes, and general stimulation of the RE system have some effect on the destruction of normal erythrocytes. All important in the development of lesions is the condition resembling shock that leads to stasis of the circulation and packing of erythrocytes in small blood vessels. Convincing evidence that this condition in malaria is caused by a rise in certain biologically active peptides has been reported (Onabanjo and Maegraith, 1970a,b,c) and that similar mechanisms will be eventually proved in babesiosis appears a foregone conclusion. If parasite antigens stimulate the production of these substances, immunization with this antigenic material should at least delay the onset of clinical signs and give the host time to respond in a way that will affect the parasites themselves.

Another approach to the mechanism of immunity is to consider how the animal limits the multiplication of parasites. This question has been more closely studied in *B. argentina*-infected cattle than in other systems and the following discussion is based on this parasite. Infection of a clinically immune cow is characterized by a succession of relapses of parasitemia each maintained at an apparently harmless level. The parasitized erythrocytes of each relapse population contain a different surface antigen from that of predecessors and these changes of antigen probably explain, at least partially, the cyclic nature of parasitemia. If protection relied solely on the production of antibodies to each new antigenic type, relapses should resemble initial parasitemia in severity and cause repetitive illness. As this does not happen, there must be some kind of immunological effect that generally retards parasite multiplication in order to allow the host time to respond to each variant before parasitemia reaches a dangerous level.

An important question is the possible antigenic origin of such a response. This basic effect is, by its very nature, inefficient, and may be the result of a generally poor fit between a population of antibodies and antigen in a state of constant variation. Thus, continued retardation of multiplication might be caused by degrees of cross-reaction between any particular variant antigen and existing antibodies to preceding variants. Only the crisis of parasitemia would be caused by production of the specific variant antibody. Reactions of calves to heterologous, homologous, and isologous challenge after immunization with *B. argentina* parasites (Figs. 6a,c) supported this idea as the experiments demonstrated an increasing degree of protection which correlated well with the degree of antigenic disparity between immunizing and corresponding challenge material. However, protection with plasma antigen was species-specific and varied little in degree with changes in the antigenic relationship between immunizing and challenge material. Comparison of these two sets of results suggested that the antigens concerned with immunity to *B. argentina* infection consist of at least two groups. One is associated with the parasites, is predominantly strain-specific, and confers strong immunity only against homologous strains of the organism. The other consists of material secreted into the plasma during infection. This is mainly species-specific, but gives only partial protection against all strains of the parasite. Perhaps plasma antigen provides the basic immunological stimulus referred to above. There is also evidence that protective substances of broad specificity are contained in the serum of infected horses (*B. caballi*), dogs (*B. canis*), and rats (*B. rodhaini*), and, although less specific than those in cattle, they could belong to the same group. Protective antibodies demonstrable in serum by passive transfer tests appear to be mainly strain-specific, but this does not preclude the existence of other immunological systems. However, even if nonvariable protective antigen can be isolated for each species, successful immunization depends also on the duration of protection induced because, under natural conditions, exposure to infection may be infrequent.

Administration of living parasites is still the method of immunization available in practice. It relies on maintaining infection for a time, and safety and efficiency have been achieved by attenuation and numerical standardization of parasites. However, the factors that influence duration of infection are poorly understood although the ability of the parasites to continue changing antigenic structure in the host seems to be an important mechanism of survival. The production of only a small number of antigenic variants might therefore result in short-lived infections and in weak strain-specific immunity. The means of determining the potential number of variants in a parasite population would be advantageous in the selection of strains for immunization as those organisms that produce a high number of such variants should possess many of the characteristics required of an efficient living vaccine.

Acknowledgments

I wish to thank Mr. P. H. Durie, Officer-in-Charge, CSIRO Long Pocket Laboratories, Dr. C. G. Ludford, Animal Research Institute, Yeerongpilly, Brisbane, Australia, and Dr. Bridget M. Ogilvie, National Institute for Medical Research, London, for criticism of the manuscript and also Messrs. B. V. Goodger and I. G. Wright, CSIRO, Long Pocket Laboratories for access to unpublished material.

References

Anderson, D., Billingham, R. E., Lampkin, G. H., and Medawar, P. B. (1951). *Heredity* **5**, 379.

Babes, V. (1888). *C. R. Acad. Sci.* **107**, 692.

Bazurto, G. R. (1967). *Proc. Pan-Amer. Congr. Vet. Med. Zootech., 5th, 1966* Vol. 1, p. 212.

Bowman, I. B. R., Grant, P. T., and Kermack, W. O. (1960). *Exp. Parasitol.* **9**, 131.

Boyden, S. V. (1951). *J. Exp. Med.* **93**, 107.

Brocklesby, D. W., Harness, E., and Sellwood, S. A. (1971). *Res. Vet. Sci.* **12**, 15.

Brown, I. N., Brown, K. N., and Hills, L. A. (1968). *Immunology* **14**, 127.

Brown, K. N., and Brown, I. N. (1965). *Nature (London)* **208**, 1286.

Bungener, W. (1967). *Z. Tropenmed. Parasitol.* **18**, 463.

Callow, L. L. (1964). *Nature (London)* **204**, 1213.

Callow, L. L. (1965). *Parasitology* **55**, 375.

Callow, L. L. (1967). *Parasitology* **57**, 455.

Callow, L. L. (1968). *Aust. Vet. J.* **44**, 268.

Callow, L. L., and McGregor, W. (1969). *Aust. Vet. J.* **45**, 408.

Callow, L. L., and McGregor, W. (1970). *Aust. Vet. J.* **46**, 195.

Callow, L. L., and Mellors, L. T. (1966). *Aust. Vet. J.* **42**, 464.

Callow, L. L., and Parker, R. J. (1969). *Aust. Vet. J.* **45**, 103.

Callow, L. L., and Tammemagi, L. (1967). *Aust. Vet. J.* **43**, 249.

Ceithaml, J., and Evans, E. A. (1946). *J. Infec. Dis.* **78**, 190.

Christophers, S. R. (1907). *Sci. Mem. Med. Sanit. Dep. India* No. 29.

Corradetti, A., Verolini, F., and Bucci, A. (1966). *Parassitologia* **8**, 133.

Cox, F. E. G., and Turner, S. A. (1970). *Ann. Trop. Med. Parasitol.* **64**, 167.

Cox, F. E. G., and Young, A. S. (1969). *Parasitology* **59**, 257.

Cox, H. W. (1959). *J. Immunol.* **82**, 209.

Cox, H. W., and Milar, R. (1968). *Amer. J. Trop. Med. Hyg.* **17**, 173.

Cox, H. W., Schroeder, W. F., and Ristic, M. (1966). *J. Protozool.* **13**, 327.

Cox, H. W., Milar, R., and Patterson, S. (1968). *Amer. J. Trop. Med. Hyg.* **17**, 13.

Crowe, M. W., and Pullen, P. L. (1968). *Amer. J. Vet. Clin. Pathol.* **2**, 263.

Curnow, J. A. (1968). *Nature (London)* **217**, 267.

Curnow, J A., and Curnow, B. A. (1967). *Aust. Vet. J.* **43**, 286.

Dalgleish, R. J. (1965). *Queensl. Agr. J.* **91**, 658.

Daly, G. D., and Hall, W. T. K. (1955). *Aust. Vet. J.* **31**, 152.

D'Antonio, L. E., von Doenhoff, A. E., and Fife, E. H. (1966). *Proc. Soc. Exp. Biol. Med.* **123**, 30.

Davidson, K. B. (1969). *Vet. Rec.* **85**, 391.

Davies, S. F. M., Joyner, L. P., and Kendall, S. B. (1958). *Ann. Trop. Med. Parasitol.* **52**, 206.

Denev, I., and Kyurtov, N. (1967). *Vet.-Med. Nauki* **4**, 93; abstr. in *Vet. Bull. (London)* **38**, 374 (1968).

Dennig, H. K. (1959). *Z. Tropenmed. Parasitol.* **10**, 373.

Dennig, H. K. (1962). *Z. Tropenmed. Parasitol.* 13, 21.

Dennig, H. K. (1966a). *Proc. Int. Congr. Parasitol., 1st, 1964* Vol. 1, p. 262.

Dennig, H. K. (1966b). *Proc. Int. Congr. Parasitol., 1st, 1964* Vol. 1, p. 263.

Dimmock, C. K., and Bell, K. (1970). *Aust. Vet. J.* 46, 44.

Dixon, F. J. (1966). *Mil. Med.* 131, 1233.

Dorner, J. L. (1967). *Amer. J. Vet. Clin. Pathol.* 1, 67.

Dresser, D. W. (1962). *Immunology* 5, 161.

Dumag, P. U., Reyes, P. V., and Castillo, A. M. (1962). *Philipp. J. Anim. Ind.* 23, 1.

Duranov, V. S. (1968). *In* "Raboty Molodykh Uchenykh" (M. F. Rostovtsev, ed.), p. 365. Izd. Kolos, Moscow [abstr. in *Vet. Bull. (London)* 39, 771 (1969)].

Duxbury, R. E., and Sadun, E. H. (1969). *J. Parasitol.* 55, 859.

Enigk, K., and Friedhoff, K. (1962). *Z. Parasitenk.* 21, 238.

Enigk, K., Friedhoff, K., and Wirahadiredja, S. (1964). *Z. Parasitenk.* 24, 309.

Ewing, S. A. (1965a). *Amer. J. Vet. Res.* 26, 727.

Ewing, S. A. (1965b). *Vet. Med. & Small Anim. Clin.* 60, 741.

Ewing, S. A., Buckner, R. G., and Stringer, B. G. (1964). *J. Parasitol.* 50, 704.

Francis, J. (1966). *Brit. Vet. J.* 122, 301.

Francis, J., and Little, D. A. (1964). *Aust. Vet. J.* 40, 247.

Frerichs, W. M., Holbrook, A. A., and Johnson, A. J. (1969a). *Amer. J. Vet. Res.* 30, 697.

Frerichs, W. M., Holbrook, A. A., and Johnson, A. J. (1969b). *Amer. J. Vet. Res.* 30, 1337.

Frerichs, W. M., Johnson, A. J., and Holbrook, A. A. (1969c). *Amer. J. Vet. Res.* 30, 1333.

Friedhoff, K. (1969). *Z. Parasitenk.* 32, 191.

Fulton, J. D. (1939). *Ann. Trop. Med. Parasitol.* 33, 217.

Garnham, P. C. C., and Voller, A. (1965). *Acta Protozool.* 3, 183.

Garnham, P. C. C., Donnelly, J., Hoogstraal, H., Kennedy, C. C. and Walton, G. A. (1969). *Brit. Med. J.* 4, 768.

Gasanov, A. A. (1965). *Veterinariya (Moscow)* 42, 56.

Goodger, B. V. (1970). *Clin. Chim. Acta* 29, 429.

Goodger, B. V. (1971). *Aust. Vet. J.* 47, 251.

Goodwin, L. G., and Richards, W. H. G. (1960). *Brit. J. Pharmacol. Chemother.* 15, 152.

Graham-Smith, G. S. (1905). *J. Hyg.* 5, 250.

Halberstaedter, L. (1938). *Brit. J. Radiol.* 11, 267.

Hall, W. T. K. (1960). *Aust. Vet. J.* 36, 361.

Hall, W. T. K. (1963). *Aust. Vet. J.* 39, 386.

Hall, W. T. K., Tammemagi, L., and Johnston, L. A. Y. (1968). *Aust. Vet. J.* 44, 259.

Hirato, K., Ninomiya, M., Uwano, Y., and Kutil, T. (1945). *Jap. J. Vet. Sci.* 7, 204.

Hirsh, D. C., Hickman, R. L., Burkholder, C. R., and Soave, O. A. (1969). *Lab. Anim. Care* 19, 205.

Holbrook, A. A. (1965). *Proc. 11th Annu. Conv. Amer. Ass. Equine Practitioners* 11, p. 157.

Holbrook, A. A. (1970). *Proc. Int. Conf. Equine Infec. Dis., 2nd, 1969* p. 249.

Holbrook, A. A., Anthony, D. W., and Johnson, A. J. (1968a). *J. Protozool.* 15, 391.

Holbrook, A. A., Johnson, A. J., and Madden, P. A. (1968b). *Amer. J. Vet. Res.* **29**, 297.

Hoyte, H. M. D. (1961). *J. Protozool.* **8**, 462.

Hoyte, H. M. D. (1965). *J. Protozool.* **12**, 83.

Hugoson, G., Vennstrom, R., and Henrikkson, K. (1968). *Bibl. Haematol.* **30**, 157.

Hunt, J. S. (1897). *Queensl. Agr. J.* **1**, 404.

Ishihara, T. (1968). *Jap. Agr. Res. Quart.* **3**, 23.

Iturri, G. M., and Cox, H. W. (1969). *Mil. Med.* **134**, 1119.

Jahiel, R. I., Vilcek, J., Nussenzweig, R., and Vanderberg, J. (1968). *Science* **161**, 802.

Johnston, L. A. Y. (1967). *Aust. Vet. J.* **43**, 427.

Johnston, L. A. Y., and Tammemagi, L. (1969). *Aust. Vet. J.* **45**, 445.

Joyner, L. P., and Davies, S. F. M. (1967). *J. Protozool.* **14**, 260.

Karput, I. M. (1966). *Veterinariya (Moscow)* **42**, 60.

Kemron, A., Hadani, A., Egyed, M., Pipano, E., and Neuman, M. (1964). *Refuah Vet.* **21**, 112.

Kolabskii, N. A., Gaidukov, A. K., Tarverdyan, T. N., and Peskov, N. M. (1961). *Sb. Rab. Konf. Protozool. Probl.* p. 202; abstr. in *Vet. Bull. (London)* **33**, 435 (1963).

Krylov, M. V. (1964). *Acta Protozool.* **2**, 97.

Kyurtov, N. (1967). *Vet.-Med. Nauki* **4**, 23; abstr. in *Vet. Bull. (London)* **38**, 87 (1968).

Kyurtov, N., and Denev, I. (1967). *Vet.-Med. Nauki* **4**, 33; abstr. in *Vet. Bull. (London)* **38**, 374 (1968).

Langford, G., Knott, S. G., Dimmock, C. K., and Derrington, P. (1971). *Aust. Vet. J.* **47**, 1.

Laser, H. (1948). *Nature (London)* **161**, 560.

Legg, J. (1935). *CSIRO (Counc. Sci. Ind. Res.)*, *Pam.* No. 56, pp. 1–48.

Levine, N. D. (1971). *Trans. Amer. Microsc. Soc.* **90**, 2.

Lohr, K. F. (1969a). *Zentral. Veteringermed., Reihe B* **16**, 40.

Lohr, K. F. (1969b). *Zentralbl. Veterinaermed., Reihe B* **16**, 158.

Lohr, K. F., and Ross, J. P. J. (1969). *Z. Tropenmed. Parsitol.* **20**, 287.

Ludford, C. G. (1967). Ph.D. Thesis, University of Queensland, Brisbane, Australia.

Ludford, C. G. (1969). *Exp. Parasitol.* **24**, 327.

Ludford, C. G., Corwin, R. M., Cox, H. W., and Sheldon, T. A. (1969). *Mil. Med.* **134**, 1276.

McHardy, N. (1967). *Nature (London)* **214**, 805.

Madden, P. A., and Holbrook, A. A. (1968). *Amer. J. Vet. Res.* **29**, 117.

Maegraith, B. G., Gilles, H. M., and Devakul, K. (1957). *Z. Tropenmed. Parasitol.* **8**, 485.

Mahoney, D. F. (1962a). *Aust. J. Sci.* **24**, 310.

Mahoney, D. F. (1962b). *Aust. Vet. J.* **38**, 48.

Mahoney, D. F. (1964). *Aust. Vet. J.* **40**, 369.

Mahoney, D. F. (1965). Ph.D. Thesis, University of Queensland, Brisbane, Australia.

Mahoney, D. F. (1966). *Nature (London)* **211**, 422.

Mahoney, D. F. (1967a). *Exp. Parasitol.* **20**, 119.

Mahoney, D. F. (1967b). *Exp. Parasitol.* **20**, 125.

Mahoney, D. F. (1967c). *Exp. Parasitol.* **20**, 232.

Mahoney, D. F. (1969). *Ann. Trop. Med. Parasitol.* **63**, 1.

Mahoney, D. F., and Goodger, B. V. (1969). *Exp. Parasitol.* **24**, 375.

Mahoney, D. F., and Mirre, G. B. (1971). *Ann. Trop. Med. Parasitol.* **65**, 309.

Markov, A. A., and Abramov, I. V. (1968). *Tr. Vses. Inst. Eksp. Vet.* **35**, 87.

Martin, L. K., Einheber, A., Sadun, E. H., and Wren, R. E. (1967). *Exp. Parasitol.* **20**, 186.

Matson, B. A. (1964). Ph.D. Thesis, University of Cambridge, London.

Moulder, J. W. (1962). "The Biochemistry of Intracellular Parasitism." Univ. of Chicago Press, Chicago, Illinois.

Muller-Eberhard, H. J. (1968). *Advan. Immunol.* **8**, 1.

Neitz, W. O. (1938). *Onderstepoort J. Vet. Sci. Anim. Ind.* **10**, 33.

Netiz, W. O. (1956). *Ann. N.Y. Acad. Sci.* **64**, 56.

Neitz, W. O. (1969). *J. S. Afr. Vet. Med. Ass.* **40**, 419.

Newton, L. G., and O'Sullivan, P. J. (1969). *Aust. Vet. J.* **45**, 404.

Nilsson, O., Nordkvist, M., and Ryden, L. (1965). *Acta Vet. Scand.* **6**, 353.

Nugera, D., and Fernando, W. W. H. S. (1963). *Ceylon Vet. J.* **11**, 123.

Nuttall, G. H. F., and Graham-Smith, G. S. (1908). *Parasitology* **1**, 220.

Onabanjo, A. O., and Maegraith, B. G. (1970a). *Ann. Trop. Med. Parasitol.* **64**, 227.

Onabanjo, A. O., and Maegraith, B. G. (1970b). *Ann. Trop. Med. Parasitol.* **64**, 237.

Onabanjo, A. O., and Maegraith, B. G. (1970c). *Advan. Exp. Med. Biol.* **8**, 411.

Overdulve, J. P., and Antonisse, H. W. (1970a). *Exp. Parasitol.* **27**, 310.

Overdulve, J. P., and Antonisse, H. W. (1970b). *Exp. Parasitol.* **27**, 323.

Paget, G. E., Alcock, S. J., and Ryley, J. F. (1962). *J. Pathol. Bacteriol.* **84**, 218.

Phillips, R. S. (1967). *Parasitology* **57**, 11P.

Phillips, R. S. (1969a). *Parasitology* **59**, 357.

Phillips, R. S. (1969b). *Parasitology* **59**, 637.

Phillips, R. S. (1970). *Nature (London)* **227**, 1255.

Phillips, R. S. (1971a). *Nature (London)* **231**, 323.

Phillips, R. S. (1971b). *Parasitology* **62**, 221.

Pipano, E. (1969). *Refuah Vet.* **26**, 11.

Ray, H. (1938). *Indian J. Vet. Sci.* **8**, 183.

Raynaud, J. P. (1962). *Rev. Elevage Med. Vet. Pays Trop.* **15**, 167.

Riek, R. F. (1963). *In* "Immunity to Protozoa" (P. C. C. Garnham, A. E. Pierce, and I. Roitt, eds.), pp. 160–179. Blackwell, Oxford.

Riek, R. F. (1964). *Aust. J. Agr. Res.* **15**, 802.

Riek, R. F. (1966). *Aust. J. Agr. Res.* **17**, 247.

Riek, R. F. (1968). *In* "Infectious Blood Diseases of Man and Animals" (D. Weinman and M. Ristic, eds.), Vol. 2, pp. 219–268. Academic Press, New York.

Ristic, M. (1962). *J. Amer. Vet. Med. Ass.* **141**, 588.

Ristic, M., and Sibinovic, S. (1964). *Amer. J. Vet. Res.* **25**, 1519.

Roberts, J. A. (1968). *Aust. J. Exp. Biol. Med. Sci.* **46**, 807.

Rogers, R. J. (1971a). *Aust. Vet. J.* **47**, 237.

Rogers, R. J. (1971b). *Aust. Vet. J.* **47**, 242.

Ross, J. P. J., and Lohr, K. F. (1968). *Res. Vet. Sci.* **9**, 557.

Roy-Smith, F. (1971). *Aust. Vet. J.* **47**, 418.

Ryley, J. F. (1964). *Res. Vet. Sci.* **5**, 411.

Schiffo, H. P., and Lombardero, O. J. (1964). *Gac. Vet.* **26**, 146.

Schindler, R., and Dennig, H. K. (1962a). *Berlin. Muenchen. Tieraerztl. Wochenschr.* **75**, 111.

Schindler, R., and Dennig, H. K. (1962b). *Z. Tropenmed. Parasitol.* **13**, 480.

Schindler, R., Schroeder, G., Stieger, R., Wirahadiredja, S., and Kessler, W. (1970). *Z. Tropenmed. Parasitol.* **21**, 182.

Scholtens, R. G., Braff, E. F., Healy, G. R., and Gleason, N. (1968). *Amer. J. Trop. Med. Hyg.* **17**, 810.

Schroeder, W. F.(1966). Ph.D. Thesis, University of Illinois, Urbana.

Schroeder, W. F., Cox, H. W., and Ristic, M. (1965). *J. Parasitol.* **51**, No. 2, Sect. 2, 30.

Schroeder, W. F., Cox, H. W., and Ristic, M. (1966). *Ann. Trop. Med. Parasitol.* **60**, 31.

Schuberg, A., and Reichenow, E. (1912). *Arb. Gesundheitsamte, Berlin* **38**, 415.

Seed, J. R. (1963). *J. Protozool.* **10**, 380.

Sergent, E. (1963). *In* "Immunity to Protozoa" (P. C. C. Garnham, A. E. Pierce, and I. Roitt, eds.), pp. 39–47. Blackwell, Oxford.

Shortt, H. E. (1962). *Symp. Zool. Soc. London* **6**, 157.

Shortt, H. E., and Blackie, E. J. (1965). *J. Trop. Med. Hyg.* **68**, 37.

Sibinovic, K. H., Ristic, M., Sibinovic, S., and Phillips, T. N. (1965). *Amer. J. Vet. Res.* **26**, 147.

Sibinovic, K. H., MacLeod, R., Ristic, M., Sibinovic, S., and Cox, H. W. (1967a). *J. Parasitol.* **53**, 919.

Sibinovic, K. H., Sibinovic, S., Ristic, M., and Cox, H. W. (1967b). *J. Parasitol.* **53**, 1121.

Sibinovic, K. H., Milar, R., Ristic, M., and Cox, H. W. (1969). *Ann. Trop. Med. Parasitol.* **63**, 327.

Sibinovic, S., Sibinovic, K. H., Ristic, M., and Cox, H. W. (1966). *J. Protozool.* **13**, 551.

Sibinovic, S., Sibinovic, K. H., and Ristic, M. (1969). *Amer. J. Vet. Res.* **30**, 691.

Skrabalo, Z., and Deanovic, Z. (1957). *Doc. Med. Geogr. Trop.* **9**, 11.

Smith, T., and Kilborne, F. L. (1893). *U.S., Dep. Agr., Bull. Bur. Anim. Ind.* No. 1, pp. 1–301.

Spindler, L. A., Allen, R. W., Diamond, L. S., and Lotze, J. C. (1958). *J. Protozool.* **5**, Suppl., 6.

Spira, D., and Zuckerman, A. (1962). *Science* **137**, 536.

Sprent, J. F. A. (1963). "Parasitism." pp. 31–33. Univ. of Queensland Press, Brisbane, Australia.

Starcovici, C. (1893). *Zentralbl. Bakteriol. Parasitenk. Infektionsk. Hyg. Abt. 1: Orig.* **14**, 1.

Stauber, L. A., and Walker, H. A. (1946). *Proc. Soc. Exp. Biol. Med.* **63**, 223.

Stepanova, N. L., Gorbatov, V. A., and Petrovskii, V. V. (1969). *Veterinariya (Moscow)* **46**, 45.

Suleimanov, S. A. (1965). *Tr. Vses. Inst. Eksp. Vet.* **31**, 309.

Swisher, S. W. (1965). *Ann. N.Y. Acad. Sci.* **127**, 901.

Taliaferro, W. H. (1955). *In* "Some Physiological Aspects and Consequences of Parasitism" (W. H. Cole, ed.), pp. 50–75. Rutgers Univ. Press, New Brunswick, New Jersey.

Taliaferro, W. H., and Cannon, P. R. (1936). *J. Infec. Dis.* **59**, 72.

Todorovic, R., Ferris, D., and Ristic, M. (1967). *Exp. Parasitol.* **21**, 354.

Tsur, I. (1961). *Refuah Vet.* **18**, 110.

Tunkel, B., Richter, S., and Romic, Z. (1961). *Vet. Glasn.* **15**, 93.

Uilenberg, G. (1969). *Rev. Elevage Med. Vet. Pays Trop.* **22**, 237.

Wallace, A. L., Osler, A. G., and Mayer, M. M. (1950). *J. Immunol.* **65**, 661.
Watkins, R. G. (1962). *J. Amer. Vet. Med. Ass.* **141**, 1330.
Watts, R. M. (1969). *Aust. Vet. J.* **45**, 437.
Wellde, B. T., and Sadun, E. H. (1967). *Exp. Parasitol.* **21**, 310.
Wellde, B. T., Briggs, N. T., and Sadun, E. H. (1966). *Mil. Med.* **131**, 859.
Western, K. A., Benson, G. D., Gleason, N. N., Healy, G. R., and Schultz, M. G. (1970). *N. Engl. J. Med.* **283**, 854.
Whitlock, J. H. (1949). *Cornell Vet.* **39**, 146.
Wright, I. G. (1971). Ph.D. Thesis, University of Queensland, Brisbane, Australia.
Zuckerman, A. (1964). *Exp. Parasitol.* **15**, 138.
Zuckerman, A. (1966). *Mil. Med.* **131**, 1201.
Zuckerman, A., Abzug, S., and Burg, R. (1969). *Mil. Med.* **134**, 1084.

13 IMMUNE RESPONSE TO INTRACELLULAR PARASITES

I. Leishmania

G. A. MAEKELT

I. Introduction

Leishmaniasis is a parasitic infection of animals and man, which occurs in many tropical and subtropical areas of the world. In Middle Asia, East Africa, South and. Central America, it occurs in enzootic form with wild natural foci. The reservoirs are rodents, small carnivores, and wild canids. In Middle Asia and the Mediterranean region it is seen in rural endemic foci, representing a zooanthroponosis in which the principal reservoirs are dogs. In the Mediterranean region, Transcaucasia, Middle Asia, and Eastern China it occurs in urban endemic foci, representing an anthropozoonosis and in which the reservoirs are dogs and man. In India it occurs in an endemic or occasionally an epidemic form in man, representing a true anthroponosis (see World Health Organization, 1967).

The immune responses of animals and man to different "species" and strains of the genus *Leishmania* are multiple and complex, depending on numerous factors which may be related to the infecting species and/or the infected host. All species of the genus *Leishmania*, Ross, 1903, are morphologically similar and not differentiable in either the amastigote or the promastigote development stages. The species *L. enriettii* (Adler, 1964) is an exception to this.

Species differentiation has been proposed and attempted by many investigators, using several criteria and characteristics such as colony morphology (Mayer and Malamos, 1936), clinical pathology in animals (Kirk, 1949, 1950), chemical tests (Senekji, 1939; Senekji and Zebouni, 1941), thermosensitivity (Biagi, 1953; Hall, 1953; Lemma, 1963, 1964), promastigote physiology and metabolism (Bell, 1966, 1968), epidemiology (Biagi, 1953), and nucleic acid base ratio (Schildkraut *et al.*, 1962; du Buy *et al.*, 1965).

Perhaps the clearest separation of *Leishmania* spp. is obtained by serological and cross-immunity tests. Noguchi (1924, 1926) was the first, using agglutination and complement fixation tests and culture growth characteristics in presence of immune sera, to differentiate the species *Leishmania donovani, Leishmania braziliensis,* and *Leishmania tropica.* Subsequently, numerous other investigators repeated these findings and attempted to obtain better results (Chang and Negherborn, 1947; da Cunha and Chagas, 1937; da Cunha, 1942; da Fonseca, 1932; Kligler, 1925; Sen and Mukherjee, 1961).

Using an improved technique based on the growth characteristics of promastigotes cultured in presence of immune sera, Adler (1964) was able to differentiate between *L. tropica* and *L. donovani,* and also between the different "species" of American *Leishmania* such as *L. mexicana, L. braziliensis,* and *L. pifanoi.* Furthermore, he was able to differentiate between *L. donovani,* and *L. infantum* and between *L. tropica major* and *L. tropica minor* by absorption of sera.

Several simple and sensitive serological techniques (e.g., indirect hemagglutinaiton test, indirect immunofluorescence antibody test, agar double diffusion test, passive agglutination test) have been introduced for the indentification of "species" and "strains" (Bray and Lainson, 1965, 1966, 1967; Bray and Rahim, 1969; Camargo and Reronato, 1969; Schneider and Hertig, 1966). However, to the present, none of these have been satisfactory enough to permit a clear differentiation of the *Leishmania* species (see Hoogstraal and Heyneman, 1969). Speciation among leishmanial agents is still based on clinical criteria, especially on the organotropism of the parasite in man and the epidemiological features of the infection (Moshkovsky, 1967 (See Table I). At first glance it would seem easy to differentiate between visceral leishmaniasis and the cutaneous and mucocutaneous leishmaniasis. However, the parasites are not always exclusively located in the skin or the viscera. Thus in the early phase of *L. donovani* infection, a skin lesion (indurated papule) may appear at the site of parasite inoculation. During the visceral stage, leishmanial bodies are frequently found in the skin, without any lesions being present (Manson-Bahr, 1959). Rohrs (1964) found parasites in nasal mucosa in 14 of 20 patients with kala azar, and after the cure of Indian kala azar up to 10% of the patients may develop a post-kala azar dermal leishmanoid, characterized by an exclusively nonulcerating, long-lasting skin lesion. Dogs infected with *L. donovani* generally show heavy skin parasitism without any superficial cutaneous lesions.

The clinical picture of cutaneous leishmaniasis may vary. The "wet" ("moist") and "dry" type of Oriental sore of Turkestan, the Middle East, and Central Asia may be identical or similar to the South or Central American cutaneous leishmanias which are characterized by a single ulcer and are variously referred to as the Mexican, British Honduras, or Guatemala type of "Chiclero's ulcer," the Peruvian "Uta" or the Guyanesian "Forest yaws." All these skin manifestations have been considered to be caused by different "species" of *Leishmania* (Pessôa, 1961). The South American mucocutaneous form of leishmaniasis, "Espundia," may begin as a typical "Oriental sore." Weeks, months, or years later, frequently when the primary sore has disappeared, metastatic destructive lesions of the oral, nasal, and pharyngeal mucosae may follow.

Very different skin lesions are produced in the so-called "diffuse cutaneous leishmaniasis" which resemble lepromatous leprosy. Reports of this type of leishmaniasis have come from Venezuela, Brasil, Bolivia, Mexico, Honduras, Ecuador, Panama, Texas, and Ethiopia (see Bryceson, 1969). Some authors consider the lesion as caused by a different species, called *L. pifanoi* (Medina and Romero, 1959, 1962) but Bryceson (1969, 1970c), argues that the clinical picture may be produced as the result of a different immune response of Ethiopians to a *L. tropica* infection.

Unfortunately, species differentiation of the genus *Leishmania*, based on the pathological manifestations in man cannot be applied to experimental animals. The behavior of leishmanial infection may be quite

TABLE I

Species Differentiation of *Leishmania* According to Their Organotropism in Man

Species	Cutaneous lesions		Lesions of		Visceral lesions	Disease
	Nodular	Ulcerous	Mucosa	Cartilage		
L. infantum	(+)	–	–	–	++++	Mediterranean infantile kala azar
L. donovani	(+)	–	–	–	++++	Classical kala azar
L. donovani	++++	–	–	–	–	Indian post-kala azar-dermal leishmanoid
L. pifanoi (Venezuela)	++++	–	(+)	–	–	Diffuse cutaneous lepromatous leishmaniasis
L. tropica (Ethiopia)	++++	–	–	–	–	Diffuse cutaneous lepromatous leishmaniasis
L. tropica (major, minor)	(+)	++++	–	–	–	Oriental sore
L. tropica	+	+	–	–	–	Leishmaniasis recidiva
L. mexicana	++	+++	–	++	–	Chicleros' ulcer
L. peruviana	++	+++	–	–	–	"Uta"
L. braziliensis	++	+++	–	–	–	Leishmaniasis tegumentaria americana
L. guyanensis	++	+++	(+)	–	–	"Forest yaws"
L. braziliensis	++	+++	+++	+++	–	"Espundia" L. mucocutanea

different in each animal. For example, *L. tropica* or *L. mexicana,* which have strong skin tropism in man, may produce a diffuse visceralization in hamsters (Adler and Zuckerman, 1948; Chung and Wang, 1939; Mata *et al.,* 1968).

Moreover, various investigators have observed differences in the behavior (e.g., infectivity, tissue parasitism, and virulence) of a single species of *Leishmania* in the same species of laboratory animal. Many of these differences may be due to a lack of standardized techniques (Stauber, 1962, 1963, 1966). Thus, few investigators have standardized the variety of factors related to infection by the parasite. These include size and route of inoculum, the infectivity and virulence of the development stage inoculated, and the age, weight, sex, genetic composition, etc., of the experimental animal. Thus, it is difficult to compare the variable results obtained by numerous investigators.

The immune response of man to leishmania infection shows two main forms. The first is characterized by a marked delayed cutaneous hypersensitivity, typical for the infections with the "species" *L. tropica, L. mexicana, L. peruviana,* and *L. braziliensis.* The second is characterized by the absence of a delayed cutaneous hypersensitivity, typical for infection with the "species" *L. donovani* and *L. pifanoi* (*L. tropica* of Ethiopia). (See Table II.)

Neither of these main forms of immune response is stable in degree, duration, or specificity. During the course of leishmanial infection and especially after clinical and parasitological cure, the type and intensity of immune response may vary, probably depending on both host and parasite factors.

To date, the immune response of man to *Leishmania* has been studied mostly by conventional clinical methods. Very little experimental work has been done to explain the different responses, the immunological mechanisms of which are still largely unknown. An excellent fundamental contribution to the immunopathology of leishmaniasis was recently published by Bryceson *et al.* (1970), who used *Leishmania enriettii* infection of guinea pigs as the parasite–host system. This seems to be a suitable model for investigating certain human types of cutaneous leishmaniasis of a similar pattern, such as Oriental sore, caused by *L. tropica.*

In the present paper an attempt is made to evaluate the knowledge of the immune response of man and animals to *Leishmania* infections by analyzing the experimental results of *L. enriettii* infections in guinea pigs and summarizing the abundant clinical and few experimental data on *L. tropica, L. braziliensis, L. donovani,* and *L. pifanoi* (*L. tropica* of Ethiopia) infection of man.

TABLE II

IMMUNOLOGICAL FEATURES OF *Leishmania* INFECTIONS IN MAN

Species	Disease	Delayed cutaneous hypersensitivity		Humoral antibodies
		During infection	After cure	
L. infantum	Kala azar infantil	−	+ +	+ + + +
L. donovani	Clasical kala azar	−	+ +	+ + + +
L. donovani	PKADL[a]	(±)	+ +	+ +
L. tropica (Ethiopia)	Diffuse cutaneous leishmaniasis	−	(±)	(+)
L. pifanoi (Venezuela)	Diffuse cutaneous leishmaniasis	−	(±)	(±)
L. tropica (*major, minor*)	Oriental sore	+ +	+ + + +	(+)
L. tropica	Leishmaniasis recidiva	+ + +	+ + + +	(+)
L. mexicana	Chiclero's ulcer	+ +	+ + + +	(+)
L. peruviana	"Uta"	+ +	+ + + +	(+)
L. brasiliensis	Leishmaniasis tegumentaria americana	+ +	+ + + +	(+)
L. brasiliensis	"Espundia" *L. mucocutanea*	+ +	+ + + +	+ +

[a] PKADL = Post-kala azar dermal leishmanoid.

II. Immune Response of Guinea Pigs to *Leishmania enriettii* Infections

An intracutaneous primary infection of guinea pigs with *L. enriettii* usually is followed by a single skin ulcer, which heals in 2–3 months (Paraense, 1953). Cutaneous metastases appear only in a low percentage of animals (Adler and Halff, 1955). Exceptionally, visceralization may be produced by reinoculation of animals cured by medication (Ercoli and Coelho, 1967). Superinfection leads to an "isophasic lesion," which heals simultaneously with the lesion of the primary infection (Bryceson *et al.*, 1970). At 5 weeks after primary infection, the isophasic lesion is possibly an expression of a partial acquired immunity. When superinfection is attempted 8–9 weeks after the primary infection, a delayed cutaneous hypersensitivity reaction occurs. Thereafter, a long-lasting immunity to reinfection follows (Coutinho, 1955, Kretschmar, 1965).

Immunization with a soluble or an insoluble *L. enriettii* antigen, in Freund's complete adjuvant, may stimulate a marked immunity to a subsequent homologous infection. Heterologous antigens, prepared from *L. donovani*, *L. mexicana*, and *L. braziliensis*, do not produce cross-immunity to *L. enriettii* infection. Recently, Preston and Dumonde (1971) showed that immunity may be enhanced by the use of a ribosomal antigen of *L. enriettii*, which elicits a strong immunity to challenge infection and a strong delayed hypersensitivity. Antigens prepared from low speed particles such as mitochondria, nuclei, and flagella obtained by differential centrifugation did not produce good immunity, while vaccination with the cell sap of promastigotes stimulated precipitating antibodies and immediate hypersensitivity and, moreover, impaired resistance to challenge infection.

Intravenous inoculation of high doses of purified soluble *L. enriettii* antigen produced immunological paralysis (Bryceson *et al.*, 1970). This was characterized by a marked diminution of the defense mechanisms to a subsequent infection 1 week later resulting in a severe ulcerating skin lesion and early cutaneous metastases.

The immunization of guinea pigs with soluble and insoluble antigens in Freund's complete adjuvant may stimulate both immunity to *L. enriettii* infections and circulating antibodies. The later response seems to be of no importance for the immune defense, since convalescent animals, which usually acquire a solid immunity to reinfection, do not produce humoral antibodies, (at least, not on concentrations demonstrable by passive cutaneous anaphylaxis or by the indirect hemagglutination test). Furthermore, Kretschmar (1965) failed to protect guinea pigs with immune sera. However, Bryceson *et al.*, (1970) demonstrated active, immediate, and cutaneous anaphylaxis in convalescent animals 8–10 weeks after primary infection. The authors suggest the importance of this type of immune response may be to produce, on challenge infection, an alteration of the microvascular system leading to a rejection of a *L. enriettii* inoculum and to the state of "sterilizing" immunity.

Cell-mediated immunity seems to be of major importance for the development of acquired immunity by guinea pigs to *L. enrietti* infection. Bryceson *et al.* (1970), demonstrated a delayed cutaneous hypersensitivity reaction in infected animals 4 weeks after infection, and also in animals 3 to 4 weeks after being immunized with a mixture of soluble and insoluble *L. enriettii* antigen in Freund's complete adjuvant. The delayed sensitivity could be transferred passively by lymphoid cells to normal animals. The reaction was not species-specific because it could also be provoked by antigens prepared from *L. donovani*, *L. mexicana*, or *L. braziliensis*, and, surprisingly, to a lesser degree, by Freund's complete adjuvant alone. Considering that animals immunized with the heterologous strains of *Leishmania* showed no

cross-immunity to *L. enriettii* infection, it may be concluded that the
delayed cutaneous hypersensitivity cannot be accepted unconditionally
as a sign of a specific immunity.

Various *in vitro* correlates of cell-mediated immunity have been
demonstrated when lymphoid cells from infected, convalescent, or immunized animals are exposed to *L. enriettii* antigen. Thus, enhanced
phagocytic activity of macrophages, inhibition of macrophage migration,
and lymphocytic transformation have been shown, and the soluble lymphokines or their reactions, such as macrophage migration inhibition

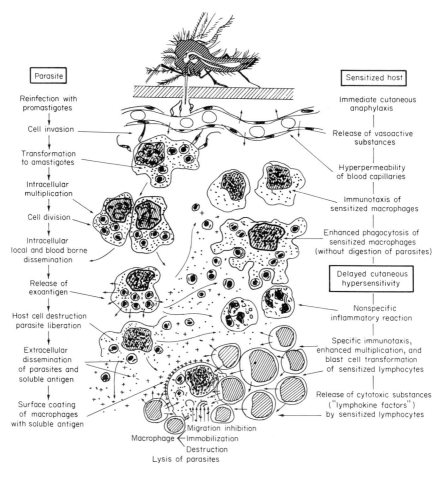

Fig. 1. Model of immune response to *Leishmania* infection (according to data
of Bryceson *et al.*, 1970).

factor (MIF) and a mitogenic factor (MF), have been demonstrated. Bray and Bryceson (1968) demonstrated that while the phagocytic activity of macrophages of convalescent animals was 2 times greater than that of normal animals, the subsequent multiplication of ingested intracellular amastigotes was not supressed. This observation agrees with what is known about histological and cellular aspects of acute lesions, in that intracellular parasite destruction is generally missing in spite of the high degree of phagocytic activity by macrophages.

The role of the specifically sensitized lymphocyte in the immune mechanisms to *L. enriettii* infection is further illustrated by the action of such cells on a monolayer of *L. enriettii*-infected macrophages. Such an infected cell culture is selectively destroyed by a cytotoxic action of sensitized lymphocytes obtained from immunized or convalescent animals. Moreover, uninfected macrophages, pretreated and coated with soluble antigen so as to serve as target cells, are similarly destroyed by the sensitized lymphocytes of convalescent animals. However, the immunological specificity of this phenomenon could not be demonstrated; thus, lymphocytes from animals immunized with Freund's complete or incomplete adjuvant alone showed a similar cytopathic effect on parasitized and on antigen-coated macrophages (Fig. 1).

III. Immune Response of Man to *Leishmania tropica* Infections

Leishmania tropica infection generally is followed by a single cutaneous ulcer, known as Oriental sore. Multiple cutaneous lesions are less frequent. Visceralization never occurs in man.

Natural or experimental superinfections during the active lesion of a primary infection are followed by "isophasic lesions," which cure simultaneously with the lesion of the primary infection (Dostrowsky *et al.*, 1952; Moshkovsky, 1942).

Acquired immunity to natural or experimental infection with *L. tropica* is developed progressively over a period of 3–18 months after primary infection. After spontaneous cure of the lesion, a solid immunity is usually acquired. It has been demonstrated that reinfection may be possible after surgical removal of an active lesion, and this may be interpreted as a sign that immunity was not fully established (Marzinowsky and Schorenkova, 1924). Acquired immunity after spontaneous cure may persist for life and this would be of the postinfection sterilizing type (Sagher *et al.*, 1955). Reinfections, after healing of the primary infection, have been observed 5 or more years later (Adler, 1963, 1964; Biagi, 1953).

Exceptionally, immunity may not always be complete. Thus, in 0.5% of cases in Iraq (Bray *et al.*, 1967), there is the reappearance of long-lasting lupoid papules near the old scars of an Oriental sore ulcer that may have healed years ago. This form is known as "Leishmaniasis recidiva." Bray and Rahim (1969), using indirect hemagglutination tests together with absorption experiments, were unable to demonstrate any antigen variations or strain differences in the causative agents of the "recidiva" forms.

In Middle and Central Asia, vaccination with material from an active Oriental sore has been practiced for centuries to prevent destructive skin lesion of the face. The effectiveness of this procedure was confirmed by Wenyon (1912) by means of a self-inoculation and by Lawrow and Dubojski (1937) in a comparative study with a living vaccine prepared from promastigote culture forms.

Subsequently, it has been confirmed by various investigators that artificial vaccination with living culture forms of *L. tropica* may be useful to prevent Oriental sore (Adler and Katzenellenbogen, 1952; Berberian, 1939, 1944; Katzenellenbogen, 1942; Senekji and Beatie, 1941), and in recent years these procedures have found large-scale application (Serebryakov *et al.*, 1968; Shuikina *et al.*, 1968). Postvaccination immunity develops slowly and needs 4–18 months to become established. Different degrees from partial protection up to solid protection may be obtained and lifelong immunity can be achieved.

The reaction to the vaccine as measured by the ulcer development and protection to challenge infections seems to be related to the virulence of the strain (Kellina, 1966), and not apparently to the dosage and the age of promastigote culture (Lawrow and Dubojski, 1937; Senekji and Beattie, 1941). The more virulent strain *L. tropica major* may protect against an *L. tropica minor* reinfection (Rodjakin, 1957), [references by Adler (1964) and by Manson-Bahr (1963)] but apparently not vice versa (Ansari and Mofidi, 1950). Vaccines prepared of killed promastigote culture forms are not able to stimulate an acquired immunity (Berberian, 1944).

Cross-immunity has been demonstrated between *L. mexicana* and *L. tropica*, two "species" that are serologically different (Adler and Gunders, 1964). Moreover, *L. tropica* may protect against experimental inoculation of culture promastigotes of *L. braziliensis* (Adler and Theodor, 1927). Cross-immunity has not been shown to exist between *L. tropica* and *L. donovani* (Manson-Bahr, 1961; Napier, 1946; Patton, 1922).

The immunity mechanisms to *L. tropica* infection, without doubt, are predominantly of the cell-mediated type. Though circulating antibodies may be stimulated in experimental animals by immunization procedures, Adler (1963, 1964) has shown that this does not have any appreciable parasiticidal properties.

However, in contrast to this, Rezai *et al.* (1970) demonstrated that promastigote-induced immune sera of rabbits, with agglutination and complement fixation antibody activity of the IgG type, had growth inhibitory activity against promastigotes of *L. tropica*, but they failed to affect the course of leishmanial infection in mice. In natural infections, humoral antibodies are not present (Adler, 1964), or are demonstrable only in very low concentration. They may be detected by certain sensitive serological procedures, such as the indirect agglutination of hemagglutination tests, the indirect immunofluorescence antibody test (Bray and Lainson, 1965, 1966, 1967; Bray and Rahim, 1969; Camargo and Reronato, 1969), and the leptomonad immobilization test (Rodjakin and Khanmamedov, 1967).

Nevertheless various authors have reported that individuals who have previously suffered an Oriental sore may respond to an inoculation of promastigotes of *L. tropica* with an acute inflammatory reaction of Arthus-type (Berberian, 1939; Senekji and Beattie, 1941; Katzenellenbogen, 1944; Adler and Katzenellenbogen, 1952; Ansari and Mofidi, 1950). Consequently, it seems that some humoral antibodies are involved and these react with an antigen in presence of complement. Probably these antibodies are produced to the soluble exo- or endoantigens of the parasite, and they may not be capable of destroying the inoculated parasite. Thus, Adler and Zuckerman (1948) demonstrated that following injection of promastigotes it was possible to isolate the parasites by culture methods for up to 24 hours from the site of the inoculation. This would indicate that a slowly acting immunity mechanism was operative, and more likely to be of the cell-mediated type than one mediated by humoral antibody. In fact the early development of a strong and long-lasting delayed cutaneous hypersensitivity response in *L. tropica* infection is an indication that immunity is intimately related to cell-mediated immunity mechanisms.

A delayed skin reaction is demonstrable before immunity is fully established (Adler and Zuckerman, 1948). It develops in response to a small inoculum of promastigotes [10^3], to a soluble antigen of the parasite, and to a culture exoantigen (Adler, 1964). According to Senekji (1941) the parasite antigen responsible for eliciting the delayed skin reaction seems to be a polysaccharide acting as a hapten. Cortisone inhibits the delayed cutaneous hypersensitivity reaction (Dostrowsky and Sagher, 1957; Dostrovsky and Cohen, 1957).

Delayed cutaneous hypersensitivity is not *Leishmania* species-specific and is evoked by antigens, probably polysaccharide in nature, prepared from *L. tropica, L. mexicana, L. donovani, L. infantum, L. braziliensis, L. enriettii, L. adleri, L. gymnodactyli* (of lizards), *Trypanosoma cruzi,* and *T. equiperdum* (Adler, 1964; Ranque *et al.,* 1958; Cahill, 1970).

As is the case with *L. enriettii* infection of guinea pigs, the immunity to Oriental sore is probably associated with sensitized and cytotoxic lymphocytes. Indeed, 20 years ago, Adler (1964) demonstrated that the disappearance of the parasites from a lesion occurred only when local mobilization of lymphocytes had taken place. The quantitative and qualitative requirements of this local mobilization are not yet known.

It is possible that an early, specific, mobilization of immune competent cells may be elicited by a soluble, incomplete, antigen (e.g., polysaccharides), and this may antecede the full development of immunity. Adler (1964) has suggested that the mobilized lymphocytes "are effective only after immunity has been established." The quantitative consideration of this would be that a sufficient number of sensitized lymphocytes, with cytotoxic properties, have to be present to eliminate the parasitized macrophages and the parasites.

The immune response to *L. mexicana* and *L. peruviana* infection resembles that of *L. tropica* infection. The appearance of a strong delayed cutaneous hypersensitivity, the lack of high titers of circulating antibodies, the self-healing tendency, and the long-lasting and apparently residual immunity are features typical for both Oriental sore and simple skin lesion of American cutaneous leishmanias. Thus the immunity mechanisms of both are probably similar.

IV. Immune Response of Man to *Leishmania braziliensis* Infection

The immune response to *L. braziliensis* infection which produces the clinical picture of "Espundia" or South American mucocutaneous leishmaniasis, is different from that of *L. tropica* infection.

A characteristic feature of the infection is the destructive metastatic lesions of the oral, nasal, and pharyngeal mucosae and cartilages (Pessôa and Barreto, 1948). This may occur early in the infection or, more frequently, a long time after healing of the cutaneous lesions of the primary infection. Pessôa (1941) found this complication in 80.9% of cases 1 year after the initial skin lesion was observed.

The lesions of mucosa show little self-healing tendency and a resistance to chemotherapy. The histological picture is predominantly characterized by histocytic proliferation with scant lymphocytic mobilization and few parasites.

In contrast to a *L. tropica* infection, circulating antibodies are generally detectable (Ulrich *et al.,* 1968). These are not species-specific and may also react with *T. cruzi* antigen (Bittencourt *et al.,* 1968; Camargo and Reronato, 1969; Pessôa and Cardoso, 1942). The delayed skin test [first described for leishmaniasis by Montenegro (1926)] is positive in the early stage of the lesions (Echandi, 1953). It, too, is not species-specific and may be evoked with antigens prepared from *L. tropica, L. braziliensis, L. mexicana, L. enriettii,* and *T. cruzi* (see Adler, 1964). Furtado and Pellegrino (1956) demonstrated that delayed cutaneous hypersensitivity may be elicited equally well by polysaccharide antigen prepared from *L. braziliensis* as by crude water soluble extract of the parasite. A crude promastigote antigen (10^7/ml) showed weaker reactions. A linear relationship between the area of skin induration and the logarithmic concentration of a soluble crude antigen of *L. braziliensis* was shown by Pellegrino *et al.* (1960).

The clinical and epidemiological studies have shown that a primary infection is followed by a long-lasting immunity to reinfection (Furtado, 1969; Ulrich *et al.,* 1968) at the skin level. However, cell-mediated immunity mechanisms do not appear to be effective in the nasal and oral mucosae. Garnham and Humphrey (1969) have explained the failure of immune protection in the cartilage of the nasopharynx by the fact that cartilage cells are protected from lymphocytes by a covering of chondroitin sulfate. They emphasized that cartilage can be transplanted easily and is not subject to homograft rejection, a reaction caused by cell-mediated immunity.

V. Immune Response of Man to *Leishmania donovani* Infection

L. donovani and *L. infantum* infections of man are the causative agents of the visceral leishmaniasis or kala azar.

A massive natural infection is generally followed by a severe disease without any self-healing tendency. The defense mechanisms are unable to halt the spread and multiplication of the parasite within the macrophages, particularly of the spleen, liver, and bone marrow. However, individuals cured of the infection by chemotherapeutic agents develop an acquired immunity to reinfection (Napier, 1946). This is not always of high degree or long-lasting. Recidivisms have been observed in *L. infantum* infections (Adler, 1964). Relapses after 6–12 months may appear in 11.3% of cases of East African kala azar (Manson-Bahr, 1959) and about 10% of Indian kala azar cases develop a post-kala azar dermal leishmanoid 1–2 years after the cure of the primary infection. In such individuals acquired immunity would seem not to be of a postinfection permanent type; but rather an indication for immunity of the premunition type (Napier, 1946; Prata, 1957).

No cross-immunity exists between L. tropica and L. donovani infections. Natural and experimental L. tropica infections of patients cured of kala azar are well documentated (Napier, 1946; Manson-Bahr, 1961), and previous infections with Oriental sore do not protect against kala azar (Patton, 1922).

A close antigen relationship apparently exists between Kenyan and Indian strains of L. donovani and the "species" L. infantum and L. donovani, and between an East African species of Leishmania isolated from a gerbil and a human strain of L. donovani.

The immunity mechanisms to L. donovani infection has yet to be adequately clarified. The marked hyperplasia of the reticuloendothelial and lymph-plasma-cell systems seen in the viscera seems to be "an unsuccessful tissue response" to the L. donovani infection. The proliferation of highly active phagocyting histiocytes is not accompanied by the capacity to destroy the intracellular parasites. The lack of a delayed cutaneous hypersensitivity response of patients with active kala azar (de Alencar, 1958; Barros and Rosenfeld, 1944; Manson-Bahr et al., 1959; Pessôa and Barreto, 1948; Rosenfeld, 1945; Sen Gupta and Mukherjee, 1962), is an additional sign that cell-mediated immunity has not been established, has been prevented, or has been nullified. Sequelae of the hyperproduction of plasma cells are the characteristic hyperglobulinemia and the increased concentration of immunoglobulins, especially those of the IgG and IgM types (Araujo and Mayrink, 1968; Chaves and Ferri, 1966; Ferri and Chaves, 1968; Irunberry et al., 1968). There is, however, no quantitative relationship between concentration of globulins and antibody titers (da Cunha et al., 1959). Though the antibodies may have no antiparasitic action against the intracellular parasites, they may have an antiparasiticidal effect against culture promastigotes (Jadin et al., 1970). Antibodies are usually non-species-specific and may react to high titers with heterologous antigens, for example, with T. cruzi (Camargo and Reronato, 1969) or acid-fast bacilli, like Mycobacterium butyricum, M. tuberculosis, and Kedrowskys bacillus (Mayrink, 1961; Nussenzweig, 1957; Pellegrino et al., 1958; Sen Gupta, 1943, 1945; Sen Gupta and Adhikari, 1952).

The persistence of intracellular organisms in the face of a markedly increased immunoglobulin response and a hyperplastic reticuloendothial system might suggest an ability to undergo antigenic variation. However, Bray (1969), in an extensive study, was unable to demonstrate this phenomenon.

The humoral response in L. donovani infection is not permanent since therapeutic treatment of kala azar causes a diminution of the immunoglobulin and the nonspecific antibody production concomitant with an enhancement of cell-mediated immune mechanisms. The appearance of delayed cutaneous hypersensitivity at the time of the development of acquired immunity shows that, as in *L. donovani* infections, cell-mediated immunity mechanisms are the principal mediators for the defense mechanisms. To date there is little information on how the cell-mediated immunity mechanisms are bypassed or abrogated during the acute stage of kala azar. Garnham and Humphrey (1969) have suggested that immune deviation and/or the presence of enhancing antibodies may be concerned in this.

Humoral antibodies may play a role in the immunity of the skin to challenge infections. For example, Manson-Bahr (1959, 1963) has observed that a second injection with *L. donovani* into an immune person may produce an Arthus-like reaction. In contrast to the observation of Adler and Zuckerman (1948) in *L. tropica* infection, he found that *L. donovani* cannot be recovered in the site of a challenge inoculum in such individuals.

In post-kala azar dermal leishmanoid, the tissue tropism of *L. donovani* has changed from one of the internal organs to one of the skin. It is an unexplained phenomena that immunity is now more pronounced to the visceral form of the disease than to the skin form. Thus, new visceral involvement is prevented, but the cutaneous lesions are long-lasting, granulomatous, and nonulcerating, and parasites though usually scanty are present in the lesion. The skin test is usually positive (Manson-Bahr, 1959; Sen Gupta and Mukherjee, 1962), and complement fixation antibodies may be present, with gamma globulin levels at 2.7% or more (Nath and Sen Gupta, 1967).

Another unsettled problem is the suceptibility of man to *L. infantum* infection. Mediterranean kala azar occurs in children up to the age of 2 in 90% of cases and is very seldom seen in adults (Adler, 1963). It was suggested by Taub (1956) that a nonspecific parasiticidal serum factor of gamma globulin type, which appears in children after the age of 5 or 6, might be responsible for the age prevalence.

VI. Immune Response of Man to *Leishmania pifanoi* Infections

Infection of man with *L. pifanoi* (*L. tropica* of Ethiopia) is followed by multiple disseminated, apparently blood-borne (Deane *et al.*, 1966), metastatic skin lesions. The latter are characterized by nonulcerating lepromatous leprosy-like nodules, called "diffuse cutaneous leishmaniasis" (Convit and Lapenta, 1948; Barrientos, 1948; Convit et al., 1959; Medina and Romero, 1959; Bryceson, 1969, 1970c).

There is no invasion of the viscera in this form (Convit et al., 1962), nor is there a previous history of kala azar (Bryceson, 1969). These clinical manifestations are important because very similar or identical skin lesions have been observed as post kala azar dermal leishmanoid. However, in 96% of cases of the latter, there was a history of L. pifanoi infection (Sen Gupta, 1962). Leishmania pifanoi produces a slow, progressive, spreading disease which shows very few self-healing tendencies. Mobilization of macrophages, heavily parasitized with mastigotes, is marked, while a few lymphocytes also may be mobilized into the nodular lesions of the skin. The intracellular amastigotes are relatively resistant to chemotherapeutic agents, such as antimony, and relapses occur frequently (Convit et al. 1959).

The most striking immunological feature of this infection is the almost complete absence of a delayed cutaneous hypersentivity to L. braziliensis (Medina and Romero, 1959; Convit et al., 1959) or to L. donovani (Bryceson, 1969). A few patients may show a very weak skin induration under 5 mm in diameter. There is not, however, a general failure of cell-mediated cutaneous hypersensitivity. It was shown by Medina and Romero (1959) and Bryceson (1969) that patients with diffuse cutaneous leishmaniasis are able to mount a skin reaction against other antigens, such as Myobacterium leprae ("Lepromina" de Mitsuda), M. tuberculosis (PPD and old tuberculin), Schistosoma mansoni ("Bilharzina"), and tissue antigens of sarcoidosis (Kveim-test).

Bryceson (1969) has shown that there is not immediate skin hypersensitivity or Arthus-type immune response in patients with diffuse cutaneous leishmaniasis, but also there is not any diminution in the production of immunoglobulin of the IgG and IgM types which might have explained a supposed depression of the humoral immune mechanisms. In few cases, a higher IgA level has been observed (Bryceson, 1970b).

Some authors have failed to find circulating antibodies, using complement fixation or immunofluorescent antibody tests (Convit and Kerdel-Vegas, 1965; Deane et al., 1966), but others using immunofluorescence did detect antibodies (Bittencourt et al., 1968; Bittencourt and Guimaraes, 1968; Ulrich et al., 1968). Very low hemagglutination antibody titers were found in sera of patients with diffuse cutaneous leishmaniasis by Bray using L. tropica (Israel) and L. tropica (Ethiopia) as antigens (Bryceson, 1970b). These showed no appreciable differences from the serum titers of patients with Oriental sore, and Bryceson (1970c) concluded that a specific depression of humoral immune mechanisms can be excluded as a causal mechanism in diffuse cutaneous leishmaniasis.

In a study of 10 patients with leishmaniasis, who had responded favorably to a chemotherapeutic treatment, Bryceson (1970a) found that 7 of them converted from an initial negative leishmanin skin test to a positive one. Similar observations have been made by Venezuelan investigators (Convit *et al.*, 1959; Medina and Romero, 1959).

Bryceson (1970a,b,c) has also observed that "immune conversion" of the skin test from negative to positive during prolonged chemotherapeutic treatment is accompanied by a change in the histological picture of the lesions. Prior to immune conversion the infiltrating cell is the macrophage, which contains many phagocytized amastigotes, but after conversion a lymphocyte and epithelioid cell infiltration predominate with tuberculoid formation, and this is accompanied by disappearance of parasites. Bryceson states that the immune conversion is a "prerequisite of cure." Attempts by Bryceson (1970b) to transfer delayed hypersentivity from leishmanin skin test positive donors to leishmanin skin test negative recipients resulted only in a transient hypersensitivity for up to 3 weeks. Failure to establish a long-lasting hypersensitivity by cell transfer may be a problem of cell numbers.

VII. Conclusion and Summary

The immune response to the different *Leishmania* spp. is predominantly of the cell-mediated type. Experimental studies of *L. enriettii* infection in the guinea pig by Bryceson *et al.* (1970) have greatly extended knowledge of the immune responses in leishmanial infections and it is probable that this experimental model will assist in the understanding of the immune response to *L. tropica, L. mexicana, L. peruviana, L. braziliensis* (single ulcer), and *L. guyanensis* (single ulcer) infections in man.

With *L. donovani* and *L. pifanoi* (*L. tropica* of Ethiopia) infections, cell-mediated immunity mechanisms in nontreated patients seem to be absent, prevented, suppressed, nullified, or insufficiently developed. The appearance of a marked delayed cutaneous hypersensitivity and the corresponding cellular changes in the lesions following effective chemotherapy strongly suggest that cell-mediated immunity mechanisms are decisive factors in the cure and resolution of these particular clinical forms of leishmanial infection.

In kala azar, "immune conversion" may be an indication of immunity to reinfection. However, insufficient data are available to confirm that a similar relationship exists between immune conversion and immunity as is seen in diffuse cutaneous leishmaniasis. It would seem that the level of immunity in L. *donovani* or L. *pifanoi* infections is not of a very high or stable character.

There is still no satisfactory explanation for the tendency for relapse in cases of diffuse cutaneous leishmaniasis that have been improved or apparently cured by therapeutic treatment. A similar comment is applicable to the late appearance of post-kala azar dermal leishmanoid and to the late appearance of mucosal lesions in L. *braziliensis* infection, in spite of the existence of a delayed cutaneous hypersensitivity response.

Several hypotheses have been advanced for the specific failure of cell-mediated immunity mechanisms in leishmaniasis (Garnham and Humphrey, 1969; Bryceson, 1970c). Experimental evidence is available for some of these, but more experimental work is required on the many, as yet unexplained, phenomena in leishmaniasis.

References

Adler, S. (1963). *In* "Immunity to Protozoa" (P. C. C. Garnham, A. E. Pierce, and I. Roitt, eds.), pp. 235–245. Blackwell, Oxford.

Adler, S. (1964). *Advan. Parsitol.* **2**, 35–96.

Adler, S., and Gunders, A. E. (1964). *Trans. Roy. Soc. Trop. Med. Hyg.* **58**, 274.

Adler, S., and Halff, L. (1955). *Ann. Trop. Med. Parasitol.* **49**, 37.

Adler, S., and Katzenellenbogen, I. (1952). *Ann. Trop. Med. Parsitol.* **46**, 25.

Adler, S., and Theodor, O. (1927). *Ann. Trop. Med. Parasitol.* **21**, 62.

Adler, S., and Zuckerman, A. (1948). *Ann. Trop. Med. Parasitol.* **42**, 178.

Ansari, N., and Mofidi, C. (1950). *Bull. Soc. Pathol. Exot.* **43**, 601.

Araujo, F. G., and Mayrink, W. (1968). *Rev. Inst. Med. Trop. Sao Paulo* **10**, 41.

Barrientos, L. P. (1948). *Mem. Inst. Oswaldo Cruz* **46**, 415.

Barros, O. M., and Rosenfeld, G. (1944). *Rev. Clin. Sao Paulo* **15**, 97.

Bell, E. J. (1966). *Proc. Int. Congr. Parasitol., 1st, 1964* Vol. 1, p. 355.

Bell, E. J. (1968). *In* "Medicina Tropical" (A. Anselmi, ed.), pp. 109–132. Fournier, Mexico City.

Berberian, D. A. (1939). *Trans. Roy. Soc. Trop. Med. Hyg.* **33**, 87.

Berberian, D. A. (1944). *Arch. Dermatol. Syph.* **49**, 433.

Biagi, F. F. (1953). Thesis, Universidad Nacional Autónoma de Mexico, Mexico, D.F.

Bittencourt, A. L., and Guimaraes, H. A. (1968). *Medna Cutanea* **2**, 395.

Bittencourt, A. L., Sodre, A., and Andrade, Z. A. (1968). *Rev. Inst. Med. Trop. Sao Paulo,* **10**, 247.

Bray, R. S. (1969). *Trans. Roy. Soc. Trop. Med. Hyg.* **63**, 378.

Bray, R. S., and Bryceson, A. D. M. (1968). *Lancet* **2**, 898.

Bray, R. S., and Lainson, R. (1965). *Trans. Roy. Soc. Trop. Med. Hyg.* **59**, 535.

Bray, R. S., and Lainson, R. (1966). *Trans. Roy. Soc. Trop. Med. Hyg.* **60**, 605.

Bray, R. S., and Lainson, R. (1967). *Trans. Roy. Soc. Trop. Med. Hyg.* **61**, 640.

Bray, R. S., and Rahim, G. A. F. (1969). *Trans. Roy. Soc. Trop. Med. Hyg.* **63**, 383.
Bray, R. S., Rahim, G. A. F., and Tajeldin, S. (1967). *Protozoology* **2**, 171.
Bryceson, A. D. M. (1969). *Trans. Roy. Soc. Trop. Med. Hyg.* **63**, 708.
Bryceson, A. D. M. (1970a). *Trans. Roy. Soc. Trop. Med. Hyg.* **64**, 369.
Bryceson, A. D. M. (1970b). *Trans. Roy. Soc. Trop. Med. Hyg.* **64**, 380.
Bryceson, A. D. M. (1970c). *Trans. Roy. Soc. Trop. Med. Hyg.* **64**, 387.
Bryceson, A. D. M., Bray, R. S., Wolstencroft, R. A., and Dumonde, D. C. (1970). *Clin. Exp. Immunol.* **7**, 301.
Cahill, K. M. (1970). *Trans. Roy. Soc. Trop. Med. Hyg.* **64**, 107.
Camargo, M. E., and Reronato, C. (1969). *Amer. J. Trop. Med. Hyg.* **18**, 500.
Chang, S. L., and Negherborn, W. O. (1947). *J. Infec. Dis.* **80**, 172.
Chaves, J., and Ferri, R. G. (1966). *Rev. Inst. Med. Trop. Sao Paulo* **8**, 225.
Chung, H. L., and Wang, C. W. I. (1939). *Chin. Med. J.* **56**, 519.
Convit, J. (1958). *Rev. Sanid. Assitenica Soc.* **23**, 28.
Convit, J., and Kerdel-Vegas, F. (1965). *Arch. Dermatol.* **91**, 439.
Convit, J., and Lapenta, P. (1948). *Rev. Policlin. Caracas* **18**, 153.
Convit, J., Alarcon, C. J., Medina, R., Reyes, O., and Kerdel-Vegas, F. (1959). *Arch. Venez. Med. Trop. Parasitol. Med.* **3**, 218.
Convit, J., Kerdel-Vegas, F., and Gordon, B. (1962). *Brit. J. Dermatol.* **74**, 132.
Coutinho, J. D. (1955). *Folia Clin. Biol.* **23**, 91.
da Cunha, A. M. (1942). *Mem. Inst. Oswaldo Cruz* **37**, 35.
da Cunha, A. M. and Chagas, E. (1937). *Hospital (Rio de Janeiro)* **11**, 148.
da Cunha, R. V., Xavier, F. S. A., and de Alencar, J. E. (1959). *Rev. Brasil. Malariol. Doencas Trop.* **11**, 45.
da Fonesca, F. (1932). *Amer. J. Trop. Med.* **12**, 453.
de Alencar, J. E. (1958). *Proc. Int. Congr. Trop. Med. Malar., 6th, 1958* Vol. 3, p. 718.
Deane, M. P., Chaves, J., Torrealba, J. W., and Torrealba, J. F. (1966). *Gac. Med. Caracas* **74**, 367.
Dostrowsky, A., and Cohen, H. A. (1957). *J. Invest. Dermatol.* **29**, 15.
Dostrowksy, A., and Sagher, F. (1957). *J. Invest. Dermatol.* **29**, 15.
Dostrowsky, A., Sagher, F., and Zuckerman, A. (1952). *AMA Arch. Dermatol. Syphilol.* **66**, 665.
du Buy, H. G., Mattern, C. F. T., and Riley, F. L. (1965). *Science* **147**, 754.
Echandi, C. A. (1953). *Rev. Biol. Trop.* **1**, 172.
Ercoli, N., and Coelho, M. V. (1967). *Amer. Trop. Med. Parasitol.* **61**, 488.
Ferri, R. G., and Chaves, J. (1968). *Arq. Gastroenterol.* **5**, 169.
Furtado, T. A. (1969). *In* "Imunopatologia Tropical" (C. da Silva Lacaz, E. Mendes, and V. A. Neto, eds.), pp. 57–70. Livraria Atheneu, Rio de Janeiro.
Furtado, T. A., and Pellegrino, J. (1956). *J. Invest. Dermatol.* **27**, 53.
Garnham, P. C. C., and Humphrey, J. H. (1969). *Curr. Top. Microbiol. Immunol.* **48**, 29.
Hall, R. P. (1953). *In* "Protozoology," pp. 574–582. Prentice-Hall, Englewood Cliffs, New Jersey.
Hoogstraal, H., and Heyneman, D. (1969). *Amer. J. Trop. Med. Hyg.* (Suppl.) **18**, 1091.
Irunberry, J., Benalleque, A., Grangaud, J. P., Mazouni, M., Knati, B., and Khedari, M. (1968). *Arch. Inst. Pasteur Alger.* **46**, 102.
Jadin, J., Le Ray, D., and Fameree, L. (1970). *Bull. Soc. Pathol. Exot.* **63**, 334.
Katzenellenbogen, I. (1942). *Ann. Trop. Med. Parasitol.* **36**, 28.

Katzenellenbogen, I. (1944). *Arch. Dermatol. Syph.* **50**, 239.
Kellina, O. I. (1966). *Med. Parazitol. Parazit. Bolez.* **35**, 455.
Kirk, R. (1949). *Parasitology* **39**, 263.
Kirk, R. (1950). *Parasitology* **40**, 58.
Kligler, I. J. (1925). *Trans. Roy. Soc. Trop. Med. Hyg.* **19**, 530.
Kretschmar, W. (1965). *Z. Tropenmed. Parasitol.* **16**, 277.
Lawrow, A. P., and Dubojski, P. A. (1937). *Arch. Schiffs- Trop.-Hyg.* **41**, 374.
Lemma, A. (1963). *J. Parasitol.* **49**, 62.
Lemma, A. (1964). Sc.D. Thesis, Johns Hopkins University.
Manson-Bahr, P. E. C. (1959). *Trans. Roy. Soc. Trop. Med. Hyg.* **53**, 123.
Manson-Bahr, P. E. C. (1961). *Trans. Roy. Soc. Trop. Med. Hyg.* **55**, 550.
Manson-Bahr, P. E. C. (1963). *In* "Immunity to Protozoa" (P. C. C. Garnham,
    A. E. Pierce, and I. Roitt, eds.), pp. 246–252. Blackwell, Oxford.
Marzinowski, E. J., and Schorenkova, A. (1924). *Trans. Roy. Soc. Trop. Med.
    Hyg.* **18**, 67.
Mata, A. D., Ruiz, C. B., Gasca, E. F., and Morales, M. C. (1968). *Salud Publ. Mex.*
    10, 159.
Mayer, M., and Malamos, B. (1936). *Zentralbl. Bakteriol. Abt. Parasitenk., Infek-
    tionskr. Hyg., Orig.* **136**, 412.
Mayrink, W. (1961). References by Adler (1964).
Medina, R., and Romero, J. (1959). *Arch. Venez. Med. Trop. Parasitol. Med.* **3**,
    298.
Medina, R., and Romero, J. (1962). *Arch. Venez. Med. Trop. Parasitol. Med.* **4**,
    349.
Montenegro, J. B. de F. (1926). *An. Fac. Med. Univ. São Paulo* **1**, 323.
Moshkovsky, S. D. (1942). *Med. Parazitol. Parazit. Bolez.* **11**, 66.
Moshkovsky, S. D. (1967). References by Adler (1964).
Napier, L. E. (1946). *In* "The Principles and Practice of Tropical Medicine,"
    p. 134. Macmillan, New York.
Nath, R. L., and Sen Gupta, P. C. (1967). *Bull. Calcutta Sch. Trop. Med.* **15**, 59.
Noguchi, H. (1924). *Proc. Int. Congr. Health Probl. Trop. Amer., 1924* pp. 455–478.
Noguchi, H. (1926). *J. Exp. Med.* **44**, 327.
Nussenzweig, V. (1957). *Hospital (Rio de Janeiro)* **51**, 217.
Paraense, L. W. (1953). *Trans. Roy. Soc. Trop. Med. Hyg.* **47**, 556.
Patton, W. S. (1922). *Indian J. Med. Res.* **9**, 496.
Pellegrino, J., and Furtado, T. A. (1960). *Dermatol. Ibero Latinoamer.* **2**, 37.
Pellegrino, J., Brener, Z., and Santos, M. M. (1958). *J. Parasitol.* **44**, 645.
Pellegrino, J., Furtado, T. A., and Memoria, J. P. (1960). *Dermatol. Ibero
    Latinoamer.* **1**, 38.
Pessôa, S. B. (1941). *Rev. Biol. Hyg., Sao Paulo* **11**, 1.
Pessôa, S. B. (1961). *Arq. Fac. Hyg. Sao Paulo* **26**, 41.
Pessôa, S. B., and Barreto, M. P. (1948). *In* "Leishmaniose Tegumentar Americana,"
    p. 527. Min. Educ. Saude, Serv. Doc., Rio de Janeiro.
Pessôa, S. B., and Cardoso, F. A. (1942). *Hospital (Rio de Janeiro)* **21**, 187.
Prata, A. (1957). Thesis, Faculdade Medicina, Bahia.
Preston, P. M., and Dumonde, D. C. (1971). *Trans. Roy. Soc. Trop. Med. Hyg.*
    65, 18.
Ranque, J., Depieds, R., Collomb, H., Mathurin, J., and Faur, E. A. (1958). *Bull.
    Soc. Pathol. Exot.* **51**, 504.
Rezai, H. R., Behforouz, N., and Gettner, S. (1970). *J. Parasitol.* **56**, 350.

Rodjakin, N. F., and Khanmamedov, N. M. (1967). *Vestn. Dermatol. Venerol.* 41, 49.

Rohrs, L. C. (1964). *Amer. J. Trop. Med. Hyg.* 13, 265.

Rosenfeld, G. (1945). *Rev. Paul. Med.* 26, 9.

Sagher, F., Verbi, S., and Zuckerman, A. (1955). *J. Invest. Dermatol.* 24, 417.

Schildkraut, C. L., Mandel, M., Levisohn, S., Smith-Sonneborn, J. E., and Marmur, J. (1962). *Nature (London)* 196, 795.

Schneider, C. R., and Hertig, M. (1966). *Exp. Parasitol.* 18, 25.

Sen, A., and Mukherjee, S. (1961). *Ann. Biochem. Exp. Med.* 21, 105.

Senekji, H. A. (1939). *Amer. J. Trop. Med.* 19, 601.

Senekji, H. A. (1941). *Amer. J. Hyg.*, Sect. C 34, 63.

Senekji, H. A., and Beattie, C. P. (1941). *Trans. Roy. Soc. Trop. Med. Hyg.* 34, 415.

Senekji, H. A., and Zebouni, N. (1941). *Amer. J. Hyg.*, Sect. C 34, 67.

Sen Gupta, P. C. (1943). *Indian Med. Gaz.* 78, 336.

Sen Gupta, P. C. (1945). *Indian Med. Gaz.* 80, 396.

Sen Gupta, P. C. (1962). *Sci. Rep. Ist. Super. Sanita* 2, 124.

Sen Gupta, P. C., and Adhikari, S. L. (1952). *J. Indian Med. Ass.* 22, 89.

Sen Gupta, P. C., and Mukherjee, A. M. (1962). *Ann. Biochem. Exp. Med.* 22, 63.

Serebryakov, V. A., Karakhodzhaeva, S. Kh., Ni, G. V., Belozerova, O. D., Safarov, G. I., and Yakubov, O. Ya. (1968). *Med. Parazitol. Parazit. Bolez.* 37, 651.

Shuikina, E. E., Sergiev, V. P., Triers, I. I., Scherbakov, V. A., and Diveev, S. K. (1968). *Med. Parazitol. Parazit. Bolez.* 37, 648.

Stauber, L. (1962). *Sci. Rep. Ist. Super. Sanita* 2, 68.

Stauber, L. (1963). *Ann. N.Y. Acad. Sci.* 113, 409.

Stauber, L. (1966). *Exp. Parasitol.* 18, 1.

Taub, J. (1956). *Bull. Res. Conc. Isr.* 6, 55.

Ulrich, M., de Pinardi, M. E., and Convit, J. (1968). *Dermatol. Venez.* (Caracas). 7, 483.

Wenyon, C. M. (1912). *J. London Sch. Trop. Med.* 1, 224.

World Health Organization. (1967). "WHO Inter-regional Traveling Seminar on Leishmaniasis, USSR, 22 May–10 June, 1967," Mimeo. Gen. Rep. WHO/LEISH/68.7. World Health Organ., Geneva.

14 IMMUNE RESPONSE TO INTRACELLULAR PARASITES

II. Coccidia

M. ELAINE ROSE

I. Introduction

The coccidia are intracellular protozoa and the immune responses of the host to these parasites are probably very similar to those developed against other intracellular organisms—the bacteria, viruses, and other protozoa. The coccidia, during the endogenous stages of the life cycle are parasitic in epithelial cells, and undergo a complicated life cycle which has been generally considered to be self-limiting in the absence of reinfection. They are remarkably host-specific and even site-specific within the normal host, but this behavior can be modified.

This review will be limited to a consideration of immune responses to the *Eimeria* since there is little experimental work on this aspect of host–parasite relationships in the other genera. Much of the recent work has been confined to those species that parasitize the domestic animals, especially poultry and cattle, as coccidiosis is an important cause of economic loss in these animals. Consequently, these studies have suffered from the limitations imposed by the lack of precise information on immune responses in general of these animals and, in the case of the larger domestic mammals, the problem of maintaining adequate numbers of them for significant results.

Earlier reviews include those by Augustin and Ridges (1963), Horton-Smith (1963), Horton-Smith and Long (1963), Horton-Smith *et al.* (1963a), and Rose (1963, 1968a, 1971a). Particular emphasis will be given in this review to the relative roles and interactions of humoral and cell-mediated immune responses. The possible implications of immune responses in parasite behavior, i.e., host and site specificity and life cycle, will also be discussed.

II. Life Cycle

The life cycle is complicated, involving, within the host, a period of asexual development (schizogony) followed by a sexual phase (gametogony). During schizogony succeeding generations of schizonts are formed which contain invasive forms, the merozoites. These eventually form gametocytes and the fertilized macrogametocyte (zygote) becomes encased within a resistant cyst wall (oocyst). The oocysts passed out of the host undergo exogenous development (sporogony) culminating in the formation of the infective forms, the sporozoites. With the release of sporozoites within the host after the ingestion of the sporulated oocyst, the cycle recommences.

The life cycle is usually considered to be self-limiting, consisting of a more or less fixed number of generations of schizonts. This aspect of development may be modified experimentally, but, in the normal hosts, it is usually standard, and thus the outcome of infection—duration of prepatent and patent periods and the numbers of oocysts produced per oocyst given—may be predicted. Oocyst production may be used as a measure of infection and, by comparison with a standard, of immunity.

The different stages of the life cycle probably differ in antigenic structure and also in immunogenicity (see Section III,B), thus presenting the host with different antigenic stimuli throughout infection. There is no published evidence of antigenic variation by the coccidia, although it is now established that other members of the Sporozoa, the *Plasmodia* (see Brown, 1969) and *Babesia* (Phillips, 1972), react in this way to the host's immune response. The normally self-limiting aspect of the coccidial life cycle would tend to suggest that this is not likely, but the possibility cannot be discounted.

III. Acquisition of Immunity

Immunity to the coccidia is fairly readily acquired, differs with species, even within the same host species, and depends greatly on the manner of immunization (age of host, size, and intervals between the immunizing inocula, etc.). Clinical immunity usually results from a single immunizing infection, but absolute immunity, i.e., no oocyst production resulting from an infective inoculum, may require one, two, three, four, or more immunizing infections depending on species. For example, in the fowl, *Eimeria maxima* is a very immunogenic species and a single inoculation with 50 oocysts usually results in complete immunity, whereas four or more inocula with fairly large numbers of oocysts of *Eimeria necatrix* will be necessary. Nevertheless, immunity results even after moderate infections with species of low immunogenicity, and is seen as a reduction in the numbers of oocysts produced per occyst fed (see Rose and Long, 1962).

A. Species Specificity of the Immune Response

Immunity is generally regarded as being species-specific and use has been made of this to establish new species (Levine, 1938, 1942; Moore and Brown, 1951) and to determine the prevalence of various species in the field (Reid, 1964). There have been reports of some cross-immunity between closely related species, especially where oocyst production has been used as a measure of infection (Lee, 1967; Rose, 1967a,b; Rommel, 1970a), but there is conflicting evidence (Hein, 1971).

B. Site Specificity of the Immune Response

Early investigators of immunity to the coccidia concluded that immunity was very localized and confined to sites that had already supported parasite development. The strong site specificity of many of the coccidia precluded experimental investigation for some time but, by taking advantage of the paired nature of the cecum in the fowl, Burns and Challey (1959) and Horton-Smith *et al.* (1961) showed that immunity was generalized and not confined to previously parasitized areas. This has also been shown to be true for *E. necatrix* infections of fowl (Rose, 1967a) and *Eimeria bovis* infections of cattle (Hammond *et al.*, 1964).

C. Stages That Stimulate Immunity

Experimentation on the roles of the various stages of the life cycle in the induction of protective immunity is difficult since, in many species, there is some overlap in the timing of the different stages, and, unless a very effective or selective coccidiostat is available, growth of some stages in the absence of others is not easily achieved. However, it is possible in some instances to induce infections in which gametocytes predominate by inoculating the appropriate merozoite generation. Even so, comparisons of the efficacy of the various stages may be invalid because of quantitative differences.

The asexual stages of *E. tenella* can immunize very effectively as has been shown by Horton-Smith (1947, 1949) and Kendall and McCullough (1952). The gametocytes of this species and especially of *E. necatrix* do not immunize well, even against the homologous stage (Horton-Smith *et al.*, 1963a; Rose, 1967a). Despite their large size, the first generation schizonts of *E. bovis* are not essential for the stimulation of immunity as shown by Hammond *et al.* (1964) who successfully immunized calves, by intracecal inoculation of first generation merozoites, against subsequent oral challenge with oocysts.

Although the low immunogenicity of gametocytes of *E. tenella* and *E. necatrix* has been confirmed, this is not necessarily true for all species.

Clearly the schizogony stages of *E. tenella* and probably of *E. necatrix* contain antigens that elicit a protective immune response. Their nature is not known but they may well be labile enzymes or metabolic products since immunization with nonviable schizogony stages, although inducing a complex antibody response, does not protect (Rose, 1961, 1963; Horton-Smith *et al.*, 1963a) and in recent experiments has even resulted in enhanced oocyst production, possibly due to the production of enhancing antibodies (see Kaliss, 1958) which may have blocked the host's own active response or modified the cell-mediated immune (CMI) response (see Mackaness and Blanden, 1967; Gray and Cheers, 1969).

D. STAGES AFFECTED BY THE IMMUNE RESPONSE

The particular stages of the life cycle that are inhibited by the immune host probably depend upon the immune status of that host. It is likely that progressively earlier stages will be affected as immunity develops and thus account for the progressive reduction in oocyst yield (due to elimination of some of the multiplicative stages) seen in successive immunizing infections with species such as *E. tenella*, *E. necatrix*, or *Eimeria acervulina*. In thoroughly immune hosts (i.e., no oocyst production resulting from an infective inoculum), the very earliest invasive stage, the sporozoite, is affected and much of the experimental evidence relates to observations made in these completely immune hosts.

Irrespective of the immune status of the host, excystation of sporozoites occurs, and probably attempted invasion; viable sporozoites of *E. tenella* capable of infecting susceptible hosts can be recovered from the lumina of immune ceca (Horton-Smith *et al.*, 1963b). There are indications of a partial "block" on invasion in highly immune hosts as sporozoites are very difficult to find (Morehouse, 1938; Augustin and Ridges, 1963; Hammond *et al.*, 1964; Leathem and Burns, 1967). The majority of sporozoites which invade the highly immune host do not develop any further, growth and division being inhibited (Tyzzer *et al.*, 1932; Horton-Smith *et al.*, 1963b). The ability of sporozoites to develop if recovered and transferred to fresh susceptible hosts may be retained for up to 24 hours after penetration of the immune host but not thereafter (Leathem and Burns, 1967). In chickens slightly less immune to *E. tenella*, development proceeds a little further and some abnormal schizonts may be found at 72 and 96 hours (Leathem and Burns, 1967). Merozoites inoculated into highly immune hosts are similarly affected (Roudabush, 1935; Horton-Smith *et al.*, 1963b; Rose, 1967a). Both asexual and sexual phases of *E. bovis* are affected in immunized calves (Hammond *et al.*, 1964). In partially immune hosts the challenge inocula probably act as boosting antigenic stimuli, the response to which affects the latter part of their own developmental cycles.

IV. Antibody Responses

Antibodies to coccidia were sought by some of the early workers (see earlier reviews) but were not convincingly demonstrated until the 1950's (McDermott and Stauber, 1954; Heist and Moore, 1959; Rose, 1959) since when they have been detected by a variety of tests including precipitation, agglutination, lysis, complement-fixation, immobilization, neutralization, and indirect fluorescent staining (Rose, 1961, 1963; Rose and Long, 1962; Pierce *et al.*, 1962, 1963; Long *et al.*, 1963; Augustin and Ridges, 1963; Andersen *et al.*, 1965; Burns and Challey, 1965; Herlich, 1965; Černá, 1966a,b, 1967, 1969, 1970).

A. HUMORAL ANTIBODIES

1. Antibody Production Detectable by Soluble and Particulate Antigens

Antibodies are usually detectable in serum from 1 to 2 weeks after oocyst inoculation, reach a peak value between 1 to 2 months, and then decline but persist from 2 to 3 months to up to 7 months. Antibody levels recorded in rabbits have in general been higher and persist longer than those found in chickens and cattle, probably reflecting the greater sensitivity of the tests used, e.g., complement fixation. In addition, *Eimeria stiedae* has been the species most studied in the rabbit, and its development site in the hepatic bile ducts may be a contributing factor. The true persistence of antibody in the complete absence of reinfection is probably not known since it is extremely difficult to prevent autoreinfection, but attempts to reinfect immune animals have usually little effect on serum antibody (Rose, 1961; Rose and Long, 1962). An anamnestic response may be obtained in partially immune animals (Burns and Challey, 1965) and also when a heterologous infection (to which the animal is susceptible) is given to an animal immune to a species which possesses common antigens (Rose and Long, 1962). This suggests that detectable antibodies are produced only as a result of infection and are not elicited by challenge attempts. It is known that in thoroughly immune animals development is blocked at a very early stage, and it is possible that in these instances local immunity is such as to limit greatly the antigenic stimulus. Complete immunity to infection may be found in the absence of detectable humoral antibody.

2. Neutralizing Antibodies

Serum antibodies which cause marked morphological changes in various stages of the parasites, e.g., lysis or agglutination, might be expected to affect their viability or infectivity and thus be considered neutralizing antibodies. Sporozoites or merozoites of *Eimeria meleagrimitis, E. tenella, E. bovis,* and *E. acervulina* which have been incubated in immune serum have been shown to cause very much reduced infections when transferred to susceptible hosts (Augustin and Ridges, 1963; Long *et al.,* 1963; Herlich, 1965). The severity of the changes in morphology and immobilization noted by other authors (Andersen *et al.,* 1965; Burns and Challey, 1965) indicate that infectivity would probably be affected, although this was not tested. Thus, coccidial infections induce the production of neutralizing circulating antibodies.

3. Opsonizing Antibodies

Information on opsonizing antibodies in coccidial infections is very scanty, as the role of macrophages in immunity has been but little investigated.

Huff and Clark (1970) injected sporozoites of *E. tenella* into the coelomic cavities of chickens and found that after 30 minutes incubation the macrophages from immune birds contained significantly fewer sporozoites than those of susceptible animals and that this effect was enhanced by the intraperitoneal injection of serum derived from immune birds. No differences were observed after incubation for 15 minutes (Huff, 1966). The authors concluded that intracellular destruction in immune macrophages was greater and was enhanced by immune serum. It is difficult to interpret these data since, clearly, phagocytosis was not increased by immune serum although the intracellular destructive effect was; thus, the possible role of an opsonin in immunity remains equivocal. The role of the macrophage will be further discussed in Section VI,A.

Natural antibodies, enhancing antibodies, and autoantibodies to coccidia are discussed in another review (Rose, 1972a).

B. LOCAL ANTIBODIES

Attempts to demonstrate local antibodies in coccidial infections have been largely unsuccessful. No antibodies to *E. meleagrimitis* and only traces of immunoglobulin were found in extracts of feces of turkeys taken from 0 to 12 days after oocyst inoculation (Augustin and Ridges, 1963). Tests for the infectivity *in vivo* of merozoite or sporozoite stages which had been incubated in extracts of intestinal tissue of immune hosts either gave equivocal (Horton-Smith *et al.*, 1963a) or negative results (Herlich, 1965), and the infectivity of stages harvested from the intestinal lumina of immune fowls has been unaffected (Horton-Smith *et al.*, 1963a). Sporozoites recovered from cells of immune hosts up to 24 hours but not later after oocyst inoculation remain infective. However, preparations of chicken cecal contents have been shown to contain immunoglobulins and, when derived from immunized hosts to moderate infections with *E. tenella* or *E. maxima* when transferred to young susceptible chicks; precipitating antibodies were not demonstrable. Two immunoglobulins have been constantly found in these preparations, IgG and another, which resembles mammalian IgA (Orlans and Rose, 1972). The exact nature of the apparent analog of mammalian IgA requires confirmation.

V. Protective Effects of Antibodies

Although antibodies may be demonstrable and may even be shown to have deleterious effects on parasites *in vitro,* their role in immunity can only be established with certainty if they can be shown to moderate infections, preferably *in vivo.* This is especially true of an infection caused by an intracellular organism. Successful passive transfer of immunity with cell-free material is the criterion for the effectiveness of free antibody.

A. PASSIVE IMMUNIZATION WITH HUMORAL ANTIBODIES

Passive immunization with serum has only recently been demonstrated after numerous reports of negative results (see earlier reviews; also Pierce *et al.*, 1963; Fitzgerald, 1964). Long and Rose (1965) were able to protect birds from infections induced by the intravenous inoculation of sporozoites of *E. tenella* provided that the intervals between serum and parasite inoculations were short. If these were prolonged, no protection ensued. Presumably, serum was effective only when in fairly direct contact with the parasite; if antibody injections were deferred until the parasite had entered the cells, they were ineffective.

Protection against infection with *E. maxima* by the administration of serum from immunized birds is possible, but the time of bleeding the donors in relation to oocyst inoculation is fairly critical. Serum taken

2–3 weeks after oocyst inoculation is the most effective; thereafter, activity declines although the serum donors remain immune. Some but less protection is given by serum taken after two, three, or more infections, at which time the donors are highly immune. Protection is not invariably given by transferred serum and has never been complete (Rose, 1971b). In these experiments, serum was usually injected daily, the effect was dose dependent, and there was some indication that it was greater when serum was injected during the earlier part of the life cycle. Protection was species-specific; antisera obtained from birds infected with *E. maxima* did not modify infections with *E. acervulina* or *Eimeria praecox*.

Passive immunization against infection with *E. tenella* has also been shown using the chick embryo as test host (Rose and Long, 1971). Globulin fractions of serum from the infected donors were injected into the embryo and the effects on subsequent infection of the chorioallantoic membrane (CAM) induced by sporozoite inoculation measured. Significant protection was obtained only with sera taken after the third inoculation of the donors with oocysts, i.e., the time at which the donors were beginning to become immune. Failure to obtain protection with the sera of completely immune donors has not yet been reexamined.

Thus, humoral antibodies are protective; the effect is at its maximum when the host is becoming completely immune, but thereafter declines although the donors are immune.

B. LOCAL ANTIBODIES

The result of recent work on immunoglobulin preparations from the cecal contents of infected chickens encouraged further attempts to demonstrate local protective antibodies. Preliminary work, on *E. maxima* infections in chicks and *E. tenella* infections in chicks and in chick embryos, has shown that these immunoglobulin preparations may be protective, indicating a role for locally produced antibodies in immunity to these infections of the intestinal mucosa. No precipitating antibodies were found in the extracts and the effects of viability and infectivity of invasive stages after incubation in the extracts have yet to be investigated, but the protective effect of antisera to *Trypanosoma gambiense* is unrelated to its agglutinating activity (Seed and Gam, 1966).

C. MATERNALLY TRANSMITTED ANTIBODIES

From published work there is little evidence for the maternal transmission of immunity to the coccidia. Long and Rose (1962) found that the chicks of hens completely immune to *E. tenella* which were receiving fortnightly doses of infective oocysts did not differ in susceptibility to challenge infection from those of control hens. Heckman *et al.* (1967) similarly found the progeny of rats immune to *Eimeria nieschulzi* to be susceptible to challenge inoculation. However, the young were challenged at approximately 6–7 weeks of age, when any maternally transmitted immunity should have waned.

The results with passive transfer of immunity with serum in *E. maxima* and *E. tenella* infections in the fowl, indicating the temporal relationship between time of inoculation of donors (hence its immune status) and protection, led to a reexamination of maternally transmitted immunity in chickens. Embryos or batches of chicks hatched from eggs laid by hens at different stages during the acquisition of immunity were compared with those from control hens. There was some moderation of infection in the chicks, judged by oocyst production, and in the embryos, judged by the numbers of coccidial foci present on the CAM (Rose and Long, 1971). In addition, yolk immunoglobulin preparations from eggs laid by hens infected with *E. maxima* partially protected chicks (Rose, 1972b). The times at which maternally transmitted protection was demonstrated correlated well with the protective activity of serum.

D. Suppression of the Antibody Response

Many of the methods used in immunosuppression have far-reaching effects and tend to affect both Ig and CMI systems. In the fowl, however, the immune response is dissociated, cells derived from the bursa of Fabricius being involved in immunoglobulin responses and those of the thymus in CMI responses (Warner *et al.*, 1962; Warner, 1967). Thus, immunity studies in bursectomized birds, theoretically in the absence of Ig responses, should determine the relative importance of the two systems. It is, however, extremely difficult completely to eliminate the bursa-dependent system, especially its response to multiple antigenic stimuli or to particulate antigens (Janković and Isaković, 1966; Rose and Orlans, 1968; Stiffel *et al.*, 1968).

1. Hormonal and Surgical Bursectomy

Hormonal bursectomy (HBX) *in ovo* coupled with neonatal irradiation is the most effective method (Warner *et al.*, 1969), but most workers have experienced difficulty in producing adequate numbers of completely bursectomized birds. The results obtained must therefore be interpreted with this in mind. Where no complementary tests of the efficacy of bursectomy in suppressing Ig responses have been done, evaluation of the results is very difficult.

The results of the effect of bursectomy on coccidial infections and the development of immunity are not conclusive but, in summary, infections were somewhat enhanced. The significant increase in mortality due to *E. tenella* observed by Challey (1962) in birds surgically bursectomised (SBX) at 2 weeks was not confirmed by Rouse and Burns (1971), and these authors also found no differences in body weights, hematocrit values, or mortality in neonatally SBX chicks. Long and Pierce (1963) and Pierce and Long (1965), using the more effective HBX technique, reported that HBX and control birds equally resisted the final challenge with oocysts but, histologically, parasites were present in a greater proportion of HBX birds than in controls, and there was slightly increased oocyst production during immunization. Serum lysins to *E. tenella* were practically absent, serum Ig values were very low, and secondary lymphoid foci and pyroninophilic cells were much reduced in the HBX birds. In view of these findings, the authors concluded that the enhancement of infection in the HBX birds might have been due to additional effects on thymus development. Rose and Long (1970) also found some increase in oocyst production during primary infections with *E. burnetti* and *E. maxima* in neonatally SBX birds which had been sublethally X-irradiated.

2. *Use of Anti-bursa Serum*

Euzèby *et al.* (1969) found that challenge inoculations with *E. tenella* oocysts given to immunized fowls treated with rabbit anti-bursa serum produced similar results to those obtained in susceptible untreated controls; control untreated immunized birds were resistant. Treatment with anti-thymus serum yielded intermediate results (discussed in Section VI,C). Despite this, they concluded that immunity was cell-mediated. No tests for antibody formation were made. Janković *et al.* (1970) found that treatment with rabbit anti-bursa serum injected together with guinea pig complement [since rabbit antibody is not cytolytic in the presence of fowl complement, see Rose and Orlans (1962)] depressed precipitating antibody formation but had no effect on experimental allergic encephalitis, caused by a CMI response. It is therefore likely that the effects noted by Euzèby *et al.* were due to suppression of the bursa-dependent Ig response.

VI. Cell-Mediated Responses

There are few publications relating to CMI responses to coccidial infections, probably because of the greater difficulty involved in this type of experimentation. This is a field of work that should be more extensively investigated in the coccidial and other protozoal infections, since, with the exception of *Leishmania* infections (Bryceson *et al.*, 1970), it has not been carefully studied (see Soulsby, 1970). In many instances, conclusions that CMI mechanisms are responsible for immunity have been based on circumstantial evidence or the absence of evidence for the participation of Ig factors.

A. PHAGOCYTOSIS

The macrophage is thought to be a potential, but not obligate host cell for a limited part of the life cycle of some species of coccidia; at least a proportion of the sporozoites of *E. necatrix* and *E. tenella* is transported through the lamina propria in cells described as macrophages (Van Doorninck and Becker, 1957; Challey and Burns, 1959; Pattillo, 1959). The macrophage plays an important part in cellular immunity to microorganisms (see Mackaness and Blanden, 1967), and this transport phase might provide an opportunity early in the life cycle for the expression of immunity (Challey and Burns, 1959), but there has been little experimentation until recently. Scholtyseck *et al.* (1969) found damaged merozoites in cells considered to be macrophages.

Cellular immunity, in one form, is induced by a specific stimulus but, once activated, the microbicidal activity of the macrophage becomes nonspecific. There are recent reports of cross-immunity between intracellular bacteria and protozoa (Ruskin and Remington, 1968; Gentry and Remington, 1971; Barrett *et al.*, 1971) and between unrelated protozoa (Cox, 1968), but there are also conflicting opinions (Frenkel, 1967). Immunity to the coccidia is fairly species-specific and it is therefore unlikely that this type of immunity is active, but it cannot be ruled out.

Patton (1970) investigated the phagocytosis of sporocysts of *E. tenella* by macrophages from heparinized blood. He found this to be increased in infected birds with activity rising from 10 days after infection to a peak value at 12–19 days and declining to normal at 27 days. Huff (1966) and Huff and Clark (1970) did similar work on sporozoites which they injected into the coelomic cavities of birds stimulated to produce exudates. Initial infection rates of macrophages in immunized and susceptible birds were similar, but the survival of sporozoites in immune macrophages was shortened since they contained fewer sporozoites after 30 minutes incubation. Thus, in Patton's work phagocytosis was increased (sporocysts are nonmotile, therefore their presence in macrophages must be due to phagocytosis), whereas in Huff and Clark's the numbers of organisms in cells were similar but they were destroyed more readily. Huff and Clark tested the effects of serum (discussed in Section IV,A,3) and found some evidence for the participation of antibodies. Patton did not specifically test for this, but, as the macrophages in his experiments were derived from blood, they may have been sensitized with cytophilic antibody.

B. Adoptive Transfer of Immunity

The transfer of immunity with cells per se is not unequivocal evidence for its cell-mediated nature as the transferred cells may produce effective antibodies in the recipient. These antibodies may not be detected because (a) an inappropriate test antigen or test systems may be used, (b) production may be local due to the "homing" of the transferred cells, or (c) they may be avidly cytophilic. These points have been stressed by Soulsby (1970) and it is pertinent to do so since assumptions of the CM nature of cell-transferable immunity are commonly made. Failure at the same time to transfer immunity with cell-free media is not necessarily corroborative evidence; this is notoriously difficult because of the quantitative, temporal, and qualitative factors involved.

With these reservations in mind, transfer of immunity to the coccidia with cells will now be discussed.

There is little published work on cell-transfer experiments in coccidial infections, possibly due to the difficulties in obtaining sufficiently inbred hosts of the species commonly used for coccidiosis experimentation. Heydorn (1970) found that oocyst production of *E. nieschulzi* in rats which had received mesenteric lymph node cells from immunized donors was significantly less than in recipients of cells from control rats; cells from Peyer's patches of the same donors were without effect. Protection of chick embryos against infections with *E. tenella* by cecal tonsil cells has also been shown (Rose and Long, 1971). The use of the chick embryo as host obviated difficulties of cell acceptance and eliminated (or greatly reduced) any effects attributable to the host's own active response. Cells from susceptible hosts provided a smaller degree of protection, probably due to a primary response. The mode of action of the cell suspensions is not known, but some of the schizonts surrounded by the proliferating cells appeared to be degenerate. In some instances, cells and serum from the same donors were tested, and found to be protective. Cecal tonsil cells are known to be capable of synthesizing antibody (Janković and Mitrović, 1967; Orlans and Rose, 1970). Antibody production by the transferred cells cannot be eliminated as the cause of protection.

C. Thymectomy

In fowls, the thymus is generally acknowledged to govern CMI responses (Warner *et al.*, 1962; Warner, 1967); thymectomy in this species should specifically depress these responses while leaving the bursa-dependent, antibody response system unimpaired. Theoretically, this host should be ideal for experimentation on the relative importance of CMI and Ig systems in immunity, but complete thymectomy is even more difficult to achieve than complete bursectomy and results obtained so far have been fairly inconclusive.

Pierce and Long (1965) noted an increase in oocyst production of *E. tenella* during immunization of neonatally thymectomized birds, but resistance to the challenge infection was unaffected. Rose and Long (1970) working with the more immunogenic *E. maxima* found some oocyst production resulting from a second (challenge) infection in a group of thirteen neonatally thymectomized and irradiated birds; two members of this group were subsequently found not to have become sensitized to avian PPD, indicating that the CMI responses had been suppressed, but these were fully resistant to a third oocyst inoculation. In the same publication, oocyst production during immunizing infections with *E. maxima* was hardly affected by combined thymectomy and irradiation or by thymectomy with irradiation and cortisone acetate treatment although body weights and lymphocyte counts were severely depressed and tuberculin sensitivity decreased. Rouse and Burns (1971) also found no significant differences in mortality, body weight, or hematocrit values in neonatally thymectomized birds during *E. tenella* infections when moderate numbers of oocysts were given at 5 weeks or after the challenge of immunized birds at 6 weeks, but they did note "subtle differences" in thymectomized birds given large numbers of oocysts as a primary infection at 6 weeks of age.

Thus, results have been equivocal and, when differences attributable to a depression of immunity have been noted, they have been very slight.

D. Treatment with Anti-lymphocyte Serum

It has been claimed that treatment with anti-lymphocyte serum (ALS) preferentially suppresses CMI responses (Levey and Medawar, 1967), but it also affects immunological memory and the production of circulating antibody, presumably by affecting precursors of antibody-forming cells since it does not affect plasma cells already producing antibody (see review by Sell, 1969). Its effects on immunity to coccidiosis will nevertheless be considered in this section.

ALS has not been widely used in experimentation on coccidiosis immunity, possibly because the production of an effective reagent presents difficulties which vary with the host species, but there are reports of its use in pigs and fowls. Rommel (1970b) found that it did not affect already established immunity to *Eimeria scabra* in pigs but suppressed the development of immunity and reduced the "crowding effect" (considered to be immunological). Somewhat conflicting results were obtained in fowls by Euzèby *et al.* (1969) who, utilizing the concept of the dissociation of immune responses, prepared an anti-thymus serum in rabbits and injected it shortly before challenge of fowls immunized with *E. tenella*. They found infection in anti-thymus-treated birds to be greater than in controls, but not as great as in an anti-bursa-treated group. In this laboratory somewhat enhanced oocyst production of *E. maxima* has been found in fowls treated with duck ALS, pig ALS plus normal pig serum, or guinea pig complement. In one instance, this was accompanied by prolonged skin graft retention, but the increase in oocyst production has never been more than approximately doubled.

The results of experiments with ALS have not therefore yielded unequivocal evidence of the nature of immunity.

VII. Suppression of the Immune Response

Suppression of immunity by specific procedures known to affect one or the other of the immune responses should provide an indication of their respective roles in immunity. The effects of the immunosuppressive methods which have been shown to be reasonably selective have been discussed in the relevant Sections (V,D and VI,C and D); those which have more general effects will be discussed here.

A. SPLENECTOMY

The spleen is known to be active in antibody production and in phagocytosis, and its removal has a profound effect in exacerbating certain protozoal infections, in particular the blood-borne ones. Latent infections may be activated (Raynaud, 1962), hosts made susceptible to species to which they are not normally so (Garnham and Bray, 1959), and the severity of infections with many spp. of *Plasmodium* increased (see reviews by Taliaferro, 1956; Brown, 1969; Longenecker *et al.*, 1966). However, the spleen plays a relatively minor part in immunity to the coccidia as infection and immunity have not been influenced by its removal (Becker *et al.*, 1935; Rose, 1968b; Rommel, 1969; Haberkorn, 1970; working with species of coccidia in the rat, fowl, pig, and mouse, respectively). There is one report of the greater susceptibility of neonatally splenectomized cockerels to a primary infection with *E. tenella* given at 5–6 weeks of age, but these animals became immune to reinfection, and already existing immunity was unaffected by splenectomy (Rouse, 1967).

The spleen is known to respond very actively to single intravenous injections of antigens (Draper and Süssdorf, 1957); repeated antigenic stimuli tend to cause the formation of antibody at nonsplenic sites, and the spleen may be more of a hindrance than a help to antibody formation in response to prolonged immunization (see Taliaferro, 1956). Infection with coccidia is more likely to represent prolonged immunization, of which circulating antigen is probably a minor component, hence the minor role of the spleen. Its phagocytic role is again probably of paramount importance only in the clearance of blood-borne particles.

B. Influence of Intercurrent Infections

Intercurrent infections often have a depressing effect on immunity which may be due to a variety of causes, most of which are nonspecific. Increased and prolonged incidence of coccidiosis in the field especially in fowls, has often been associated with other infections, but there has been little experimental work in this connection except in the case of Marek's disease. This is a lymphoproliferative condition caused by a herpes-type virus and chickens infected with it are more susceptible to primary and subsequent coccidial infections (Biggs *et al.*, 1968). Infection with Marek's disease causes a slight depression in humoral antibody response to a variety of antigens (Purchase *et al.*, 1968). Its effect on CMI responses is difficult to evaluate since Purchase *et al.* obtained conflicting results in that the graft versus host response was enhanced whereas skin graft rejection time was delayed.

Thus intercurrent infections with Marek's disease virus provides little information on the mechanisms in coccidial immunity.

C. Effect of Treatment with Corticosteroids

1. Effect on Immunity

Of all the attempts to date experimentally to modify immunity to the coccidia, treatment with corticosteroids has been the most effective. Primary infections with *Eimeria mivati* in fowls are greatly enhanced and already existing immunity abolished by treatment with betamethasone, a powerful derivative of cortisone (Rose, 1970); treatment with cortisone acetate, used in earlier work, had little effect on infections with *E. brunetti* even when combined with thymectomy and irradiation (Rose and Long, 1970). This may be due to insufficient dosage, a critical factor in immunosuppression, since small doses may even enhance humoral antibody responses; conflicting reports on the effects of corticosterone treatment are common (Gabrielsen and Good, 1967; Herbert and Becker, 1961; Sherman and Ruble, 1967). Rommel [1969; briefly reported by Rommel (1970b)] has also shown that existing immunity to *E. scabra* in pigs can be suppressed by paramethasone and dexamethasone treatment. Treatment with cortisone and its derivatives has diverse effects and the possible ways by which it might influence resistance to infection have been reviewed by Kass and Finland (1953) and Gabrielsen and Good (1967). The inhibition of inflammation and of antibody production and alterations in the function of the reticuloendothelial system (see Vernon-Roberts, 1969) are all possible candidates for the causation of lowered immunity to the coccidia. The invasion of gut epithelium by sporozoites is accompanied by an increase in local capillary permeability leading to leakage of plasma proteins which is particularly marked in the intestines of immunized animals, but can be suppressed by betamethasone treatment (Rose and Long, 1969). Thus corticosteroid treatment could affect immunity by depressing antibody formation (known to be at least partly concerned in the immune response) and by limiting the access of antibody to the parasite by inhibition of the inflammatory response. In addition to this, CMI responses may also be affected, e.g., by interference with macrophage function. There is a severe depletion of lymphoid tissue, both diffuse and in the form of foci, in the intestines of corticosteroid-treated chickens infected with *E. mivaii*, but, as the whole spectrum of lymphoid elements is affected, no conclusions can be drawn as to the relative roles of CMI or antibody responses. Graft rejection is generally considered to be a CMI response, and this is affected by corticosteroid treatment in chickens (Aspinall and Meyer, 1964).

2. Disruption of Host and Site Specificity and Effect on the Life Cycle

Although no conclusions as to the respective actions of humoral and CMI responses in immunity to the coccidia can be drawn from the results of corticosteroid treatment, it has provided some interesting information leading to speculation as to the immune basis for host and site specificity, and life cycle determination.

McLoughlin (1969) overcame the species specificity of *E. meleagrimitis* for turkeys by treating chickens with dexamethasone but *E. tenella* did not complete its life cycle in treated turkeys; histological examinations that might have revealed partial development were not made, and Long (1971) has recorded the growth of schizonts of *E. tenella* in the CAMs of dexamethasone-treated goose embryos.

Site specificity can also be altered by corticosteroid treatment; the distribution of *E. mivati* in the intestines of treated chickens is very much wider than in normal birds (Long and Rose, 1970), but other tissues were not examined. An even more remarkable deviation from normal behavior is seen in the growth of *E. tenella* in the livers of treated chickens and chick embryos (Long, 1970, 1971).

The life cycle of *E. mivati* in treated chickens was considerably different from that normally found; schizogony continued for a very much longer period than usual leading to prolonged oocyst output. The numerous extra generations of schizonts formed were not due to autoreinfection of immunosuppressed hosts (Long and Rose, 1970). This finding suggests that the life cycles of the coccidia may be influenced by the immune responses of the host with asexual development continuing for longer periods in the absence or suppression of immunity. Prolonged oocyst discharge has also been noted in calves treated with dexamethasone (Niilo, 1970).

VIII. Discussion

The aim of this review has been to present the results of experimentation on immunity to the coccidia in so far as they indicate the nature of the immune responses. Ogilvie (1970) has pointed out that the limitations of experimental design in immunity to parasites has tended to produce two opposing groups of workers; those who claim antibodies and those who claim CMI responses to be the mediators of immunity respectively. Ogilvie (1970) and Soulsby (1970) have stressed that, in the complex, constantly changing relationship which exists between host and parasite, a single basis for immunity is unlikely, and that both types of responses are probably active with the balance changing throughout the infection. The data given in this review fully support this concept.

A. ROLE OF Ig SYSTEM

1. Humoral Antibodies

Humoral antibodies are protective as shown by the results of experiments involving the passive transfer of sera, as are yolk antibodies, in the case of coccidiosis of the fowl, shown by maternal transfer and inoculation of yolk Ig preparations. There are also indications that Ig preparations of intestinal contents of immunized chickens, containing what appears to be an analog of mammalian IgA, are protective when passively transferred. In the case of serum and yolk transfer there is a temporal relationship between protection and the immune state of the donors; protection is greatest when immunity is becoming complete. In the hyperimmune state, protection by humoral or yolk antibody may have waned or may even be absent. At this time, clearly, these antibodies are not responsible for the immunity of the donors, and its mediation must lie elsewhere, perhaps in local Ig or in CMI responses. Even when humoral and yolk antibodies can be shown to be protective, they may be only one of several factors operating.

2. Locally Produced Antibodies

Local Ig responses have not been very fully investigated as yet; it would be interesting to determine whether they are active and protective in the hyperimmune state when humoral antibodies are less so. It could be postulated that, in this state, local immunity is so strong as to inhibit parasite development at a very early stage, thus preventing the release of enough antigen to provoke a humoral response.

3. Possible Mode of Action of Antibodies

The mode of action of protective antibodies is not known; that of muco- or coproantibody may perhaps be more readily visualized than that of humoral antibody. A high concentration of mucoantibodies might prevent cell penetration by invasive stages; immobilization, agglutination, or lysis of sporozoites, sometimes seen after treatment with humoral antibodies, might take place in the lumen of the gut or on the mucous surface, but this has yet to be demonstrated. Alternatively, anti-enzyme or anti-metabolite antibodies might affect penetration and/or subsequent development.

Serum-derived antibody may also contact the parasite in its extracellular phases since a marked extravasation of plasma proteins into the intestinal submucosa, mucosa, and lumen accompanies cell invasion.

An effect on development within the cell is not so readily explicable. Antibodies which may have coated the parasites in their extracellular phases could accompany them into the cells and exert their action there. These antibodies would be more likely to be directed against enzyme systems than cell membranes. However, a function of this kind is contra-indicated by the work of Leathem and Burns (1967) who found that parasites that were recovered from immunized hosts within 24 hours of invasion were able to complete their development on transfer to susceptible animals. Any antibody bound to the parasite should have continued to exert its effect, irrespective of the immune status of the harboring host. Whether antibodies can penetrate in an effective form into living cells is still controversial (see Humphrey and White, 1965), but parasitization may well change cell permeability. It is, however, believed that humoral antibodies to *Plasmodium knowlesi* have little effect upon the growth of intracellular stages but prevent reinvasion (Cohen and Butcher, 1970).

Another possible way in which Ig responses may protect is in conjunction with the CMI system in promoting phagocytosis. Work on this aspect of immunity requires confirmation and extension.

B. ROLE OF CMI RESPONSES

It is obvious from the foregoing that Ig responses are only partly the effectors of immunity and the remainder must be due to CMI responses. It is, however, much more difficult to fulfill completely the criteria required for the unequivocal demonstration of the effectiveness of CMI responses. Soulsby (1970) has pointed out that the conclusion, commonly made, that immunity transferable with lymphoid cells but not with serum must be due to CMI responses, can be false; such experiments should be carefully controlled to ensure that the transferred cells are not effective by virtue of their antibody-forming capacity. Immunity to coccidiosis is transferable by lymphoid cells (Heydorn, 1970; Rose and Long, 1971) and, as a consequence, has been claimed to be CMI in nature (Heydorn, 1970), but this is not necessarily so. This work should also be extended; it would, for instance, be interesting to know whether the hyperimmune state, not readily transferable by Ig, can be transferred with lymphoid cells.

Procedures considered selectively to depress either Ig or CMI responses may not always have such straightforward effects, and there may be variations in the responses to different antigens and between species (see Soulsby, 1970). Such procedures have been widely used in experimentation on immunity to the coccidia, partly because the fowl, a much-studied host, has separated bursa-dependent Ig and thymus-dependent CMI systems.

The results are difficult to evaluate because completely effective thymectomy and bursectomy are rare and, often, independent checks of the functioning of the two systems, e.g., development of delayed hypersensitivity to tuberculin or antibody production to unrelated antigens were not made. However, the data obtained indicate that both systems are involved.

Other immunosuppressive procedures, while less selective than bursectomy or thymectomy, have provided some information on the role of CMI responses. Treatment with ALS predominantly affects CMI, and there are a few reports of partial suppression of immunity to the coccidia by this means.

Many aspects of CMI responses have not been investigated in immunity to the coccidia and attention should be paid to these. The results of such work might provide more corroborative evidence of the role of CMI responses and perhaps some indication of their mode of action. Studies of macrophage activity and lymphocyte sensitization and the interactions of these cells are potentially rewarding topics for research.

Some preliminary work on delayed hypersensitivity responses has been carried out, and an observation suggesting the participation of transfer factor (Lawrence, 1969) has already been made by Long, in this laboratory. These studies require confirmation and extension.

C. Possible Effect of Immune Responses on Parasite Behavior

The most effective suppression obtained has been with corticosteroid treatment, perhaps the least defined and selective of any method since metabolic processes, inflammatory reactions, antibody synthesis, and CMI responses are affected. Thus, its use has not provided irrefutable evidence of the predominance of one immune system over the other but it has contributed some interesting information on aspects of the host–parasite relationships such as host and site specificity and host influence on the life cycle.

References

Andersen, F. L., Lowder, L. J., Hammond, D. M., and Carter, P. B. (1965). *Exp. Parasitol.* 16, 23.

Aspinall, R. L., and Meyer, R. K. (1964). In "The Thymus in Immunobiology" (R. A. Good and A. E. Gabrielsen, eds.), pp. 376–392. Harper, New York.

Augustin, R., and Ridges, A. P. (1963). In "Immunity to Protozoa" (P. C. C. Garnham, A. E. Pierce, and I. Roitt, eds.), pp. 296–335. Blackwell, Oxford.

Barrett, J. T., Rigney, M. M., and Breitenbach, R. P. (1971). *Avian Dis.* 15, 7.

Becker, E. R., Hall, P. R., and Madden, R. (1935). *Amer. J. Hyg.* 21, 389.

Biggs, P. M., Long, P. L., Kenzy, S. G., and Rootes, D. G. (1968). *Vet. Rec.* 83, 284.

Brown, I. N. (1969). *Advan. Immunol.* 11, 267.

Bryceson, A. D. M., Bray, R. S., Wolstencroft, R. A., and Dumonde, D. C. (1970). *Clin. Exp. Immunol.* 7, 301.

Burns, W. C., and Challey, J. R. (1959). *Exp. Parasitol.* 8, 515.

Burns, W. C., and Challey, J. R. (1965). *J. Parasitol.* **51**, 660.
Černá, Z. (1966a). *Zentralbl. Bakteriol., Parasitenk., Infektionskr. Hyg., Abt. 1: Orig.* **199**, 264.
Černá, Z. (1966b). *Folia Parasitol. (Prague)* **13**, 332.
Černá, Z. (1967). *Folia Parasitol. (Prague)* **14**, 13.
Černá, Z. (1969). *Acta Vet. (Brno)* **38**, 37.
Černá, Z. (1970). *Folia Parasitol. (Prague)* **17**, 135.
Challey, J. R. (1962). *J. Parasitol.* **48**, 352.
Challey, J. R., and Burns, W. C. (1959). *J. Protozool.* **6**, 238.
Cohen, S., and Butcher, G. A. (1970). *Immunology* **19**, 369.
Cox, F. E. G. (1968). *Nature (London)* **219**, 646.
Draper, L. R., and Süssdorf, D. H. (1957). *J. Infec. Dis.* **100**, 147.
Euzèby, J., Garcin, C., and Grosjean, N. (1969). *C. R. Acad. Sci.* **268**, 1616.
Fitzgerald, P. R. (1964). *J. Protozool.* **11**, 46.
Frenkel, J. K. (1967). *J. Immunol.* **98**, 1309.
Gabrielsen, A. E., and Good, R. A. (1967). *Advan. Immunol.* **6**, 91.
Garnham, P. C. C., and Bray, R. S. (1959). *J. Protozool.* **6**, 352.
Gentry, L. O., and Remington, J. S. (1971). *J. Infec. Dis.* **123**, 22.
Gray, D. F., and Cheers, C. (1969). *Immunology* **17**, 889.
Haberkorn, A. (1970). *Z. Parasitenk.* **34**, 49.
Hammond, D. M., Andersen, F. L., and Miner, M. L. (1964). *J. Parasitol.* **50**, 209.
Heckmann, R., Gansen, B., and Hom, H. (1967). *J. Protozool.* **14**, Suppl. 35.
Hein, H. (1971). *Exp. Parasitol.* **29**, 367.
Heist, C. E., and Moore, T. D. (1959). *J. Protozool.* **6**, Suppl. 7.
Herbert, I. V., and Becker, E. R. (1961). *J. Parasitol.* **47**, 304.
Herlich, H. (1965). *J. Parasitol.* **51**, 847.
Heydorn, A. D. (1970). Inaugural Dissertation, Free University, Berlin.
Horton-Smith, C. (1947). *Vet. Rec.* **59**, 645.
Horton-Smith, C. (1949). *Vet. Rec.* **61**, 237.
Horton-Smith, C. (1963). *Brit. Vet. J.* **119**, 99.
Horton-Smith, C., and Long, P. L. (1963). *Advan. Parasitol.* **1**, 68.
Horton-Smith, C., Beattie, J., and Long, P. L. (1961). *Immunology* **4**, 111.
Horton-Smith, C., Long, P. L., Pierce, A. E., and Rose, M. E. (1963a). *In* "Immunity to Protozoa" (P. C. C. Garnham, A. E. Pierce, and I. Roitt, eds.), pp. 273–295. Blackwell, Oxford.
Horton-Smith, C., Long, P. L., and Pierce, A. E. (1963b). *Exp. Parasitol.* **13**, 66.
Huff, D. K. (1966). Ph.D. Thesis, Michigan State University, University Microfilms Inc., Ann Arbor.
Huff, D. K., and Clark, D. T. (1970). *J. Protozool.* **17**, 35.
Humphrey, J. H., and White, R. G. (1965). *In* "Immunology for Medical Students," 3rd ed., p. 414. Blackwell, Oxford.
Janković, B. D., and Isaković, K. (1966). *Nature (London)* **211**, 202.
Janković, B. D., and Mitrović, W. (1967). *Folia Biol. (Prague)* **13**, 406.
Janković, B. D., Isaković, K., Petrović, S., Vujić, D., and Horvat, J. (1970). *Clin. Exp. Immunol.* **7**, 709.
Kaliss, N. (1958). *Cancer Res.* **18**, 992.
Kass, E. H., and Finland, M. (1953). *Annu. Rev. Microbiol.* **7**, 361.
Kendall, S. B., and McCullough, F. S. (1952). *J. Comp. Pathol. Ther.* **62**, 116.
Lawrence, H. S. (1969). *Advan. Immunol.* **11**, 195.

Leathem,W. D., and Burns, W. C. (1967). *J. Parasitol.* **53**, 180.
Lee, H. H. (1967). *Diss. Abstr.* **28**, No. 5, 2052-B.
Levey, R. M., and Medawar, P. B. (1967). *Ciba Found. Study Group* [*Pap.*] **29**, 72–90.
Levine, P. P. (1938). *Cornell Vet.* **28**, 263.
Levine, P. P. (1942). *Cornell Vet.* **32**, 430.
Long, P. L. (1970). *Nature (London)* **225**, 290.
Long, P. L. (1971). *J. Protozool.* **18**, 17.
Long, P. L., and Pierce, A. E. (1963). *Nature (London)* **200**, 426.
Long, P. L., and Rose, M. E. (1962). *Exp. Parasitol.* **12**, 75.
Long, P. L., and Rose, M. E. (1965). *Exp. Parasitol.* **16**, 1.
Long, P. L., and Rose, M. E. (1970). *Parasitology* **60**, 147.
Long, P. L., Rose, M. E., and Pierce, A. E. (1963). *Exp. Parasitol.* **14**, 210.
Longenecker, B. M., Breitenbach, R. P., and Farmer, J. N. (1966). *J. Immunol.* **97**, 594.
McDermott, J. J., and Stauber, L. A. (1954). *J. Parasitol.* **40**, Suppl., 23.
Mackaness, G. B., and Blanden, R. V. (1967). *Progr. Allergy* **11**, 89.
McLoughlin, D. K. (1969). *J. Protozool.* **16**, 145.
Moore, E. N., and Brown, J. A. (1951). *Cornell Vet.* **41**, 124.
Morehouse, N. F. (1938). *J. Parasitol.* **24**, 311.
Niilo, L. (1970). *Can. J. Comp. Med. Vet. Sci.* **34**, 325.
Ogilvie, B. M. (1970). *J. Parasitol.* **56**, 525.
Orlans, E., and Rose, M. E. (1970). *Immunology* **18**, 473.
Orlans, E., and Rose, M. E. (1972). *Immunochemistry* (in press).
Pattillo, W. H. (1959). *J Parasitol.* **45**, 253.
Patton, W. H. (1970). *J. Parasitol.* **56**, Sect. II, 260.
Phillips, R. S. (1971). *Parasitology* **63**, 315.
Pierce, A. E., and Long, P. L. (1965). *Immunology* **9**, 427.
Pierce, A. E., Long, P. L., and Horton-Smith, C. (1962). *Immunology* **5**, 129.
Pierce, A. E., Long, P. L., and Horton-Smith, C. (1963). *Immunology* **6**, 37.
Purchase, H. G., Chubb, R. C., and Biggs, P. M. (1968). *J. Nat. Cancer Inst.* **40**, 583.
Raynaud, J. P. (1962). *Ann. Parasitol. Hum. Comp.* **37**, 755.
Reid, W. M. (1964). *Amer. J. Vet. Res.* **25**, 224.
Rommel, M. (1969). Dissertation, Free University, Berlin.
Rommel, M. (1970a). *Berlin. Muench Tieraerztl. Wochenschr.* **83**, 236.
Rommel, M. (1970b). *J. Parasitol.* **56**, Sect. II, 846.
Rose, M. E. (1959). *Immunology* **2**, 112.
Rose, M. E. (1961). *Immunology* **4**, 346.
Rose, M. E. (1963). *Ann. N.Y. Acad. Sci.* **113**, 383.
Rose, M. E. (1967a). *Parasitology* **57**, 567.
Rose, M. E. (1967b). *Parasitology* **57**, 363.
Rose, M. E. (1968a). *In* "Immunity to Parasites" (A. E. R. Taylor, ed.), pp. 43–50. Blackwell, Oxford.
Rose, M. E. (1968b). *Parasitology* **58**, 481.
Rose, M. E. (1970). *Parasitology* **60**, 137.
Rose, M. E. (1971a). *Poultry Dis. World Econ., Brit. Egg Marketing Board Symp. 7th, 1970* pp. 93–108.
Rose, M. E. (1971b). *Parasitology* **62**, 11.

Rose, M. E. (1972a). In "The Coccidia" (D. M. Hammond, ed.), Univ. Park Press, Baltimore, Maryland (in press).

Rose, M. E. (1972b). Parasitology 65 (in press).

Rose, M. E., and Long, P. L. (1962). Immunology 5, 79.

Rose, M. E., and Long, P. L. (1969). Experientia 25, 183.

Rose, M. E., and Long, P. L. (1970). Parasitology 60, 291.

Rose, M. E., and Long, P. L. (1971). Parasitology 63, 299.

Rose, M. E., and Orlans, E. (1962). Immunology 5, 633.

Rose, M. E., and Orlans, E. (1968). Nature (London) 217, 231.

Roudabush, R. L. (1935). J. Parasitol. 21, 453.

Rouse, T. C. (1967). Diss. Abstr. 28, 3.

Rouse, T. C., and Burns, W. C. (1971). J. Parasitol. 57, 40.

Ruskin, J., and Remington, J. S. (1968). Science 160, 72.

Scholtyseck, E., Strout, R. G., and Haberkorn, A. (1969). Z. Parasitenk. 32, 284.

Seed, J. R., and Gam, A. A. (1966). J. Parasitol. 52, 395.

Sell, S. (1969). Ann. Intern. Med. 71, 177.

Sherman, I. W., and Ruble, J. A. (1967). J. Parasitol. 53, 258.

Soulsby, E. J. L. (1970). J. Parasitol. 56, 534.

Stiffel, C., Perini, A., Passos, H. C., Bier, O. G., and Biozzi, G. (1968). Pathol. Biol. 16, 67.

Taliaferro, W. H. (1956). Amer. J. Trop. Med. Hyg. 5, 391.

Tyzzer, E. E., Theiler, H., and Jones, E. E. (1932). Amer. J. Hyg. 15, 319.

Van Doorninck, W. M., and Becker, E. R. (1957). J. Parasitol. 43, 40.

Vernon-Roberts, B. (1969). Int. Rev. Cytol. 25, 131.

Warner, N. L. (1967). Folia Biol. (Prague) 13, 1.

Warner, N. L., Szenberg, A., and Burnet, F. M. (1962). Aust. J. Exp. Biol. Med. Sci. 40, 373.

Warner, N. L., Uhr, J. W., Thorbecke, G. J., and Ovary, Z. (1969). J. Immunol. 103, 1317.

AUTHOR INDEX

Numbers in italics refer to the pages on which the complete references are listed.

SUBJECT INDEX